PHILIP AND ALEXANDER

ALSO BY ADRIAN GOLDSWORTHY:

Cannae: Hannibal's Greatest Victory

Hadrian's Wall

Roman Warfare

Pax Romana

Augustus

Antony and Cleopatra

How Rome Fell

Caesar

The Complete Roman Army

In the Name of Rome

The Punic Wars / The Fall of Carthage

The Roman Army at War

PHILIP

=== AND ===

ALEXANDER

KINGS AND CONQUERORS

ADRIAN GOLDSWORTHY

BASIC BOOKS
New York

Basic Books
Hachette Book Group
1290 Avenue of the Americas, New York, NY 10104
www.basicbooks.com

Printed in the United States of America

First Edition: November 2020

Published by Basic Books, an imprint of Perseus Books, LLC, a subsidiary of Hachette Book Group, Inc. The Basic Books name and logo is a trademark of the Hachette Book Group.

The Hachette Speakers Bureau provides a wide range of authors for speaking events. To find out more, go to www.hachettespeakersbureau.com or call (866) 376-6591.

The publisher is not responsible for websites (or their content) that are not owned by the publisher.

Print book interior design by Jeff Williams.

All maps by Jamie Whyte

Library of Congress Cataloging-in-Publication Data

Names: Goldsworthy, Adrian Keith, author.
Title: Philip and Alexander : kings and conquerors / Adrian Goldsworthy.
Description: First edition. | New York : Basic Books, 2020. | Includes
    bibliographical references and index.
Identifiers: LCCN 2020017515 | ISBN 9781541646698 (hardcover) | ISBN
    9780465095506 (ebook)
Subjects: LCSH: Alexander, the Great, 356 B.C.–323 B.C. | Philip II, King
    of Macedonia, 382 B.C.–336 B.C. | Greece—Kings and rulers—Biography. |
    Generals—Greece—Biography. | Greece—History—Macedonian Expansion,
    359–323 B.C. | Macedonia—Kings and rulers—Biography. |
    Macedonia—History—To 168 B.C. | Armies—Macedonia—History. |
    Macedonia—History, Military.
Classification: LCC DF233.8.A44 G65 2020 | DDC 938/.070922 [B]—dc23
LC record available at https://lccn.loc.gov/2020017515

ISBNs: 978-1-5416-4669-8 (hardcover), 978-0-465-09550-6 (ebook)

LSC-C

10 9 8 7 6 5 4 3 2 1

To Dorothy with thanks

CONTENTS

PART TWO: ALEXANDER AND PERSIA

PART THREE: LORD OF ASIA

MAPS AND FIGURES

CHRONOLOGY

All dates are BC. The timing of many events is often uncertain, especially for Philip's reign, as explained in the main text.

499–494	Ionian Revolt against Persia.
498/7	**Death of Amyntas I of Macedon** (date of start of reign unknown)
498/7–c. 454	**Reign of Alexander I of Macedon**
490	Darius sends army to invade Greece. Victory of Athenians and Plataeans over the Persians at Marathon.
480	Xerxes leads second invasion of Greece. After forcing the pass at Thermopylae, his fleet is defeated at Salamis.
479	Defeat of Persian army at Plataea.
454–413	**Reign of Perdiccas II of Macedon**
431	Outbreak of Peloponnesian War.
415–413	Disastrous Athenian expedition to Sicily.
413–399	**Reign of Archelaus of Macedon**

404	End of Peloponnesian War. Athens's Long Walls demolished and tyranny established.
403	Restoration of democracy at Athens.
399–398/7	**Reign of Orestes of Macedon**
398/7–395/4	**Reign of Areopus II of Macedon**
394–393	**Reign of Pausanias**
393–370/69	**Reign of Amyntas III**
386	Persian "King's Peace" established in Greece.
382	Spartans seize Theban citadel.
c. 382	Birth of Philip.
379/8	Thebans destroy Spartan garrison.
371	Epaminondas and Pelopidas lead Theban army to victory over the Spartans at Leuctra.
370/69–367	**Reign of Alexander II of Macedon**
c. 368–365	Philip held hostage in Thebes.
367–365	**Reign/Regency of Ptolemy**
365–359	**Reign of Perdiccas III**
362	Tactical defeat of Spartans at Mantineia proves strategically indecisive, in part because of the death of Epaminondas.
359	Death in battle of Perdiccas II. Philip becomes leader of Macedonia, either as king or regent. He fends off and defeats several Argead challengers.
359–336	**Reign of Philip II of Macedon**
358	Philip subdues Paeonia. He then defeats Illyrian king Bardylis. Intervention in Thessaly(?).
357	Philip captures Amphipolis. Athens engaged in war with rebellious allies. Philip marries Olympias. (If Philip initially rules as regent for his nephew Amyntas, then he became king in his own right around this time.) Philip allies with Chalcidian League.

356	Philip captures Pydna and other cities. He defeats a loose coalition of Thracian, Illyrian, and Paeonian leaders. Philip captures Potidaea and hands it over to his Chalcidian allies.
356	Birth of Alexander.
355	Philip active in Thessaly (?). He starts to besiege Methone. Start of Sacred War.
354	Philip wounded during the siege and loses an eye. Methone falls. Autumn campaign in Thrace (?).
353	Philip once again in Thessaly and becomes involved in the Sacred War. He is defeated by Onomarchus.
352	Philip returns and wins victory at the Crocus Field. The pass at Thermopylae is occupied by a strong coalition force, blocking the Macedonians from advancing into southern Greece. By the end of the year, Philip campaigns in Thrace, where he is taken ill.
351	Operations in Thrace near the Gallipoli Peninsula and in Illyria.
350	Philip intervenes in Epirus.
349	Philip attacks the Chalcidian League.
348	Philip captures Olynthus.
347	Philip besieges Halus. Athenians attempt to create an anti-Macedonia alliance, but fail to raise much interest. Philip probably begins to campaign in Thrace.
346	Philip campaigns in Thrace. Continuing negotiations with Athens and other states. He marches south and skillfully manipulates the situation to accept the surrender of Phocis. End of the Sacred War. In the autumn he presides over the Pythian Games.
345	Philip campaigns against the Dardanians.

344	Philip campaigns against the Illyrians. Activity in Thessaly. Negotiations with Athens.
343	Philip sends envoy to Athens. Demosthenes prosecutes Aeschines.
342	Philip deposes the king of Epirus and replaces him with Olympias's brother Alexander of Epirus. Aristotle begins to tutor Philip's son, Alexander.
341	Philip campaigns in Thrace.
340	Sieges of Perinthus, Selymbria, and Byzantium. Seizure of Athenian grain fleet. Alexander is left as regent and defeats Maedi. He founds Alexandropolis.
339	Amphictyonic League declares Sacred War on Amphissa and appoints Philip as its leader. Philip abandons siege of Byzantium and launches campaign against Scythians. He is wounded in an encounter with the Triballi on his way home. After recovering he marches south and by the end of the year has seized Elatea.
338	Philip defeats Thebes, Athens, and their allies at Chaeronea and imposes peace terms on them.
337	Philip summons Greek leaders to Corinth. He is appointed leader of a Panhellenic war to be waged against Persia. There is friction at court following his marriage to Cleopatra, prompting Alexander to flee. He is subsequently recalled.
336–323	**Reign of Alexander III (the Great) of Macedon**
336	Parmenio and Attalus sent to Asia Minor at the head of some 10,000 men. Philip prepares to follow, but is murdered. Accession of Alexander amid executions and political murders. He responds quickly to crush initial opposition in Greece and is appointed *hegemon* of Panhellenic forces for the Persian War.
335	Alexander campaigns against Thracians and Illyrians. Thebes declares war, prompting his

rapid return. Thebes is stormed and abolished as a political entity.

334	Alexander marches overland to the Dardanelles and crosses to Asia in May. He defeats the local satraps at the Battle of Granicus. Capture of Miletus and siege of Halicarnassus.
333	Memnon launches naval offensive, but momentum is lost when he dies and then Darius recalls most of the mercenaries serving with the fleet. Alexander campaigns in Asia Minor and cuts the Gordian knot. Reaching Cilicia late in the summer he falls seriously ill, but eventually recovers. He defeats Darius III at the Battle of Issus.
332	Siege of Tyre. Persian fleet fragments, much of it joining Alexander. After the fall of Tyre Alexander besieges and captures Gaza. By the end of the year he takes Egypt, which is not defended against him.
331	During the visit to Egypt Alexander founds Alexandria and visits the oracle of Zeus Ammon at the Siwah Oasis. He returns to Tyre and launches offensive into the Persian heartland. He defeats Darius at the Battle of Gaugamela, and takes Babylon. Late in the year (or possibly in the next) news arrives of the rebellion and defeat of Agis of Sparta.
330	Alexander loots and burns Persepolis. Campaign against the Mardi. Alexander resumes pursuit of Darius, who is arrested and murdered by his own nobles. Plot by members of Alexander's court. Philotas accused of treason and executed. Bessus declares himself king of kings.
329	Macedonians advance into Sogdiana and Bactria. Alexander leads army over the Hindu Kush. Bessus captured. Widespread rebellion against the Macedonians in Bactria and Sogdiana.
328	Brutal campaigning against various rebel leaders. During a rest period at the end of the year, Alexander kills Cleitus in a drunken argument.

328 or 327	Alexander captures the Sogdian Rock and the Rock of Chorienes.
327	Continued campaigning against rebels. Plot of the pages discovered, leading to executions. Advance to the Indus.
326	Alexander defeats Porus at Battle of Hydaspes. He advances to the river Hyphasis, but his Macedonian troops refuse to cross it. Alexander returns to the Hydaspes and leads expedition downriver toward the sea. Any community refusing to submit is treated as an enemy and attacked. Late in the year (or early in the next) Alexander is badly wounded during the storming of a city of the Malli.
325	In spite of his injuries, there is no more than a brief delay in the advance. A revolt led by Brahmans is suppressed. Alexander reaches the Indian Ocean and sacrifices. He divides his forces for the march back to the Persian heartland. Craterus sets out first, then Alexander, and finally Nearchus and the fleet, delayed by adverse weather. Alexander and his men endure the hardships of the Gedrosian desert.
324	Army and fleet once again concentrate in Carmania. Alexander orders the dismissal of mercenaries employed by his satraps. He also sends an envoy to the Olympic Games declaring the return of exiles to the Greek cities. His veterans mutiny at Opis, but Alexander imposes his will. Mass marriage of his Companions to Persian brides. A large contingent of veterans begin journey home under command of Craterus. Death of Hephaestion.
323	Alexander at Babylon. Preparations for major expedition to Arabia, but Alexander falls ill and dies before it can be launched.

LANDS AROUND THE AEGEAN
356 BC

Danube

BLACK SEA

Mt Haemus

ILLYRIA

Philippopolis

THRACE

Strymon

Axius

MACEDONIA

LYNCESTIS
Pella
Mieza
ORESTIS
Aegae
Dion
Mt Pindus
ELIMIOTIS
Mt Olympus

Perinthus
Byzantium
SEA OF
MARMARA

Amphipolis
Stagira
Philippi
Mt Pangaeum
Olynthus
THASOS
SAMOTHRACE
Potidaea
Mt Athos

HELLESPONTINE
PHRYGIA
TROAD

Sestos

THERMAIC GULF

EPIRUS

Larissa
THESSALY
Dodona

AEGEAN SEA

ASIA MINOR

LESBOS
Mytilene

LYDIA
Sardis

Thermopylae

Delphi
EUBOEA
Chaeronea ✗
Thebes
Corinth
Athens

CHIOS

Ephesus
SAMOS
Priene
Miletus

Olympia
Argos

CARIA
Halicarnassus
COS

Sparta

RHODES

MEDITERRANEAN

CRETE

SEA

0   100   200
Miles

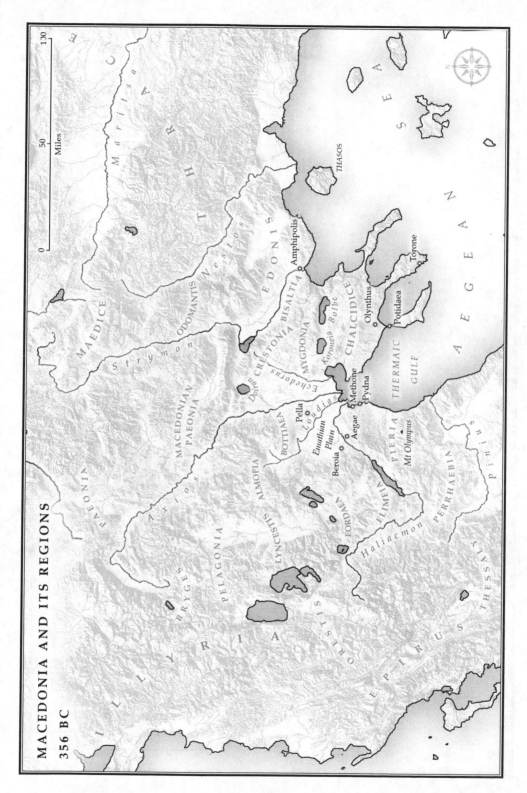

MACEDONIA AND ITS REGIONS
356 BC

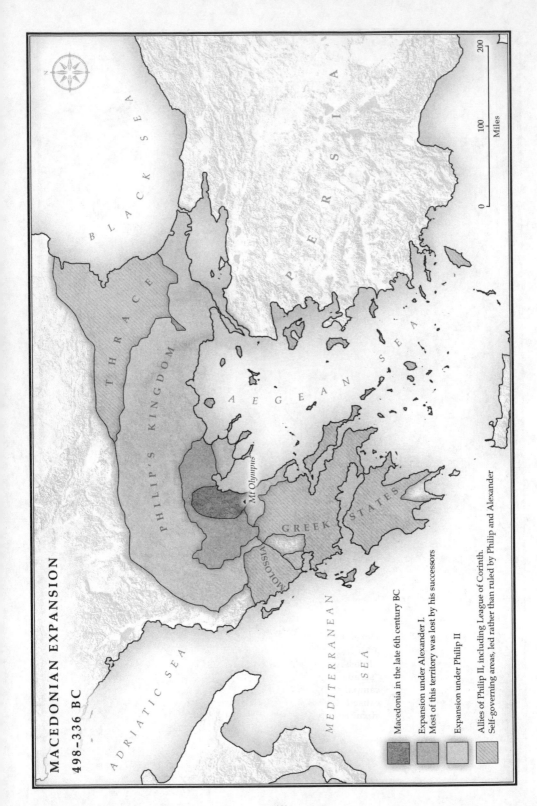

MACEDONIAN EXPANSION
498–336 BC

Macedonia in the late 6th century BC

Expansion under Alexander I.
Most of this territory was lost by his successors

Expansion under Philip II

Allies of Philip II, including League of Corinth.
Self-governing areas, led rather than ruled by Philip and Alexander

BLACK SEA

THRACE

PHILIP'S KINGDOM

PERSIA

AEGEAN SEA

Mt Olympus

MOLOSSIA

GREEK STATES

ADRIATIC SEA

MEDITERRANEAN SEA

Miles
0   100   200

A wedge of 55 cavalrymen. The leader is at the front of the formation. His deputy is in the center of the rear flank and flank guards at each end of the rank.

Uncertainty over the precise size of an *ilè* and its internal organization make it impossible to be precise regarding any "standard" formation. The realities of campaigning must inevitably have then caused the theory to be modified by circumstances.

FIGURE 1B

Conjectural diagram of a Macedonian *ilè* formed into four separate wedges. This is more likely than a single wedge of 200 or more riders and conforms to the eventual formal division of the *ilè* into four subunits. How the individual wedges were arranged is nowhere mentioned, and probably varied. In most cases some initial reserve would have been sensible.

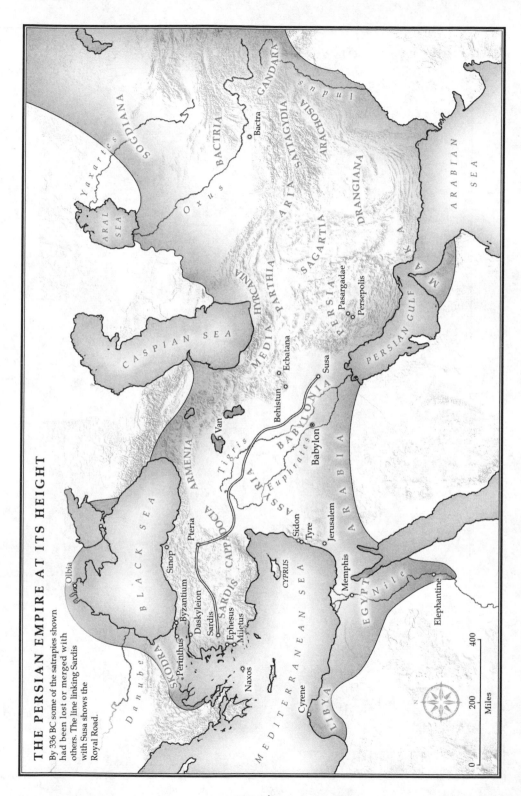

THE PERSIAN EMPIRE AT ITS HEIGHT

By 336 BC some of the satrapies shown had been lost or merged with others. The line linking Sardis with Susa shows the Royal Road.

ARAL SEA

SOGDIANA

Yaxartes

Oxus

BACTRIA

Bactra

GANDARA

INDUS

ARIA

SATTAGYDIA

ARACHOSIA

ARABIAN SEA

DRANGIANA

PARTHIA

HYRCANIA

SAGARTIA

PERSIA

Pasargadae

Persepolis

MEDIA

CASPIAN SEA

Ecbatana

Behistun

Susa

PERSIAN GULF

CARMANIA

ARMENIA

Van

Tigris

BABYLONIA

Euphrates

Babylon

ASSYRIA

ARABIA

BLACK SEA

Sinop

Olbia

Perinthus

Byzantium

Daskyleion

Sardis

Ephesus

Miletus

Pteria

CAPPADOCIA

SKODRA

Danube

Naxos

CYPRUS

Sidon

Tyre

Jerusalem

Memphis

EGYPT

Nile

Elephantine

MEDITERRANEAN SEA

Cyrene

LIBYA

N

0   200   400

Miles

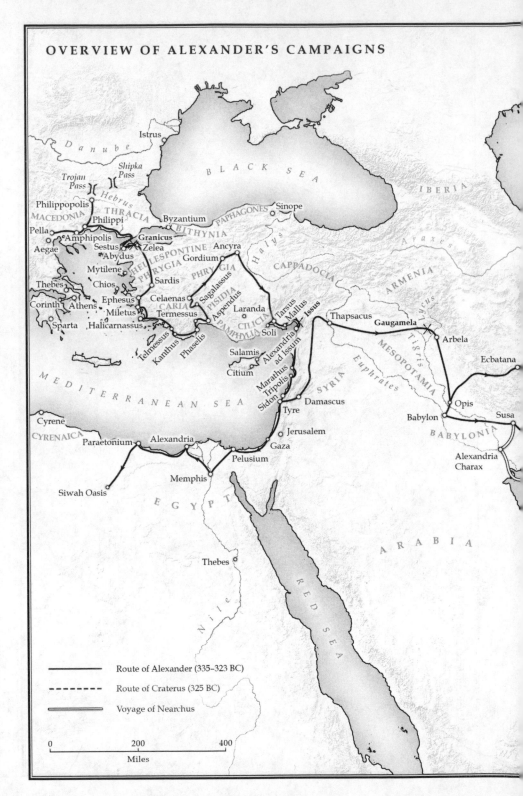

OVERVIEW OF ALEXANDER'S CAMPAIGNS

Danube

Istrus

BLACK SEA

Shipka Pass

Trojan Pass

Hebrus

IBERIA

Araxes

Philippopolis

MACEDONIA THRACIA

Philippi

Byzantium

BITHYNIA PAPHAGONES

Sinope

Pella

Amphipolis

Aegae Sestus Zelea **Granicus**

Abydus HELLESPONTINE Ancyra

Mytilene PHRYGIA Gordium

Halys

CAPPADOCIA

ARMENIA

Thebes Chios Sardis PHRYGIA

Lycus

Corinth Athens Ephesus Celaenas Sagalassus PISIDIA

Miletus CARIA Aspendus Laranda Tarsus Mallus **Issus**

Sparta Termessus Soli CILICIA Thapsacus **Gaugamela**

Halicarnassus PAMPHYLIA

Arbela

Telmessus Kanthus Phaselis

Ecbatana

MEDITERRANEAN SEA Salamis

Alexandria ad Issum MESOPOTAMIA

Citium

Euphrates

Opis

Susa

Marathus Tripolis SYRIA

Cyrene Sidon Damascus Babylon

CYRENAICA Tyre BABYLONIA

Paraetonium Alexandria Jerusalem

Alexandria Charax

Gaza

Pelusium

Memphis

EGYPT

ARABIA

Siwah Oasis

Nile

Thebes

RED SEA

─────── Route of Alexander (335–323 BC)

- - - - - - - Route of Craterus (325 BC)

─────── Voyage of Nearchus

0   200   400

Miles

xxii

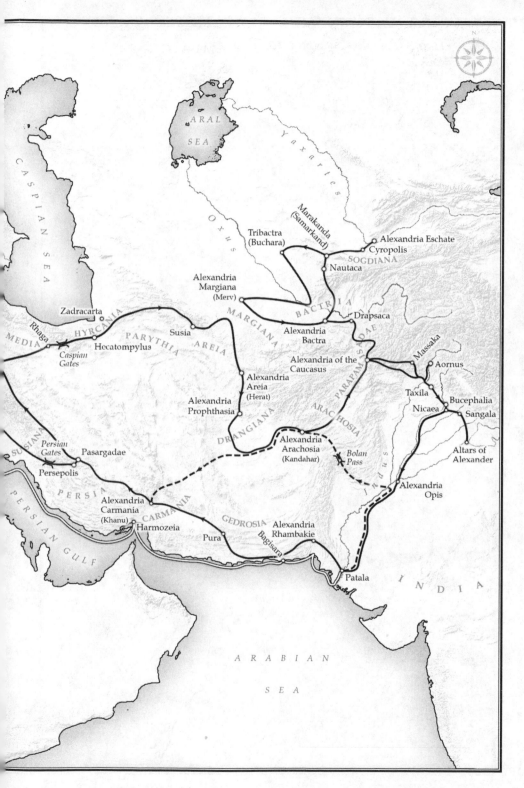

CASPIAN SEA

ARAL SEA

Oxus

Yaxartes

Tribactra (Buchara)

Marakanda (Samarkand)

Alexandria Eschate
Cyropolis

SOGDIANA

Nautaca

Alexandria Margiana (Merv)

MARGIANA

BACTRIA

Drapsaca

Alexandria Bactra

Zadracarta

Rhaga

HYRCANIA

Caspian Gates

MEDIA

Hecatompylus

PARYTHIA

Susia

AREIA

Alexandria of the Caucasus

PARAPAMISADAE

Massaka

Aornus

Alexandria Areia (Herat)

Alexandria Prophthasia

DRANGIANA

ARACHOSIA

Taxila

Nicaea

Bucephalia

Sangala

Persian Gates

Pasargadae

Alexandria Arachosia (Kandahar)

Bolan Pass

Indus

Altars of Alexander

SUSIANA

Persepolis

PERSIA

Alexandria Carmania (Khanu)

CARMANIA

Harmozeia

GEDROSIA

Pura

Bagisara

Alexandria Rhambakie

Alexandria Opis

PERSIAN GULF

Patala

INDIA

ARABIAN SEA

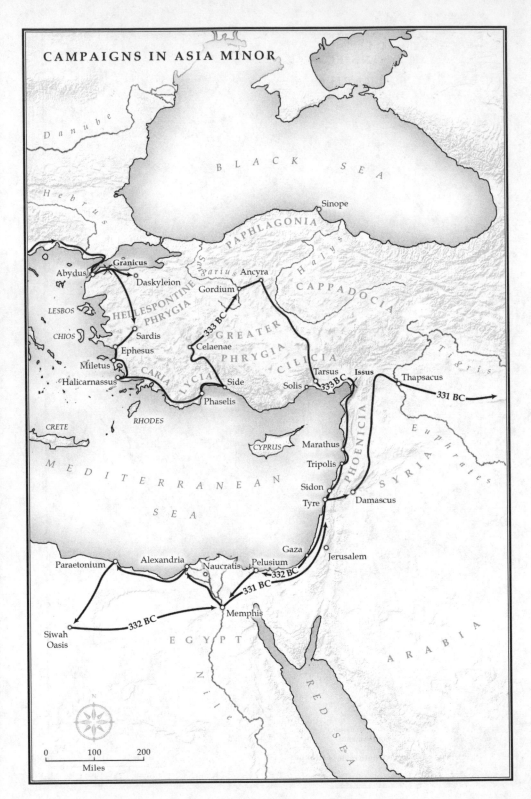

CAMPAIGNS IN ASIA MINOR

Danube

Hebrus

BLACK SEA

Sinope

PAPHLAGONIA

Sangarius

Halys

Granicus

Abydus

Daskyleion

Ancyra

CAPPADOCIA

HELLESPONTINE PHRYGIA

LESBOS

Gordium

333 BC

Sardis

CHIOS

GREATER PHRYGIA

Ephesus

Celaenae

Tarsus

Thapsacus

Miletus

CARIA

CILICIA

Issus

331 BC

Halicarnassus

LYCIA

Side

Solis

333 BC

Tigris

Phaselis

Euphrates

CRETE

RHODES

CYPRUS

Marathus

PHOENICIA

SYRIA

MEDITERRANEAN

Tripolis

Sidon

SEA

Tyre

Damascus

Gaza

Paraetonium

Alexandria

Naucratis

Pelusium

Jerusalem

332 BC

331 BC

Siwah Oasis

332 BC

Memphis

EGYPT

Nile

ARABIA

RED SEA

N

0   100   200

Miles

xxiv

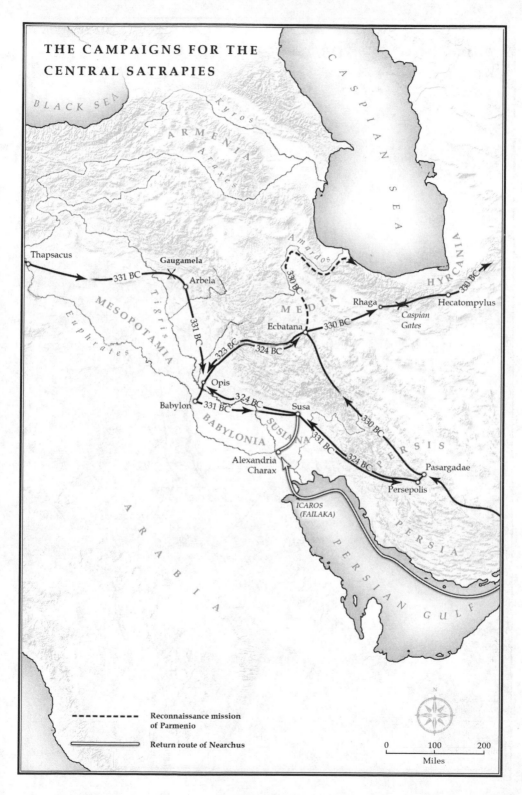

THE CAMPAIGNS FOR THE
CENTRAL SATRAPIES

BLACK SEA

CASPIAN SEA

ARMENIA

Kyros

Araxes

Amardos

HYRCANIA

Thapsacus

Gaugamela

Arbela

331 BC

MESOPOTAMIA

Tigris

Euphrates

331 BC

330 BC

330 BC

MEDIA

Rhaga

Hecatompylus

330 BC

Caspian
Gates

Ecbatana

330 BC

323 BC

324 BC

Opis

Babylon

331 BC

324 BC

Susa

330 BC

BABYLONIA

SUSIANA

Alexandria
Charax

331 BC

324 BC

PERSIS

ARABIA

*ICAROS
(FAILAKA)*

Pasargadae

Persepolis

PERSIA

PERSIAN

GULF

- - - - -   Reconnaissance mission
of Parmenio

———   Return route of Nearchus

N

0   100   200
Miles

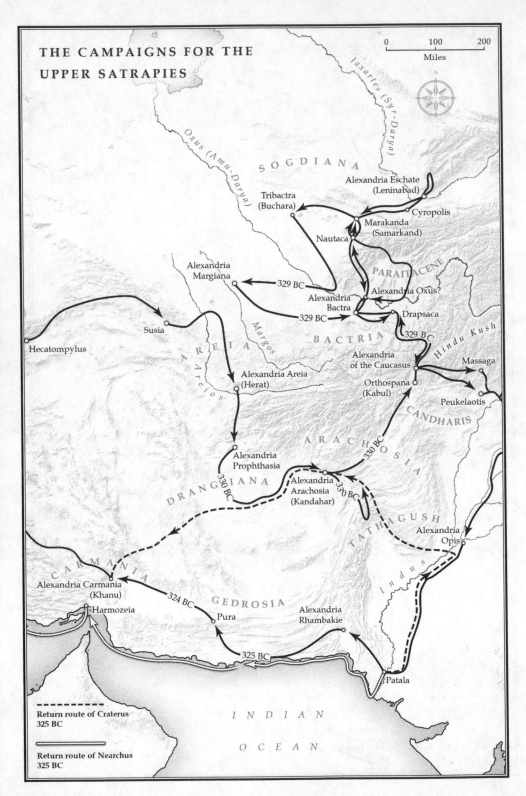

THE CAMPAIGNS FOR THE UPPER SATRAPIES

0   100   200
Miles

Iaxartes (Syr-Darya)

Oxus (Amu-Darya)

SOGDIANA

Alexandria Eschate
(Leninabad)

Tribactra
(Buchara)

Cyropolis

Marakanda
(Samarkand)

Nautaca

PARAITACENE

Alexandria
Margiana

329 BC

Alexandria Oxus?

Alexandria
Bactra

329 BC

Drapsaca

Susia

Margos

BACTRIA

329 BC

Hecatompylus

A R E I A

Areios

Alexandria
of the Caucasus

Hindu Kush

Massaga

Alexandria Areia
(Herat)

Orthospana
(Kabul)

Peukelaotis

CANDHARIS

A R A C H O S I A

330 BC

Alexandria
Prophthasia

330 BC

Alexandria
Arachosia
(Kandahar)

330 BC

D R A N G I A N A

T A T H A G U S H

Alexandria
Opis

CARMANIA

Alexandria Carmania
(Khanu)

324 BC

Pura

G E D R O S I A

Indus

Harmozeia

Alexandria
Rhambakie

325 BC

Patala

- - - - - **Return route of Craterus
325 BC**

———— **Return route of Nearchus
325 BC**

INDIAN

OCEAN

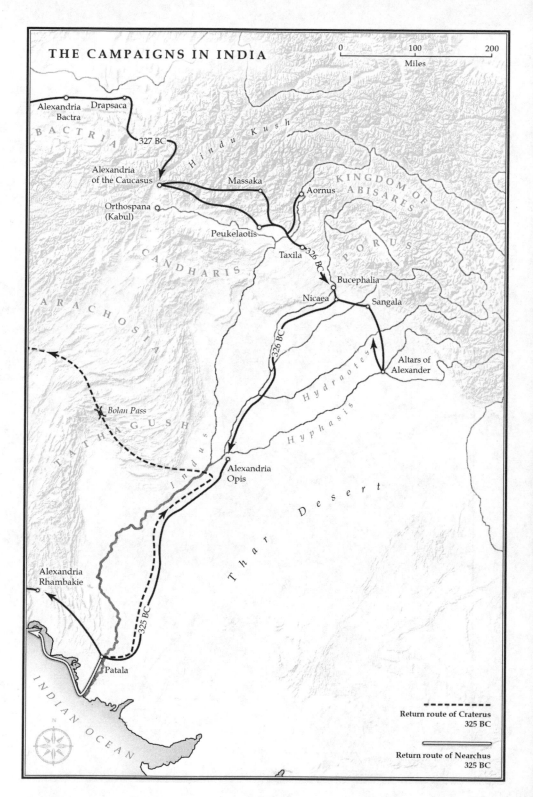

THE CAMPAIGNS IN INDIA

0   100   200

Miles

Alexandria
Bactra   Drapsaca

B A C T R I A

327 BC

Hindu Kush

Alexandria
of the Caucasus

Massaka

Aornus

K I N G D O M
O F
A B I S A R E S

Orthospana
(Kabul)

Peukelaotis

Taxila   326 BC

P O R U S

Bucephalia

Nicaea

Sangala

C A N D H A R I S

A R A C H O S I A

326 BC

Altars of
Alexander

Hydraotes

Bolan Pass

T A T H A G U S H

Indus

Hyphasis

Alexandria
Opis

T h a r   D e s e r t

Alexandria
Rhambakie

325 BC

Patala

I N D I A N   O C E A N

N

- - - - - - - - - -
Return route of Craterus
325 BC

———————
Return route of Nearchus
325 BC

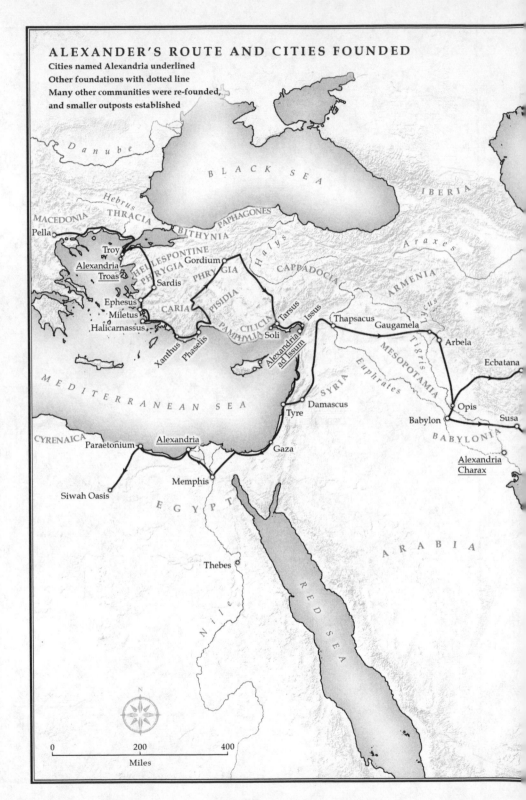

ALEXANDER'S ROUTE AND CITIES FOUNDED

Cities named Alexandria underlined
Other foundations with dotted line
Many other communities were re-founded,
and smaller outposts established

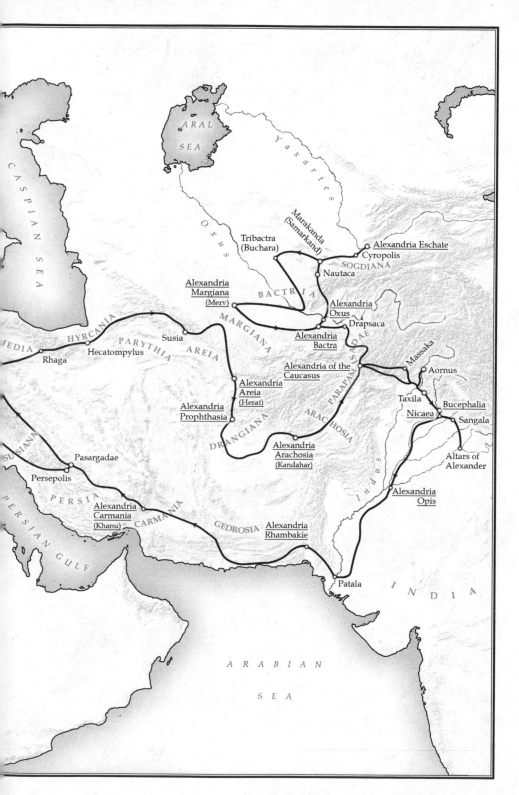

come to dominate see if then attacked the greatest superpower of

---

"SOME TALK OF ALEXANDER"

Some individuals change history. Perhaps all do in at least a tiny way, but some leaders make a much greater difference to events that shape their own world and what follows. Saying this in no way denies the importance of wider factors. Contemporary society, the economy, demographic trends, and technology underlie the rise and fall of nations and create context, limiting what is possible. The actions and characters of human beings still matter, and leaders inevitably have the greatest influence of all. To take an obvious example, there were many factors that encouraged the rise of dictatorship in Germany after the First World War, but the personality of Hitler was critical in determining how Germany's tragic history played out. At the same time the United States and Britain would have had other leaders if Roosevelt and Churchill had died in their cradles, but the course of the Second World War would have been different without the decisions each man made. Leaders matter in any age for good or ill, and there are times in history when a few individuals make a profound difference, even if much of it is unintentional.

Philip and Alexander were such leaders, and between them they changed the course of history, and did it remarkably quickly. In less than forty years the fractured, backwater kingdom of Macedonia came to dominate Greece, then attacked the greatest superpower of the day and won. They created and led the finest fighting force yet seen in history, humbling Athens and Sparta, destroying Thebes, burning down the palace of the Persian king, crossing the Hindu Kush, and marching into what is now Pakistan. These were no mere raids, and both men founded many cities and settled them with their soldiers to control the conquered territory. While the empire Philip and Alexander forged did not survive them as a single entity, they played a key role in spreading Greek language and culture over a vast area, and a different sort of Greek culture, its ideas no longer dominated by the leading city-states. The consequences of this were many and profound, for it led to the New Testament being written in Greek, and a Greek-speaking "Roman" empire surviving in the eastern Mediterranean for a thousand years after the last emperor to rule from Italy.

Alexander the Great is famous, one of that handful of leaders for whom the epithet has stuck. Few now remember Pompey Magnus at Rome, so of "the Great" we are left with Alfred in England, Charlemagne in France, and much later Peter and Catherine in Russia, and Frederick in Prussia—the last three from a relatively short period of time. Alexander's victories and sheer importance dwarf those of the others, and he never suffered the catastrophic military disasters of the likes of Napoleon—partly through his own luck and talent, and more because he died before his thirty-third birthday.

Alexander has done much to shape the Western image of the youthful hero: small, fair-haired, pale-eyed, and boyish, he was unconventional, impatient, swaggeringly confident, always proven right when he defied the wisdom of his elders, and a man who fought in a way that was as clever as it was ferocious. Leading from the front, he won more victories than any fictional hero, in a spectacular "live fast, die young" career that briefly made him master of much of the known world. If in reality he never wept because there were no more worlds to conquer or sheathed his sword for lack of argument, it does not diminish what he did in such a short time. Only in the modern mechanized era have a few armies managed to advance so fast for such a long period as Alexander's men.[1]

Philip was not dubbed "the Great" (nor indeed was Alexander until the Roman period), and he was inevitably overshadowed by his son. When Philip is remembered, it is as part of Alexander's story, the old man too drunk to cross the floor when he lost his temper with his son. One-eyed and limping from his many wounds, he can seem worn out and little more than an obstacle to his dazzlingly talented child. In contrast none of Alexander's wounds were permanently disfiguring and he never got the chance to grow old. Centuries later the Emperor Augustus permitted no sculpture, statue, painting, or coin to show him aging beyond his twenties, but this was tight control of his public image and not an accurate reflection of a man who lived into his seventies and had bad teeth. Alexander also tightly controlled his image, but unlike Philip or the Roman emperor, he died before old age became an issue.

Yet without Philip there could have been no Alexander, for Philip reshaped Macedonia, making it bigger, stronger, and more united, and also created the army from scratch and even the plan to attack Persia. His son inherited all of this at the perfect moment and age for him to chance his luck and win far greater glory. Philip died at forty-six, and it is too easy to forget that he was at most twenty-three when he became king. Then he was the young, handsome, unscarred, and charismatic monarch, with only modest military achievements in his own right, but with the confidence and energy to save a kingdom on the brink of dismemberment and turn it into a military and economic powerhouse. The story of how he did this is well worth telling in its own right, apart from being essential to understanding what his son did.

Still, Alexander casts a very long shadow. Another youthful hero, let alone his father, does not easily fit with his image: just as Julius Caesar must always be the elderly lover of Cleopatra and Mark Antony the dashing younger man, even if the latter was in his middle fifties when he took his own life—at most a couple of years younger than Caesar on the Ides of March. On the whole the Romans get far more attention than the Greeks in fiction, screen dramas, and even documentaries. The discovery in the 1980s of the royal tombs at Vergina in northern Greece and the possible identification of one set of remains as Philip briefly produced a surge of attention, but otherwise even Alexander receives no more than occasional coverage on television, usually connected with his battles. Two Hollywood epics have tried to tell his story, with Richard Burton playing the role in 1956 and Colin Farrell in 2004, but each film struggled because the sheer breadth of the tale is very hard to fit into a few hours of screen time. In both we have Philip as the old man, more or less a spent force, and a story that gets going only when he is murdered and makes way for Alexander.

My own love of the ancient world began with the Romans, and specifically the Romans in Britain and the Roman army, although as my interest grew, like everyone else I soon realized that Rome can only be understood in the context of Classical and Hellenistic Greece. In my childhood Alexander was little more than a name, and my fondness for cinematic epics meant that I avidly watched the Richard Burton movie on TV, though little of it stayed with me apart from Philip tripping as he attacked his son, and Burton delivering the speech before the battle, ending in, "Kill Darius, kill Darius, kill Darius." Aged seventeen, I first studied Alexander in any depth, and it was not until a few years later that I really encountered Philip, not least when as a young lecturer I was tasked with teaching seminars on father and son.

The pull of Greek history and culture is a strong one, as the Romans understood. There remains something almost unbelievable about the burst of creativity coming from the people living in this small area, who in such a short time came up with the idea of democracy (and discussing politics), developed philosophical ideas, and laid much of the basis of scientific thought, while producing plays and literature that remain moving and provocative to this day. They also portrayed human beings in art in a way that was both more lifelike than ever before and at the same time idealized. More than anything else, Classical Greece is a microcosm of humanity, for alongside all the wonders and greatness there was savagery and cruelty, selfishness and prejudice, and a willingness to despise the rest of the world as barbarians and accept slavery as normal. The Greeks were both great and terrible, just as people throughout the ages have shown themselves capable of the extremes of good and evil. In many ways Philip and Alexander represent this paradox, as men who both built and destroyed, and who acted from a very Greek desire to excel for the sake of doing it—as well as for personal advantage, of course.

This book is about Philip and Alexander and aims to tell each man's story in as much depth and detail as possible, because no book has so far done this for the general reader. Books on Alexander abound: for every year there is at least one new biography or study of some aspect of his campaigns. Some of these are very good and I have no desire to add to the pile, but in contrast Philip is neglected, only rarely written about in his own right and usually as little more than a prologue to his son. This is unfair to Philip's importance, but also weakens our understanding of how Alexander behaved, for the similarities in the way father and son waged war and made politics are highly revealing. Looking at both men offers a far better way to place them into context, and if anything makes their achievement all the more striking.

The sheer scale of what Philip and Alexander achieved is staggering. This is not to say that this was a good thing for the wider world or to claim that their motives were even remotely altruistic. The historian's job is to discover and understand the past, and that is no easy thing, especially when dealing with the ancient world. This book is not about judging Philip and Alexander or their contemporaries in moral terms, but about trying to establish what happened, how it happened, and, where possible, why it happened. As well as telling the reader what is known about this era, it is equally important to say what is not known, and to make clear that conjecture and surmise are just that and not fact. Alexander has appeared in many guises down the ages, from saint to monster, military genius to efficient thug, and even recently as a gay or bisexual icon. Those looking to the past to justify their views about the present will readily see what they wish to see, but this is not good history for it brings us no nearer to understanding what really happened or the world of these human beings.

A true biography of Philip or Alexander is impossible, for there is so much about them, and especially their thoughts, emotions, and ideas, that cannot be known. Unlike Caesar or Augustus, virtually nothing survives in their own words, and nothing at all hinting at private thoughts, at least that we can be sure is genuine. This book tries to tell the story of their lives as far as the sources permit, and to this end it is vital to remember that they and those around them were simply people, like us, albeit products of very different cultures. It is well worth asking some of the questions a biographer might, in spite of the fact that most cannot be answered with any certainty. However, one of the biggest mistakes anyone can make in this sort of book is to create their own Philip or Alexander and then fill in the gaps by deciding that this is the sort of thing they would have done in the circumstances. Honesty is important, especially when admitting what is unknown.

In many ways this book is old-fashioned history, with the emphasis on war and politics because these were the preoccupation of the ancient sources (and indeed of Philip and Alexander), and with the story presented as a narrative. I make no apology for this. Narrative history is the test for understanding any era, for the best theories of social or economic history, let alone other academically fashionable approaches, fail if they do not match—and ideally help to explain—the wider course of events. One aim is to work out where Philip and then Alexander were at any time and what they were doing. This means that there is a lot of discussion of campaigns, battles, and sieges, for both men spent most of their adult lives fighting wars. There is a lot of killing in this book, a lot of storming cities and massacring or enslaving their populations, and the details can become repetitive as well as grim. It was tempting to skim over much of this, and sometimes I have summarized weeks or months of operations in a few lines, but on the whole I have tried to resist this urge, for the danger is that it lets us forget just how much time both men devoted to fighting small-scale skirmishes.

Philip and Alexander led their armies in a style that put them personally at far more risk than Roman commanders such as Julius Caesar, let alone the generals of more recent centuries. Both men suffered multiple wounds, and both came closest to death in combat when fighting against communities and peoples that were obscure even in the ancient world. Both spent most of their adult lives marching in all weather over all terrain, in the many little combats and dangers, while living in camp with the army all around. Neither Philip nor Alexander had prolonged periods of rest in which to formulate policy with care and consideration, for they were rarely still. Envoys are supposed to have been amazed when they were brought before Alexander, conqueror of Persia, to find him in armor, stained with sweat and covered in dust, rather than the splendor and ceremony associated with royalty. Sometimes there was luxury and excess, but danger, hardship, and fatigue were even more familiar.[2]

It is impossible to say what all this meant to either man, or to do more than guess at how the experience changed them, or the toll taken by fatigue and injury. Most of the time, the king's key advisors were men sharing these experiences, hardships, and dangers, so apart from the pressures of kingship, little of their life was unique. There is a good deal that we cannot know. Alexander's mother, Olympias, was clearly a strong personality, and it would be revealing to know far more about her, and to understand her relationship with her husband and her son, but the evidence does not exist. Women tend to be a shadowy presence in much of ancient history, and although it is obvious that they were often highly influential, their own voices are not preserved and they are seen solely through the prism of others. Lamenting this fact does not change it.

Macedonian kings were polygamous by tradition, and Philip took at least seven wives, fathering five children who reached adulthood. It was claimed, admittedly by Greek observers contemptuous of his character if not his achievements, that he also had many affairs, taking both women and young men as his lovers. Alexander married three times, all in the last few years of his life, and the tradition about him is very different, asserting that he did not sleep with a woman until he was twenty-three and first took a mistress. A homosexual relationship is alleged with Hephaestion, a friend since his youth, and later with the eunuch Bagoas, as well as hazily with others, but the emphasis is always on his restraint and self-control, exceptional by contemporary standards and most of all compared to the promiscuous Philip. In general, the sources suggest that many Macedonian kings and aristocrats took lovers of both sexes, although some caution is required since these are accounts written by outsiders portraying their subjects as barbarians. They were also influenced by the deeply entrenched idea that excessive, sometimes aggressive, sexual activity was the mark of kings and tyrants. Each case must be considered in turn, even if the truth can rarely be established. Yet what stands out is how little any of the sources deal with either man's love life—or that of any other major figure from the ancient world. Sexuality was a minor concern when the Greeks or Romans tried to understand someone's character, which ought to put the modern obsession into some sort of perspective.

The sources present many problems, even by the standards of studying Greek and Roman history, and not simply because they do not discuss many things of interest to us. (See Appendix 1 for a fuller list of the sources.) Plenty was written about Philip during his lifetime and soon afterward, apart from his own public letters and decrees, but none of this has survived intact. The only contemporary or near contemporary evidence we have consists of snippets of such works quoted by later authors, a small number of inscriptions, and the speeches of Athenian orators, delivered to an audience who understood far more of their own world than we ever can, in a political environment where truth was of minor importance. The only surviving narratives for Philip's life were written far later, and the most complete are by Diodorus Siculus, who wrote his *Library of History* in the first century BC, and Justin, who produced an *Epitome* of the earlier Pompeius Trogus's general history at some point between the second and fourth centuries AD. In each case Philip was not their main concern, and his career was just a fairly brief episode in their wider surveys of the past. Neither source would be a scholar's first choice when it came to reliability if anything better was on offer.

Far more material survives for Alexander, often focused on him to the exclusion of wider history, and yet here the problem of distance in time is even more marked. Traditionally, historians have relied heavily on Arrian and Plutarch, both of whom wrote in the second century AD, more than 400 years after Alexander's death—as distant from him as we are from Elizabeth I and the earliest days of Colonial America. Greeks writing under the Roman Empire—both men were Roman citizens and Arrian was a distinguished senator—they lived in a very different world, and it is hard to tell when they interpreted the past by the standards of their own day. This is even more true of Curtius, a Roman who wrote in the first century AD and was clearly influenced by his experience living under Rome's emperors. Diodorus devotes more space to Alexander than Philip, although substantial sections of his work are missing, as is a significant part of Curtius dealing with Alexander's early years and some of the months near the end of his life.

The surviving authors all made use of accounts that have not survived, some of them written by eyewitnesses or others living far closer to the events. Arrian tells us that he relied most on Aristobulus, a member of Alexander's court, and Ptolemy, one of Alexander's officers who later became ruler of Egypt, because they were in a position to know the truth; in the case of Ptolemy, it would be "shameful" for a king to lie. Scholars have devoted immense effort and great ingenuity into mining the surviving sources in the hope of reaching their ultimate sources, and on that basis judging the accuracy of the material they contain. The results are precarious houses of cards, tottering from so many guesses and assumptions. Thus many have contrasted the "official" version of Alexander's career, which tends to be sober and flattering to the king and is represented by Arrian, with the "vulgate" of Diodorus and Curtius, which is hostile and sensationalist. In this way, and from the best of motives, they have tried to create certainty from the confusion and contradictions in the evidence, ignoring the flimsy basis for their underlying assumptions and the ease with which the whole lot can come crashing down. It is both more honest and simply better to acknowledge that our sources are all far later, and that we cannot be sure how accurate the information that they had at their disposal was, or how well they used it. What survives is all that we have to go on, and all we can do is make the best of them, judging each author on his own merits.[3]

The sources restrict what we can say about Philip and Alexander, and generations of scholarship still leaves us with a good deal of disagreement and uncertainty. Another reason for writing this book is to bring some of this work to an audience outside specialists in the field, and at the start I ought to acknowledge the massive debt owed to them. The literature on Philip and Alexander is vast and ever growing, asking new questions and adopting new forms of analysis. One eminent scholar noted that she began studying Alexander's history and found that gradually she and her colleagues were redefining the field as Macedonian studies and raising a far broader range of themes than in the past. The notes and bibliography will give interested readers initial access to the academic literature. Neither is exhaustive, for to cite every work on the subject would result in references that dwarfed the main text of the book.[4]

My own work has in the main been concerned with the Romans, so I am an outsider to the study of the fourth century BC; I do not presume to answer all the unanswered questions or revolutionize the academic understanding of the period. Hopefully this has the advantage of a wider perspective, and an approach that is both fresh and useful. Hindsight is one of the greatest problems for any historian, as is long familiarity with a period: it can lead to taking far too much for granted. The rise of Macedonia under Philip and Alexander was as unexpected as it was rapid, and it is all too easy to forget this. When Alexander died, there were still plenty of people around who had been adults during the chaotic years before Philip's accession. Those years really were not that long before, but the knowledge that Philip's reforms fundamentally changed the nature of Macedonia, turning it into a formidable power, and that his son would march all the way to India, can make it hard to appreciate just how shocking and baffling this was to contemporaries.

Philip was murdered at the age of forty-six, and Alexander died a few weeks short of his thirty-third birthday without a clear successor. These are the facts, and it is vital to remember that no one knew these events were going to happen, or that Philip and Alexander would lead the Macedonians to so many victories against a wide range of opponents in very different conditions. One of the keys to understanding these men is to bear in mind how much they did and how quickly they did it. As far as possible this book will approach the story as if the ending was uncertain and, while once again admitting my profound debt to all the work that has been done on them and their era, also go back to the sources with an open mind and see what sort of story they tell.

PART ONE

PHILIP II

359–336 BC

"Your thoughts reach higher than the air"

I

IN THE BEGINNING

Long before Philip or Alexander there was Macedonia, a kingdom in northern Greece ruled by the Argead dynasty. The nature of the family is important, for their sole right to become king was never challenged by the aristocracy. One justification for this was that the Argeads claimed to be distinct, originally outsiders to the region, descendants of a nobleman exiled from the city of Argos in the southern Greek Peloponnese, who in the seventh century BC took his family and household north and conquered a new kingdom. As aristocrats of Argos, they claimed Hercules, the demigod and son of Zeus, as the founder of their line, often worshipping him as *Herakles Patruoüs* (the "ancestor" or "father"). Such stories were common in the ancient world; the Romans famously boasted that their city was founded by Romulus—son of Mars and descendant of Aeneas, himself son of Venus, who had led away a party of Trojans after the sack of their city and eventually settled in Italy. By the first century BC, the Aedui, a large tribe living in Gaul, claimed to be the offspring of other refugees from Troy, making them "brothers" of the Romans, and smoothing the alliance between the tribe and Rome's Republic.[1]

Ancient communities were fond of such stories, happily inventing them when convenient, making it hard to know whether any of these tales contained the slightest shred of truth. Perhaps the Argeads were originally from elsewhere—a chief and his band of warriors forced to leave their homeland or migrants seeking new opportunities—but it is impossible to know. For whatever reason, only an Argead could be king of Macedon, a rule that was never broken until the final extinction of the line with the murder of Alexander IV, son of Alexander the Great, in 310 BC. Something in the Argead bloodline was seen as special and sacred, for the king had an important role as somehow more closely connected to the gods. Tradition claimed that one of Philip's ancestors, newly become king on the death of his father, was carried as a babe in arms to join the Macedonian army as it faced the Illyrians, turning defeat into victory. More routinely, an adult king led the army on any important occasion and presided over major festivals, while each royal day began with the king personally cutting the throat of the sacrificial animal.[2]

The Argeads were special, alone possessing the right to rule, but this had failed to grant Macedonia any great stability, since any male Argead could be king if enough people supported him, or at least were willing to accept him. As far as we can tell there was no fixed rule as to who should succeed when the king died. If his oldest son was an adult, then there would probably need to be a good reason not to choose him, but this was certainly possible. Brothers might be preferred, or members of another line of the wider clan. Although a gathering of adult males representing the people in arms, or at least the most significant among them, acclaimed a new king by clashing weapons against shields, there is no sense of an election where royal candidates were chosen. Instead a man claimed to be king and then saw whether he was supported and able to survive. There were sometimes plenty of other options available, for the Argeads bred prolifically, helped by a tradition of polygamy. They also tended to be long-lived, at least if they did not come to a violent end.[3]

In the earliest days the names of kings are known, including the first Philip, but little else is certain, and the dynasty begins to emerge into recorded history in the second half of the sixth century BC, under the rule of Amyntas I, who was succeeded c. 498 BC by his son, Alexander I, and then in 454 BC by his grandson Perdiccas II. After these three long reigns, the kingdom became less stable, with many of the next monarchs assassinated by those around them. In 399 BC Archelaus I was murdered during a hunt, the conspirators not quite managing to make it look like an accident. The philosopher Aristotle judged that the king was killed because of his own vices, dying at the hands of a disappointed young lover, although he explains that politics as well as personal grudges played a role. Archelaus had ruled fairly successfully for fourteen years, strengthening his kingdom, but he had risen to power in the first place through assassinations and executions. He was the son of King Perdiccas II, but the philosopher Plato alleges that his mother was no more than a slave owned by his uncle. This may simply be a slur, a misunderstanding of royal polygamy, or could even true, confirming that the child of a concubine might be recognized as legitimate. Archelaus killed his uncle, the uncle's son, and also a half brother as he made himself king.[4]

Amyntas III became king in 393 BC, the fifth king in the six years since the murder of Archelaus. One of his four predecessors may have died of disease, but the rest were murdered, and the precise details and lengths of their reigns are hard to decipher. Amyntas most likely assassinated his immediate predecessor. The new king was a great-grandson of Alexander I. The first Alexander had lived a long life and fathered at least six children, including Amyntas's grandfather, but neither this man nor Amyntas's father had been king. For whatever reasons the line had so far been overlooked, for Amyntas was already a mature man and yet had clearly not been seen as an obvious candidate for the throne up to this point. Yet in spite of the heavy Argead death toll during the last few years, rivals survived and would soon resurface. Apart from the threat posed by Amyntas's own relatives, his kingdom was surrounded by foreign enemies.[5]

The first to act were the Illyrians, old adversaries of the Macedonians, who lived to the northwest. They were a numerous and warlike people divided into many different tribes and following different kings and chieftains. *Illyrians* was the name given by the Greeks to the "barbarians" living in this area, much as they dubbed other groups Celts, Thracians, or Scythians because they felt them to be similar and it was easier to use such blanket terms than to understand the complicated reality of tribes and clans. There is little reason to believe that the Illyrians felt much sense of corporate identity, and they certainly had no idea of nationhood. However, by the start of the fourth century BC a leader named Bardylis, most likely a king of a tribe called the Dardanians, had united not simply his own people, but also many of their neighbors under his rule. He may have been behind the major invasion that struck the heartland of Macedonia just a few months after Amyntas III became king. Whichever group of Illyrians was responsible, the new king was forced to flee, probably taking refuge in Thessaly, Macedon's southern neighbor.[6]

Eventually Amyntas III returned, aided by Thessalian allies; usually the Illyrians were interested more in plunder and extortion than permanent occupation, so Amyntas did not have to drive them out. A man named Argaeus may have exploited the king's flight to seize the throne for himself, for according to Diodorus some of his sources claimed that the man ruled for two years, but the whole episode is obscure and hard to interpret. A decade later there was another major Illyrian attack, and this was soon followed by hostility from some of the Greek communities in the Chalcidice, the triple-pronged peninsula to the east. These latter were led by Olynthus, a city-state that Amyntas had tried to appease in the past. Once again, the king was forced to flee, and this time it took aid from Sparta to restore him in 382 BC.[7]

It is hard to know how much of Macedonia Amyntas actually controlled during his reign. The heartland of the kingdom was Lower Macedonia, the rich plains north of Mount Olympus and around the Thermaic Gulf on the Aegean coast. This was good farming country, with a more settled population dwelling in towns and villages. Most important were the old royal center at Aegae, the "place of goats" (modern-day Vergina), and the even larger city of Pella, which had grown in size and importance under Archelaus I. Lower Macedonia was encircled by mountains. Upper Macedonia lay beyond, also enclosed by mountain ranges crossed by only a few passes. Its population was still predominantly pastoralists, and it was divided into several independently minded regions, such as Lyncestis and Elimiotis, each with its own royal dynasty. These local kings never appear to have challenged the Argeads for the rule of all of Macedonia, but staunchly resisted central control and were willing to fight to maintain their independence, even allying with Illyrians and other neighbors such as the Molossians of Epirus to the west. The stronger Argead kings imposed their will on most or all of Upper Macedonia. Weaker monarchs, like Amyntas, had to do their best to conciliate and persuade.[8]

Amyntas III had at least two wives, and as far as we can tell he was married to both women simultaneously rather than in succession. Polygamy was alien and repellent to most Greeks—or at least to educated Athenian males, who overwhelmingly shape what we like to consider to be Greek opinion. Taking more than one wife was seen as barbaric, as indeed was monarchy itself. In the Greek world polygamy was the mark of a tyrant, who was expected to be sexually predatory, and generally immoral and cruel. (All of which would later be said of Philip by critics in Athens.) Foreign monarchs, notably the king of kings in Persia, tended to be polygamous, reinforcing the sense that this was something foreign and inherently wrong. Athenians were uncomfortable with the idea of queens having any political influence at all, so having more than one queen at a time, all of them vying for power, was especially sinister.[9]

Our best evidence for Macedonian polygamy comes from Philip himself, who took seven—or possibly eight—wives. His father's two wives and the sheer quantity of Argeads suggest that this was an established tradition, since otherwise our sources would surely have criticized Philip for what they would see as so distasteful an innovation. There is no direct evidence for polygamy among Macedonians in general, so it may have been exclusive to the Argeads, or more probably the sole right of the ruling king. One result was that there were often plenty of potential kings, some willing to challenge the incumbent. As we have seen, most Macedonian kings died violent deaths, usually at the hands of someone close to them; the same was true of other Argeads, who were killed because they had, or it was feared that they might, seek kingship.

One of Amyntas III's wives, Eurydice, gave birth to Philip in 382 BC, or perhaps a little earlier in 383 BC, based on a source saying that he was forty-six and another that he was forty-seven when he died. The discrepancy may be down to different methods of counting, and whether from birth the individual is considered to be one year old. To add to the confusion the Greeks used a number of ways of measuring time, usually based on lunar months, and none of them correspond to the modern solar calendar of twelve months, derived as it is from the system introduced by Julius Caesar in 46 BC. This means that even when a source actually gives us a date for something, it may have occurred late in what would be for us the preceding year. In fact, more often than not, ancient historians and biographers did not bother to go into much detail about someone's birth, unless it happened to coincide with a major event or later became surrounded with stories foretelling a great destiny. As a result, we cannot be sure in which year Caesar, Cleopatra, or Mark Antony was born, let alone many other less famous figures from the ancient world, since none of our sources tell us.[10]

None of our sources preserve any stories about Philip's birth or early childhood. Once again, this is not uncommon, save for a handful of individuals like Alexander and the Emperor Augustus, and in these cases much is the product of later romantic invention. The lives of women and children rarely occupied the attention of our sources. For Caesar and other aristocratic Romans of his era we can get some idea of the rituals surrounding childbirth common among their class and paint a generic picture of the event. Similar information on the practices of the Macedonian royal family in the fourth century BC simply does not exist or is of little value; Philip is said to have dismissed one of his army officers for taking hot baths, a luxury the Macedonians did not even permit to women in labor, while we know that Artemis Eileithyia, goddess of childbirth, was venerated at the sacred site of Dium. Since ritual and sacrifice permeated every aspect of life in the ancient world, especially for the kings of Macedon, we may safely assume that the birth of a son to Amyntas III was marked with due ceremony, at least within his household. In the wider world few would have paid much attention, for Macedonia lay on the fringes—some would say beyond—the world of the Greeks, and was not a great power or considered an important cultural center.[11]

Childbirth was a dangerous time for both mother and infant. Philip's mother had already survived the ordeal at least twice, for she had presented her husband with two other boys, Alexander and Perdiccas. At some point the couple also had a daughter, Eurynoë, but it is unclear where she came in the sequence, although she was most likely older than Philip. These four are the children who survived to reach adulthood, and it is quite possible that there were others who did not. Infant mortality rates were shockingly high in the ancient world, while some believe that the heartland of Amyntas's kingdom was plagued by malaria-bearing mosquitoes, adding to the risks for all ages. In spite of this, the mother and these four children all survived and would outlive her husband.[12]

Amyntas III was also married to a woman named Gygaea, with whom he had another three sons, all of whom reached adulthood. Philip's mother, Eurydice, outlived her husband, and all three of her sons were preferred as candidates for the throne before the sons of Gygaea, which may suggest that the latter were younger, unless there was some other reason for their being overlooked. It is possible that another wife or wives has gone unrecorded, for yet another son of Amyntas is mentioned by Diodorus. Nor was it wholly unthinkable that an illegitimate son might be recognized as rightful successor. Thus from birth it was possible that Philip would one day become king, but unlikely ever to be straightforward or unchallenged, and had his older brothers lived longer, he might never have ruled.[13]

Eurydice came from one of the Upper Macedonian dynasties, for her maternal grandfather was king of Lyncestis. Yet her father's name was Sirras and he may have been an Illyrian. Upper Macedonia was most at risk from Illyrian raiding and it would have made perfect sense for a local dynasty to form a marriage alliance with a powerful leader among the tribes. Philip would in due course take an Illyrian wife for the same reason, so there is nothing inherently impossible in this, although some scholars prefer to believe that Eurydice was wholly Lyncestian. Plutarch calls her an Illyrian, "so thrice barbarian," and claims that she was illiterate until as a mature woman she learned to read and write in Greek alongside her children. He quotes a now lost inscription she dedicated to the Muses, "when she gained her soul's desire to learn, mother of young and lusty sons was she, and by her diligence attained to learn letters."[14]

Two inscriptions commissioned by Eurydice have survived from Aegae, both dedications to Eucleia at the temple dedicated to this goddess of good reputation. In Athens Eucleia's temple was set up to commemorate victory over the Persians at the Battle of Marathon, but in other Greek cities the shrines do not appear to have had any warlike association. Instead the goddess was linked to Artemis (the virgin huntress and twin of Apollo) and sometimes claimed to be daughter to Hercules, with her temples located near marketplaces and often visited by courting couples who made offerings before getting married. Whatever the precise nature of the cult of Eucleia at Aegae, Eurydice is the first royal Macedonian woman who has left any trace of a public presence, although this may only have developed after the death of her husband.

Some Illyrian women were believed to train as warriors, prompting speculation that—if she was in fact the daughter of one of the tribes' leaders—Amyntas's wife was far more forceful than most Macedonian royal women. Since we know so little about the latter it is unwise to do more than speculate, and it may simply be that Eurydice was a strong character and that the circumstances allowed her to assert herself. Many Greeks, and especially Athenians, revolted at the thought of a woman wielding power, so it is no coincidence that some of the sources describe her in an extremely hostile way as treacherous and enslaved by her passions. Similar themes will recur when we encounter other forceful royal women.[15]

Amyntas III died in 370 BC. By recent standards among the Argead family he had lasted a long time and survived threats from all sides, albeit often at the cost of making major concessions to outside powers and leaving his kingdom weak and vulnerable. His death was apparently from natural causes, which was an achievement in itself in the bloody politics of the Argeads. Justin in his *Epitome* repeats a story claiming that Eurydice plotted to murder her husband. In this version she was having an affair with her daughter's husband, and planned to marry him and make him king in Amyntas's place. What was to happen to Eurynoë is not explained, but she uncovered the plot and revealed it to her father. The conspiracy fell apart, and the king is supposed to have spared his wife for the sake of their children. No other source contains this bizarre and implausible anecdote, and it is the sole evidence for the existence of Philip's sister, Eurynoë.[16]

Alexander II, Eurydice's eldest son, succeeded to the throne. Philip was about twelve and his brother eighteen or more, since it was unlikely that anyone younger would have ruled without a regent. He was certainly active and bold, soon leading an expedition to intervene in a power struggle within Thessaly. Yet Macedonia remained weak, threatened on every side. The Illyrians were once again active, and Alexander II may have bought peace by paying them tribute, much like Anglo-Saxon kings paid Danegeld to keep away the Vikings or people offering protection money to mobsters. In each case such desperate measures give no permanent respite, for the aggressor soon returns. Philip may have been sent as a hostage to cement the agreement. Thebes, newly dominant after inflicting a stunning defeat on the Spartans at Leuctra in 371 BC, was also active in Thessaly at the time, and Macedonia could not on its own hope to compete with a major Greek power. In 369 BC the Theban general Pelopidas imposed a peace on Macedonia and the warring cities of Thessaly, and as part of this agreement Philip definitely was sent as hostage to Thebes along with thirty sons of Macedonian nobles.[17]

Philip spent almost three years in Thebes, much or all of the time living as a guest in the house of Pammenes, a wealthy and well-connected aristocrat. Although he was not free to leave, this was a very loose and comfortable confinement. For generations the Argeads had embraced Greek, and especially Athenian, culture, so that Philip was already well read and familiar with the great works of literature and drama. A Macedonian boy was also prepared for war, learning to ride and fight from a young age. Hunting was both the great joy of the aristocracy and further training for war. It was said that a Macedonian had to sit rather than recline on a couch at dinner until he had killed a boar without trapping it in a net. No doubt such a custom only applied to aristocratic males, and may have been less rigid in practice than outsiders liked to think, but courage and skill at arms were expected of a young Argead male.[18]

Greek city-states saw monarchies such as Macedonia as inherently backward. Even so, aristocratic culture in most cities remained a little closer to these old-fashioned ways. Aristocrats could afford to keep horses to ride for pleasure, for travel, and for the thrill of hunting. In Athens and elsewhere, the wealthiest class was known as *hippeis*—horsemen or knights. They also had the leisure time to study and discuss, and to devote themselves wholeheartedly to the physical training, competition, and display of the gymnasium. Pelopidas was renowned for his obsession with physical training and bodybuilding. Thus although the experience was different, it was not wholly alien to Philip's upbringing. In later life his attitude toward Thebes was pragmatic, suggesting neither great love nor particular hatred. He treated Pammenes as a friend, and although it was politically convenient to do so, the emotion may well have been genuine. Accepting the hospitality of an aristocrat, whether simply visiting his homeland as a private individual, as a representative of the state, or even as a hostage, was believed to create a bond on both sides, guest friendship of the sort familiar from Homer's poems. One source claims that Pammenes and Philip were lovers, but stories of this sort are common enough whenever a youth came into contact with a famous man and it is impossible to know whether or not there is any truth in them.[19]

Pammenes was an important man who had already made something of a military reputation and would go on to lead Theban armies. He was on very good terms with Epaminondas, who alongside Pelopidas had led the recent Theban resurgence, commanding the army and fighting in the front rank when the Spartans were beaten at Leuctra. Through his host, Philip thus came into contact with the most famous commander of his day. Epaminondas was a serious man, a devotee of Pythagorean philosophy, which apart from its interest in numbers and formulae made him refuse to eat meat or participate in animal sacrifice. Although an aristocrat by birth, he was not wealthy and was seen as something of an eccentric because he seemed to revel in a simple life devoted to learning and virtue. Plutarch says that Philip "comprehended his [i.e., Epaminondas's] efficiency in war and campaigns," but was neither by nature nor choice inclined to copy his "restraint, justice, magnanimity and gentleness, wherein Epaminondas was truly great."[20]

Some ancient sources say that the years in Thebes had an important influence on Philip, but they do not go into detail. Modern scholars have often gone much further, claiming that in these years he learned about military equipment and training, tactics, strategy, politics, and diplomacy. All we can definitely say is that for several years he experienced life among the elite in a leading Greek city-state. He had the chance to witness the vagaries of politics within Thebes and among the wider community of city-states, for in these years Theban prestige was at its height. Politics and war would have filled as much or more of the conversation among his hosts than ideas and culture. How much he understood and learned from all this is pure speculation.[21]

In late 368 BC or early in 367 BC—we cannot be certain given the systems of dating—Alexander II of Macedon was stabbed to death during a ritual war dance (*telesias*) held as part of a festival, a situation which inevitably put the king close to a number of armed young men. Although one man was executed for the murder, most people seem to have believed that the conspiracy was led by Ptolemy of Alorus, who is mentioned as a prominent member of Amyntas III's court on an inscription in Athens. Diodorus says that Ptolemy was a son of Amyntas, and brother to the young king. Perhaps he was the child of a third, otherwise unknown wife to Amyntas, or simply an Argead from another branch of the family, but as usual we simply do not know. Justin blames Eurydice for the murder of her own son, so some historians have identified Ptolemy as the unnamed son-in-law and lover with whom she was supposed to have conspired a few years earlier.[22]

Perdiccas was not yet old enough to succeed, so Ptolemy took charge as his regent or guardian (*epitropos*). He did not mint coins in his own name, and opinion is divided over whether or not he actually proclaimed himself king, but there is no doubt that he became in all important respects the ruler of Macedon. He may have married Eurydice, and she appears to have had a fairly public role in these years. While this might appear to confirm Justin's story of illicit and murderous passion, she may equally have had little or no choice in the matter and simply have done what was necessary to protect herself and her remaining sons. That we happen to have evidence for her dedicating a statue in a temple to a goddess of good repute may be mere chance, an attempt to quash the lies being told about her, or even bold defiance of the truth.[23]

The position of Macedonia remained weak. Pelopidas of Thebes intervened soon after the murder of Alexander II, but moderated his stance and came to terms after Ptolemy managed to bribe some of the mercenary soldiers serving with the Thebans. Another fifty hostages, including Ptolemy's son, were dispatched to Thebes, but Ptolemy remained in power. A more direct threat appeared in 367 BC when Pausanias, an exiled Argead probably from another branch of the royal family, invaded with his own force of mercenaries. This pretender mounted his campaign from the Chalcidice to the east and found substantial support, whether because of his own reputation or dislike of Ptolemy. Several Macedonian communities were swiftly captured or decided to welcome the challenger. Ptolemy lacked the strength to defeat him, so he did what so many Macedonian rulers had done in the past and looked for outside help.[24]

Iphicrates was a famous Athenian commander who had spent a lot of his life campaigning in the north as a representative of his home city and a mercenary leader. He had married a Thracian princess and at some point had dealings with Macedonia and Amyntas III, who was said to have adopted him. At the moment he happened to be in command of a squadron of Athenian warships, hovering around the coast near the city of Amphipolis, trying to reestablish an Athenian presence in the Chalcidice in spite of the hostility of the cities there. Ptolemy appealed to him for help, although our sources suggest that the lead was taken by Eurydice, who asked Iphicrates to come to her aid. Decades later the Athenian orator Aeschines boasted that he had reminded Philip of this past favor, claiming that his mother "put your brother into the arms of Iphicrates, and set you upon his knees—for you were a little boy." Then she reminded the Athenian general of her late husband Amyntas, who "made you his son and enjoyed the friendship of the city of Athens." In honor of this relationship, she begged for his protection now for her sons and Macedonia. The appeal worked and Iphicrates chased Pausanias "out of Macedonia and preserved the dynasty for you."[25]

Aeschines told the story decades later, when he was defending himself against charges of misconduct during a subsequent embassy to Philip and was keen to show that he had reminded the Macedonian monarch of Athens's past services to him and his family. Speeches, especially those made in a heated atmosphere of Athenian politics, were not noted for strict adherence to the truth, and some of his account is distinctly odd. Philip was fourteen or fifteen at the time, Perdiccas at least a year older, so that neither was little and the image of them sitting on the Athenian general highly unlikely. Apart from that, Philip was a hostage in Thebes at the time and nowhere near the royal court. On the other hand, the speech was designed to convince fellow Athenians of Philip's past goodwill, and it would have been strange and personally dangerous for Aeschines to say all this if there was no basis for the claim that Athens had helped the king's family during this crisis. Most likely he embellished rather than invented. A little earlier in the speech, Aeschines said that this was a time when Philip and Perdiccas were at risk and Eurydice "had been betrayed by those who claimed to be their friends." Perhaps this was an allusion to the murder of Alexander and takeover by Ptolemy, suggesting that the queen was a pawn caught up in a power struggle rather than the adulterous conspirator. The only mention of Ptolemy in the speech is far from positive, for almost as soon as Pausanias had been driven away, the regent collaborated with Thebes and allied with the city of Amphipolis against Athens. Aeschines called this "ungrateful and outrageous," although it was characteristic of the rapid switches of alliance made by earlier Macedonian monarchs—and by Athens itself.[26]

Ptolemy was murdered in 365 BC by Perdiccas or someone acting on his behalf, and the second of Philip's brothers now became sole ruler no longer controlled by a regent. Perhaps he had simply reached an age where he was old enough to rule without a regent or could no longer be easily controlled, prompting a power struggle which culminated in assassination. His policies did not differ from those of the dead regent and at first did not favor Athens. Instead he renewed the alliance with Thebes, and as part of this agreement Philip returned home. He would never again find himself in the hands of enemies or any foreign power.[27]

2

CRISIS

Philip was free after years as a hostage at Thebes, was now around seventeen years old, and returned to a Macedonia ruled by his brother, Perdiccas. This was an important moment, although it is impossible to say how he felt, what his character was at this age, or even much about his appearance. Few images of Philip survive, and all depict him late in life, his face lined and missing an eye. In 1977 archaeologists working at Vergina, the site of ancient Aegae, dug into a great tumulus and concluded that one of the sealed tombs within belonged to Philip and contained his cremated remains. From this a famous reconstruction was made of the features of this man in the hope of gaining a sense of the person who turned Macedonia into such a formidable kingdom. The identification is not certain, but the case is a good one.

This tomb, Tomb II, was one of three hidden by the tumulus, and all three are likely to be royal and date from the latter part of the fourth century BC, which narrows down the possibilities when it comes to who was interred in each one. Tomb I had been broken into and plundered in antiquity, and among the bones were those of a man in his forties, who was some six feet high, which was unusually, although not exceptionally, tall for the ancient world. These remains had not been cremated and many believe that they were not the original occupant of the tomb. The man in Tomb II was also middle-aged, but at five foot seven or five foot eight, he was very much average size for a Greek or Macedonian. The initial analysis of the bones suggested a serious injury to the right eye and perhaps a leg wound, although a minority of those to examine the remains subsequently have disagreed. On balance, the occupant of Tomb II probably is Philip II, which means that the reconstruction of his face may give a hint of his real appearance. Yet caution is needed, for much about any such reconstruction must be conjectural in the circumstances, whether it be the shape and size of the nose or ears or the complexion and coloring. No ancient source mentions the color of Philip's hair or eyes. As an adult he sported a thick beard, which was normal for an adult Macedonian male and was fairly universal throughout the wider Greek world, so the seventeen-year-old may already have grown one.

More is known about Alexander's appearance, which helps to suggest some possibilities, for the father may have resembled the son. Alexander's hair was said to be blond or tawny like a lion's, and several monarchs from the dynasties set up by his Successors were also described as golden-haired. A mosaic from Pompeii copied from a fourth century BC Greek original depicts Alexander with medium brown hair, although it is quite possible that the color on the mosaic did not match the original or had faded over time. The paintings from the royal tombs at Aegae show a wide range of hair colors, from black and dark brown through to fair and even distinctly chestnut. All of this suggests that Macedonians were not of any single complexion or coloring and that Philip's hair and eyes could have been almost any shade.[1]

In 365 BC the young Philip was not yet grown to full maturity, although he was surely fit and strong from his active life and time in the gymnasium. He would not have had the marks of a hard life and a succession of injuries, so he was not yet the stern, commanding presence suggested by the reconstruction of the dead man. All in all the young Philip remains a shadowy figure, and we can only guess at his appearance, let alone his attitudes to his older brother and mother when he returned to his homeland. Eurydice is only mentioned once more in our sources, in a passage from Justin that is even more dubious than usual, and we do not know when she died. An especially rich tomb made for a female burial at Aegae in the fourth century BC has been dubbed the Tomb of Eurydice. While this is perfectly possible, as yet there is no direct evidence to associate it with her.[2]

Philip had returned to his homeland and his family, and at some point he was given charge of a region by his brother. Scholars speculate that this was in the east, including the border facing the Thracians and the Greek colonies on the coast. If this is right, then the suggestion that he was given command of some troops as well would make sense to defend royal control against these possible threats. Perdiccas III had an infant son, and it is impossible to know whether Philip was the trusted brother and friend happy to serve the family interest or seen as a potential rival to be placated and watched carefully, albeit less of a threat than the others waiting in the wings. The king was a devotee of Plato, and greatly honored one of the philosopher's pupils, a man named Euphraeus. He chose as dinner companions men able to discuss geometry and philosophy. Philip may well have been able to do this, but little in his later life suggests that he relished such earnest gatherings, and there are hints of squabbles between the brothers.[3]

Perdiccas III decided to back Amphipolis and other cities in the Chalcidice against the Athenians. Around 364 BC an Athenian force struck back and the king was forced to accept peace terms imposed by Athens, so that he switched sides and contributed soldiers to aid an unsuccessful Athenian attack on Amphipolis. After this, he abandoned the new alliance and sided with the Chalcidian cities once again, only to be defeated by another Athenian expedition. Perdiccas begged for peace, was granted it, but within a few years was flouting the agreement. He dispatched soldiers to help garrison Amphipolis, which was under renewed attack from the Athenians.[4]

We have more evidence for relations with Athens than other matters during these years, but this was far from being Perdiccas III's only concern, and there were several bouts of fighting against the Illyrians. At one stage, the king came to believe that his men were surrendering too readily, confident that they would be ransomed and return home. Perdiccas sent ambassadors to discuss the terms of this, but he does not seem to have wanted to secure the men's release. When the delegation returned empty-handed, he had them tell everyone that the Illyrians had refused to take payment and executed the captives instead. The deception is supposed to have stiffened the resolve of the rest of Perdiccas's troops to fight rather than surrender.[5]

In 360 BC a large army of Illyrians invaded Molossia, one of Macedonia's close neighbors and equally exposed to the predations of the tribes. The Molossians managed to save many of their people and ambushed a substantial number of raiders, but just like paying tribute, this did not end the threat. In the past the Illyrians had inflicted heavy defeats on the Molossians of neighboring Epirus, and they kept coming back. King Bardylis was now well into his nineties but remained tightly in control of his territory and able to field large numbers of warriors. While it may seem unlikely that such an elderly man actually took the field, around the same time a King Agesilaus II of Sparta died aged about eighty-four while bringing his army home from a campaign in Egypt. Life expectancy was low in the ancient world, but some tough individuals beat the odds and remained active into old age.[6]

Upper Macedonia was Bardylis's next target, and Perdiccas responded by mustering a large army and confronting the invaders. A battle was fought in the late summer of 360 BC or perhaps spring of 359 BC; there is the usual uncertainty over the precise date according to our calendar. Nor are any details known of this battle, and whether it was an open encounter or an ambush, but there is no doubt of the catastrophic defeat suffered by the Macedonians. Perdiccas was killed—the first Macedonian monarch known to have died at the hands of a foreign enemy, and we cannot say whether the defeat began with his death or whether he fell when his army was already beaten. Either way, some 4,000 of his men died alongside him, and in the aftermath the cowed survivors could do nothing to stop the Illyrians from plundering freely. Macedonia's other enemies also scented weakness.[7]

Perdiccas III's son Amyntas was a very small boy, unable to take over. Instead, Philip was acclaimed as leader. Initially this may have been as *epitropos* on behalf of his nephew, a claim made by Justin and perhaps implied elsewhere. Yet he may have been named king from the start, perhaps with the assumption that Amyntas was earmarked as his successor until he had produced a son of his own. Sadly there is no detailed description of how Philip became leader of the Macedonians, which makes it even harder to settle the question of his precise status after the death of Perdiccas. Most of the evidence for choosing a new king comes from the era of Alexander and especially the events after the latter's death without an obvious heir, making it hard to know how much was well-established tradition and how much a product of a wholly new situation for an army whose conquests had taken it so far from home. Scholarly debate has a tendency to polarize between those who believe that the Macedonians had strongly entrenched constitutional practices and others who prefer to see everything as far looser, dependent on the strength or weakness of individual kings. No doubt the truth lies somewhere in between, since it is hard to imagine any society lasting so long without creating strong and deep-seated traditions and conventions. The most obvious of these was the belief that only an Argead could become king.[8]

An assembly (*ecclesia*) of the Macedonians, adult men who when called upon served in the royal army or had done so in the past, gathered to acclaim a new king, marking their approval by clashing spear shafts against shields. How this all worked is impossible to say, and we simply do not know whether this was little more than a formality or in any meaningful way a forum for genuine debate and decision making. Some scholars have suggested that the assembly showed a strong preference in favor of the late king's eldest son as successor, perhaps because they felt that the monarch's sacred aura passed most strongly to his closest blood relation. Others deny this, or at least feel that in the desperate situation following Perdiccas's disastrous defeat, common sense would overrule any sentiment of this sort when an adult brother of the king was available.[9]

In favor of a period as *epitropos* is an inscription from Boeotia, the Theban-dominated region of central Greece, which recorded visitors and donors to an oracle. The inscription includes an "Amyntas, son of Perdiccas, king of the Macedonians" and could refer to Philip's nephew. Otherwise we have Justin's explicit state-ment and differing versions of the length of Philip's reign, which can be interpreted to support around two years or so as regent before he became king. Although Justin is far from the most reliable of sources, the claim of a regency is an odd one to invent. Against this, if Amyntas was named as king, then no coins were minted bearing his name, nor is it clear how and when he was removed and formally replaced by Philip as monarch in his own right rather than as *epitropos*. Amyntas was clearly not seen as too dangerous a rival, for he remained at court and when old enough married one of Philip's daughters. Given the willingness of other Argeads to kill their close kin this is surprising, most of all if he had actually been king, although it may simply tell us of Philip's growing self-confidence as over time success followed success.[10]

Hindsight makes Philip the obvious choice to succeed his brother, but we should remember that he was just twenty-two or twenty-three and as yet unproven. He had administered a region for his brother, and as a result commanded some troops. Control of an organized force, however small, strengthened his hand in the aftermath of the death of the king and the costly rout of his army. While it is possible that Philip had taken an active part in some of Perdiccas's campaigns, there is no direct evidence of this and we cannot assume that he was able to boast of any personal military achievements. Apart from his nephew, there were other Argeads to consider, not least his three half brothers, the sons of Gygaea. If these made a bid for power then it was quickly defeated. The eldest, Archelaus, was executed by Philip, most likely around this time, and the other two escaped into exile. More serious challenges came from outside the kingdom, so were not on the spot to chal-lenge the decision of the assembly. Pausanius, the man defeated with the help of Iphicrates, reappeared, this time backed by a Thracian king. Argaeus, most likely the same man who had briefly supplanted Philip's father Amyntas, also renewed his claim to rule and was backed by Athens with ships, men, and money.[11]

Philip was chosen to lead Macedonia, presumably with sup-port from the majority of influential men at court and by the acclamation of the assembly. Rarely did the Macedonians refer to their monarch as king (*basileus*), and instead he would simply be Philip, son of Amyntas. Although we cannot be sure of his status, the Macedonians knew who Philip was and what powers he held and what influence he wielded. In many ways it does not matter whether he was regent or king, for either way it was up to him to deal with the usurpers and defend the kingdom. Bardylis of Illyria had overrun and occupied large parts of Upper Macedonia and was well placed to raid further afield. The Paeonians, another neighboring tribal kingdom, also began to send plundering expeditions across the border.[12]

The bigger threats took a while to develop, since no one had expected Perdiccas to be killed or Macedonia to be plunged into the uncertainty inevitable at the start of a new reign. If the defeat happened late in 360 BC, then autumn and winter soon followed and warfare was rarely continued during these months, giving Philip a breathing space. Even if the king died in early 359 BC, then there was still bound to be a lull before the storm. Both of the pretenders needed time to find allies, who then assisted them in raising armies. The Illyrians had won a great victory, and no doubt wished to return home to celebrate and enjoy the spoils of success. This was simply one glorious episode in the long predatory conflict with Macedonia and other vulnerable regions; it was never a war to the death, but rather an ongoing source of profit. Bardylis took some territory but could look forward to a renewal of payments of tribute from whoever succeeded Perdiccas, with the option of launching fresh attacks if the Macedonians failed to comply. Whatever the details of his status, Philip was now in charge of a kingdom that seemed on the verge of being torn apart by its neighbors.[13]

Philip had a short breathing space to consolidate his hold on power and prepare to meet the onslaught. That it would come from a disparate and mutually hostile array of opponents did not make it any less daunting. Nor was the condition of Macedonia encouraging after long decades of weakness. The 4,000 soldiers who had died with Perdiccas represented at least a third of the royal army, and most likely included many of the best men. The survivors were understandably demoralized, while the quality of

Macedonian soldiers was mixed even in more stable times. For well over a century Macedonia had enjoyed a reputation for producing fine cavalrymen. These were drawn from those wealthy enough to afford a mount and body armor, men who learned to ride at a young age. In contrast, Macedonian infantry were viewed with contempt as a poorly armed and unskilled rabble. Archelaus I (413–399 BC) had tried to address this weakness by issuing his soldiers with standard equipment paid for by the state, but any improvements achieved by this do not seem to have outlived him. Philip's brother Alexander II made another attempt, organizing his infantry into a close-order phalanx like that used by the Greek hoplites who had dominated the battlefield since the fifth century BC; he also granted them an honorific title to foster their morale. He suffered too many defeats and was murdered too soon for there to be any lasting improvement.[14]

The weakness of Macedonia in this era cannot be overstressed. Alexander II had only minted coins in bronze, and Perdiccas III mainly in bronze with some issues of silver coins conforming to Persian weights. This is in marked contrast to the plentiful silver coinage minted by Bardylis, and the rich gold, silver, and bronze issues from the cities of the Chalcidian League. The wider region was rich in natural resources. In the early fifth century BC Alexander I had controlled a silver mine that yielded one talent of precious metal a day, but this now lay in territory no longer ruled by the kings of Macedon. Iron and other minerals were still readily available, although it is clear that access to silver was greatly reduced. Gains made in recent years scarcely compensated for the scale of such losses. An exiled Athenian politician helped Perdiccas III to reform the sale of the franchises to collect harbor duties, doubling the income from twenty talents to forty a year, a gain that was sufficiently large to be worth noting. Philip's brothers were not poverty stricken, but they did bequeath a treasury far weaker than those of earlier monarchs.[15]

Yet Macedonia had the potential to be very wealthy. The climate even of Lower Macedonia is more continental than Mediterranean, giving it greater annual rainfall and less extreme heat in the summer. Olive trees, one of the central pillars of Greek agriculture, grew in only a few small areas within the kingdom, but most other crops, including cereals and vines, flourished, and there were extensive areas of good pasturage. In Upper Macedonia, the balance shifted more in favor of animal husbandry than agriculture, but even so there was plenty of fertile farmland. In all regions the population was reasonably large by ancient standards and able to feed itself from local produce.

In southern Greece decent arable land was in such short supply that woods had long since been felled as even marginal ground was put under cultivation. In contrast Macedonia had plenty of good farmland and extensive forests survived, with a useful mix of deciduous and evergreen trees. These provided fuel and building material for the population, but were a very valuable resource for export. Any major building project required long timbers for roof beams, and such things were simply not available locally in most of Greece. Timber was even more vital for shipbuilding, with keels, frames, masts, and oars all needing the right size and quality of wood. The forests also provided the pitch used to seal the hulls. The philosopher Theophrastus wrote that "the best timber which comes into Greece for the carpenter's use is Macedonian."[16]

Timber, pitch, and minerals all appear to have been royal monopolies. Much of the land was also owned by the king, although he might grant it to individuals in small or large estates and permit them to take the revenue from it. All this meant that in stable times a strong king controlled substantial and highly profitable resources, which provided a generous income. Insecurity and instability eroded this, weakening each king and making it harder for them to assert control. Under Alexander I, Upper and Lower Macedonia were united. By the end of the fifth century BC, the regional kingdoms of Upper Macedonia were loose allies of the king of Macedon, sometimes willing to accept his rule but at other times joining his enemies to fight for their independence. Since 399 BC prolonged weakness had loosened the bonds even further. The kings were simply not strong enough to be worth courting for the regional monarchs, nor powerful enough to assert control. Over time the regions became more and more independent. Some looked elsewhere for friends better able to offer protection against the Illyrians and others.

The Orestae joined the Molossian tribes, describing themselves as Orestae Molossi rather than Orestae Macedones. There were also old links of culture and alliance to neighbors like the Molossians, many as strong or stronger than the bonds to Macedonia. Similarly, Greek cities on the coast that had at times acknowledged the king asserted their own independence, often marking this by minting coins in their own name.[17]

Philip took charge of a shrunken and impoverished kingdom surrounded by enemies, all of whom gave every impression of being much stronger. Later it was claimed that a prophecy foretold that Macedonia would become great under the rule of a son of Amyntas. At the time, most people doubtless expected a continuation of brief reigns by kings dominated by external powers. For its neighbors and the Greeks to the south, the death of one Macedonian king and the creation of a new regime were of interest only because they offered opportunities for gain. Neither Perdiccas, nor at the moment Philip, held any great significance in the wider sweep of things. Macedonia mattered to outsiders only because of its location and access to natural resources. This, rather than any sentiment, was the reason why stronger states and leaders were willing to back pretenders and intervene in the politics of the kingdom.[18]

In 359 BC Macedonia was weak, and Philip simply could not hope to confront and beat all the threats facing him simultaneously. Fortunately, his opponents needed time to prepare almost as much as he did. Diodorus Siculus claimed that he began by talking, "bringing together the Macedonians in a series of assemblies and exhorting them with eloquent speeches to be men. . . . He was courteous . . . and sought to win over the multitudes by his gifts and his promises." Even Philip's enemies would later admit that the king was charming and charismatic, and this was an early display of the force of his personality, when he most needed to exude confidence. Leadership is never simply about a leader imposing his will on others, and the audience of Macedonians desperately wanted to be inspired and to believe that there really was hope of success.[19]

Encouragement was accompanied by practical preparation to confront the Macedonians' enemies in battle. The development of the army that would win Philip's later battles and under Alexander sweep across the world was not instant, but the process began in these early months. Diodorus tells us that Philip introduced new tactics and equipment, specifically forming his infantry in a phalanx, but one that was unlike anything seen before. Macedon lacked a hoplite class—the mainstay of the armies of Greek city-states—composed of men able to provide their own equipment and hone their skills in the gymnasium. Instead of relying on armored spearmen fully capable of fighting as individuals, Philip issued a new weapon, the *sarissa*, a pike some sixteen to eighteen feet long and held in both hands. It had a large iron spearpoint and, crucially, a heavy counterweight on the butt, allowing it to be held far back so that most of the weapon projected in front of the man wielding it.[20]

The sarissa was cumbersome, almost useless for an individual and designed for a group of men in close formation, standing shoulder to shoulder. Because of its size, it could not be used with the large and heavy *hoplon*, so this was replaced by a smaller shield, no more than two feet in diameter, which was strapped to the left arm and shoulder. At least at this early stage, few men in the Macedonian phalanx wore armor, and even helmets may have been rare. A pikeman in the front rank stood with his sarissa held underarm. He was able to jab at the enemy, but could do little to defend himself. In the meantime the sarissa kept the enemy at a distance, because even if an opponent managed to break it or dodge past, the spearheads from the pikes of the next four ranks projected in front of the formation. A hoplite would have to get past all of these spearpoints before he brought his own spear in reach of the pikemen in the front rank. Later on, the standard formation for the Macedonian variant of the phalanx was eight ranks deep, and it is quite likely that this was true from the start. The men in the ranks behind the fifth angled their pikes forward to offer some protection against thrown missiles.

There was nothing subtle about Philip's pike phalanx, which was designed to attack the enemy head on, confronting them with serried rows of pike heads. In this formation the individual soldier did not need great skill with his weapon. What mattered was the strength with which he delivered each thrust and, crucially, keeping in rank so that no gaps developed in the phalanx. The sarissa was awkward and far from the handiest weapon for attacking, especially compared to a spear or sword. That did not really matter. The enemy were held off at a distance where it was hard for them even to strike at the Macedonians, while the sarissas could and did inflict wounds, especially to the face. The mere approach of a dense phalanx with its hedgehog of glittering spearheads was itself intimidating; in the second century BC one experienced Roman commander described it as the most terrifying thing he had ever seen.

In the early days Philip had to train his men to stay in formation during the advance, to keep their ranks and files, and then for the front rank to jab and keep on jabbing at the enemy. The basics of what was required could be achieved in weeks. After a few months of drill, confidence and familiarity would grow. In later years Philip's and Alexander's phalanxes drilled and drilled until they became highly flexible, but that took a long time and required the creation of new drills. The first steps were much simpler, suitable for training men who were not full-time soldiers but farmers, herdsmen, and craftsmen who answered the king's call to muster.[21]

Philip may well have invented the sarissa, at least in the form it was adopted by his army. The Thracians sometimes used exceptionally long spears, and Iphicrates had also given longer-than-usual spears to the mercenary soldiers he had led with great success. In neither case does it seem that these weapons were held two-handed, so the sarissa was clearly distinct and new. Philip had seen military training at Thebes, most notably of the Sacred Band, an elite formation of 300 semiprofessional hoplites. He may have copied some of their techniques for his infantry bodyguard, who appear to have fought as hoplites and not adopted the sarissa or the smaller shield. Otherwise, it may simply have taught him the value of practicing for war as much as possible rather than offering specific methods to copy.[22]

Apart from the close-order infantry, the better-off provided cavalry for the Macedonian army and there may well have been archers and other specialist troops, and perhaps a few mercenaries.

All could be trained, and Philip could do his best to instill confidence. Yet he was unproven as a commander and so was the army, while battle was always a risk. The simplicity of the tactics of the sarissa phalanx ultimately depended on the willingness of the soldiers to keep ranks, close with the enemy, and stay in contact until the other side gave way. Even a moment of panic could quickly cause the whole formation to collapse. Greek generals led from the front, and all the indications are that Macedonian kings did the same, which meant that even victory could come at a high price; Epaminondas died at Mantineia, while the famous Spartan Brasidas was one of only a handful of fatalities on his own side when he routed an Athenian army outside Amphipolis in 422 BC.[23]

More than seventy years later the Athenians still coveted their former colony of Amphipolis, which had allied with Sparta and thrown off Athenian rule. Sensing that regaining the city was their real goal, and that backing Argaeus in his bid for the Macedonian throne was merely a means to this end, Philip decided to weaken their resolve. He recalled the garrison sent to the city by his brother and formally declared that the city was autonomous. Ostensibly this renounced any Macedonian claim to Amphipolis, so that even if Argaeus succeeded in becoming king he would not be able to hand over the city to Athens. In the meantime, envoys went to the Paeonian king and also to the Thracian king; they were backing Pausanias, the other pretender to the Macedonian throne. Philip gave both monarchs substantial bribes. The gifts were enough to persuade the Paeonians to cease raiding his territory, at least for the moment. Like a lot of successful leaders, Philip was lucky; in Thrace the formidable King Cotys, who had united the tribes, had just died, and because several of his sons were battling to succeed him, they did not present a unified threat. The prince who was supporting Pausanias preferred to take Philip's gold and silver rather than risk war on the pretender's behalf in the hope of gaining plunder and influence. Pausanias vanishes from our sources at this point, so perhaps the deal was sealed with his death.[24]

In 359 BC an Athenian expedition landed at their ally Methone, a city near Pydna on the coast of Macedon. Argaeus brought his own mercenaries, and there was also a force of 3,000 hoplites supplied by

Athens: many mercenaries, but at least some of whom were citizens, all backed by a squadron of warships. This was a substantial force, its scale in keeping with earlier Athenian expeditions to the region. After disembarking, they divided their strength. The bulk of the Athenians remained under their commander, Mantias, at Methone, while Argaeus advanced with his own men and some Athenian observers. He force-marched to Aegae, some eighteen or nineteen miles away, and it is just possible that the decision to leave the main force behind was to avoid making his reliance on foreign aid too obvious. Arriving outside the traditional capital of the kingdom, he declared himself king, hoping that the locals would come out and acclaim him. They ignored him, whether from trust or affection for Philip, dislike of Argaeus, or plain doubts about his chances.

Argaeus retreated, but his men must have been tired and dispirited, and by this time Philip knew of his presence. It was his turn to move quickly, and he caught and defeated the pretender before he could get back to Methone and his allies. Although it was little more than a large skirmish, Philip had won his first victory. He was generous to those Athenian citizens with the column, allowing them to return to Methone. Argaeus and any exiled Macedonians serving him were not so fortunate, and Philip insisted that they be handed over to him, presumably for execution. Meanwhile Mantias and his men tried to capture Amphipolis, but failed.[25]

Luck is one thing, but successful leaders need to be good at exploiting the opportunities that come their way. Soon afterward, the Paeonian king died. Philip had bought peace from him, but he now realized that the Paeonians would more than likely be preoccupied in squabbling over the succession. He mustered a large army and advanced against the Paeonians, defeating them in battle and forcing their leaders to swear allegiance to him. Buoyed by this second success, Philip now turned to deal with Bardylis's Illyrians, and—most probably early in 358 BC—he summoned the Macedonians to muster under arms after a winter spent in their homes. At an assembly, he made a speech encouraging them and promising victory, before advancing at the head of an army of 10,000 infantry and 600 cavalry.[26]

This time it was not Philip but his opponent who preferred to talk. Bardylis sent to propose peace on the basis that each monarch would hold on to the territory he controlled. Philip rejected the offer, demanding that the Illyrians retire entirely from Upper Macedonia, and in response Bardylis gathered his forces, which suggests that he was more than half expecting to fight. He had 10,000 infantry and 500 cavalry, although the latter appear a lot less capable than their Macedonian counterparts. On the other hand, he and his men remembered their great victory over Perdiccas and were bound to be confident that they could rout the same enemy once again.[27]

In the fifth century BC the Spartan general Brasidas had been dismissive of Illyrian warriors, claiming that they were far less formidable than they looked to inexperienced eyes. Their battle cries were frightening, and they postured and waved their weapons in the hope of frightening their enemies, but he dismissed this as empty bluster. Steady troops would ignore all this, and whereas civilized Greeks fought in ordered ranks, each man dependent on his neighbors and unwilling to let them down, the Illyrian warriors were a loose mob. Brasidas assured his men that "since flight and attack are considered equally honourable with them, their courage cannot be put to the test. Besides a mode of fighting in which everyone is his own master will provide a man the best excuse for saving himself." Several generations later, it was possible that the Illyrians had adopted closer formations in battle, and there is some evidence that many wealthier warriors adopted hoplite-style helmets and armor, but even so their style of warfare continued to favor individual heroism.[28]

The two armies met in fairly open country, most likely near Lyncus. Bardylis had waited for the Macedonians to come to him, perhaps still hoping that Philip would make concessions rather than risk battle. A lot of the Macedonian troops were the sort of inexperienced soldiers that Brasidas had claimed were most easily intimidated by the noisy demonstrations of tribal warriors. Philip trusted to the training his men had received and, unwilling to talk, deployed his army to face the Illyrians. For a while the Macedonians yelled their own challenges back at the enemy; some ancient commentators claimed that you could tell the outcome of a battle by listening to the shouts raised by each side.

Philip advanced, ordering his cavalry to sweep around the Illyrians' flanks. Bardylis's cavalry are not mentioned, which suggests that they either gave way or dismounted to join the infantry. The Macedonian infantry were formed with the royal bodyguard on the right. Seeing the threat of encirclement, Bardylis pulled his men back until they formed a large hollow square—a difficult maneuver that may suggest that the warriors still formed up in a fairly open order. Philip led his bodyguard, which moved faster than the rest of the line, most of which consisted of pikemen. This may have been deliberate, mirroring tactics pioneered by the Thebans Epaminondas and Pelopidas when they defeated the Spartans at Leuctra in 371 BC, or simply a reflection of the better training and confidence of his elite troops. He struck on the enemy's flank, on the vulnerable corner of their formation.

Diodorus tells that the battle was hard fought and that the combat swayed back and forth for some time, with heavy casualties on both sides. There is no reason to disbelieve him. Even Philip's best troops were not especially experienced, while the Illyrians were confident of beating the Macedonians once again. The sarissa kept the warriors at a distance, but unless the pikemen were very determined and had great stamina, they would soon tire and struggle to inflict many wounds. Combat tended to be over quickly or bog down into a slogging match as each side became exhausted. The side most able to hold on and keep going forward to renew the fight was most likely to win.

Philip and the bodyguard fought well, and after some time his cavalry managed to break into the square. This was no mean achievement in an era when horsemen were not expected to defeat determined men on foot in a head-to-head encounter. Fatigue, and the continued aggression of the Macedonians, meant that this time it was the Illyrians who started to give way. Once the formation was broken, it quickly dissolved into panicked flight. Diodorus claims that 7,000 Illyrian warriors died in the battle or in the vigorous pursuit launched by Philip's men. The square formation would have made it harder than usual for men to escape once the army collapsed, so that a good many of these casualties are likely to have fallen close to the battlefield. Philip eventually recalled his men and began to deal with his own wounded. In properly Greek fashion he set up a trophy on the spot to mark his victory. Showing a similar understanding of how things were done—and an acknowledgment of his appalling losses—Bardylis sent envoys to beg for peace. Philip reclaimed all the lost territory of Upper Macedonia as the price of granting it.[29]

This was a major victory against a truly formidable opponent, and although we know of the successes to come, we should not forget that Philip had taken a big gamble. For the moment all the pretenders were defeated or in exile, and the immediate threats had been beaten off. In the process Philip had begun to recover lost regions and assert his dominance over neighbors. He had survived the first crisis. That did not mean that he was secure.

3

MACEDONIAN, GREEK, AND BARBARIAN

For the first time in generations, the Macedonians had smashed an Illyrian army, but that did not make Philip safe or his kingdom secure. To understand the threats and pressures he faced, it is important to pause the narrative for a moment and look at the place of Macedonia, its kings and people in Greece as a whole, and also at the wider world. This means going back in time, for few cultures are truly static, and the dynamism of the Greek city-states meant that there was constant political change and shifts in the balance of power.

Macedonia lay on the fringe of the Greek world, and opinion was divided over whether the Macedonians were Greeks or barbarians. Linguistically it ought to have been simple. The Macedonians spoke Greek, their names were Greek, and whenever they committed anything to writing it was in the Greek language. In Lower Macedonia they spoke a dialect with a distinct accent and many unusual expressions, which although definitely Greek was barely intelligible to outsiders. The peoples of the Upper Macedonian regions mainly used a form of western Greek, much like the Molossians and other communities in that area. The royal family and most aristocrats also knew the more widely spoken Attic Greek, and when Macedonian embassies went to Athens they did not require the services of translators to understand and be understood. No doubt many Macedonians also were more or less fluent in the tongues of their neighbors, such as the Illyrians and Thracians. Ethnically the population was a mix, and this would only increase under Philip's rule. When it came to religion, Mount Olympus, the legendary home of the gods, lay on Macedonia's southern border, and the Macedonians worshipped Zeus, Dionysus, and the other Olympian gods and goddesses just like other Greeks. In all these ways they stood apart from the Thracians and Illyrians, but there were also profound differences in culture and society between the Macedonians and the wider Greek world.[1]

As always, the evidence is heavily weighted in favor of Athens, skewing our sense of what was normal. The idea of what it meant to be Greek no doubt varied a great deal over time and from region to region. In its origins it was a simple division between those who spoke a form of the Greek language and everyone else—the barbarians whose words sounded like the bleating of a flock of sheep. Many cultures throughout history have seen themselves as normal and the rest of the world as different and inevitably inferior. (I am reluctant to employ the overused and far too simplistic catchall term "the other," since this really explains very little and ignores the subtle degrees of attitude in most human beings.) Greek observers like Herodotus could note the great antiquity of Egyptian culture, marvel at its monuments and the old secrets of its religion, yet still see the Egyptians as barbarians. The same was true of the population of the Persian Empire for all its might and wealth. Early on the sense of what it meant to be Greek grew far beyond mere language.[2]

It was not simply ethnic, although there was a strong sense of ancestry and past history, which blurred with what we would see as myth. Tradition maintained that there were distinct groups of Greeks, notably Dorians like the Spartans and Ionians like the Athenians, who spoke distinct dialects and had their own cults. Every community also had its foundation story, often involving heroes and divine assistance, and any mention of a people in Homer's epics was especially treasured. The community in the specific form of the city-state (*polis*, plural *poleis*) became central to Greeks' sense of their own identity early on. A linguistic element and some of the ethnic element remained, since other peoples, such as the Etruscans or Latins in Italy, also had urban cultures and their own versions of the city-states, but they were never considered Greek.

The development of the polis is not at all well understood, but it emerged as a self-governing state with its own laws, constitution, magistrates, and official cults. Physically it was a city, usually fortified, and always controlling an area of territory outside the walls. There might be villages within that territory, but none of these had a significant separate identity: they were part of the polis. The smallest city-states had populations numbering in hundreds, but most boasted several thousand people, while a handful grew to be even larger. In most cases one or more other independent—even rival or hostile—cities lay within sight and certainly within a couple of hours' walk. No one is quite sure, but there were at the very least more than 400 Greek poleis. Most lay in the Greek peninsula itself, but over the centuries colonists had gone out to found new city-states on the Black Sea shore and widely across the Mediterranean coastlines. In Philip's day southern Italy and much of Sicily had been Greek for centuries, and there was also the great city of Massilia (modern Marseilles) on the south coast of Gaul, Emporion and other communities in Spain, as well as cities in Asia Minor. Some colonies failed or were wiped out by the indigenous peoples while others flourished, so that the wider Greek world covered a large area.

A polis was not a community of equals. Slavery in various forms was omnipresent and its existence never seriously questioned. Slaves were not citizens, had no political rights, and were rarely given their freedom. Sparta's remarkable military machine relied on work being done by the helots, a subject serf population descended from the existing inhabitants of the area when it was conquered by the Spartans. Many cities were reluctant to grant citizenship to foreigners living and working there, even when these became permanent residents. Freeborn women were citizens, and their rights varied from community to community, but while they might participate in some official cults, they were barred from politics, unable to vote or hold office. There was an intimate connection between political rights and the obligation to fight in the army whenever the polis went to war, and this was one major pretext for the marginalization of citizen women.

Monarchy was rare by the fifth and fourth centuries BC. Where it survived—as in Sparta, which had two kings at a time—it tended to be part of a mixed constitution, involving councils of elders and popular assemblies. There were tyrants, men who had seized or inherited supreme power and who were more or less restrained by the law depending on local circumstances. Such men tended to thrive overseas but were rare in southern Greece. Some cities were oligarchies, where the greatest power was in the hands of a restricted group, usually a clique of wealthy aristocratic families. Others were democracies, in which the people or *demos* were supposed to be supreme, electing magistrates and voting directly on many matters great and small. Just who constituted the demos varied considerably, and the right to vote, let alone stand for election, was usually tied to wealth. Distinctions between types of constitution were often blurred, so that a tightly restricted demos of the better-off was akin more to oligarchy than to some of the more radical democracies. Internal revolution was fairly common as different groups seized power and the constitution changed.

Greek city-states were inherently unstable. They were also warlike: a sense of shared Hellenic culture never prevented city-states from frequently and enthusiastically going to war with each other. This had helped to create, and then continually reinforced, the importance of military service as a central part of citizenship. Political rights were the preserve of those who were willing to fight for the state in the most important and dangerous role. Opinion is divided as to how much warfare shaped the polis, or whether the polis created a distinct form of warfare. At its heart was the pitched battle, decided by a clash of heavily armed and armored hoplites formed up in a dense line or phalanx. The name hoplite came from the *hoplon*, a bronze-faced circular wooden shield some three feet in diameter. This sheltered the man carrying it, but also helped to protect the man on either side as long as they kept close together in line. In addition, a hoplite wore a bronze helmet sometimes covering his face apart from eye slits, wore a metal or heavy fabric cuirass, and sometimes greaves on his lower legs. He was primarily a spearman, wielding a seven-to-eight-foot spear that he used to thrust.[3]

In the fifth century, Herodotus has a Persian commander express amazement at the Greeks' style of fighting, claiming that they fight wars "most senselessly . . . in their wrongheadedness and folly. When they have declared war against each other, they come down to the fairest and most level ground that they can find and there they fight." Exaggerating wildly, he then claimed that the losses in such battles were catastrophic, with the victors suffering heavily and the losers virtually annihilated. More reasonably, he argued that since they all spoke the same language, Greeks ought to be able to settle their differences peacefully rather than through war, but if they had to fight, at least they ought to use cunning and fight from strong positions.[4]

All this is a caricature, written for Greeks proud of their subsequent triumph over the mighty Persian Empire, but there are elements of truth within it. A hoplite panoply was fairly expensive, and it was the duty of each man to equip himself. This meant that under normal circumstances poorer citizens could not be hoplites or join the city's phalanx. Originally most hoplites were farmers who owned a decent-sized plot of land and were aided by their family and a number of slaves. Such men were not professional soldiers and did not wish to be away from home for too long, especially at labor-intensive times like harvest. There was little collective training, so the simple tactics of a phalanx were ideally suited. Each side's hoplites deployed in a single long line, eight or more ranks deep, before one or both advanced into contact. An army reliant on such part-time soldiers was best suited to a fairly brief and ideally decisive campaign. In southern Greece the open plains needed by a phalanx are rare, which meant that battles tended to occur on or near the same sites generation after generation, at the most convenient spots on the routes between cities. Both sides formed up, advanced to contact, and within an hour or so one or the other tended to collapse and flee. The hoplite panoply was heavy and uncomfortable; combined with the stress of combat and the heat of the day, this meant that men were soon exhausted. Victory went to the side left in possession of the field and able to set up a trophy of victory. The losers acknowledged defeat by ask-ing permission to recover their dead, a task that needed to be done quickly in the heat of the Greek summer.[5]

Tactics were simple, and after forming the phalanx and decid-ing how deep it would be, most generals stationed themselves in the front rank, unable to do much more than set an example and inspire the men closest to them. Skirmishers and cavalry rarely played much part on the day of battle. A properly formed phalanx would not be broken by any horsemen fielded by a city-state, and the missiles of skirmishers were little more than a nuisance to the well-protected hoplites. Skirmishers were drawn from the poor, and their marginal role in a pitched battle justified their marginal role in politics. Cavalrymen tended to be drawn from well-to-do aristo-crats, men not only able to afford a horse, but the time to learn to ride properly. Yet the glory in battle went to hoplites, so that many men who could have afforded to serve as horsemen chose instead to join the phalanx and fight on foot.

At least in the early days of democracy in the sixth century BC, the demos was effectively the hoplite class, even if we cannot say whether it was the political or military reform that came first. Hoplite farmers elected their civil and military leaders and went out to do battle against a phalanx of their counterparts from rival cities. Aristocracies adapted to the new situation, joining the pha-lanx in battle, and through their money and connections provided a disproportionately large share of elected magistrates.

City-states were aggressive and unstable, and even democracies were grossly unequal societies by our standards, yet still in this era Greek communities could boast so many staggering achievements. Among the Greeks and nowhere else was the idea of democracy created and put into practice. They discussed and analyzed the con-cept as well as other political ideas, just as they began to study and dissect abstract concepts and the world around them in a way no one else had done. They produced art, architecture, literature, and theater unlike anything that had come before. Familiarity should not obscure just how extraordinary this explosion of creativity was.

The same innate competitiveness, the desire to win glory (*aristeia*) by showing yourself to be better than those around you, fueled the good and the bad of Greek culture. Honor and status mattered for cities and for individuals. The Olympic Games are famous in part because of their modern revival, but they were just one of a cycle of major Panhellenic festivals involving competitions in artistic performances as well as sport. Homer's heroes raced and dueled against each other, and the "anger of Achilles" that shapes the story of the *Iliad* began with a slight against his honor. Tradition maintained that the first Olympic Games were held in 776 BC and repeated every four years, providing one of the most widespread systems of dating. For a set period before and after this and the other major festivals, a truce was imposed on any conflict between Greeks to permit travel and participation in the games. That quintessentially Greek institution, the gymnasium, was a place not simply for promoting personal fitness, but was designed deliberately to do this in public, so that even training was competitive. Pelopidas, the man who sent Philip as hostage to Thebes, was renowned as a bodybuilder in the gymnasium before he made a name as a soldier and commander. Excellence in anything was little valued unless it was acknowledged by others.[6]

Reputation and honor mattered, and were shaped both by how someone saw himself and how others treated them. Citizens who felt themselves poorly treated by their home community readily plotted revolution to set things right. A group that considered themselves superior would genuinely believe that it was right for them to seize power, and the individual confident in his talents could aspire to leadership or even tyranny. Cities went to war when they felt slighted by another community, even when their actual military resources were far weaker than the new enemy. It was taken for granted that a polis would dominate others if it was sufficiently strong, while the philosophers who considered the issue of relations between states came very close to seeing war rather than peace as the natural condition.[7]

It is wrong to exaggerate and see the desire to excel as obsessive or as the sole driving force in Greek politics and society. Not everyone was an Achilles, obsessed with personal honor above all else, nor so spectacular as a warrior—or anything else—that their behavior had such a profound impact on those around them. Most of the time, the ambitions of politicians within a community balanced each other. Yet the revolutions kept on occurring, and it is striking just how many Greek politicians spent time in voluntary or forced exile from their home cities.

At the same time, warfare between city-states always was common, over real or imagined slights as well as for more tangible advantages. Many wars were decided by the clash of rival phalanxes, but things were not always so simple. Even in Homer, it was not the face-to-face heroism of Achilles that got the Greeks into Troy, but the cunning of Odysseus in devising the wooden horse. There were raids, ambushes, piracy, and surprise attacks, and on occasions one side gained sufficient advantage to take and destroy the rival community. When this occurred any sense of shared Greek identity did nothing to prevent massacre and mass enslavement.

Being Greek set someone apart from the barbarians, but a man generally identified far more with his city. Some cities maintained long-standing ties of friendship with other communities, but all also had historic rivalries and enmities, and by their very nature, Greek poleis did not readily cooperate. The pressure of the great Persian invasions in the early fifth century BC changed this to some extent, at least for a brief period. These were epic victories in which the Greeks against all odds threw back the invaders, prompting Herodotus to write the first prose history in Greek and fostering the greatest flourishing of Athenian culture.[8]

Persia was the mightiest empire of its day, controlling territory, population, and wealth that dwarfed all the Greek communities combined. By the end of the sixth century BC, the Persian kings were pushing their dominance westward into Europe, coming ever closer to mainland Greece, but the spark for the first invasion came from Athens. Greek cities of Ionia in Asia Minor (modern-day Turkey) rebelled against Persian rule, and democratic Athens answered their request for help in the war. The Athenian aid was limited and did not prevent the utter defeat of the rebels, but it drew Persian attention. In 490 BC, King Darius sent an expedition to punish the impudent Greek city. Sparta promised aid, but delayed sending an army because it was celebrating a religious festival. This meant that only the Athenians and their allies from the city of Plataea formed in a phalanx and charged the Persian army at Marathon. It was the first real sign of the superiority of the hoplite in hand-to-hand fighting, for the Persians were routed with heavy loss and the invasion defeated.

A decade later Darius's son Xerxes returned with an enormous army and fleet, preceded by ambassadors demanding fire and water, the traditional symbols of submission. Preparations for the expedition took several years and were deliberately as visible as possible to convince anyone considering resistance that defeat was inevitable. In 480 BC the Persians bridged the Hellespont, the narrow strait of the Dardanelles between Europe and Asia, and marched their army into Europe. Herodotus later claimed that it numbered a million men, which is logistically impossible but provides an early example of our sources' fondness for portraying Persian armies as vast hordes. This was a far more serious effort than the first invasion, and the aim was formal conquest.

For a while, the enormity of the threat overcame the instinctive Greek reluctance to cooperate. Resistance was led by Athens and Sparta, the two largest city-states, and each contributed in its own way. Sparta was the land power, its army acknowledged as the finest in Greece. At its heart were the Spartiates, the small caste of Spartan male citizens raised from earliest youth to be soldiers. Professionals in a world of amateur hoplites, they trained constantly both as individuals and as units, freed from the need to work for a living because all laboring tasks were performed by helot serfs. Spartan society was brutal. Every year the state formally declared war against the helots, and in their late teens Spartiates took to the hills, descending at night to beat up or murder any helots they could find.

In contrast Athens was a democracy, with a society that was outward-looking and innovative, unlike the staunchly conservative Spartans. The city had a large population, which meant that it could field a large number of hoplites, but its main contribution was its navy. In the last generation Athens had turned itself into the greatest naval power in Greece, the state building a fleet of triremes, sleek and maneuverable warships rowed by three banks of oars, each oar operated by a single rower. This navy was funded by state-owned silver mines at Laurion in southern Attica, and the ships were probably built mainly from timber from Macedonia. Ships were one thing, but to be truly effective the crews needed regular training and this meant they had to be paid.

Once again, the Spartans were occupied with a festival and unwilling to commit their full army at the start of the campaign in 480 BC. Famously, they sent Leonidas, one of their two kings, and 300 Spartiates to defend the narrow pass at Thermopylae. Less famously, they were supported by a larger number of non-Spartan citizens, as well as allies from other states. For days they held the pass against Xerxes, proving again and again the superiority of hoplites—especially Spartan hoplites—in close combat. At the same time the combined Greek fleet held the larger Persian navy to a draw at Artemisium. The end came when the Persians were shown a route through the mountains around the pass itself. There were not enough men to defend this properly, so the Greeks withdrew, covered by the Spartans, who were wiped out in the process.

Xerxes had broken through to Boeotia, and there were few natural obstacles left to hinder his advance until he reached the isthmus of the Peloponnese. Thebes was one of several communities to submit to Persia rather than risk the devastation of its homeland. In contrast Athens evacuated most of its population and let the enemy sack the home city. Although there were severe strains, somehow the spirit of cooperation endured among enough of the poleis for them to re-muster their fleet and face the Persians at Salamis, a restricted stretch of water where numbers could not be brought to bear fully and skill and seamanship would be critical. Led by a Spartan commander as part of a political deal even though the largest contingent of ships were Athenian, the Greeks triumphed. Like Trafalgar, the Battle of Britain, or Midway, Salamis was a victory that meant that the defenders would not lose for the moment, rather than a battle to win the war. Xerxes returned home, leaving behind a general in command of a very large army to complete the conquest. A year later, in 479 BC, this force was routed on land at the Battle of Plataea.

Sparta and Athens emerged from this epic struggle against a superpower with their prestige at a new height. Spartan hoplites had held the limelight in the glorious defeat of Thermopylae and the victory at Plataea, while Athens could boast that it had made Salamis possible and had borne the brunt of the fighting. That victory was less straightforward and could not be attributed solely to the courage of hoplites, for each trireme's crew of just under 200 men consisted primarily of rowers, recruited from the poorest. Soon, Athens would extend the right to attend and speak in the Popular Assembly to all citizens, including those registered as owning little or no wealth. This was democracy in its most radical form, and although the better-off and more educated were disdainful of what they saw as the fickle nature of the mass of the people, it was under this system that Athens reached the height of its power and prosperity.

Athens with its flourishing cultural life was better placed to celebrate its achievements than Sparta. As importantly, its navy gave it the chance to pursue the enemy and continue to prosecute the war by raiding Asia Minor and aiding the Greek cities there. In order to do this effectively, it formed the Delian League of coastal cities, which contributed ships or money to the common effort of aggressive defense against Persia. As the Persian threat receded, the League gradually transformed into an Athenian empire, where the allies were clearly subordinate, contributing only money that Athens then used to maintain its own massive fleet. Yet tension with Sparta bubbled away, each city seeing the other's prestige and power as a challenge to its own status. Larger cities like Corinth and Thebes in turn resented Spartan and Athenian eminence. Smaller cities made alliances with more powerful ones for protection against local rivals. This meant that a petty dispute between two minor cities could provide the pretext for larger states to seek advantage. The second half of the fifth century was dominated by the struggle for preeminence between Athens and Sparta, with short lulls interrupting longer periods of open warfare, culminating in what is called the Peloponnesian War (431–404).[9]

The fundamental differences between the land power Sparta and the naval power Athens made it hard for each side to use its main strength to inflict fatal damage on the other. Pitched battles between phalanxes were rare, raiding by land and sea more common. No Greek state had much skill at siege warfare, so taking an enemy city was a matter of long and difficult blockade. Unless the city was small, or a faction within it was willing to betray the others and admit the enemy by stealth, it was a question of waiting for the inhabitants to starve. Athens was a huge city by Greek standards, which had long since been unable to feed its population from local produce. Instead the Athenians relied on imports of staples, especially grain, much of it from the Black Sea. Lines of fortification known as the Long Walls connected the city itself to its harbor at Piraeus. Sparta formed armies of 30,000 or so to invade Attica, the wider country around Athens. These were forces on a scale not seen since the muster at Plataea. The Athenians simply retreated behind their walls, leaving the Spartans to ravage the countryside while staring impotently at the fortifications. For a decade the Spartans did this each summer for a month or so. Athens hoped to win the war elsewhere by stripping Sparta of allies and nibbling away at her strength. Other states could not avoid getting caught up in the conflict, but their interests were their own, and they were willing to switch allegiance whenever it seemed to their advantage.

The cost of decades of warfare was appalling. Cities were destroyed, their populations slaughtered or enslaved. Athens was especially brutal in the treatment of allies who turned against her, although in truth there was little to choose between the savagery of each side. Natural disaster added to the horrors inflicted by human beings when plague broke out in overcrowded Athens, killing a large proportion of the population. The unfocused strategy of both sides is shown especially in the Athenian decision to commit huge resources to an attack on Syracuse, the greatest Greek city on Sicily. Poorly planned and even more poorly executed, this resulted in a humiliating and costly disaster at the hands of the Syracusans, who were aided by a Spartan military advisor. Yet the war lumbered on. Sparta, realizing that it needed to defeat the Athenian fleet to bring its enemy down, created its own squadrons of warships to add to the triremes provided by its allies. In a great irony, this was all made possible by an alliance between Sparta and Persia, the current Great King sending large subsidies to pay for the creation of the fleet. Athens was close to exhaustion and was not helped by some of the more quixotic decisions of the Popular Assembly, most notably executing some of their best admirals for failing to save all the sailors from triremes sunk during a battle.[10]

In 404 BC, after one too many defeats, Athens capitulated, its subjection marked by the Spartans with the demolition of the Long Walls to the music of pipers and scenes of celebration. Yet to the surprise of many, Sparta did not choose to eradicate its rival altogether. Radical democracy was replaced by a narrow oligarchy, the Thirty Tyrants, and for the moment Spartan dominance was unchallenged. At first some welcomed this, hoping that the new great power would prove less arrogant and self-centered than the Athenians had done in the past. This hope swiftly faded. In 401 BC the Spartans aided the formation of a mercenary army of hoplites to assist Cyrus, brother of the Persian king, in a bid for the throne. These men, the Ten Thousand, won a victory at Cunaxa deep in Persian territory, but it was rendered meaningless because Cyrus was killed while seeking out his brother on the battlefield. The Greek mercenaries then fought the long way back all the way to the coast of Asia Minor. Some were still there a few years later to aid King Agis of Sparta when he led a Spartan army into Asia Minor in a campaign supposedly to liberate the Greek cities of the region from Persian rule.[11]

By this time Athens was recovering after a period of bitter internal power struggles that led to civil war. In 403 BC, little more than a year after the creation of oligarchy, King Pausanias of Sparta reestablished a degree of stability and paved the way for the restoration of democracy. Gratitude for his generosity did not last very long as Athens started to recover its confidence and strength. A little later the Athenians accepted Persian funding to build warships to be used against the Spartans, while the latter were proposing a treaty with the Persian king acknowledging his right to rule the Greek cities in Asia. Short-term advantage motivated every Greek city in this era, with little or no concern for others or consistency, and in turn all the major powers went to Persia for financial backing. In 387 BC, the Persians acted as the guarantors of a universal peace treaty, ostensibly to end warfare between the city-states of Greece. Anyone violating the truce of the "King's Peace" would find their opponents aided by plentiful supplies of Persian gold. In practice, this did little more than entrench the power of the most dominant state at any one time, which for the moment was still Sparta.

Athens grew strong again, rebuilt the Long Walls, and in 378 BC began to create a second league of allies, pledging to treat them with more respect than in the past. At first, the Athenians lived up to their word and relations with the allies were good. Before long the Athenian navy once again outstripped that of any other state in sheer size, and her power was felt throughout the Aegean. Spartan hegemony started to decay, the process encouraged by her clumsy diplomacy and the internal weaknesses of Spartan society, which meant that there always needed to be sufficient Spartiates at home to keep the helots under control. In 382 BC Sparta had treacherously installed a garrison in Thebes and created a puppet government. Just over three years later, a bold coup was achieved by Epaminondas, Pelopidas, and their confederates when they killed the leading Spartans and their allies in the city.

Thebes, Athens, and Sparta were the major players in the ongoing power struggle, but other states and leagues of states were also significant. None was able to achieve lasting dominance, and the result was near constant warfare, whether direct or waged by proxy against allies. Sparta's reputation as invincible in pitched battle was shattered at Leuctra in 371, but formal hoplite battles remained uncommon. Most campaigns were smaller-scale and lasted longer than the month or so a hoplite farmer was keen to spend away from home. A city either paid and fed its own citizens to stay in the field for months or even years on end or hired mercenaries. Both methods required substantial funds, making warfare more and more expensive, and only rarely would plunder and other spoils come at all close to covering the cost. There were plenty of mercenaries available, for generations of warfare and internal strife had produced large numbers of men whose cities had been destroyed or had sent them into exile, as well as those who simply discovered that they had a taste for fighting. Triremes were also costly to build and maintain, while their crews needed frequent training, which in turn meant that ideally they were paid to do the job full time.

War was expensive and risky, but old grudges, perceptions of honor, the instinctive urge to compete, and the hope of victory kept fueling conflict, with no one able to gain a permanent advantage. Thebes was dominant for around the decade after 371 BC, and during this time it launched several major invasions of the Spartan homeland and founded and fortified the city of Messene as a new home for Sparta's Messenian helots. Many escaped to join the new community, and others returned from generations of exile. Aided by a Theban garrison, the new polis beat off all Spartan attacks and soon flourished as a constant reminder to other helots. In 362 BC Theban and Spartan phalanxes, each bolstered by large contingents of allies, clashed again at Mantineia. There were heavy casualties, including Epaminondas, but neither side gained clear victory or any real strategic advantage. The historian Xenophon, an Athenian aristocrat who had led the Ten Thousand and later settled in Sparta, ended his history at this point on a deeply pessimistic note, for after the battle "the opposite of what all men believed would happen was brought to pass." He claimed that most of the Greek states had joined the conflict, expecting clear winners to dominate. Instead both sides claimed victory, without really gaining power or territory or being significantly "better off . . . than before the battle took place; but there was even more confusion and disorder in Greece after the battle than before."[12]

Philosophers searched for the underlying cause of this unending and indecisive cycle of warfare. Many, Plato among them, had decided that oligarchy and especially democracy fueled conflict, and began to fantasize about the advantages of rule by a wise and good tyrant. Other voices felt that the Greeks needed a great cause to unite them and spoke of joining together to invade Persia. Few listened to any of these theorists, and the conflicts between poleis went on as they always had.

MACEDONIA WAS ALWAYS different, in country and culture, and from a southern Greek perspective it was backward. City-states did not develop there, and the only recognizable poleis in or near the kingdom were colonies settled by people from outside. There were urban communities in Macedonia, but they were not independent or truly self-governing, and many were unwalled. The rule of kings in itself was archaic and foreign, save to that tiny handful of philosophers eager to explore the possibility of rule by an enlightened monarch. Thessaly's city-states were dominated by aristocrats and prone to the emergence of tyrants, but it still appeared more obviously Greek than its northern neighbor. Political institutions mattered more than language, and from an Athenian perspective Macedonia was far off, closer to Thrace and Illyria culturally as well as geographically than it seemed to their homeland.

Other Greeks at other times may have felt differently, and a fragment written by the Greek poet Hesiod around 700 BC speaks of a Macedon, son of Zeus, a lover of horses who lived near Mount Olympus and Pieria. Such a mythical ancestor suggests inclusion within the broad family of Greek peoples. Two hundred years later the Persians were pressing into Europe, years before Athens went to the help of the Ionian rebels. Darius campaigned in person in Thrace and Scythia. By about 500 BC he set up an inscription listing his subject peoples, ending with "countries which are across the sea." Another specified the "Scythians which are across the sea, Skudra, and the petasos-wearing Ionians." Skudra was probably Thrace, although it may also have extended into Macedonia as well, while the petasos was the distinctive Macedonian hat. Describing them as Ionians suggests that the Persians saw them as akin to the Greek cities of Asia and Greece itself. There is no reason to doubt Darius's claim to control these areas. Less clear is whether or not Macedon formed part of a Persian satrapy—effectively a province controlled by a Persian governor. There is no evidence for Amyntas I or his son Alexander I being satraps themselves, and on balance it is more likely that they were recognized as subject dynasts, much like some of the monarchs in Asia Minor.[13]

When Xerxes marched against Greece in 480 BC, Alexander I as his loyal ally brought Macedonian troops to join the royal army—just as the Thebans would do after their capitulation. According to Herodotus, the night before the Battle of Plataea a lone horseman rode up to the Athenian outposts and asked to see their commanders, because he too was a Greek by descent and feared for the Greek cause. When these arrived, the rider told them of the Persian battle plans for the next day before riding away, saying simply that he was Alexander the Macedonian. This treachery was supposed to have helped the Greeks alter their own tactics and win the battle.[14]

Alexander I later became known as the philhellene for his passion for all things Greek (and the nickname suggests that a Macedonian king was not thought of as purely Greek in the first place). Herodotus tells us that at some point he attended the Olympic Games and competed in the one-stade sprint (a distance of 200 yards or about 180 meters). We do not know when this occurred, although 500 or 496 BC are good candidates, since this was an event for the fairly young; the matter is complicated because we do not know when Alexander was born, although he was old enough in 498 BC to become king. At the time there were complaints from other competitors that the Macedonian was not eligible because he was not Greek. However, the organizers accepted the tradition that the Argead family was originally from Argos as proof that he was. Alexander took part and tied for first place. Since he is not mentioned in any surviving list of victors, he may well have lost a retrial, and there is no good reason to reject the story. What is interesting is the implication that simply being Macedonian was not enough to prove that a man was Greek, at least in the tense environment of the Olympic competition. If, as seems likely, it all occurred while Macedon was part of the Persian Empire, this may well have added to the uncertainty.[15]

Herodotus tells another story about Alexander I that is a good deal less plausible. This claims that while he was young and his father still king, a delegation of Persian ambassadors came to the royal court. During a feast, the guests drank heavily and began to treat some of the royal women as if they were courtesans. The Macedonians were outraged at this, and the teenage Alexander devised a plan. A group of youths donned women's clothes, replaced the real women, and then at a given moment murdered the Persians.

Most likely the king later invented and circulated the tale to prove that his heart had never been with the Persians in all the years of forced alliance. Apart from anything else, there is no evidence of Darius's responding angrily as he must surely have done had news reached him of the slaughter of his envoys. Instead, we learn that Alexander's sister was married to an important Persian commander, while the king himself was sufficiently trusted to be sent as the Persian envoy to Athens in the winter of 480–479 BC. This was a mark both of his perceived reliability and Persian awareness that the king had an existing connection with Athens, and had been honored by the city for his goodwill and benefactions. We do not know what had prompted these honors, but by far the most plausible explanation is that Alexander had provided a lot of the material used to build Athens's new fleet. The Persian Empire was far too vast for its king or his satraps to micromanage every region, let alone the more distant territories. Macedonia lay on the fringes. Alexander could neither ignore the power of Persia nor fail to seek opportunities for trade and good relations with nearer states.[16]

After Plataea, Persian power retreated and that of Athens flourished—as did that of Sparta, but at first the Spartans showed little interest in Macedonia. In contrast the Athenian navy grew ever larger with the transition of the Delian League into the Athenian empire. Macedonia was one of the best sources for the raw materials of shipbuilding and maintenance, and this alone made it very important. In addition, the wider region offered mineral resources on a scale that was very appealing to any state, and especially one determined to possess something as expensive as a fleet. Strategically, the coast of Macedonia, the Chalcidice, and the Chersonese were vital links to the many coastal and Aegean island communities forming the Athenian empire. Triremes had very large crews for their size and little space to store the food and water these men needed. Their range was short, for they needed to make a secure landing for the night at least every two to three days, and ideally more often. Coastal cities with harbors and landing places were essential for the fleet to operate in an area. For Athens, the route to and from the grain-rich Black Sea colonies was a vital lifeline that needed to be kept secure.[17]

All of this meant that Athens, and in time other cities, took an ever greater interest in Macedonia and its neighbors. Much could be achieved by alliance, which meant that the kings of Macedon were cultivated by other states, but the idea of securing a permanent presence in the region was also very appealing. This was not always easy. The Thracians destroyed more than one Greek colony set up to exploit mineral resources in the region. Two attempts by Athens to found a community at Amphipolis, close to a good port and surrounded on three sides by the river Strymon, failed. A third attempt succeeded in 437–436 BC and allowed them good access to timber and minerals brought down the river. It was a great prize, but inevitably what was important to Athens also gained new significance for her enemies. In 424 BC the citizens of Amphipolis, most of whom were from allied communities rather than actual Athenians, switched sides and admitted the Spartan general Brasidas and his forces into their city.[18]

Macedonia and the neighboring lands became one more theater of operations in the sprawling conflict of the Peloponnesian War. Athenians, Spartans, and their respective allies added to the Thracian and Illyrian leaders who had long intervened in the kingdom. Later the Thebans and Thessalians would join them, for the formal end of the great war did nothing to reduce the attractions of the area to bigger states. All were motivated by self-interest, as were the Argead kings, the monarchs of the Upper Macedonian cantons, and the Molossian tribes, which meant that alliances were often brief, yesterday's enemy becoming today's friend and vice versa as the situation changed. Perdiccas II (454–413 BC) and his son Archelaus I in particular appear as fickle and devious in our sources, which is simply to say that they switched sides, made and broke alliances at will, and generally behaved as unscrupulously as everyone else. Skill at playing off other competing interests, and a good deal of luck, allowed them to survive, just as it had allowed Alexander I to steer a path between Persia and the Greek states to the south.[19]

It helped that no one was able to gain any lasting dominance in the region, at least after the withdrawal of Persia in 479 BC. Indeed, the growth of one power automatically inclined most others to treat it with suspicion and hostility. Athens, Sparta, Thebes, and the rest all had many other concerns apart from this area, while the local groups and leaders were not strong enough to see off all rivals. It meant that the instability persisted for generations and steadily eroded the strength of the Argead monarchy, not least because there was almost always an external backer to support family members who challenged the king. Athens never went completely away, and the coast was always exposed to her squadrons of triremes. The loss of Amphipolis remained a sore, deeply emotional grievance for many Athenians, but repeated attempts to retake it failed. At other times they made alliances with or gained control of coastal cities such as Pydna and Methone.

Alexander I celebrated Greek culture, even if it had required a ruling to accept him as Greek enough to participate at Olympia. He had gold statues of himself set up at Olympia as part of dedications to Zeus and Apollo. At this date portraits of specific people rather than gods were exceptionally rare among the Greeks, so this behavior marked him out as revering Hellenic culture while being not quite part of it. Yet the famous poet Pindar was one of a number of well-known Greek writers who visited Macedonia and were lavishly entertained at the royal court. In the fifth century BC both Herodotus and Thucydides were among the guests. This enthusiasm for the best of Greek culture remained strong to Philip's day, and generous royal patronage brought painters and sculptors as well as writers to Macedonia. Archelaus I created a great festival at Dion, which included dramatic contests in honor of Zeus and the Muses, as well as "Olympian" games styled after the Olympics. He also lured Euripides to his court, and the famous Athenian playwright wrote and staged at least one play while he was at Pella. His *Archelaus* was the tale of the king's ancestor and namesake, and it recast the foundation story of the Argeads in a suitably Greek setting. The *Bacchae* may also have been created while he was in Macedon, as it dealt with a cult especially important to the Macedonians.[20]

Euripides never returned to his homeland and died in Macedon in 406 BC. Although the Athenians requested that his remains be sent back, each time the Macedonians refused—presumably a decision made in an Assembly—and he was instead given a tomb there. Not everyone accepted invitations to the royal court; Socrates is said to have declined, although his reasons are unclear. For all the enthusiasm the royal family and leading Macedonians displayed for Greek and especially Athenian culture, they remained different from the aristocrats in the city-states to the south. Ultimately they were first and foremost Macedonians, and whether or not they were considered "Greek" depended on the viewer's perspective. The same was true of Philip, but over time he would force himself into the heart of southern Greece and confront its greatest city-states.[21]

4

ALLIANCES AND WIVES

In 358 BC it was still the early days of Philip's reign, and his and Macedonia's positions remained precarious. Philip had tasted victory and defeated the same Illyrians who had killed his brother, and for the moment the Illyrian tribes were deterred from fresh attacks. Bardylis the Illyrian vanishes from the sources after accepting the treaty imposed by Philip, and given that he was a very old man he probably did not live much longer. One charismatic leader had gone, but the Illyrians remained numerous and warlike, and as the years passed other chiefs and kings would emerge and lead raids to the south. For the moment Philip and his army were to be feared, but that would not last forever. To help cement the new peace for as long as possible Philip married for the first time, taking as his bride Audata, an Illyrian presumably close kin to an important tribal leader, perhaps to Bardylis himself.[1]

In addition to a wife, Philip gained a lot of territory, adding all the land as far as Lake Lychnitis to his kingdom. This included not simply the Upper Macedonian tribes, but a number of communities of Illyrian speakers. The new western frontier of his kingdom would be shielded by a double line of mountains, crossed by just two passes suitable for an army. Internal communications were good, and work soon began to fortify existing settlements and found new walled cities to act as garrisons.

No Argead king had asserted his claim to rule Upper Macedonia as strongly since the days of Alexander I. During Philip's reign the local dynasties of this region disappear altogether. Instead, the leading men of Upper Macedonia came to Philip's court as "Companions" of the king. His favor, and the status they possessed at court and as senior men in the Macedonian army, became far more important than old titles. As usual we cannot trace this process so we do not know whether the petty kingdoms were ever formally abolished or slowly withered in the face of the new opportunities on offer. Philip may well have seemed a more attractive proposition than domination by the Illyrians, and his victory had demonstrated his strength.

The young king was enthusiastic, confident, and charming. He took a second wife, Phila, who was from the Upper Macedonian region of Elimeia and most likely a member of its royal house. There is no sign of concerted resistance to Philip's takeover of Upper Macedonia, but that does not mean that all welcomed it. One of Phila's brothers went into exile and would fight against the king in years to come. On the other hand even more of her relatives did very well through serving Philip. Probably the same pattern was reflected in the other kingdoms, with the vast majority accepting service with him, at least for the moment while his power was growing.[2]

The encouragement for the leaders of the Upper Macedonian tribes to look to Philip for rewards and honor was just one aspect of major social change. The pastoralists of the area were made to move to the newly important walled cities and towns and cultivate the land. Years later Alexander the Great is supposed to have reminded his truculent soldiers that Philip had changed them from wanderers into to city dwellers, herdsmen to farmers, and replaced their animal-skin clothes with respectable cloaks. All of these things were marks of civilization rather than barbarism. At the same time, the king shifted the population around. Settlers from Lower Macedonia were brought in to add numbers to the new and existing cities, and men from the regions of Upper Macedonia would later be sent as colonists elsewhere. The royal army was itself one of the main engines of social change, for Philip's control of all this territory greatly increased the manpower available to him. From now on half of the regiments of the pike phalanx and half of the Macedonian cavalry were recruited from Upper Macedonia in units named after the regions. These formations mixed the settlers from outside with local men, who would fight alongside each other, all looking to Philip to give them victory, glory, and plunder.[3]

None of this was instant, and none of it was inevitable. Philip's early success could easily have turned into failure, just as it had for several of his predecessors, and he was still only about twenty-four. Assassination remained as great a danger as it was for any Argead, and there were plenty of foreign leaders and states ready to attack whenever they sensed an opportunity. If Philip was to bond the Upper Macedonian cantons to him, then his successes needed to continue, confirming his strength and also giving him the chance to reward loyal followers. All this meant that more warfare was almost inevitable, and the king's conspicuous bravery put him at risk; one well-aimed arrow or spear thrust could end his life or leave him crippled and highly vulnerable to challengers. Philip was an enthusiastic diplomat, and it was later said that he was prouder of his successes in negotiation than his victories in battle. Yet this was the fourth century BC, and diplomacy without the threat of force was toothless.[4]

Philip could not afford time to rest and soon began to search for ways to make his kingdom more secure by dominating his neighbors instead of waiting for them to threaten him. Thessaly lay on his southern border, and there was a long history of Thessalian leaders intervening in Macedonia, not least aiding the return of his father. Thessaly was in some ways much more like southern Greece, yet prone to the emergence of tyrants. One reason was that its aristocratic families dominated the city-states in a way that had long since ceased to the south. A visible sign of this was that it produced some of the finest cavalrymen anywhere in the Hellenic world, for the aristocracy wanted to remain distinct from the wider hoplite class. In 358 BC Thessaly was divided into two camps. The first was centered around the city of Pherae and its allies and controlled the coastline. Against it was ranged the self-proclaimed Thessalian League, led by the city of Larissa and originally formed with aid from Thebes, which was concerned by the growing power of its former ally Pherae.

At the time of Philip's birth, Pherae was led by a charismatic tyrant named Jason, whose career in many ways foreshowed his own. Xenophon dubbed Jason the "greatest man of his times," admiring him as a skillful commander. His large army consisted primarily of mercenaries, which meant that as long as they were paid they were available for campaigning at any time. Like Philip, Jason was even more adept in negotiation than warfare, and his ambition may even have gone as far as planning an expedition to Persia. Others had ambitions of their own, and in 370 BC Jason was murdered. Two of his brothers succeeded to his power but were in turn murdered, the second by Jason's son Alexander, who was ruthless, a gifted opportunist, and who switched alliances as readily as any Argead king. Although never able to match his father's military might, Alexander held on to power for more than a decade until he was murdered in 358 BC in a conspiracy led by his wife.[5]

Thessaly was unstable, just as Macedonia had been during Philip's youth, but like Macedonia it had the potential to be rich and powerful. The young king began to involve himself in Thessalian affairs very early on, probably in 358 BC, although the details are obscure. The most visible consequence was to add to his list of wives. A fragment of Satyrus, who wrote a generation after the death of Alexander the Great, appears to list Philip's wives in chronological order, although inevitably some scholars have disagreed. If the names really are given in the order in which they were married, then Philip wed Nicesipolis from Pherae as his third wife and then Philinna of Larissa as his fourth. That the wives each came from the two leading cities in Thessaly was surely not coincidence. Philinna was already a widow and is dismissed in one source as of obscure birth, while others accuse her of being a dancing girl and prostitute, but this may be no more than later propaganda. Most likely she was from an aristocratic family, perhaps a member of the Aleudae, the leading clan in Larissa and an established ally of the Argeads. A very late source claims that Nicesipolis was the niece of Jason of Pherae.[6]

These two marriages gave Philip connections with the aristocracy of Thessaly and were no doubt part of a quest for allies, which perhaps included offering military support to factions connected to his new wives. For the moment this achieved little more than making any Thessalian aggression against him less likely in the short term. It also meant that in less than two years he had taken four wives, all for political advantage. As far as we can tell, no other Argead had married as many women in so short a time. Only one, Phila, was in any sense Macedonian, and she was from Upper Macedonia, which had effectively been independent of the Argeads for more than a generation. Each of the marriages looked outward rather than within the heartland of the kingdom. Philip gave every impression of being in a hurry, and of possessing aims on a scale far surpassing his predecessors. Deliberately or not, he was marking himself out as different.

Before the end of 357 BC, Philip had taken yet another bride. His fifth wife was Olympias, daughter of the late king of the Molossians and niece of the current ruler, Arybbas. The marriage alliance helped secure the relationship with this close and very similar neighbor. The Molossians were the largest of the three main tribal groups of Epirus to the west, and although a useful ally, they were not a match for the power of Philip's resurgent Macedonia, so the alliance was very much in his favor. Either now or in the previous year the Orestae who had defected to the Molossians when Macedonia was weak became formally Macedonian again. Olympias's younger brother, also named Alexander, came to Philip's court to be raised.[7]

There are only a few glimpses of life at the royal court, mainly seen through the jaundiced gaze of southern Greeks and focusing on the king. Yet Philip went on campaign almost every year, so he was away at least as often as he was present; his wives did not accompany him but stayed at home, usually either at Pella or Vergina. Both cities possessed a substantial palace as well as other large houses, although the archaeology does not make clear whether or not there were specific women's quarters occupied by the king's wives. As we have seen, most Greeks were puzzled by the rarity of slaves in Macedonia, and the royal court was no exception to this. Of course servants can exist where there is no slavery, and all the indications are that there were plenty of men and women employed at court. If the royal women wove clothes and supervised the running of the household they did not do it alone. The excavations at Aegae/Vergina show that the palace was capable of mounting feasts for hundreds of guests, in itself an indication of the number of staff whose work made this possible.[8]

There were doubtless cooks, sweepers, and cleaners; grooms and stable hands; nurses for the children and tutors for those who were older; maids for the king's wives; and carpenters, leather workers, weavers, and other craftsmen, apart from the visitors to the court—ranging from ambassadors to traders and guests—and the entertainers. The vast majority of the servants were freeborn and, apart from some of the specialists, likely to be Macedonians. One distinct group whose role included waiting on the king were the Royal Pages, the teenage sons of distinguished men sent to court to be raised. Fosterage was a common institution in many tribal societies, and something of this sort most likely was traditional in Macedonia. Philip drastically increased the number of pages and made the whole thing far more organized. Boys from all over his kingdom were included, perhaps as many as fifty in each of the age years of the pages, and this helped integrate the aristocracies of Upper Macedonia. In one sense the pages were hostages for their fathers' behavior, but they also offered a promise of future favor. They were raised to be soldiers and schooled as potential leaders.[9]

All in all there were a lot of people in and around the court even when the king was away on campaign, and the royal women were part of this community. Athenian women of well-to-do families lived rather secluded lives, the paleness of their skin seen as an honorable mark of how little they had been exposed to the sun. They appeared in public only in certain circumstances, such as participation in state festivals. This seclusion was extreme, albeit far from unique. Philip's mother, Eurydice, proved that royal women could have a public role in Macedonia, which implies that at times they were visible and politically active. Yet they did not attend the hard-drinking and raucous symposia that formed a central part of the social life of the court whenever Philip was present, for the only women to appear at these events were entertainers, whether musicians, dancers, or straightforward prostitutes. The wearing of veils by women was common in many Greek communities and it is possible that the practice was followed in Macedon. Such veils varied from ones that covered most of the face to others that were more like a scarf.[10]

If Eurydice was still alive in the 350s BC, then she was surely the senior and influential woman at court. Otherwise there was no formal hierarchy of wives, or any recognized first wife. Philip married to secure alliances and to father children. Sons were potential heirs, at least if they survived into their teens, while daughters could be employed in marriage alliances once they were old enough. In such circumstances any emotional attachment to a wife was not of primary concern, which is not to say that it did not ever happen. Philip was still just twenty-five and a man of strong passions. Although he took numerous lovers, some of whom bore him children, it is not impossible that he felt affection and even love for some or all of his wives. Scholars who are determined not to assume any of the aspects of modern ideas of romantic love can sometimes forget that we are dealing with human beings. Each of Philip's wives was an individual just as he was, with a personality more or less determined, abrasive or charming. The king's attitude toward them at any time more than anything else determined their influence.

Audata the Illyrian is unlikely to have been a meek person. She gave Philip a daughter, Cynane, who after the death of Alexander the Great would lead an army into battle and fight at its head. She in turn had a daughter, Adea, whom she trained as a warrior. It was said to be an Illyrian custom for some noblewomen to fight, and there is a good chance that Audata was part of this tradition, although there is no evidence for her ever actually fighting. Given his mother's ancestry, Philip understood something of Illyrian culture and certainly did not prevent Cynane from training with weapons.[11]

Phila of Elimeia is a shadowy figure. She did not have any children, or at least none who lived long enough to be recorded in our sources, and we do not know whether she perished young or lived on, losing prestige because of her childlessness. Those of her male relatives who joined Philip flourished throughout his reign, so there is no sign of a loss of favor as far as they were concerned. The two Thessalians each gave him a child. Nicesipolis of Pherae had a daughter named Thessalonice, or "Victory in Thessaly," but since Philip had not won any notable engagement there as yet the girl was probably not born until a few years later. Philinna of Larissa bore a boy, Arrhidaeus (later also called Philip), in 357 BC or early 356 BC. These are the recorded children, and there may have been others who died young.[12]

Olympias from Epirus became by far the most important of Philip's wives, although according to Plutarch her real name was Polyxena, and Olympias was just a nickname. He says that she was also sometimes called Myrtale and Stratonice. Justin says that she was called Myrtale as a little girl, but otherwise all our sources refer to her as Olympias and it remains the convention to use this name. There are far more stories about her than any of the other wives because in due course she would become the mother of Alexander the Great. As he became the favored heir and then king, she became more important, while after his death Olympias was one of the main players in the bloody struggle to succeed him. At this time she led an army, executed rivals, and was finally killed. Alexander's own self-promoted image, let alone the propaganda from the years after his death in 323 BC, inevitably created or distorted the tales of his mother and her relationship with Philip. Plutarch says that "we are told that Philip, after being initiated into the mysteries of Samothrace at the same time with Olympias, he being himself still a youth and she an orphan child, fell in love with her and betrothed himself to her at once with the consent of her brother Arymbas."[13]

Apart from the minor error that Arybbas (which is the correct spelling) was her uncle rather than brother, many scholars reject the whole story as a romantic invention, letting Alexander's parents meet in more dramatic circumstances than simply as part of an arranged marriage. In this version, Philip fell in love with Olympias before he even saw any of the four women he took as wives before her. Their union was special because it would produce Alexander, and needed to be passionate since it was said that their love later turned to bitter hatred. All in all it makes for a very good story, worth telling and repeating even if it was not true. The advantages of an alliance with the Molossians were obvious enough in 357 BC not to require Philip to have fallen in love. Caution is wise, although it is just possible that the pair did encounter each other and that Philip was struck by the girl—Plutarch does not say that the attraction was mutual. Possible does not mean likely, and if there was a betrothal it would be puzzling that he waited so long to marry her and confirm the alliance.[14]

Further doubts are raised by the passage that follows. Plutarch claims that the night before Philip first slept with Olympias to consummate their marriage she dreamed that "there was a peal of thunder and that a thunder-bolt fell upon her womb, and that thereby much fire was kindled, which broke into flames that travelled all about, and then was extinguished." A little later Philip in turn dreamed of putting a seal shaped like a lion on Olympias's womb, which his seers interpreted as a sign of pregnancy, and that she would bear a son who was lion-like and brave. For the ancients, the conception and birth of a man who did as much as Alexander would do must have been accompanied by omens. When he was born in 356 BC, the great temple of Artemis in Ephesus in Asia Minor burned down. The two events are unlikely to have occurred on the same day, but the coincidence was close enough to be irresistible. A Greek seer explained that the goddess had been too busy bringing Alexander into the world to look after her own temple, while Persian magi despaired and said that one had been born who would bring a great calamity to Asia. Hindsight is a wonderful thing, and while the accidental destruction of a famous shrine was bound to be seen as an omen, in later years it was all too easy to link things together and remember the past as it ought to have been.[15]

Philinna's son Arrhidaeus was most probably born before Alexander. The two boys were the only legitimate sons fathered by Philip to survive long enough to appear in our sources. Both would reach adulthood, but at the time no one could have known this. Many children died in infancy and no one knew that there would be no other royal princes to come. In each case the birth enhanced the status of each mother, even if only a little. To say any more is speculation, for the lives of Philip's wives and their relationships with him and each other sadly remain a mystery.

It is revealing that no source records when or under what circumstances most of Philip's wives died, just as they do not tell when his mother died. None of this is unusual for Greek or Roman history. Matters improve a little under the Successor dynasties established after the death of Alexander the Great, for especially under the Ptolemies royal women played a more open role. It is no coincidence that this family culminated in Cleopatra VII, surely the most famous woman from Classical Antiquity. Yet even her fame is based on the affairs with Caesar and Mark Antony, and the sources reveal far less about her life during the years she was not with one of them. Thus the paucity of information about the women in Philip's and Alexander's lives is in no way exceptional, but typical for Greek and Roman history. Ancient authors concerned themselves with the deeds of kings and statesmen, in part because these left far more trace in the records. Therefore war and politics dominate the surviving accounts, which equally make it unsurprising that these are the areas in which we know most about Philip's life.[16]

5

WAR AND ITS PRICE

Early in 357 BC Philip went to war again, this time as the aggressor. His enemy was Amphipolis, and he claimed that the people there were "ill disposed toward him and offered many pretexts for war." Two years earlier he had withdrawn the soldiers stationed in the city, a measure that can only have damaged the standing of any factions favorable to Macedonia. Most likely others had risen to prominence who had no reason to feel affection toward him. At the same time, Philip had assured Athens that he had no interest in Amphipolis. Thus the change was drastic and transparently self interested, and the supposed provocation a cynical excuse for war.[1]

Amphipolis did not possess a large army and relied on its very strong natural and man-made defenses. In the past, this had proved sufficient for the city to maintain its independence from every opponent. The Spartan Brasidas was admitted as an ally not an overlord during the Peloponnesian War, but repeated sieges by the Athenians had all ended in failure. With good access to the sea as well as to rivers and land, the city was difficult to blockade, especially for an Athenian expedition operating a long way from home. Greek history up to this point suggested that a city of this size and strength could only be captured by treachery from within or a blockade lasting years.

Philip had other ideas. He had a large army and Amphipolis lay not far from home, which made supplying his men far easier than it was for past Athenian expeditions that had to bring everything in by sea. Rather than adopting the standard approach of blockading the city, which took a long time and even then might not be successful, he opted for a direct assault. This meant either climbing the city walls by ladders or some other means, knocking a hole in them so that the rubble formed a ramp that men could scramble up, or undermining the fortifications to make them collapse. The last option required suitable geology and skills in military mining that at this stage no one in Greece possessed, including Philip. Assaults were rare unless the city was small and had weak fortifications, for the poleis balked at the probable heavy casualties and high risk of failure in escalading a high wall defended by determined men. Although simple catapults were well known and widely used in defense, no one had so far developed any artillery capable of knocking a hole in a well-built city wall.[2]

During the course of his reign Philip would recruit a large corps of engineers and technical experts; many were from outside Macedonia and drawn to the king because he paid them well. Amphipolis was his first siege, and already there were signs of an army learning how to deal with fortifications. Diodorus tells us that Philip brought "siege-engines against the wall," although he does not describe them. He does mention battering rams, quite probably on wheels and protected by solid roofs, and there were probably mobile sheds to shelter pioneers as they came up to the wall and tried to prize out stones using crowbars and other tools. Perhaps the attackers also built towers to allow them to shoot down onto the walls, although as yet they may not have possessed the skill to make mobile siege towers able to be rolled up to the defenses. Amphipolis was sheltered by the river, which can only have reduced the sections of wall that the Macedonians could readily reach. That made it easier for the defenders to concentrate their strength to meet each attack, which in turn meant that Philip's men had to do everything possible to suppress them. Archers and slingers shot missiles at anyone visible on the battlements, as did catapults shooting both sharp bolts and stones. Ideally all of these operated from within shelters that protected them as much as possible from the defenders' missiles.[3]

It took time to construct the siege works needed to bring rams and other things up to the wall and provide cover for them and the supporting troops, although far less time than was required to mount a blockade. It also required a large and willing labor force directed by skilled engineers, and here Philip's Macedonians proved themselves willing workmen. At every stage the defenders did their best to hinder and delay the attackers, although in this case they can have had no experience of dealing with such aggressive besiegers. Apart from throwing and shooting missiles, they could sally out to burn siege engines and kill the men operating them. This meant that both day and night formed bodies of Macedonians needed to be stationed close enough to meet any sudden sortie. In turn, Philip's men launched "severe and continuous assaults" to wear down the defenders and keep them too busy to counterattack. This meant maintaining a deluge of missiles to make it dangerous to be on the battlements, and attacks by parties of men with ladders.[4]

This sort of fighting was hard work for both sides, and such a siege became a test of endurance, willpower, and logistics. Philip needed to keep his army fed and as free from disease as possible, all the while inspiring the soldiers to keep pressing the siege in spite of the casualties. Evidence from the better-documented sieges of Alexander's time suggest that far more men were wounded than killed in such fighting, but as the days and weeks passed the numbers grew steadily. Philip had to convince his soldiers that their suffering was worthwhile because they would win in the end and enjoy the glory and rewards of victory. Although the Macedonian losses were inevitably higher than those of the better-protected defenders, there were far fewer Amphipolitans in the first place. Every loss, whether a man killed, badly wounded, or merely weakened, was proportionally far more serious for them. Philip had a large enough army to allow soldiers to rest while others prosecuted the siege. Fatigue was far worse for the citizens of Amphipolis, who did not have this luxury, and as the attacks continued the prospect of defeat loomed ever larger.[5]

From the start it was obvious that this attack was far more violent and determined than anything ever attempted by the Athenians. Philip showed no sign of quitting, and gradually his battering rams ate into a section of the city wall. Defenders who surrendered before a final assault was launched had reasonable hope for securing better treatment than if they waited for the city to be stormed and sacked. Sieges placed immense strain on any polis and pushed at the fractures within its political class. Treachery was so great a risk that a fourth century BC theorist on siege warfare devoted more space to dealing with this than any threat from outside. As defeat loomed, the temptation to cut a deal with the attacker in return for personal safety for the leaders, their families, and supporters grew very strong, especially as any deal was likely to be sweetened by reward and the promise of winning political supremacy. Philip later quipped that he could "storm any fort to which an ass laden with gold could climb."[6]

There was an alternative to surrender—whether by the whole community or a treacherous faction—and that was to seek aid from outside. Before the siege began, two aristocrats from Amphipolis had traveled to Athens, although it is not clear whether they went with official approval or on their own initiative. Once there they invited the Athenians to "sail and take over the city," begging for help from their old enemy after almost seventy years of staunchly resisting the restoration of Athenian control. Around the same time, envoys from the Chalcidian League were also in Athens seeking alliance to strengthen their hand against the bullishly confident Macedonian king.[7]

While Athens had an opportunity to regain the great prize of Amphipolis, she also had other concerns: tension was growing with her allies and by the end of the year it would erupt into war. There were also practical problems. Not so long ago their expedition to support Argaeus had ended in utter failure. If Athens were to confront Philip again, then substantial numbers of men and ships were needed to give any chance of victory. The prevailing seasonal winds were not in their favor in the early summer, so depending on when precisely the siege began and how long it lasted, it may have been impractical to sail.

Instead of military aid, the Athenians sent two ambassadors, Antiphon and Charidemus, to talk to the king. They found Philip heavily engaged in the siege, but apparently welcoming and willing to negotiate. Precisely what followed is very hard to reconstruct, since most of what is known comes from the highly distorted version offered eight years later by the Athenian orator Demosthenes. He claimed that Philip "won our simple hearts by promising to hand over Amphipolis to us and by negotiating that secret treaty once so talked about." Other sources claim that in the "secret treaty" the Athenians promised to give Philip the allied city of Pydna in return, and such treachery would explain the need for secrecy. No formal treaty was possible without a public vote in the Athenian Assembly, which cannot have happened if the whole affair was believed to be secret. This suggests there were private talks about a deal and only hints in public, sufficient to persuade Athenian citizens that everything was in hand and that there was no need for war with the Macedonians.[8]

As the summer wore on, Philip's men created a viable breach in the city wall. He attacked—almost certainly leading the assault in person—and broke into Amphipolis. In the ancient world this did not in itself guarantee the end of resistance. Greek cities tended to have very narrow streets between rows of tall houses and other buildings, as well as a citadel within the walls. Determined defenders could continue the fight and sometimes drive the attackers out once more. This time Philip's men were not to be denied; they inflicted heavy losses on the Amphipolitans before they capitulated. The Greeks expected the fall of a city to be accompanied by massacre and rape, and the enslavement of the survivors. While the assault may well have been extremely brutal, once the city was secure Philip was unusually lenient. The men who had led the opposition to him were exiled along with their supporters, but the remainder were not harmed and allowed to stay in their homes and keep the bulk of their property. Although now part of Philip's kingdom, the polis continued to function on a day-to-day basis under its own laws and democratic institutions. There was to be a

Macedonian garrison, and a number of Macedonian settlers were introduced; some land—or at least its produce—was confiscated to provide for these. In addition Philip controlled all matters of foreign policy, was paid taxes, and took the lion's share of profits from the nearby mines at Mount Pangaeum.[9]

Whatever he had said before and during the siege, Philip clearly never had any intention of handing Amphipolis over to the Athenians. As this truth began to sink in, salt was rubbed into the wound when he followed up his success by besieging and taking Pydna as well. Late in the day, the Athenian Assembly voted to declare war on the king. For the moment this was little more than an empty gesture, but Athens was too occupied elsewhere to do any more. The rebellion of their allies was the more immediate priority, and without allies in the area it would be hard to mount an effective campaign against Macedon.[10]

Philip had enjoyed another year of victories, but his success was beginning to worry his neighbors. By the end of 357 BC, threats were growing on all sides. (Some scholars have suggested that this was the time "when dangerous wars threatened," and Justin claims that Philip was named king instead of regent by the Assembly, assuming that the author was right about this in the first place.) Illyrians led by King Grabus were preparing for war with Macedonia, as were the Paeonians led by King Lyppeius. To the east, Cetriporis, who controlled almost a third of the Thracian tribes, saw an opportunity to strike. These three kings formed an alliance, although the object was less about direct cooperation than to present Philip with a number of threats simultaneously. He was already at war with Athens, and the Athenians began to search for allies. For the moment they focused on the cities of the Chalcidian League, the same cities whose envoys had received no encouragement when they offered alliance not long ago. Together, the league cities fielded much stronger forces than Amphipolis, and both Philip and Athens saw them as the decisive factor in the coming struggle.[11]

Philip offered to grant the Chalcidians the city of Anthemus, which was part of his kingdom, and also to give them Potidaea, which he would first capture. Originally a Corinthian colony, Potidaea had at times been part of Athens's empire and had been retaken by the Athenians in 363 BC. It stood on the isthmus of the western finger of the Chalcidice, within easy striking distance of Olynthus, the leading city of the League. Philip asked little in the way of direct aid from the Chalcidians, merely that both parties promised not to make a separate peace with Athens. As an offer it was extremely generous, always supposing that he was sincere. Perhaps the rumors of the "secret" deal with Athens over Amphipolis fed suspicion, or perhaps the Chalcidians were simply cautious. Both they and Philip consulted the oracle of Apollo at Delphi, asking whether the treaty was wise. Although relatively common in earlier periods, this is the only recorded occasion when this happened in the fourth century BC, and we do not know which side insisted on the precaution. In the event, the oracle's answers were clearly satisfactory, for the treaty was signed and copies inscribed on stone and erected at Delphi, Dium in Macedonia, and Olynthus. This last copy partially survives, albeit mainly with clauses threatening divine punishment for anyone who broke the terms.[12]

In the spring or early summer of 356 BC, Philip marched to Potidaea and began the siege. Athens, having failed to ally with the Chalcidians, now turned to Philip's tribal enemies, but once again she moved slowly and no agreement was reached with the three kings until July. By then the situation had changed so drastically as to render the alliance meaningless. The Paeonians—or at least those following Lyppeius—were defeated and their resistance collapsed. A Macedonian force commanded by a general named Parmenio beat Grabus's Illyrians in battle and ended that threat. This is the first time we hear of a man who would serve Philip and Alexander as a senior and highly able subordinate. He was already most likely in his forties and may have served under Philip's father or brothers, but little is known about his earlier career and origins. He may have come from Upper Macedonia or he may not, and it is hard to tell whether his family's rise to prominence was due to Philip's favor or whether they were already wealthy and important.[13]

At some point Philip received an appeal for aid from the citizens of Crenides, who were exposed to Thracian raids by bands loyal to Cetriporis. Founded as a colony by the island city of Thasos around

360 BC, Crenides was set up to exploit the rich silver deposits and other minerals in the area. In the past the Thracians had destroyed more than one Greek effort at securing these and similar resources, which explains the willingness of Crenides to sacrifice its independence for the sake of survival. Philip hurried to its aid in person, presumably taking some of his forces while others remained to keep Potidaea under blockade at the very least. He drove off the Thracians and took control of Crenides, which he soon refounded and named Philippi—the same place later famous for the defeat of Brutus and Cassius and whose Christian community received one of Paul's letters. Combined with Amphipolis, Philip had hugely increased his income, giving himself a steady flow of precious metals. At some point in the next year or so he besieged and took three smaller Greek colonies in the region to ensure that all this was kept firmly under his control.[14]

Philip returned to the siege of Potidaea. It had taken Athens two years to blockade the place into submission during the Peloponnesian War, while Olynthus and the Chalcidians had failed to capture it in spite of living so close and possessing a sizeable army. Philip took the city in a matter of months, and it may have surrendered to avoid the final assault. True to his word Potidaea and its lands were transferred to the Chalcidians. Philip gained some personal profit by selling the Potidaeans as slaves, but he was once again generous to the Athenians garrisoning the city, who were allowed to go home without having to pay a ransom. An Athenian expedition had arrived off the coast just after the city had fallen, and once again Athens had dithered and ended up taking no effective action. The instinct for historians is to speak of the Athenians missing another great opportunity, just as they had missed their "last chance" to take Amphipolis. This is to forget that Philip was just one of Athens's problems; by this time Athens was focused far more on defeating its rebellious allies, and on internal bickering over where the blame lay for the failure of a recent campaign in the Gallipoli Peninsula that led to putting a number of their own generals on trial. There was also no good reason to expect the Macedonian resurgence to last or to doubt that there would be opportunities to reestablish their presence in the area. For the moment, their only toehold within reach of Macedonia's heartland was the allied city of Methone.[15]

Philip had enjoyed another good year. Just after the fall of Potidaea he is supposed to have received three messages on the same day. The first was a report of Parmenio's victory over the Illyrians, and the second of another victory, this time of one of his horses at the Olympic Games; by this time, we do not hear of any question over whether or not the king of Macedon was eligible to compete. The third message informed him of the birth of Alexander. Given that he was born in July and the Games were held at the end of that summer in August or September, the chances of the news arriving on the same day are slim in the extreme, but once again it made for a good story.[16]

Macedonian settlers were introduced to the newly named Philippi, but neither the Greeks nor the Thracians already there were wholly supplanted. Workers began draining nearby marshland so that it could be cultivated, and this is surely an indication of similar developments throughout the kingdom. Soon the mines near the city were providing Philip with 1,000 talents of silver every year. Combined with the yield from the workings at Mount Pangaeum, Philip was now very wealthy indeed, and this was marked by an increase in the quality and quantity of his coinage. Gold coins were produced on the Attic standard, while the silver conformed to Thracian weights, a balance that helped trade. Most of the goods that passed into Europe, whether through Thrace or Illyria, from now on also passed through Macedon. This gave more revenue from tolls as well as access to a wide range of commodities. One coin issue in 356 BC depicted the race horse and jockey that had triumphed at the Olympics. The Macedonian aristocracy had long had a fondness for finely made vessels and ornaments, and this was reflected in their increasingly conspicuous lifestyle, most of all in the palace.[17]

His greatly increased income also allowed Philip to hire mercenaries to supplement his army. In particular he attracted growing numbers of specialists such as engineers and funded their research. At some point pay was introduced for the Macedonian soldiers, and the higher ranks within the phalanx were marked not just with prestige and responsibility, but with higher rates of pay. His new settlements allowed him to grant soldiers the right to a share of the produce from set areas of land, and this combined with their pay freed them to be virtually professional soldiers. Philip's men trained even when there was no war, drilling in formation, practicing with weapons, and marching long distances—route marches of 37.5 miles in a day are mentioned by one writer. Philip banned the use of wheeled transport for ordinary baggage and reduced the number of servants, making the soldiers carry their own equipment and food. Cumbersome though the sarissa was, the rest of the pikeman's equipment was light in comparison to the hoplite's panoply. Less burdened and toughened by their training, Philip's army became highly mobile; its sheer speed of movement was something that would surprise one enemy after another.[18]

Those closest to the king benefited greatly from his newfound wealth. All Argead kings had their Companions (*hetairoi*), who feasted with them, fought by their side, or were given important commands, and whose advice they sought. These men included both members of established aristocratic families and the newly favored. Under Philip their numbers increased dramatically, as did their responsibilities and the rewards available. Companions were granted the rights to a share of the produce from large estates surrounding his new communities. Many were from Upper Macedonia and some from further afield, but the key was royal favor, for the king granted estates in his territory to bind outsiders to him and Macedonia. They were all tied to Philip, who rewarded them generously, and his success became their success. The relationship was personal, an echo of older traditions of a chieftain and his warrior household, who shared the dangers and the rewards. Tradition allowed the Companions to address the king freely and to disagree with him; they expected him to respect them as they respected him, and to lead them in battle.[19]

The Royal Pages also had a close, albeit more clearly subordinate, relationship with Philip, since they were so much younger and not yet fully considered to be adult. The older boys guarded the king's tent on campaign, waited on his table, hunted with him, and fought by his side. They could be beaten, but only by the king himself. Even so, Athenians and other southern Greeks found it baffling to see young noblemen serving at table or submitting to a flogging, as if they were slaves. There was also concern that surrounding a king with so many young men and boys invited their sexual exploitation. Apart from affairs with women, Philip was said to have had numerous young men and boys as lovers, including a number of pages.[20]

Gossip inevitably surrounded a man like Philip who had such a spectacular career and was also hated and feared by so many people, so we must not simply accept all the stories as genuine. At this distance the truth is impossible to establish. What we can say is that a lot of people believed that the king was promiscuous, perhaps predatory in his relations with women and youths alike. Aristotle, who knew the king, accepted as fact at least one of Philip's flings with a young man. The king's power was not absolute, but it was considerable, and he was rumored to have beaten one boy to death for disobeying him on campaign. If the rules were different, it was still the case that pages expected to be treated in a certain way by the king, just like their fathers and the other Companions. Failure to meet these expectations was risky, and a number of conspiracies aimed at assassinating both Philip and later Alexander involved pages. An Argead king's relationship with those around him, including the rank and file of the army, was essentially personal; it worked in both directions and conformed to a strong sense of what was acceptable.[21]

Delivering victory and then sharing its benefits was central to the king's role, and so far Philip had an unbroken record of success. We know little about his actions for most of 355 BC. Probably he campaigned to secure the gains around Philippi and Amphipolis, and he may also have intervened in Thessaly. Late in the year he marched on Methone, the last Athenian ally on the doorstep of Lower Macedonia, and a bare six miles from Pydna, which had already fallen. In spite of the fate of their neighbor and the failure of Athens to help, the citizens of Methone resisted staunchly against the fierce assault of the Macedonians. On one occasion, Philip's men escaladed the city wall, and the king ordered the ladders to be taken away once the men were on the battlements, thinking that this would force them to conquer or die. It was a drastic tactic, and in this case failed.[22]

Supplying an army over the winter months was difficult, and that he succeeded is testament to the logistical organization underlying Philip's operations even at this fairly early stage. Even on the coast, the season can be cold and wet, and in this respect Methone may well have been the toughest siege yet undertaken by his army. The city held out into the spring of 354 BC, hoping for an Athenian relief force, for by this time there was a lull in the struggle between Athens and her rebellious allies. During an inspection of the siege works, Philip was wounded. The earliest source says that the missile was an arrow and struck his right eye. In later centuries the whole story was embellished, with the man who inflicted the wound named as one Aster. In some versions it was a javelin and not an arrow, while another claims that it was a bolt fired by a catapult. Several say that Aster inscribed his own name and Philip's on the projectile, while one even claims that Philip had another message scratched onto it before shooting it back into the city.[23]

An arrow shot from a bow seems the most likely instrument, especially as it is mentioned by the sources closest in date to the event. The greater power of a bolt from a catapult would most likely have been fatal, unless almost spent or robbed of a lot of its power by deflecting off something else. (Analysis indicating damage to the right eye socket on the male skull from Tomb II at Aegae/Vergina is one of the main reasons for identifying the remains as Philip.) The strike caused permanent blindness in that eye, but according to a Roman author Philip's doctor "Critoboulus achieved great renown for having extracted the arrow from the eye of King Philip, and for having treated the loss of the eyeball without causing disfigurement to the face." It could easily have been different, but Philip survived, although the pain can only have been terrible and must have lasted for some time. It was not enough to persuade him to give up the siege. As the months wore on without adequate help coming from Athens, the citizens of Methone eventually capitulated.[24]

By Greek standards Philip was surprisingly generous to the defenders, whether through a desire to get the siege finished or to demonstrate that he was not prone to revenge for personal injuries. All the citizens were allowed to leave, albeit wearing only the clothes on their backs, and to go wherever they wanted. Their property, including presumably their slaves, became plunder. The polis was abolished, the physical city was razed, and its land was distributed in plots to his Companions and soldiers. Still only in his twenty-eighth year, Philip had already more than doubled the size of his kingdom, eradicated the independent cities close to its heartland, vastly increased his wealth, married five wives, and fathered several children. There had been many dangers along the way, but his luck had held—if narrowly when he was shot in the eye. In the process of his rise Philip had highlighted the limitations of Athens's will and the capacity of its fleet to defeat a land-based power. More and more people began to notice Macedonia and its king and wonder whether they needed to challenge him or seek his friendship.[25]

6

"I DID NOT RUN AWAY": DEFEAT IN THESSALY

Philip's power was growing. In the early days he and his men had fought with their backs against the wall, struggling simply to survive. Such victories staved off disaster, while each one made the king a little stronger, more secure and confident. Turning to expansion, even on a local level, marked a major change, for the rewards of success were greater. The scale and sheer speed of Philip's early victories is hard to exaggerate, for in little more than five years he had made the Macedonian kingdom at least as large as it had ever been, and far stronger in terms of resources and manpower. Apart from the Chalcidice, he now controlled all of the ports along his coastline, making it far harder for Athens to attack him, while his northwestern frontier was far better protected than it had been in living memory. Yet in the past other Argead kings—and indeed rulers in Thrace or Illyria—had flourished for a while without managing to make their power permanent, let alone pass it on to an heir. If Philip died, then there was no obvious adult successor, for his sons were infants and his nephew still a boy. Equally, no one could predict what would happen if Philip's run of successes came to an end, or be sure that he could hold on to the newly conquered territory.

Exploiting all of these gains also took time and effort, and it is a mistake to think in terms of Philip instantly becoming wealthy or having far more soldiers ready for service. New and refounded communities had to be set up, populations established, and farming, mining, and other industries developed as appropriate. Philip was not one to wait for resources to accumulate into a surplus before he spent them, and there was little or no pause in his activity. At some stage during these early years he constructed and manned a flotilla of small warships. He had plenty of material for shipbuilding readily available, and no doubt the Greek cities brought under his control had plenty of crews and experienced mariners. This was not a grand fleet designed to challenge the Athenian navy or anyone else in massed battle; such a project would have taken years and most likely still been unable to match the enemy. Instead Philip built light vessels for raiding, whether independently or in support of his forces on shore. It was a way of harassing the Athenians, by snapping up merchant vessels and forcing them to defend their outposts and allies within his reach. This kept the war going, and might eventually persuade the Athenians to negotiate.[1]

Raiding on this scale was a fairly cheap method of making war and could be profitable, but in the meantime crews had to be paid. The same was true of soldiers, especially mercenaries and specialists. Philip spent as rapidly as he acquired new sources of income, lavishing rewards on his men and especially the Companions, entertaining on a grand scale, and giving gifts and bribes to win friends and allies abroad. At times, no doubt especially in the early years, spending outstripped his means. On one occasion a crowd of angry soldiers confronted him over their arrears of back pay. Philip was exercising at the palace by wrestling with a man named Menegetes, who was presumably a foreign athlete. Sweating heavily and covered in dust, the king finished the bout and then ran toward the soldiers, saying, "You are right, comrades, I have been practicing with this barbarian in order to thank you properly for the credit you have extended to me!" Barging through them, he dived into a pool and swam up and down until the men got bored and wandered away, none the wiser as to when they would actually be paid. In later years Philip was supposed to have been very fond of telling this story of how he had avoided paying his men yet still kept their loyalty.[2]

His army continued to obey and fight, and there was no pause in campaigning. However, the events of the years after the fall of Methone in 354 BC are poorly covered by our sources, so the chronology is unclear even for major events. Quite often we do not know what Philip was doing at any one time. At best we tend to hear only of the highlights, usually based on their significance to Athens. Such accounts give no real idea of how much time Philip spent in administration, hearing petitions and making rulings and all the dull routine of government. They also display little interest in his dealings with the Thracians, Illyrians, and other northern neighbors, even though Philip spent a lot of his time negotiating with or fighting against the leaders of these peoples. As the Macedonian kingdom expanded, so did Philip's commitments, which meant that he had to manage his affairs in several areas during the same year. Although at times he concentrated a large part of his total military strength into a single army, more often his soldiers were split into several different commands, whether led by the king or trusted subordinates like Parmenio. Thus some campaigning seasons saw wide-ranging activity that would have been complicated to recount even if our sources had possessed the interest.

Nothing definite is known about Philip's actions for the remainder of 354 BC. Since we do not know at what point during the siege of Methone he was wounded, we have no idea of whether he was still convalescing for much of the year. Diodorus follows his description of the fall of the city by saying that the king then subdued Pagasae, and the most natural reading is to see this as happening in the same year. Pagasae was the port of Pherae, the rival city of Larissa in Thessaly and formerly home of tyrants like Jason and Alexander. So it is possible that Philip led a force into Thessaly in 354 BC, continuing the long-standing alliance of the Argeads with Larissa, but there is no hint of this intervention in any other source. Since we know that from 353 BC onward Philip was heavily involved in Thessaly and that at some point he

captured Pagasae, some have concluded that Diodorus was anticipating events. Others argue that the text is corrupt and that he was
speaking of another city altogether, an unidentified Pagas or Pagae
perhaps somewhere along the Thracian coast.[3]

None of these interpretations is implausible in itself. As we have
seen, Thessalian and Macedonian affairs had long been deeply inter-
twined, with frequent military interventions in both directions by
whoever happened to be the strongest neighbor at the time. Demosthenes tells us that Pagasae fell to Philip before help sent from
Athens reached the beleaguered city, but gives no more details about
when this occurred. Otherwise, he and our remaining sources show
almost as little interest in Thessaly as they do in Thrace and Illyria.
Although definitely Greek, the Thessalians did not fully conform
to the ideals and political habits of Athenians and other southern-
ers. Theopompus of Chios, writing in the later fourth century BC,
was characteristically scornful of the aristocrats who dominated
Thessaly, claiming that they "wile away their lives in the presence of
dancing girls and flute-girls. Some waste their days at dice, drinking,
and similar incontinence. They are more concerned to furnish themselves with a table full of every sort of delicacy than to have their
own lives well ordered."[4]

For all his admiration for Philip's achievements, Theopompus
had a similarly jaundiced view of the king and his Companions'
habits, and while he may have exaggerated, he did not wholly
invent. Later a shared fondness for raucous feasting and drinking helped to bond many Thessalian noblemen with Macedonia
and its monarch; quite a few ended up among the ranks of his
Companions. A fondness for parties went alongside a fondness for
war and conflict for Macedonians and Thessalians alike, and the
one common thread running through the recent history of Thessaly
was the almost constant power struggles within and between cities. Conflict between Pherae and Larissa was more likely than not
in 354 BC, and Philip might have been asked to intervene, but we
cannot be sure.

Either way, Philip was in Thrace early in the campaigning season
of 353 BC, attacking the Greek coastal cities of Maronea and Abdera
and pushing toward the Gallipoli Peninsula and the Dardanelles

Strait. Also in the area was Pammenes, the man in whose house he had lived during his captivity in Thebes. The Theban was at the head of 5,000 mercenary hoplites on their way to aid a satrap in Asia Minor who had rebelled against the Persian king. Although no one specifically mentions the agreement, Thebes must have arranged with Philip for these men to march through Macedonia to get this far and there may have been a formal alliance between the king and the Thebans. In fact Philip went further, assisting Pammenes by negotiating with the Thracian Cersobleptes so that the hoplites could continue on their journey unmolested. The presence of these mercenaries as well as his own Macedonian troops meant that the talks were backed up by the threat of considerable force, and they were able to defy another Thracian ruler who was hostile. Pammenes crossed the Dardanelles and for a while served the satrap well, until doubts were raised about his loyalty and he and his men were sent home. A few years later the Thebans hired out another mercenary contingent, this time to fight on behalf of the Persian king against rebels in Egypt.[5]

In the meantime Philip had received a desperate appeal from Larissa for aid against Pherae and decided to answer it. This was no easy matter, for he was some 500 miles away, which in itself is an indication of just how far his kingdom and his commitments had grown since he came to power. The quickest way was by sea, with transport ships guarded by his small navy, but an Athenian squadron led by Chares was near Neapolis, waiting to intercept. Philip chose his four fastest warships and gave them strong crews of all his best sailors and oarsmen. Then he sent them on ahead, with orders to sail closer than usual to the shore by Neapolis. Chares took the bait and led his triremes in the chase until they were far out to sea. Seizing the moment, Philip and the rest of his fleet went through. By the time the Athenians realized that they could not catch the fast ships, they were a long way out to sea and unable to turn and attack the other Macedonians.[6]

The Athenians had missed a chance to inflict a severe defeat on Philip and perhaps even to kill or capture the king himself. Yet this was not the primary reason why Chares had been sent to the region, and in the rest of the year he operated with great success on and around the Gallipoli Peninsula. He captured Sestus, a Greek city, massacring the defenders and selling the surviving women and children as slaves. In due course they were replaced by Athenian settlers. Chares brought the peninsula firmly back under Athenian control, forcing Cersobleptes to accept this reality. At some point he defeated a force of mercenaries in Philip's pay and commanded by a man named Adaeus, or "the cockerel."[7]

For the moment Philip had other priorities: leading an army into Thessaly. Although the struggle between Larissa and Pherae was an old one, it had recently become part of a much broader conflict involving many Greek city-states, which scholars term the Third Sacred War. Philip's intervention would in due course involve him more and more with the affairs of southern Greece and eventually to greater conflicts and victories there. He may well have scented opportunities in marching against Pherae, but it would be wrong to see this as part of some deeper plan aimed at the domination of Greece. Philip was allied with Larissa, had a long association with its leading family, the Aleudae, while marriage to a wife from the city and another from Pherae emphasized his connection with Thessaly. The appeal was an opportunity to add to his power and status, while failing to aid an ally would have reflected badly on him and led other allies to doubt his reliability. All around there was no good reason not to intervene in 353 BC.

Yet Thessaly was already involved in a much wider struggle involving most of the major Greek cities and many lesser ones, with the shrine at Delphi the original pretext for a spiraling power struggle. Delphi was the greatest of the sacred sites revered by all Greeks and sometimes by kings and states from the wider world. The oracle of Apollo was widely trusted for its authority, the judgment of the god delivered in often cryptic phrases spoken by the priestess. While it had been unusual for Philip and the Olynthians to consult the oracle before confirming their treaty, no one would have doubted the power and solemnity of this gesture. Delphi was special, the navel (*omphalos*) of mother earth, and every four years competitors came there from all over the Greek world to compete in the Pythian Games, which was part of the cycle including the Olympic Games. At other times pilgrims went to Delphi, as did formal delegations wishing to consult the oracle. There was also a constant flow of wealth as states and individuals made dedications to the god and paid for monuments on which their name would be inscribed. Victors often sent trophies from the battlefield to be dedicated and displayed as permanent commemoration of their triumph—in almost every case, of triumph over fellow Greeks. In Philip's day Delphi, and especially the sacred precinct of Apollo, was one of the most grandly built sites anywhere in the Greek world.[8]

As a city, Delphi was not militarily or politically powerful, and given its Panhellenic significance, it had traditionally been overseen by a "council of neighbors," the Amphictyonic League. This consisted of twelve tribes, each with two votes, and over the centuries the definition of a neighbor had broadened and been shaped by the power struggles of Greece. The Thessalians were part of the council, as was Thebes and Boeotia, and by the fourth century BC Athens had one vote as part of the Ionian tribe. Both it and Thebes were given preferential status, so they had a shorter wait before any question was put to the oracle.[9]

Inevitably, city-states being what they were, any organization of this sort became a forum for political maneuvering, but most of the time the balance between the various voting members prevented anything too drastic. This changed in the years after the Spartan defeat at Leuctra, and while Thebes was dominant it managed to convince a majority to vote as it wished, especially when conflict in Thessaly went against the leaders of Pherae and shifted Thessaly's two votes in Thebes's favor. Sparta was fined for its illegal seizure of Thebes's citadel of Cadmeia and its occupation of the city back in 382 BC at a time when the two cities were allies. Phocis, another long-term rival of Thebes, which although smaller than Sparta was a good deal closer, was also fined, in this case for cultivating sacred land. The resolutions were passed and—in a manner reminiscent of the United Nations—nothing happened.

In 356 BC the Amphictyonic League met and not only renewed the fines, but doubled them and threatened war if they were not paid. Opinion was divided at Phocis as in any Greek city, but eventually the more militant voices prevailed and a small army led by Philomelus marched the short distance to Delphi and occupied the city. Phocis had an ancient, albeit disputed, claim to be guardian of the shrine, and ambassadors went around Greece reasserting this and also pleading the injustice of the fines imposed on them. Several major cities, including Athens and Sparta, allied with Phocis, in part because they realized that there was some justice in the Phocian case, but mainly because they wished to weaken Thebes. For a while, most states were too busy with other problems for anything more to happen, but in late 355 BC a council of the Amphictyonic League met again, although clearly not at Delphi and without all of its members, for Phocis and its allies did not see this as a legitimate session. A majority of those who were present voted to declare Sacred War against Phocis for seizing the shrine.

Philomelus responded by using some of the wealth held in the sacred precinct to hire mercenaries. Many cities, including Athens, sometimes used temple funds in this way to finance major wars, normally calling it a loan even if it was not always repaid. So while Phocis's right to control Delphi was questionable, at this stage its actions were relatively restrained. In 354 BC Philomelus and his hired soldiers defeated a mixed force of Boeotians and Locrians, from the city of Locri, and then 6,000 Thessalians. More Thebans and Boeotians arrived, and Philomelus was in turn defeated and either died in the battle or committed suicide in its aftermath.[10]

With the Phocians' main army smashed and its leader dead, the war seemed virtually over, and it was in the aftermath of this victory that Thebes decided to send Pammenes and his men off to Asia. Wars were expensive, even when successful, and hiring soldiers out might bring some profit as well as political advantage, but it relieved the state of the need to pay, feed, and clothe them in the meantime. Hopefully these experienced men would be available when they were next needed by the polis. Phocis was smaller than Thebes, lacking its manpower and wealth, but it still held Delphi and its treasures, which gave it the funds to wage war on a scale that would not otherwise have been possible. The Phocians elected Onomarchus as their new commander, and he exploited the sacred treasuries on a far greater scale than his predecessor. During the course of the war the Phocians went from paying one and a half times to twice the normal rate of pay for mercenary service; there was never any shortage of recruits willing to sign on under these terms. Delphi's wealth also allowed the Phocians to sweeten offers of alliance with substantial gifts. Onomarchus sent money to the Athenian general Chares, allowing him to pay for a feast at Athens to celebrate his defeat of Philip's commander Adaeus.[11]

In 353 BC Onomarchus went on the attack. Thebes was weak after sending away the pick of its own and its mercenary hoplites, and hampered because Phocis lay in between it and its allies in Thessaly. The latter were also distracted when the tyrant Lycophron emerged at Pherae and decided once again to challenge the dominance of Larissa and the Thessalian League. As was natural in Greece, local struggles fed into the wider conflicts, so Pherae allied itself with Phocis, the enemy of its enemies and perhaps also an old friend. Thus when Philip marched against Pherae in support of Larissa, it was almost inevitable that he would become caught up in the wider Sacred War, especially since he was already at war with Athens, another ally of Phocis.[12]

Philip and his Thessalian allies began to press Pherae, prompting Lycophron to ask Onomarchus for help. The Phocian commander sent his brother, Phayllus, with 7,000 men, but Philip routed him. Next Onomarchus came in person with the greater part of his forces, and this time the Macedonians and their allies were outnumbered. Philip was beaten twice, and in a brief description of one of these battles it is evident that he was also outfoxed. Onomarchus deployed his hoplites in front of a crescent-shaped mountain. On the high ground on each tip of the crescent he concealed stone-throwing catapults with their crews and plenty of ammunition. Philip saw the phalanx and deployed his own men to meet them, but did not spot the ambush. Onomarchus then advanced to meet the Macedonians and Thessalians, but before they came into contact his hoplites pretended to give way. The stress of hand-to-hand combat when phalanxes met was so terrible that sometimes one side would collapse before any fighting. As the Phocian mercenaries retreated back onto the lower slopes of the mountain, Philip's men gave chase. A rapid advance tended to make any close formation become ragged. Then they came in range of the artillery, which removed whatever camouflage they had employed and began to lob stones down onto the dense target offered by the Macedonians. Onomarchus gave the prearranged trumpet signal and his hoplites halted, formed up, and charged.[13]

The Macedonians broke. Some of them abandoned Philip altogether and made their own way home. The king managed to rally others and keep them together in a more organized retreat, but for the moment their morale was shattered and with it their belief in their king. Philip's unbroken run of successes had at last come to an end, when at long last he had faced a large Greek army. Some of the Macedonians openly blamed him for the defeat, and it was undeniable that he had walked into the trap. Onomarchus's use of artillery in a pitched battle was unprecedented and never repeated with anything like the same success. Catapults were cumbersome, unsuitable for use in the field, which has led scholars to suggest that the Phocians only had them with the army because they were planning to lay siege to cities in Thessaly. This might be right, although they may also have brought the artillery to give to allies wanting them for use in defending their own cities—as much a psychological urge as a practical one, for the use of artillery even in siege warfare was something new to most Greeks. Either way, Onomarchus used them and his well-drilled troops decisively, leaving Philip with no choice but to lead his sullen troops back to Macedonia. He tried to reassure them by declaring that he was not running away, but deliberately going backward just like a ram when it prepares for another, harder charge.[14]

News of the defeat spread quickly. For all his success up to this point, Philip might prove to be just another of those Macedonian kings who had flourished briefly before it all went wrong and he died at the hands of his own people. There were alternatives to him as king, and around this time his two surviving half brothers reappeared at Olynthus. Olynthus had led the Chalcidian League into its alliance with Philip when Athens seemed the greater threat, but now the Athenian enclaves had all gone and Philip was close, strong enough to be dangerous but perhaps now vulnerable. Some leading citizens went to Athens seeking friendship and even alliance, even though the latter was specifically banned by the treaty they had signed with Philip. There are hints that leaders in Epirus, Illyria, and Paeonia all began to wonder whether Philip really was invincible after all. He had narrowly escaped in the seas off Neapolis and then suffered a major defeat in Thessaly. It was a critical moment, and another failure could easily begin to unravel all that Philip had achieved.[15]

7

THE AVENGER

Philip could not afford another failure, nor could he let the defeat at the hands of the Phocians go unavenged and allow doubts about his power and prospects to grow. That meant that he had to continue the war and hope that he could win next time. Thus in 352 BC he returned to Thessaly, and this time he and his allies mustered no fewer than 20,000 infantry and 3,000 cavalry. How many were Macedonian and how many Thessalian is hard to say, although the latter certainly provided a large proportion, and perhaps the majority, of the mounted troops. In the meantime Onomarchus and the Phocians had won another victory, this time over the Boeotians, but he duly responded to a fresh appeal for aid from the Thessalian tyrant Lycophron and marched north with 20,000 foot and 500 horsemen. He may have hoped to join up with the tyrant, who apart from more mercenaries would have had good cavalry of his own.

Some scholars would place Philip's capture of Pagasae as part of this campaign, while others suspect a direct attack on Pherae itself. The battle that followed occurred near the Gulf of Pagasae, most likely in a stretch of gently rolling land known as the Crocus Field for the flowers that bloom there. Philip may have managed to slip away from Pherae and force march to intercept Onomarchus and the Phocian army. This was good cavalry country, but hoplites and not cavalry were usually the key players in battles in mainland Greece, and Onomarchus's men were veterans and had the added confidence of knowing that they had beaten the Macedonians in the last encounter. No doubt Philip had spent much of the winter training and encouraging his men to counter the memory of defeat, just as he had done before marching against Bardylis back in 358 BC. This time he gave his soldiers a special cause, ordering them to wear crowns of laurel on their helmets. Laurel was closely associated with Apollo and with the wreathes of victory and celebration. The symbol proclaimed that the soldiers were the servants of the god in this sacred fight and not merely allies of Thebes in an everyday war between city-states. Philip may well have hoped that his soldiers would feel that they were fighting with the god's aid, and thus bound to win even against the same men who had chased them away the year before.

Justin claims that the mere sight of the laurel leaves made some of the Phocian hoplites drop their weapons and flee as they understood the impiety of their actions. More prosaically, Diodorus says that after a tough fight Philip won because of the numbers and bravery of the Thessalian cavalry. The Phocian army collapsed, and many of the fugitives headed for the beach because Athenian ships were in clear sight offshore. This squadron was led by Chares, back from the Thracian coast, and it is unclear whether he chanced to be there or the Athenians were meant to rendezvous with their Phocian allies. If so, then they were late once again, albeit this time by a matter of hours. Onomarchus was one of many who stripped off armor and tried to swim to the ships. Few if any made it. Most drowned or were killed by missiles; 6,000 men died, while another 3,000 were taken prisoner.

The fate of these captives is disputed, for Diodorus can be read as saying that Philip had them all drowned as punishment for their sacrilege. Both sides had executed prisoners during the early stages of the conflict, albeit not on this scale and only for a short while. Yet achieving such a mass slaughter by drowning does seem unlikely, unless there were convenient cliffs where anyone falling or pushed from the top was bound to perish. The mercenaries might have been killed and their bodies afterward thrown into the sea, or perhaps there was some confusion with the men who died in the water trying to reach the ships. Whatever happened, Philip cannot have risked letting so many trained hoplites go free or be ransomed, especially given the enemy's willingness and ability to pay mercenaries. The corpse of Onomarchus was retrieved and crucified to deny proper burial to the despoiler of Apollo's temple.[1]

Philip was hailed as the avenger of the god and protector of religion, at least by those inclined to side against Phocis and its allies. His wife Nicesipolis gave birth to a daughter, although the mother died some twenty days later. The baby girl was given the name Thessalonice, or "Victory in Thessaly," and the defeat of Onomarchus is most likely the success that was being celebrated, for it was the greatest Philip ever achieved in that region. Soon afterward Pherae capitulated, with Lycophron accepting terms that allowed him and his supporters and 2,000 mercenaries to depart. For much of the summer Philip lingered in Thessaly, helping to reestablish the communities after years of conflict. Our sources differ over how he approached the task, and whether he was mild or very active in plundering and punishing any community or individuals who had opposed him. He was accused of favoring popular movements within cities, which in the long run weakened the hold on power of the established aristocracy. No doubt there was a difficult balancing act in keeping Thessaly's fractious aristocrats happy. His marriage alliances with Larissa and Pherae helped—and some scholars would have his wedding to Nicesipolis occur now rather than earlier. More likely his engagement with both of the major cities of the region had begun far earlier.[2]

Allies of Pherae suffered, perhaps severely, and a few cities may have been abolished, even though in the past they had been loyal members of the Thessalian League. Mainly Philip's decisions resulted in the reorganization of communities and changes in their political balance. Gomphi was renamed Philippolis sometime in the next few years, the second city to take Philip's name. Yet the vast majority of Thessalian cities remained independent and not part of his kingdom, with just a few exceptions, such as Magnesia and the port of Pagasae. Perrhaebia—an area to the north and not truly part of Thessaly although for a long time under the control of the League—did come under Philip's direct control for he appointed one of his men to administer it. We cannot say whether the king could and did call on Thessalian troops in the following years other than to defend Thessalian interests, but this seems unlikely at this stage.

For the moment his popularity was high, at least with those on his side, and it may well have been now that the Thessalians conferred an unprecedented honor and named him *archon*. This was the supreme war leader and magistrate of all Thessaly, and he certainly gained the title at some point, even though no source actually tells us when. Many scholars argue that the euphoria following the victory over the Phocian army and the surrender of Lycophron was the most likely occasion for this honor. Something is certainly needed to explain a league of Greek cities setting aside their instinctive jealousy over citizens' rights and control of their own communities to award the post to a foreigner. Jason of Pherae had been *tagos*, a similarly wide-ranging magistracy held for life, and archon may have been a version of this traditional post. In practical terms it gave Philip the right to call on Thessalian troops and some income from specific levies, including harbor duties and market taxes, but it also gave him responsibility for settling disputes and dealing with problems throughout the area. Justin claims that the reason the Thessalians chose Philip to lead them against Pherae and the Phocians was because their aristocrats feared that if one of them was in charge and won the war then this would be a springboard to tyranny. During and after the war a substantial faction of noblemen decided that it was for the common good—and no doubt their own good—to have Philip as leader.[3]

All of these matters took time, so it was late in the year when Philip began to march south and continue the war against Phocis. By this time the Phocians had appointed Onomarchus's brother as their new commander, and he was busily hiring more soldiers after the loss of almost half the army. The delay also gave time for allies to send help, their enthusiasm encouraged by yet more generous gifts from the treasures of Delphi as well as a reluctance to let the Thebans and Thessalians win an outright victory. Sparta sent 1,000 men, Achaea 2,000, and Athens—for once acting with speed—no fewer than 5,000 infantry and 400 cavalry. The main Phocian army campaigned in Boeotia against the Thebans and their allies, winning some skirmishes and losing others.

Philip's army might have made the difference if it was able to join up with the Thebans and other Boeotians, or at least attack Phocis itself, but he had waited too long. The main route from Thessaly into Phocis went through the pass of Thermopylae, and before he reached it the enemy was already there in force, including the Athenians. There was no reason to think that Philip's men were any more capable of storming the narrow pass head-on than the Persians had been, and this time the route around the flank was securely guarded by the Phocians. From the start Philip's priority had been Thessaly and his allies there, and after the failure in 353 BC he had returned and won an outright victory. Larissa and the Thessalian League were restored to supremacy and this in turn appears the primary goal of its leaders, with the Sacred War as something of a sideshow. Blocked at Thermopylae, Philip turned around and went back to Macedonia. Several years would pass before he returned to central Greece, and the Sacred War ground on indecisively, mainly fought between Phocis and Boeotia as the allied contingents went home. Although Philip withdrew, his involvement with Thessaly was now far closer than before and this did not change. In the meantime he had plenty of other business in the north, and by the autumn of 352 BC Philip was campaigning in Thrace.[4]

Alliances had shifted among the Thracian tribes and leaders as they so often did; Philip like everyone else switched whenever it seemed in his best interest. Therefore in a reversal of the previous year, he was on good terms with King Amadocus (possibly the son and successor of the earlier king of the same name who had been an enemy) and fighting against Cersobleptes. In November news reached Athens that he was not far from the Dardanelles, besieging a Thracian stronghold called Heraion Teichos whose precise location is unknown. The Athenians, dependent on grain from the Black Sea and nervous that Chares's success in the area was about to be undone, voted to send forty triremes manned by citizens up to the age of forty-five, and to introduce a special tax to raise the sixty talents needed to fund the operation. Campaigns in winter were never undertaken lightly and this was a significant force, indicative of Athenian concern. Then, before the expedition was ready, news arrived saying that Philip was seriously ill. Soon afterward another report claimed that he was dead. Mightily relieved, and thus all the more eager to believe such good tidings, the Athenians canceled the operation and the tax.[5]

Philip was not dead, although it does look as if he fell seriously ill, for the campaign in Thrace ended indecisively in 352 BC and he does not seem to have returned there for several years. He was thirty or a little more, but even the young sometimes died of disease, and aggressive leaders like the king most certainly could fall in battle. The reports of his real illness—and even the false story of his death—reminded everyone that he was mortal, just as the defeat of Adaeus and the far more serious personal defeat in Thessaly showed that he was fallible. A world without Philip was a recent memory, as was a Macedonia crippled by internal power struggles. For the moment he was successful and strong enough to prompt jealousy and suspicion in his neighbors, without being so invincible that he was obviously too strong to challenge. If Philip died then all his gains might rapidly wither. His closest adult relations were his two exiled half brothers, who were bound to face a hard struggle if they tried to become king.

Nothing definite is known about Philip's activity in 351 and 350 BC, but this background of doubt may hold the key. A little later, the Athenian orator Demosthenes mentions "campaigns against Illyrians and Paeonians and King Arybbas," and in an earlier speech claims that Philip was building fortresses in Illyria. Although each is an aside, offering no detail whatsoever or any precise date, they fit best at this time. Plenty of leaders resented being forced to submit to Philip, since for the Greeks and war leaders elsewhere, acknowledging the greater power of someone else was a constant irritation, sometimes necessary and occasionally made palatable by tradition or even personal charm. Former enemies and allies alike were bound to wonder whether Philip was about to fall, and if he did then it was always better to make new friends earlier rather than later. Assertions of independence on the part of some Illyrian and Paeonian leaders is highly likely in the circumstances, leading to raiding. Philip had to respond promptly and forcefully if the contagion was not to spread. With nothing to go on, we cannot say how serious and hard-fought the resulting campaigns were, and we should be wary of dismissing them as minor simply because they failed to draw the attention of our Greek sources.[6]

A little more is known about affairs in Epirus, ruled by King Arybbas of the Molossians, the uncle of Philip's wife Olympias. There may not have been any actual fighting, and instead merely a demonstration of the strength of the Macedonian army and its ability to march at will into Epirus. Olympias's younger brother, Alexander of Epirus, went with Philip and the army when it returned home. Arybbas remained on the throne, but one sign of Macedonian dominance is that for the moment the Molossians stopped minting their own coinage and used Philip's currency instead. Alexander of Epirus stayed at Pella or wherever the Macedonian court happened to be, and almost inevitably there were rumors that the boy was seduced by Philip. What mattered for the moment was that Arybbas had not only received a sharp reminder of Macedonian power, but also knew from now on that Philip had a replacement for him on hand if ever he chose to back the claim of Olympias's brother.[7]

As we have seen, Philip's two half brothers had been offered a welcome by the city of Olynthus, the head of the Chalcidian League. This was provocative, and much like the League's ongoing flirtation with Athens, was meant as a clear signal that Philip should not take the Olynthians for granted, for they were wealthy, reasonably powerful, and had other options for allies. More than likely these actions reflected the rise in domestic politics of men who were rivals of those who had favored Philip, and they naturally adopted an assertive pose to emphasize that they were different and would lead their city and the League to better things. In response Philip seems to have made a demonstration of force on their borders in 351 BC, though like his dealings with the Molossians this stopped short of actual war. Any impression this made was temporary, for tension continued to build. International relations in the Greek world were generally shaped by blinkered self-interest and very short memories, so perhaps there was an inevitability about what followed. The Chalcidian League had come to fear Philip more than any other state, while he in turn no longer needed to be at peace with them and was confident in his own strength. We do not hear of direct provocation on his part, nor is there any sign of reluctance, and by 349 BC Philip and the Chalcidian League were at war.[8]

Much of the evidence for this conflict comes from the published speeches of Demosthenes, which were celebrated in antiquity for their style and passion. Three centuries later Rome's greatest orator, Cicero, declared that he was modeling his own attacks on Mark Antony on these famous speeches—willfully ignoring the fact that Demosthenes's arguments led Athens to defeat. This admiration for the artistic merits of Demosthenes's words can disguise the fact that his was merely one voice among many in the Athenian Assembly, and that others whose works have not survived were far more influential at the time. In these years Athens struggled to fund its instinctive ambition, and at times voted for wars that it simply could not afford. In 355 BC the prudent Eubolus was elected to control the Theoric Fund, and came effectively to direct state finances, making it far harder for the Assembly to direct money to overseas adventures. Neither he nor his sympathizers were rigid, for when the need seemed real they were prepared to pay for major commitments, like the force that had helped the Phocians seal Thermopylae shut against Philip's advance.[9]

Prudence was never a feature of Demosthenes's rhetoric. Although born to wealth, his factory-owning father died when he was young and his inheritance was squandered by his guardians. Once old enough Demosthenes successfully sued the men, but that did little to recover what he had lost. A sickly and thin child grew into a serious young man who drank little and was averse to luxury in food and everything else, who devoted years of hard slog to develop his voice and his skill with words. For a long time he made a living writing speeches for others to deliver in legal cases, and he did not speak in the Assembly until he was thirty. His early speeches there make no mention of Philip, until the *First Philippic* (the name is a modern one) delivered in 351 BC. From then onward the king of Macedon became an obsession, a theme to which he returned again and again, assuring Athenians that if they did not fight Philip in the north, then they would end up fighting him in Attica itself—"Because, men of Athens, I want you to know and realize two things: first, what an expensive game it is to squander your interests one by one; and secondly, the restless activity which is ingrained in Philip's nature. . . . Seriously, is anyone here so foolish as not to see that our negligence will transfer the war from Chalcidice to Attica?"[10]

Demosthenes spoke to those Athenians who resented the loss of their northern allies and settlements and still yearned to recover Amphipolis, which had gained a talismanic hold on many of his fellow citizens. In a sense this was a nostalgia for past glories, and he pushed this much further to paint Philip as their inevitable enemy in a life and death struggle. This premise lay behind all his speeches, and filled them with an urgency as well as the remarkable emotional force that this otherwise cold and reserved individual only let loose when he spoke in public. Thus for Demosthenes, Philip must be fought and beaten, and the Athenians needed to realize this and take the necessary action, seize the initiative and take the war to the king. In the *First Philippic* he likened Athens to an ignorant "barbarian" trying to box. "The barbarian, when struck, always clutches the place; hit him on the other side and there go his hands. He neither knows nor cares how to parry a blow or how to watch his adversary." The image is vivid, and all the more powerful for its shock value of suggesting that Athenians, in their own estimation the epitome of all that was best about Greeks, could behave so clumsily.[11]

Philip never saw himself as the inveterate foe of Athens, only as competitor for control of the areas nearer to his kingdom, and it was a competition he was well on the way to winning, at least for the moment. It is impossible to say whether Demosthenes truly believed his own message from the start or came to believe it in time. Opposing Philip gave the orator a cause to champion and a means of making himself better known in the Assembly, and he latched on to this and let it shape his life. Genuine conviction and a convenient opportunity were not—and are not—mutually exclusive in politics, and the repetition of a message can convince the speaker as much as the audience. Demosthenes at the very least contributed to a wider Athenian suspicion of the king and the sense that Athens ought to become strong again, although he was not a lonely voice in this cause. He had less idea about how to defeat Philip, for at heart the orator was not a practical or constructive man. Fond of proposing to form expeditions and increasingly direct in suggesting the use of money from the special Theoric Fund to pay for them, even though using the money in this way was a crime punishable by death, Demosthenes was vague about what these forces were to do. His message was essentially to send men and ships, make allies, and somehow Philip would be defeated. Like plenty of other eloquent politicians, Demosthenes was eager to wage war without feeling the need for even the vaguest strategic idea of how to win.

Ultimately Athens did not possess an army to defeat Philip's men on land or capture cities back from the king, while its navy could neither reach the king nor be defeated by him. Macedonia's small squadron of warships was active, raiding islands and shipping, seizing goods and Athenian citizens as hostages, and managing a great propaganda coup by capturing Athens's sacred trireme while it had paused at Marathon so that the delegation on board could offer a sacrifice in Apollo's temple there. All of this was deeply embarrassing for a naval power like Athens, although the actual damage was no more than pinpricks. When Demosthenes suggested sending triremes to counter Macedon's warships, he argued that a mere ten would do the job. Time and again Philip was generous in his treatment of Athenian prisoners, suggesting a desire for peace. Most of the time, war with Athens was an unnecessary distraction from his other ambitions, offering him little advantage for considerable effort.[12]

In 349 BC Philip attacked the Chalcidian League, targeting its smaller cities rather than striking at Olynthus itself. Even by Greek standards, some of these communities were very small indeed, with little prospect of withstanding a siege directed by Philip's engineers, so most surrendered. One community was stormed and razed, but its name is so garbled by successive scribes copying Diodorus's text that it cannot be identified. Perhaps Philip hoped to intimidate Olynthus into negotiating or had other concerns and was unable to focus his mind and resources solely on the League. There also seems to have been trouble in Thessaly during this year, when one of the tyrants who had been allowed to leave in 352 BC returned and seized control of a city. Philip went in person to deal with this, expelling the man and then reasserting peace, and his leadership as archon, in the wider region.[13]

In the meantime the Olynthians managed at long last to secure an alliance with Athens, which then acted with uncharacteristic energy, at least for a while, sending Chares to the Chalcidice with 2,000 soldiers, most if not all of them mercenaries, and thirty-eight triremes. Later, another Athenian commander brought 4,000 more mercenaries across from the Gallipoli Peninsula, and 150 citizen cavalrymen were also sent to the Chalcidice. These were substantial numbers, even though most were likely the lighter-armed peltasts rather than true hoplites. In addition the Chalcidian League was said to muster 10,000 hoplites and 1,000 cavalry. It was enough over the winter and spring of 349–348 BC to permit the allies to go on the offensive and raid Philip's territory and the lands of the cities that had defected to him. Yet they were not strong enough to attack the Macedonian heartland or to challenge Philip's power base, even while he was away in Thessaly. Athens had other concerns, especially rebellion by its remaining allies on the island of Euboea, and could not risk reducing its forces in Thrace for very long.[14]

Philip returned to the Chalcidice in the summer of 348 BC, by which time most of the Athenian troops had left. Athens debated what to do and eventually decided to form a new expedition to aid the Chalcidian League. It was too small to have made any difference even if it had managed to arrive before the fall of Olynthus, but once again the prevailing winds of these months were in Philip's favor and the Athenians were late. The king advanced, taking city after city, aided by the realization that his power was overwhelming and also by generous gifts to leaders willing to change sides. Soon, Olynthus was surrounded and largely cut off from the sea. The Olynthians sent ambassadors to ask for peace, and were given the blunt reply that "for the rest of time it is not possible for you to live on in Olynthus and me in Macedonia"—or so Demosthenes claims.[15]

At some point two of the aristocratic commanders of the Olynthian cavalry defected to Philip, bringing many of their men with them. Further treachery aided the Macedonians during the siege, and it is unclear whether the city was stormed or eventually capitulated. Either way it was sacked, the survivors sold into slavery, and the polis abolished, along with the Chalcidian League. In effect, Olynthus ceased to exist, and refugees were granted asylum and citizenship in Athens if they wished. Athenian captives were not sold, but were imprisoned. No such clemency could be expected by Philip's half brothers who were captured and executed, removing the closest adult rivals for the throne.[16]

Before the city fell, Philip sent word to Athens claiming that he wanted peace, although it is hard to gauge his sincerity. There was no letup in the assaults on Olynthus, while Philip's squadron of little ships was snapping up Athenian merchants whenever they had the opportunity, and freelancing pirates joined in. This led to a formal complaint from a man taken prisoner by these raiders during the truce surrounding the Olympic Games, who had paid his own ransom and raised the matter on his return to Athens. A delegation was sent to Macedonia, where it was assured of Philip's desire for peace, but moves to begin negotiations failed when the Assembly changed its mind. Instead, Athens sent ambassadors all around Greece seeking allies for a grand coalition against Macedon. No one was interested, so the war lumbered on with neither side prosecuting it with any great energy.[17]

In the early autumn of 348 BC Philip returned home and celebrated Macedon's own Olympic-style festival at Dium, held in honor of Olympian Zeus. Artists, writers, and athletes from much of the Greek world attended, lured by the prizes and the king's generous hospitality. At least one Athenian actor attended, a man named Satyrus, and he is unlikely to have been alone, reminding us of the importance of the truces surrounding such games and the prestige of competition. Demosthenes claims that Philip asked the actor what gift he would like. Satyrus requested the freedom of the two daughters of an old friend, Apollophanes of Pydna, who presumably had moved to Olynthus after the fall of his home city. Both girls were approaching marriageable age, and the king granted them freedom and suitable dowries.[18]

Such generosity came easily, for Philip was riding high once more. In just over a decade he had made his kingdom secure against all the closest threats and vastly expanded his territory and resources, with the occupation of the Chalcidice being another rich gain. As importantly, he had recovered from his defeat and seemed once again secure and powerful. As the Athenians found out, no one else was keen to confront the king or saw a pressing need to do so. While this was in part based on well-entrenched suspicion of Athens, it also showed that few saw the king as vulnerable or more threatening than other, nearer neighbors.

8

PEACE

Athens failed to rally support for its struggle against Philip, and he was in no hurry to escalate the war with the Athenians. The defeat in 353 BC had shown him that major battles against a Greek army were risky affairs. A decade of fighting had secured and enlarged Macedonia, making it far less vulnerable to any likely Athenian expedition, so that conflict with the city was not a life or death struggle for Philip, as it could have been in the first few years of his reign. The Macedonian king could afford to wait, which did not mean that he was inactive or ignored Athens, although the details are hazy. The sources for his activities after the fall of Olynthus in 348 BC are vague, at least until the middle of 346 BC, when Philip began to negotiate with the Athenians. Justin writes that he seized "gold mines in Thessaly, and silver mines in Thrace," encouraged piracy, and intervened in power struggles between Thracian kings. Since there are not and have never been gold mines in Thessaly, this mistake has led many scholars to dismiss the whole passage as another instance of Justin garbling his source. A few years later, Philip asked Athens to provide ships and crews for a Macedonian-funded campaign against piracy, which seems to conflict with the suggestion that he was promoting it now.[1]

Yet care is needed. Philip had created a small fleet, and no doubt continued to prey on Athenian and allied merchant ships as well as coastal communities, activities that might well have been labeled as "piracy" by Athenian sources even though they were simply part of the ongoing war between Athens and the king. Nor is there anything at all implausible in the suggestion that he was active in Thessaly and Thrace in 347 and 346 BC. Indeed, we know that he did campaign in Thrace in the second half of 346 BC. Although Philip was archon of Thessaly, it is unwise to see this post as effectively granting him the rule of the region or seeing his position as instantly secure. Thessalian history was a catalog of rivalries within and between cities, of interminable conflict, revolution, and the emergence of tyrants. Bringing this under control took time and effort, involving more negotiation and arbitration of disputes than direct force. Some of the talking could be done wherever Philip happened to be or carried out by his representatives, but at times he would have had to go to Thessaly in person.[2]

Thrace was even more unstable and a good deal more threatening. Rivalry between the tribal kings and other leaders was exacerbated by Athenian and Macedonian interventions and produced frequent shifts in alliances and bursts of aggression. Justin says that "two brothers, kings of Thrace" asked Philip to arbitrate in a dispute, not through faith in his sense of justice, but from mutual fear that the other would enlist Macedonian aid. The arbitrator came to the agreed meeting accompanied by an army strong enough to intimidate the brothers, and the arbitrator decided to dethrone both of them. Justin is the only source to mention the incident and does not name the kings, so we cannot say how much or how little basis there was to it. King Cersobleptes is far better known than other Thracian leaders, and was at various times ally and enemy of both Athens and Philip. In the summer of 346 BC, Athenian ambassadors saw the Thracian king's son as a hostage at Pella, and reported this as if it would come as a surprise to their fellow citizens. At this time Cersobleptes was allied to Athens and had been cooperating with its commander in the Gallipoli Peninsula. The boy's presence at Philip's court suggested a new degree of alliance with Thracian leaders and subordination to Macedon, which does suggest that force—or diplomacy backed by force—had enforced this on Cersobleptes sometime late in 347 or early in 346 BC.[3]

Philip had claimed to want peace with Athens while he was besieging Olynthus, but had been rebuffed. If he was indeed active in Thrace in these years, then this reinforced Athenian fears over the security of their vital supply route through the Dardanelles. The war between the two continued, although neither made a major effort to win it. Instead both concentrated on securing territory and allies in Thrace. Many Athenians still referred to the struggle as "the war over Amphipolis," and naively clung to the hope that they could still recover the city. Such optimism was unrealistic, but instinctive. Athens had been the greatest power in the Hellenic world until its defeat by Sparta in the Peloponnesian War in 404 BC. Accepting that she would never again rise to such glory was too bitter for citizens obsessed with honor, which meant that setbacks were seen as temporary. Athens should not back down, least of all to an upstart leader of a kingdom only recently seen as at all important. Against this the war was getting nowhere and costing a lot of money. A feeling grew that Athens needed strong allies to defeat Macedon or a spell of peace so that the city could build up her own strength once again.[4]

In much the same way, the Sacred War sputtered along indecisively, and by 346 BC was in its tenth year, the fighting now mainly between the Phocians and Boeotians led by Thebes. Everyone was exhausted, and the war consisted of raids, skirmishes, and attempts to seize smaller cities; none of these actions offered any prospect of final victory. By now the treasures of Delphi—at least the ones easily convertible into coin or gifts—were at long last running out, giving even less chance of breaking the stalemate as the Phocian ability to hire ever more mercenaries petered out. As in any Greek community, there were rival factions waiting for any hint of weakness on the part of the current leaders. Phalaecus, son of Onomarchus and the main Phocian general, was accused of siphoning off wealth for his own use and was dismissed as a new regime took charge.[5]

Philip had made no more than token contributions to the Sacred War since he had withdrawn from Thermopylae in 352 BC. Much the same was true of Phocis's allies, leaving the war to be waged primarily by the Phocians' mercenaries against the Boeotians' citizen soldiers and mercenaries, their strengths too evenly balanced for either to gain a decisive advantage. Substantial aid from outside was needed to break the stalemate, and at some point late in 347 BC Philip decided to supply it. Justin says that the Thessalians and Boeotians begged him to act on behalf of the Amphictyonic League and lead them against Phocis. Appeals of this sort are likely enough, although we cannot say whether this was something new or simply that it suited Philip to act at this point. Opinion in Thessaly mattered a good deal if he was to cement his leadership there, and perhaps after years of internal bickering he had created enough of a lull for the Thessalians to remember old and recent grievances against Phocis.[6]

The news that Philip would march south in 346 BC soon spread, prompting the Phocians to appeal to Athens, Sparta, and her other allies to send troops to secure the pass at Thermopylae. They hoped to stop the Macedonian advance in its tracks just as had happened in 352 BC, and as added incentive Phocis promised to give to its allies several strategically placed strongholds. Athens and Sparta had demonstrated little enthusiasm for direct involvement in the raiding and skirmishing with the Boeotians, but they did not want to see Phocis overwhelmed. Nor did they wish to see Philip at the head of a grand coalition army loose in southern Greece, able to reach Athens with ease and Sparta and the Peloponnese if he chose. Blocking the pass would keep Philip at arm's length and Phocis in the war, which would in turn help to occupy and weaken Thebes, an old rival of both cities, and prevent her from becoming too strong once again. The decision to aid was quickly made and as quickly acted upon. A Spartan king led 1,000 men to the area, while the Athenian Assembly voted to send triremes and raise a levy of citizen hoplites.[7]

They did not arrive in time, although this had nothing to do with Philip—at least nothing directly. Instead the Phocians turned their allies away, for between the sending out of the appeal and the response there was another internal revolution, this time bringing Phalaecus back into power. He may not have wanted to accept aid summoned by his rivals, lest they receive the credit and depose him for a second time. More likely he realized that the Sacred War was unwinnable and was searching for a way out for himself and his loyal mercenaries, and for a means of mitigating the punishment likely to be inflicted on Phocis. While there is no evidence that he was already negotiating with Philip, this is more than likely. For what little it is worth, Justin claims that Philip had thrice received gifts from the Phocians to refrain from intervening in the Sacred War. More openly, the king once again tried to start negotiations with Athens, releasing an Athenian captured at Olynthus to carry the message home and giving the same response to an envoy who arrived soon afterward from Athens seeking the release of all the remaining prisoners.[8]

Athens felt threatened and unsure whether the Phocians would block the Macedonians at Thermopylae. In this mood the Athenians approved a motion proposed by Philocrates to send him and nine other ambassadors to Philip to discuss peace. Demosthenes was chosen, and for all the invective he had aimed at Philip in the past, he was sincere in his desire for peace because he was one of those who felt that Athens needed time to rebuild her strength before resuming the struggle. Later he would do his best to disassociate himself from the treaty that was negotiated and launched fresh verbal attacks on the king. This subsequent reworking of events is important because unusually we have four long speeches discussing the talks, two by Demosthenes and the others in answer by his fellow ambassador and subsequent rival, Aeschines. At least from the Athenian perspective, this means that these months in 346 BC have fuller sources than any other moment in Philip's life.

Sadly, the routine exaggeration and distortion of political dialogue at Athens is exacerbated by the context. The first pair of speeches was delivered when Demosthenes prosecuted Aeschines in 343 BC, accusing him of taking bribes and betraying Athens during the negotiations, and the second pair in 330 BC when Aeschines prosecuted another former ambassador for proposing an honor for Demosthenes. Both speakers abused their opponent and anyone associated with him, made unsubstantiated accusations, and reshaped events to fit their cases. Wildly inaccurate allusions to Athens's past suggest considerable ignorance of history among Athenian citizens. All in all, the truth is very hard to separate from the partisan distortion and downright lies, making these difficult sources to use. Here we are only concerned with the broad outline of events and in particular what we learn about Philip, but as always we must remember that nearly everything is debatable. However, for once it is not a question of having little or no evidence for events, and instead we struggle to judge how much we can trust from these lengthy accounts.[9]

Most Athenians wanted an end to their "war over Amphipolis" and the Sacred War, but they wanted what they felt to be peace with honor, defined first by their own self-image and then with regard to their allies. Not long before the Assembly voted to send the embassy to Philip, it had also decided to dispatch embassies seeking allies in a war against Macedon in the hope that there was more enthusiasm for this than there had been after the fall of Olynthus. There was not, but it would take time to learn this, and subsequently it would be yet another element in the struggle to shift the blame among the men who went to Pella.

The Athenians were received with great courtesy and entertained lavishly, as was to be expected of important visitors to the royal court. All ten had prepared speeches, to be delivered in order of age and experience, and Philip listened with patience to them all, something that took at least several hours. Aeschines was the ninth speaker, and claimed to have reminded Philip of past goodwill shown to his family by Athens, including the story about Iphicrates helping Eurydice when Philip was a teenager. More boldly he repeated the Athenian claim to Amphipolis.

Demosthenes, as the youngest and most junior, spoke last. He was well known for the care with which he prepared and scripted any speech, not trusting himself to speak off the cuff unless he could not avoid it. Aeschines, who as a former actor was always more comfortable in the limelight, claims that Demosthenes had a fit of nerves, and after a bad start dried up altogether. Philip is supposed to have shown sympathy, encouraging him to take his time and continue when he was ready. According to his rival, the famous orator stumbled on for a while, becoming ever less coherent until he fell silent. A herald led the Athenians out of the room, presumably while the king and his advisors discussed the matter.

When they were summoned again, Philip spoke graciously, answering each argument in turn, often naming the orator in question—though never Demosthenes, at least according to his rival. The king concluded with warm expressions of his goodwill toward Athens—proof, according to Aeschines, that the mention of Amphipolis had in no way enraged him. He agreed to send his own ambassadors to Athens to continue negotiations, while he went off to fight against Cersobleptes in Thrace. As a further mark of friendship, Philip promised not to take any action against the Gallipoli Peninsula unless the talks failed. This campaign was to be his main effort in the spring of 346 BC, although Parmenio was also dispatched with a force to besiege Halus on the Gulf of Pagasae (an Athenian ally), which was in conflict with the Thessalian city of Pharsalus. Philip was thus showing his support of the interests of some Thessalians, while promising to return later in the year to lead them all against Phocis and resolve the Sacred War once and for all.[10]

Parmenio left the siege of Halus for a while to serve as ambassador to Athens. He was joined by Antipater (later a very important man) and Eurylochus. All three were distinguished Macedonian noblemen, and Demosthenes was among those who entertained them while they were in the city, boasting that he did so in a generous style appropriate to the welcome shown by Philip to the Athenians and to Macedonian fashion. On his suggestion the Assembly voted to give the envoys front seats in the theater. More practically, two days (by modern reckoning in April) were set aside for the Assembly to debate the question of peace with Macedon, in a rare exception to the usual practice of deciding any matter in one session.[11]

Philip claimed to want not simply peace, but peace without any time limit and with an alliance of equality between Macedonia and his allies and Athens and her allies. The prospect was tempting, but other indications were less flattering to Athenian honor. Philip made clear that this must be on the basis of each side holding all that they currently controlled, slamming the door to Athenian dreams of recovering Amphipolis and other lost territory. In addition Athens's allies were to be restricted to only those formal members of her confederation. Phocis was excluded, as was Halus, which the Athenians had been supplying, and also in due course King Cersobleptes. On the first day of debate much hot air was expended discussing what Athens would prefer to have. There was talk of past greatness, with the implication that this entitled them to better treatment, and tub-thumping boasts about Athenian might and the strength of her fleet.

On the next day, since Philip's envoys did not shift in their statements of his position, Eubolus concentrated his fellow citizens' minds by a blunt statement that they must either accept Philip's demands or resolve to fight against him, with all the cost in blood and bullion that implied. There was a little wriggling, and measures were proposed in the hope of improving the terms in further negotiation, but a motion by Philocrates to accept was passed comfortably, and Philip's ambassadors were helped on their return journey to carry the news. Demosthenes played an important part in making sure that Philip's terms were accepted, specifically refusing to add Cersobleptes to Athens's formal allies when an attempt was made to do this a little later. His close involvement in what became known as the Peace of Philocrates was one of the reasons why he worked so hard to distance himself from it as soon as it was convenient.

The Athenians and their allies swore solemn oaths to abide by the treaty, and then sent the same ten ambassadors to Philip so that he and his allies could do the same and complete the process. Since the king was still in Thrace, this was to take some time. Philocrates and the others made their leisurely way to Pella, and then waited for Philip to return, all of which took the best part of two months. The Athenians were not the only envoys there, and discovered deputations from all over Greece, including Thessalians, Thebans, Spartans, and Phocians. Such a gathering is unlikely ever to have happened in Macedonia before, demonstrating Philip's influence and how many other states were eager to win his favor.[12]

Athens's democracy conducted all its public business in plain view to a degree rarely equaled in any large society. This was a great source of pride, although it also meant that attempts to out-maneuver others during negotiations were transparent from the start. At Pella everything was ultimately determined by Philip's decision, often made by him alone or in consultation with chosen advisors behind closed doors. The deputations from the various cities and leagues waited nervously, suspicious that others knew more than they did. In particular the Thebans worried about the presence of the Phocians, and wondered whether the Thessalians knew more about Philip's plans than they did. None of them knew what Philip intended, while all realized that his will would be very difficult to oppose unless two or more of the great cities combined, and that was not likely. Sparta was primarily concerned with the Peloponnese and the threat to her entire system posed by the freed helot communities established by Epaminondas during the years of Theban dominance. Thebes wanted the destruction of Phocis, ide-ally in a way that restored her own dominance in central Greece. Each of them saw the other as more of a danger than Philip, and their attitude to Athens was similar.

Philip came back from Thrace sometime in the second half of June 346 BC, well content to find himself at the center of every-thing. The campaign had gone well in pressuring King Cersobleptes to accept his place as subordinate ally once more and establishing some new forts to help maintain Macedonian dominance. Philip and the army now prepared for operations against Phocis, while Philip began to receive the waiting ambassadors. His precise inten-tions remained opaque, and rather than speculate about these it is better to see what actually happened before returning to the ques-tion. Listening to the various deputations took time and Philip was in a hurry to begin the war. Very soon, he and his army began the march south and the ambassadors had to go with him and wait to be summoned.

He received the Spartans and the Athenians early on. Philip had promised to release without ransom the Athenians captured at Olynthus in time for a festival later in the year, but had not yet done so. Alone of the ten envoys, Demosthenes raised the matter, offering to pay a token ransom for their release. His colleagues were unimpressed, or so Aeschines later claimed, and the gesture was clearly meant far more for the audience at home than for Philip. Demosthenes spoke of the king being praised for his looks, drinking capacity, and memory, but said that such compliments were unworthy of him; to praise beauty was only right for a woman, the ability to consume wine fitting only for a sponge, and great memory appropriate for a professional orator or sophist. There was a lot of talking, a lot of speeches, some witty and most not. So far the king and his allies had not taken the oaths required to complete the alliance with Athens. As this and other public decisions were delayed, rumor flourished, swinging between fear and hope. Some of the Athenians came to believe—in part because they wanted to believe—that Philip aimed to break Theban power and was ready to turn against his ally in the Sacred War. The Thebans in turn felt excluded, fearing that Phocis was to be let off the hook so that their old enemy would remain a threat. Around this time they raised an army in preparation for the attack on Phocis, and perhaps also as a reminder to Philip of their strength.[13]

Later Demosthenes claimed that the Theban ambassadors also took a tough line with Philip, refusing to be bribed and demanding that he fulfill his obligation as ally and military leader of the Amphictyonic army. According to the orator, the king gave in to the Theban demands whereas he did not to the suppliant approach of his fellow Athenians, proving that Philip was a barbarian and a bully at heart, full of empty bluster. An important aspect of their cases in both confrontations was Aeschines's and Demosthenes's differing portraits of Philip. Demosthenes described the king as a brooding presence, alien in every way to sound Athenian statesmen and citizens. In contrast Aeschines spoke of a king who was well mannered, generous, and eloquent, all admirably aristocratic and Greek qualities. His Philip is still clever and cunning, backed up by subtle Companions, which all meant that there was no shame if the ambassadors were misled. Demosthenes claimed that on their way to Pella for the first time, Aeschines had dismissed Philip as a barbarian, and that he changed his tune only later, after being bribed by the king. Gift giving was a normal part of diplomatic exchange and of traditional hospitality, and accusations of bribery were common in Athenian political disputes, so this was probably no more than routine abuse of an opponent.[14]

Another aspect of this was the portrayal of each other's behavior with the Macedonians. Aeschines more than once explained that he and Demosthenes were never likely to be close, because he drank wine and the other man only water. His Demosthenes is nervous, alternating between hostility to and fawning attempts to befriend his fellow ambassadors, and ridiculous as well as misguided in his insistence on raising the issue of the Athenian prisoners. Demosthenes accused Aeschines of attending a sacrifice and feast where the defeat of their Phocian allies was celebrated. The reply was that diplomats were expected to be diplomatic and accept hospitality from their hosts, that the feast was part of a wider festival, entirely respectable and Greek, and that he had kept silent during the part where the victory was hailed.

Another charge was that Aeschines and a colleague had accepted dinner at the house of the son of an Athenian exile, one of the hated Thirty Tyrants who had held power when democracy was suspended at the end of the Peloponnesian War. They were waited on by a young woman, a freeborn Olynthian of good family now a slave, and treated her like an entertainer rather than a respectable woman. When she resisted, Demosthenes claims that the drunken men stripped off her dress and had her flogged. Aeschines maintained that his character was so well known in Athens that no one would believe any of this, and that the crowd had shouted his rival down when the accusation was made.[15]

Such rows came later, and for the moment Philip, his court, and the army made a brief stop at Pherae, where at long last he and representatives of his allies swore their oaths to confirm the peace with Athens. Delaying this while he held secret talks with all sides had suited Philip, and there was another slight delay before the Athenians set off to report home. The Macedonian army was in Thessaly, no more than a couple of days' march from Thermopylae. Philip's intentions remained unclear, although there was talk, which he surely encouraged, hinting that the punishment

for looting the sacred funds at Delphi could fall on those responsible and not on all Phocians. This suggested milder treatment
than many of the members of the Amphictyonic council (who had
declared the Sacred War in the first place) were demanding, but
could be imposed by Philip, especially if he was directly supported
by Athenian and Spartan troops.

Philip reached the approaches to Thermopylae and halted. At
Athens the Assembly listened to their ambassadors and, encouraged by their reports of Philip's promises of goodwill and future
benefits, once again confirmed the alliance. The ambassadors were
sent to the king for the third time to inform him of this, although
this time Demosthenes declined to go and was beginning to criticize
Philip once again. Aeschines pleaded ill health so that he could stay
in Athens and answer any claims made by the other man. Before
the ambassadors reached Philip, he dispatched envoys of his own
requesting that the Athenians send a force to assist in the settlement of Phocis. Demosthenes argued against it, saying that these
citizens would simply become more hostages, like the captives from
Olynthus, and plenty of Athenians believed him. Aeschines failed
to persuade the Assembly otherwise, and the request was refused.[16]

The news was a disappointment, although it is arguable how
far it altered Philip's plans. By now he had clearly done a deal with
Phalaecus the Phocian commander, who was allowed to depart and
take his 8,000 mercenaries with him. The Macedonians marched
through Thermopylae unopposed and occupied Phocis, where
Philip summoned a meeting of the Amphictyonic council to decide
what punishment to inflict. There was talk of executing all males,
but it was obvious that Philip did not intend anything so brutal and
had most likely made the agreement with Phalaecus on that basis.
Phocis and all its cities were demolished, except for a single community that had opposed the occupation of Delphi. All weapons
were ritually destroyed, all horses were sold, and the Phocians were
banned from obtaining replacements in the foreseeable future. The
population was settled in new villages too small and undefended
ever to become poleis, and a large sum was to be paid back to
Delphi each year until the amount stolen had been replaced. Given
the wanton cruelty of victors in Greek warfare, let alone in the

context of a sacred war, this was mild, although we should never downplay the severity of political extinction to a Greek. Theban and Macedonian garrisons were established in Phocis to ensure that the terms were enforced.[17]

Philip had avenged the insult to Apollo, and the prestige this earned him in many Greek cities should not be blurred by hostile Athenian opinion. He was given—or more likely in a strict sense— the Macedonians were given Phocis's two votes on the Amphictyonic council and the Athenians' priority for consulting the oracle at Delphi. Shortly afterward he was honored by the appointment to oversee the Pythian Games in the autumn; the festival had not been held since before the Sacred War. A sulking Athens refused to take part, complaining that the treatment of Phocis was cruel and feeling that Athens itself was not being held in sufficient respect. Given that neither she nor Sparta, as the Phocians' two greatest allies, suffered any real punishment, this was as unrealistic as it was predictable. Demosthenes and others raised fears of imminent Macedonian invasion and there was certainly little to stop Philip if he chose to march against the city. He did not, and although the Athenians did not attend the games, they did vote as members of the Amphictyonic council to approve all of its decisions.[18]

We do not know how large a force Philip had led into Phocis and whether he had the strength to besiege as large a city as Athens, which was easily supplied from the sea. Such a move, or intervention in the Peloponnese, risked alienating the goodwill he had gained, and might perhaps even persuade other Greeks that Macedonia was a real threat and needed to be fought. Athens was not the center of Philip's world, and the following years demonstrate that he felt he had a lot of work to do on his northern and eastern borders. The Macedonian army had plenty of enemies without starting another major war. Some scholars have taken seriously the rumors about his hostility to Thebes and claimed that he did plan to move against the Thebans, only to be thwarted by lack of support from Athens and others, and by the mustering of the Boeotians. None of this makes sense, for any Athenian contribution was bound to be of minor importance. Attacking Thebes and its allies, even by surprise, was unlikely to produce a quick victory, for wars in

Greece tended to last a long time and victors soon became feared, prompting others to turn against them. Ending the Sacred War was neat and simple by comparison, allowing Philip to turn to other matters.[19]

There is no doubt that Philip's conduct throughout 346 BC was calculated, self-interested, and sometimes devious—in other words just like that of all the other participants. He had manipulated events, delayed when it suited him, spread rumors and vague promises. All this was made easier because his hand was so strong in the first place, for his military force was likely to be decisive unless Athens and Sparta gave effective support to Phocis. He was lucky as well as skillful, for the internal struggles among the Phocians eventually opened the pass at Thermopylae. Victory was bloodless, Apollo avenged, and the king of "barbarian" Macedonia was now a leading member of an organization at the heart of Greek culture. He had also secured Thessalian aims by capturing Halus and giving it to the leaders of Pharsalus, who promptly enslaved the entire population. The garrisons in Phocis served a double purpose, for as long as his Theban alliance remained sound, then the route into southern Greece would be open to his army whenever it was needed. Since he had ensured that the Thebans had achieved much of what they wanted—notably removing fortifications from three Boeotian communities that had more or less willingly joined the Phocians—such goodwill was likely. Athenians could and did speak ever more loudly of the threat he posed to them, but at least from now on they did so fully aware that their city was not beyond his reach.[20]

Philip was not yet forty, so the scale of his success in 346 BC should not be downplayed in expectation of his later, more complete domination of Greece and the attack on Persia. We cannot know how far ahead Philip planned or how fixed his ideas were, but he was still young, more successful than any earlier Macedonian king, about as secure as any Argead could be, and able to work to his own timetable.

9

THE PRINCE

Since the defeat and death of Perdiccas in 359 BC, Philip had fought, negotiated, and coerced his way to this position of strength, exploiting the opportunities that came his way. While he had made mistakes and suffered setbacks—and might have died at Methone—his luck had held out and he had learned from his errors, never repeating them. He was stronger than any Argead king in living memory, and perhaps even stronger than any of his predecessors, for none had created such a confident and effective army. Philip might still fail, and all that he had created collapse, but his defeat was now harder for any enemy to accomplish.

Reinforcing his security was the gradual emergence of an heir, old enough to have survived the most dangerous childhood years and still too young to be a rival. Aeschines spoke of the Athenian ambassadors being entertained during a feast at Pella by the ten-year-old Alexander, who played the harp-like kithara and then engaged in formal debate with another boy. The skills were appropriate for a young Greek aristocrat, although appearing at a party was not, for this was the business of professional entertainers. This, and supposed sycophancy on the part of Aeschines, was mocked by Demosthenes in the Assembly, who implied a sordid role for the young prince, although his claims were clearly nonsense.[1]

Philip's son Arrhidaeus was older than Alexander but was kept out of the limelight and already seen as unfit to succeed because he was physically, or more probably mentally, weak. Malicious rumor later claimed that Alexander's mother Olympias had tried to poison the boy and failed to kill him, instead inflicting permanent harm. Justin makes a vague reference to Philip having other sons, perhaps with lovers rather than wives, which did not mean that he could not decide to recognize them if he chose. None appear clearly in our sources, so they either died young or lacked favor if they truly existed.[2]

Through his father, Alexander was an Argead descended from Hercules. Olympias and the Molossian royal house boasted Achilles, the greatest warrior of all the Greeks in the Trojan War, as ancestor. There is no doubt that she was strong-willed to the point of ruthlessness—as was Philip and subsequently Alexander. Her passionate nature went naturally with devotion to the cult of Dionysus in the local form, which included keeping tame snakes in imitation of the maenads, female companions of the god famed for their wildly ecstatic behavior. Plutarch tells a story of Philip peeking—or dreaming that he peeked—into Olympias's bedroom and being horrified to see a snake lying with her, invoking all the myths of gods appearing in various forms to seduce mortal women. Later on he sent a representative to the oracle at Delphi for explanation, and was told to sacrifice to and revere Zeus Ammon, and that the eye that had peeked through the opening would be taken as forfeit—a tale neatly tying in with his wound at Methone. The whole episode is suspicious, since Alexander later claimed Zeus Ammon as his true father, and is surely invented. Olympias is said either to have given hints of encouragement in the belief, or chided her son for making Hera (Zeus's wife) jealous. Plutarch also says that Philip feared Olympias would work magic or was the lover of a god, and lost his enthusiasm for sleeping with her and visited her less often. As well as Alexander, the couple also produced a daughter, Cleopatra, so for a while at the very least the relationship maintained a sexual element. Philip had his other wives and his lovers, and apart from that spent most of each year away from Pella.[3]

For the young Alexander, his father was surely a distant figure, while his mother was far more familiar and important to him,
even if her role was primarily to supervise his upbringing. His
nurse was named Lanice and came from an important and favored
family, for her brother "Black" Cleitus was a Companion of both
Philip and later Alexander. Three of her own sons would serve
and die in Alexander's campaigns. One of the prince's tutors was
Leonidas, a relative of Olympias, although kinship did not stop
him from searching the boy's belongings and removing any treats
secreted there by his mother. Another teacher was Lysimachus of
Acarnania, who flattered the boy by calling him Achilles, naming
Philip Peleus, the hero's father, and himself Phoenix, who in the
stories had taught the young Achilles. As the Athenian delegates
had witnessed, Alexander's education included music, something
for which he displayed a keen interest throughout his life. There
was also study of famous texts, starting with Homer and paying
particular respect to the glories of Athenian literature and drama.[4]

All this was appropriate for the liberal education of any Greek
aristocrat, as was an emphasis on physical training, although this
may have been given a distinctly Macedonian slant. Leonidas was
a hard taskmaster and in later life Alexander quipped that his
tutor's idea of breakfast was "a night march, and for his supper,
a light breakfast." Formal athletics and the world of the gymnasium were not as celebrated in Macedon as elsewhere, and as an
adult Alexander showed rather less enthusiasm for them than he
did for Hellenic culture and music, which does not mean that he
did not promote them or value them at all. Physical fitness was a
central part of his training, if not competition; he later said that
he was unwilling to take part in a race unless he could compete
against other kings. Equally important was the ability to fight and
hunt. If the supposed custom that a Macedonian nobleman could
not recline at a meal until he had killed a boar single-handed was
really followed, no source mentions Alexander performing this
feat of courage, skill, and strength. Most scholars simply assume
that he did this and everything else expected of him as he grew up,
although the silence has also been used to claim that he did not,
and to suggest that he had a sheltered, overprotective childhood.[5]

We are not told how much or little time the prince spent with other boys of his age. Friends who became ever more prominent during his reign are often declared the friends of his childhood; this is possible, perhaps likely, but never attested by the sources. Similarly, many assume that once he was old enough Alexander learned alongside the royal pages, or at least with selected members of the corps, although once again we are never told whether or not this happened. As an adult he displayed considerable skill at arms, understanding of tactics and drill, as well as superb horsemanship, all of which were the product of long practice; we cannot be sure of the context of all of this.

The most famous story about Alexander's childhood is the taming of the horse, Bucephalus, which, whether or not Plutarch's account is true, celebrated his ingenuity, immense self-confidence, and skill as a rider. There is no firm date, although a good guess would place it when he was about twelve. A Thessalian merchant came to Philip's court, bringing with him a large stallion called Bucephalus or "ox head," sometimes a generic name or perhaps reference to the shape, size, or markings on the animal's head. The horse was magnificent, tall and dark, and the man asked the immense sum of thirteen talents for him, far more than the cost recorded for any other mount in the ancient world. Philip was interested, but when his grooms tried to put Bucephalus through his paces he refused any control, would let no one stay on his back, and seemed to be unbroken and perhaps unbreakable. The king decided that such a horse was not worth buying.

His son was of a different opinion, saying loudly that they were losing a great horse because they did not know how to handle him properly. Philip ignored him, but the young Alexander would not let the matter go and kept on telling his father, the grooms, and anyone else in earshot that they were all making a big mistake. The king demanded to know whether the boy thought he knew better than his horse-loving elders. The boy replied that he could manage that horse better than anyone. His father turned it into a challenge and a wager—something no doubt common at court—asking his son what he would pay if he lost the bet. Alexander pledged the thirteen-talent price asked for the stallion, and amid amused laughter the stakes were set.

Plutarch told the story in some detail. "Alexander ran to the horse, took hold of his bridle-rein, and turned him toward the sun; for he had noticed . . . that the horse was greatly disturbed by the sight of his own shadow falling in front of him and dancing about." Then he spoke to the horse, stroking his head, before finally putting down his own cloak and jumping onto Bucephalus's back. Gently, making sure he did not put enough pressure on the reins to make the bit dig into the animal's mouth, he rode gently, "but when he saw that the horse was rid of the fear . . . and was impatient . . . he gave him his head, and at last urged him on with sterner tone and thrust of foot." Philip went from fear for his son's safety to tearful pride as Alexander galloped away, before turning and coming back. The king kissed his son, and then supposedly told him that Macedonia was too small for him, so that he would need to find a greater realm.[6]

This praise sounds suspiciously like a later invention. Bucephalus became famous as Alexander's favorite horse, ridden in all the key battles; his death in India was marked by the founding of a city, Bucephalia, so people would want to believe that their first meeting was dramatic. Yet the story is plausible in itself. Horses can spook at the oddest things, although his own shadow seems inadequate for this on its own. Perhaps the strange environment of so much attention and noise and other strange horses made Bucephalus nervous and his own and other shadows of people and cloaks made it worse. Some horses do take strong likes—and indeed dislikes—to individual humans in a way that is hard to explain. There is nothing odd about the stallion and Alexander being attracted to each other, and the boy's calmness, soothing the animal with sounds and touch before he mounted, then collecting the animal before riding off, are all good practice. It is a story that could be true, and anyone of sentiment will feel it ought to be true, which does not mean that it is.[7]

Philip is supposed to have decided that his son was too stubborn to be compelled, so it was better to "persuade rather than command him." When the boy was thirteen or fourteen a new tutor was needed, and after some consideration the king chose Aristotle. A native of the Chalcidice, the philosopher was forty and not yet as celebrated as he would become. His father had been royal physician to Amyntas III, so there was acquaintance and a connection with the family. Aristotle had studied under Plato, although he did not succeed him as head of the Academy and left Athens soon after Plato's death. He went first to Asia Minor, to the court of the tyrant Hermias, whose adopted daughter he later married. The move to Macedon around 342 BC was no doubt financially attractive, and also meant that he was not caught up a few years later in the torture and execution of Hermias for rebellion against the Persian king.[8]

Aristotle and Alexander were set up in a precinct at the shrine of the nymphs at Mieza, which removed them from the court at Pella. Once again, we do not know whether any friends or some or all of the similarly aged pages were taught alongside the prince. Probably learning under the philosopher went alongside continued training in arms and other physical pursuits such as hunting. Aristotle taught politics, ethics, and sparked or encouraged in Alexander an interest in the natural world, especially medicine and healing. For the best part of three years, the philosopher taught the prince, although how gifted a pupil he was depends mainly on how each modern scholar views Alexander. Inevitably the meeting of two of the most famous names from the ancient world excites our interest, but as usual the meager evidence prevents us from saying anything definite on what passed between them. Aristotle prepared a condensed and annotated text of the *Iliad* for his pupil, which Alexander took on all his campaigns, keeping it—alongside a dagger—under his bed.[9]

As a man Alexander was much shorter than the average for Greeks and Macedonians in the fourth century BC. Although small in stature, Alexander was well proportioned, strong, and a good sprinter, all of which reinforces the sense of constant physical training. His complexion was fair, skin sometimes ruddy, and his hair described as tawny like a lion's (and so not quite the peroxide-blond of Hollywood). His eyes were odd-colored, one blue-gray and the other brown, which may have contributed to his unusual and sometimes off-putting gaze: at some stage he developed the habit of leaning his head a little to the left and staring upward—presumably higher than the taller men often standing around him.[10]

Most, perhaps all, of the stories about his youth were embellished or invented in later years. The exchanges with Philip center around Alexander's desire for honor and glory, that here was an even greater son of a great father, and they make use of well-worn aphorisms—for instance, that the king's wounds were visible badges of courage more to be prized than other trophies. Another theme is the boy's instinctive challenge to any attempt to restrict him. Leonidas is said to have chided Alexander for using too much expensive incense during a sacrifice. A decade later the conqueror of Asia sent his former tutor a staggering eighteen tons of frankincense and myrrh with the advice that he should no longer be mean in his offerings to the gods. Determination, restless ambition, and absolute faith in his own abilities, which usually was backed by proof that he was right, run through these tales; there are no stories of Alexander failing. There is also impatience. He is supposed to have complained whenever news came of Philip's latest victory that his father was leaving less and less for him to achieve. When a Persian delegation arrived at Pella in the king's absence, Alexander received them, impressing the ambassadors by asking precise and pertinent questions about Persian military strength as well as roads and communications.[11]

The young prince of these stories displays the same qualities—or at least the ones thought admirable to Greeks—as the king who would conquer so much of the world. Given what the man did, it would be no surprise if the boy was so precocious, focused, and talented, and also entirely natural for people to invent such stories to flesh out what little was actually known.

PHILIP MAY WELL have been pleased and proud of Alexander, which did not mean that his attitude toward him could not change or that another son could be born and eventually supplant Alexander. Little of Philip's time was devoted to thoughts for the long-term future, let alone the succession, for he always had plenty to do and the present was his priority. He was always busy and some of his acts can only have taken a long time and a lot of care. Justin says that Philip embarked on major reform once he returned home from the Sacred War, establishing new communities, often in border areas, and moving much of the population: "As shepherds drive their flocks, sometimes into winter, sometimes into summer pastures, so he transplanted people and cities," causing widespread misery among those ripped from their ancestral homes. As we have seen, he had begun this process early in his reign, so perhaps there was an especially intensive burst of activity from late 346 BC onward, or Justin or his source chose to describe a longer-term plan at this point. Willingly or not, the people were moved, and as far as we can tell Philip's new communities with their mixed populations all succeeded; many became recruiting and training centers for the army.[12]

In 345 BC Philip led a major expedition against the Illyrians, fighting a number of tribal kings included Pleuratus, in operations that may well have lasted into the next year. Past Macedonian victories and the death of Bardylis had inevitably influenced local rivalries as different leaders and groups rose and fell. Whenever any became strong enough, or Macedonia seemed weak enough, then raids were likely. Philip was determined to dominate and terrify the Illyrians rather than risk them doing the same to him. He ravaged tribal lands and stormed many settlements, gaining a rich haul of plunder, no doubt including captives and livestock as well as treasure. Diplomacy and treachery accompanied military force. On one occasion Philip went to meet with a group of warriors. The enemy and his own escort of soldiers carried no weapons, but the Macedonians were equipped with concealed ropes or leather thongs. At his signal, they suddenly turned on the Illyrians and tied their arms together, leading them off as prisoners. Our source's claim that 10,000 were captured in this way is hardly credible, and perhaps only leading men were taken and the rest forced to give in.[13]

Not everything went Philip's way, and some of the fighting was hard, for in one engagement one of his Companion cavalrymen was killed and no fewer than 150 were wounded—another example of a huge disparity between the number of fatalities and the number of wounded. Philip received a blow that broke his collar bone. Elsewhere Diodorus claims that in one engagement against the Illyrians, the king was saved because one of his bodyguards, a youth named Pausanias, stood over him when he fell and saved Philip at the cost of his own life. This may relate to this episode or have occurred in a later, otherwise unrecorded campaign in the area. The Macedonians may still have won this encounter, and if not then they soon won an overall victory and dominated a large part of Illyria, almost to the Adriatic coast. More mining areas came under Philip's control, adding revenue and resources to meet his ongoing demands.[14]

Recovery from the injury presumably took some time and was another testament to Philip's tough constitution. The details and chronology of his activities in these years are poorly recorded, since once again our Greek sources display limited interest in the affairs of the peoples to the north. More than one visit to Thessaly is likely, to arbitrate in the continuing rivalries of its noble families and cities. There were inevitably winners and losers, the ones who gained his favor and the ones who did not, and their views about him and what he had done varied accordingly. He feigned illness in one attempt to lure some of the Aleudae family from Larissa to come to him so that they could be arrested, but word reached them of the deception and they did not show up. At least one of them later appears serving the Persians against Alexander, and quite a few may have chosen exile. By 342 BC, if not before, Philip reformed the Thessalian League, dividing it into four regions, each overseen by a tetrarch appointed by him rather than elected. Yet for all the rhetoric of Philip's critics, even they admitted that the king treated the cities and the League as independent allies and not as subjects.[15]

His use of power to enforce his will was more blatant when at some point around this time he marched into Epirus and deposed King Arybbas. Olympias's younger brother, also named Alexander, was now twenty years old and replaced his uncle as king in a bloodless campaign. Arybbas went into comfortable exile in Athens, which welcomed him and made him a citizen. Afterward Philip led his army beyond Epirus's borders to attack three or four Greek cities near the Ambracian Gulf. The pretext for this is unknown, although no doubt there were old disputes easy enough to revive. The aim was to secure Epirus's border and enrich the kingdom because these cities—all originally colonies of Elis—controlled the maritime trade to and from the wider world. Philip made them slaves to King Alexander, much as he had taken over cities like Amphipolis to add to his own wealth and power. Once again, outside of his interventions, the Molossian-led kingdom of Epirus ran its own affairs and was another independent, if close and clearly subordinate, ally.[16]

From 342 BC onward for the next three or four years, Thrace once again occupied much of Philip's time and resources. For instance, in 341 BC Demosthenes reported that Philip had already been fighting in Thrace for ten to eleven months consecutively. There was fresh war with Cersobleptes, and Philip appears to have resolved to bring much of the region under more or less direct control. At the start he posed as protector of the Greek cities in the area, but his aim was clearly conquest of a wide area and there was heavy fighting. Demosthenes spoke disparagingly of the king marching without the phalanx that was the heart of a "proper" army, and instead leading cavalry, peltasts, archers, and mercenaries.[17]

Much of the terrain was mountain and forest, ripe for ambush. On at least one occasion Philip used hunting dogs to sniff out the warriors hiding in the trees, and there were careful arrangements to cover withdrawal in the face of enemy pursuit. Such operations were protracted and grueling, making heavy demands on the king as well as his soldiers, and both showed great tenacity. As always, diplomacy went hand in hand with warfare. Reviving his practice from the start of his reign, Philip married a sixth wife, Meda, daughter of King Cothelas of the Getae, a similarly warlike people living north of the Thracians. No children are recorded from this union, and she is not mentioned elsewhere, but the marriage appears to have served its function in cementing the alliance.[18]

Athenians were naturally sensitive about activity around the Thracian coast, and for Demosthenes and those who thought like him, Philip's campaigns were proof of his deep hostility to Athens. The fractious approval of the Peace of Philocrates was merely the start of protracted wrangling over relations with Macedonia and its king. As early as 346 BC, Demosthenes and an associate named Timarchus announced that they were prosecuting Aeschines for betraying his city by taking bribes and aiding Philip. Probably satisfied to have blackened his name, they did not press for the issue to come to trial. Before they managed to do this Aeschines responded by indicting Timarchus on a charge of gross immorality, and this did come to court. The trial occurred in 345 BC with accusations of prostitution, pimping, and other shameful behavior sufficient to render him unfit to address the Assembly. The charges stuck, and Timarchus was stripped of his citizenship, ending his political career. In 344 BC Philocrates, the architect of the peace treaty, was charged with the capital offense of betraying the city; he decided to go into voluntary exile rather than risk trial. Demosthenes finally prosecuted Aeschines, who stayed and fought it out, narrowly being acquitted by a margin of 30 votes out of around 1,500.[19]

Bribery was a common-enough slur in Athenian politics, and for Demosthenes something of an obsession; anyone who disagreed with him regarding Philip must have been bribed. The message was simple, that Athens was no longer great because she had been betrayed by her leaders. True patriotism in citizens and leaders alike, stern resolve, and sound allies would change all this, would defeat Philip and restore Athens to her rightful prominence. A simple idea repeated often enough can be very powerful, most of all when it is what the audience dearly wants to believe, and it can be even stronger when there is a kernel of truth, however small. The interests of Philip and of Athens were sometimes in conflict, and these confrontations had gone his way. Realists accepted this as a sign that the king was too strong to fight, at least in the immediate future, and that returning to war and escalating its scale was bound to go badly. The orator dismissed such voices as those of the corrupt and came back to his message again and again.[20]

Demosthenes's influence grew in these years, although once again we should remember that he was not alone and some of his prominence is due to the survival and veneration for his speeches. He insisted that Philip was Athens's inveterate enemy—"All his activity and all his organization is preparing the way for an attack on our city." How could anyone believe that Philip really coveted "Drongilus and Cabyle and Mastira," obscure Thracian strongholds captured in these years, and "does not covet the Athenian harbours and dockyards and war-galleys and silver mines and the like sources of wealth" if he was willing to toil through harsh winters to win the meager spoils in Thrace? Other Athenians were nervous about some of the king's activities. His capture of the cities near the Ambracian Gulf prompted the Athenians to send an expedition to the support of communities in Acarnania on its southern shore. Philip withdrew without advancing against Athens's allies, whether because he was deterred or had never planned to attack there in the first place.[21]

Euboea—a large island close to the eastern coast of Greece and a former ally of Athens that had forcefully won full independence—was another sensitive area, so the appearance there of Macedonian-paid mercenaries gave Demosthenes more fuel to attack Philip. They came to support local leaders in factional struggles within the cities, and where they were successful it inevitably meant that the new regimes were well disposed to the king. Mercenaries supplied by the king also appeared in the Peloponnese, although their presence attracted less concern at Athens. A little earlier Philip had not answered the appeal of one ambitious Euboean who declared his intention of forming a tight league in the area; Philip's support was not automatic and had more to do with estimates of local support for a leader. The same man later appealed to Athens, and the Athenians intervened in Euboea several times, clashing with leaders backed by Philip.[22]

Yet these years are more striking for how rarely Philip chose to intervene in southern Greece, especially with troops, and how rarely he appears to have initiated rather than responded to appeals. Euboea was deeply divided, and the assistance given to some leaders by Macedonia and Athens merely added fuel to an already raging blaze. The choice of mercenaries over actual Macedonians was perhaps tactful, but may simply have been a question of availability, for he did send Parmenio and other senior officers. Sending hired troops to join in foreign wars was common enough in these years. Athens turned down an appeal from the Persian king for hoplites to serve in the reconquest of Egypt, although Thebes agreed. A Spartan king and army went to fight in Italy. Phalaecus of Phocis and his army went to Italy and then Crete for employment, while tens of thousands of individuals and smaller groups were in Persian pay.[23]

Athens was fond of sending out its generals with largely mercenary forces, as the careers of Iphicrates and Chares demonstrated. There was always the expectation that these operations would fund themselves, and lack of reliable support from Athens often meant that such commanders had little choice save to plunder and raid, making alliances or war with locals simply so that they could pay their men. Sometime around 343 BC a man named Diopeithes was sent to the Gallipoli area with such a force and proved especially ruthless. He was known to be close to Hegesippus, one of the influential if less eloquent voices repeating the same arguments as Demosthenes.[24]

Open debate in the Assembly ensured that Philip was aware of what was being said about him at Athens, of the voices accusing him of bribery and declaring that another war was inevitable. Similarly, attempts by formal and informal representatives of Athens to recruit allies against Macedon were not secret. In 343 BC the famous orator Python of Byzantium came to Athens on Philip's behalf to make a formal complaint about his critics in the Assembly. This able speaker claimed that the king had honored every part of the Peace of Philocrates. He assured the Athenians of Philip's earnest desire for their friendship, beyond that of any other state, and was ready to listen to their suggestions if they wished to modify the alliance. Many Athenians applauded and an embassy was sent to Philip to negotiate. Nothing was achieved, not least because Hegesippus was one of the envoys and made excessive demands, reviving claims to Amphipolis and other possessions long since lost to Athens. Talk of a new Common Peace between all Greek states, like the treaty after Leuctra in 362 BC, went further, not least because Philip gave it his support, but it was not clear that the wider world was that interested.[25]

All of the Gallipoli Peninsula was Athenian, apart from the city of Cardia, which had never fallen to them. Now it was an ally of Philip's, but this did not prevent Athens from desiring it. In 342 BC Philip wrote a letter offering to submit to outside arbitration over the question of Amphipolis, Cardia, and the tiny island of Halonnesus, once part of the Athenian empire, then a pirate stronghold, and more recently captured by the Macedonians. This was a common enough technique of resolving disputes without warfare, and also helped to honor and strengthen friendships with the community asked to arbitrate. Philip had already offered to give the island to the Athenians, who were persuaded to refuse because he had not said that he was restoring what was already theirs. Those wishing to avoid war with Macedonia pragmatically accepted that keeping the peace would cost a measure of pride. Demosthenes, Hegesippus, and their associates saw even the slightest compromise as undermining Athens's whole position, effectively arguing that to give up anything was to give up everything.[26]

The Athenian general Diopeithes appears to have held similar views, and also needed to fund his army. Backed by Athenian settlers, he threatened Cardia, prompting Philip to send troops to garrison it as well as a suggestion that they seek arbitration. Late in 342 BC or early in 341 BC Diopeithes captured an envoy sent by Philip and sent the prisoner to Athens, where the dispatches he was carrying were made public. In 341 BC Diopeithes raided Thracian communities, taking plunder and slaves, which no doubt helped support his army. Philip sent another representative to complain, and he was not only taken prisoner, but tortured before he was ransomed. Diopeithes also preyed on merchant vessels, including those of Macedon and its allies. Demosthenes defended the general, assuring his fellow citizens that the inevitable war against Philip had already begun, even if it had not been declared formally. Athens's ally in Euboea gained the upper hand, possibly because there were no longer any Macedonian paid mercenaries there, and began raiding the coast of the Gulf of Pagasae. Since these were Macedonian allies, this was in direct violation of the Peace of Philocrates.[27]

Demosthenes always claimed that many Greeks feared and resented Philip, and that Athens would find ready allies if they were bold enough to take the lead in fighting him. For generations now it was no longer strange for an orator to revel in the past glories of Athens at Marathon and Thermopylae while suggesting that the Athenians seek assistance from Persia. Demosthenes supported this and in 341 BC an Athenian embassy went to the king of kings. There were signs that the Persians were becoming nervous about Philip's Thracian conquests, and although they were unwilling to make an alliance, they sent encouragement and money. Others were also nervous as Philip advanced to the European side of the Hellespont. Well-established Greek colonies like Byzantium and Perinthus had been his allies for some time, glad of the protection this offered against ambitious Thracian kings, but they found the alliance less appealing now that he was so successful and on their doorstep. Demosthenes went to Byzantium in 341 BC and reported that they had come to fear Philip. Former allies of Athens, such as Rhodes and Cos, which had not so long ago led the revolt of the Athenian allies, similarly were now more worried about the Macedonians than their old mistress.[28]

Diopeithes died around this time and was replaced as commander in the Dardanelles region by Chares, who at least knew the region well, although his record against Philip was patchy. At some point Byzantium and the other coastal cities openly declared themselves against Macedon, encouraged in this by pledges of aid from Athens and also from Persia. Philip attacked with some 30,000 men in 340 BC and targeted Perinthus, which was closer and smaller than Byzantium. The professional engineers in his army had come up with a new artillery design, the far more powerful torsion catapult. These were used along with static and mobile towers to gain a height advantage over the city walls, but in spite of this and the soldiers' long experience of siege warfare, progress was slow. Chares's squadron of triremes prevented the Macedonians from blockading the city's port, which meant that aid was never shut off. Persian satraps sent both supplies and mercenaries to assist the defenders, as did Byzantium and other allies. The defenders still used the old-fashioned catapults, which remained effective, and more artillery was brought into the city.[29]

Perinthus lay on a slope, with tiers of tightly packed houses climbing upward. When Philip's men breached the outer wall with battering rams, the defenders built another line just behind it and the whole process had to begin again. Day after day the Macedonians made attacks on different sectors of the defenses, trying to wear the defenders down as they had often done in the past. Artillery, no doubt backed by archers and slingers, shot down from the towers onto the wall, trying to make it untenable for the defenders, while the rams kept up their work. Repeated attacks using ladders forced the Perinthians to come out onto the walls and repulse them as casualties mounted on both sides. The secondary wall was breached and taken, only for the Macedonians to discover that the streets and alleys between the houses were solidly barricaded. Effectively they were faced with another new wall, and could only bring rams and other engines against it if they demolished any structures on the ground in front. When the Macedonians breached this line of defense the Perinthians pulled back to the next tier of houses and yet another improvised line. As they drew back and upward into the city, Philip's towers were negated and the advantage of shooting or throwing missiles downward passed back to the defenders.[30]

More than adequate supplies kept reaching the city and the Perinthians remained confident. Philip gambled that aiding Perinthus had stripped Byzantium of its best men, engines, and leaders. Dividing his army into two halves, he force-marched with one section of it in the hope of taking the bigger city. Once there he began another siege and discovered that he was partly right, for the defense was less energetic than normal. Early on luck favored him when he discovered that a vast convoy of grain ships had gathered at nearby Hieron on the Asiatic side of the Bosporus, waiting for an escort to take it to Athens. Chares was away for a conference with the Persians, so Philip—combining the small Macedonian fleet with soldiers ferried across to attack the port from the land—captured the entire convoy. Some fifty neutral ships were released, but he had taken 180 Athenian vessels. (Merchant vessels in this period tended to be relatively small, with trade relying on lots of small ships rather than some of the larger grain ships that later operated in the Roman Empire.) The grain they carried fed his army, while the ships themselves were broken apart and any suitable timbers used in the siege works.[31]

Yet Byzantium's fortifications were formidable, and once again the Macedonians were incapable of cutting the city off from the sea. Reinforcements soon came from Rhodes, Cos, and Chios, swelling the numbers and raising the spirits of the defenders. A night attack during torrential rain almost succeeded, achieving surprise until barking dogs woke enough men to rush to the spot and repulse the Macedonians. This gamble had failed, as had the bigger one in splitting his forces, and eventually Philip decided to call off both sieges.[32]

Athens smashed the stone inscribed with the treaty agreed in 346 BC. Opinion is divided over whether or not Philip had already effectively declared war, and if so when this happened. Statements in a letter to the Athenians in 341 BC might be taken as an ultimatum that would naturally lead to war if Athens did not make redress. Demosthenes had constantly assured his fellow citizens that war with Philip was inevitable. His words and actions, along with those of Hegesippus and all the others of like mind, had gone a long way to making this come true. By 340 BC Athens had found some allies, unlike its earlier appeals, but these remained few. It was unclear whether others would join, and even less clear whether there was any real prospect of defeating Philip. Demosthenes's promises were about to be put to the test.[33]

———

ONE MORE EVENT of note occurred in 340 BC, although it was a minor affair compared to the operations on the Thracian coast. In his absence, Philip had appointed the sixteen-year-old Alexander as regent, bringing an end to his years of formal study. Trouble broke out among the Maedi, a group on the borders of Paeonia and Thrace, and the teenager gathered whatever forces he had under his command and marched against them. Plutarch provides few details of the affair, other than to say that he captured their main settlement, expelled the population, and refounded it. Copying his father, he settled a mixed population there, and again like his father named it after himself—Alexandropolis. This was the first time the prince had gone to war, and we cannot say how serious the fighting was. There is no doubt that it was yet another sign of his confidence.[34]

10

OLD AND NEW ENEMIES

By 340 BC Philip was stronger and far harder for Athens to damage, but success came at a cost. He had made Macedonia secure and powerful, which meant that other states were bound to see it as more dangerous. For the moment, the majority remained inclined to see the conflict with Philip as Athens's concern. Balance was better for outsiders than letting either Macedonia or Athens shatter the other. Other states watched and waited, looking for opportunities to gain and warily sniffing for threats. There was the potential for the conflict to broaden and grow in ways hard to predict.

Yet not everyone at Athens welcomed the renewal of open war with Philip. Aeschines and his allies argued that the war was unnecessary and dangerous, that the king was not a threat, or at least not an imminent one or the most important problem facing Athens. For the moment such opinions were in the minority, and the majority of voters approved the war. An even smaller minority saw Philip as a great leader who might prove the savior of all the Greek states. Since the end of the Peloponnesian War, plenty of people had deplored the unending succession of wars and revolutions as Greek fought Greek, and a few believed that they had discovered the cure. The key was poverty; too many citizens lacked sufficient land or other sources of income to be comfortable and secure. The less well-off envied the wealthy and the wealthy competed with each other, fueling power struggles within a city and attacks on other poleis. This handful of thinkers claimed that all this could change if the Greeks joined together in the Panhellenic cause and attacked Persia to take land and wealth. Once conquered, Asian barbarians would work the fields and tend the cattle as slaves or helot-like serfs, leaving their Greek overlords to live in comfort and harmony, at last capable of elevation to all that was finest about Hellenic civilization.[1]

Victory was taken for granted, for the philosophers voicing these ideas shared the common belief that Persians and other Asians were naturally inferior, cowards who would easily be defeated as long as the Greeks united. The easterners were also former enemies, so there was no need for any other reason for turning on them. Ideally the inevitable triumph would be the product of the Greeks willingly joining together through mutual goodwill and the realization that such a war would benefit every city. When their impassioned speeches and pamphlets failed to bring the states together, advocates instead urged the dominant city of the time to set an example and persuade others to join. Sparta, Thebes, and Athens were all addressed in this way, but many philosophers, and not simply those preaching a great war against Persia, began to lose faith in city-states and especially democracies, and instead placed their hopes in charismatic rulers. Tyrants in Sicily, Jason of Pherae, and his son Alexander were all urged to lead the great war, and, as his power grew, so was Philip.

One of the most persistent voices raised in this cause was Isocrates of Athens, head of the rhetorical school, the great rival of Plato's Academy. By this time aged about ninety, in 346 BC (or possibly 344 BC) he wrote an open letter to Philip, tailoring the well-tried arguments for a Panhellenic "crusade" against Persia to this new hero. It was a great cause, bound to bring honorable glory so that his reputation would rise as one of "the foremost men of history, while if you fall short of your expectations you will at any rate win the good will of all the Hellenes." This was far better than trying to dominate the Greek cities by force, since even success in such an endeavor was bound to make him hated.[2]

Philip was urged to persuade the Greek cities, and especially the most prestigious of them all—Athens, Sparta, Thebes, and Argos—to serve together under his leadership in the greater cause. With the Peace of Philocrates freshly agreed, Isocrates claimed that Athens would readily join the king, and lamented that his city had not already led the way. He challenged the many critics of the Macedonian king, dismissing the claims of Demosthenes and like-minded politicians for falsely painting Philip as a tyrant out of sheer jealousy and the desire to stir up conflict. Such men were selfish and irresponsible to present him as enemy of the Greeks rather than an obvious leader of the willing.[3]

In the meantime Isocrates argued that Philip should not be wasting his time and efforts fighting tribes in Illyria and Thrace—too distant from Athens to be worthy of much concern—and taking great personal risks in the process. "I assert that it is incumbent upon you to work for the good of the Hellenes, to reign as king over the Macedonians, and to extend your power over the greatest possible number of the barbarians." If Philip acted in this way then all men would be grateful; Greeks would love him for his "kindness" and the foreigners because they had been "delivered from barbaric despotism and are brought under the protection of Hellas."[4]

Isocrates was a very elderly philosopher, not a politician or a typical citizen farmer, but he was not the only Athenian intellectual urging Philip to unite the Greeks against the Persians. Speusippus, successor to Plato as head of the Academy, criticized Isocrates's advice on how Philip should win the support of the Greeks, while fully endorsing the call for the king to lead a Panhellenic crusade. Aristotle also expressed support, and there is good reason to believe that the basic idea appealed to many Greeks of all classes. For all the rationalization of the need to end conflict between and within communities, at its heart was a primitive call: "Consider also what a disgrace it is to sit idly by and see Asia flourishing more than Europe and the barbarians enjoying a greater prosperity than the Hellenes," Isocrates wrote. Greeks despised barbarians and knew themselves to be inherently superior, thus it was simply not fair that Persians should have the greater wealth. Similar feelings prompted many tribal peoples in the ancient world to attack foreigners, and we should not forget that beneath the veneer of high culture most Greeks felt similar urges. Probably it was no more strong than that, and certainly other concerns and ambitions were far more important in day-to-day life and politics, while pride in the polis and a wish to uphold its honor militated far more strongly against letting some other state or king take the lead.[5]

Macedonia lay closer to the Persian Empire than southern Greece. The Persians still laid claim to Thrace, although it is hard to know whether this was ever in any sense a reality during the fourth century BC, and Macedonia had been part of the Persian Empire for at least a generation. Its role in the Persian invasion of 480–479 BC was at best ambiguous, and the Macedonians had played no part in subsequent conflicts against Persia, nor provided any of the mercenary hoplites who figured so much in subsequent campaigns. There is no trace of long-term hostility between Macedonia and Persia or any real hint of this in the early years of Philip's reign. Artabazus, the satrap who had hired and then dismissed the Theban Pammenes, fled to Macedon after the failure of his rebellion against the great king and was treated as a guest by Philip. Conventions of hospitality were widely understood, and welcoming aristocratic refugees was rarely seen as an act of war or even of hostile intent. Persian ambassadors went to Philip's court now and again, and a few years later the former satrap returned home and was treated well.

By 346 BC Isocrates felt able to appeal to Philip openly, but it is less clear whether the king had already hinted of plans for taking up the idea of a great Panhellenic war or was simply addressed because he was powerful. While negotiating for peace during these years he did make promises of future benefits to Athens, and presumably to other cities. According to one of his Athenian critics, Philip stated in a letter preserved on public display "that if peace were made [Philip] would confer such benefits on you as would stop the mouths of us, his opponents, benefits which he said he would put down in writing, if he were sure that peace would be made." When peace was made and no benefits actually appeared, Philip kept referring to them, making some wonder whether these were cryptic references to his willingness to lead the Greeks against Persia so that they could win rich plunder. All this is guesswork, and it is hard to say what even Isocrates read between these lines. The Persians are unlikely to have seen Macedonia as much of a threat at this time, while their relations with the major Greek city-states continued to be good.[6]

Deeper instincts as well as more immediate grudges and ambitions all made it almost impossible for the city-states to unite willingly under Philip's leadership or that of anyone else. By this time the threat posed by Persia was too distant. Isocrates had railed against the Persian sponsored King's Peace earlier in the century, but most had accepted it for as long as it lasted. In many respects it was easier for Demosthenes to suggest seeking aid from Persia against Philip than it was for him or anyone else to speak favorably of recent and closer enemies such as Thebes. Too many Athenians resented the Peace of Philocrates far more strongly than they yearned to humble Persia, and Isocrates's calls were drowned out, although no one considered prosecuting him, which is a clear indication of his political insignificance.

Demosthenes and his allies had their long-called-for war against Macedonia, even if no one had any real idea of how to win it, for the strategic situation was no more favorable now than it had been in 346 BC. As long as the Theban alliance remained secure, Philip could march his army south and invade Attica in such strength that Athens was bound to be defeated unless she acquired more than the handful of allies willing to support her at present. In contrast Athens could not hurt Philip seriously. During the sieges of Perinthus and Byzantium in 340 BC, an Athenian squadron had raided the Macedonian coast. In command was Phocion, a stern and capable general whose terse speech and integrity—both rare in Athenian public life—had won him respect at home and abroad, so that communities who refused to deal with the rather slippery Chares eagerly accepted him. Yet these attacks were never more than pinpricks, and the chief result was that Phocion was wounded in one of the forays ashore and returned to Athens.[7]

Athens's naval might meant little when she lacked the capacity to capture any significant stronghold, even when it was on the coast. Philip's own navy remained far too small to challenge the Athenians at sea, so it was not going to offer itself up to be smashed and was unlikely to let itself be cornered. According to a passage in a collection of stratagems compiled by a Roman general at the end of the first century AD, there was a chance that the Macedonian squadron would be caught soon after Philip abandoned the sieges. These ships had gone to the Black Sea, so must come through the Bosporus to escape back into open water, but Chares along with ships from Rhodes and Chios was guarding the straits, waiting for them. Philip "wrote to Antipater that Thrace was in revolt, and that the garrisons which he had left there had been cut off, directing Antipater to leave all other matters and follow him." Making sure that the letter would be captured, he then waited. The Athenians took the bait, convinced that the message was genuine and Philip had gone inland, and withdrew their ships, so that the Macedonian squadron was able to sail through the straits unmolested.

Chares had been tricked once again. The account goes on to claim that Philip had returned captured vessels to Rhodes and Chios, who were allies of Byzantium and only indirectly of Athens. He also negotiated with the Byzantines, prolonging the talks by shifting his arguments over minor details. This helped lull the waiting allies, so that they failed to react when he sailed through. The story is late and garbled, but if it is true, then Philip had avoided losing most or all of his little navy, and avoided suffering a fresh defeat to add to the failures at Byzantium and Perinthus. Each dented his prestige, but even collectively they were not enough to weaken his power seriously. If taken literally, the wording would imply that Philip was onboard one of the trapped ships, which would have been different had the Athenians succeeded, for his death or capture would have thrown Macedonia into chaos, but we probably should not assume this. Nor is it clear whether peace talks really did occur at this point or later. There is no record of any further hostility between Philip and Byzantium and Perinthus, while Athens's former allies in the islands also played little or no part in the years to follow, so an agreement of some sort is likely enough.[8]

Although he had failed to take the two cities, Philip's three years of operations in Thrace had been otherwise successful, greatly expanding the territory under his control, establishing new colonies, and absorbing considerable numbers of Thracians as subjects or close allies. Macedonia was stronger and more secure as a result. Set against this, renewal of war with Athens was a minor concern, especially as the Athenians had few allies and no effective means of taking the war to the king. After supporting Perinthus, the Persians do not seem to have continued to involve themselves in the conflict, in part because the assassination of the great king and succession of a minor prompted a period of internal weakness. Due to our sources, the war with Athens looms large, but Philip's attitude is made clear by his actions over the winter of 340–339 BC. Ignoring Athens for the moment, he continued the task of securing his recent conquests in Thrace by attacking a new enemy, the Scythians.[9]

The Scythian king, Atheas, had carved out a kingdom to the northeast, including much of Dobruja, an area of fertile land stretching toward the Danube (and including parts of modern Bulgaria and Romania). Philip's recent conquests meant that his own territory now lay close to Atheas's kingdom. Nomads from the steppes, the Scythians were famous as horsemen, archers, and formidable warriors. In the late sixth century BC some of their tribes had repulsed a major invasion led by Darius of Persia, drawing the attackers on and on until they were exhausted and vulnerable. More recently, Atheas had carved out a kingdom, overrunning the inhabitants of the area, forcing settled communities to accept his rule, and minting high-quality silver coins bearing his name. By 340 BC he was ninety, yet another of those tough old warlords who appear in these years. Although the area was wealthy, competition with Byzantium was hurting Atheas, probably militarily and in terms of trade, so Philip's siege of that city was welcome.[10]

At some point Atheas was at war with a king of the "Histrians"—presumably a group living near the Danube—and sent envoys to the Greek colony of Apollonia to ask them to approach their ally

Philip on his behalf. The Scythian king requested soldiers and promised in return to adopt Philip—most likely through a marriage alliance—and bequeath his kingdom to him. The offer was accepted and troops dispatched, but before they arrived the king of the Histrians died and the threat appears to have died with him. Atheas sent the troops back to Philip, refusing to pay them and baldly claiming that he had never asked for aid nor made any promise. As proof of this claim, he stated that his Scythians were far better warriors than any Macedonians so could not have needed help, and that his own son was his heir and he had no need of anyone else. Macedonian ambassadors were sent to ask that Atheas cover the costs of the pay and supplies for the soldiers sent to him, and some of the expenses of the siege of Byzantium. No money was forthcoming: the Scythian king protested poverty, for his people were rich only in their valor and hardiness rather than possessions. Philip may already have been set on attacking the Scythians, hoping for a victory to help erase the disappointment of recent failures. He also needed money, wanting, as Justin wrote, to "make up the expense of one war by the profits of another."[11]

Philip now informed Atheas that he wished to honor a vow made during the siege of Byzantium to his ancestor Hercules, by traveling to the Danube and erecting a statue of the demigod at the mouth of the great river. He asked for free and unhindered passage for his army as he advanced to perform this act of piety, assuring the Scythians of his continuing goodwill. Understandably dubious about Philip's sincerity, Atheas demurred and suggested instead that the statue be sent to him, promising to set it up with all due respect. No enemy army could be permitted onto his lands, and should the statue ever be set up by invaders, then once they were gone the Scythians would melt the bronze down and turn it into arrowheads.[12]

Justin supplies this uncharacteristically detailed account of the diplomatic exchanges before skimming over the war that followed in just a few terse sentences. The Macedonians attacked, and "though the spirit and numbers of the Scythians were superior, Philip prevailed through his cunning." Another source tells us that when the Macedonians became nervous fighting against Scythians,

Philip stationed his best cavalry behind the main line with orders to kill anyone who tried to flee. Even the most timid preferred the risk of battle to certain execution, so the threat worked and the fight was won. This incident may refer to this campaign, or it may be garbled. However the battle was won, the victory was overwhelming. Atheas's claims of poverty were borne out in the lack of silver and gold, but the other spoils were substantial. The Macedonians took a vast number of cattle, 20,000 brood mares, and 20,000 women and children as slaves.[13]

The Scythians were usually hard to defeat. While it was not the vast grass sea of the steppes, Atheas's kingdom consisted of open and gently rolling country, well suited to the mobile tactics of these superb horsemen. Philip would cram a lot of activity into 339 BC, following this campaign with another conflict, during which he was badly wounded, and yet he still managed to recover and lead his army into southern Greece by the autumn. We do not know precisely when he abandoned the sieges, how long any negotiations took in their aftermath, but it makes a good deal of sense if the attack on Atheas was launched before the end of the winter of 340–339 BC. Philip's army had long experience of operating in all seasons, showing that it was capable of supplying itself even in winter. As Demosthenes had said, the king often traveled fast with cavalry, peltasts, and other quick-marching units rather than his massed army.

The Scythians were nomadic, and even if Atheas's kingdom included villages and other settled communities, the warriors on which his power rested kept to the old lifestyle. For most of the year they were mobile, perhaps trading and interacting in other ways with the farming settlements, but then moving on to feed their horses and herds. In winter the grazing was poor and the weather harsh, and for those months they camped in a favorable spot, most likely gathered together in larger groups than the rest of the year. At this time—and usually only at this time—the population was concentrated. By the end of the winter horses were at their weakest, lacking exercise and good feed. More importantly, the large camps with families and herds could not move quickly if they were to survive in the winter weather. All this made them vulnerable to a sudden attack, as was true of many nomadic and seminomadic peoples throughout history. Philip's "cunning" may well have been to strike at their camps or perhaps the main camp of Atheas before winter was done. This faced the Scythians with the stark choice of fleeing, which meant abandoning their families and possessions, or fighting to defend them in a situation that did not permit them to make the most of their mobility and traditional tactics. Philip would not need his entire army to win in such circumstances, and may well have been outnumbered by the Scythians, just as Justin claims.

There is no proof that this was what happened, but a rapid attack in February or March would leave plenty of time for the other events of the year, and the speed of the victory and sheer numbers of prisoners and captured animals all suggest that the Scythians were concentrated and unable to escape. Alexander's campaigns offer many examples of similar lightning strikes against tribal enemies, and the young prince was with Philip "to learn the rudiments of warfare from his father."[14]

Force-marching a small column to mount a sudden attack was far easier than returning home with so many prisoners and animals. The mares may have gone back to Macedonia separately, for they were easier to drive, while Philip took another route, whether to ease the problem of supply or to parade his power over a wider area. Even if the initial strike force had been joined by parts of the main army, there is still a good chance that there were more prisoners than there were Macedonians to guard them, and the soldiers and their servants also had to watch the captured herds. Unlike their captors, the prisoners were not hardened to long marches and had only the incentive of fear to make them hurry.[15]

Philip and his encumbered column approached the territory of the Triballi, a Thracian or related people who had raided Macedonia in the past. He may have hoped that his reputation, reinforced by his recent victory, would overawe the tribal leaders, so he asked for free passage through their lands. The Triballi were more impressed by the sight of so many slaves and cattle, and demanded a share. Philip refused, and then faced the difficult task of marching through hostile territory, some of it well suited to ambush, all the while guarding his spoils. Soon there was fighting, during the course of which virtually all of the Scythian captives and herds were lost. Where they met enemy warriors, the Macedonians probably dominated, but the Triballi were more interested in plundering than fighting, and there were simply not enough soldiers to protect the entire column, while the ambushers had plenty of time to wait for favorable opportunities.[16]

Philip was on horseback, most likely trying to respond to each new attack in turn, when he was struck by a spear. One source calls the weapon a sarissa, leading to suggestions that he was accidentally hit by one of his own soldiers, but it is far more likely that the author was not at all concerned about technical precision. Some Thracians also employed long spears, and whatever its length or shape and whoever struck the blow, it was with immense force, driving through the king's thigh to kill the horse he was riding. Demosthenes says that his hand was also hurt, perhaps in this incident or maybe he broke it during the fall. Philip fainted and was feared dead before he was found to be still alive.

Once again his hardy constitution pulled him through, although the price was a permanent limp. Philip had survived when he might easily have been killed or succumbed to infection in the days that followed. For all the confusion, which ensured that even more of their spoils were taken by the Triballi, the Macedonian army did not fall apart. Considerably poorer, the Macedonians marched back home, and may even have felt that they had defeated the Triballi. Philip was well enough to be moved and does not seem to have lost control of the situation for any significant length of time. Even so, it was most likely several months before he was fit enough to ride and fight once again. By then the situation in Greece had changed, shifting the balance of power against him.[17]

11

CHAERONEA

Hindsight encourages us to see the rise of Philip as a profound change in the history of Greece, and thus see every action as shaped by this. Yet at the time few were aware of what this meant, and the city-states went about their rivalries as they had always done. Attitude toward Philip was only one concern among many for most politicians, let alone ordinary citizens, and rarely at the forefront of their minds. Nor was Philip in control of all the goings on in Greece. Few states chose to join Athens in the war with Macedonia because to most it simply did not seem any of their business, being a conflict over the distant Thracian coast. Justin later claimed that the states of Greece were too busy trying to dominate each other to pay enough attention to Philip, who watched "as it were from a high tower" and eventually "forced victor and defeated alike to submit to his rule." That is to put Philip at the center of everything and ignore the ambitions of the other states. Thebes had allied with Philip for its own advantage and did not see this as challenging its own status.[1]

In 339 BC Philip's Theban allies decided to supplant the Macedonian garrison and Thessalian-backed regime at Nicaea, one of the strongholds controlling the route through Thermopylae. There does not appear to have been any fighting and we do not know the details of what happened. At the very least it was a reminder that Thebes saw itself as a powerful state, fully independent and in no way subordinate to Macedonia; the road through Thermopylae might still be open to Philip, as long as the Thebans approved of his actions.[2]

Amphissa was a Locrian city of no great importance, and during an internal power struggle, a leadership favorable to—and perhaps aided by—Thebes came to power. In the autumn of 340 BC, these leaders took a complaint to the regular meeting of the Amphictyonic council, charging Athens with improperly rededicating trophies at Delphi, presumably either during the Sacred War or before the temple had been reconsecrated in its aftermath. They were spoils of the Persian wars, bearing the inscription "from the Medes and the Thebans when they fought against the Greeks." The Amphisseans were confident of Theban support, perhaps expecting the council to welcome the chance to condemn Athens after its support for Phocis, and asked that a fine of fifty talents be imposed.[3]

The sum was largely symbolic for a state the size of Athens, but accepting a reprimand would be a humiliation. Aeschines was one of the Athenian ambassadors to the council meeting and decided that attack was the best form of defense. He accused the Amphisseans of cultivating fields belonging to the temple at Delphi and thus sacred to Apollo. Convinced that this was a serious charge—and swayed by the orator's well-chosen words, his rival Demosthenes claiming that the delegates were "simple folk"—the council decided to investigate. The council members went to explore, for the land in question was in easy walking distance. Discovering that the charge was true, they began burning farm buildings on the sacred land, until they were chased off by a band of Amphisseans and fled back up the rocky path to Delphi. Soon afterward sacred war was declared on Amphissa, with a Thessalian nobleman appointed to lead the council's forces, although neither Athens nor Thebes sent delegates to this extraordinary meeting. Even so, the regime at Amphissa was supplanted by another faction, its old rivals, who capitulated before any fighting occurred. In the spring of 339 BC the Amphictyonic council met again and decided to impose a fine on the Amphisseans. The new leaders of

Amphissa lost face and were in turn supplanted by the faction who had brought the original charge and who now refused to pay the fine. When the Amphictyonic council met again in the autumn, it appointed Philip to command their forces and continue the Sacred War against Amphissa.[4]

Demosthenes later declared that Philip was behind everything from the start and that Aeschines was his willing and well-paid tool. Certainly the outcome was that the king marched into Greece as the head of all those who rallied to the call of the Amphictyonic council, just as he had done during the earlier Sacred War. In itself this was unlikely to persuade any state not otherwise inclined to join him, but at least it softened his arrival, for he did not march simply as the enemy of Athens. Yet this is once again to see Philip as the center of everything and also implies an inevitability about events. Amphissa expected and clearly received Theban support and encouragement for its actions, and the Thebans refused to join the war declared on them, in contrast to its willingness to fight Phocis.

Like the occupation of Nicaea, which occurred at some point during the process, this was a Thebes wanting to assert its own strength and status, sending a message not simply to Philip but to all Greek states, while stopping short of openly declaring alliance with Amphissa in the war. Demosthenes helped to persuade the Athenian Assembly not to answer the call to the extraordinary meeting of the Amphictyonic council, which declared war on Amphissa. Secretly he was eager not to offend Thebes, in the hope of allying with the Thebans. Aeschines accused him of manipulating the system, sneaking through an artfully worded decree after most people had left the Assembly—and for good measure alleged that the orator was being paid by the Amphisseans.[5]

After convalescing from his injuries at Pella, Philip marched south in the autumn of 339 BC. As winter closed in, the weather became harsh, especially in the mountains, and most likely he came at first with only part of his army. His allies from Thessaly and other states willing to answer the call to sacred war were slow in arriving. Thebes controlled the route through Thermopylae, and it was unlikely that the Thebans would grant him passage to attack their ally Amphissa. Philip did not take the chance of being blocked by his allies, so instead he led his men into the mountains. This was harder, especially given the season, and offered plenty of positions where even a relatively small force would be able to stop him, but there were no defenders. Some were active allies in the Amphictyonic cause, and he was able to station troops at Cytinium, close to the high Gravia Pass that led to Amphissa. When he did not push on south across the pass against the declared enemy, and instead went southeast into Phocis, the Phocians were in no position to resist. As far as we can see they welcomed the Macedonians, remembering Philip's mild treatment of them in 346 BC and probably encouraged by promises of greater rewards to come. Philip occupied the city of Elatea, which had been unfortified since the end of the Sacred War and offered welcome shelter and a good strategic position.[6]

For the moment there was nothing to stop him from marching into Boeotia and then on into Attica. The Boeotians had not mustered, nor had the Athenians, both conveniently forgetting the lesson of history that Thermopylae could be bypassed if the route through Phocis was not securely held. Added to that, Thebes was not at war with Macedon, nor had the Thebans committed to resisting the Amphictyonic army moving against Amphissa, so there was no reason for them to have raised an army, especially outside the normal campaigning season. The road to Athens appeared to be open, although taking it risked provoking Thebes and the other Boeotians to turn against Philip, as well as shifting opinion against him in other cities including his Amphictyonic allies. Philip did not have the bulk of his forces with him, and most likely led the same sort of fast-moving strike force he had used in Scythia and on many other occasions. Surprise was often effective, but it is doubtful that he had the capacity to force his way to Athens and besiege the city unless the Athenians' morale collapsed altogether. There were sound military reasons for not pressing onward, and it is unlikely that this was ever Philip's intention. He had shown his enemy—as well as neutral and allied states—that he could reach southern Greece if he wanted, and hoped that this would soften their attitude and make them far more willing to compromise. Diplomacy was always Philip's preferred approach, especially in dealing with the big states of southern Greece, so hc rested his men at Elatea, started building fortifications, and sent ambassadors to Thebes.[7]

The news that Philip was at Elatea reached Athens as the sun was setting, spreading panic throughout the city at the thought that Macedonian soldiers would soon be outside its walls, most likely with Thebans alongside them. Magistrates left the dinner table and ordered the marketplace cleared of stalls and the barriers set up that formed approaches to the Pnyx, the place of Assembly, for a meeting the next day. Soon after dawn the news was read to the gathered citizens and speakers were invited to have their say. According to Demosthenes, who saw what followed as one of the greatest moments of his life, no one stepped forward, even though the question was repeated over and over again. None of the magistrates or city councillors or the usual orators fond of their own voices came forward, at least in part because the Athenians had a nasty habit of later blaming anyone associated with bad news. "But, it seems, the call of the crisis on that momentous day was not only for the wealthy patriot but for the man who from first to last had closely watched the sequence of events, and had rightly fathomed the purposes and the desires of Philip." Only Demosthenes had understood the king and studied him. "On that day, then, the call was manifestly for me. I came forward and addressed you . . . I, alone among your orators and politicians" knew what to do and had the courage to speak.[8]

Demosthenes assured his fellow citizens that the situation was not hopeless, for only a few Thebans—the scoundrels and the men bribed by Macedonian gold—were aligned with Philip, and the king was hoping to intimidate the rest. Athenians must put aside all the old grudges against Thebes to seek alliance with it now. Mustering their own army and extending the hand of friendship, the Athenians would inspire all those decent Thebans by pledging to fight alongside them for the safety and independence of Thebes. This was to be a war for the liberty of all Greek states, that precious liberty threatened by Philip's repeated interventions with money or mercenaries in internal politics and his conquests. Ambassadors were once more to go to many communities, "but first of all to the Thebans, because Philip is nearest their territory and exhort them not to be dismayed at Philip, but to hold fast to their own liberty and the liberty of the other Greeks." They were to make clear that Athens held no grudges for past disputes and would help with "troops, money, supplies, and arms, knowing that, while it is an honourable ambition for Greeks to dispute with each other for the hegemony," it was shameful to be supplanted by a foreigner like Philip.[9]

Philip was once again a barbarian, and Demosthenes went on to cite mythological examples of friendship between Athens and Thebes as good reasons for forgetting about recent hostility from the Thebans. He offered the Athenians a plan of action and more importantly hope, and was greeted by thunderous applause and the approval of his motion. Demosthenes was among the ten ambassadors sent to Thebes.[10]

The Athenians found Philip's envoys already in Thebes, along with envoys from the Greek cities aligned with him in the war against Amphissa, and these were permitted to speak to the Theban Assembly first. The Macedonians asked the Thebans to join their king in marching against Athens, promising them full share in the spoils to come from their inevitable victory. If they were unwilling to fight, then all he requested was that they permit his forces to go through Boeotia as friends. However, he also wanted the Thebans to give up Nicaea, although not to him directly or the Thessalians, but to the Locrians, also his allies now, whose better claim to the place had been ignored by everyone in 346 BC. This was in accordance with the decision of the Amphictyonic council.

Demosthenes nowhere records what he said in any detail, but it was widely held that his words convinced the Thebans to ally with Athens. No doubt his oratory was as smooth and impassioned as ever, although we should note that Theban pride was also involved. Destroying or humbling Athens had some appeal, but not if it strengthened Philip more than it did Thebes, or suggested to the world that the Thebans were subordinate to Macedonia. Demosthenes also agreed to—and perhaps offered from the start—extraordinarily generous terms. Athens would foot the bill for the entire war effort at sea, and pay two-thirds of the combined expenses of operations on land, with supreme command of the joint army being given to a Theban. In addition, the Athenians agreed to support Thebes against not simply Philip, but any Boeotian city who ever opposed her, which effectively meant support for Theban dominance of the entire area and the Boeotian League.[11]

Philip now found two of the most powerful city-states aligned against him. Thebes was all the more significant because, although often short of funds and lacking the natural resources and trade of Athens or the helot workforce of Sparta, it fielded a large army of very good hoplites. Once again hindsight readily misleads us into the belief that Philip's remodeled Macedonian army was so markedly superior to the traditional phalanx that its triumph was inevitable. So far the Macedonians had defeated plenty of tribal armies and shown themselves highly skilled in sieges and assaults. Yet only twice, in 353 and 352 BC, had Philip fought a major pitched battle against a Greek army; he had been routed on the first occasion, though he had won a decisive victory in the second encounter at the Crocus Field. These fights had been against mercenaries serving a dubious cause, and he had never faced the well-motivated citizen phalanxes of major city-states. Athens had a poor record in big battles on land, apart from its successes in the Persian wars, for its strength had always lain at sea and in quick raids. In contrast the Thebans had twice humbled Sparta in living memory, and plenty of their leaders could recall their interventions in Macedonia, and the time when Philip was a hostage. Deep down, most Thebans must have struggled to see the king as a serious rival, while the Athenians were offering generous support and treating Thebes in an appropriately respectful manner.

The Athenians had begun to muster their citizens for war before they knew the outcome of the embassy to Thebes. Once ready, they joined with the Thebans and then took up a line of positions on the frontier of Boeotia, prepared to meet Philip if he advanced from Phocis. In the meantime some 10,000 mercenaries were sent to hold the Gravia Pass and protect the road to Amphissa. These were in Athenian pay and led by Chares and Proxenos, who may have been Theban or a fellow Athenian. Greek armies rarely took the field in such numbers during the winter months, and that they were able to do is testament to the resolve of Athens and Thebes, and also of Athenian wealth and organization in the ability to feed them all. Philip remained stationary, not making any aggressive moves but continuing to try diplomacy, if mainly now directed toward neutral states. The Athenians and Thebans were similarly doing their best to win more allies. Achaea in the Peloponnese sent them hoplites, Corinth and Megara expressions of strong goodwill. Others remained strictly neutral, whether persuaded by Philip's envoys or because they did not see the war against him as in their own interest.[12]

There were skirmishes during the winter and early spring of 339–338 BC, suggesting some raiding on each side. Demosthenes claims that Athenians played a key role in two of these little victories, and although no doubt these were small-scale affairs, it was widely believed that such successes were important, as they showed which side was bolder and more confident. In practical terms Philip was most likely still outnumbered, for it was well into 338 BC before he was reinforced by his remaining troops, while the allied contingents were especially slow in joining him. Tardy or not, far more significant was the fact that they came, accepting that the war had gone beyond the formally sanctioned punishment of Amphissa and now extended to the Amphisseans' supporters.[13]

By the summer Philip had gathered some 30,000 infantry and 2,000 cavalry. He was still in no hurry to provoke a massed battle, especially by attacking the good defensive positions chosen by the main Athenian and Theban forces. Instead he looked toward the Gravia Pass and once again is supposed to have resorted to stratagem. Writing a letter ostensibly to Antipater, he said that he was abandoning the war for the moment so that he could return north and deal with rebellion in Thrace, and made sure that the dispatch was captured. Then, no doubt watched by scouts from the mercenary force, the Macedonians duly trooped out of Cytinium and marched away. Proxenos and Chares relaxed and gave their men a rest from permanently outposting the high pass, even though the Athenian at least ought to have been more suspicious having fallen for a similar trick in the recent past. Perhaps the divided command did not make for good decision making, for a few nights later Philip's men came under cover of dark, surprised and over-whelmed the weakened guards still in the pass, and sent the rest of the mercenaries into panicked flight. He occupied Amphissa, ban-ishing all those involved in the sacrilegious use of Apollo's land and the attack on the Amphictyonic representatives.[14]

From Amphissa Philip was able to outflank the positions of the main enemy army. The Thebans and Athenians withdrew, in due course moving to Chaeronea. Both sides were still reluctant to risk battle, and we must remember that pitched battles were rare events, even if they inevitably attract far more attention than the small-scale raids and skirmishes. Battles were unpredictable and tended to have dramatic consequences, winning or losing the whole campaign in an hour or so. In this case the Theban high command appeared determined that Philip should attack them on ground of their own choosing and were unwilling to force a battle by launching an attack of their own. In the past, plenty of cam-paigns had been decided when one side withdrew after days or weeks of confrontation rather than chance a battle on equal, let alone unfavorable, terms, and this was surely their hope. Again we should remember that the reputation of the Theban army was very high, not least in the Thebans' own minds, and Philip was merely the leader of a hitherto poorly regarded northern kingdom.[15]

For several months Philip made no serious aggressive move, no doubt reinforcing the Thebans' confidence. Instead he sent envoys to Thebes and Athens asking for peace. He was probably sincere. Failure to take cities on the Thracian coast was unfortunate, as was losing his plunder to the Triballi, but a defeat in a battle on this scale against these opponents would be far more damaging, perhaps undoing all the work of the last two decades. While he was unwilling to concede anything significant, he is unlikely to have made any major demands and simply wanted peace, with all sides keeping what they held. Some of the leaders in the two cities were as aware of the stakes and doubted that the potential gains were worth the risk. At Athens Phocion, the same man who had led the fleet against Philip in 340 BC, recommended acceptance, and there were probably other voices echoing his views, as there were in Thebes. If Philip withdrew and peace was agreed, then this would be an honorable outcome in a war in which the Athenians and Thebans had made it clear that they were willing to face him. Unsurprisingly, Demosthenes did not agree and led the criticism. Opinion in Athens shifted his way, and he even proposed sending ambassadors to the Thebans to ask them to let the Athenians march through Boeotia and fight Philip on their own, denouncing the Theban leaders as "traitors to Hellas." Whether shamed into fighting on or seeing the king's caution as fear, both cities rejected Philip's offer of peace.[16]

In early August 338 BC the two armies were camped a mile or so apart near Chaeronea. Allied numbers are uncertain, but most scholars follow Justin's statement that Philip was outnumbered and estimate the allied infantry at some 30,000–35,000, supported by some cavalry, who may have matched the Macedonians in numbers but were inferior in quality. Athens sent perhaps 10,000 men as its contribution, Thebes probably somewhat more, and there were mercenaries and allied contingents from several cities. Among the ranks of the Athenians was Demosthenes, carrying a shield with the slogan "Good Fortune" in gold lettering, and Phocion, as one of the commanders. The Thebans included the 300 men of their elite Sacred Band, one of the few units of full-time soldiers outside Sparta or Macedon. Later tradition claimed that they were recruited from 150 pairs of lovers, the special bond between partners stronger than mere comradeship, but this is unlikely to have been strictly true, and may be simply part of the largely Athenian tradition that depicted the Boeotians as odd. In practical terms it is difficult to see how this could have worked after the first batch of recruits, and most likely the story grew from discussions of the ideal phalanx. For Greeks, or at least Athenian aristocrats, a phalanx of such men ought never to flee, for not only would there be the passion of love, but even more importantly—at least in their eyes—the desire that neither lover be shamed by abandoning his partner by flight. The imagery is powerful, which may explain why the Sacred Band figures far more prominently in modern discussions of Greek warfare than the meager evidence for it should ever justify.[17]

In a similar vein, much has been said about the Battle of Chaeronea even though almost nothing is actually known about it, for our sources are more than usually limited for such a pivotal event. Two monuments—a mound containing the cremated remains of the Macedonians who fell, and a burial topped by a statue of a lion that was held to be a Theban monument and covered the skeletons of at least 255 men—help to confirm the general area of the battlefield. It is a considerable leap of faith to use these to establish positions of the battle lines, since monuments of this sort are rarely tied precisely to the locations of actual fighting. We have far fuller descriptions of Alexander's army in the major battles of the Persian war just a few years later. Using these to guess at the composition of Philip's army is more justified, at least if done with caution, but it is still rash to take the tactics adopted against the cavalry-strong Persians and assume that these were employed in much the same way against the very different opponent of a hoplite army in the far less open country of Greece. We cannot even be sure how much our sources actually knew, for the account in Diodorus is vague even by his standards. Plutarch was a native of Chaeronea and preserved a few local traditions: of Alexander's tree, where the prince is supposed to have pitched his tent, and a stream renamed the Haemon because it flowed with blood. After more than four centuries it would have been hard for anyone to know the truth behind such tales, especially as Chaeronea had witnessed other major battles in the years in between that might easily confuse the tradition.[18]

The Allies seem to have chosen a position where their flanks were protected by streams and broken terrain on the valley sides. This would have made it hard for Philip to outflank them. Given the Theban fondness for deploying unusually deep phalanxes, this position may have been relatively narrow for an army of this size, and some contingents formed in significantly more depth than the standard eight ranks. Diodorus says that the Thebans were on one flank and the Athenians on the other, but he does not specify which, just as he vaguely has Alexander on one flank and Philip on the other. The Lion Monument is on the right of where most scholars position the Allied line, and the right was traditionally the place of honor, so appropriate in a Theban-commanded army, while Athenian fugitives escaped over the Kerata Pass, which is on the left of the valley. Therefore a reasonable case can be made that the Thebans were on the right and the Athenians on the left. No mention is made of either side's cavalry during the battle; often-repeated descriptions of Alexander charging at the head of the Companion cavalry are wholly conjectural. The most common position for cavalry was on the wings, but it is possible that they were held back. Alexander is credited with breaking the Sacred Band, thus allowing the above scholars to put him on the Macedonian left and usually place the Sacred Band on the extreme right of the Theban line, so that Philip was stationed on the right since he seems to have faced the Athenians.

Two stratagems are attributed to the king in the battle. In one he is supposed to have feigned a withdrawal, drawing the inexperienced Athenians forward just as Onomarchus had lured Philip's men on in 353 BC. Stratcoles, an Athenian general, is supposed to have urged those around him to chase the enemy back to Macedon. Pushing forward, the Athenians gave up their strong position, while the Macedonian phalanx pulled back in good order until it was standing on higher ground. Having declared that the Athenians did not know how to win a victory, Philip counterattacked and drove the enemy back. If this occurred at all, then like William the Conqueror at Hastings, he may have made a virtue out of what was initially a genuine retreat, realizing that the enemy were being lured out of a strong position and losing their formation in the process.

Another story has Philip deliberately drawing the battle out, believing that his well-trained men could endure longer than the inexperienced Athenians. In general this was no doubt true, for as Demosthenes was wont to complain, Athens had relied far more on mercenaries than citizen hoplites for some time. Although highly motivated, many of the citizen soldiers were past their prime and unlikely to have been especially fit, while few had experience of fighting in a phalanx. Diodorus also has the armies deploying at dawn and the fighting raging "for a long time" with the fortunes swaying back and forth. No source hints that the Allies broke quickly, so a prolonged fight seems likely.[19]

A high proportion of Philip's infantry were armed with the sarissa, although we cannot say how many of his 30,000 foot soldiers were light troops or hoplites provided by his allies, while it looks as if some of the elite infantry of the Macedonian Army, known in Alexander's time as the hypaspists, usually wielded spears rather than pikes. The sarissa had a much longer reach than a hoplite's spear. It was unlikely to penetrate a hoplite's shield, at least with sufficient force to wound the man carrying it, but when wielded well could strike at the face and neck. By this period the majority of hoplites wore open-faced helmets rather than the enclosed Corinthian type usually associated with them.

The Macedonian pikemen could reach their hoplite opponents, but unless they could break or push aside several sarissa heads in succession, it is hard to see how the Allied hoplites could harm their enemies. Yet prolonged fighting and the significant number of Macedonian dead attested by the burial mound—to which must be added a far greater number of wounded, judging from other battles—make it clear that they did. A spear could be thrown, and it is a mistake to assume that some hoplites did not carry additional spears or javelins in some circumstances. Pikemen had smaller shields and less chance of shifting them to catch a missile, but were offered a degree of protection by the shafts of the sarissas carried by the men in the ranks behind. Perhaps there were some archers among the phalanx or close behind it, for the practice was certainly common in earlier centuries and would have made sense in the context of Chaeronea. In the years that followed it is known that Athenian youths went through a period of training in their late teens that included archery, and the practice may have been established earlier, so even among the hoplite class there were men with some basic familiarity with bows. Overall, the impression is of a slogging battle with losses on both sides, all suggesting local retreats and lulls as men gathered their breath.[20]

Alexander is said to have first broken the enemy line, although this may be no more than inevitable praise for the eighteen-year-old prince who would two years later become king. Plutarch says that he broke the ranks of the Sacred Band and perhaps he did, if it was not simply too tempting for later authors to resist connecting the young hero with the defeat of the famous elite unit. The Allied line broke up and eventually collapsed, leaving 1,000 Athenians dead and some 2,000 as prisoners, and Theban losses on a similar scale. Demosthenes was one of the fugitives who fled over the Kerata Pass. No figures are given for Macedonian casualties, and the losing side tended to suffer far more heavily than the victors as men were cut down in the initial stages of flight. There does not seem to have been a prolonged pursuit of the sort Philip employed against tribal enemies.[21]

The men of the Sacred Band died where they stood, whether unwilling to retreat, surrounded and unable to do so, or choosing to cover the flight of others by deliberate sacrifice. The 255 corpses buried under the Lion Monument are often assumed to be from this unit; the total is certainly close enough and would have represented catastrophic casualties sufficient to justify talk of annihilation even if this was not literally true. Monuments were not normally set up by the losers, so something needs to explain why the Thebans did this, and commemoration of famous heroes, perhaps decades later when symbols of past glory were of use in contemporary politics, makes sense. Yet no ancient source associates the Lion Monument with the Sacred Band, and it is possible that it covers a larger graveyard, for only some of the ground has been excavated. The surviving remains testify to the brutal realities of combat with edged weapons; one man had most of his face sliced off by a sword cut.[22]

Philip had won the largest battle of his career, but there are conflicting traditions about his conduct in the aftermath of the battle. Justin has the king behaving with great restraint and refusing to exult at his success, while Plutarch says that he wept at the sight of the Sacred Band lying dead almost in formation. Yet Diodorus reports an alternative where Philip held a wine-fueled celebration before processing around in the company of similarly drunken friends, dancing and mocking prisoners and enemy dead alike. Demades, a captured Athenian, sobered him by saying that he ought to be acting like Agamemnon, the leader of the Greek army in the Trojan War, not Thersites, the ugliest and least heroic warrior in the *Iliad*.[23]

Winning the battle was a great achievement, but Philip knew that the key was making a permanent peace. He needed to secure his own position and ensure that there were no more serious challenges from the city-states, and this required a balance between threats and persuasion. History showed that Greek communities resented anything they saw as humiliation, nursing the grudge until they felt that they had even the slightest chance of avenging themselves. They also expected victors to show little or no restraint and exploit their power to inflict the maximum injury on the defeated. Philip had smashed the army led by Thebes and Athens, and they and their allies fearfully awaited his next move. If Philip punished them severely, then this would entrench their hatred and lay up problems for the future, while if he destroyed or severely crippled them he could not be sure that the new balance of power to emerge in southern Greece would favor him. The instinctive independence of the Greeks that made it so hard for them to come together in a cause also made it all the harder to deal with them, for how each city was treated had an impact on how others were likely to behave in the future. Even for a man who took such pride in his diplomatic achievements, this was a challenge.

12

LOVE AND PERSIA

Athens's influence as a great trading city and naval power spread over a very wide area, making it especially important for Philip to get right his settlement in relation to the Athenians. He chose as his initial envoy Demades, the same captured Athenian who had reprimanded him after the battle, according to Diodorus. For the moment the Macedonian army remained at Chaeronea and did not advance. Their own dead were cremated and the monument erected over them, while the wounded needed care. Athenian corpses were also burned, the remains gathered up and escorted to Athens by Alexander, Antipater (presumably having arrived from Macedonia at some point before the battle), and another prominent Macedonian nobleman. They carried the message that the Athenian prisoners were to be returned without ransom. In contrast the Thebans would have to pay to get their fellow citizens back and even to retrieve their dead. Judging from the Lion Monument, some—probably all if Philip's men camped nearby for any length of time under the hot August sun—were hastily buried.[1]

Before the messengers arrived, Athenians responded to the panicked tales of fugitives by preparing for a desperate siege. The countryside was to be evacuated; all citizens eligible for military service up to the age of sixty called to arms; and a plan approved to free slaves working in the mines or fields, make them citizens, and arm them for the fight. In a characteristically Athenian way, a scapegoat for the defeat was sought and soon found, in the person of their senior elected general, who was tried, condemned, and executed. Over time, Athenians readily shifted the blame to the Theban commanders, damning them as incompetents. Demosthenes and his allies continued to sway the assembly, and a last-ditch stand appealed to more people than abject capitulation. The mood began to change when the envoys arrived—for the return of their dead was a rare honor from an enemy in Greek warfare—and when they heard the tone of Demades's message that the king wished to discuss peace. Demosthenes preached unrelenting hostility to the king, but the ever pragmatic and respected Phocion argued that they should at least find out what Philip's specific terms would be. The Assembly listened to him, although they also chose Demosthenes to give the traditional oration at the ceremony to bury the ashes of their honored dead. Mocked by rivals for his cowardice, and clearly not a natural fighting man, Demosthenes cannot have been the first to run at Chaeronea, even though run is what he and many others certainly did.[2]

Philip's terms to Athens were generous. There was to be no Macedonian garrison in Athens, nor was the city to be forced to abandon its democratic constitution or to hand over the politicians who had inspired the war against the king. Athens also kept its fleet and its few remaining allies, if not the formal structure of the confederation binding them. The recall of colonists from the Gallipoli Peninsula was a rare and mild punishment in a settlement that allowed Athens to continue flourishing as an independent state and great trading power. Phocion's support helped secure acceptance of the terms, but there was widespread relief among the voters. Philip and Alexander were made citizens of Athens, and a statue of the king erected. As far as we can tell, Philip never actually visited the city, and this was the only time in his life that Alexander went to Athens.

In contrast Thebes suffered. Some leaders were exiled or chose to flee, while exiled noblemen were allowed home and, all of them grateful to Philip, formed a significant element in a new council of 300 that was to rule as an oligarchy under the watchful eyes of Macedonian soldiers garrisoning the Cadmeia, the city's ancient citadel. The Boeotian League was restructured so that Thebes no longer dominated, while cities she had destroyed were rebuilt and restored as poleis. In addition, Phocis was rewarded by similar restoration, with its debt to Delphi being drastically reduced. Corinth also received a garrison, and there may have been others as Philip took his army into the Peloponnese, but overall Greece was scarcely occupied territory, and most communities there found it timely to seek the king's friendship. Sparta stayed aloof, but its hostility did not extend beyond bad manners, and it was no longer the power it had once been. Many small states welcomed the dominance of Philip as preferable to that of closer states like Corinth, for he asked little in return. Philip's policy was deliberately mild, as "he would rather be called a good man for a long time, than master for a short one."[3]

Philip had always shown surprising lenience toward Athens in spite of getting little goodwill in return, and many wonder why he did not now choose to break the city's power. In part this was because besieging the city—or any other major community— was likely to take a long time and prove costly. The task was less easy than many scholars imagine and, even if successful, would bring him few gains to compensate for the risk and cost, as well as damage his prestige. Athens was a great symbol of much that all Greeks admired, as the greatest Hellenic cultural and intellectual center, and for its defiance of Persia in the fifth century BC. The Athenians were not always popular and sometimes hated, but while many Greeks would happily see them humbled, few would rejoice in their utter destruction. More practically, destroying or crippling Athens would create a power vacuum and unbalance the politics of much of Greece, whereas an Athens willing to maintain the peace was a far greater force for stability, its fleet the best able to keep the sea lanes open and restrict piracy.[4]

The king of Macedon also had greater projects in mind. At some point late in 338 BC or early in 337 BC representatives from all the Greek states were invited to meet with Philip at Corinth. Sparta did not attend, but everyone else accepted the call. The outcome was a treaty and an alliance known to scholars as the League of Corinth, although debate continues over its precise technical nature. A representative council was created and a peace treaty established between all Greek states that recognized their right to choose their own constitution and to be independent, while threatening united war against any state seeking to deprive another of these things. There were elements in the treaty of the King's Peace once sponsored by the Persians and earlier attempts at a Common Peace, given more power because the might of Macedon was there to intervene and enforce the rules. No attempt was made to force Sparta to join, demonstrating that participation was voluntary, although of course the choice was influenced by the simple fact that Philip's army was the most powerful then in existence. He had already made individual alliances with most of the communities involved and these continued, for effectively the purpose was to maintain the status quo of domestic politics and in relations between states. Either at this stage or a little later, all members swore to keep their oaths to and treaty with Philip and his descendants. Past experience suggested that permanent stability did not come naturally to the city-states, whatever the terms of any alliance, but for the moment Philip was strong.[5]

At the first gathering of the council, Philip proposed a united war against Persia to punish the Persians for their destruction of Greek shrines during the invasion of 480–479 BC. The delegates approved, electing Philip as leader (*hegemon*) for this war with supreme authority to do as he saw fit and agreeing to raise troops and supplies to participate. Their vote was then ratified by oaths taken in each member state. Justin claims that the combined armies of the members amounted to 200,000 infantry and 15,000 cavalry, but if these figures mean anything, they represented the theoretical total of every citizen eligible to bear arms. Philip's requests for contingents were far more modest than this. In the spring of 337 BC an advance guard under Parmenio, his most trusted and reliable subordinate, crossed to Asia Minor and the war began. Philip planned to follow a year later with the main army, for the preparations all took time.[6]

The dream of the Athenian philosopher Isocrates and the other Panhellenists had finally become a reality. We cannot say how early Philip had begun to consider a Persian war, let alone when he decided to embark on one as soon as was practical. Isocrates openly wondered whether he had inspired the king or simply reinforced a plan already formed in his mind, but at the age of ninety-eight he had discussed the matter with Antipater when the Macedonian nobleman came to Athens after Chaeronea. Thrace was still claimed by the Persians, if no longer under their control, so in one sense Philip's Macedonia was always closer to the Persian Empire than the southern Greeks were. He had helped the Theban Pammenes take his army to aid a satrap against the Persian king, while everyone knew of the successes won by Greek hoplites time and again over far larger eastern armies, a fact endlessly repeated by the Panhellenists. Asia Minor and the empire in general were wealthy, accessible, and appeared vulnerable. Philip was in his forties, fit and active in spite of his wounds, the head of a greatly enlarged kingdom and leader of an excellent army. For all his diplomatic skill, his rise was due to military force, for he had campaigned with little break for his entire reign. The regime he had created and now led needed more victories, more glory, more spoils to reward soldiers and aristocrats alike, and, to fund his new settlements, more displays of power and gifts to win support throughout Greece. Attacking Persia offered wealth and glory to surpass everything he had already done.[7]

Philip may well have pondered a Persian expedition for many years before he launched it. His Thracian campaigns had prepared the way, giving him secure control of the shortest crossing points to Asia, but it is a mistake to see him working to a clear long-term plan, with everything little more than preparation for a great war with Persia. The expansion into Thrace was a worthwhile end in itself that added to his territory, wealth, and manpower while securing the heartland of his kingdom from attack. More immediately, his settlement of Greece after Chaeronea, and probably his attempts at a peaceful settlement beforehand, were surely made with the Persian War in mind. Perhaps the Panhellenists would be right and Hellenes would unite enthusiastically to defeat and despoil the "real" enemy of Persia. Choosing as pretext for war an offense committed a century and a half earlier seems thin to modern eyes, but was less so to the Greeks, who were used to dredging up ancient feuds or friendships when it was convenient. Destruction of temples was a fitting cause for the man who had avenged Apollo and punished Amphissa for sacrilege. No doubt deliberately, Philip's mild treatment of Athens, one of the victims of Persian misbehavior in 480 BC, and his harsher punishment of Thebes, which had joined the invaders and fought against the other Greeks at Plataea, were all the more fitting as this history was revived.[8]

The Greeks had little choice in agreeing to the war and choosing Philip to lead them, which does not mean that some, perhaps many, did not thrill at the prospect. The king did not announce his ultimate goals for the war or say just what would represent suitable revenge for Persia's insult to the gods of Greece. Most likely his plans were not fixed and would have developed over time, shaped by how well the war went. For the moment Philip had won a great victory, shaped a peace that in the short term at least seemed secure, and was about to embark on a grand expedition.

The king had every reason to feel content at his prospects. If our sources are right, he was also in love, and late in 337 BC the forty-five-year-old Philip married again. His bride was a teenager, and unlike all his other wives she came from Lower Macedonia, the heartland of the old kingdom. Her name was Cleopatra, and since this name appears more than once in the royal family, it is possible that she was an Argead and certain that she came from an important aristocratic family. Although her father was dead, she was the niece and ward of Attalus, a middle-aged nobleman. Cleopatra was young and beautiful, and our sources tell us that Philip was besotted, marrying for love instead of political advantage.

Some scholars are reluctant to believe that the hard-headed Philip would suddenly be swayed by emotion and prefer to see this as a carefully calculated move. Unless he was killed, the longevity of his family made it more than likely that the king had decades more to live. At present Alexander was showing talent and was openly favored as successor, but the only other son of Philip's marriages was incapable, and by this time most of his wives were getting too old for any more children to be likely. Fathering another son or two was a wise precaution in case Alexander failed to outlive him or proved a disappointment. While this is reasonable, we should note that since Philip planned to go to the east in 336 or at latest 335 BC, there was only time for perhaps two pregnancies even in the best of circumstances, and it was not his custom to take his wives with him on campaign.[9]

Apart from the succession, if politics was behind his latest marriage, then for the first time it was for domestic concerns rather than aimed at securing his borders. Since Philip expected to be in Asia for at least a few years and perhaps longer, he needed to be sure that Macedonia was secure from challenges to his rule. Unfortunately we know so little about the influence and identity of the Macedonian aristocracy that we can only guess at Philip's relationship with them throughout his reign and presume ever present tension between different groupings, not least between the clans of Upper and Lower Macedonia. The bride's uncle Attalus may well have led a faction or extended family in the country and at court, making it attractive for him to have a personal interest in maintaining Philip's rule. Yet he is not mentioned in our sources before 337 BC, so we really know almost nothing about him, making it impossible to know whether his prominence at court was long-standing or the result of the king marrying his niece. Political calculation does not exclude emotion, and Philip may have loved Cleopatra, just as Plutarch claims Philip had once loved Olympias. Nor, even in such a male-dominated society, need we see either woman as wholly passive in all this rather than determined and ambitious. There is nothing implausible about a middle-aged man, especially one about to embark on the rigors of a great war, falling head over heels for a much younger woman.[10]

Alexander attended the great feast celebrating the union and reclined on a couch close to the king. Olympias was not there, nor was Cleopatra, since well-born women did not take part in these raucous and hard-drinking affairs. As the evening progressed, the wine flowed and tongues loosened as they usually did at these parties. Attalus raised his cup and proposed a toast, beseeching the gods that the union provide the kingdom with a legitimate heir, by implication one of pure, Lower Macedonian blood, rather than the son of foreigners like Olympias and Philinna. We cannot know whether the words were carefully chosen or came from a man too drunk to know what he was doing. Alexander heard them clearly— or at least thought he did—and understandably flew into a temper. He flung his own cup at Attalus and demanded to know whether he was calling him a bastard. Philip now intervened. Whether or not he had been following closely and had heard what was said, he was the host and it was his job to keep the peace and prevent violence, let alone against the guardian of his new bride. He rose and even drew his sword, but was so drunk that as he lurched toward his son, the king tripped and fell flat on his face. Alexander taunted him—"Look, everyone! Here is the man who was preparing to cross from Europe to Asia and he is upset in trying to cross from one couch to another!" Philip's friends managed to hold him back while his son left. Alexander fled not only from the feast but left Macedonia, taking his mother to Epirus and then going on himself to seek refuge with an Illyrian leader.[11]

In itself Philip's latest marriage was not a direct challenge to either Olympias or Alexander. She was still mother of the obvious successor should the king die, and even if Cleopatra gave Philip a son, it would be years before everyone could be confident that the boy would survive and be suitable as an heir under a regent's guidance. Nothing suggests that Philip was about to withdraw his open favor for Alexander. After Chaeronea he commissioned a grand monument at the shrine of Zeus at Olympia. Known as the Philippeion, it was circular in shape (a *tholos*), the tiled roof supported by an outer circle of eighteen Ionic columns and an inner ring of nine Doric columns. In the heart, at least partially visible from outside for there were no walls, were five statues, each one of marble decorated with gold. In the center stood Philip, with his parents on one side and Alexander and Olympias on the other. This was his monument—the name means simply "Philip's building"— for his glory, and placed him at the heart of the dynasty. Situated at one of the greatest and most frequently visited Panhellenic shrines, the unusual circular shape and splendor of the monument ensured that it stood out, honoring the leader of the Greeks in the war of vengeance against Persia.[12]

Alexander and Alexander alone represented a future after Philip in the Philippeion. There was no statue of his other son Arrhidaeus, nor of Philip's nephew Amyntas, even though around this time the latter was married to the king's daughter, Cynane. Olympias and no other wife was there as mother of the heir apparent. Yet Philip was at the heart of it all and Philip had no plan to die any time soon, so he anticipated a substantial future of his own. There was no formal position of heir to the throne, nor any fixed rule dictating the order of succession. Alexander would become king if he managed to outlive his father and if he retained Philip's favor over any other potential choices. The longer the king lived, then the more chance that Alexander would die, be crippled, or find himself the fading hero compared to a younger half brother. No source tells us whether Philip planned to take Alexander with him to Asia or leave him as regent in Macedonia, and the many positive statements one way or another in modern books are wholly speculative. Either way, he would be overshadowed by his still vigorous father.[13]

Alexander was bound to resent this. The nineteen-year-old prince was impatient, quick-tempered, determined, and obsessively competitive. All of his future career testifies to these traits, as well as a strong streak of suspicion and jealousy. Whether or not the story is true of his regretting each success won by his father as one less victory he might win, Alexander's relationship with Philip was made all the more complicated and tense because both craved glory. Even by the standards of their age, they were fiercely competitive, the father because he had already done so much and craved even more, and the son because the father's deeds had set the bar for being the best even higher than before. For all his prodigious talent, we should not expect exceptional emotional maturity from the young prince who struggled to cope with playing a supporting role. He knew that his future depended on his father. Rationally, we can see that neither Arrhidaeus nor Amyntas can have been serious rivals, but the latter's marriage was a mark of favor. The enigmatic

Caranus, mentioned only by Justin as another brother, presumably illegitimate if he existed at all, may have seemed to be one—that is if he was in his teens and Philip appeared to like him. We do not know enough about Argead history to be certain that no bastard was ever recognized and perhaps even ruled. To us it is obvious that Alexander would become king if anything happened to Philip in the foreseeable future, and Philip surely thought the same thing. That does not mean Alexander knew this and was free from fear of real or imagined rivals.[14]

Feasts were a traditional venue for praising the king, and also often for mocking others. They served a role in displaying and testing the pecking order at court and relations between the king and his leading men. Angry, usually drunken exchanges were common enough, but always the king was at the center, above everyone else, including his son. Philip is said to have expressed great pride in his son, especially when his courage at Chaeronea was praised, but at the same time he may also have wanted to remind Alexander that he was the son of the king and not yet king. For all his personal charm and diplomatic skill, Philip sometimes made mistakes and did not win over everyone all of the time. No one comes out of the row at the wedding feast very well, and it is possible that the king mishandled the whole affair and perhaps was not good at reassuring his son. Our sources say that Alexander fled through choice, with no hint of exile or threat of punishment. There is also no suggestion that Alexander or Olympias tried to stir up a war against Philip. Epirus was too small to challenge the might of Macedonia, and the days were gone when an Illyrian-backed claimant to the throne stood much chance.[15]

Plutarch tells us that Demaratus, a Corinthian guest-friend of Philip, persuaded the king to recall his son, the brusque words of a decent Greek a reassuring solution for the author and his Greek audience. Whatever the reason, after a relatively short time—a few months at the very most—Philip sent men to invite his son home. Alexander returned and continued to be treated with the same favor by his father. Yet everyone knew that Philip had allowed him to return, a reminder of the king's authority. No one tells us whether Olympias remained in Epirus, but then the movements and activities of the royal women are rarely mentioned in our sources. Attalus continued to enjoy considerable favor, and Philip chose him to go alongside Parmenio as joint commanders of the 10,000–man advance guard who were the first to cross to Asia in 337 BC. By the end of the year Cleopatra was pregnant, potentially reinforcing her status.[16]

Weddings continued to feature in Philip's diplomacy, and at some point it was arranged that Alexander's sister Cleopatra was to marry their uncle, Alexander of Epirus, further reinforcing the alliance between the kingdoms. It was a good match in political terms, and meant that she would not marry a Macedonian noble-man, and thereby create another line of the Argead family. Scholars tend to see it either as a sop to Olympias for the insult offered to her by Attalus and her subsequent flight, or at the other extreme as circumventing her altogether by tying Alexander of Epirus to Philip independently and rendering her irrelevant. Both views overcomplicate matters.[17]

After Alexander's return to court, an envoy came to Philip from Pixodarus, ruler of Caria in Asia Minor and one of the sons of Mausolus, famous for his lavish tomb or mausoleum. The Carians were not Greeks, but had long shown a fondness for many aspects of Greek culture and architecture. They were part of the Persian Empire, although rebellions by and against the satraps of Asia Minor ensured that the relationship was complex, and in day-to-day affairs, including diplomacy, they had a great deal of independence. Plutarch claims that Pixodarus was looking for an ally against the Persians and offered his daughter as a bride for Arrhidaeus. Philip expressed interest, for Caria was a large enough state for this to be honorable and would offer a useful ally in his forthcoming campaign.

Alexander was worried, feeling left out as his father now arranged a marriage for his half brother just as he had done for Amyntas. His circle of friends and his mother (wherever she was) fueled his suspicion of being marginalized. Choosing as his repre-sentative a well-known actor named Thessalus, he sent the man to Caria to offer himself as prospective bridegroom instead of his brother. Pixodarus was delighted.

Philip was not. Royal marriages were controlled by the king and no one else, not even a favored son. Accompanied by Parmenio's son Philotas, who was a little older than Alexander and his friend, the king went to Alexander's room to have a stern word with his son. According to Plutarch he told him that he was a fool and not behaving in a manner befitting his status. Marriage to the daughter of mere local dynast—"a Carian and a slave to a barbarian king"—was far beneath him. Negotiations were broken off, the prospective alliance dead. A little later Pixodarus married the girl to a Persian satrap. Orders were sent to arrest Thessalus and send him to Macedonia in chains, but the actor wisely decided to pursue his career elsewhere and was not caught. Four of Alexander's close friends—Ptolemy (later king of Egypt and chronicler of Alexander's campaigns), Harpalus, Nearchus, and Erigyius—were banished, presumably because they were believed to have encouraged him.[18]

Plutarch is our only source for this story and appears to date it after Alexander's recall from Illyria. In it the young prince is deeply insecure, impetuous, and surrounded by friends and a mother encouraging him to assert independence from his father. This was all about politics and apparent status, and not any urge on the part of the nineteen-year-old to marry and father children. After he had become king, Alexander would wait many years before taking a wife. His sex life attracts a lot of interest but is attested only by a few fragments in our sources, many of which are dubious. Later in life he is supposed to have said that he hated sleep and sex because they reminded him that he was mortal, not least because he evidently could not do without either. During his teens his parents are supposed to have been worried that he showed no interest in women, so they hired a famous Greek courtesan to pique his interest. The experiment failed, and compared to his notoriously promiscuous father, Alexander had far fewer lovers.[19]

Hephaestion was a friend of his youth and would rise to great prominence later; his death would be marked by an extraordinary and excessive display of mourning by Alexander. The bond between the two was close, perhaps closer than any Alexander had with anyone else, but the precise nature of the relationship is elusive. In later centuries they were believed to be lovers, a pair of heroes to match Achilles and Patroclus from the Trojan War, who were similarly portrayed, even though this required a good deal of reading between the lines of the *Iliad*. The idea of two famous warriors who fought side by side, trusting and loving the other utterly, exercised a powerful appeal to the minds of Greek aristocrats, making it hard to tell whether it was an ideal or ever a reality in general let alone specific cases, rather like the case of the Sacred Band. Alongside this is the tendency to interpret every relationship, especially involving kings, as sexual. The simple truth is that we do not know, and can say only that many later believed that this was part of the relationship. Hephaestion is barely mentioned until his promotion ever higher by Alexander. He was taller than his friend, and more conventionally handsome, but he also had an abrasive manner that made him plenty of enemies.[20]

Hephaestion was not exiled after the Pixodarus affair, and it is significant that three of the named friends were Greeks rather than Macedonians. Ptolemy was from Upper Macedonia, although later claims of a link to the Argeads, let alone the rumor that he was Philip's bastard son, were concoctions of the power struggles after Alexander's death. The inclusion of non-Macedonians in the prince's inner circle reflects the cosmopolitan nature of Philip's court, where men who served him well were rewarded with lands, honor, and rank. Foreigners may have been easier to send away than other friends who had connections with established aristocratic families. Philip's purpose was once again to remind Alexander of his superiority, not to demote him or undermine his status as favored heir. Later events make it clear that the prince still had plenty of friends and allies at court. For the moment, and for many years to come, Alexander was bound to be seen as the natural successor to Philip.

13

"WREATHED IS THE BULL": PASSION, AMBITION, AND REVENGE

P hilip had every reason to feel pleased with life in 336 BC. As usual the sources are hazy concerning what he was doing and where he was for much of this and the preceding year, and on very slender evidence some scholars have suggested an Illyrian campaign around this time. The great project was preparing for his Persian expedition, and this occupied much of his time and even more of his resources. The Pythian priestess at Delphi responded to his question by speaking of a sacrifice: "Wreathed is the bull. All is done. There is also the one who will smite him." Philip had no doubt that the Persian king was the garlanded bull and he the man wielding the sacrificial blade. In the spring the advance guard crossed the Hellespont and pushed into Asia Minor. As usual the Persian response was slow and at first ponderous, for no satrap had substantial forces at his immediate disposal and there was still more intrigue and murder at the royal court. Cities, especially the Greek communities of the area, readily defected rather than risk fighting the invader. At Ephesus a new democratic regime assumed control and set up a statue of Philip in the precinct of the great temple of Artemis, and all in all this was an excellent start.[1]

Before the expedition departed a brutal episode occurred at court that was to change everything, even though neither Philip nor Alexander was directly involved. Cleopatra's uncle Attalus held a drinking party, and one of the guests was Pausanias, who came from Orestis in Upper Macedonia. Years before, probably as a page, he had caught Philip's eye and for a while became his lover. Ever fickle, the king had soon switched his attention to another youth, coincidentally also named Pausanias. In Athens it was felt inappropriate to maintain an affair once a youth's beard grew properly, but such attitudes may have been different elsewhere. The discarded lover was jealous and angry, and took it out on the new favorite, calling him easy and as much woman as man. Convention maintained that a youth should be courted before giving himself to an older lover, and that the older man should teach the youth and give him gifts. Reputation and honor mattered greatly to aristocrats, especially young men eager to win a name as fighters. The second Pausanias decided to prove his manhood beyond doubt by dying in battle, and got his chance in Illyria in 345 BC when Philip was knocked down with a broken collar bone. Pausanias saved him and died in the act.

Attalus was a friend of the dead youth, who was said to have told him of his plan. Sometime during the winter of 337–336 BC he took revenge, now that he enjoyed royal favor. He got the other Pausanias drunk, something not too hard to do in the culture of the court. When the young man was helpless, the noblemen and his other guests beat him up and may have raped him. Afterward, to deepen the pain and especially the humiliation, he was given to Attalus's muleteers who gang-raped him. Apart from revenge this was a gesture of power on the part of Attalus, for there was no attempt to hide what had been done.[2]

Pausanias complained to Philip, who was reluctant to punish the uncle of his expectant new wife and one of the two nominated commanders for the advance guard. He did not want a breach with Attalus over a matter that did not directly affect him. Instead Philip hoped to placate the young man, so promoted him to be one of the seven royal bodyguards, a position of both trust and honor. Attalus was soon sent off to war, and no longer had a chance to taunt his victim, but Attalus's associates, including his niece Cleopatra, remained at court, favored and disdainful. Olympias offered Pausanias sympathy, as did Alexander, whether genuinely moved or from dislike of Attalus. They fed the sense of outrage and of the inadequacy of punishment as Pausanias brooded, angry not just at the man who had attacked him, but at Philip, the king who had failed to give justice to someone who had once been a favorite.[3]

The wedding of Alexander of Epirus and Olympias's daughter Cleopatra was to take place at Aegae during a festival, and both events were used as an occasion for Philip to celebrate and parade his success and popularity. Guests came from all over Greece: official delegates and guest-friends of the king, and even of those his noblemen, were all welcome. This was to show his generosity and add to the picture of the leader chosen by the league of Greeks to take them off to the great war. The Athenian delegation brought word of new honors, including a pledge never to aid or give refuge to anyone who had plotted against the king, but instead to hand such an enemy over. They also presented Philip with a golden crown, a symbolic and valuable present to add to his funds, as did the representatives of other Greek cities, who were equally sycophantic in their eagerness to assure the king of their loyalty. There is debate over whether the event occurred in summer or in the early autumn, but the Olympian festival around October seems likely. Whenever Philip planned to take the main army across to Asia Minor, he expected to wait until the following spring before launching the main offensive.[4]

There were lavish sacrifices of animals followed by feasting, for it was common in the ancient world to serve the meat of the sacrifice in a ceremonial banquet. A well-known and popular actor entertained the guests with a selection of works felt appropriate for the occasion. One verse began, "Your thoughts reach higher than the air: You dream of wide fields' cultivation," but warned against taking the future for granted. For "death, mortals' source of many woes" strikes suddenly from nowhere "and robs us of our distant hopes." Philip approved, taking this as warning for the Persian king of kings who, in spite of his might and glory, was doomed to fall and die. The next day was for the start of the festival proper, with competitive performances staged in the theater. This was to be another spectacle, and the crowd assembled before dawn and took their seats. Among the procession to open the events was a parade of statues of the twelve Olympian gods—the gods of Greece to witness and approve the expressions of Greece's high culture. They were closely followed by a statue of Philip, not to claim divine status, but to show the Olympians' favor and approval of him.[5]

The culmination of the procession was the arrival of Philip in person, and he had stage-managed this with great care, so that he would be the last to arrive. The crowd was already there, the images of the gods reminders of their blessing. Unlike a Persian king, Philip did not intend to ride or be surrounded by serried ranks of guards and courtiers. The seven royal bodyguards, Pausanias among them, stood off to the side, holding their javelins. Finally, at the perfect moment Philip approached the theater, with Alexander on one side of him and Alexander of Epirus on the other. Then Philip stopped and let the two younger men precede him to their seats.

Philip II, king of Macedon, archon of Thessaly, and *hegemon* of the Greeks stood alone. His cloak was bleached to a dazzling white, but otherwise the insignia of kingship were few, unlike the magnificent robes of a Persian king. Philip did not need such finery to puff himself up. His achievements and power were shown by all those who had traveled to the ceremony, and by all the things he had done in the last twenty or so years. He did not need armed men to protect him, and for all his glory remained an Argead, dressed only slightly differently from his Companions, and happy to feast with them, drinking and laughing freely, just as he did with his guests from Greece.

The forty-six-year-old king reveled in the moment as the crowd cheered. Leaders tend to have a strong theatrical streak and this was especially true in the ancient world. Philip waited, soaking up the acclaim, before he began to walk forward. He walked with a limp, but like his lost eye this was not something he tried to conceal, which again was in contrast with the kings of Persia, where it was expected that the monarch should be perfect physically. Philip was the center of the day's celebrations because of who he was and what he had done. The resounding cheers were expressions of all that he had done and achieved, and of promise for all the glory he hoped to win in the future. Never before had the Greeks of so many cities gathered to celebrate any man. Only Philip had achieved this, just as only Philip had made Macedonia so strong. This was his moment, and he alone would take the credit as he walked toward his seat. The cheers of thousands echoed around the theater.

Then, without any warning, Pausanias broke away from the other bodyguards and ran at the lone figure. Philip had no time to react as the young man reached him. Pausanias dropped his javelin and produced a "Celtic" dagger, which had been hidden under his cloak. He thrust once, stabbing the king between the ribs. Philip fell and was dead within seconds before anyone could react, really before anyone understood what had happened. The assassin ran to where horses waited for his escape. He was closely pursued by three of his fellow bodyguards, men who must have known him well. Pausanias had a good lead, until he tripped on a vine root and fell. The bodyguards caught him and killed him with the javelins they carried. His body was crucified as punishment, but the assassin had said no final words of triumph or justification. The vicious treatment he had received from Attalus and his people was well known—indeed the publicity of it made the offense all the deeper. Everyone understood that he acted out of anger, because Philip had failed to give him the justice he deserved as loyal subject and former lover. Aristotle later cited the assassination as an example of one motivated by a perceived personal wrong.[6]

Quickly, perhaps within hours, Antipater presented Alexander to a gathering of officers and soldiers who proclaimed him as king in the traditional way. Around sixty-three years old, Antipater had lived through royal murders and successions before, and was an important commander during Perdiccas III's reign, if not before. With Parmenio and Attalus away in Asia, he was the most prominent of Philip's senior subordinates on the spot, allowing him to act decisively. Father of at least ten children, one of his daughters was married to Alexander of Lyncestis, who was probably from one of the royal lines of Upper Macedonia and possibly an Argead. Either way, this Alexander and his two brothers were well enough connected to be considered as rivals. Antipater's son-in-law joined him in acclaiming the new monarch to prove his loyalty. One king was dead and Macedon had a new king, but past history of the Argeads made clear that succession was rarely simple or uncontested. However, the kingdom was no longer weak enough to be easy prey to interventions by foreign powers backing claimants to the throne, for Philip had changed that as he had changed so many things.[7]

Pausanias is supposed to have asked a sophist how to become famous, and got the answer that the killer of the man who achieved most would have his name preserved along with the victim's. Diodorus tells us this story and he supplies the fullest account of Philip's assassination, with details that appear broadly reliable. Yet there was uncertainty even at the time, fueling rumor and gossip and, more recently, academic speculation. Pausanias's motive was clear enough, and by Macedonian standards more than adequate to prompt regicide. Murder was one of the commonest forms of death for the Argeads, and other killers had acted on personal motives and chosen to do the deed in public, for instance the killing of Philip's brother Alexander II during a ritual dance. Yet mystery and uncertainty surround almost every aspect of Philip's death. Personal revenge prompted the assassin, but was he encouraged or aided by anyone else? In short, was there politics behind the passion and anger?[8]

Pausanias had prepared more than one horse for his escape. That could mean that there were accomplices who were supposed to flee with him, or simply that he had a servant waiting and wanted a spare mount or mounts to keep ahead of any pursuit. The three bodyguards who slaughtered the assassin before he could reach this means of escape may have acted out of ferocious rage, for the king they served had been murdered and they had not saved him. On the other hand they might have killed Pausanias to make sure that he never spoke and could not implicate anyone else, making the assassin a mere pawn in a deeper game.

Antipater acted very quickly. His support ensured Alexander's immediate acclamation and meant that he was trusted and favored by the new king for the rest of the reign. This could be no more than a skillful politician thinking on his feet and making the best of the situation, and need not mean premeditation. The same is true of Alexander. Even if his father's death took him wholly by surprise, Philip was gone, a new king was needed, and it was natural for him to do everything he could to ensure that he was that new ruler. Indecision was never one of Alexander's faults, so a rapid response was entirely in character. He benefited the most from the death, for at twenty he was now king, at the head of a powerful state and army, and with a war already begun that offered the prospect of glory and plunder far surpassing any of Philip's victories. With hindsight we know that he took full advantage of the situation, waging the war with a restless energy that the middle-aged Philip is unlikely to have matched. Olympias also saw a great leap in her status, switching from being one wife among seven or so (depending on how many were still alive) to the unique position of the beloved mother of the king.

Both Alexander and Olympias were accused of being behind the murder, or at least of having encouraged Pausanias's desire for revenge. Justin claims that Olympias crowned the corpse of the crucified assassin, having come to Aegae under the pretext of attending her husband's funeral. She had orchestrated the plot, providing the horses to be used for the getaway, and later blatantly honored the remains of the murderer. A vicious, wild, yet calculating and murderous woman struck a chord with the prejudices of Greeks and later the Romans, and a lot of the blame was fixed on the wife rather than the son. While our sources exaggerated, it does seem likely that Olympias and Philip had come to dislike each other, and that she and Alexander both became nervous about his future, whether or not this was really justified. Justin says that Alexander knew of the plot, while happily smearing the memory of Olympias rather than the great conqueror; others also claim that Alexander was involved to some degree, if only by encouraging Pausanias to extend his hatred to Philip and Cleopatra as well as Attalus. Plutarch tells us that at the time Olympias was blamed more than her son. After Alexander's death, Olympias's role in the

wars between his generals meant that there was even more reason to slander her while preserving his reputation, since each side
wanted to be seen as his true heir.[9]

Others were also held responsible. A few years later Alexander
accused the Persian king of being behind the murder, even stating
that he had admitted the charge. More immediately Philip's was
the first of a number of deaths in the days, weeks, and months that
followed. Alexander of Lyncestis had sided with his father-in-law
and backed Alexander, but his two brothers were less shrewd or
perhaps less quick off the mark. They were accused of involvement
in the plot and were executed, although it is less clear whether this
was after formal trial or on the new king's orders. Also killed was
the royal diviner who had overseen the morning sacrifice on the day
of the murder and proclaimed the omens good, although this was
for his failure rather than any suspicion of deliberate disloyalty.
Amyntas, the nephew Philip had displaced and kept in comfortable obscurity for decades, was now killed; by 335 BC his widow
Cynane was available for a new marriage. Other Argeads fell victim to the purge; some were the shadowy relatives of the king,
perhaps including an illegitimate son or sons of Philip. Arrhidaeus
survived, presumably because he was seen as incapable of ruling
and therefore not a threat.[10]

Attalus was in Asia with Parmenio, and what they did mattered.
Like Antipater, both men had already lived through the aftermath
of a king's assassination or sudden death. Shortly before the murder, Philip's new wife Cleopatra had given birth to a daughter. If
not the son Philip had no doubt been hoping for, the baby was
healthy and an addition to the royal family who could be useful in
the future for cementing an alliance. He gave her the grand name
of Europa, but with Philip dead, Attalus's position was weaker, for
his niece would not have the chance to produce any more children.
When news reached Asia of the murder of Philip and accession of
Alexander, Plutarch claims that Attalus exchanged messages with
Demosthenes, discussing the prospects for a rebellion against the
new king. At some point the Macedonian changed his mind, and
instead sent one of Demosthenes's letters to Alexander with assurances of his complete support. The new king was unimpressed, and

sent a party led by Hecataeus to Asia to bring Attalus back with
him or to arrange his death.[11]

Attalus was married to one of Parmenio's daughters, which
suggests a level of closeness between the two in the last years of
Philip's reign. What Parmenio decided to do was critical, for he
was by far the most prominent of Philip's marshals and very popular with the soldiers. Yet only a small part of the army was with
him: he was in hostile territory and challenging Alexander, who
was backed by Antipater, was risky. Parmenio preferred to sacrifice his son-in-law Attalus, who was promptly killed by Hecataeus.
The reward was continued favor for the old general and a number
of important commands and posts for his family.

At some point Cleopatra and her baby were murdered. This is
the first recorded case of the political killing of a woman or baby
in Macedonian power struggles, although both would become
common after Alexander died. We cannot know whether this was
an unprecedented savagery, or whether women and infants were
simply ignored in the brief accounts of earlier in-fighting among
the Argeads. Olympias was held responsible, and it was even
claimed that she had it done while Alexander was away because
he would not have approved. Grisly details were added in a way
that was rarely the case when a man committed a political murder, claiming that they were killed by being dragged over a heated
bronze vessel, so that they were scorched to death. Neither the
mother nor the baby was a serious threat to the new king, so
their deaths suggest personal hatred, but whether from Olympias,
Alexander, or both cannot be known. Blaming Olympias was natural given the attitudes of the age, and convenient for Alexander.
The stories about Attalus suggest a man who was provocative,
vindictive, and hard to like, and few seem to have lamented him
or his family. (A desire to be dispassionate and analytical sometimes leads historians to deny the importance of personalities. At
the same time media coverage of contemporary politics stresses
the personal rivalries and friendships within political parties let
alone outside them, reminding us that it is a mistake to view the
past as if everyone acted pragmatically and personalities did not
play a great part.)[12]

Rumor and accusation are not proof, and ultimately we cannot know what was really behind the deaths that followed Philip's. In his case we cannot know whether anyone else was behind the assassination or whether it was the work of one poor, damaged man. If the brothers of Alexander of Lyncestis were behind the plot, then their handling of it was inept. This does not exonerate them, since competence is not essential for those embarking on crime, but it does make it less likely that they were the key players. From the Persian point of view, removing Philip by assassination had great appeal, for it offered a cheap way of taking the heart out of the war launched against them, and might even end it—they could not then know the ferocity of his successor. The Persians had gold to bribe and some connections at the Macedonian court and among the Greek states, although this does not mean that they had the capacity to arrange the murder. Antipater was well placed to pull strings behind the scenes, whether in concert with Alexander or independently, but that assumes he desired the death of the man he had served loyally for so long and believed that he would be better off with a new king.[13]

Alexander would order many deaths during his reign, and drunkenly kill with his own hands a man he had known all his life. Yet killing one's father was felt to be one of the most appalling acts of impiety by the Greeks, and throughout his life Alexander paraded his respect for the gods. Some see this as proof that he could not have been complicit in the assassination, although it is really to guess at his inner character, for the truth is that we do not know. If our sources for this were as meager as those for the violent deaths of earlier Argead kings, then Olympias as a woman would probably not be mentioned at all, and historians would simply assume that as the beneficiary, Alexander or those close to him were responsible. Having more information robs us of such simple—and unjustified—certainty, but denies us any clear answer. Alexander may have been involved in Philip's murder, or he may have been wholly innocent. Whatever suspicions there were did not prevent the overwhelming majority of Macedonians from accepting his leadership. After all the uncertainty, the truth was simple: Philip was dead, and Alexander was king, at least for the moment.

The news of the assassination reached Athens a few days after the death of Demosthenes's daughter, but according to Plutarch a private report reached the orator first. Publicly he declared that he had had a dream foretelling a great blessing for his city. When the assassination was generally reported, he set aside his mourning, put on a garland, and led the celebration and sacrifices. At his urging, the Assembly voted a crown to Pausanias, in stark contrast to the recent Athenian assurances of loyalty to the king. For Demosthenes Philip had been the bugbear for so many years—the great menace to Athens and other Greeks, the man who had smashed the allies at Chaeronea—and if he had treated the Athenians mildly in its aftermath, he still represented an insult to their honor because he had the power to decide their fate. Now he was gone, succeeded by an unproven twenty-year-old. Perhaps this was a chance to set things right and let Macedon revert to its traditional chaos and impotence, so that Athens could once again become the preeminent city in the Greek world.[14]

A change as great as the death of Philip was bound to make plenty of people consider the opportunities now on offer. In Thessaly some noblemen saw a chance to assert independence, most likely from personal ambition rather than feelings for or against Macedonia. Other communities wondered what to do; factions and leaders appeared who saw change to their advantage. There was no massed rebellion against Alexander, just a mood of uncertainty. The Athenians talked and sent ambassadors in search of allies. Cities in Aetolia re-formed their league, challenging the treaty of 338 BC that guaranteed the status quo. In Ambracia a group expelled the Macedonian garrison and proclaimed a democratic constitution. These few wanted to test the resolve and ability of the new king, but most were more inclined to watch, let others take the lead, and then make up their minds.[15]

Alexander spent some time securing his rule, beginning the elimination of rivals, and giving his father a proper funeral. The corpse was laid in state on a pyre, dressed in armor with his weapons by his side, before being cremated. The bones were cleaned, placed in a casket, and installed in a tomb, which was subsequently covered by a great mound. The Lyncestian brothers had been executed nearby, along with the horses on which Pausanias planned to escape, and their remains were also burned. In Tomb II at Vergina, sometimes identified as that of Philip, the remains of a woman were also interred in the chamber, but the age is too old for Cleopatra (and some would also feel such an honor unlikely), adding to the many questions about the find.[16]

His father decently interred, Alexander promptly showed that he was just as capable as Philip when it came to rapid action. Mustering an army, he marched south to Thessaly. Local forces blocked the main pass so he went around it, at one point having his men cut steps in the mountainside so that the rest could follow. Resistance collapsed, and soon Alexander was appointed archon of the Thessalian League. Thessaly would send a large and important contingent of their excellent horsemen for his war against Persia and never again wavered in its loyalty during his lifetime.

Pressing on and never having to fight, Alexander marched to the Peloponnese and summoned representatives of the Greeks to a meeting at Corinth, just as his father had done. They came and duly voted to make him the leader of the League and reaffirmed their approval for the war of vengeance against Persia. The only exception was the Spartans, and Alexander just like his father chose to use this to emphasize the unity of everyone else. By the end of 336 BC, without bloodshed, there was no more open resistance in Greece. In the next year Alexander would turn north to deal with the Thracians and Illyrians, just as Philip had so often done.[17]

PHILIP CAME TO power at a time of crisis, after his brother was cut down by the Illyrians and the army routed. Only two or three years older than Alexander was in 336 BC, he'd had even less military and political experience. His son grew up in a Macedonia that was constantly expanding, where the king had the wealth to lavish on paying the army, building monuments, living in luxury, and buying favor at home and abroad. When Alexander joined him on campaign in Thrace and for Chaeronea, he was part of a large, well-trained, and most of all confident army, buoyed by twenty years of almost unbroken success. Alexander had never been a hostage, nor was there a serious invasion of Macedonia during his lifetime. Whatever his doubts about his father's favor, Alexander never had to worry about the survival of the kingdom or doubt its continued success. In such an environment it was natural to dream of future success—though perhaps only a man like Alexander would dream on such a scale.

All of this was because of Philip. When Perdiccas III was killed, no sane observer would have predicted the revolutionary change in fortunes under his successor. Somehow, Philip survived the challenges to his rule, preserved the kingdom, and then systematically defeated each of the threats facing it. None of this was inevitable and none of it was easy, and as part of it he created a state and an army geared to constant war. Sheer talent played a key part in everything, and if we knew more we might well speak of the king's ability in finding and giving responsibility to capable subordinates like Parmenio and Antipater. Philip was an exceptionally gifted general and diplomat, while his alleged feasting, drinking, and love affairs never seem to have reduced the relentless energy and determination with which he put his plans into action. Like all successful men and women, luck played a part; Athens and the other Greek states failed to produce any truly able commanders to oppose him, and the most powerful warlords in Illyria and Thrace died early on. Again like other successful leaders, Philip had the ability to take advantage of fortune and rode his luck well, at least until he failed to spot the resentment in one of his bodyguards.

Philip's success surprised everyone—perhaps even himself. One of the difficulties for many Greeks, especially the likes of Demosthenes, was forcing themselves to believe that this northern "barbarian" king was so capable and successful. It can never have felt right, that such a leader did not make more mistakes, or that despised and obscure Macedonia was suddenly so powerful. Once the serious threats were removed, Philip turned to expansion, seizing territory and resources and then exploiting them for the wealth and manpower to fuel further expansion. Halting to consolidate was never part of the plan, and may well have been impossible. Philip created a machine for expansion that had to keep moving. Spending increased with each success; victory kept the army happy and loyal, and gave him enough wealth to move on to the next target. This at least was something Greeks understood, seeing it as natural. Any leader or polis that had become as powerful would never have been satisfied, and would have continued to strive for ever greater dominance. Competition for glory and status could not end, and it was equally natural for others to resent Philip's rise and see his prominence as diminishing their own.

The scale of Philip's success was unprecedented. His son would carve out a vastly greater empire, and his deeds are described far more fully, while so much of what Philip did must remain a mystery. One noticeable contrast is that throughout Alexander's reign we know where he was and what he was doing. There was surely far more to Philip's reign than we can now reconstruct, but what we cannot doubt is that without Philip, the story of Alexander would be very different.

PART TWO

ALEXANDER AND PERSIA

336–329 BC

A Good King and a Strong Spear Fighter

14

THE EXAMPLE

Plutarch says that when Alexander became king, Macedonia was "exposed to great jealousies, dire hatreds, and dangers on every hand," but in 336 BC he had managed to put down all the immediate challenges with great speed. The same author tells us an anecdote about Alexander's visit to Corinth in that year, when the representatives of the city-states and any prominent men who happened to be there queued for the chance to assure the young king of their loyalty and admiration, and no doubt often to ask for largesse. The praise was fulsome, had little to do with actual sentiment, and was inevitably long-winded in a society so very fond of oratory. Many philosophers spoke a lot about the ideal ruler, and no doubt did their best to portray Alexander in this way. Yet the most famous thinker then present at Corinth did not appear. This was Diogenes the Cynic, a longtime exile from his home of Sinope after he and his father were accused of adulterating the city's coinage. As his ideas developed, Diogenes challenged conventional respect for law, city, and family, claiming that actions were more important than any theory, and that life should be lived in as simple and natural a way as possible. For Diogenes this meant wearing no more than a coarse cloak and carrying a staff and a small satchel for coins and food. He had no house, although at times he lived in a large barrel, and like an animal he ate, slept, and defecated in public—the word *cynic* literally means "dog-ish" or "dog-like." Even so he wrote several tragedies and at least one philosophical text, which mocked Plato's and conventional philosophers' concern for politics.[1]

Diogenes prompted fascination, horror, disgust, ridicule, and admiration in fairly equal measures. Alexander, realizing that the philosopher was not coming to see him, went with a group of friends to pay a visit. They found Diogenes dozing in the late autumn sunshine. As they approached, the philosopher sat up a little and looked at the king, but said nothing. Finally, Alexander asked him whether he wanted anything. "Yes," said Diogenes, "stand a little out of my sun." As they left the king's companions began laughing at the old man. Their leader did not mock, and was so impressed by the pride and sincerity of the philosopher, that he announced, "If I were not Alexander, I would be Diogenes."[2]

At the very least the story is embellished, and may be wholly apocryphal, but true or not it illustrates the fundamental difference between our meager sources for Philip and the abundant material about Alexander. Often the focus is on his character, or at least on making a point about the young king's overwhelming self-assurance. In this case Diogenes is also held up for admiration, but generally others appear merely as foils and everything centers on Alexander. Thus after his accession his older advisors urged caution, conciliation, and even retreat in the face of the hostility in Greece and to the north. Alexander did the opposite, and as we have seen the opposition in Greece quickly collapsed. After his encounter with Diogenes, the king went to seek guidance from the oracle at Delphi. Plutarch tells us that he came at a time when the oracle did not speak, but Alexander refused to accept this. He grabbed the Pythian priestess, demanding that she consult the god, and pulled her toward the temple. Exasperated, she shouted, "You are invincible, my son!" Alexander let go, happy to take this as if it were the god's answer. Once again, there is a chance that the whole story is romantic invention, with the impetuous young king breaking all the rules but still getting what he wants, demonstrating his spirit as well as the favor of the gods. Alexander could do these things and win, just as he would go on to conquer a large part of the world.[3]

While the Greek cities appeared settled in their alliance with him, this was less true of the peoples living on Macedonia's northern borders. In the spring of 335 BC Alexander mustered a large army and advanced from Amphipolis against those Thracians who remained independent of Macedon. The operations that followed are described in some detail by Arrian and hint at the many campaigns fought by Philip against the tribes on his northern and eastern borders. For the first time we gain a far better sense of how the army created by Philip operated in the field. The units and tactics were the product of two decades of development during his reign, so we cannot say when it had reached this stage, but there is no suggestion that it operated under Alexander in a fundamentally different way, at least in the early years. Although Alexander's friends had returned from exile, at this early stage few of his contemporaries were promoted to important positions. These were still Philip's soldiers, led by Philip's officers, the vast majority experienced and accustomed to victory. The army was in little need of further training, and in many ways the fighting was more important for allowing the twenty-one-year-old Alexander to practice supreme command, and to ensure that all ranks had confidence in him.

For all the detail, Arrian does not tell us everything we should like to know and is somewhat vague on the route taken and the composition of the army. By the end of the year Alexander had massed some 30,000 men under his direct command, but he may well have led a smaller force of 10,000 to 20,000 in the initial campaigns, for supply was never easy in this country. Units that would become very familiar in the coming years were there, most notably the elite infantry hypaspists, as well as professional archers—mostly mercenaries from Crete—and the Agrianians, tough mountain tribesmen accustomed to moving quickly over even the most difficult terrain to strike hard and fast. Backing them were several regiments of the main phalanx and squadrons of Companion cavalry, as well as a range of other troops, including engineers, and artillery with catapults.[4]

After ten days Alexander reached the area of Mount Haemus, where Philip and his lieutenants had campaigned in the past. A large force of Thracians occupied a pass ahead of the column and the slopes above the army's line of march—most probably the Shipka Pass in Bulgaria. They had women and children with them, a common enough practice among some tribal peoples when they went to war, and had carried them in wagons. Most of these vehicles, probably fairly light carts given the mountainous country, were lined up to form an improvised rampart, while some were ready to be rolled down the slope if the Macedonians tried to march up it and attack.

Alexander and his officers saw what the enemy was planning, as did the soldiers, suggesting either that the positioning of the wagons made it obvious or that the tactic had been used in the past. The danger was to the infantry's formation as much as life and limb, making any advance by a phalanx likely to split apart as men dodged and fled to avoid the rushing vehicles, leaving them vulnerable to a downhill charge by the warriors. Panic was less likely if everyone knew what to do, so Alexander ordered his men to split and create a lane to let each wagon run past and then to re-form quickly. If there was not space for them to do this, then they were to hunker down and hold their shields up and as close together as possible to create a roof or ramp so that the cart would run or bounce over them—a formation a little like the famous Roman *testudo*. The hypaspists seem to have led the advance, at least on the left where there was no room to open lanes, for these picked soldiers were equipped with a shield much like the one used by hoplites, significantly larger and easier to maneuver than the little shield strapped to the shoulder and arm of each pikeman. Their confidence buoyed because they knew what to expect and what they were to do, the Macedonians pressed up the slope, then followed their orders as the carts came rumbling down. No one was killed, injuries apparently were few, and the soldiers quickly re-formed, raising their battle cry as they closed with the enemy.

The Thracians were dismayed by the failure of their carefully prepared plan, then saw the Macedonians getting ever closer, coming on noisily, full of confidence and in good order. Alexander sent orders for his archers to push ahead of the main line where it was easier to shoot and pick off the bolder warriors who were trying to charge. He then led the elite infantry, including the hypaspists and Agrianians, in a charge. The Thracians broke and fled, dropping their weapons to run faster. For some it was too late, and the Macedonians claimed to have killed some 1,500 but far more escaped, abandoning their families; almost all the women and children were taken as slaves.[5]

It was a good start to the campaign, and Alexander and the main army moved on to attack the Triballi who had wounded his father and stolen much of the army's plunder just a few short years earlier. This time the Macedonians sent their captives and other spoils under escort back to the coastal cities before pushing on for three days until they approached the Danube. The Triballi knew that they were coming and, along with their neighbors, evacuated their families to the island of Peuce in the midst of the river. Some of the warriors under King Syrmus stayed to guard them, but others crossed back to the south bank. Knowing the country well, this large force marched around behind the advancing Macedonians. Alexander's scouts discovered what was happening, and the column turned back and caught them before they were ready. As Philip had found, one of the hardest parts of campaigning in this area was luring the enemy warriors into the open. Alexander had his archers and slingers pushed close to the Triballi, stinging them with missiles until this provoked a wild charge. Companion cavalry from Upper Macedonia then struck against their right, more squadrons of Companions hit their left, and the phalanx and yet more cavalry drove against their center. Ptolemy—who probably served in this campaign—later claimed that the Macedonians had 11 cavalry and 44 infantrymen killed, but cut down over 3,000 of the enemy.[6]

Anticipating operations on the Danube, Alexander had arranged for warships from Byzantium—now once again firmly an ally of Macedon—to meet him. He put soldiers on board and tried to force a landing on Peuce, but the landing places on the island were restricted and there were too few men on the vessels to overcome the determined defense. In the meantime, the news of his presence had prompted the Getae on the north bank of the Danube to muster an army of some 4,000 cavalry and 10,000 infantry. This was a natural reaction for most peoples in the ancient world to the approach of armed strangers, not necessarily anything more than a precaution, since attacks might come without warning or any prior history of conflict. Equally naturally, mustering an army was seen as provocative in a world obsessed with honor and the visible signs of respect. Throughout his life, Alexander was rarely willing to ignore a challenge.

Philip had reached the Danube, the first Macedonian king ever to do this, but he had not crossed the river. Arrian tells us that Alexander was seized with "a craving" (*pothos*) to go beyond the river. This is the first appearance of a recurring theme in his account, explaining many of the king's actions as the result of an overwhelming and deeply personal urge to do something never before attempted or previously seen to be impossible. Men were sent to scour the riverbanks and settlements for the log canoes used by the locals. Others packed leather tents with straw to make rafts. The method was mentioned by Xenophon in his account of the Ten Thousand's escape from the heart of the Persian Empire. Alexander—or one of his officers—may have remembered reading about this, or perhaps the technique was used more widely than we know. Using all the ships, boats, and rafts, he took 1,500 cavalry and 4,000 infantry over the Danube under the cover of darkness, landing amid fields of high wheat or barley so that they were hidden even when the sun rose.[7]

Unlike the defenders of Peuce, the Getae were not really expecting a sudden attack and remained oblivious to the presence of the Macedonians. Alexander's men formed up and advanced, infantry leading, the soldiers in front using their sarissas to beat down the tall crops so that the rest could follow more easily. When they emerged into untilled open ground, the phalanx stood with its left sheltered by the river and the cavalry under Alexander's direct command on the right. The Getae were dismayed by the sight—amazed that the enemy were there and seeing the disciplined advance of a Macedonian army for the first time. Numbers mattered far less than the shock of the attack, and the Getae fled, streaming back to a nearby settlement. Its defenses were rudimentary—perhaps a simple stockade or bank—and as the Macedonians continued their well-ordered advance, no one was in any mood to stay there. The warriors fled, taking with them as many of their women and children as their horses could carry. Alexander's men plundered the settlement of all that was left and burned it. On the riverbank he sacrificed to Zeus the preserver, his ancestor Hercules, and the river god himself. After less than twenty-four hours, he took his troops and the spoils back across the river to rejoin the main army.[8]

This demonstration of force proved highly effective. King Syrmus sent ambassadors offering his submission, aware now that his island refuge was less safe than his people had hoped. Other tribal groups from the far shore of the Danube sent representatives asking for friendship, a gesture that in itself acknowledged Alexander's superiority, so it was most welcome. Among them were Celts, a blanket term used by Greek writers for many of the occupants of Europe, and Alexander had them asked what they feared most in the world "hoping that his own great name had reached the Celts . . . and that they would say that they feared him more than anything else." Instead the noblemen declared that their greatest fear was that the sky would fall on them. In spite of this disappointment, friendship was duly pledged, although after they had gone the king dismissed them as braggarts.[9]

Alexander next went westward to confirm the loyalty of the Paeonians and Agrianians by meeting with their leaders, but news reached him of an alliance between two Illyrian kings, Cleitus and Glaucias. The former, who was the son or grandson of Bardylis, had seized a well-fortified city called Pellium. The place is otherwise unknown, but was near or perhaps even inside Upper Macedonia. Accepting the promise of the Agrianian king to deal with another hostile tribe, Alexander hurried toward Pellium, catching the enemy before the two kings had joined forces. He camped outside, next to the river Eordaicus, and gave orders for an assault the next day. Cleitus had men on the walls, and many more gathered on the wooded heights above the city, but he was still waiting for his ally, King Glaucias, to arrive. Presumably according to custom, the Illyrians sacrificed three boys, three girls, and three black rams, seeking divine aid in the battles to come.[10]

Alexander attacked as planned, but the tribesmen outside the city fled after minimal resistance, so the Macedonians found the grisly remains of their sacrifice. The army camped outside Pellium, preparing for blockade and assault in due course, but the arrival the next day of Glaucias and his army behind them threatened to take the Macedonians from two sides. A foraging party led by Philotas, the son of Parmenio, was almost surrounded and only extricated when Alexander led a force to their rescue. The situation was dangerous. Alexander did not have enough men to attack the city and simultaneously fight off Glaucias, and could not stay for long where he was because finding food and forage would only leave detachments open to ambush. Yet escape would not be easy, for there was only a narrow route, broken by patches of woodland and enclosed by higher ground, held by Glaucias on one side and the river on the other. Arrian claimed that at times the track was barely wide enough for four men to march abreast—some four yards if they were in battle order or twice that if in open order, which was usual on the march.[11]

Withdrawal in the face of the enemy is rarely an easy thing to do, especially in mountainous terrain against highly mobile bands of warriors accustomed to the country and inclined to see retreat as a sign of cowardice. Alexander decided to put on a display. His close-order infantry formed up 120 ranks deep. Most likely this was not in single phalanx, but rather each unit of 500 or so men in its own distinct column. They were not yet at the narrowest parts of the route, so there was enough room for 200 cavalry on either side. The Macedonians then commenced a display of discipline and drill, raising sarissas then bringing them down into the charge position. Next they turned ready to thrust to the right, then to the left, before marching forward and wheeling in each direction in turn and going through a series of formation changes. All of this was done in silence, save for the brief shouted orders and inevitable thumps of shields, armor, and equipment. It was uncanny, even inhuman, proof of a discipline and control the tribesmen not only did not possess, but probably could not imagine wanting.

Slowly, jerkily as it went through the maneuvers, the head of the army's long column came closer and closer to the first positions occupied by the Illyrians. Already some warriors were slipping away, deciding against confronting such uncannily silent soldiers. Alexander changed the formation so that the head turned to attack toward the left, ordered his men to raise their battle cry and clash spear and sarissa shafts against their shields, and the sudden noise panicked those facing them, as well as some who had come from Pellium to pursue. For the moment the way was clear and the Macedonians moved on, but they were far from safe and the awe they had created would not last long. Any mistake or any sign of weakness was bound to revive the spirits of the Illyrians to return to the attack. A hillock stood in the army's path, close to where Alexander planned to ford the river, and he led some of the hypaspists and Companions to seize it, the defenders fleeing up the valley sides to even higher ground. Archers and Agrianians were brought up to hold the position and all the hypaspists then sent to lead the way over the river. The rest of the army—horse, foot, and baggage train—followed them over. On the far side the hypaspists formed ranks facing back the way they had come, and each unit of the phalanx crossed and deployed to their left to make a battle line.

Gradually, the bulk of the army was across, leaving an ever smaller number of men—including Alexander—as rear guard. The Illyrians surged down from the high ground, hoping to cut off and overwhelm them, but stopped short when Alexander charged and some of the phalanx raised a shout and began to recross the river. There was a short breathing space, and the Agrianians and archers were ordered to race for the river. Alexander was ahead of them and gave orders for some of the siege engines in the baggage train to be set up on the far bank. Once again the Illyrians rushed forward, but the catapults began to hurl missiles farther than any bowman or slinger could shoot and the Macedonians' archers stopped before they were fully across and added their arrows to the volleys. Under this barrage the tribesmen beat a hasty retreat, allowing the remainder of the Macedonian army to retire across the river.[12]

Alexander had escaped from a difficult situation without losing a single man. The ground on the far bank was more open, better suited to his army, and the enemy had no inclination to risk attacking across such an obstacle. For the moment Cleitus and Glaucias contented themselves with joining forces, happy in the knowledge that they had frightened off their enemy and still held Pellium. Alexander learned that they were camped in no sort of order, without throwing up any defenses or setting outposts and guards, confident that the Macedonians would continue to retreat. As at the Danube, he decided to exploit the cover of night and led a strike force of the hypaspists, Agrianians, archers, and some picked units of the phalanx back across the much smaller obstacle of the river Eordaicus. The rest of the army was to follow, but when his strike force reached the enemy camp, the young king decided not to wait for them. Surprise was total as the small force launched a concentrated attack from one side. Warriors were caught fast asleep or still groggy, and were cut down or captured before they could escape. There was no serious resistance. Glaucias escaped deep into the mountains. Cleitus tarried long enough to burn Pellium before joining him.[13]

In 335 BC Alexander asserted Macedonian dominance on his frontiers. When he set out the following year for the eastern war, he left a strong garrison to protect the kingdom, but there is little evidence of its needing to fight any major campaigns against the Illyrians or Thracians. Philip's army had once again shown that it could reach out and strike almost at will into the most difficult and inaccessible places. The death of the old king and accession of his son had not blunted its effectiveness in any way. Some scholars speak of Alexander's genius even in these early campaigns, but this is premature. On the whole, this was a well-trained and experienced army doing things it had often done before. At twenty-one, he showed every sign of settling into supreme command, and this was no slight achievement. Frontier warfare of this sort required confidence and careful handling of the army, and these he had shown. The use of artillery in a field action was unusual, only recorded in the past when Onomarchus employed his catapults against Philip in 353 BC, but it was not to become a common tactic and is not highlighted as an innovation. Alexander had failed in his attempt to take Peuce and got himself surrounded by Cleitus and Glaucias, but in each case he recovered and brought the campaign to a successful conclusion. All in all his performance was competent, and he had made good use of the superior tactics, equipment, and discipline of his army. At the very least, the Macedonians had been shown that they would still win, even now that Philip had gone; the son was showing that he had learned a lot from his father.[14]

Alexander spent six or seven months campaigning in Thrace and Illyria, and at the same time the king of the Agrianians lived up to his promise and pacified and suppressed resistance elsewhere. An old friend of Alexander's, his reward was the offer of marriage to Alexander's half sister, the now widowed Cynane, although in the event he died of natural causes before the wedding could take place. For all their importance to the security of Macedonia, as usual the cities of southern Greece had limited interest and even less knowledge of what was happening in the far north. In similar circumstances during Philip's reign rumors had spread that the king of Macedon was fatally sick or wounded, and now the same thing happened: Alexander was dead, without an obvious and competent successor, and surely the Macedonian weakness expected after Philip's murder would finally become reality. Demosthenes assured the Athenian Assembly that the story was true, bringing forth an injured and bandaged man who claimed to be a survivor of the disaster in which Alexander had fallen. Opponents said that Demosthenes was using Persian gold to persuade leaders in other cities that now was the time to throw off the dominance of Macedon.[15]

At Thebes, a group of aristocrats exiled after Chaeronea returned home and were not only admitted, but allowed to address the Assembly. Inspired by the famous heroes led by Pelopidas and Epaminondas who had come back to slaughter the Spartan garrison of the Cadmeia, they convinced the majority of their fellow citizens to throw off the alliance with Macedon. Two officers from the garrison were caught in the city and killed, the rest blockaded within the Cadmeia. Some leaders in other cities expressed sympathy, and a few prepared to raise troops to assist the Thebans. The Athenians as usual talked a lot while doing very little. Still, if Alexander were truly dead, then they were likely to have plenty of time.

Reports of the rebellion—and his own death—reached Alexander soon after the rout of the Illyrian kings. Showing that he could match his father for speed, he hastened south and reached

Thebes in thirteen days, averaging somewhere between fifteen to twenty miles a day, some of it through very difficult country. Unwilling to believe the first reports of his approach, the leaders of the Theban revolt first claimed that it was Antipater rather than Alexander, who after all was surely dead, and then suggested that it was some lesser Macedonian leader who also had the common enough name of Alexander. Only at the last moment did they face the reality that Alexander was outside their walls with some 30,000 infantry and 3,000 cavalry, including allied contingents, many with long-standing grudges against Thebes.[16]

In 335 BC displays of force had been enough to end all open resistance in Greece, so Alexander called on the Thebans to surrender. He demanded that the two key leaders be handed over to him, but promised amnesty for anyone who immediately went over to him. Unsurprisingly the returned exiles, who had staked everything on this revolution, were determined to fight, but they were not alone. Thebes was a proud and famous city. While we hear that the Athenians blamed Theban leadership for the defeat at Chaeronea, no doubt the Thebans blamed their allies and remained confident in their own prowess and courage. The assembled citizens voted to fight and freed large numbers of slaves, equipping them with weapons sent by the Athenians—the only practical support to come from this vocal ally. In a show of bravado, the Thebans sent envoys demanding that Alexander give them Antipater and Philotas as hostages, and then issued a proclamation inviting all Greeks to join them and the Great King of Persia to defeat the tyrant Alexander. Soon afterward they sallied out against the Macedonian camp, killing a few soldiers.

Thebes was a large, well-fortified city, and under normal circumstances would have required a long and difficult siege. Yet now it was vulnerable, for the Cadmeia citadel formed part of the outer defenses, and it remained in Macedonian hands. In the days before Alexander arrived the Thebans had done their best to surround it, building a palisade outside the walls to enclose the citadel and barricading the streets leading to it inside the city. They then raised a second palisade facing outward to protect the one surrounding the Cadmeia, but the vulnerability remained, for these quickly constructed lines could not match the strength of a proper city wall. Alexander deployed his army to threaten these weak spots. He still hoped that the Thebans would back down, sparing him casualties and the uncertainty of an assault.[17]

Ptolemy later claimed that the phalanx regiment commanded by Perdiccas attacked the outer palisade without orders, which was always a risk with troops deployed so close to the enemy. They hacked through the flimsy defenses, came up against the Thebans inside, and were supported by the neighboring regiment of the phalanx. Whether deliberate or accidental, a full-scale assault developed, and the advantage of numbers and ability to choose where he attacked allowed Alexander to keep strong reserves of fresh troops. The fighting was bitter, with no space for tactical subtlety as the Thebans resisted with the grim determination of proud men defending their homes. Gradually they were forced to give way. Some broke, and as they fled through the gates into the city itself, Macedonians streamed in behind them. Other Macedonians linked up with the garrison of the Cadmeia. There was fighting in the streets and marketplaces, cavalry joining the infantry on both sides, and with no one able to see everything it is unsurprising that accounts are confused and conflicting. Yet once large numbers of Macedonians were inside the defenses the outcome was never in doubt. Some Thebans escaped, especially aristocrats with horses, but Diodorus and Plutarch both claim that 6,000 died.[18]

The Macedonians sacked the city. They had done this before, when cities had failed to surrender to Philip and forced him to take them by assault, but never before had they taken a Greek city as large and as famous as Thebes. Storming fortifications was dangerous, and they had lost 500 dead as well as no doubt many others wounded, including Perdiccas. The survivors—their blood up, anger at the enemy still fresh, and in the narrow streets and dark houses of the city able to do what they wished, judged only by the opinion of their comrades—killed, raped, and plundered at will. The officer in charge of a unit of Thracians occupied the house of Timocleia, who was a nobleman's wife and the sister of one of the generals who had fallen at Chaeronea. First he raped her, then demanded that she hand over her valuables. Timocleia led him to a well in the garden, assuring him that she had hidden everything in it. As he leaned over to look, she pushed him in and then, helped by her maids, flung down stones until the officer was dead. The Thracians bound her and took her to Alexander, whether because they were impressed by her courage or perhaps had been none too fond of their former commander. The king made a show of admiring her dignity, and the pride with which she spoke of her family. Timocleia and her children were given protection and allowed to go free.[19]

Murder and rape were accepted as inevitable when a city was stormed. While it is doubtful that Alexander and his officers could have controlled the army fully and entirely prevented such things, it is equally unlikely that they even thought to try, beyond protecting some households and individuals who were considered important or otherwise favored. This was just part of war, and from a pragmatic point of view, Philip and Alexander both recognized the power of terror. At Thebes Alexander consulted his Greek allies over how to treat the captured city and they were not inclined to leniency, which surely suited him well but also helped to present a veneer of proper justice rather than simple revenge.

Priests were spared out of respect for the gods, and mercy was extended to guest friends of the king and other Macedonians, as well as to people with similar ties to his allies, and to the descendants of the poet Pindar who had praised the king of Macedon. The other survivors were sold as slaves, and one source claims that these numbered no fewer than 30,000. Thebes was abolished as a city-state, its walls to be demolished apart from the Cadmeia, which would remain as a garrison supplied by the allies. As the Phocians had shown, such extinction need not be permanent, and another result of the fall of Thebes was that Plataea and Orchomenus, states destroyed in the past by the Thebans and their allies, were refounded. History was again invoked to remind other Greeks that the Thebans had joined Persia in 480 BC, making this punishment an appropriate start to the great war of vengeance.[20]

When not assuring his fellow citizens that Alexander was dead, Demosthenes was dismissive of the young king, calling him a mere boy or dubbing him Margites—the ridiculous hero of a parody of

Homer's *Iliad*. Once again, he and others had urged the Athenians to war with Macedon as if rhetoric alone would bring victory. They had sent very little aid and no soldiers to support Thebes. In contrast the Arcadians had mustered a force to send, but it did not arrive in time. They now voted to execute the men who had proposed and led the expedition, while the Aetolians sent ambassadors apologizing for voicing support for Thebes. As the first Theban fugitives reached Athens with news of the fall of the city, the Athenians called off one of their great religious festivals and prepared for a siege, but also sent an embassy led by Demades to seek peace. Demosthenes was supposed to go, but found an excuse to fall out.[21]

Alexander responded much as Philip had always done. He did not want to besiege Athens, nor did he wish to destroy another of Greece's most important communities, for with Thebes and Athens gone there was no knowing what a new balance of power in southern Greece would look like. He demanded that the Athenians hand over about ten leading men into his custody—the sources differ over the precise total and some of the names, but they included Demosthenes and other leading opponents. Demades brought the ultimatum back to Athens. Phocion suggested that the men go for the greater good, while unsurprisingly Demosthenes was less keen, claiming that this would mean giving up the "sheepdogs who guarded the flock" and even argued that if the Athenians surrendered him and the others, then they were really surrendering themselves. Demades agreed to return to the king and ask for leniency, persuaded—or so it was claimed—by a bribe of five talents of silver from Demosthenes and the rest. Alexander relented, letting off all save one of the men on his list. This was Charidemus, a Euboean with long experience as a mercenary commander who had been granted Athenian citizenship; he may have been an easier sacrifice for the Athenians to accept than a member of an established family. He fled and took service with the king of Persia and would fight against Alexander. In public the vast majority of Athenians deplored the savage destruction of Thebes and the Assembly formally voted to give sanctuary to the numerous refugees from the city. One prominent Athenian also purchased a young Theban noblewoman enslaved after the sack of the city and kept her as a mistress, so there were limits to their sympathy in some cases. Past experience showed how tolerant Philip had been of open criticism and support for exiles or refugees, so the Athenians knew this was unlikely to have any repercussions. No one—not even Demosthenes—urged open or active hostility to Alexander.[22]

The destruction of Thebes demonstrated to all that Alexander was ruthless as well as capable. His treatment of Athens was mild, especially since this was the latest in so many Athenian moves against Macedon. As on the northern borders, it was enough to confirm Macedonian dominance, and during his lifetime there would be only one serious rising in Greece, which was supported by a small number of states and, very significantly, did not include Athens. While the disinterest of Greek sources in the affairs of Illyria and Thrace must always be borne in mind, the groundwork of Philip was confirmed by the operations in 336–335 BC, which left the kingdom secure from internal and external threats. Significant numbers of warriors from Illyria and Thrace as well as hoplites and sailors from Greece would serve at one time or another with Alexander in the east, removing many of the more active spirits from these areas. This service appears willing enough, and was not an oppressive burden. Although their support was demanded in other forms as well, the great war of revenge against Persia did not impose too high a burden on the Greek states, sufficient to make them risk Macedonian retribution. Alexander had found the right balance: involving them, making acceptable demands of money and resources, and in time sharing the glory. Perhaps it helped that he was to be so far away, but the majority of leaders in the vast majority of poleis were able to accept Macedonian domination, at least for a while.[23]

It was time for Alexander to embark on the great adventure and resume the war his father had begun in 336 BC when Philip sent Parmenio and Attalus over to Asia.

15

THE ARMY AND THE ENEMY

P hilip's war against Persia had stalled and been delayed for well over a year by his murder and Alexander's need to secure himself. Yet it was a mark of Philip's success that the advance guard he had sent to Asia under Parmenio and Attalus consisted of some 10,000 infantry and perhaps 1,000 cavalry, at least equal in size to the army he had mustered when he marched against Bardylis the Illyrian at the start of his reign. By 336 BC an army of this size was merely a small part of Macedonia's military might. Nothing is known about the composition of this force, and at first it was highly successful given such modest numbers. The delay in reinforcement, let alone the execution of Attalus, robbed the campaign of momentum, and cities that had defected to join the invaders began to have second thoughts. A battle was fought, perhaps involving only a portion of the Macedonian forces, who lost. Revolutions broke out, replacing regimes that had welcomed Parmenio and his men with ones eager to show their loyalty to Persia. By the end of 335 BC, the Macedonians held on to little more than a bridgehead on the Asian side of the Hellespont.[1]

This would prove to be enough for the main force was finally on its way, but before discussing the first campaign, it is worth taking a look at the army Alexander would lead to the great war, an army created by his father. Its evolution is impossible to trace, nor can we really judge how far the invasion force was organized specifically with the Asian campaign in mind. In at least one respect it certainly was different than the armies seen so far, for it was significantly larger and had a much higher proportion of cavalry. Just how big the expedition actually was is unclear, for our sources varied. Plutarch said that in the accounts he read the numbers varied from 30,000 infantry and 4,000 cavalry to 43,000 infantry and 5,000 cavalry, and he did not care to state which seemed most likely. Some of the disparity may be due to whether the advance guard was included. What follows reflects the broad consensus among modern scholars of the army's composition and size.[2]

In all of the major battles and many minor actions, Alexander led the Companion cavalry in person. The basic tactical unit was the squadron (ilê) of 200 men, which was made up of four troops (tetrarchiai) of 50. Alexander took eight squadrons of Companion cavalry to Asia, one of them the royal squadron, which seems to have been twice the normal size, so there were 1,800 of these elite horsemen in his army. Other squadrons, including several recruited or based in Upper Macedonia, remained behind at home with Antipater. The Companion cavalry rode larger horses than was normal in the rest of Greece, although these unarmored mounts suffered a far higher casualty rate than their riders, and in due course more and more would ride captured Persian animals, which were lighter and faster. Early saddles were in use among the Scythians, so it is just possible that the Macedonians adopted them, but good evidence for the use of the saddle among Mediterranean armies does not come until the third century BC. The Companions did use saddlecloths; for those who were wealthy, often the pelt of a lion or other big cat, which helped pad and protect the animal's back and gave a slightly better seat. Philip and Alexander's men relied on exceptionally high standards of horsemanship to keep their seat without the aids familiar to modern riders. Philip's largesse in giving parcels of land to favored supporters had greatly expanded the class of men who did not need to labor and therefore could concentrate on training for war. In wartime, a groom accompanied each rider to keep his horse and equipment in good condition.[3]

Shields do not appear to have been carried as a matter of course by Companion cavalrymen when they were mounted and are not depicted in art. Instead they relied on a helmet, invariably open faced so that the rider could see and hear well, and a leather, fabric, or metal cuirass to protect the body. High boots offered some protection to feet and lower legs and might be supplemented by metal greaves. The primary offensive weapon was a spear (*xyston*) of slim cornel wood, which although long, was shorter than the sarissa and could be wielded in one hand. It was usually thrust underarm and was significantly longer than the spears employed by Persian cavalry. The slimness of the shaft kept it light enough to carry, but also meant that it frequently broke or shattered on impact. There was a butt-spike that could be reversed and used to stab with what was left of the shaft, but most often the rider relied on his sword. The standard formation remained the triangular wedge introduced by Philip, with the commander of the unit at the apex. The entire squadron did not form a single wedge, and instead deployed as several small wedges to retain the advantages of this maneuverable attacking formation.

Next in association with the king were the hypaspists, and there were three regiments/battalions (*chiliarchies*) of these, each numbering some 1,000 men, in turn divided into two companies (*lochoi*) with a theoretical strength of 512. At least one of the regiments was probably derived from the picked men and guards mentioned in Philip's victory over Bardylis in 358 BC. The hypaspists were the most fully professional soldiers in the army, recruited for their bravery and ability, and were also the most frequently engaged. Although it is possible that they sometimes used the sarissa and a small shield, their standard equipment was a shield that was effectively a *hoplon* and a spear some eight feet or so in length, making them fairly standard fourth-century BC hoplites. What made them so effective was the selection of recruits, high standards of drill and training, and long experience of victory.

The mass of the Macedonian infantry consisted of the Foot Companions (*pezhetairoi*) of the main phalanx, which was equipped with the sarissa. There were six regiments (*taxis*) of these, known usually by their commander's name and sometimes by region, and units from Upper Macedonia figure prominently in the campaigns to come. Each regiment mustered some 1,500 men at the start of the campaign, divided into three *lochoi*, which were in turn subdivided into two 256-man units (which was later known as a *syntagma*). The *dekas* or file of sixteen soldiers was the basis of all drill and formations, and had an important role in administration and day-to-day living. There was a commander at each level of unit, down to the *dekadarchos* who was in charge of the file and whose station in battle was at its head in the front rank. There was also a "double-pay man" (*dimoirites*) who stood in the ninth rank, which would join the front rank on those occasions when the phalanx was formed eight deep, and the "ten-stater man" (*dekastateroi*), paid more than standard but less than double, at the rear in the fifteenth and sixteenth ranks. Having reliable men at the front and back to keep proper pace during drill movements was important, while Greek military theory held that the bravest soldiers should be at the front and back of the formation, making it more difficult for the others to flee as long as these picked men stayed in place.[4]

There may well have been some contingents of the phalanx with the advance guard in addition to the 9,000 soldiers brought by Alexander, perhaps as many as 3,000. If so, then these were either already subunits of the six regiments or were merged with them. Some Macedonian light infantry may have served, although the evidence is poor. Better recorded are the light cavalry *prodromoi*, consisting of four *ilai*. Some or all of these are also called *sarissophoroi*, suggesting that they were armed with the sarissa or at least a longer than normal spear that required two hands to wield properly. Mentioned often, their ethnicity is unclear and they may have been Macedonians. With the Paeonian and Thracian cavalry that often operated alongside them, they appear to have numbered some 900 men.[5]

Pride of place among the allied contingents must go to the Thessalian cavalry, whose numbers appear equivalent to the Companion cavalry and who were also organized into *ilai*. They carried a shorter spear than the *xyston* and used a rhomboid formation rather than a wedge, but they appear just as capable of launching a shock charge as the Macedonian heavy cavalry. Our sources concentrate so much on Alexander and the Companions that the vital contribution made by these men is often overlooked. This is generally true of all the allies, with rare exceptions like the Agrianians, who may have numbered 1,000, although this total may also include archers such as the Cretans who often operated with them. Greek cavalry supplied by other allies is rarely mentioned, although we know it existed; even the actions of the 7,000 allied Greek infantry that formed part of the main army in 334 BC are obscure. As with Philip, extensive use was made of mercenaries, and there were at least 5,000 of these at the start, but they also receive little attention. In addition there were 7,000 Illyrians, Triballians, and other Thracians, mainly infantry but with some cavalry. Greek allies also provided large numbers of warships. The land army was accompanied by engineers as well as many more noncombatants, from servants to scholars. Philip had taught his men to march hard and travel light, and Alexander kept to the same discipline, but there were still many extra mouths to feed, extra animals to help carry this food, and a wide range of baggage to be brought along. Compared to a Greek army, let alone a Persian one, Alexander's supply train was relatively small, but it was still substantial.[6]

In terms of the combat arms, the Macedonians supplied the largest single contingent in the army. The pike phalanx was the most numerous troop type, and together with the hypaspists, allied and mercenary hoplites, and the more heavily armed northern tribesmen, close order infantry made up the majority and the heart of the army in a way that was essentially Greek. Unlike a hoplite army, there was some variety of equipment, and a good deal of variety when it came to formations and mobility, but this remained at heart an infantry force best designed for close combat in the tradition of hoplite phalanxes. However, strong contingents of other troops ensured that this was a far better balanced and more flexible force than any army previously raised by a Greek state or states. In particular, it had a lot of cavalry, with around one in seven or eight of its soldiers a horseman, and the ratio was higher in some battles after numbers of infantry were detached as garrisons and escorts. (Late in the third century BC Hannibal managed a ratio of one-to-four in the army that virtually annihilated a much larger Roman force at Cannae, but such a high ratio was exceptionally rare in European armies before the medieval period.) Similar numbers of Macedonian infantry and cavalry were left in Macedon under Antipater's command, and he had access to allies, although these were not permanently embodied.[7]

The invasion army was large, well balanced, and at its core had many units and leaders who were used to operating together and accustomed to winning. To modern eyes accustomed to most combat soldiers being in their late teens or early twenties, this was not an especially young army. Justin claims that Alexander took care to select veterans to take with him, and although he exaggerates, there was a kernel of truth to this. A significant number of the hypaspists were men in their forties or even older. Probably they were a minority, but a large enough one to be visible and to give an air of immense experience and invincibility to the corps. Most pikemen and cavalrymen had served in some of Philip's campaigns, and a few in most or all of them. Without exception, unit commanders and senior officers at the start of the expedition had made their names under Philip.[8]

There was little or no permanent command structure above the infantry regiments and cavalry squadrons. Temporary groupings were formed as needed, under the command of someone appointed by the king rather than holding a specific rank or post. Parmenio, now in his mid-sixties, remained fit and active and was the first choice for any important mission or task. Antipater was just a few years younger and would be equally vigorous as the commander of the troops in Macedonia and regent in the king's absence, living on until he was almost eighty. Parmenio's son Philotas was in charge of the Companion cavalry, and another son, Nicanor, led the hypaspists. There was no permanent overall commander of the main phalanx, but the officers in charge of each regiment were important men and were sometimes given independent commands. The core of the army consisted of men who had served together for many years under Philip, and now his son, and knew their trade well.

Such a large army—not to mention the troops left to protect Macedonia—was not mustered without considerable effort and vast expense. Like Philip, Alexander spent in anticipation of future success and, in spite of the profits from the sack of Thebes, had reduced his reserves almost to nothing. Plutarch mentions accounts claiming that only seventy talents were left and that there were sufficient funds to pay and supply the great army for no more than thirty days. Alexander was generous in giving land and other rights to his followers, and especially the Companions of his court. Failure might well have bankrupted him and the monarchy, but this did not concern him, since it was likely also to mean his death, whether at the hands of the enemy or of aristocrats intolerant of defeat. The expedition was a huge gamble, and we should not let our knowledge of its spectacular success blind us to the scale of the risk. Self-confidence is common enough for the young, and the boldness of his decision to lead the war Philip had planned was rightly seen by our sources as reflecting the unlimited assurance of Alexander, providing them with more stories.[9]

Before setting out, Antipater and Parmenio—presumably by letter unless the latter had returned from Asia—are supposed to have urged the young king to marry and father an heir to the throne. Alexander refused, and some see this as a sign of the precarious balance between the noble houses of the kingdom, something all too easily upset by a choice of bride. More practically, taking a wife did not guarantee that she would immediately fall pregnant, let alone bear a healthy son, and even then it would be many years before the boy grew into a plausible successor. Alexander declared that it would be shameful to wait on such domestic matters when the glory of a great war beckoned. In the autumn of 335 BC he celebrated the Dium festival on a grand scale, holding a feast under canvas in a tent large enough to cover 100 couches, each with three guests. Huge sacrifices provided meat for not only these honored guests but the entire army. Once again like his father, the growing shortage of funds did not in any way deter the king from spending. After doling out so much largesse, he was asked by Perdiccas what he was keeping for himself. The reply was supposedly, "My hopes."[10]

By the spring of 334 BC preparations were complete and Alexander at last began the great expedition against Persia. He was never to return to Macedonia, although no one could have known that, nor would he ever again see his mother Olympias or his sister Cleopatra. The latter was soon to become a widow, for her husband, Alexander of Epirus, set off on an expedition to southern Italy around the same time and died on campaign a couple of years later without achieving very much.[11]

For all the excitement of the moment, we should not think of Alexander abandoning his homeland and only thinking of the great adventure. He was king of Macedon and there was much that only the king could do. Throughout his life Alexander remained in touch with what was happening at home and elsewhere via a flow of letters and messengers. In the early months and years this was no great feat, but as the distances increased, and hundreds stretched to thousands of miles, the chain of correspondence was never interrupted for any great length of time, even if it did become much slower.

Antipater was formally in charge as the king's senior representative, tasked with much day-to-day administration as well as maintaining Macedonian dominance on the frontiers to the north and over Greece. Yet he did not wield power in his own right but as the king's representative, and any decision could be overruled, even if this took time, while decisions made by the king had to be enforced. His task was complicated because he was not the only one sending reports, opinions, and requests to Alexander. There was an independent commander in Thrace and perhaps others elsewhere, and other noblemen and Companions were also able to write directly to the king. Most of all Olympias's and Cleopatra's messages would receive prompt and sympathetic consideration. As the king's mother, Olympias had some official role—for instance standing in for her son at some sacrifices and other ceremonies— but more important was her obvious influence, which at times would lead to tension with Antipater. The interplay of a wide range of interests and factions was nothing new in Macedonian politics, and as usual we can do little more than guess at the details.

Although complicated by the prolonged absence of the king, on the whole the system functioned well.[12]

Rumor claimed that before her son departed, Olympias secretly told Alexander the truth of his conception and his "true" divine father—though rumor did not bother to explain how anyone else had learned of this. More directly, the memory of Philip hovered around the army. The expedition marched via Amphipolis, crossed the river Strymon, passed Mount Pangaeum with its busy mines, and then went through Abdera and Maronea on its way to the Dardanelles. It was the natural route, following the coastal plains, and Xerxes's Persians had used it when they launched their invasion of Greece in 480 BC. Now Alexander as *hegemon* of the Greeks was heading the opposite way, and this was an appropriate start to his war of vengeance, but the Macedonian veterans surely recalled their campaigns under Philip in this region. Those operations had taken many years and utterly turned around the fortunes of the kingdom. As proof there was not only the size of their army, but the ease with which in twenty days it covered some 300 miles and reached Sestus, a little over halfway down the Gallipoli Peninsula.[13]

Parmenio was put in charge of ferrying the army across to the Asian shore, with the aid of 160 triremes provided mainly by the Greek allies and a supporting fleet of merchant ships and other transports. It was not an opposed landing, as the advance guard had clung to its bridgehead on the far shore. Those scholars who express surprise at the absence of the Persian navy fundamentally misunderstand the capabilities of naval power in an age of oared warships. Triremes had a short operational range, since they had very little cargo space to carry the quantities of food and fresh water required by their crews. The Macedonian advance guard still controlled all the ports around the Dardanelles and could prevent any Persian ship from landing anywhere else to draw supplies from the countryside. In addition an attack had to be timed to catch a significant portion of the Macedonian army while it was actually crossing, for the fleet alone could not face the enemy on shore. There was nothing to stop Alexander's men from waiting until the enemy ships had to leave to replenish their stores and rest their crews. The theory that most of the warships available to the Persian king were far away, having suppressed a rebellion in Egypt, is possible but irrelevant. Even if they had been on the spot, Persian squadrons could not have stopped Alexander's army from crossing.[14]

The Dardanelles are close to their narrowest near Sestus, less than a mile broad in some spots and never more than two, although the currents remain strong. Triremes could transport only a small number of soldiers, and if merchant vessels offered more space, loading and unloading took time. Cavalry mounts and baggage animals in particular were valuable assets and had to be treated with great care since they were of no use if seriously injured. Food and other supplies had to be stored while waiting to be embarked, and then stored again on the far shore. Crossing the straits took time and required considerable planning and organization, so Alexander left it in the capable hands of his father's most trusted general, Parmenio, and instead went to the southernmost end of the peninsula to add grandeur to the start of the expedition.

The king went to Elaeus, where the Greeks were said to have embarked for the siege of Troy. There was a tomb there said to be that of Protesilaus, the first Greek to charge ashore and the first to die: in the *Iliad*, "a Dardan man had killed him as he leapt from his ship, far the first of all the Achaians." Alexander sacrificed at the tomb, honoring the dead hero and seeking better fortune for his own enterprise. Altars were set up and offerings made to Zeus for safe landings, and to Athena (who was associated with the region) and his ancestor Hercules (who had once waged his own war against Troy). Then he and his escort embarked on sixty triremes and put out to sea, the king personally steering his ship in the manner of Homer's heroes. Halfway across they paused, and he sacrificed a bull to Poseidon and the Nereids—sea nymphs, one of whom was Thetis, the mother of Achilles. A libation of wine was poured into the sea from a golden cup as an offering before they resumed the crossing and landed on the Asian shore at the bay where the Greeks were said to have arrived. Alexander led the way, fully armed for war, wading through the surf just like Protesilaus, although this time there was no one to oppose him. Some said he threw his spear hard into the ground, claiming Asia as "spear-won," or his by right of conquest.[15]

Alexander raised altars to the same triad as at Elaeus and then went the few miles to Troy—or at least the place incorrectly believed to be Troy by everyone at the time and filled with shrines, places, and artifacts linked to the story. Naturally, he went to the tomb of Achilles, where he laid a wreath, and one tradition has his friend Hephaestion also laying a wreath on the tomb of Patroclus. The king and his youthful companions stripped naked to run a race, just like the competitive heroes of the stories, although it is unlikely that anyone risked surpassing Alexander. He sacrificed in the famous temple of Athena Ilium, and when shown a panoply said to have belonged to Achilles he exchanged it with a set of his own and had it carried into battle beside him in the years to come. However, he spurned the offer to see the lyre of his namesake Alexander or Paris, whose abduction of Helen caused the war but whose conduct during it was far from heroic. This was not a rejection of all things Trojan, nor did he paint the Trojans as simple predecessors of his Persian enemy. Neoptolemus, son of Achilles and his direct ancestor, had killed King Priam of Troy while he clung to the altar of Zeus of the Enclosures, before carrying off and marrying his granddaughter. Their descendant went to the shrine and sacrificed to propitiate the spirit of the murdered king.[16]

After he had paid his respects and seen the sights, Alexander went to join the main force, which had by this time crossed the straits and camped at Arisbe. Parmenio had displayed all his usual efficiency, and the pilgrimage to Troy was a mark of the king's faith in his subordinates, not a disinterest in the practical aspects of the campaign. It would have been strange indeed for a descendant of Achilles—or almost any educated Greek—to pass so close and not visit the sites of the Trojan War. How much wider interest there was in the king's visit at the time is impossible to say. Wherever he went, Alexander conspicuously honored the gods, and at the very least his conduct was respectful and proper. In 480 BC Xerxes had ordered a bridge of boats made across the Dardanelles, and when it was smashed in a storm he had men whip the sea and drop fetters into it to make the waves themselves submit to the king of kings. He had also plundered the shrine of Athena at Ilium, the tomb of Protesilaus, and other sacred places well before he robbed the temples of Athens itself. Alexander's army was too small to justify a bridge of boats, even if he had wanted one, but the manner of his crossing and the respect he displayed to shrines and the distant past were in deliberate contrast.[17]

———

THE MAIN INVASION had at last begun, in spite of the death of Philip and the troubled early days of Alexander's succession. This was surely a disappointment to the Persians, but it was hardly a crisis. Greek armies had come to Asia Minor before and all had failed in the long run and retreated. Alexander's army was larger than any past invader from Greece, but the resources available to him were still dwarfed by the money and manpower of Persia, even assuming he managed the unlikely feat of maintaining the unity and support of his Greek allies. At this early stage the invasion was simply a problem, and King Darius III was content to let his local representatives deal with it. In truth he had little choice, for the heartland of the empire was more than a thousand miles away from the Dardanelles and it would take a long time to muster a royal army, arrange to feed it, and then lead it to the war zone. There was never a realistic possibility of this occurring before the year was out. Head of such a vast empire, the Persian king had to delegate.

Darius III was twice Alexander's age but had only been king for about the same time, and like Alexander he ascended the throne in the aftermath of murder, the latest in a succession of assassinations. It began in 338 BC, when the eunuch Bagoas is supposed to have poisoned Artaxerxes III Ochus. He was replaced by his infant son, Arses, who was then named Artaxerxes IV. The father had proved himself capable and utterly ruthless, killing off all obvious rivals and suppressing the revolt of the satraps and communities in Asia Minor and along the Mediterranean coast, prompting Artabazus and his household to seek sanctuary in Macedonia. Artaxerxes IV's greatest victory was recovering Egypt, a wealthy province that had successfully rebelled against Persia near the end of the fifth century BC.[18]

Bagoas eliminated Ochus's other sons to protect the new king, but as the boy grew up he began to show signs of independence and a natural suspicion of his manipulative and murderous advisor. In 336 BC, the eunuch poisoned him and arranged for the nobleman Codomannus to become king, who took the name Darius III. In time Bagoas changed his mind, but the king found out about the plot and made the eunuch drink his own poison. Such at least is the story told by Diodorus, reflecting the Greeks' entrenched suspicion and contempt of kings and their courts, barbarians in general, and the eunuchs who simultaneously fascinated and repelled them. We cannot say how much truth there is in these tales, although there seems little doubt that Ochus and his son were murdered and that these years heavily culled the main line of the Achaemenid royal family.[19]

Darius must have belonged to the family, and it was claimed that he was grandson of a brother of Ochus's father, King Artaxerxes II. If so, then it was surprising that he had survived Ochus's purges, although since it was claimed that Artaxerxes II had 115 sons by various concubines there were no doubt plenty of other victims. This lineage is possible, but equally may have been invented after Darius's succession. More likely he was an obscure member of the royal clan, not considered enough of a threat to be worth killing. Instead he won Ochus's favor for his bravery in battle, most notably when he defeated an enemy champion in single combat. He was a tall handsome man, even among the Persians who were famed for their good looks, and had a son and a daughter from an existing marriage. Probably after becoming king he married Stateira—reputedly the most beautiful woman in all Asia—who was said to be his sister, although this may be part of a fabricated lineage created as more suitable for the king: if his wife/sister was from the true royal line, then Darius was too.[20]

Much about Darius is uncertain, and our sources give no real indication of his character. Given the circumstances of his elevation to the throne, the death of Philip and the delay to the Macedonian expedition had given him something of a breathing space, which he surely needed to consolidate power. The Achaemenids ruled over many communities with strong identities and memories of past independence. A rebellion in Babylon is possible, as is another in Egypt, although we cannot be sure. If they occurred then both had been suppressed by the time Alexander crossed to Asia, but they would have been rightly seen as far more serious than any threat from Macedonia. Revolts had occurred in the past and sometimes lasted for years or even decades, as in Egypt, before they were eventually overcome. Darius III ruled over an empire that was no longer at its height but was certainly not in deep or terminal decline. Indeed, the robustness of its administration and organization was one important reason why Alexander was able to take over and hold it all together.[21]

Darius ruled over an empire that was far bigger, wealthier, and more populous than any Greek state—even including Macedonia and its allies combined. Herodotus claimed that Xerxes had led a million men in his invasion of Greece, so many that they drained rivers dry and had to be counted by area rather than by head. Logistically, such a force was an impossibility; Napoleon had just over half that number in the Grande Armée when he attacked Russia in 1812, and this was by far the largest army fielded by any European state or alliance up to that date, and would rarely be matched, let alone surpassed, until the twentieth century. Our sources make similar claims about some of Darius's encounters with Alexander, alleging great hordes of a million or more soldiers. The numbers mean little more specific than "vast" by Greek standards, proving that one Greek was superior to many barbarians, and making the glory of victory all the greater. Repetition of these wild estimates meant that a Greek audience would struggle to accept the idea of a Persian army that was not truly massive. Thus the historians accompanying Alexander and their successors who wrote later had little choice but to speak of great hordes of enemies, which does not mean that the young king was not as eager to inflate Persian numbers to add to his own reputation.[22]

The available manpower was considerable, even if not on the alleged scale, but the Persians did not maintain a large standing army—as with most ancient states it is better to talk of individual Persian armies rather than a single institution of the Persian army. So vast was the empire that a large trained force kept at the king's immediate disposal would have made little military sense, apart from being culturally unlikely; sheer distance meant that it would have taken too long for such an army to get to where it was needed in time to be useful. The empire was not permanently at war, and conflicts tended to occur on distant borders or result from internal rebellion. Each situation called for an appropriate response, prepared for that campaign, drawn first from neighboring regions and then in time from further afield if this proved necessary. It was hard to prepare in advance for such warfare, but this did not matter. No opponent was seen to threaten the empire's existence, which meant that even if there were initial defeats the consequences were not fatal, and there would always be time to bring ever greater resources to bear. Persian wars of conquest were very rare by the fourth century BC, although the recovery of Egypt in many ways fell into this category; other conflicts tended to be reactions to an enemy.

There were few professional soldiers. The Immortals of Xerxes's day—the 10,000 picked Persian infantry who were elite, full-time soldiers—seem no longer to have existed, at least in such numbers and skill at arms. There were royal troops, more or less full-time, but in the main the army was recruited from leaders and communities obliged to send men in answer to a royal summons. The best tended to be cavalrymen, drawn from noblemen and their households with the leisure time to hunt on horseback, ride and practice with weapons, and the obligation to justify their status through their valor. These were available in numbers far greater than in any Greek state, even in the cavalry-heavy army created by Philip and Alexander. Their weapons, armor, and costume varied from region to region. Some were primarily skirmishers armed with javelins or sometimes bows, while the majority were willing both to throw javelins or close and fight hand to hand with short spear, sword, or axe, especially if the enemy showed signs of wavering. In this they were much like the cavalry of most Greek city-states, but better mounted and usually better riders.

Infantry were numerous but poorly armored compared to hoplites and even Macedonian pikemen. There was simply no equivalent to the hoplite class in Persia, and the only foot soldiers who could really match Greek armies in close combat were hired Greek mercenaries. As always, we have to be cautious of numbers, especially numbers attributed to the enemy, but it does seem that there were significantly more Greeks taking Darius's pay than there were as allies or mercenaries under Alexander. Isocrates and the other Panhellenists dismissed the Persians as effeminate and decadent, alleging that they hired Greek soldiers because Greeks were simply superior. This was true only in the sense that hoplites were better than any other infantry of the era when it came to massed close combat. Such a verdict ignored the fine Persian cavalry and, even more importantly, that warfare consisted of a good deal more than pitched battle: the Persians had plenty of troops suited to the far more common activities of raiding and sieges. Greek hoplites added an extra element to the mix, which was very useful in some situations. Mercenary troops had the added advantage of being full-time soldiers who could be sent anywhere by the king, whether as garrisons or to operate in the field. As importantly, hiring warlike and restless Greek soldiers was better than letting someone else recruit them.

In addition to the armies he could summon, Darius had access to substantial numbers of warships, although once again there was no such thing as a Persian navy, but rather individual fleets raised for each operation. Like each army, fleets were multiethnic and drawn from the communities along the Mediterranean coast, including Greek cities of Asia and the nearer islands who provided triremes and crews as part of their obligation to the king. Most of these peoples had strong maritime traditions, notably the Phoenicians from the great cities of Tyre and Sidon who were accounted some of the finest shipbuilders and sailors in the ancient world. This meant that the ships in a Persian fleet tended to be well made, maintained, and manned. They were also numerous, which was why Athens had needed to mobilize its allies when it contested naval supremacy with the Persians in the fifth century BC. Later in 334 BC, a fleet of 400 warships is mentioned, and even if exaggerated, such numbers surely represented the potential strength available to Darius. This was a far greater fleet than anything Alexander could find or afford, and equal or even better when it came to seamanship.[23]

When it came to size, the same was true of land forces. In the longer run, Darius could field many more soldiers than Alexander, but the delay mattered and shaped Persian war making. Each Persian army or fleet took time to muster and each was unique, for there was no permanent organization or command structure. Generals were appointed whenever the king was not present, and usually they were satraps or other officials and nobles from the wider area. Alexander's army had at its core soldiers and officers who had fought alongside each other for up to twenty years, creating a well-trained team confident in themselves and each other. In contrast, any Persian force had to learn to work together, to convey and follow orders, and to maneuver en masse after it had mustered. On land or sea, there were plenty of skilled and courageous individuals and contingents, but the challenge lay in coordinating all the different elements to a common end. This meant that the Persian response was likely to be slow, but would steadily grow stronger. Alexander had the advantage of having his well-tempered army ready, but the task facing the young king and his men remained daunting.

16

THE RIVER

In 334 BC the initial response to Alexander's invasion lay with the local satraps and commanders, who gathered at Zeleia, some ten miles south of the sea. Our sources are unclear, but it is likely that Darius placed in charge Arsites, satrap of Hellespontine Phrygia (the north coast of modern Turkey, which included the territory held by the Macedonians), who had sent aid to Perinthus when Philip besieged the city in 340 BC. Even if he was formally in charge and not simply first among equals because the campaign happened to be in his region, his authority over the other commanders was considerably less than Alexander's, for the army included a large number of important noblemen. Foremost were Arsames, satrap of Cilicia; Spithridates, satrap of Lydia and Ionia (the western coast including most of the Greek communities of Asia Minor), along with his brother Rhoesaces; Rheomithres, whose son later became a satrap; Petenes; Niphates; and Mithridates, who was married to Darius's daughter from his first marriage.

Little is known of these men, and our sources give most attention to another commander, Memnon of Rhodes, although this may be because he was a Greek rather than because he was genuinely more competent than the rest. One of that company of mercenary officers who figure so often in this era, he and his brother, Mentor, had a long association with the Persians, their sister having married Artabazus, one of the main leaders in the satrap revolt suppressed by Ochus. During those years Memnon had fled with Artabazus and taken refuge at Philip's court, giving him the chance to get to know Macedonia and its leaders. Mentor had remained loyal to the Persian king, and distinguished service in the recovery of Egypt won him royal favor and the granting of a request to permit the exiles to return. Perhaps in gratitude, Artabazus married his daughter, Barsine, to the condottiere Mentor, even though she was her new husband's niece. When Mentor died a little later, Memnon married the widow, with whom he had at least one child. At some point he was granted substantial estates, mainly in the area close to where the Macedonians had landed. In 335 BC, at the head of 5,000 Greek mercenaries, he had done more than anyone else to hem in Parmenio and the advance guard. Then it had been enough, but such a force was far too small to face Alexander and the full invasion.[1]

A year later the satraps and noblemen had between them managed to raise some 10,000 to 20,000 cavalry, which meant that even taking the lower figure they had a substantial advantage over Alexander. Arrian, our most reliable source, claims that there were 20,000 infantry, most or all of them Greek mercenaries, but many scholars see this as far too high, and are inclined to reduce it to the 5,000 of the previous year. While that number is possible, for Arrian's own source may well have exaggerated to add luster to Alexander's success, there is no actual evidence to support it, and there had been plenty of time to reinforce the troops in Asia Minor. Substantial numbers of cavalry from distant Hyrcania, Media, and Bactria had joined the army at Zeleia at some point, so additional detachments of mercenaries may well also have come. Some local infantry were surely with the army and their presence is hinted at in the sources. On balance, it is safe to say that overall the Persians did not enjoy a marked numerical advantage. They had more horsemen, and past experience suggested that these would also be better than any fielded by a Greek army, but of their infantry only

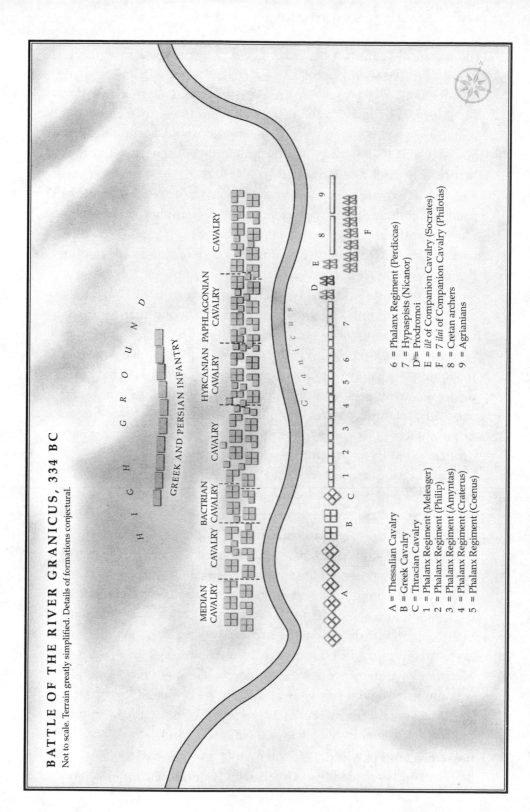

BATTLE OF THE RIVER GRANICUS, 334 BC

Not to scale. Terrain greatly simplified. Details of formations conjectural.

HIGH GROUND

GREEK AND PERSIAN INFANTRY

MEDIAN CAVALRY

BACTRIAN CAVALRY

CAVALRY

CAVALRY

HYRCANIAN CAVALRY

PAPHLAGONIAN CAVALRY

CAVALRY

Granicus

A   B   C   1   2   3   4   5   6   7   D   E   8   9   F

A = Thessalian Cavalry
B = Greek Cavalry
C = Thracian Cavalry
1 = Phalanx Regiment (Meleager)
2 = Phalanx Regiment (Philip)
3 = Phalanx Regiment (Amyntas)
4 = Phalanx Regiment (Craterus)
5 = Phalanx Regiment (Coenus)

6 = Phalanx Regiment (Perdiccas)
7 = Hypaspists (Nicanor)
D = Prodromoi
E = *ilē* of Companion Cavalry (Socrates)
F = 7 *ilai* of Companion Cavalry (Philotas)
8 = Cretan archers
9 = Agrianians

the mercenaries, however many there were, could hope to go toe-to-toe with the enemy phalanx.[2]

Memnon urged caution, arguing that until Darius raised a royal army and came to the theater of operations, they could not match the enemy's infantry and so should avoid battle. He suggested a scorched-earth policy, trampling or burning the tall crops before they could be harvested in a month or so, even evacuating and destroying their own cities to deprive the Macedonians of food and fodder. Starve Alexander's army of supplies, and eventually he would be forced into a humiliating withdrawal. According to Diodorus, Memnon also wanted to counterattack by raiding the coast of Macedonia. Arsites disagreed, not least because it was his satrapy that would suffer the most from such a policy, and the other noblemen supported him, suspecting that Memnon wanted to prolong the war and with it the trust and responsibility he received from Darius. The Rhodian was not popular, whether from simple jealousy or because he was a Greek. By chance or deliberate stratagem, Alexander's foraging parties had so far not touched Memnon's estates and only plundered those belonging to other noblemen, encouraging suspicions of collusion, since it was no secret that he had spent time in Macedonia.

Instead of starving Alexander, the Persians would advance with their field force and confront him. Only hindsight makes this appear unwise, not least because the sources were so eager to show a Greek as wiser than barbarians. Holding back and destroying crops and houses might make some military sense, but was politically dangerous for it would make the Persians seem weak. Few local communities had a strong emotional attachment to the empire, and the demand that they make such a sacrifice was likely to prompt defections—better to welcome the invader and give up some of your food than lose everything. Implementing Memnon's strategy would be extremely difficult, for Alexander was unlikely to wait passively as his army starved. Talk of attacks on Macedonia itself at this early stage is likely a later invention, but even if Memnon did suggest them, all the indications are that there was not yet a fleet available to undertake such an operation. There was little real choice other than confronting Alexander and seeking battle, at least if this could be fought in favorable circumstances. Finding the right place and the right moment for battle were key arts of generalship.

Alexander needed to advance and make gains to encourage his men and impress upon the locals that this Macedonian army was here to stay and worth befriending. Supply was a never-ending problem, and in this at least Memnon had been right. The harvest was not yet ripe, so little could be foraged by the Macedonians from the land around them, which at this stage was only a small area. Cities and villages inevitably ran down their stores of food over the winter months and had not yet replenished them, so they had little to give. It was unlikely to encourage defections if Alexander's men stripped occupied territory bare. On the way to the Dardanelles the army had marched along a predictable route in friendly territory and was thus able to be fed from prepared stores as well as grain and other provisions brought by sea. However, once he began to march inland, the lifeline to the sea was cut and from then on he had to carry everything he needed with the army. A little could be carried on the backs of his soldiers—the Macedonians were accustomed to this—but with the weight of weapons and equipment there were severe limits to how many days' rations could be carried. The rest required transport by wagon, pack animal, or human porter, which in turn added to the amount of food, fodder, drink, and wood for cooking required by the army. The thirty days of supplies Alexander possessed at the start of the campaign gave just a month of operations, but even these stores were of little use if he could not get them to where they were needed.[3]

Alexander had a lot of soldiers and a lot of cavalry horses, even before the baggage train was added. As long as they stayed near the crossing place they could still be fed by sea, as could the fleet, which increased the supply requirements by more than two-thirds, but staying where he was achieved nothing and devoured his limited reserves. The Persians were at Zeleia and Alexander knew this, although he may not have known their precise strength or intentions. That did not really matter, as he had to deal with the threat of the local satraps as soon as possible regardless of how strong they were. Delay would only make him seem weak, perhaps allow them to add to their forces, and certainly make any other operation he attempted very difficult.

The Macedonians advanced toward Zeleia. Mountains rose to the south, so it was obvious to everyone that they would follow the main route along the coastal plain, a well-established path and part of the empire's communication system. Alexander did not take his entire army, instead forming a field force just as Philip had often done in the past. Virtually all the cavalry went with him but less than half of his infantry, which consisted of the Macedonians and a few favored specialists like the Agrianians. Altogether he had a little under 20,000 men, not including servants, porters, and other noncombatants. Some suggest that the Greek allies were left behind because the king did not wholly trust them, although this does not explain why the mercenaries and tribal infantry from the Balkans also remained. Practical concerns are more likely. The Macedonian infantry had learned under Philip to travel light and march quickly and far. Allied troops lacked this training and discipline, while Greek hoplites in particular usually traveled at a modest pace and wanted plenty of slaves to carry for them. Taking less than half of his forces meant that any supplies carried would last longer. At this stage, Alexander may not have possessed enough transport animals and porters to carry enough for everyone for more than a very short period. With the pick of his forces he had the chance to move quickly and aggressively, rather than lumbering along.

A scouting force of *prodromoi* light horsemen backed by a squadron of heavy Companion cavalry led the way. The cities en route offered no resistance, being either already under Alexander's control or willing to submit. A deputation came from Priapus, which lay away from the route on the coast itself, and a small detachment was sent there to accept the citizens' surrender. The city was the center of a cult to the phallic god Priapus, whose fame would spread widely in the next century and especially in the Roman period. Sometimes depicted in statues pushing a wheel barrow to support his enormous penis, a whole genre of obscene comic poems was dedicated to him.[4]

By this time the Persians had advanced from Zeleia, following essentially the same route from the opposite direction. They

halted where the track forded the river Granicus, protecting communications with their base and the important city of Cyzicus.
Alexander marched with his army ready to deploy into battle
order, phalanx in the middle and cavalry on the wings. His scouts,
on this day the *prodromoi* with 5,000 light infantry, probably the
Agrianians, reported that the enemy was waiting on the far bank
of the river. Alexander pushed ahead, forming the army into line.
As he came closer he saw that the Persian cavalry was by the river,
their infantry, chiefly the mercenaries, on high ground some distance to the rear.[5]

Parmenio advised caution, suggesting that they camp for the
night and cross at dawn. He believed that the Persians would
retire from the riverbank for the night, fearing a surprise attack
by the Macedonian infantry, so that the enemy should not oppose
the crossing. Attacking directly across the river was risky, because
it was unlikely to be fordable everywhere, so that their formation
would break up, and then they would have to climb the steep
bank on the far shore in the teeth of the enemy. If they lost this
first major encounter, then the consequences would be very serious for the entire war.[6]

There was truth in a lot of the arguments. Alexander could lose
the war in a day by suffering defeat and humiliation, or by getting
killed or badly wounded. In contrast beating the Persians would
only be a first step toward victory. Most commanders would balk
at attacking any position where the ground favored the enemy,
whether that meant crossing a river or advancing up a slope. The
convention in such circumstances was to avoid battle, unless there
was no other choice. Philip had waited for weeks before attacking
at Chaeronea against a far weaker position. It is highly likely that
the Persians did not expect Alexander to attack them, at least not
so late in the day and at the end of a long march. Instead they were
making a show of force.

Alexander saw the situation differently, declaring that he would
be ashamed of stopping at this "petty stream" after crossing the
Dardanelles, for this would be unworthy of the Macedonians and
their king, while liable to encourage the enemy. Parmenio was sent
to take charge of the left wing and orders were issued for an attack.

The story conforms to a number of anecdotes where the veteran general urges caution and has his advice rejected by Alexander, who then proves to be right by winning a great victory. All may be invented to showcase the boldness of the young hero, although as we have seen the decision to attack across the Granicus defied conventional military thinking. Curiously, Diodorus does not mention the incident, but has the Macedonians camp for the night and then cross the next day to fight the battle. Although a few scholars have accepted this, his narrative is confused and implausible, and it is better to accept our other sources.[7]

On the right were seven squadrons of Companion cavalry under Philotas, with the Agrianians and archers in support. To their left were the *prodromoi*, Paeonians, and the remaining squadron of Companions. Then came the hypaspists under Nicanor, with the six regiments of the main phalanx to their left, and finally the Thessalian, allied, and Thracian cavalry on the wing. Arrian, the most detailed and plausible source for the battle, gives the Persians 20,000 horsemen, although as we have seen some scholars prefer the figure of 10,000 given by Diodorus. These were on the bank of the river, a claim that has provoked even more debate and is not helped by the strange assumption that they deployed in a single great block. Cavalry did not operate like a solid phalanx, for this would have robbed them of any chance of maneuver and made them more inclined to stampede. Instead, just like the Macedonians and their allies, they were broken up into small tactical units of a few hundred men at most formed up with space around them and usually in more than one line. Cavalry combats were fast-moving, whirling affairs, as each side advanced, charged, and retreated in turn as fresh reserves joined in until a decisive advantage was gained. Practical considerations and Arrian's narrative suggest that what he meant was that the Persian cavalry were arranged on the plain beyond the river, the forward squadrons actually on the high banks, and the rest ready to support with plenty of space between each unit. They were also divided into seven or so larger contingents, partly on an ethnic basis.[8]

Arrian claimed that there were 20,000 infantry on the high ground, while Diodorus gives the absurd figure of 100,000. Throughout his narrative Arrian supplies detailed breakdowns of units and especially dispositions of Alexander's forces, suggesting that at least one of his key sources had access to official records. Estimates of enemy numbers were always likely to be guesswork. Leaving the infantry behind in this way was unusual, and reinforces the sense that this was a show of force and that the Persian leaders did not expect a battle on that day. All of the satraps and key commanders, including Memnon, were among the cavalry, some or all perhaps in consultation, which meant that it was questionable whether any would have the opportunity or perspective to commit the infantry. For a while there was a lull, the two armies staring at each other across the river, and such confrontations were common and often did not lead to battle. The Persians did not retreat, which would have meant losing face, nor did they make any major changes to their deployment, most likely still not expecting to fight.

The topography of the battlefield is disputed, mainly because opinion is divided over whether or not the modern river near the village of Dimetoka flows along the same line as it did in the fourth century BC. More likely it does not, and centuries of flood control and agricultural irrigation systems have altered the course, resulting in clearly defined and heavily overgrown banks. In 334 BC there was little or no vegetation, for the armies were in plain sight of each other, and the river itself flowed in the middle of a wider channel that might fill during high flood. At the time of the battle, the current would have been fast and fairly full, flowing north from the mountains. There must have been at least one main crossing place, and probably several others where the banks were a little less steep and fording the river itself possible. Elsewhere the banks were higher—taller than a man on horseback—and often steep. Some of the gravel patches forming ramps to be seen today may have existed, but the bulk of the bed was hard clay, which could become slippery when churned into mud by heavy use, as happened during the battle with so many horses in and around the eastern bank.[9]

Alexander mounted his horse—perhaps Bucephalus, although by the end of the day he was riding another mount—and with his attendants, close companions, and bodyguards moved to the right wing. Apart from his distinctive cloak, armor, and the crowd around him, his helmet marked him out, for as well as a central crest it had a white plume on either side. The Macedonians could easily spot him, as could the Persians, and Arrian says that they deliberately massed squadrons opposite where the king was. Alexander gave orders to start the attack, which was led by the *prodromoi*, Paeonians, and the squadron of Companion cavalry whose turn it was to lead the advance on this day, supported by one *taxis* of infantry, presumably from the hypaspists, and all under command of Amyntas, son of Arrabaeus. At the very least they would show whether or not the river was fordable and the far bank could be climbed. As this spearhead force started across, Alexander reached the main body of Companions and gave the trumpet signal for a general advance. In the meantime, the spearhead splashed through the river, probably using the most clearly defined ford, the horsemen outstripping the infantry. The Persians were waiting, throwing javelins down from the high banks. Other units surged down into the channel to fling missiles at closer range or to charge. Fresh squadrons came up on either side, more and more of the defenders being sucked in so that the numbers were clearly in their favor. Memnon and his sons led their horsemen into the fight. No fewer than twenty-five men from the squadron of Companions were killed and soon the spearhead units were falling back.[10]

Alexander had taken the main force of Companions into the channel and then the river, heading to the right, against the strong current. Searching for a way across, he was also keen to form them into a line as they crossed, rather than being funneled into one of the obvious access points in the far bank. At the head of the royal squadron, he charged headlong into the thickest concentration of Persians who had just driven back the spearhead. Elsewhere the remainder of the army was wading over as best it could, formation no doubt ragged but spreading out into a rough battle line, searching for places to get up onto the enemy bank.

The fighting was fierce and confused, with little semblance left of ordered squadrons, with individuals and groups of horsemen intermingled, horses walking, sometimes barging forward, but with little space to charge. For the ancients such a static fight was more like an infantry than a cavalry battle. The comment of one eyewitness at

Waterloo who compared the clash of sabers to a thousand copper-smiths at work gives an idea of the noise; add to that the screams and shouts of men and horses. Some of the Agrianians and archers began to come up in support, but this remained primarily a mounted battle. The Macedonians' longer spears and their aggression gave them the edge over the enemy horsemen with their shorter javelins. They thrust at the Persians' faces, and the chests and the heads of their horses, and started to make headway, the numbers in contact probably now much closer to equal. A horse will willingly surge up a slope if at all practical, a far more natural act than standing at the top and trying to block such a rush, so more and more went up. The Persians gave way, and some of the Macedonians gathered in groups on the edge of the plain, facing the enemy's supporting squadrons that were still waiting to come up.[11]

At this point the attention of our sources narrows down just to Alexander and those immediately around him. He broke his spear and called on one of the royal grooms who was nearby to give him a new one. The man could not help, for his own had also snapped and he was busy fending off opponents with the broken stump and the spike on its butt. He told the king to look elsewhere. Demaratus of Corinth, a Greek become Companion of Philip and now Alexander (and the man credited with persuading Philip to recall his son from Illyria), gave the king his own *xyston*. There was clearly some open ground ahead, for the king then spotted a group of enemy horsemen in a dense block or wedge, well ahead of the main lines of reserves and coming forward. They were led by Mithridates, although whether or not Alexander knew who he was or simply saw a bold and well-dressed enemy nobleman is hard to say. Either way, Alexander galloped at him, streaming ahead of his followers; the Persians had no doubt who he was and determined to kill him, whether as part of a considered plan or opportunistically.

Alexander drove his borrowed spear into Mithridates's face, killing him. Rhoesaces, brother of the satrap Spithridates, was there as well and pressed close, hacking down with sword or axe and striking Alexander on the helmet. Diodorus claims the blow broke through the metal, something inherently unlikely unless the helmet was badly made. Arrian more plausibly has the blow strike off part of it, probably one of the side plumes, and perhaps the helmet twisted and gave a slight cut to his head. Alexander then drove his spearhead into his opponent's chest, felling him. In the loose mix of struggling horses and horsemen, the dead man's brother, Spithridates, had worked around the king's flank and raised his own blade to strike. Alexander did not see the threat, but fortunately "Black" Cleitus, the commander of the royal squadron, was on hand and was an instant faster than the satrap. He sliced down hard with his own sword, hacking off the Persian's arm. More and more Macedonians rode up to join them and the danger was over. At the same time, the Persians started to give way, with much of Alexander's army across the river. Apart from driving back the spearhead, they had failed to stop any of the attacks. Casualties among the leaders who faced the Macedonian left wing suggest that Parmenio and the Thessalians had also had a hard fight before they broke through.[12]

The Persian cavalry fled, along with almost all of their surviving leaders, leaving behind their infantry. Arrian has the mercenaries mesmerized by the speed of the collapse, staying in place when they should have withdrawn. They were soon surrounded, pressed by the phalanx in front and cavalry to flanks and rear. Arrian baldly reports the massacre, while Plutarch attributes it to Alexander's rage and claims that there was heavy fighting to defeat them, during which the king's horse was killed. Two thousand mercenaries were taken prisoner, but as Greeks fighting against the great Greek alliance and its *hegemon*, they were enslaved and sent back to Macedonia in chains to labor in the mines or fields. A literal reading of Arrian would imply that 18,000 were massacred, but we cannot really know and some may have escaped. The Persian cavalry lost 1,000 dead, including eight of its senior commanders. Arsites escaped but committed suicide soon afterward, presumably accepting blame for the defeat. Memnon got away and would soon fight the Macedonians again.

The twenty-five Companion cavalrymen from the leading squadron who were killed were commemorated by bronze statues Alexander commissioned and had erected in the sacred site at Dium in Macedonia. Arrian says another sixty horsemen died along with about thirty infantry. Modern historians, who are always inclined to be bloodthirsty, have often doubted these figures as too low, but they reflect casualty patterns in ancient battles and are entirely plausible. In addition, there would have been at least as many, and probably several times as many, wounded. Casualties among cavalry mounts were likely even higher. Alexander spent time visiting the wounded and discussing their treatment, and giving proper burial to the dead. He also treated the corpses of the Greek mercenaries (now that they were dead) and Persian nobles with respect.[13]

The Granicus was a small battle compared to the big encounters with Darius in the years to come. It was not tactically subtle. Alexander needed to fight, did not want to wait and risk the enemy withdrawing to another, perhaps better position, and trusted to the skill and ferocity of his men. He set a personal example, and after ordering the general advance could do nothing to influence wider tactics, trusting to his subordinates to do the right thing. Convention as much as real difficulty cautioned commanders against attacking across an obstacle. Alexander trusted the quality of his men, their prowess and weaponry, the willingness to push on, and the ability of their leaders to seize control of whoever was nearby and deal with the chaos better than the enemy. It was a gamble, and if Cleitus had been slow off the mark then the king might well have died and the campaign failed there and then. Luck and skill were with the Macedonians and the gamble paid off.

Alexander had his first battle and first major victory, and one that could be described in pleasingly Homeric style. Three hundred captured panoplies were sent back to Greece to be dedicated at the Temple of Athena in Athens—the most prominent victim of Xerxes's depredations. Alexander personally dictated the inscription to be set up with them—"Alexander son of Philip, and the Greeks, except the Spartans, set up these spoils from the barbarians dwelling in Asia." In practical terms, the only field force the Persians possessed in the area was beaten, dispersed, and deprived of most of its leaders. An officer who had served with Parmenio and the advance guard was named satrap in place of Arsites, showing that Alexander intended to make use of the Persian administrative structures. The king paraded his mildness, announcing that he would not punish the citizens of Zeleia because they had been forced to support the enemy. Other cities were occupied without resistance in the days and weeks that followed. The Persian commander of the garrison at Sardis led a deputation of its leading men to surrender the city and its well-filled treasury. Alexander announced that they and the other Lydians would be free and allowed their own customs. This was not a change, since they appear to have enjoyed these things under Persian rule, and as under Persia, they were expected to contribute money and food to their new master.[14]

Ephesus had declared for Philip in 336 BC, setting up his statue before tearing it down when the Macedonians retreated the next year and a group of oligarchs seized power. Four days after accepting the surrender of Sardis, Alexander came to the city to find that the Persian garrison had fled and a welcoming crowd was waiting for him. There were riots, but only against the oligarchs, several of whom were lynched before Alexander's men restored order and he forbade any more reprisals. A new democracy was established with his approval and similar systems were set up in other cities after Persian-backed oligarchies were expelled. Like Philip, Alexander's attitude to different forms of government was entirely pragmatic, favoring in every case whatever regime was most likely to support him. The king's piety continued to be public. In Lydia he ordered construction of a temple to Zeus on a site struck by lightning, while at Ephesus he did not take over the levies formally paid to the Persian king, and instead ordered that they be used to restore the great temple of Artemis, which had burned down at the time of his birth and was still awaiting reconstruction. However, an offer to undertake and contribute to this work on Alexander's part was refused by the Ephesians.[15]

Alexander paused at Ephesus for several weeks, making offerings to Artemis and holding a formal parade of celebration, while detachments went out to accept the surrender of other cities. During this time he sat for a portrait by the famous Greek painter Apelles. The brash young king was friendly but inclined to voice strong opinions about artistic technique, in spite of his scant knowledge. Eventually the artist quietly suggested that Alexander had better stop, because even his junior assistants were laughing at his ignorance. An early version of the portrait with the king astride Bucephalus did not receive royal approval, but when modified to show him wielding a thunderbolt like Zeus, the king was delighted, prompting him to give no less than twenty talents to the painter and announce that from now on only Apelles was allowed to paint his official portrait.[16]

The Persians were regrouping, with a fleet now gathered and on the way. The Persian commander at Miletus on the coast had written offering to surrender, but changed his mind when he heard that help would soon come by sea. Alexander took a column and went there, overrunning the outer city without resistance but being held by the strong inner walled area. His own ships came to support him and arrived three days before the Persian navy, securing the approaches to the harbor and the island of Lade. Arrian claims the enemy navy had 400 warships to Alexander's 160, and then for once tells a story where Parmenio urged the reckless course, saying that they should risk a naval battle that he offered to command. The king refused, as must surely have been correct unless Arrian's estimates of the relative strengths are wildly off the mark. At sea the prowess of the Macedonian army and its king mattered little, while any serious defeat would be damaging.[17]

Miletus was where the Ionian Revolt against Persia had begun in 499 BC, which had led eventually to Athenian intervention and the subsequent Persian invasions of Greece. The city had eventually fallen after the rebels suffered a catastrophic defeat in a naval battle off Lade. This time the "Greeks" refused to fight, and the Persians were not inclined to attack into the narrow waters around the harbor, where their numbers could not be brought to bear. They could not reach the defenders, and had to base themselves on the shore near Mount Mycale, some ten miles away, and had to go even farther to find enough fresh water. A representative from Miletus was sent to Alexander proposing that the city become neutral, open to both sides. Unsurprisingly the proposal was rejected, and the Macedonians set about making a breach in the city wall. Once this was created, an assault was launched and was quickly successful. Active defenders, especially units of Greek mercenaries, were massacred as they tried to escape. One group of

300 packed themselves into small boats and reached a tiny island near the harbor. Alexander prepared ships with ladders to assault its rocky sides, but unlike at Granicus he accepted their surrender and enlisted them in his own forces. Citizens who had not fought or survived the initial massacre were pardoned and their famous city allowed to continue as his subjects.[18]

Unwilling to challenge the enemy at sea, Alexander sent Philotas with three regiments of infantry and the cavalry to harass the Persian camp. In an illustration of the vulnerability of ancient fleets without secure bases on shore, the Persians were soon deprived of food and water and sailed away to the island of Samos. Once there, the Persian commanders decided on one last aggressive act, heading back to Miletus in the hope that this time the Greek fleet serving with Alexander would come out and fight. This was partly in the hope of a battle, but also because they had heard that most of the crews in Alexander's fleet had themselves gone ashore to forage. Five galleys slipped into the sea between Lade and the harbor to find out the truth, and burn the Greek warships if they were undefended. The attackers were spotted and sufficient crewmen scraped together to put ten triremes to sea, chasing the Persians away and capturing one vessel.[19]

Soon afterward Alexander decided to send the ships of his own fleet back to their homes, keeping only some twenty vessels, mainly as transports. Among these was an Athenian squadron, whether as a compliment to their fame as a city and naval power or as hostages— or indeed as both. In the short term this made sense. While they were with him, sailors had to be paid and fed, something always difficult, especially with winter approaching, and in spite of gains he had made in the last months the available food and money was limited. They could not face the stronger Persian fleet and needed to be protected lest the next enemy attack prove more successful. On balance the fleet as it stood cost more than it was worth to him—or at least more than he could readily afford. Instead of beating the Persians at sea he said that he would capture all the remaining harbors and "overcome the ships from dry land."[20]

Following the coast southward he set about this task, capturing a number of small cities until he came to Halicarnassus, capital of

Caria. Pixodarus, the dynast who had so recently sought marriage alliance with Macedonia and failed after Alexander's intervention, had by this time died and been replaced by a Persian satrap. The latter married the Carian ruler's daughter who had earlier been offered as bride to Philip's sons. Pixodarus was one of five siblings, children of Hecatomnus: the others had all ruled before him, with his two older brothers marrying and ruling with his two sisters. Most recently, Ada had ruled with her brother/husband Idreius, and then held power alone for four years after he died in 344 BC. This ended when she was supplanted by Pixodarus, but Ada escaped and held out in the stronghold of Alinda. She outlived him and was still holding out when Alexander arrived. Middle-aged and childless, Ada went to the young king asking for reinstatement and promising her support. Alexander not only agreed, but accepted "adoption," addressing Ada as mother and letting her call him son. Plutarch says that she made a great display of affection, sending him treats and other presents as if to a child; this was the occasion when he said that he was used to the frugal life taught by his tutor Leonidas. The alliance with Ada put a dignified front on her submission, and was a practical piece of politics from Alexander's point of view.[21]

An attempt to rush Halicarnassus failed, and Alexander then had to wait for heavy siege equipment to be brought down the coast. The convoy avoided the attentions of the Persian fleet, but now that his navy had disbanded, Alexander could not prevent the supply of the city by sea. This, combined with its very strong natural and man-made defenses, aided the vigorous defense led by Memnon and a number of other bold leaders, including two experienced Athenian mercenary generals. Early on, Alexander took a force away in the hope of capturing nearby Myndus, but failed. In the meantime the siege of Halicarnassus ground on, the defenders sallying out to destroy the siege engines. One evening drunken posturing by a couple of men from Perdiccas's battalion escalated into a major fight, as many more soldiers joined them in a spontaneous attack on the walls, at the end of which Alexander had to ask to recover his dead, thus admitting defeat for the first time. Yet the reverse did not change the balance of power. The Macedonians persisted and there was more heavy fighting, in the course of which one of the Athenian generals was killed. Eventually the defenders retreated into the inner citadels. These were even harder to attack, and as the campaigning season was over Alexander left a mainly mercenary force to complete the siege and divided the remainder of the army into detachments so that it was easier to supply them over the winter.[22]

The siege of Halicarnassus was incomplete, but did little to tarnish the achievements of this first campaign in Asia. Alexander now controlled the Aegean coast and a lot of territory inland. Overall, the balance of resources between him and Darius had not fundamentally shifted, but Alexander had won enough to keep funding and supplying the war. With the theater of operations still relatively close to home, he sent all of his soldiers who were recently married back to their wives in Macedonia for the winter. This was a mark of his care for men's welfare, much like his concern for the wounded, so it was good for morale. He also stated that he wanted them to sire the next generation of soldiers, which was in contrast to his own disinterest in becoming a father for the moment. More immediately, the officers who led the leave party were ordered to make new levies of recruits and bring them back with them when they returned in time for the start of operations next year. Alexander had made a good start to his war but was a long way from victory, and it was clear that this would not be easy to achieve. He could still lose everything in a single day.[23]

17

THE GORDIAN KNOT

Alexander did not rest as the year 334 BC came to an end. Neither the Greeks nor the Persians conducted major campaigns during the winter months except in the most exceptional circumstances. There might be raiding and the odd skirmish, and the blockade of a city would be enforced, but the problems of finding food and fodder, the bad weather that made traveling hard, and the reassurance that enemies would usually face all the same restrictions meant that sizeable armies did not take the field again until the spring. Philip changed all this, giving his opponents no relief by waging war regardless of season, and his son was no different. Time was not on Alexander's side.

For the moment he had shattered the Persian forces in Asia Minor, but already resistance to him was starting to reorganize, as the defense of Halicarnassus had shown. Memnon would soon launch an offensive in the Aegean, using ships from the coastal communities carrying Greek mercenaries. Other small forces loyal to Darius started to appear inland—too small to challenge Alexander in battle, but still big enough to make local communities think twice about whether it was worth the risk of joining the invaders. Eventually the king of kings was bound to muster greater and greater numbers of soldiers and commit them to the fight. Resting and waiting would only make the enemy stronger, so Alexander did neither.

Arrian writes of Alexander pushing into Lycia and Pamphylia, "so as to gain control of the coast and render the enemy's navy useless." Although it may seem puzzling since this meant that he was actually advancing inland away from the sea, this is to misunderstand the situation. The major coastal cities were large and tough nuts to crack if they did not surrender. Even if Alexander had taken them all, and thus acquired all or most of the coastal strip, they would remain vulnerable to Persian counterattacks from land as well as the sea. He needed to control enough territory beyond the coast to make these cities secure, reducing the risk that a sudden attack or internal revolution would hand some or all of the ports back to Darius. Alexander also needed access to food and other supplies, including replacement mounts and transport animals to support the army and make possible the operations to come. Thus for most of the next year, the Macedonians overran as much of Asia Minor as they could, their focus mainly on the highlands of Anatolia. Winters there are harsh, but the Macedonians were used to cold weather and rugged country, as were allies like the Thracians and Illyrians. Parmenio took the other main division of the army into Phrygia, and smaller forces operated elsewhere.[1]

Most of our sources skim over the remainder of 334 and the first half of 333 BC quickly, and modern historians tend to do the same, for the operations were small in scale and lacked dramatic pitched battles or sieges of famous cities. Arrian is the only one to describe these months in any detail at all, and even he deals only with Alexander and ignores Parmenio and the rest of the army. A snippet gives a flavor of the narrative. Alexander "first took in his stride Hyparna, a strong place with a mercenary garrison; the mercenaries received terms and marched out of the citadel. Then on entering Lycia he took over the Telmisseans by surrender, and after crossing the Xanthus he received Pinara and the city of Xanthus and Patara in submission with about thirty smaller towns. By the time he had completed all this it was the depth of winter."[2]

Many of the places mentioned during these operations remain unidentified, so we cannot trace the route Alexander followed or understand most of the details of the campaign. The local response to the invaders varied a good deal, since this was a region of many fiercely independent communities, always difficult for any power to control—as the Romans would discover in later centuries. Some of the inhabitants were enthusiastic raiders, trusting to the strength of their walled strongholds to avoid retribution. The Marmares ambushed the Macedonian rear guard, managing to get among the baggage animals and steal some of them. Alexander rounded on them, and spent two days assaulting their hilltop city. According to Diodorus the warriors massacred their own families, burning some alive along with their houses, before slipping over the walls and through the Macedonian lines to escape.[3]

A direct attack could not go unavenged, but otherwise Alexander did not feel compelled to capture every settlement where the people failed to welcome him. Syllium was strongly fortified and garrisoned by mercenaries loyal to Darius, so he judged it unlikely to fall to a hasty assault and moved on. The Telmissians mustered to defend the mountain pass leading to their city. Alexander camped for the night in plain sight, judging that the locals would relax their vigilance. He was proved right, as many wandered home rather than spend a cold and uncomfortable night in position. The king rushed to the spot with a picked force, and a few volleys from his archers were enough to put the remaining defenders to flight. Even so, their city was too strong to fall without a proper siege, so he passed it and moved on. A neighboring community and longtime enemy of the Telmissians asked him for an alliance and agreed to keep them in check. This did not prevent some Telmissian warriors going to aid the next community in his path. Trusting in a strong position on high ground in front of their city, the warriors of Sagalassus formed for battle. Alexander led an infantry assault uphill. His archers were driven back, their commander and twenty soldiers killed, but the hypaspists and phalangites pressed on, routing the poorly equipped and undisciplined enemy. Most escaped, but their city fell easily. In the aftermath, other strongholds surrendered or were stormed.[4]

Alexander kept advancing, willing to assault if there was the prospect of a quick success, but refusing to halt and prosecute a formal siege. Celenae in Phrygia was garrisoned by 1,000 Carian and 100 Greek mercenaries in the pay of the local satrap. These men sent envoys to Alexander offering to surrender if relief did not reach them within sixty days, something that both sides knew was unlikely to happen. Alexander accepted the deal, leaving 1,500 men to watch the city and keep the mercenaries honest. During these months his decisions were pragmatic, although a lot depended on how communities chose to approach him. Early on in the campaign, the city of Phaselis sent envoys bearing a golden crown asking for his friendship. Alexander accepted the alliance, and his soldiers stormed a hostile stronghold used by raiders to attack the city's territory. Those who submitted were protected and treated moderately as long as they stayed loyal and agreed to supply whatever Alexander demanded to feed the war effort.[5]

The leaders of Aspendus sent envoys offering to surrender if they were not required to accept a garrison. Alexander agreed, but demanded the substantial sum of fifty talents in return, as well as the horses the city was obliged to supply to Persia. When the envoys went home, their fellow citizens balked at this, refusing to give anything to the men sent to collect and instead preparing to defend their city. Alexander hurried back, his determination to punish them for breaking the deal so obvious that resistance collapsed and the city surrendered. As a warning to its population and others, they now had to pay 100 talents and submit to the authority of his local representative, although it is not clear whether this also meant accepting a garrison as well. As territory was overrun, Alexander appointed his own satraps and other officials and left behind some troops, usually allies or mercenaries. The alliances made with local communities were not equal, for they were required to give him whatever he demanded, so once again this was really a case of exchanging one master for a new one. Rule by Macedon was probably no more burdensome than rule by Persia, although at the moment the Macedonians were present in force, consuming resources, and also close enough to strike against any open resistance.[6]

The majority of local communities recognized the strength of the invaders and made peace with them, and most of the resistance came from those communities in the wilder areas that had similarly asserted a fair degree of independence from Persia and waged war against their neighbors. Most were defeated, and the remainder, like the bypassed cities, were no more than small enclaves in regions controlled by the Macedonians, and their resistance was local and uncoordinated.

Earlier Greek attacks against Persia had never amounted to much more than raids, and the contrast with Alexander's systematic conquest is great. He did what Philip had done in Illyria and especially Thrace, and once again this was a case of his father's army doing what it had done so many times before. As always it did it well, and for all the new names and places, much will have seemed the same, the tactics and techniques of this warfare familiar and well practiced; in one incident Thracian warriors once again made a decent track through the mountain passes when Alexander needed one. He led from the front, fighting when necessary, marching or riding through all weathers and all terrains just like his men. The young king directed operations of his main force in person, involving himself in what were sometimes very small operations against obscure opponents. It was the pattern set by Philip and one his son followed throughout his life. While the drama of leading the charge at Granicus was an important step in confirming his men's trust, there were many less famous moments, as month after month Alexander campaigned, always advancing and always winning.

In the course of these campaigns, the king led part of his column along a stretch of the coastline of Pamphylia. At one point they waded through the surf, helped because the wind veered from its normal direction and blew out to sea, making the water shallow enough for them to pass. Callisthenes, nephew of Aristotle who accompanied the expedition and wrote the first history of Alexander almost as soon as the events occurred, claimed this was a sign of heavenly favor and the story quickly grew into a miracle, with even the waves bowing before Alexander, just as easterners did obeisance before the Persian king. Plutarch was dismissive, noting that Alexander made no mention of any of this in his letters and simply stated that he marched along the coast. Just before this incident, he was said to be encouraged when a spring near Xanthus threw up a bronze tablet inscribed in an ancient language. Conveniently, someone was on hand to translate, and even more conveniently the text prophesied that Greeks would one day bring the Persian empire to an end.[7]

Other signs were less welcome. Arrian says that during the siege of Halicarnassus a chattering swallow flew around the king while he was taking a siesta, finally perching on Alexander's head. A seer in the royal entourage interpreted this as a sign of a plot among the king's friends, but one that would be revealed. Arrian recounts the story as encouraging Alexander to believe accusations made during the winter against Alexander of Lyncestis, who had so publicly backed Alexander's claim to succeed in the chaotic hours after Philip's murder and thus avoided the fate of his brothers. Loyalty had been rewarded with more than being spared execution, most recently by placing him in charge of the Thessalian cavalry when their existing commander was made a satrap after the Battle of Granicus.

Our sources contradict each other over major details of what happened in 333 BC. Court intrigue by its nature is secretive, the truth known to few and readily distorted by gossip and deliberate fabrication. Arrian's version has Parmenio sending a message to Alexander along with a Persian named Sisenes. The latter had been arrested and confessed to carrying a letter from Darius to Alexander of Lyncestis, who had already contacted Darius via a Macedonian exile at the Persian court. The Persian king offered to pay 1,000 talents in gold and help him become king of Macedonia if he assassinated Alexander. When consulted, the king's friends and advisors were not inclined to speak up for the accused, whether through genuine suspicion, personal dislike, or a sense that the man was already compromised, whatever the truth of the matter. Alexander decided to act, sending an officer disguised in local dress to Parmenio with verbal instructions. The accused man was stripped of his command and arrested, remaining a prisoner for three years. This was odd, for long-term captivity was rare in the ancient world, with execution or exile the usual immediate punishments, and may suggest doubt or lingering affection on the king's part.

Arrian has all this occurring while Alexander was at Phaselis during the winter, whereas Curtius and Diodorus place it much later in the year, after Alexander and Parmenio had rejoined their forces. Diodorus also claims that Olympias wrote to her son warning him not to trust Alexander of Lyncestis, while Curtius speaks of two accusers but does not name them. According to Curtius, Sisenes had been at the Macedonian court since Philip's reign, and was well trusted, only to be executed some time later after he failed a test that had been staged to prove his loyalty.[8]

The conflicting traditions have allowed much scope for speculation, while making it impossible to be certain about almost any aspect of the affair other than to know that Alexander of Lyncestis was arrested and much later executed. Perhaps he had plotted to murder the king, since such conspiracies were common enough at the Argead court, although as noted earlier we do not know whether or not he was a member of the royal family and could seek to rule. On the other hand, Alexander may not have trusted him after executing both his brothers and simply waited until it was safe to dispose of him under the pretext of treachery. Alternatively the king and his victim may both have been innocent, and the plot fabricated by someone else, whether to dispose of a rival or simply to prove loyalty—perhaps even by the Persians to encourage distrust among Alexander's officers. Parmenio has been suspected, although this is pure speculation and we cannot see clear evidence that the arrest improved his status and position. Similarly, there is no hint of a deterioration in the relationship between the king and Antipater back in Macedonia, who was Alexander of Lyncestis's father-in-law, either as a result of his arrest or eventual execution. So much depends on what we think Alexander was like, and even then there remains the puzzle of why someone was arrested, only to be kept alive and killed so much later, which suggests that the king was either unwilling to have the man killed or felt too weak politically to do this. Given the prevalence of assassination in Argead history, the easiest interpretation is that the man really was or at least was believed to be plotting, but easiest does not necessarily mean correct.

Parmenio brought his troops to rendezvous with Alexander's column at Gordium in Phrygia, which makes Arrian's detailed account of the communications during the alleged plot more likely than the suggestions elsewhere that the affair happened after the army had reunited. By this time it was well into the spring, probably late May 333 BC, and also joining the army were the newly raised reinforcements and the men returning from winter's leave in Macedonia who had completed a round trip of almost 1,000 miles. The fresh troops numbered some 3,000 Macedonian infantry and 300 cavalry, along with 200 Thessalian horsemen and 150 from Elis. Around the same time, additional mercenaries also joined the army.[9]

In the temple of Zeus at Gordium was a yoked wagon, said to have belonged to Gordius, father of Midas, the mythical founders of the dynasty that had ruled Phrygia, most recently as Persian representatives. The yoke was fastened by a cord of cornel bark, tied with a complicated knot that left no end visible. Legend, presumably local and never mentioned in any surviving source before Alexander's visit, proclaimed that whoever undid the knot would be master of Asia. The young king was once again seized with a longing (*pothos*), this time to see the sacred relic and meet the challenge. Aristobulus claimed that Alexander pulled out the pin fastening the wagon pole and was able to slide the yoke free. Everyone else said that he drew his sword and slashed through the knot, perhaps because this is a far more dramatic story of boldness and strength rather than cunning—more Achilles than Odysseus. Either way he sacrificed to Zeus Basileus (Zeus the King), and the thunderstorm that raged that night was taken as the god's approval.[10]

It was a good story, especially in hindsight and for Macedonians and Greeks who would not worry too much about whether or not there really was such a prophecy. There is no sign of a flood of envoys seeking alliance after hearing about it, but there was respect for Macedonian force. Alexander continued the campaign to overrun Asia Minor, accepting submission whenever it was

offered, fighting if a quick victory was in prospect, and bypass-
ing anything else. A Paphlagonian delegation offered allegiance
while asking him not to advance into their territory. This was
agreed, although Alexander made clear that they must obey his
satrap. He pushed into Cappadocia, appointing another satrap
for the region, although in this case his choice appears to have
been either a defecting Persian or a local nobleman rather than a
Macedonian. By now most of Asia Minor was under his control
and reasonably secure, at least from anything less than a major
attack, and while he was seen as strong, Alexander kept moving,
going south into Cilicia.[11]

The Persians had not been idle. After Halicarnassus, Darius had
appointed Memnon to be overall commander on the Aegean coast,
having first taken the precaution of summoning his family as a
guarantee of loyalty. The Rhodian was given ships and men, including many mercenaries and money to hire more. Unchallenged at
sea, Memnon began to target Alexander's Greek allies. Chios fell
quickly, as did most of the major cities on Lesbos. Mytilene defied
the Persians, falling only after a prolonged siege in 333 BC. Victory
came at a price in casualties, including Memnon, who fell ill and
died, and command passed to his nephew Pharnabazus, who continued to act with vigor. Lesbos lay close to the Dardanelles—and
would be the main Allied base in the Gallipoli campaign in the First
World War—which allowed the Persians to threaten the straits.
This risked severing Alexander's communications with Macedonia
and opening up the coast of Greece itself to attack. This was serious, and instructions along with money went back home to raise
naval squadrons once more. All that would take time and for the
moment Persia dominated the seas, with all the key seafaring communities still obedient to Darius. A local success by a dozen or so
hastily gathered ships from Euboea fighting on Alexander's behalf
did not change this, but at least it was encouraging.

Yet for all their naval might, the Persians ultimately faced the
same problem as the Athenians had when they had fought Philip and
his son. Galleys needed bases—or at least secure landing places—
so independent fleets had a short strategic range. They could attack
the coastlines and a little way inland, which meant that the Aegean

islands were highly vulnerable; Arrian claims at least one community yielded to necessity and surrendered to the Persians even though its citizens would have preferred to remain loyal to Alexander. Closing the Dardanelles altogether was difficult, and by this time Alexander controlled enough territory to meet his immediate requirements for food and money. No fleet on its own could strike at the Macedonian heartland or overrun the Greek mainland. For that, an army was needed and neither Memnon nor his successor had sufficient mercenaries to constitute a sizeable army, even assuming that they would have been willing to disembark them all in hostile territory for a prolonged campaign.[12]

Like the Athenians in the past, the Persians needed allies to provide an army that they could then assist and fund. Thebes no longer existed, while Athens remained a sea power and had little enthusiasm for war. Demosthenes expressed the hope that Darius would deal with Alexander and his army, but did not dare to urge his fellow citizens to direct action against the Macedonian king. In addition there were Athenians among the allies serving under Alexander as *hegemon*, as well as on board the warships he had retained when the rest of the fleet was dismissed. Most poleis were in the same situation, with citizens serving in Asia with Alexander who might readily become hostages. An Athenian delegation came to Alexander in 333 BC asking for the release of their fellow citizens among the 2,000 captive mercenaries sent to Macedonia after the Battle of Granicus. He declined their request, at least until the coalition war against Persia was won. Fear played a part, but more importantly there is no sense of any great appetite among the Athenians and other Greeks for war against Macedon, least of all for the benefit of the Persian king. The exception was Sparta, which had stood apart from the war. Although the Spartans had not fought Philip, their allies in the Peloponnese had eagerly sought his support to preserve their independence. In 333 BC Sparta was the only major city willing to negotiate with the Persians.[13]

Yet Sparta rarely acted quickly. For the moment the offensive in the Aegean was disturbing enough for Alexander to reverse his decision to manage without a fleet, something it was easier for him to afford now that he had the revenue from Asia Minor. Otherwise his strategy was unchanged, his army still overrunning more and more territory and not showing the slightest inclination to return home. Darius could not ignore this. By the summer of 333 BC he had amassed a large army near Babylon in the heartland of his empire. The sources estimate its size as from 400,000 to 600,000 men, and he had not had the time or inclination to call on some of the most distant regions in the east of his empire to supply troops. Although such numbers must be taken with more than a pinch of salt, this was a far larger and more formidable force than the one Alexander had encountered at the Granicus. In the fifteen months or so since crossing to Asia, Alexander had overrun an area as large as all of Philip's conquests in Thrace and the Balkans, but this was still no more than a tiny part of Darius's empire.[14]

Darius began the long journey toward an enemy who was still hundreds of miles away on the Mediterranean coast. With him went his close family, including his mother, wife, and children, and there were also families following many of his officers and soldiers, as well as servants and attendants; these noncombatants added to the number of mouths to feed, perhaps equaling or even surpassing the total of soldiers. The ability to control and supply this great mass of humanity illustrates the power of the Persian Empire and its capacity to organize, although there is a good chance that it split into several sections, at least for the early stages of the march. However it was done, the journey of some 700 miles took months to complete and the news of the king's advance soon spread. By the autumn it was known at Athens, and Demosthenes gleefully predicted that the Macedonians would be trampled under the hooves of the Persian cavalry.[15]

Assembling a great army was one thing, and using it successfully was another. Hindsight tells us—as it did many ancient authors—that facing Alexander the Great and his Macedonians in a pitched battle was unwise. Just as Memnon was supposed to have recommended avoiding battle and starving the enemy in 334 BC, other Greeks are credited with voicing similarly "wise" counsel a year later. Charidemus, the mercenary leader become Athenian citizen who had fled to Persia rather than surrender to Alexander after the fall of Thebes, was especially vocal. He urged Darius and the bulk of his army to stay well away from the Macedonians and to instead send a detachment—allegedly 100,000 men including 30,000 Greek mercenaries—to deal with the enemy, hinting that he was the best man to command. Doubts were raised about the Greek's loyalty as well as his plan, and it would have been strange after raising such a great army only to employ part of it. Numbers were on Darius's side, however large his army actually was, and in many ways were his greatest advantage. Charidemus responded with more vigor than sense to the noblemen who spoke against him, doubting Persian manhood and courage. Abuse was every-day in Athenian public life but was not the etiquette of the king of king's court, and Darius ordered his execution. Diodorus claims that the mercenary was defiant to the end and shouted out that the king would regret killing him and soon witness the destruction of his own kingdom.[16]

The route into Cilicia chosen by Alexander followed one of the main Persian roads and led to the Cilician Gates, a pass through the mountains where at one point the track was barely wide enough for three or four men to march abreast. There were Persian troops already there, so Alexander halted his march some distance away and gave every sign of settling down for the night. The place was known as the camp of Cyrus, for it had been used by the usurper's army at the end of the fifth century including Xenophon and the Ten Thousand, and the association probably pleased Alexander and his officers. (It certainly pleased Arrian, who in another work styled himself as "Xenophon.") Hoping that the enemy would relax their guard, under cover of darkness Alexander led out the usual strike force of the hypaspists, Agrianians, and archers, and hurried straight at the pass. They did not go unnoticed, but the aggression and allegedly the realization that Alexander was coming in person broke the nerve of the garrison. The Persians were outnumbered, and more importantly had no prospect of relief by a larger force however long they managed to hold out, so quite reasonably they fled. News arrived from the citizens of Tarsus that the local satrap also planned to flee, and they feared that he would sack the city before he went. Alexander took cavalry and light troops and appeared so quickly that the satrap ran off before he could do any harm.[17]

The river Cydnus flows through Tarsus to the sea. Almost three centuries later Cleopatra would come here on her fabulous barge to meet Mark Antony, in a scene so wonderfully conjured by Plutarch and Shakespeare. In the ancient world the river was known for its clear and very chilly water. Tired, sweat-stained, and hot from the hard ride to secure the city, Alexander plunged in for a swim, only to be seized by cramps, and by the time he was hauled out he had succumbed to fever. Perhaps the shock was too much for his system after more than a year of marching, riding, and fighting over rugged country in all weathers, or perhaps an infection he had already caught happened to break out at this moment. Either way the king was seriously ill, unable to sleep properly, and seemed on the brink of death. There was no clear heir with the army and it was deep in enemy territory, adding to all the nervousness inevitable at a time of succession to the Argead throne. Harpalus, one of Alexander's friends who had been exiled by Philip after the Pixodarus affair, was prevented from fighting due to poor health—perhaps a physical handicap—and instead served as the senior treasurer. In these uncertain times, he chose to flee, taking some of the money with him. In the long run Alexander did not hold it against his old friend, for Harpalus returned and was reinstated in 331 BC.

That was for the future, and for the moment the treasurer was not the only one to despair of Alexander's life. We are told that all save one of the royal physicians was unwilling to treat the king, fearing that they would be blamed and punished when he died. The exception was Philip, an Acarnanian who had tended to the king since he was a boy. He suggested the drastic remedy of a purge and the king, always fascinated by medicine, agreed. As is so often the case, the tradition for what happened is confused, but it claims that Parmenio sent a message warning Alexander of a report that Philip had been bribed by Darius to assassinate the king. This is supposed to have arrived as the doctor was making up a potion. Alexander took the cup and handed the letter to Philip. As the doctor read the accusation, the king drained the draft to show his trust in a man he had known since childhood. At first the patient grew much worse, and Philip applied poultices and other treatments; after a little while Alexander recovered, whether from the cure or simply through his robust constitution.[18]

Illness kept Alexander off his feet and inactive for a month or so as summer faded into autumn 333 BC. Apart from the sieges of Miletus and Halicarnassus, it was the longest he had stayed in one place since landing in Asia. The Cilician plain, although encircled by mountain ranges, was famed for its rich soil, and as the harvest had come in, there was plenty of food to provide for the army. By the end of September Alexander was active once more, overrunning more of Cilicia, extracting 200 talents from Soli for its alleged Persian sympathy, while treating Mallus far more generously. He passed Anchialus, founded by an Assyrian king, whose great monument lay near the decaying walls. The king was shown clapping or snapping his fingers, the inscription boasting that he had built Anchialus and Tarsus in a single day, and advised onlookers to eat, drink, and make love, for in comparison anything they did would not amount to the sound the king made with his hands. Alexander spent a week putting on a show of force for the tribes of the Taurus Mountains, who were often enthusiastic raiders, before returning to Soli to celebrate a festival and sacrifice to Aesculapius, the god of healing, for his recovery. News had arrived that Darius had formed a great army and was advancing, but the current location of the Persians was unknown. However, there was good news of local victories by the Macedonian officers tasked with protecting Asia Minor. Encouraged, and from the start eager to meet the Persians head on, Alexander resumed his advance.[19]

18

"THEN TRULY THERE WAS GREAT BLOODSHED": THE BATTLE OF ISSUS, 333 BC

A narrow strip of coastal plain led into Syria, fringed by mountain ranges that an army could only cross via one of three routes. Parmenio had gone ahead to secure the entrances to these, taking with him most of the non-Macedonian troops. Alexander busied himself in Cilicia, clearly feeling it safe for his army to be divided for the moment, until news arrived that Darius and his army were at Sochi in Syria, far nearer than he had suspected, and not far from the pass near the Pillar of Jonah. He hurried to reunite the army, and then together with Parmenio's men he advanced to Issus, where a depot was established for the heavier baggage, and the wounded and sick left behind. The king discussed with his officers whether it was better to wait for the Persians to come to them or to advance, and all seem to have favored aggression. That meant taking one of the three passes, and Alexander decided to head to the southernmost, perhaps because this would keep him by the sea for the longest, allowing bulkier supplies to be brought by water. The Macedonians reached Myriandrus, where a savage overnight storm stalled the advance short of the pass. Then the news came in that Darius and his army were behind them, only some 100 stades (about 12.5 miles) away.[1]

Alexander did not believe it and sent trusted Companions aboard a thirty-oared light warship to investigate. Sailing north, they sighted the vast Persian encampment near the mouth of the river Pinarus, and only when they returned did the king accept the fact that the enemy had outmaneuvered him. It was not by design, for neither side had had much idea of what the other was doing or intending. Darius had waited for some time at Sochi, planning to let the Macedonians come to him so that he could pick a battlefield in the open plains of Syria, where his far greater numbers, especially in cavalry, should give him the advantage. Had he waited even longer, then Alexander probably would have obliged, but the Persians were puzzled by the Macedonians' long halt at Tarsus and the operations in Cilicia, and wondered whether the enemy was frightened to engage. Darius had a much larger army, which made it all the harder to be cautious, especially as the autumn was passing. Even the bureaucracy of the Persian empire would struggle to supply so many people and animals if they stayed for a long time in one place, or remained in the field during the winter.[2]

A Macedonian exile still urged caution, arguing that to push into the narrow coastal plain was likely to favor Alexander's smaller and more nimble army—or at least so it is claimed by our sources. Darius would not listen and refused to wait any longer. He sent much of his cumbersome baggage train and treasury away to safety at Damascus, although this still left the royal household and many other luxuries and noncombatants with the main force. Then he advanced, heading through the northernmost of the three passes and not realizing that Alexander had already passed by until he reached the coastal plain. At Issus he captured the Macedonian depot, executing or maiming the sick and wounded he found there. Like Alexander's massacre of the mercenaries at Granicus, such atrocities were risky, since they might as easily enrage as terrify the enemy. Then Darius followed the Macedonians, looking for a good place to fight.[3]

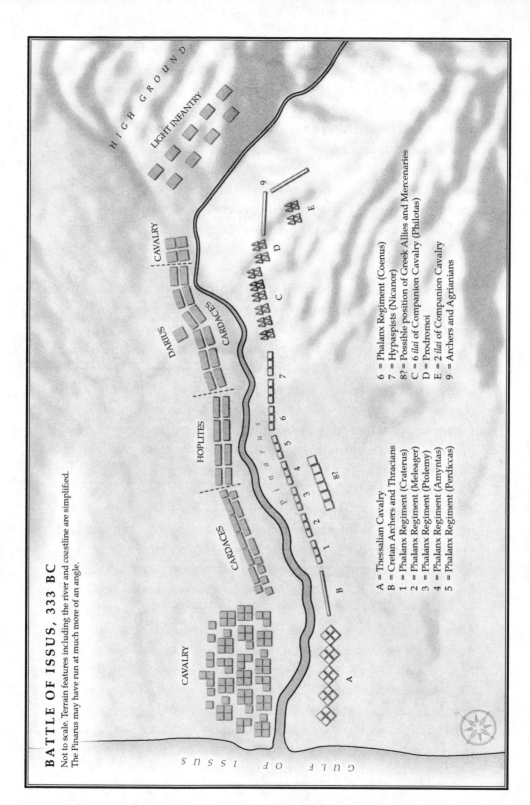

BATTLE OF ISSUS, 333 BC

Not to scale. Terrain features including the river and coastline are simplified.
The Pinarus may have run at much more of an angle.

A = Thessalian Cavalry
B = Cretan Archers and Thracians
1 = Phalanx Regiment (Craterus)
2 = Phalanx Regiment (Meleager)
3 = Phalanx Regiment (Ptolemy)
4 = Phalanx Regiment (Amyntas)
5 = Phalanx Regiment (Perdiccas)

6 = Phalanx Regiment (Coenus)
7 = Hypaspists (Nicanor)
8? = Possible position of Greek Allies and Mercenaries
C = 6 *ilai* of Companion Cavalry (Philotas)
D = Prodromoi
E = 2 *ilai* of Companion Cavalry
9 = Archers and Agrianians

When the presence of the enemy was confirmed, Alexander summoned his senior officers and unit commanders and gave them a pep talk. He assured them that the narrow ground between the mountains and the sea was in their favor, big enough for their pike phalanx and too small for the enemy hordes. These were Persians, men they had beaten before, and more than that mere slaves instead of free men, while even Darius's Greek mercenaries lacked the motivation of those fighting for their own just cause. If the famous Ten Thousand had routed the Persians so many times, what could they not do with their greater numbers, and the might of Macedonians, Thessalians, and Greeks united with the most martial tribes of Europe. Victory over Darius would bring far greater rewards than beating his satraps. Arrian records that "he also told them of anything else which at such a time, before dangers, a brave general would naturally tell brave men by way of encouragement. They crowded round and clasped their king's hand, and with cries of encouragement urged him to lead them on at once."[4]

Alexander had no real choice other than to fight, for retreating with the enemy so close was dangerous, and would shatter his prestige and lower morale, not to mention risk running out of supplies. His aim was to face Darius and thrash him, not to escape like Xenophon and the Ten Thousand. The confidence he exuded was genuine, based on trust in himself and his soldiers and the simple fact that there would have been no point launching the invasion if he refused the chance to fight when Darius had at last appeared. A battle there must now be, and it was bound to come soon with the armies such a short distance apart. That did not mean that he had to rush. Alexander dismissed his officers and ordered the men to rest and eat a good hot meal. Scouting parties were sent north to the Jonah Pass to see whether the enemy was approaching. Learning that they were not, as the sun set he led the army out of camp. After about eight miles the pass was secure and the Macedonians halted. Outposts were set to maintain a careful watch, while everyone else slept as best they could.[5]

At dawn the Macedonians started to descend onto the flat plain beside the sea, so that they were some five miles away from the Persians. Darius had not moved from his position on the north of the river Pinarus. (The identity of this waterway has attracted a good deal of debate, but by far the best candidate is the modern Payas. In spite of the modern name for this battle, it was not fought near Issus itself.) It is not clear when the Persian king realized that Alexander was planning to attack him, although at some point his men began to strengthen the north bank of the river with some simple field fortifications, perhaps no more than lines of sharpened stakes. According to our sources Darius had massed no fewer than 30,000 Greek mercenaries, including the ones who had served with the fleet under Memnon and his successors. This seriously weakened the offensive in the Aegean, but that would not matter if Darius defeated Alexander's army, so it was sensible for him to have as many hoplites as he could get. There is a fair chance that these forces of "Greek" mercenaries included contingents of Carians and others who had adopted hoplite equipment and tactics and were equally formidable. Even so, the total may be exaggerated, and the figure of 60,000 Kardakes, Persian infantrymen who fought in close order, is probably also too high. There were also supposedly 30,000 or more horsemen, many of them heavily armored, and even more numerous contingents of light infantry and archers.[6]

The sources say little about Alexander's numbers, although they do tell us that most of his field army was present, leading scholars to estimate a force of between 30,000 and 45,000, usually working on the assumption that most contingents remained at full strength. The problem is that there is no information about the rate of attrition suffered by the army since the start of its operations, of how many men were detached or how many were left behind—not just at Issus but elsewhere—until they recovered from injury or disease. Therefore we have no idea whether the new contingents brought from Macedonia were sufficient to replace losses or were an actual reinforcement. The lesson of history is that few military units manage to stay at their theoretical strength for very long, and we should be wary of assuming that Alexander's army was an exception. Whatever the details, the balance of probability is that Alexander's men were heavily outnumbered by an enemy army perhaps two or three times larger at the very least.[7]

Where the Macedonians came down the coastal plain was narrow, forcing them to keep to a marching column. Neither army could see the other, although before too long the Persians saw the cloud of dust rising above their opponents as they advanced. Alexander's scouts rode ahead and spotted the waiting enemy when they were some thirty stades distant (3.75 miles). Darius made no aggressive moves, other than to send cavalry and light infantry to screen his army. Gradually the open country widened and the Macedonians could start to deploy. Alexander led with his heavy infantry, confident that a phalanx had little to fear from a frontal attack by horsemen, even if the Persian screening force became aggressive.[8]

Once there was sufficient space, each individual regiment of hypaspists and pike phalanx formed up thirty-two ranks deep. At full strength this would give a regiment (*taxis*) a frontage of forty-eight men. Contrary to most modern accounts, the entire phalanx was not in a single block, and the maneuvers that followed only make sense if the units were distinct, each with room on either side to change into shallower and wider formations. As the plain widened, more and more regiments were able to come up alongside. There were frequent halts to dress formations and keep the proper distances as well as to judge better the space available. Alexander and his officers closely supervised the march. Undulations in the ground meant that for much of the time they remained invisible to the waiting enemy. At some point the formations halved their depth to sixteen ranks, and then finally to the standard eight ranks, a move that again required more than adequate empty space between each unit before the drill was performed. The march was one of distinct blocks, with plenty of space between them, marching, halting, re-forming, marching again, and was a testament to much practice and skill on the part of soldiers and officers. Few armies in the ancient world could have managed such an ordered advance anywhere near as well as Alexander's men. As they pushed forward, the Persian screening force withdrew to rejoin the rest of Darius's army.[9]

This was a narrow battlefield given the number of soldiers on both sides. Callisthenes said that the distance along the river

Pinarus from the mountains in the east to the sea was fourteen stades (1.75 miles) and that the river ran diagonally across the plain. If the identification with the modern Payas is correct, then the shoreline has changed, for the distance is nearer 2.7 miles and near the sea the river's line is straighter; but it still remains a better fit than any of the other possibilities, and the river itself conforms well to the ancient description. Where it comes down from the mountains it flows quickly and "the sides of its bed were torn away." Except in a few places the banks were not much of an obstacle and the river was readily fordable, although the number of large and small boulders amid the sand and gravel of its bed meant that a horseman would need to go slowly and pick his way across. In the middle section of the plain the ground no longer slopes and the riverbed is more clearly defined, with banks that are higher and sometimes steep or overhanging, especially on the north side. After that it widens and flows more gently into the sea and is easy to ford, even for troops in formation.[10]

As the Persian covering screen withdrew, Darius concentrated the bulk of his cavalry on his right wing, nearest the sea, where the river was not a significant obstacle. His center was formed from the mercenary hoplites, with Kardakes on either flank, each group supposedly numbering 30,000 men. Archers supported them, where possible on rising ground behind the formed infantry. The king, resplendently clad and riding in an ornate chariot, was also in the center, for this was the proper place for a Persian king, and he had some 3,000 of his best cavalry nearby as escort. There were some cavalry on the Persian left, as well as light infantry, and behind the main line supposedly hordes of lesser troops. Very large numbers of skirmishers were on the high ground on the extreme left, poised to edge around the Macedonian flank. Both these men and the concentrated cavalry by the sea were ordered to make the only offensive moves, threatening Alexander on both wings. Everywhere else, the posture was entirely defensive. Darius planned to use the obstacle of the river and the dense formations of his close order infantry to stop the Macedonian attack. He did not need to destroy or rout Alexander, merely to stop him, for the young king had to win and win decisively. A draw, especially one with heavy losses, would leave the invaders stranded and discredited.

The sources claim that both sides modified their deployment as the Macedonians approached, but given the constricted plain, the sheer numbers of Persian troops, and the inexperience of the Persian army in operating together, Darius was surely unable to do very much. Alexander's advance took hours and his plan and deployment developed in careful stages. At its heart was the traditional and familiar marching order, the hypaspists in the lead, then the phalanx regiments in order of precedence for that day. These formed the center of the army, the hypaspists in the place of honor on the right, then the pike regiments; once they were eight deep, they stretched for a mile or so depending on how close they were to the theoretical strength of 12,000 and the size of the small intervals maintained between each unit. For a long time the cavalry kept behind the phalanx, partly because the ground was so restricted and perhaps also to avoid an early combat with the Persian screening force. Then Alexander sent the mercenary and allied cavalry to form his left wing, nearest the sea, supported by Thracian infantry and Cretan archers. For a while he kept the Thessalians and Companions together on the right, a concentration of his best horsemen not seen on any other occasion.

Seeing that Darius had placed so many of his own cavalry near the sea, and perhaps also realizing that the ground on his right flank was not ideal for cavalry, at least in the initial attack, Alexander sent the Thessalians to reinforce his left wing. They went behind the phalanx, and this and the dead ground kept them out of sight until they were in their new position. There were light infantry, including the tough Agrianian mountaineers and archers on his right, but seeing the Persians threatening this wing he reinforced them with mercenary hoplites backed by two squadrons of Companion cavalry. So far the Persian attempt to come around Alexander's right wing was cautious and the Agrianians, confident after so many victories and well used to operating on rough ground, pushed up into the foothills. This, and the menace of the Macedonian cavalry if these Persians came down from the hills onto the level ground, to all intents and purposes ended the threat on this wing.

The two armies were still some way apart, as the rest of the Persian army waited in its positions as instructed. Alexander kept his men in hand, still halting frequently to rest and tidy up the formation. It is impossible to march in perfect formation for any distance even over perfectly flat terrain, so this was sensible, allowing ranks to be dressed and units kept properly in line. The Persians waited and watched, the enemy sometimes disappearing into folds in the ground or hidden by dust, in the center the long sarissas held upright so that these could sometimes be seen even when the men could not. Alexander's men filled most of the width of the plain, so the Persian advantage in numbers would not seem so obvious, while the order and precision of the slow advance was in itself eerie and intimidating. Arrian says that when Alexander saw that the Persians were staying put and had strengthened the north bank with defenses, he realized that Darius was "in spirit a beaten man." Strategically the Persian king needed to do no more than not lose the battle, but such an attitude is scarcely inspiring. Morale counts for a great deal in warfare, and most of all in battles fought at such close range.[11]

That did not mean that the task confronting the Macedonians was an easy one. As at the Granicus, the Persian occupation of the riverbank would have been enough to deter most ancient armies from attacking at all. Darius may even have expected Alexander to halt and wait a day or more before attacking in the hope that the Persians would trust to their numerical superiority and attack him. Numbers and the ground were in the Persians' favor, but Alexander had nowhere to go and had either to fight here or retreat, aware that supplying his men would be extremely difficult with the Persians straddling his lines of communication. Always inclined to meet any real or imagined challenge, he could not decline this one. So the twenty-three-year-old Alexander rode up and down his line, talking to each unit in turn, addressing commanders by name, encouraging all ranks. Cheers greeted him, soldiers urging him to order the attack. Satisfied, the advance resumed, but he continued to restrain his men from surging forward and kept to a slow, steady pace "to avoid any part of the phalanx fluctuating in a more rapid advance and so breaking apart." Only when they came within range of the Persians' bows—200 yards at the most and less for effective range—did the attack begin.[12]

Alexander was in the lead, and almost every modern historian describes how he spurred his horse through the river at the head of the royal squadron and slammed into the Kardakes on the opposite bank. As at Chaeronea, it is simply assumed that Alexander always charged on horseback—just as he supposedly always tried to extend his right and open a gap in the enemy line (as he would do at Gaugamela two years later). Yet Arrian's account suggests that this time he began the battle differently, as "those with Alexander and Alexander himself, stationed on the right, were the first indeed to rush into the river at a run . . . so that the rapidity of the attack terrified the Persians and the speed of coming to grips lessened the damage done by the archers." The Greek word for "at a run" (*dromo*) strongly suggests an infantry charge, and the logic of Arrian's entire description is that this was at the head of one of the battalions of hypaspists, consisting of Philip's own former royal guard. Infantry running to close with enemy archers and accepting that their formation would become ragged as the price for taking fewer missiles was a recognized tactic for the Romans. In this case the archers were protected behind the formed Kardakes, described as hoplites by Arrian, although elsewhere styled as peltasts, which probably means that they had slightly lighter armor and equipment than proper Greek hoplites. Almost as importantly, they did not come from a society with a long tradition celebrating the aggression of phalanx fighting, nor did they have the personal experience of war and victory of the veterans they faced. "Alexander rushed impetuously into the river, engaged in hand-to-hand fighting, and was already pushing out the Persians who were stationed there."[13]

In the center the Macedonian phalanx had a tougher time as they attacked the mercenaries ensconced behind the strongest parts of the bank. A large phalanx was always inclined to break up in a long advance, and now the charge—and even more the crossing of the river—disrupted their formation. Gaps opened and units became confused as they tried to find a way up the north bank and reach the defenders. Exploiting the opportunity, in some places groups of mercenaries counterattacked, their spears handier in this situation than the longer sarissas. The regimental commander Ptolemy, son of Seleucas, died here, along with 120 pikemen as the attack stalled. Near the sea the Persian cavalry came through the river to attack, and the Thessalian and allied cavalry under Parmenio had a difficult time holding them in check. The fighting swayed back and forth in the way of cavalry combats, the restricted space making it hard for the Persian numbers to come fully into play.[14]

Alexander and the hypaspists drove back the Kardakes facing them. That created space on the north bank, permitting the Companions, Paeonians, and other horsemen to walk their mounts across the river and form up on the far side. The king left the fighting line and joined the Companions, jumping onto the back of Bucephalus or one of his other horses. He then led them into a new attack, not pushing straight forward but slanting toward the enemy center, as some of the hypaspists and the closest pikemen were starting to do. Cavalry did not do well in frontal charges against decent close-order infantry—which is another reason why an initial charge on horseback is unlikely—but could be devastating coming in from the flank.

The Persian center began to break up. Alexander headed toward Darius, fighting a fierce combat against cavalry led by the Persian king's brother. It may have been here that he took a sword wound in the thigh, and it is probably the confrontation between the two kings that was depicted in the famous painting later reproduced as a mosaic at Pompeii. Interpreting art is inevitably subjective, and some would see an artist's sympathy for the Persian faced with a rampaging Alexander in the work, while others see only a celebration of Macedonian triumph. What mattered was that Darius fled, abandoning chariot, cloak, and equipment, and escaped. It was a blow to his prestige, but not a fatal one, for he remained king of kings with huge resources at his beck and call. He escaped to fight another day, as did some of his army.

The mercenaries formed into groups that stuck together and still showed fight, deterring all but the boldest of pursuers, while the other Macedonians hunted for easier prey. After the slow advance and the fighting, the day was long spent by the time the battle was over, and although the pursuit lasted into the early night, darkness and the relatively small number of Macedonian and allied cavalry limited the damage inflicted. Even so it was appalling, for the dream of any mounted soldier is a fleeing and helpless enemy who can be slaughtered at will. The memory even for the victors assumed a nightmarish quality, so that in his history Ptolemy later claimed to remember crossing a gully on a mound of enemy dead. Arrian claims 100,000 Persians died, a figure in keeping with the vast totals for the entire army and no doubt inflated. The Macedonian losses were also very heavy, although in this case Arrian does not give an overall total. Other sources suggest that about 450 died, a third of them cavalry, and 4,500 were wounded, producing overall casualties of 12–16.5 percent.[15]

Issus was not a subtle battle, but a head-to-head slog on a narrow frontage for armies of this size, where success came because the Macedonian army was more skillful, more confident, and better led. Alexander took great care in the approach and preparations for the attack, and once the breakthrough occurred, he exploited it. This was less about grand tactics than the small details of the battle. Leading an infantry and then cavalry charge in person suggests he did more than in other battles, although as always he relied heavily on his officers to do the right thing and keep on attacking on their own initiative since he could not direct them while he was doing this. They did not let him down, and neither did his soldiers, while he again displayed the courage and skill expected of the son of Philip. Compared to Granicus, this was a far more important battle and a far greater success, for Darius and his great army had been routed. For Alexander this was all another big step out of Philip's shadow.

Once again Alexander went to visit his wounded, talking to them, encouraging and praising, and listening to their stories. Given the sheer numbers this took a lot of time, but was a mark of his care and reinforced the sense—already deep-rooted in Macedonian society—that they were comrades regardless of rank. His own wound was a visible reminder of the part he had played, although it does not appear to have been serious. A parade to witness the honorable burial of the fallen gave the opportunity for mourning amid pomp and ceremony celebrating the victory.[16]

The Persian camp was overrun during the pursuit. Even though Darius had sent much of the baggage to Damascus, the luxuries they found still staggered the excited Macedonian soldiers. Alexander returned from the pursuit, bandaged and covered in dust and sweat and spent the night in Darius's tent after first washing in Darius's bath—only to be corrected by one of his Companions who pointed out that this was now "Alexander's bath." Seeing all the luxuries of Darius's campaign tent, Alexander archly commented, "This, as it would seem, is to be a king." The sound of wailing came from close by, and asking what this was, he was told that it was Darius's mother, wife, and children, who believed that he had been killed. Alexander sent one of his staff to assure the royal family that Darius was alive and free, and that they were all safe and would receive every honor from him.[17]

This encounter became famous, allowing plenty of romantic embellishment. Some said that on the next day Alexander went in person to see the women, who mistook his taller friend Hephaestion for the king. They were embarrassed when their mistake was explained, but Alexander told them not to be concerned for "Hephaestion was also an Alexander." Darius's infant son was supposed to have come boldly to the conqueror, allowing a scathing comparison with his "cowardly" father. Alexander was true to his word in treating the Persian king's family with generosity and respect, and his refusal to abuse his power was much praised as a sign of his virtue and self-control, not least because Darius's wife Stateira was accounted one of the most beautiful women of her day. In later versions, Alexander is supposed to have refused ever to see her or hear about her beauty, and there was great admiration for his restraint and respect in his dealings with women. Yet there is one jarring note in the tradition. Stateira subsequently died, and our sources date this to 331 BC, while Justin and Plutarch both claim that this was after a miscarriage. The dating may be wrong, as may the cause of death, and no source comments that the story conflicts with the earlier tales of restraint. An element of mystery must remain, and we are unlikely ever to know whether Stateira really became pregnant after her capture, whether this was seduction or rape, and if so whether Alexander or someone else was the father.[18]

There was a good deal of wealth in Darius's camp, and even larger amounts were acquired when Parmenio and a fast-moving column overran Damascus before the main treasury and baggage train could be evacuated. Among the captives taken was Barsine, Memnon's widow, and Parmenio sent her to his king. Alexander must have encountered her while she and her father were refugees at Philip's court following the satraps' revolt, and she was his own age or a little older, attractive, intelligent, and comfortable in Greek language and culture as well as those of Asia and the Persian court. Perhaps the young prince had liked or been attracted to her years before, or Parmenio was simply a good judge of his inclinations, for Alexander took her as his mistress. Plutarch preserves the tradition that Barsine was the first woman Alexander took as a lover, and she remained his mistress for a long time, giving him a son. Little more is known about the relationship, but she appears never to have altogether fallen from favor. As a rule Alexander did not welcome gifts of prospective lovers, angrily replying to subordinates when they sent him handsome boys, so the incident suggests that Parmenio had a surer feel for the king's mood than many others. It is interesting that the Issus campaign has no story of the young monarch overruling the cautious advice of the veteran, and instead Parmenio led all the most important independent operations and controlled the left of the army during the battle itself.[19]

In the months after his defeat, Darius communicated directly with Alexander for the first time. This in itself acknowledged Alexander as more than a mere barbarian raider, and the Persian offered alliance as well as a large ransom for his captured family, but not permanent grant of territory. Alexander's response was to reiterate the justice of the Greek cause in seeking vengeance and accuse Darius of involvement in Philip's murder. His victories showed that the gods approved, and the lands he had taken were now his, their inhabitants and the prisoners he had taken his subjects, to be cared for as a good king should. Asia was his, so Darius must address him as its lord, and not dare to treat him as if he was an equal, but come as a suppliant, for "if you claim the kingship, stand your ground and fight for it and do not flee, as I shall pursue you wherever you are."[20]

Philip is shown as a mature man on this gold medallion, bearded and his brow furrowed, but with none of his many battle scars.

CPA Media Pte Ltd / Alamy Stock Photo.

Pella became the main center for Macedonian king's before Philip's day. Unlike southern Greek cities, it is dominated by grand royal buildings.

DEA / ARCHIVIO J. LANGE / Getty Images.

Vergina remained an important royal center, especially for ritual. It was in the theater at Vergina that Philip was murdered. *AKG / De Agostini Picture Lib.*

The clash of two hoplite phalanxes was the grandest and most prestigious form of warfare for Greek communities, but was extremely difficult to depict artistically.

Public Domain.

For all the dominance of hoplite battles, sieges did occur, usually at great cost to the civilian population. Note the woman within the city, her arms raised in appeal.

Adam Eastland Art + Architecture / Alamy Stock Photo.

Athens was the largest and wealthiest city in southern Greece, as well as a radical democracy. Male citizens assembled here, in the Pnyx, to debate and vote.

Hercules Milas / Alamy Stock Photo.

The trireme with its three banks of oars was the dominant warship of the fourth century BC, and its fleet gave Athens great importance. *AKG / John Hios.*

Instead of hoplite spears, Philip equipped most of his heavy infantry with the sarissa, a pike held two-handed that required very close formation.

© Look and Learn / Bridgeman Images.

This bust shows the classic image of Alexander—young, clean shaven, with tousled hair and head slightly to one side.

Jastrow (2006) / Wiki Commons.

This wall painting from a royal tomb at Vergina shows Hades, god of the underworld, abducting Persephone. Both are shown with reddish-brown hair. *Public Domain.*

This ornate shield was found in Tomb II at Vergina, which is often associated with Philip.

De Agostini Picture Library / Bridgeman Images.

Is this the face of Philip? The reconstruction is based on cremated skull fragments found in Tomb II.

Creative Commons_Manolis Andronikos.

Demosthenes was revered as one of the greatest orators ever produced by Athens. In opposition to Philip he found the great cause of his life.

Ullstein bild Dtl. / Getty Images.

The Lion monument at Chaeronea stood over a cemetery containing more than 250 skeletons of men killed in the battle in 338 BC and is assumed to have been set up by Thebes. *Hercules Milas / Alamy Stock Photo.*

Alexander confronts Darius in the midst of a great battle in this Roman era mosaic copied from a Greek original, which many claim depicts the battle of Issus. *Creative Commons-Lucas.*

A mosaic from Pella showing a lion hunt. The heroically nude youths may be royal pages or perhaps even Alexander and one of his Companions.

AKG / De Agostini Picture Lib.

This depiction of Alexander in battle against the Persians comes from the so-called Alexander sarcophagus. Note the lion skin headgear, associating him with his ancestor Heracles. *Creative Commons-Ronald Slabke*.

Tyre in the early twentieth century. Over time, the mole built by Alexander's engineers to assault the city grew into a permanent isthmus. *Library of Congress*.

Remains of the circular Philippeion at Olympia. The monument proclaimed Philip's power and the strength of his dynasty and included a statue of his heir, Alexander.

Classic Image / Alamy Stock Photo.

The palaces at the Persian royal city of Persepolis were far grander than anything in Macedonia or Greece, physically representing the power and wealth of the king of kings. *Victor Sanchez / Alamy Stock Photo.*

Visitors ascended to the palace on great stairs, decorated by images of the king's many and ethnically diverse subjects bringing tribute from his vast realm.

Sergey Strelkov / Alamy Stock Photo.

Cyrus was the founder of the Persian Empire, and Alexander chose to make a show of respect to his memory, visiting his tomb. *Leonid Andronov / Alamy Stock Photo.*

There are more contemporary depictions of Alexander's victory in India than any of his other campaigns, with an emphasis on the mighty war elephants used by the enemy.

This gold quiver and bowcase from Tomb II at Vergina is of the style used by the Scythians, which may or may not have belonged to the woman interred there.

This gold medallion may depict Olympias, one of Philip's wives and the mother of Alexander. She was clearly a strong individual, but the truth is hard to find amid all the hostile propaganda. *AKG / De Agostini Picture Lib. / A. Dagli Orti.*

A terracotta from Amphipolis showing a woman with her head covered. Such coverings and fuller veils were common for noble women in many Greek communities. *Hercules Milas / Alamy Stock Photo.*

19

"MANIFESTLY A LARGE TASK": THE SIEGE OF TYRE

The war was going well. Issus was the largest battle yet fought by the army created by Philip and honed by Alexander, and the spoils of victory were commensurately huge, on a scale unlike anything won by the Macedonians—or for that matter any Greek army—in past campaigns. Arrian claims that they found 3,000 talents of gold and silver in the camp as well as the greater wealth of the main baggage train at Damascus, which Curtius lists as 2,600 talents in coin, plus 500 pounds of wrought silver, gold cups weighing 4,500 pounds, and others inlaid with jewels weighing 3,400 pounds. This may represent the official figures for the spoils acquired by Alexander, and a good deal was taken by the soldiers and may never have been collected for formal distribution. The Thessalians were said to have done especially well at Damascus, and were selected for the mission as a reward for their courage. Apart from gold and silver there were other luxuries of all kinds, including incense and silks, and ceremonial robes. During the thwarted attempt to carry off the baggage before Parmenio arrived, the bearers had wrapped themselves in purple robes in an effort to stave off the winter cold.[1]

Some 30,000 bearers and other servants were captured, along with 7,000 pack animals, all highly welcome additions to the Macedonian supply train. Less practical, if more visible, were Darius's 329 concubines, most musically trained, and nearly 300 servants skilled in preparing food and drink. One especially exquisite casket formerly owned by Darius was brought to Alexander, who after some deliberation and discussion with his Companions used it to house the manuscript of the *Iliad* prepared for him by Aristotle. From now on, this was placed under his bed at night to provide inspiration and solace, along with a sharp knife in case of more dangerous emergencies.

Like his father, Alexander was generous in sharing the spoils, and many luxuries went home, especially to his mother and sister. He also made a pointedly lavish gift of incense to Leonidas, suggesting that his former tutor no longer be so stingy in his offerings to the gods. His officers did especially well, but so did the soldiers, many acquiring slaves and especially women as companions. The women had no choice, and initial encounters were surely often rape or the acceptance of one master for protection rather than be subject to attacks from anyone. Over time, especially when the unions produced children, human nature will have softened at least some relationships, although how many of the women were ever granted something like the status of true wives is hard to say. Marriage was respected, and Alexander was severe in his judgment when two Macedonians were accused of seducing the wives of some mercenaries, but the status of mistresses was a lot less certain.[2]

Among the prisoners taken at Damascus were Theban, Spartan, and Athenian envoys to Darius, although whether the latter were formal representatives of their polis or politicians acting on their own initiative is unclear. Parmenio sent them all to Alexander given the political implications, and the king dealt with each in turn. The Thebans were released, the king declaring publicly that anyone whose city had been destroyed had a right to seek help wherever they could, and privately because they included a nobleman with ties of guest friendship to his family as well as an Olympic winner. The Athenian was the son and namesake of Iphicrates and was kept with the king, but treated with honor and friendship out of

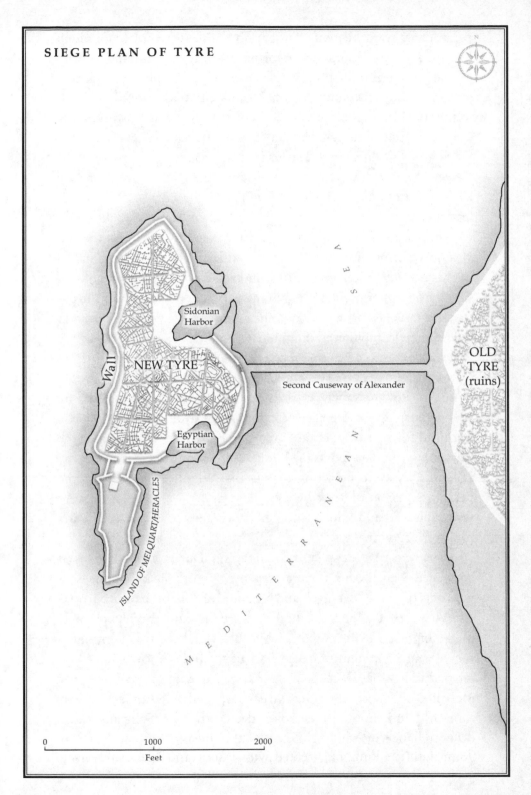

SIEGE PLAN OF TYRE

N

Sidonian
Harbor

Wall

NEW TYRE

Egyptian
Harbor

ISLAND OF MELQUART/HERACLES

Second Causeway of Alexander

OLD
TYRE
(ruins)

S
E
A

M E D I T E R R A N E A N

0   1000   2000
Feet

respect and gratitude to the father and politically prudent goodwill toward Athens. He was to die of natural causes at some point in the next few years without ever returning home. The Spartan was more formally held under arrest, for his city had not only refused to join the alliance of the Greeks against Persia, but was becoming openly hostile, although Alexander may not have known just how far Sparta's dealings with Darius had developed.[3]

Apart from the envoy at Damascus, late in 333 BC King Agis III of Sparta sailed to rendezvous with Pharnabazus and the other leaders of the Persian fleet at the island of Siphnos, asking for warships and money to use against Macedon. The unexpected and devastating news of the disaster at Issus dampened the mood of the meeting, and Agis got just ten triremes and thirty talents of silver. These were sent to his younger brother and fellow king— the Spartans always had two kings simultaneously—to be used in the ongoing campaign to dominate Crete, while Agis kept near the Persian fleet in the hope of more substantial aid. The majority of Greek mercenaries had escaped from the defeat at Issus, but only a minority of the survivors stayed with Darius. Most escaped by sea, wantonly burning the transport ships and triremes they did not need for fear of pursuit. Some 4,000 went to Egypt under the leadership of an exiled Macedonian and tried to seize it, claiming, at least at first, to be acting for Darius. Whether true or not, the Persian garrison did not believe them and the mercenaries were soon defeated and killed. Another contingent of 8,000 eventually took service with Agis.[4]

Issus was a great victory, damaging Darius's prestige as it enhanced Alexander's fame and people's faith in his chances of winning the war. Even so, and in spite of all the captured treasure, the Persian king still had vast wealth and the greater part of his empire to draw upon, while his warships still dominated the Aegean. Mainland Greece had never been known for long-term stability or peace, and if Sparta did commit to open war then it could pose a serious threat, especially if funded by Persian gold and should other poleis decide that the Spartans had a decent chance of winning. None of this meant that the war was going badly for Alexander, because it was not—it simply meant that it could still turn sour. Hindsight tells us that within a year the Persian naval offensive against the Greek islands would collapse, but Alexander and his commanders could not know this. Some of the signs were encouraging, for the withdrawal of the mercenaries to fight at Issus had taken some of the power out of the naval campaign, while the loyalty of many of Darius's naval allies was wavering as the Macedonians overran or threatened their home cities. The wealth won after Issus also meant that Alexander could hire more and more mercenaries and soak up some of the men who might otherwise be available for the Spartans or anyone else to hire. On the other hand, the Persians still controlled most of the key Aegean islands, which threatened the Dardanelles and the coast of Caria, while the Macedonians had not yet reassembled a big enough fleet to challenge them at sea.[5]

Darius retreated east beyond the Euphrates into the heartland of his kingdom and Alexander did not pursue him. Advancing so far into Persia would have been dangerous, for the distances were immense. Even the raid to take Damascus and the enemy baggage train meant sending Parmenio's detachment some 200 miles from the main force. Darius was unlikely to risk another battle until he had assembled a new army, and this was bound to take many months. Killing or capturing the king was not in itself enough to win the war and the empire, for it did not mean that all Persians would submit and most likely would simply mean the proclamation of a new king and the continuation of the war. There were also great risks in driving so deeply into the empire where the Macedonians might find themselves struggling to find food, especially in the winter months, and cut off from reinforcement.[6]

Alexander's boldness and personal heroism can all too easily mask the methodical way in which he waged war, and much that seems reckless was based on a careful judgment and balancing of the risks against the potential gains and the available options. From the initial landing in Asia it was clear that he was aiming at permanent conquest and occupation of new territory, although we cannot know how large an area he planned to take in the long run or whether he had fixed objectives in this respect. While he bypassed some cities and strongholds, these were always a small minority, and each was invariably left isolated and masked or surrounded by communities that had submitted to him. His own satraps and other commanders were appointed to oversee each region, but as the new conquests grew in size the number of soldiers who could be spared from his field army meant that garrisons were small and had to watch over wide areas as best they could. They managed to deal with local forces and small Persian detachments, including fragments of the army from Issus, albeit in the last case only after considerable effort and hard fighting. They were not sufficiently strong to have dealt with any major offensive, and as far as possible Alexander kept to a minimum the occupation of territory that would border on any serious threat.

Politics as much as military considerations shaped everything Alexander did in these years, just as it had for Philip. He needed communities to accept his rule and prefer it to renewing the war whether on Persia's behalf or for their own independence, ideally to the extent of fighting against any neighbors who were inclined to oppose him. Some of this relied on the fear of his army and the savagery of the punishments he was willing and able to inflict, and the rest on his reputation for fairness, even generosity. Centuries later the Roman commander Sulla chose as his own epitaph that there was never a better friend or worse enemy, and this was the essence of power politics in the ancient world. Communities were treated well or harshly in direct relation to the respect they showed to Alexander. His strategy of defeating Persian sea power by capturing its bases on land made this all the more urgent. The Phoenicians were at the heart of any Persian fleet, both in numbers and quality of ships and crews. After Issus, their cities were within reach and needed to be shown Alexander's power. His eyes were already looking even further toward Egypt, which had never truly accepted Persian rule, and he was probably already in contact with leaders there. Egypt was valuable in its own right, for its grain, other wealth, and sheer fame. It was also a wonderful opportunity to show that Alexander welcomed submission and treated those who came to him very well. If he ignored the appeal of leaders in Egypt, then why should other communities defect? For the moment Darius was not an immediate threat, and Alexander could focus on conquest and securing the lands he had already taken.[7]

Near the end of 333 BC Alexander took the main force south along the coast into what is now Lebanon. Parmenio stayed behind and operated on his own, as did other commanders, although as usual we hear almost nothing about their activities. Antigonus Gonatus—the One-Eyed—fought and won three actions in Asia Minor during the months to come, although we probably only know about this because after Alexander's death he became one of the key players in the struggle for succession. About fifty years old, he was another of Philip's men, old in war and still the backbone of the army, but the young king and his contemporaries were learning fast, their confidence soaring with each victory.[8]

At first the appearance of Alexander and the reports of his triumph at Issus made for speedy progress. King Straton of the island of Aradus and leader of several other Phoenician cities on the mainland nearby came to offer the conqueror a golden crown as a mark of submission. As he proceeded south, Byblus and the great city of Sidon went over to him, although in this case its king acted under pressure from the wider community. He was deposed, and Alexander had Hephaestion choose a replacement. In the end he settled on an obscure member of the royal family, who worked as a market gardener, and the story became famous as an illustration of the turns of fortune and the rewards of virtue. For the moment many ships from all these cities were still with the Persian fleet, and only time would tell whether the defection of their homeland would change this.[9]

The other major Phoenician community was Tyre, and soon afterward it sent envoys to Alexander offering submission, but when he arrived on shore opposite the island city, this was qualified as neutrality. He replied that he wished to sacrifice to Hercules— the main god of the Tyrians whom they knew as Melquart—in the temple in their city, using much the same ploy as Philip in his dealings with the Scythians. It was February, time of the main festival honoring the god and a time of great significance for the community. As usual on this sacred occasion there were envoys from distant Carthage, once a Tyrian colony and now prosperous and powerful in its own right, but still emotionally tied to the mother city. It was a reminder of Tyre's great past and its enduring importance.

Letting Alexander enter into Tyre at this time and preside over a sacrifice in the temple would acknowledge him as ruler and not simply an ally. The Tyrian king was with the Persian fleet, and his son acted in his place in the negotiations. The Tyrians were proud, and not long before had rebelled against Persia. This streak of independence more than any great loyalty to Darius—combined perhaps with fear that their king and ships might become hostages, as well as long-standing rivalry with Sidon—determined their answer. He was informed that there was a temple to Melquart in the largely derelict Old Tyre on the mainland, and Alexander should perform whatever rites he wished there, but they would not permit him to cross to the island and enter their city. Another attempt was made to negotiate, but the defenders took the Macedonian envoys up onto the city wall and killed them there, tipping the bodies into the sea in plain sight.[10]

Alexander could no more accept neutrality from Tyre than he had done at Miletus, especially since the Tyrian contingent was a major part of the Persian fleet, which was anything but neutral. If the Macedonian envoys were actually slaughtered, then this was another provocation that had to be answered. Arrian gave Alexander a speech in which the king explains why the Macedonians must take the city, both to open the road to Egypt and to defeat the Persian navy to end the threat to Macedonia and Greece, where the Spartans were hostile and Athens an unreliable friend. We cannot know whether this was based on an original source or simply what the historian later felt was appropriate for the king to have said given Arrian's assessment of the situation. Alexander reinforced his logic by announcing that Hercules had come to him in a dream and led him by the hand into Tyre, which he said meant that they would take the city, but that it would require Herculean effort. Assuring soldiers that the gods would give them victory was a recognized ploy, although this does not automatically mean that the young king did not also believe that he had dreamed a dream that could be interpreted in this way.[11]

The army needed encouragement, for the task facing it was daunting. Tyre lay about half a mile offshore, the sea shallow at first, but dropping to some eighteen feet nearer the island on which the city lay. Its walls were high, reinforced with taller towers that were well made and maintained, even if the walls were a lot lower than the 150 feet claimed by Arrian for one section. As importantly, they stood almost on the edge of the sea so that there was no significant ground in front of them where siege works could be built and battering rams brought against the wall. That assumed that the Macedonians could get that far, for the Tyrians had not sent all their warships to join the Persian fleet and had plenty of well-crewed vessels, substantially outnumbering Alexander's modest squadron. The Tyrians proudly remembered holding out for thirteen years against a Babylonian siege in the distant past, forcing the enemy to quit, and the sheer strength of the city's position and defenses reinforced their willingness to defy Persians and now Macedonians. They had plenty of food and the freedom to bring in more by sea, and from the large population plenty of well-motivated men to fight and labor.[12]

Alexander and his engineers decided that since they could not hope to approach by sea, then they must build a mole from the shore to the island. The ruins of Old Tyre provided stones, the cedar forests of Lebanon timber, and the soldiers the labor force, augmented by porters, servants, and civilians drawn more or less willingly from their allies. Stones were gathered, trees felled, and then all had to be carried to the shore and out to where they were needed as the mole slowly grew. At the same time supplies needed to be brought to feed and water everyone as they toiled. Alexander sent to Jerusalem "asking" the high priest to contribute supplies, and on the whole the communities of the region obeyed and in the main his foragers and convoys of supplies went unmolested. When some hill tribes began raiding a little later in the siege, Alexander led off a flying column in a week's campaign to punish them; he seems to have instilled sufficient fear to make sure that the

problem never again became serious. This episode is more notable for the story that he and a few others got left behind when his
old tutor Lysimachus, who had insisted on coming along in spite
of his advanced age, collapsed in exhaustion. The night was cold
and they had no fire, so Alexander crept toward an enemy camp,
stabbed two warriors, and made off with a burning branch that he
carried back so they could light their own fire. Such tales were easy
enough to invent and, true or not, were even easier to believe, especially at the time for an army growing to trust its leader's audacity
and luck. If true then there was a degree of recklessness, but it is
harder to say whether this was within the bounds of what was
expected for a Macedonian king when it came to sharing the risks
of a campaign.[13]

Weeks turned into months as the soldiers and civilians worked
and the mole slowly grew longer. The early stages were in shallow
water and over shoals that made the task easier. At first the Tyrians
did no more than row nearby and yell abuse, mocking the soldiers
because they had become no more than laborers. As the causeway
reached further out, the defenders started to shoot arrows and missiles from light catapults, both from the walls and from ships. It
was hard to work and wear armor at the same time—although the
Roman army would later train legionnaires to do this—and men
were wounded, and more often forced to take cover. Ancient sieges
were prolonged contests of ingenuity and determination, attacker
and defender in turn coming up with new ploys. This time the
Macedonians responded by building two high towers at the tip of
the mole, covering them with hides to defend against flaming missiles, and equipping them with artillery of their own. Their height
meant that they could shoot down onto the deck of any approaching warship, so these were forced to keep their distance, and at
the same time made it harder for anyone on the walls to operate.
Protected by the towers and screens to shelter the work as far as
possible, the advantage swayed back to the attackers.

Alexander's engineers were ingenious, but so were the Tyrians.
Choosing a transport ship, the defenders packed it with combustible material. More oil and other inflammable liquids were put
in cauldrons and suspended from the masts so that when these

burned through they would drop and fuel the flames. Then they weighted the whole vessel to make it stern heavy and more likely to run up onto the mole. Judging the moment with generations of knowledge of the seas around their city, they waited until the wind was right before triremes towed the fire ship toward the enemy work. The brave men on board lit the first fires, the triremes rowed hard, and then they released the lines so the ship's own sail and the men steering it carried it the rest of the way. At the last minute the sailors dived overboard and swam to safety before the ship rammed into the mole, the mast fell as planned, and the great surge of flame erupted onto causeway and towers. Animal hides and skins were little protection against the inferno, and soon the towers were blazing, as was the frame of the causeway and the shelters on it. More Tyrian ships drew alongside, shooting at any Macedonians trying to resist and landing parties of soldiers to rip up and burn anything they could.

The labor of many weeks was undone in a matter of hours, especially when nature took a hand and storms damaged what was left. Surveying the ruins, Alexander gave orders for work to recommence, only this time they would make the mole much wider and build more towers to protect it. Probably the new causeway began at a different spot on the shore and lay at a different angle to the tide, but our sources are not clear on this. Either way, it was a task that would take even longer than the construction that had been wrecked so quickly. Alexander himself went with the hypaspists to Sidon, wanting to gather as many warships as he could because he had realized that the "siege was unlikely to succeed as long as the Tyrians were masters of the sea."[14]

All successful leaders tend to be lucky, although they also do everything they can to help luck along and weight the odds in their favor. Alexander's strategy of taking the home cities of contingents in the Persian fleet bore fruit as eighty Phoenician ships from Sidon, Aradus, and Byblus defected to him. Rhodes sent another ten ships, Lycia the same number, and there was a handful of vessels from other places, although only a single small warship could be spared and was able to reach him from Macedonia. Even more welcome was the fleet of 120 ships brought by the kings of Cyprus who "had heard of Darius's defeat at Issus, and were alarmed at the whole of Phoenicia being already in Alexander's power." To all of them, Alexander let bygones be bygones, supposing that it was "rather from necessity than their own choice that they had contributed to the Persian fleet." Pragmatism was the order of the day on both sides, and Alexander had the ships he needed at just the right moment. He sailed back to Tyre, hoping that the enemy would face him at sea, but the Tyrians were too prudent to fight against hopeless odds. They retired to the two harbors—the one in the north facing toward Sidon and the one in the south called the Egyptian harbor because Egypt lay off far to the south. Triremes with rams facing outward lined the entrances, keeping Alexander's ships out, but also bottling their own in.[15]

The balance had shifted heavily in the besiegers' favor, but that did not make success inevitable. Alexander sent out for as many engineers and technicians as could be found in Cyprus and Phoenicia to join him, so that there would be far more skilled supervisors for all the construction required. Much sweat and skill meant that the new causeway edged slowly forward, although inevitably the Macedonians had to look ever further afield to find the materials, especially timber, adding to the time it took to bring it to where it was needed. The laborers were spared attacks from warships, but once within range of the walls they were subjected to darts, arrows, and stones. Macedonian artillery in the towers and on board ships tried to suppress the defenders as far as possible, and much effort was spent on both sides to protect against incoming missiles. Merchant ships and some triremes were lashed together so that they could support towers mounting artillery or be equipped with battering rams. Alexander was able to probe at different parts of the defenses, and not simply at the stretch of wall in front of the causeway. Threats and real attacks forced the defenders to reply, slowly wearing their strength down.

Not everything went the Macedonians' way. The Tyrians covered the decks of some warships with rudimentary armor so that they could sally out, protected from enemy missiles, to attack or sever the anchor cables of ships mounting siege engines. Others swam underwater to cut the ropes. As always each ruse soon prompted a counter-ruse. Alexander's men replaced anchor ropes with chains so that they could not be cut, and covered ships of their own to close with the enemy defenses and block the attacks of the "armored' Tyrian warships. The Tyrians used sacks to cover the section of wall attacked by rams, padding it and reducing the force of the blows, and made devices to strike at the enemy or block missiles aimed at the wall. They also heated up sand and poured it off the walls down onto ships and the end of the causeway; it only took a few grains slipping inside a man's clothes or armor to scorch. The choice was then to take off the armor and risk being struck by a missile or to labor on in constant pain.

The defenders devoted great care to preparing a raid by sea, and for days ahead of the attack, sails were suspended across the mouth of the Sidonian harbor so that the attackers would get used to the sight and not think anything of it. The attack came suddenly and silently in the middle of the day, without even the usual calls to keep the rowers in rhythm. Surprise was complete, and a number of ships, including several flagships belonging to the allied kings, were caught at anchor and sunk. By chance Alexander was not taking his usual siesta and saw an opportunity. Crewing as many ships as was possible in the time, he sent some to seal off the harbor again, preventing reinforcements coming out and cutting off the lines of retreat, while leading the rest to intercept. The defenders on the wall saw the threat before the raiders, but all their frantic efforts to signal to them failed and the withdrawal started too late. Nearly all the attacking ships were sunk or captured, although the crews escaped and swam back to the city. There were no more sallies, and the cost of this one surely dampened morale. Curtius claims that there was pressure to reintroduce the archaic moloch sacrifice of an infant first-born son, and that only the determination of civic leaders prevented this. A man claimed to dream that Apollo was leaving the city, so the Tyrians bound the god's statue with a golden chain to keep him with them. As the months drew on, the prospects for the defenders became ever more bleak, but they did not attempt to surrender.[16]

The capture of Tyre was the longest and most difficult siege undertaken by either Philip or Alexander. Arrian called it "manifestly a large task," while Curtius claims that Alexander also came close to despair and considered giving it up and marching to Egypt: "But he was much ashamed to withdraw . . . thinking that his reputation . . . would be impaired if he should leave Tyre as a witness that he could be defeated." If the thought ever occurred, then he did not act upon it, and the more effort and prestige he had committed to the siege the harder it became to fail. Both Curtius and Diodorus claim that a large "sea monster" was cast up onto the causeway and eventually slid back into the sea, the attackers and defenders alike choosing to see this as a good omen. The Macedonians continued to press on all sides, and weaknesses were discovered in the south, near the Egyptian harbor. A breach was made, and an assault launched from scaling ladders and ramps mounted on a ship. It failed, and two days of bad weather brought a lull. Alexander is supposed to have manipulated the calendar by adding an extra day to the month so that there was a chance to take the city within the month as his seer had predicted.[17]

The main assault was carefully prepared, spearheaded by two ships mounting ladders (like those on fire engines). One carried hypaspists and the other picked members of one of the phalanx regiments. There were probably other supporting attacks as well, to spread the defenders in the hope that somewhere the Macedonians could break through. Alexander watched from a high tower, presumably on the causeway, but quickly joined the assault as rapid progress was made. The officer leading the hypaspists was killed on top of the wall—either by a spear or when his head was split open by an axe, depending on the account. Alexander buffeted men with his shield and hacked with his sword as he fought his way to the top of a turret on the wall, and quickly the Tyrians began to retreat from the walls. Ships sailed into both harbors as the defenders abandoned the outer wall and more and more attackers poured into the city. After so much effort and so many months, and remembering the execution of the envoys and perhaps other prisoners during the siege, the Macedonians were exhilarated and vengeful.[18]

Alexander had proclaimed that anyone taking shelter in a temple would be spared, and ordered heralds to shout this out, although we cannot know how far the word had spread or was believed inside the city. No mercy was shown anywhere else, and the Macedonians in particular ran amok. Many defenders gathered near the temple of Agenor and made a last stand. Arrian says that 8,000 Tyrian men died during the assault and sack of the city, although there is another tradition that has 2,000 of these taken prisoner and then crucified along the shore. Alexander was certainly capable of ordering such a horrific punishment as a warning to others, which does not mean that the story is automatically true. Some 30,000 (for which we should probably read "a large number") women and children were sold as slaves, and others were spared, including Carthaginian envoys, who had taken refuge in the Temple of Hercules. The Sidonians serving with Alexander as allies are also supposed to have protected men and women alike. Arrian says that twenty hypaspists died in the final assault and that overall fatalities during the siege were about 400. As usual many scholars distrust these figures as far too low, but since they probably only represent the Macedonians and do not include allies and civilian laborers they are plausible enough. The wounded would amount to many more, for in most circumstances the context of a siege made it easier to recover and treat, and overall this would suggest losses at Tyre on a scale with the Battle of Issus or even heavier.[19]

Alexander celebrated the capture of the city with more than mere slaughter. One of the first things he did was to fulfill his desire to sacrifice to Hercules in the city's temple. His newly acquired navy also held a review in honor of the demigod, while the army paraded, and then there were games including a torch-lit race. With no apparent sense of irony, Alexander dedicated to Hercules and installed in his temple precinct the ram that had first broken the city wall and also the Tyrians' sacred warship. Settlers were brought in from elsewhere to repopulate the city, although it is quite possible that over time survivors of the old population returned. Certainly the culture of the city does not appear to have changed drastically and the links with Carthage endured. Tyre remained large and important, although it was never quite as prosperous and powerful again. Another change was that gradually the tide washed more and more mud against the causeway, forming a permanent isthmus.

Appalling though the cost of their brave resistance proved for the Tyrians, there was nothing especially exceptional in the punishment inflicted on them, with the partial exception of the mass crucifixion, if that occurred. Like Thebes, it was more the sheer size of the place and its brave resistance that made the sack seem so much more terrible.

20

AN OASIS AND A GOD

Before Tyre fell to the Macedonians, envoys came from Darius offering alliance and peace, and 10,000 talents as ransom for the release of his family. The Persian king offered to cede all his lands west of the Euphrates and give his daughter in marriage to Alexander. The Macedonian king consulted his close companions, and it was claimed that Parmenio declared that he would accept "if he were Alexander" rather than risk what they had so far gained, to which the young king replied that he might also accept "if he were Parmenio." Like the other stories of this sort, this one may be invented, and since Parmenio spent a lot of these months holding an independent command in Syria, we cannot be sure that he was present for the meeting. As Alexander is made to point out in the answer he sent to Darius, he already controlled all the lands Darius had ceded, had no need of money after his recent gains, and could marry the king's daughter if he chose. There were obvious risks in continuing the war, but there were also risks in halting. Ancient states had a poor record in keeping long-term promises of peace and friendship, tending to cherish grudges and resume conflict when it was convenient. For the moment the momentum was on Alexander's side, and losing this would be dangerous, especially as in terms of numbers he remained so heavily outmatched.[1]

Alexander rejected the offer and continued his march toward Egypt. The punishment inflicted on Tyre, like the sack of Thebes, was made deliberately appalling as a warning that resisting him was futile and virtually suicidal. Such terror tactics often work, but also risk making resistance all the harder since the enemy have nothing left to lose and may as well fight to the last. Gaza lay in his path, the last significant obstacle before the desert route to Egypt. A few miles in from the coast, it was held by a Persian governor named Batis (or Betis) who commanded a force including a contingent of Arab mercenaries. The city stood on a high tel, an artificial hill created over the centuries as dust piled onto the ruins of earlier settlements, and had strong walls.[2]

Arrian says that Batis was a eunuch, and a fragment of another source calls him fat and very dark-skinned, which may be no more than the usual Greek distaste for such royal courtiers. His actions suggest that he was a determined, capable leader, confident in the strength of his position and loyal to Darius. Such a challenge made Alexander all the more determined to capture the city for fear that his reputation for invincibility would suffer. He had hoped that Gaza would capitulate or fall to a rapid assault, but the siege would actually take him two months. His light siege train of equipment that could be taken apart and reassembled proved inadequate, so heavier gear had to be brought by sea from Tyre. Hephaestion supervised this in another of his rare early appearances in the sources.[3]

The siege of Gaza is recorded in much less detail than the attack on Tyre. We are told that the softness of the soil made it harder to operate siege engines and towers, for they tended to bog down in the sand, but it made tunneling easier. The Macedonians built great mounds to carry towers and rams—all around the city according to Arrian, although since this would have been a mammoth task, perhaps the height varied. They also dug mines to go under the city wall; this is the first mention of this technique on the part of Macedonian engineers, which was rare even in the traditions of Eastern siege warfare. The only way to meet the threat was by countermining, but the defenders of Gaza either did not have the ability or the awareness to do this.

All such siege works took time, and as usual there were probing attacks to weaken the defenders. On one day Alexander was conducting a sacrifice when a bird dropped something onto his head. Sources differ over whether it was an eagle or raven, and whether the projectile was a lump of dirt or excrement. His loyal seer Aristander provided a generally positive interpretation of what must have seemed a bad omen, saying that it meant that the city would be taken, but that the king should be very careful today and stay out of the fighting. Soon afterward Batis launched a determined sally, driving the Macedonians away from one of the siege mounds in an effort to set light to the siege engines. Ignoring the advice or forgetting it in this moment of crisis, Alexander led some of the hypaspists in a counterattack that drove the enemy back. Curtius says that an Arab feigned surrender only to hack at the king's neck. Alexander was faster and severed the man's wrist, and presumably he was then finished off by the Macedonians nearby. Thinking that this was the danger indicated by the omen, Alexander stayed with his men, only to be struck in the shoulder by an arrow shot by a bow or by a bolt from a catapult that penetrated both shield and cuirass. For a while he stayed with his men, but started to bleed heavily and was on the verge of unconsciousness when carried to safety. Like Philip's injury at Methone, the wound was a serious one, at least according to our sources, but skillful treatment and the king's determination and strong constitution pulled him through. Father and son alike ran risks, although the quality of their armor and sheer luck preserved them—at least so far, in Alexander's case.[4]

Soon afterward Hephaestion arrived with the heavy siege equipment, and the siege was pressed all the harder over the next weeks. Rams battered at the walls and created breaches. Mines dug underneath were completed and filled with combustible material that was then ignited, burning through the timber props. As these collapsed the roof came down and so did the section of wall above it. Batis and his men did not give in and managed to repulse three assaults. More breaches were made and the existing ones widened, until a fourth assault through the breaches and a direct escalation of the wall overwhelmed the defense. There was competition to be the first man over the wall, which was won by one of the king's Companions. Curtius claims that Alexander was fit enough to take part and was hurt again when a stone flung by hand or engine struck his leg, although this was probably no more than a cut or bruise.

Batis and Gaza had challenged Alexander, and as at Tyre he was savage in his punishment. The men were massacred, the city sacked, and women and children sold into slavery. Once again the city was to be repopulated by people brought in from the wider neighborhood. Arrian does not mention Batis's fate, but Curtius claims that he fought on heroically until exhaustion and wounds caused him to collapse. Brought to Alexander, he defied him, keeping silent and disdaining the abuse that was hurled at him. Since he would not submit or beg for mercy, the king exploded in rage and ordered the enemy commander bound by the feet and dragged behind a speeding chariot until he died. This was a conscious echo of the *Iliad*, for Achilles had treated Hector's corpse in this way, but it was far more savage to do this to a live enemy. If this was how Batis died, then it was a particularly vicious act and even Curtius notes that usually Alexander had more respect for courage in an enemy. Perhaps his wound, which could so easily have ended his life and may well have still been causing pain, along with sheer impatience at the enemy holding out for another difficult siege so soon after Tyre, provoked such an outburst, or the story may be invented. What we can say is that Batis served his king with great courage and loyalty at the cost of his life.[5]

An army taking the desert route to Egypt needed to take care organizing its supply and especially provisions of water, and could encounter great difficulties if faced by a determined enemy. Alexander was not opposed, his supply organization was well tested by this stage of the war, and when he reached the fortress city of Pelusium, the traditional gateway to Egypt, he was met by enthusiastic crowds. This is unlikely to have been a surprise. Darius's governor handed the country over to the invader in marked contrast to the stubborn resistance of Batis, albeit the lack of enthusiasm for Persian rule among the Egyptians made successful resistance unlikely. Alexander made himself pharaoh, king of the Upper and Lower Kingdoms, Son of the god Ra, and beloved of the god Amun, and was depicted in the traditional way on monuments. In marked and deliberate contrast to the Persians, he showed great respect for the Egyptians, their religion, and customs, which in turn involved generous treatment of the highly influential priestly caste. His mood may well have been helped by good news arriving from the Aegean. The Persian fleet had withered away as contingents deserted and communities rebelled against Persian control, and its commanders had been captured, although Pharnabazus subsequently escaped.[6]

Respect for local opinion only went so far, and there is no good evidence that Alexander was formally crowned as ruler or took part in any distinctly Egyptian rituals or sacrifices. When he celebrated a festival, it was as usual thoroughly Greek, and when he decided to found a great city on the coast—what would become the most famous of his Alexandrias—this was from the start to be overwhelmingly Greek in its culture: even shrines to native deities such as Osiris were Hellenized. Arrian once again speaks of a longing to found the city, with Alexander also claiming inspiration from Homer in his choice of the site, and as so often divine approval was supposedly shown through an omen. For want of anything better his staff used grain to mark out the main streets and other key features, and when birds flew down and ate it this was interpreted as a sign of future prosperity for this city would feed many people in the wider world.[7]

Late in 332 or early in 331 BC, another longing seized Alexander and he led a small column out into the desert to the west of Egypt to visit the shrine and oracle at the Siwah oasis of a god called Ammon, who was associated with Zeus by the Greeks. The choice of this, rather than any of the oracles in Egypt itself, shows that he was not primarily interested in local opinion. Ammon was far better known in Greece and further afield and less alien to Greeks. Hercules and Perseus were both said to have visited, although in the case of Perseus the context of Alexander's visit is the only time this is mentioned, and also the only time he was claimed as

Alexander's ancestor. We cannot say how famous these stories really were, or whether as with the Gordian knot the importance of the place really started when Alexander showed an interest.[8]

First going to Paraetonium (modern Mersah Matruh), where he received deputations and submission from Cyrene to the west, Alexander followed the desert trails for some 170 miles to Siwah. The oasis was isolated—in the Second World War it became the base of the Long Range Desert Group in its lonely campaign against the Germans and Italians—but not so remote that the path was not reasonably well trodden. Yet, apart from the march to Egypt, the Macedonians had no experience of deserts and found the going hard. Rainstorms buffeted the travelers and sandstorms confused them so that they lost their way, only to be saved by following a pair of crows. It was natural enough for creatures to head for the water of the oasis, but this was readily interpreted as an omen; Ptolemy even claimed that the guides were two snakes, able to cry in what sounded like words. The reverence for snakes as royal symbols in Egypt may well have influenced this passage written down years later when he ruled the country.[9]

Alexander and his party arrived, dust-stained and weary, and the mysteriousness of the shrine compound can only have been reinforced after the journey through such desolate country. The senior priest was waiting outside, and greeted Alexander as "son of Ammon" or "son of Zeus," which may have reflected his new status as pharaoh, although one tradition claimed it was a slip of the tongue by a man unused to Greek. Ptolemy and Aristobulus, both of whom were with the party, do not appear to have gone into any detail about what happened once Alexander alone accompanied the priest inside, for Arrian says no more than that he made his inquiry of the god "and received the answer his heart desired, as he said, and turned back for Egypt." Not even the means by which the oracle gave its answer is certain—whether it was the ancient Egyptian method whereby a sacred boat carried on the shoulders of priests was made to move in various ways, or a priest using gestures and facial expressions rather than words, just like in some Greek shrines. Plutarch cites a letter from Alexander to Olympias, that in itself may or may not have been genuine, claiming that he had learned secrets that he would reveal only to her and only in person on his return to Macedonia—something he was never to do, but a message at least compatible with the public version of an answer that pleased him, and hinting that this confirmed her supposed belief that his father was divine. Alexander certainly paid more attention in future to Zeus Ammon than other gods associated with his new empire.[10]

Other traditions swiftly grew up, imagined by authors unable to resist the encounter between the king and the oracle of his divine father, and tend to run along similar lines. He is supposed to have asked whether he would rule the world, to which the answer was affirmative. Another question was whether his father's murderers had all been punished, only to be told that his true father was divine but that Philip's assassins had all paid for their crime. All of these details are likely to have been invented after his death. The visit to Siwah was clearly of great personal importance to Alexander, otherwise he would not have made the long journey, and it was at the very least an additional reason for taking Egypt. Witnesses heard the priest address him as the son of the god—or at least believed this is what he had said—and for the rest of his life Alexander sometimes openly referred to himself as son of Ammon or Zeus Ammon and let himself be called son of Zeus by others, including Aristotle's nephew Callisthenes, who was writing the "official" version of the expedition. He was not invariably referred to in this way, nor did it mean a renunciation of Philip. Greek heroes could have both a divine and a human father, the god joining in the conception in some mystical way. It was another sign that Alexander wanted to be seen—and probably saw himself—as special, different from other kings including his father, something his spectacular successes proclaimed. Leaving the oasis behind him, he returned to Egypt and soon to the war with Darius.[11]

In 332–331 BC Alexander spent more than four months in Egypt, and in contrast to the previous two winters there is no sign of major campaigning. For the first time the king and his soldiers had a break from fighting, which does not mean that they were inactive. The visit to Siwah tends to dominate our sources, although it took no more than a few weeks. Nothing suggests that

the experience was marked by any visible or immediate trans-
formation in the king's character or behavior in spite of all the
fascination shown by later generations. Both before and after the
pilgrimage, most of his time was spent in administration, organizing his new conquests, preparing the next campaign, and receiving
delegations from allies and subjects alike. Two Egyptian noblemen
were selected to become senior civilian officials or nomarchs, but
one declined the honor for reasons that are not specified. It made
practical sense to secure as much goodwill as possible among the
wider population and especially the elite, and time and effort was
spent in showing them and their customs respect. Yet Alexander
was a conqueror, perhaps better behaved than some of the Persians
in the past, but still a foreign invader, and there was no reason
for Egyptians to love him. Garrisons, mainly of mercenaries, were
to stay and their commanders were drawn from his Companions,
overwhelmingly Macedonian noblemen with a handful of Greeks,
as were the financial and civilian overseers with authority greater
than the nomarch. This was the pattern everywhere, with all significant posts going to men selected from his court and each decision
made by the king and based on his willingness to trust an individual. A few months later the errant treasurer Harpalus returned
from Greece and Alexander's old friend was readmitted to favor
and high office.[12]

Some time was spent at Memphis, where numerous embassies from Greek cities were given audience by a king inclined to
be generous in his decisions. He held a festival, including a sacrifice to Zeus the King, with athletic and artistic competitions.
This quintessentially Hellenic celebration was matched by equally
Greek curiosity, and at some point an expedition was sent south
along the Nile to discover the cause of the annual inundation, and
its conclusions, no doubt passed from Callisthenes to his uncle,
led Aristotle to declare that the matter was settled. Alongside the
exploration and celebration came a moment of tragedy when a
small boat carrying some of the king's younger friends overturned
in the Nile. Hector, youngest known son of Parmenio, managed
to struggle to the bank, only to collapse from exhaustion and die.
Alexander was said to be very fond of the young man, and this,

along with his father's importance, ensured that he was given a "magnificent" funeral.[13]

In early April 331 BC, Alexander marched out, crossing the Nile and its canals on bridges he had constructed. He followed much the same route as during the invasion, no doubt with similar arrangements to supply food and water for his men, and went back to Tyre, where the army would concentrate, ready to advance once the harvest ripened in early summer. En route he learned that one of his men put in charge of Samaria had been captured by a band of Samaritans and burned alive. Alexander marched to the region and demanded that the culprits be handed over to him for execution. If there had ever been widespread unrest rather than the actions of an isolated group, this collapsed as soon as he arrived at the head of a column. The men were handed over for punishment and a replacement appointed for the dead officer.[14]

At Tyre Alexander once again sacrificed in the Temple of Hercules and held another festival. The prestige of the victorious leader of the Greeks and generous prizes on offer were attracting many famous athletes and performers to these events. One was Thessalus, the tragic actor who had acted as envoy when Alexander intervened in the negotiations between Philip and Pixodarus of Caria and scuppered the marriage alliance planned for Arrhidaeus. A past victor at several of the major Athenian festivals, he remained a friend and favorite of the young king. In spite of this, he was beaten to the prize by Athenodorus, a rival whose record was almost as distinguished, and who had broken a contract to perform in Athens in his enthusiasm to attend Alexander's event. Alexander's support for Thessalus was public, as was his willingness to accept the judges' decision regardless. A little later the Athenians fined Athenodorus for breach of contract, and the actor wrote to the king asking him to intervene. Alexander declined to overrule the city's authorities, and instead sent money to pay the fine.[15]

Alexander's enthusiasm for the ritual and competition of a Greek festival was deep-rooted and genuine, and was shared by most senior Macedonians and perhaps many soldiers. It was also politic, proclaiming that he and the Macedonians were properly Greek, and therefore fitting leaders for the great Hellenic war of revenge that had still to be won. While he did not scruple to poach participants from events at other cities—or at least not to forbid it—in every other way Alexander acted the part of the good king rather than the tyrant. Thus he did not try to influence the judges in favor of Thessalus, and subsequently accepted the Athenian authorities' ruling against Athenodorus, while at the same time ensuring the victor did not suffer any loss for his enthusiasm to come to Tyre and perform before him. Such marks of respect never altered the fact that Alexander's leadership of the Greeks relied on Macedonian military and financial dominance, but they made it easier for people to accept.

Relations with the *poleis* had always been important, and neither Philip nor his son consciously provoked public opinion unless they saw some advantage in doing so. In 331 BC, with Alexander preparing to drive deep into Persia, the mood in Greece was particularly important as Agis III made plain his determination to assert Spartan power. Thus Alexander continued to be generous in response to petitions from the other Greek cities. He ruled in favor of the leaders on several islands against the local Macedonian commanders, and accepted Mytilene's claim that it had only defected to Persia because it was unable to defend against the Persian fleet. That fleet was now gone, drastically reducing Darius's opportunities to send military and monetary aid to anyone willing to oppose Alexander. Even so, Agis had already received a little funding and more importantly a significant force of mercenaries. Alexander dispatched ships—many of them manned by Phoenicians who not long before had been on the other side—to Crete and to the Peloponnese to harass the Spartans and their allies.[16]

As far as possible Alexander needed to convince other cities that joining Sparta would be unwise, and in this he was helped by widespread distaste for the Spartans, fueled by memories of their conduct in the past. What Athens did was especially important, for it still had the capacity to form a large navy and muster substantial numbers of hoplites. An Athenian delegation reached the king, repeating the earlier request for the release of citizens captured with the mercenaries at Granicus. This time, Alexander agreed, even though the war with Persia was not over. Presumably he judged that the goodwill he would earn in this way was more valuable than keeping the men as hostages; he still had the twenty Athenian ships and their crews, as well as some of their fellow citizens among the allied soldiers with his army.

The chronology of Agis's war is confused, permitting widely divergent reconstructions, although most likely it did not begin until after Alexander had marched eastward from Tyre. Sparta had not joined the common peace or the treaty that followed Philip's victory at Chaeronea, hence Alexander's pointed comments when dedicating spoils in 334 BC, so that Agis's war was not in any legal sense a rebellion or direct attack on Macedonia. He acted to assert Spartan power, and his targets were long-standing enemies of his country, most notably Megalopolis, the city formed by freed helots. However, his enemies were part of the common peace and alliance, so that an attack on them was a violation of the treaty, which meant that other cities, and most of all Macedonia, ought to come to their aid.

Agis had prepared for war for some time and chose his moment with care, and had the backing of a strong mercenary force to add to Sparta's own army. Almost all of Sparta's allies in the Peloponnese joined him, especially when he defeated the troops led against him by Corrhagus, the first Macedonian officer to respond to the challenge. Traditional enemies, notably the Messenians and Megalopolitans, opposed him, but most of the Achaeans did join the cause. Athens did not, contentment with recent treatment by Alexander making it easier for Athenians to recall his might and their long-standing rivalry with Sparta. Before Issus, Demosthenes had hoped for a Macedonian disaster, gleefully predicting that Alexander and his men would be trampled beneath the hoofs of Darius's cavalry. After the battle, the orator had sought to be reconciled with the king, and for once did not urge his fellow citizens to join a new war against Macedon.[17]

It is possible that if more of the Greek states had joined with Agis, and if Darius had managed to send more aid in the early years of the war, that Antipater might have been thoroughly defeated, but this should not be taken for granted. Nor was it the best strategy open to Darius. Unity and cooperation did not come naturally to the poleis, especially since helping to overthrow one dominant power usually resulted in setting up another that would soon prove as tyrannical or worse. Alexander had left his lieutenant with substantial military and financial resources, as events proved. The king and his main army were in Asia, always advancing. For Darius, a decisive end to the war and proof of his own right to rule required him to defeat Alexander, not wage war by proxy in distant Greece.

21

THE BATTLE OF GAUGAMELA

Since the details and timing of Agis's war in Greece are impossible to establish, it is equally impossible to judge how speedily reports reached Alexander of what was happening and how quickly any messages or aid sent back to Antipater in Macedon arrived. Near the end of 332 BC or early in 331 BC Alexander ordered his regent to raise the biggest reinforcement yet for his field army, especially of young men who had just reached adulthood, to supply the manpower necessary to feed the ongoing and ever expanding war, this now being affordable from the spoils taken so far and the levies imposed on the territory he had overrun. Alexander never countermanded this order, which suggests either that Agis had not yet begun open hostilities in the Peloponnese, or at least that Alexander had not heard about it, unless he was simply focused on Darius above all else, and decided that Antipater could or must cope with what was left because the reinforcements were needed in Asia for the great struggle with Persia.

Alexander's information about the Persian king was also limited. Some sources date the negotiations and Darius's offer of all the lands west of the Euphrates to these months rather than the previous year, and there may have been more than one approach. The Persian king had not been idle and had raised a new army, this time drawing on the more distant provinces such as Bactria and even India, and rumors of this reached Alexander. As the months passed there was no sign of Darius embarking on an offensive, and instead, as far as Alexander could tell, the Persian king was waiting in the heartland of Persia for the enemy to come to him. Never one to shy away from such a challenge or let the initiative slip from him, Alexander was determined to find the king and defeat him.[1]

Preparations for the next stage in the Macedonian offensive had been underway for some time, but clearly not all was to Alexander's satisfaction, for he sacked the officer placed in charge of gathering supplies from Syria and replaced him with another man. We cannot say how serious the failure was and whether it influenced his plans. Driving inland meant that the Macedonians would no longer be able to transport bulky supplies and siege equipment by sea, although depending on the route chosen it might still be possible to employ barges on the Euphrates. To move on land required far more porters, pack and draft animals, and readily portable and robust containers for food and water as well as the food and water themselves, sufficient for the largest army Alexander had ever commanded in one place. Altogether he had 40,000 infantry and 7,000 cavalry for his main field force, not including the garrisons dotted around the territory he had already overrun. Securing enough grain to feed his soldiers without starving civilian communities meant waiting for the harvest, and it was not until July that Alexander set out from Tyre.[2]

An advance force had gone to Thapsacus on the Euphrates and constructed two bridges most of the way across. There was a Persian force of a few thousand on the far bank watching the Macedonians but not doing anything else, so the detachment waited for Alexander and the main force to arrive before completing the structures. Hugely outnumbered, the Persians withdrew, and in the weeks that followed Alexander lost contact even with these enemy outposts. Once across the river, he faced a choice between two routes: whether to continue down the Euphrates Valley and follow the most direct route to Babylon, or take the longer path looping through northern Mesopotamia to the river Tigris. Staying near the river offered the chance to carry supplies on barges, at least

BATTLE OF GAUGAMELA, 331 BC

Not to scale. Formations conjectural.

A = Thracian Cavalry (Agathon)
B = Greek Mercenary Cavalry (Andromachus)
C = Greek Allied Cavalry (Coeranus)
D = Thessalian Cavalry (Philip)
1 = Phalanx Regiment (Craterus)
2 = Phalanx Regiment (Simias, vice Amyntas)
3 = Phalanx Regiment (Polyperchon)
4 = Phalanx Regiment (Meleager)
5 = Phalanx Regiment (Perdiccas)
6 = Phalanx Regiment (Coenus)

7 = Hypaspists (Nicanor)
8 = Mercenary infantry
9 = Thracian skirmishers
10 = Cretan archers
E = Companion Cavalry (Philotas)
F = Prodromoi (Aretes)
G = Greek Mercenary Cavalry (Menidas)
H = Paeonian Cavalry (Ariston)
11 = Part of Agrianians and other light infantry

12 = Remainder of Agrianians
13 = Archers
14 = "Old" Mercenary Infantry
15 = Allied and Mercenary Infantry

The extent of this second line and how closely it was linked to the first line by other contingents is unclear. The army may loosely have been in a hollow square or parallelogram, with the flanking troops angled to connect the two main lines.

for a while, but meant marching under a pitiless sun across plains where the summer temperature can reach 120 degrees Fahrenheit (almost 49 Celsius). Another problem was that the gathered harvest was likely to be stored in walled cities. With the great Persian army somewhere in the area, these might not be inclined to capitulate, and sieges would be hard in such conditions and open him up to attack by Darius.[3]

Alexander chose the northern route, where it would be easier to gather stores and animals from dispersed settlements, the climate was less extreme, and he might wrong-foot the enemy by taking the less obvious path. Darius had concentrated his army at Babylon, although it is more than likely that Alexander did not know this for certain, just as the Persians had little real idea of where the Macedonians were once they were across the Euphrates and their covering force withdrew. As with the Issus campaign, where neither side knew where the other was until they were very close, the impression from our sources is of two armies maneuvering with little long-range intelligence, and most of it well out of date. Instead each commander guessed where the enemy was likely to be, based on what he must defend or attack. At some point Darius judged that Alexander was not following the Euphrates so he moved north, keeping to the east of the Tigris, perhaps in the hope of contesting the crossing and certainly to make it more difficult for the Macedonians to attack without warning.

According to Arrian, the Persians had 1 million infantry and 200,000 horsemen. Diodorus and Plutarch reduced this to 1 million of foot soldiers and horsemen combined, Justin says 500,000 in total, while Curtius gives the lowest estimate of 200,000 infantry and 45,000 cavalry, and even this would be at the summit or beyond what was logistically possible to supply in the field. There is a fair chance that the Persian army in 331 BC was substantially larger than the one defeated at Issus, and everything suggests that the cavalry outnumbered the Macedonian horsemen by a very large margin, and some would even accept a figure of 40,000 to 45,000 cavalry. Many were excellent horsemen, and Darius had issued some with longer spears and better swords, doing his best to learn from earlier defeats.

The cavalry were what mattered, for many of them were of very high quality, but the infantry's numbers mattered very little since most were incapable of standing up to Macedonian or Greek infantry in close combat. There is no mention of the close-order Kardakes in the coming battle, while the contingent of mercenary hoplites numbered no more than a few thousand, and apart from a 1,000-strong royal bodyguard of "Apple-bearers" (with a gold apple instead of a butt spike on their spears), the remainder were of little use except to pursue in the event of victory or flee and be massacred in the case of defeat. Darius's army looked impressive because of its sheer size, but this also strained resources to feed it. Yet appearances were important for a Persian king, so once again he went to war in appropriate pomp and luxury. More practically he planned to win with his cavalry, and had gathered 200 scythed chariots to assist them.[4]

Alexander marched for just under 300 miles, probably via Harran (an ancient city known from the book of Genesis and called Carrhae in the Roman period) and Nisibis until he reached the Tigris in September—probably near modern Mosul. Until the last stage he had not forced the pace, moving steadily and giving his men rest periods. The capture of some Persian scouts gave him a rare snippet of intelligence, claiming that Darius had sent men to defend the river, so he force-marched to get there first. As it turned out, the story was untrue, and the Macedonians crossed unopposed. At this time of year the river was shallow enough to ford, so there was no need to construct a bridge, although our sources claim that the men and horses struggled against the strong current. Alexander gave his men two days to rest and recover, and then took care to reassure them when there was a lunar eclipse on the night of September 20–21. The king offered sacrifices to the Earth, Sun, and Moon—for educated Greeks understood what an eclipse was—while Aristander the diviner announced that the omen was bad only for Darius and good for the Macedonians.[5]

The advance resumed along the east bank of the Tigris, and two days later patrols from the *prodromoi* light horse sighted strong forces of Persian cavalry. Alexander ordered a halt and began deploying for battle, until another rider came in to say that there were barely 1,000 Persians. Taking a squadron of Companions and the Paeonians to reinforce the *prodromoi*, Alexander headed for the enemy, who promptly withdrew, although not before one of Alexander's officers speared a Persian nobleman and brought his severed head to the king. A long chase followed and a few men whose horses gave out were killed or taken by the Macedonians, and the prisoners revealed that Darius was not far off with a very large army. After weeks of groping blindly, each side now had a clearer idea of where the enemy were. Sometime before, Darius had realized that the Macedonians were not coming down the Euphrates so he had moved up the Tigris, knowing that this was the only other viable route for an invading army. His own great host was not suited to rapid maneuver, nor could it stay too long in one place. For his plan to work, he needed open country and could not risk ending up in the same sort of restricted terrain that had hindered him at Issus. As he marched he looked for suitable battle-fields and by this time had settled on one a little north of the city of Arbela. There he halted and waited for Alexander to come to him, although it is more than likely that if the Macedonians had not been contacted, he would have moved again in due course.[6]

Alexander halted, chose a good site for a camp, and brought up the rest of his army. Men labored to fortify the camp, for he planned to leave his heavy baggage there, but otherwise he gave the troops four days to rest and prepare for the coming engagement. At the Granicus he had needed a quick battle, and at Issus Darius appeared behind him and left him no choice other than to fight. Now he did not need to hurry and could give the army time to recover after nearly three months of long marches. Taking only his fighting troops and light baggage carrying supplies for a few days, he waited until the cover of darkness before marching with the intention of being ready to fight soon after dawn. As the late September sun rose they were some 7.5 miles from the Persians. Neither of the main forces could see each other, for hills blocked their lines of sight, but the Persians were also ready for battle, either because their scouts had revealed the Macedonian advance or as a simple precaution since they knew that the enemy were close. It was not until they were less than four miles apart that the two armies saw each other, at which point Alexander halted and called his officers together.[7]

This, at least, is the essence of Arrian's version. Our other sources differ over the details, and Curtius has Darius attempt to bribe the Greeks with the army to turn against the Macedonians, then places the death of his wife Stateira at this point, followed by a final attempt at negotiation. Most of his narrative has a moral purpose, whether it is Parmenio persuading Alexander not to make public the captured letters attempting to bribe the Greeks, or declaring that he would accept the peace offer; it is here we have Alexander's quip that he would also accept "if he were Parmenio." The death of Stateira gave Curtius and others a rich seam to mine, for he has a eunuch escape to bring the news, and a Darius who is heartbroken, then suspicious when he hears how well Alexander treated his wife, until finally convinced that he had not raped or seduced her, at which point he supposedly prayed aloud that if he should fall, only the Macedonian king should succeed him. None of this seems very likely, and at the least any truth has been so embellished as to become almost unrecognizable.[8]

All the sources agree that the battle did not occur on the first day that the armies sighted each other. At almost four miles each side would see no more than clouds of dust from movement or a darker shade on the land. Patrols no doubt rode forward for a closer look, and at a little under a mile would be able to tell cavalry from infantry with confidence. The sheer size of Darius's host would have been obvious from the start, and the strength of his cavalry, which formed the bulk of his first line, was apparent on closer inspection. Then there were the chariots and fifteen Indian elephants, although in the event the latter would play little or no role in the fighting.[9]

Most of Alexander's officers were keen to press on and attack, full of confidence given that they had won every significant encounter with the Persians since the Granicus. Parmenio was a lone voice of caution, advising that they halt and reconnoiter, and this time the king agreed. They halted and made camp, while Alexander took the Companions and light troops to study the ground and the enemy. The plain was open, largely flat, and Darius's men had cleared wide stretches of any obstacles to make sure that his chariots would have a smooth run at the enemy. This and the Persian deployment made the essence of his plan obvious, for the prepared ground showed that Darius would wait for Alexander to come to him before launching a counterattack—neither chariots nor cavalry were designed for static defense. With his great line of cavalry he would aim to envelop the smaller Macedonian army. Horsemen, however brave, could not hope to break a phalanx from the front, let alone one armed with pikes, so the charge of heavy chariots was clearly meant to break up its ranks. Once scattered the infantry would become highly vulnerable to horsemen. There was nothing particularly subtle about the Persian plan, but it was sound and could easily work with their numbers. Alexander needed to negate the chariots and protect his flanks while still routing the enemy.[10]

When he returned to the camp, he once again summoned his officers and issued orders for the next day, explaining what he had in mind. Parmenio is now said to have urged a night attack to reduce the impact of enemy numbers, but Alexander refused, saying that he would not "steal a victory." This is more like some of the other stories we have encountered, although we need always to remind ourselves that the common thread is not that Parmenio was always wrong, but that Alexander was always right. In this case Arrian, himself a former army commander, praised the decision, noting the confusion inherent in any night action as well as the political value of a clear triumph rather than a defeat where Darius could blame the Macedonians' cunning and duplicity rather than their courage. He does claim that the Persians feared a night attack, so that most or all of their army stood to arms—or at least in position—overnight, making them far less fresh than the Macedonians. Highly unlikely are stories of mass panic among the Macedonians, and of Alexander spending the night performing sacrifices until both he and Aristander were satisfied with the omens, at which point the king fell into such a deep sleep that Parmenio had to shake him awake hours after the sun had risen.[11]

Instead, at dawn on October 1, the Macedonians and their king paraded and marched out of camp. Alexander performed his usual morning sacrifice, and Callisthenes said that the king spoke to the

Thessalians and other Greek allies, praying as "the son of Zeus" that the gods would protect and strengthen them all. Aristander, robed in white and wearing a golden circlet, announced that he saw an eagle high overhead, the messenger of Zeus speeding at the enemy who were thus bound to be defeated. Plutarch describes Alexander's costume on this day in greater detail than at any other battle. Over a belted tunic from Sicily, he had a two-layered linen corselet captured at Issus. His iron helmet was carefully finished and then polished so that it shone like silver, and his cloak was highly decorated, made some time ago by a famous craftsman and given as a present to him by Rhodes. His sword was another present, this time from the king of Citium in Cyprus, and was said to be finely tempered and beautifully balanced. During the marshaling of the forces and the preliminary advance he rode a horse whose name has not been preserved, switching to Bucephalus immediately before the fighting despite that his beloved companion was "now past his prime."[12]

The Macedonians probably advanced for some distance in one or more columns before forming for battle. Darius's men waited for them, and unlike at Issus did not send out a cloud of light cavalry to skirmish, so it was soon plain that the Persians were in the same formation as the day before. Arrian cites Aristobulus, who claimed that the Macedonians subsequently captured a copy of the Persian order of battle, so the details in our sources may well be accurate. The king of kings was once again in a chariot at his proper station behind the center of the line, guarded by 1,000 royal cavalry, the 1,000 Apple-bearers, and the Greek mercenaries on either side of them. Elsewhere the army was divided into ethnic contingents, the cavalry in the first line, with corresponding infantry behind in a second line. Darius's right wing was commanded by Mazaeus, former satrap of Cilicia, with Syrians, Mesopotamians, Medes, Parthians, Sacae (a nomadic tribe famous as heavily armored horse archers), Tapurians and Hyrcanians, Albanians, Sacasinians, Cappadocians, and Armenians. The left wing was equally powerful, led by Bessus, the satrap of Bactria and a member of the royal family, albeit presumably a distant one to have survived the purges. He led Bactrians, Dahae from his own territory, and more Sacae, and between him and the center were Persians, Susians, and Cadusians. Some infantry archers were in or near the front line, and a little ahead were the chariots in three main groups, 100 near the left wing, 50 in the center, and 50 more on the right.[13]

Alexander deployed so that he was facing Darius. As usual in the center was a phalanx with the hypaspists on the right next to the six regiments of pikemen. Again as usual, the king and the Companion cavalry were to the right of the phalanx and the Thessalian cavalry under Parmenio on its left—just as they had begun the battle at the Granicus and how they eventually moved into position at Issus. Even if he had placed all his units in a single line Alexander could not have matched the width of the Persian army, and in the open plain there was no feature to protect either flank. Thus for the first and only known occasion in any of Philip or Alexander's battles, the Greek allied and mercenary hoplites were arranged as a second phalanx some distance behind the main line. At the very least the second line matched the first in numbers and length, and may even have been wider, but its primary role was not as a reserve: it was to turn and face to the rear if enemy cavalry enveloped the army. Angled back were flanking forces to connect the two lines. On the right were Paeonians, the *prodromoi*, half the Agrianian infantry, archers, veteran mercenary infantry who had served under Philip, and mercenary cavalry led by Menidas, with the remaining Agrianians and some other skirmishers a little in front. The left wing was guarded by Thracians and Allied and mercenary cavalry. Thus the entire army formed as a rough square, or more precisely a sort of trapezoid, able to face a threat from any direction. Some servants, surely including many water carriers as well as grooms and others, were behind—or possibly between— the two phalanxes, while the rest stayed in the rudimentary camp pitched on the previous day.

This was not a defensive, let alone a static, formation—simply fending off the Persians was not enough, for Alexander had to close with Darius and rout his army. Getting everyone into position took some time—probably a couple of hours—and there may then have been a pause as the two sides studied each other and Alexander wondered whether the Persians would start coming to him. They did not, remaining two or three miles away, and during the lull Alexander no doubt encouraged his men; Arrian earlier on has him issue orders that were surely standard practice, telling the men to keep formation and stay silent until the moment came to shout their battle-cry and then to scream and terrify the enemy, and that they all depended on each other and would win if they worked together. Repeating the familiar while exuding confidence tends to be reassuring.[14]

Then he gave the signal to advance. Unlike at Issus, we have no account of how this was done, and whether or not from the start the phalanx and other units were in their standard fighting formations or went first in narrower columns until they got closer. Marching for two or three miles even in such open ground made it hard for individual units to keep in neat formation, let alone for the entire army to stay in alignment given its complex deployment. Quite a few halts to redress the ranks and adjust position in relation to others were inevitable, for as far as we can tell, the army had never practiced an advance in this formation. From the start Alexander angled to the right, moving away from the center of the Persian position and the middle of the carefully prepared tracks for their chariots, and this only made keeping alignment all the harder. Maneuver and drill are less dramatic than fighting, but once again the ability of Alexander and his army to do this is a great testimony to the high quality of its leaders and the discipline, confidence, and training of the troops.

Gradually the Macedonians closed with the Persians, never moving at faster than a walking pace. Darius watched as they edged away from the bulk of his chariots and toward his left flank. He responded, sending orders for his troops to move in the same direction and make sure that Alexander's right would be out-flanked. Some Sacae closed and skirmished with the light infantry moving ahead of the Macedonian right wing, but it was much harder to direct and shift the far larger Persian host, which had only completed its muster a few months before and thus had had little time to train together, as well as being so multinational. As Alexander kept on advancing and heading right, Darius became worried that soon the enemy would move away from the smooth tracks prepared for his chariots and onto slightly rougher ground. Probably sooner than he had hoped, he ordered his left wing to envelop and pin the enemy to stop their maneuver and sent the chariots into the attack.

As usual our understanding of what followed breaks down after the deployment and preliminary moves, making a reconstruction of the Battle of Gaugamela highly conjectural. (The name comes from the nearest substantial town.) This was an especially confusing battle for those involved, with great numbers of cavalry charging and countercharging by squadrons rather than in the neat blocks on our plans, and tens of thousands of hoofs throwing up clouds of dust so that visibility was often extremely poor. Arrian offers the most detailed and convincing narrative, while failing to explain much of what happened, and he and all the other sources once again fixate on Alexander and what he did. There is a fair chance than no one, least of all our sources written so long afterward, truly understood the course of the fighting. As a result, this can at best be a simplified and partial reconstruction.[15]

When some of the Persian left wing cavalry began to envelop the Macedonians, the 400 or so Greek mercenary horsemen under Menidas, stationed on Alexander's right, wheeled to charge them in the flank. Before the battle Alexander had given Menidas orders to do this on his own initiative if this occurred. The Persian envelopment halted, and instead Sacae and Bactrian squadrons countercharged. At the very least these numbered a couple of thousand, and before long Menidas and his small unit were chased back. Alexander had time to order the Paeonians to attack in turn, supported by the veteran mercenary infantry, who may well have been peltasts more lightly equipped and more mobile than hoplites. The combination of cavalry with good infantry—able to throw or shoot missiles and to form dense knots behind which tired horsemen could rally and re-form to charge again—was often highly effective in the ancient world. The Persians gave back for a while, and brought up more of their own supports, forgetting all thoughts of enveloping the Macedonian right. Even though outnumbered overall, Alexander's men held their own in very hard fighting, sucking in a disproportionately large number of opponents into a back-and-forth fight with no clear advantage on either side.[16]

The scythed chariots were heavily constructed, pulled by a team of four horses, and apart from the rotating scythe on each wheel had blades and spearheads mounted on the end of the yoke. Drivers were not expected to fight, but to flog the horses and keep them running straight at the enemy. If the enemy were infantry and held together in close formation with spears or pikes thrust out in front, then the instinct of the horses would make them pull up short, but it took a very steady nerve for pikemen to do this as the noisy teams and vehicles came bearing down. At Cunaxa in 401 BC the Ten Thousand had shown just such nerve and rendered the chariots useless. At Gaugamela Darius's chariots probably started earlier than planned so had to go farther, and the Macedonians matched the coolness of the famous mercenaries. Alexander had ordered the hypaspists and pikemen to open lanes in their formation to let the chariots through, just as they had done in the face of Thracian wagons rolled down the slopes in Alexander's first campaign as king. The horses naturally swerved to run through the gap rather than into the solid-looking walls of soldiers. Elsewhere, especially in front of the cavalry who could not easily use the same ploy, light infantrymen shot down horses and drivers. Curtius and Diodorus could not resist gruesome accounts of limbs and heads lopped off, both Macedonian and Persian, when some chariots turned around and fled, but the truth seems to be that the chariots inflicted hardly any casualties at all. Once past the phalanx the chariots—their teams beginning to tire and drivers confused—were dealt with by light infantry and the grooms waiting to support the Companion cavalry.[17]

The chief purpose of the chariots was not to kill, but to disrupt the phalanx and open the way for cavalry charges. This they utterly failed to do, and by the time the main line of Persian cavalry came forward they were confronted by serried ranks of spear and sarissa points as hypaspists and phalanx resumed their advance. Yet the shift to the right during the advance meant that the Macedonian left was threatened even more seriously than at Issus. Parmenio was soon outflanked, and the Thessalians had a tough fight against far greater numbers of enemy horsemen. Some Persians went right around the Macedonian army and attacked their camp (although the story of a deliberate raid to release Darius's family, and his mother's refusal to leave with her "rescuers" is highly unlikely, not least because such captives were surely at the strongly fortified main camp some distance from the battlefield). With the whole Macedonian left flank under threat, there was no question of advancing there, and the two leftmost regiments of the phalanx halted to keep in alignment with the cavalry and other troops on the wing. The rest of the first line pushed on, exacerbating the natural tendency for a large phalanx to fracture into its constituent units during a long advance. A wide gap opened, letting some Indian and Persian cavalry charge through. Most of the horsemen kept going, failing to wheel and attack the phalanx from side or rear, and they may even have found another gap in the second line. Servants were killed and baggage animals panicked before units from the second line responded, obeying orders issued before the battle. They turned and drove the enemy away.

Alexander had committed the *prodromoi* to the general melee on his right, and may have begun to charge with some or all of the Companions. At the start of the battle the Persian cavalry had formed a coherent line, but horsemen far more than close-order infantry are not suited to maintaining alignment in this way. Darius's orders to move to the left to match the angle of Alexander's advance, and then to try to envelop the Macedonians, disrupted the neat rows of squadrons, and order fell apart once the fighting started. Such very large numbers of horses so close together tend to excite one another, and as some units charged, more and more would surge with them, regardless of orders, and the leaders of the units were only a little less enthusiastic than their mounts. The Persian line broke up into clusters both large and small, with some squadrons in order and others scattered. There is no sign that the Persian infantry supported the horsemen effectively, still less that they formed a steady line. The first line phalanx, with the remaining four pike regiments and the hypaspists, kept advancing, pushing back infantry and cavalry alike.

A gap, or perhaps just a thinly held stretch, developed in the Persian line and Alexander led the Companions and the closest infantry straight at it. Arrian speaks of a great wedge formation, without explaining just what this meant on the day. The main force of the attack was angled toward Darius in the center. "Now for a little time it became a hand-to-hand fight, but when the cavalry with Alexander, and Alexander himself, pressed vigorously, shoving the Persians and striking their faces with spears," and at the same time the phalanx closed, ". . . Darius, who had now long been in a panic, . . . was the first to turn and flee." Around the same time, whether by chance or as word of the king of king's flight spread and men started to follow, the center and left wing of the Persian army dissolved. The *prodromoi* and other light troops, who had been clinging on against the odds, also charged one more time and routed the enemy facing them.[18]

Parmenio's wing was still hard pressed, and he sent a messenger to tell Alexander that he needed any support available. Diodorus claims that the courier could not find the young king who was already busy in the pursuit, while Arrian states that Alexander got the report and led the Companions back into the fray. They ran into a mass of Parthian, Indian, and Persian cavalry going in the opposite direction, producing some of the heaviest fighting of the battle, with sixty Companion cavalrymen killed and many more, including Hephaestion, wounded. Eventually the Macedonians prevailed, or perhaps some of the enemy broke off and were able to retreat as they had intended. Any aid to Parmenio was indirect, and his stubborn resistance at the head of the Thessalians eventually prevailed as the Persian commander, Mazaeus, realized that Darius and the remainder of the army was in flight and ordered his men to retreat.

Alexander ordered Parmenio to take the Persian camp, while he led the rest of the cavalry in pursuit. As in all ancient battles, the greatest slaughter was inflicted on a helpless fleeing enemy, although Arrian's 300,000 killed and far more taken prisoner is as wildly inflated as his estimate of the Persian numbers before the battle. Diodorus reduces this to 90,000, while Curtius says 40,000, but we have no idea whether or not these figures were based on reliable information. The spirit of Darius's army was broken, its camp and supplies overrun, and the contingents dispersed. Alexander had no body of fresh cavalry kept in reserve for the moment of pursuit, so the chase and killing was done by weary riders on tired horses, limiting just how much they could do before exhaustion forced a halt. Yet the excitement of triumph and the driving personality of the king who led them pushed what could be done to the very limit, so that 1,000 horses were lost by the Macedonians at Gaugamela, either killed in the fighting or ridden to death in the aftermath. Half of these were from the Companions, who as always were in the forefront. Fatalities among the men were once again relatively low. Arrian says just 100, which seems odd having said that 60 fell in one phase, and he may again be referring only to Macedonians. Curtius says the Macedonians had less than 300 dead, while even Diodorus's 500 represents less than 2 percent of the army. As always there were many times more wounded than dead, multiplying the total of casualties perhaps as much as tenfold. Apart from Hephaestion, the commanders of two of the phalanx regiments were wounded, as was Menidas, the man who led the mercenary cavalry in the charge that opened the battle.

―――――

AGIS III MAY already have been dead by the end of 331 BC, and if not he fell early in the next spring. After his initial victory the Spartan king had mustered an army of 20,000 infantry and 2,000 cavalry, with which he besieged—or at least blockaded—Megalopolis. For a while Antipater was busy in the north, for there was trouble with Alexander's governor of Thrace, although it is confused in our sources and we cannot tell what really happened. There was no fighting, and since the governor does not appear to have been punished, perhaps it was no more than bickering between two subordinates over authority. In time Antipater mustered 40,000 men, including mercenaries and allies. If estimates for Macedonia's population of some 500,000 are even roughly correct, then Alexander never took anything like as much as half of the adult male population on campaign, although he probably did have most of the bolder spirits and keener soldiers. Even after sending the great reinforcement to Asia in 331 BC, Antipater could call on plenty of other willing and capable soldiers, at least for a short campaign.

A battle was fought near Megalopolis, the confined battlefield chosen by Agis to make it hard for the enemy's greater numbers to come to play. There are no real details of what appears to have been a tough fight, but by the end a quarter of the Spartan king's army lay dead and he was badly wounded and killed in a skirmish soon afterward. Diodorus claims that the victory cost Antipater some 3,000 men, which seems high, and Curtius gives the lower figure of 1,000, but without knowing more details we cannot judge whether this is likely to be accurate. When he eventually heard of the battle and the success of his regent, Alexander is supposed to have spoken dismissively of a "war of mice" back in distant Greece. That was unfair if Diodorus's narrative is at all accurate, albeit understandable in a twenty-five-year-old who had overrun most of a great empire in just a few years.[19]

22

"THE MOST HATEFUL OF THE CITIES OF ASIA"

Darius was beaten once again, but escaped. On October 2, 331 BC, Alexander captured Arbela and discovered that the king of kings had already been there, abandoned another royal chariot, and departed. There was no prospect of catching him, for with the remnants of his guards, the Greek mercenaries, and some of the Bactrian cavalry, he was headed not to the rich cities of Babylonia, but took the harder route to Media. In time he might be able to build another army, although this second defeat, inflicted on his great army on ground of his own choice and well suited to their numbers, was a far greater blow to his prestige than Issus.

There were more tangible losses to follow. The camps near the battlefield and at Arbela once again were filled with luxuries to prompt scorn and delight on the part of the victors. Curtius says that there were 4,000 talents of silver at Arbela alone. Alexander brought the main army up from Gaugamela as soon as possible, not least because there were too many corpses to cope with, all rapidly decaying in the heat, and only his own dead received burial. It was probably at Arbela that he sacrificed to celebrate the victory and was proclaimed King of Asia, the celebration marked by generous gifts to friends and allies. His role as hegemon of the Greek cause remained as important, and he wrote to the poleis in Greece and Asia Minor to say that the tyrannies (presumably in the main of Persia) were abolished and that they might live under their own laws. Plataea was to be rebuilt in honor of the city's sacrifice in the greater Greek cause in 479 BC—although since Philip had already decreed this after Chaeronea, presumably this was no more than a gift to make its reconstruction all the more splendid. On the basis of the heroism of an athlete from Croton—one of the Greek cities of Italy—who had brought a trireme to fight at Salamis, he singled out the community for a gift to celebrate the Hellenic victory.[1]

When the advance resumed, Alexander headed for Babylon. There was no opposition, and before he arrived envoys came to negotiate. Mazaeus, the commander of the Persian right wing at Gaugamela, had fled to the city, for he had local connections and had married a Babylonian. The Babylonians had no great reason to love Darius or the Achaemenid dynasty for they had their own culture and religion, memories of their own former glories. In the past they had rebelled against Persian rule, provoked by real and imagined slights against their gods and their prestige, and been suppressed. As elsewhere, dislike of Persian rule did not automatically translate to enthusiasm for a Macedonian conqueror. The city had strong walls and could choose to resist the invader. Yet there was no prospect of relief and Alexander's army had shown its skill and determination at siegecraft, so in the end Babylon would probably fall and be sacked, and that was not an appealing prospect if something better was on offer. As elsewhere, pragmatism ruled. The Babylonians decided that loyalty to Darius was extremely dangerous and highly unlikely to bring them any benefit, at least in the immediate future, and Mazaeus and the commander of the Persian garrison agreed. On October 18 Alexander issued a decree guaranteeing that his army would respect the rights and possessions of individual Babylonians and not enter forcibly into their houses. Once again, displays of respect by both parties ensured that Alexander received the submission that he wanted, and his new subjects gave it in a way that made it acceptable to them.[2]

When the Macedonians reached the city later in the month, they were greeted outside by a delegation of local dignitaries and senior Persians. Crowds cheered, strewing flowers in their path as Alexander and his men paraded through the streets. Babylon was larger, far more ancient and far grander than any Greek city or any community the Macedonians had yet encountered, and can only have been a source of wonder; its Hanging Gardens were later always included in lists of Wonders of the World. Alexander offered sacrifice to the city's patron deity Bel-Marduk, was named as king, and given control of the treasury and citadel, as well as gifts ranging from luxuries to the food and supplies needed by his army. The agreements were honored and there was no looting, while the subsequent appointment of Mazaeus as his satrap for the area may suggest that other provisions had been included in the deal, even if kept secret. This was the first time that Alexander had appointed a Persian, so it marked a major step in creating his new kingdom of Asia, even though he made sure that Mazaeus's independence was limited by the presence of Macedonians in key financial and all military posts. Yet it was a sign to others that his war was with the Persian king and not with his subjects if they showed the sense to submit.

As in Egypt, Alexander respected local cults and conventions. One mark of this was his promise to rebuild the great eight-story ziggurat temple to Bel-Marduk destroyed by the Persians, although he took no concrete action to achieve this and expected the locals to direct and fund the project. For the Babylonians this was a transition from one master to another, and it was relatively seamless, just as when one king died and was succeeded by his heir. A fragmentary cuneiform tablet describes Darius as "the king of the world" on the morning of Gaugamela. Later it notes that "the troops of the king deserted him," and a little later has the matter of fact statement that "Alexander, king of the world, entered Babylon." The temple records simply continued, whoever was king.

The Macedonians upheld their side of the agreement. Denied plunder, Alexander gave a bounty to each soldier from the captured treasury, with Companion cavalrymen receiving 600 drachmae apiece (one-tenth of a talent), Allied horsemen 500, Macedonian infantrymen 200, and the mercenaries a sum equivalent to two months of pay. They also had several weeks of rest and feasting in the spectacular city, courtesy of a population eager to please their new masters. According to Curtius many Babylonian women, and not simply prostitutes and entertainers but those from respectable families, were said to be adept at a form of striptease dance.[3]

Ancient authors believed that too much time spent in the flesh-pots of a city weakened an army, but there was no sign of this when the Macedonians moved on after a few weeks. The next great city along the road was Susa, and once again negotiations were complete before he arrived. On the road Alexander was met by the son of Abulites the satrap, bringing written assurances that the city and its treasury were now his. Like Mazaeus, Abulites became satrap in service of the new overlord. The march from Babylon to Susa took the army twenty unhurried days and ended in another warm welcome. Unlike Babylon, Susa was a Persian city, the administrative center of the empire, and leaders and people alike accepted the presence of the conqueror, who in turn treated them with respect. Its treasury contained at least 50,000 talents of silver and gold coin and bullion, as well as much other wealth. Each gain to Alexander was another loss to Darius and his capacity to fund war.[4]

Respect for the locals only went so far, and there were celebrations of victory marked by sacrifices and athletic competition. Statues of Harmodius and Aristogeiton, Athenian heroes who had assassinated a tyrant, had been part of the plunder brought home by Xerxes, and were now sent back to Athens, and remained on view in Arrian's day. There was a royal throne and footstool in the palace at Susa, designed for the tall Darius, and when Alexander climbed into the chair his feet did not reach the footstool, so someone pushed the higher royal dining table over instead. A eunuch—himself part of the spoils of conquest—wept at the sight, and Alexander was supposed to have been about to order it taken away when Philotas assured him that it was a good omen.[5]

Amid the celebration, there was an awareness that the war was not over. Around this time the reinforcement ordered from Anti-pater earlier in the year caught up with the army. It was the largest ever sent, numbering some 15,000 troops, including no fewer than

6,000 Macedonian infantry and 500 Macedonian cavalry, as well as contingents from Thrace and the Peloponnese. In return Alexander sent 3,000 talents of silver from his new acquisitions on the slow road back to Macedonia for Antipater to use in the war against Agis; he was aware that this conflict had broken out but unsure how it was progressing.[6]

As the year came to an end and winter began Alexander resumed the advance, heading for Persepolis, the grand ceremonial capital of the Achaemenids and some 400 miles from Susa. The road led through the foothills of the Zagros Mountains, and a hill people known as the Uxii demanded payment for safe passage as they were accustomed to do with all travelers, including those on business of the Persian king. Alexander was in no mood to humor them, but pretended compliance and then led out the hypaspists and other picked troops during the night, ravaged the tribal lands, and then seized the pass that the locals had expected to hold against him. Some were killed, most fled, and the intervention of Darius's mother gave Alexander a pretext for mercy: he imposed an annual tribute of livestock on them since they did not employ currency.[7]

A tougher challenge came soon afterward at the Persian Gates, the key pass through the Zagros Mountains leading to the province of Persis, which was held by the satrap of the region and a strong force of at least 25,000 men. Alexander sent Parmenio with the baggage and the greater part of the army by the longer, gentler route, and took most of the Macedonians and other picked troops to the pass. An attempt at a quick assault failed in the face of a well-built rampart, which had artillery on top of it, but in an echo of Xerxes at Thermopylae, a local was captured and told them of a difficult path that led around the main pass. Craterus—an officer who began to receive more and more independent commands from now on—was left with a fairly small force to occupy a fortified camp, lighting far more fires than needed to deceive the enemy into believing that the whole army was present. Alexander took the remainder, once again using the night for a forced march, and had them rest concealed in woodland during the next day, before they set out again the following night. Persian outposts were overrun before they could give the alarm, and the main position attacked from the rear and—once Craterus heard the signals—the front as well. The defenders were routed or killed, the satrap escaping only to fall in a skirmish shortly afterward. There was now nothing between Alexander and Persepolis.[8]

The Persian official in command of Persepolis sent envoys offering surrender and urging Alexander to hurry and take control of the city and its immense treasures before they could be looted by the garrison. The Macedonians pressed on, seizing a bridge before the enemy made any attempt to contest the only significant obstacle in their path. Some of our sources claim that the advance guard then encountered a pathetic crowd of Greek prisoners, at last free from Persian captivity. Most of them were elderly, and all were mutilated, noses and ears cut off, limbs amputated as carefully judged punishment that left them just capable of performing specific manual tasks. Alexander was moved to pity and offered to return them to their homes, until after a long debate the men decided that it was easier to bear their disfigurement in isolation. He granted them a community of their own, and land to support them and the families that they had acquired during their captivity.[9]

Arrian does not mention the incident, and most modern scholars have wondered when in the prior half century so many Greek prisoners could have been taken and transported to the heart of the Persian empire. Perhaps the invaders did come across some mutilated prisoners, and perhaps there was a handful of Greeks from Ionia or even Greece itself among them, and the story grew in the telling, although it is far more likely to be pure invention. Exaggeration and myth surrounded Alexander from the start, not least because court historians like Callisthenes embellished a good deal, while later authors made up incidents to add drama to the story. The further away from Greece Alexander and his soldiers marched, the more far-fetched details and whole incidents become, partly from the lack of genuine information and also the confidence that distance would make any tale that much more plausible. Many authors claimed that Alexander was visited by the Queen of the Amazons later in 330 BC, although once again

Arrian does not even mention the tale. She had come to the bravest of men so that he could give her a child, since she was the bravest of women, promising that a boy would be sent back while a girl would stay with her. After thirteen days of passion, she left an exhausted Alexander to return to her homeland. Plutarch thought the story highly dubious, and says that in later years Lysimachus, one of Alexander's Companions and in due course a king, heard a historian read out an account of the incident, prompting him to smile and say, "And where was I at the time?"[10]

Meeting Greek victims of a Persian king's cruelty just outside Persepolis reminded a Greek audience of the need for vengeance that was the much proclaimed justification for Alexander's expedition, all adding to the probability that someone, perhaps the notoriously unreliable Cleitarchus, made it all up. Yet Persepolis was a symbol of the might and majesty of the Achaemenid dynasty, and Alexander does seem to have stoked the hostility of his army. Diodorus claims that he called it "the most hateful of the cities of Asia," and in Curtius's version he reminded his men that "it was from here that those huge armies had been poured into their country, from here that first Darius, then Xerxes, had made impious war upon Europe." Darius I had begun construction of the vast royal precinct at Persepolis, and his son had done more than anyone else to complete it, so there was some justice in the association of this place with the invaders of Greece so long ago. Unlike Susa, it was less a center of government than a place of ceremony, where the right to rule of the Persian king as representative of the god Ahura Mazda was annually reaffirmed as envoys from the entire empire came to present tribute. Its very name, "city of Perse," marked it as the heart of Darius III's empire, center of the region named Persis, the home of the Persians (today known as Fārs province in Iran), but now the king had abandoned it to the Macedonian and Greek invaders.[11]

All of this may begin to explain why Alexander treated Persepolis so differently from any other surrendering city. Although there was no resistance when he arrived at the end of January 330 BC, his soldiers were given license to run amok for a day, something they had been denied at every city since Tyre and Gaza. The details are unclear, and Arrian does not mention it at all, while other accounts specify that the royal precinct at least was excluded and speak of the plundering as especially brutal, with the soldiers fighting among themselves over spoils. Amid the familiar horrors, they claim that some of the behavior was unusual, such as women being carried off still fully clothed, the captors willing to postpone rape to save the valuable garments their victims wore. Classical authors were adept at describing terrible events whether or not they had evidence, and tend rhetorically to make their current subject more terrible than any other. Diodorus claimed that "as Persepolis had exceeded all other cities in prosperity, so in the same measure it now exceeded all others in misery." No doubt it was appalling, but it is unlikely to have created a wasteland or to have spared no one from death or enslavement, for the army remained in and around the city for the best part of four months. It is quite possible that the sack focused on the richly furnished houses of the court aristocrats.[12]

For the moment Alexander reserved the royal precinct for himself, and there he sat on another of Darius's thrones. Plutarch claims that at this sight "Demaratus of Corinth . . . burst into tears, as old men will, and declared that those Hellenes were deprived of great pleasure who had died before seeing Alexander seated on the throne of Darius." For many, taking the city seemed the happy culmination of the great war of vengeance or at least showed that the ultimate victory must be close. Babylon's monuments were magnificent and of great antiquity, stretching back long before Persia's empire, but at Persepolis everything was designed to celebrate the Achaemenids. Built on a rock terrace to be higher than the city, which was primarily there to support the court when the king was in residence, and surrounded by a high wall, the royal compound was divided into three main ceremonial sections, the *Apadana* (Audience Hall), Throne Room, and Treasury, with palaces including a complex set aside for the royal harem. Visitors entered through one of the great gates and climbed a wide stairway to the terrace, past reliefs depicting the nations of the empire coming to pay homage and offer tribute. The diversity of the king's subjects was emphasized, each with their distinctive dress, and the sculpted soldiers showed Medes as well as Persians.

Persepolis was far, far larger and grander than Aegae or Pella—indeed than anything in the Greek world. Much of it was mud brick rather than stone, but the walls were high, the great halls roofed by cedar beams held up by row after row of pillars. Colors were bright and decoration elaborate in its detail, no doubt reinforced by the richness of tapestries, furnishings, and the bright clothes of the attendants, courtiers, and visitors who thronged the place during one of the great ceremonies. Yet the overwhelming impression was deliberately one of sheer scale, constantly reminding any visitors that they were tiny and insignificant compared to the majesty of the king whose halls these were. Everything was vast, and when Alexander's men went into the Treasury they are supposed to have found 120,000 talents in gold and silver, apart from all the other precious things. There were also immense quantities of stored weapons, especially arrows and spears forged from bronze as well as iron. By the fourth century BC Persepolis appears to have had only a secondary administrative role in the running of the empire, and it looks as if its Treasury was a reserve, rarely if ever touched and instead housing the annual tribute brought from all over the empire. The great king's power was underlined by the simple fact that he did not need to call upon this wealth, nor did he spend that much time in at Persepolis, instead ruling from Susa or Ecbatana, the capital of Media and conveniently placed to supervise the eastern satrapies.[13]

Persepolis proclaimed the strength of the Achaemenid kings, their right to rule as representatives of the Zoroastrian god Ahura Mazda, and, in the emphasis on the great variety of his subjects, the Persian acceptance of local traditions and religions as long as subject peoples remained loyal and subservient. It is hard to say how much Alexander or any Macedonian or Greek understood of this or of how the empire functioned. They could certainly see the splendor and fabulous wealth, as well as the simple truth that Alexander now sat on Darius's throne, occupied his palaces and ceremonial halls, and possessed his treasures while the great king of kings was a fugitive somewhere to the east. Even after Babylon, Susa, and all the victories of the last few years, the knowledge can only have been intoxicating.[14]

The problem was what to do with it all. Persepolis was important because it was the symbolic heart of Persia and the Persians and their kings were the overlords of the empire. Nearby was Pasargadae, the capital before the far grander Persepolis was built. Alexander paid a visit, ordering the removal of the 6,000 talents in its treasury, while paying respect to the tomb of Cyrus, the founder of the dynasty. This may well have been genuine, as well as inviting contrast between the heroic first Achaemenid and the weak Darius III. His attitude toward other Persian kings and the symbols of their power was less enthusiastic, and he is supposed to have pondered raising a fallen statue of Xerxes on the basis that he had been a just king apart from his attack on Greece. After a while Alexander moved on and the statue remained in the dust.[15]

From the start it was clear that Persepolis had no place in the regime Alexander wished to create. He ordered the Treasury to be emptied, and the wealth transported to Susa, and subsequently to Ecbatana. This was a huge task, for the coin and bullion alone weighed over 7,000 tons, and Plutarch says that 10,000 pairs of mules and 3,000 pack camels had to be brought to Persepolis. Gathering the transport took time, as did collecting and packing the treasure and escorting it on the journey, so this was one reason why the army stayed at Persepolis. The difficulty of supply during the winter months was another reason, especially when so much of the available logistic support was being used to move the treasure. Alexander was not wholly idle, and took a column out on a month's punitive expedition against the Mardi living in the southern reaches of the Zagros Mountains. There was little organized resistance, but conditions were harsh and the operation may have helped introduce some of the reinforcements to the rigors of campaigning, as well as satisfied the king's restless spirit.[16]

Arrian reports a debate between Alexander and his Companions over what to do with the royal precinct, with Parmenio arguing that it should be preserved and used, since "it was not good to destroy what was now his own property." In addition he claimed that the Asians would assume he had come just to plunder and destroy rather than forge a new kingdom, and therefore would not feel it was worth joining him. However, Alexander wanted to punish the Persians and opted to destroy everything, and for once Arrian felt that the king was wrong and his old subordinate right.[17]

Plutarch and others recount another tradition, which has Alexander hold a feast where, in true Macedonian fashion, the wine flowed freely. Philip had liked to celebrate whenever the opportunity offered on campaign, and a few anecdotes make clear that Alexander did the same. Present was an Athenian courtesan (the Greek *hetaira* means literally "female companion") named Thaïs, who at some point became the mistress of Ptolemy the historian, bearing him three children and later becoming his wife. There were other courtesans, as quite a few of the officers seem to have kept lovers as well as female entertainers. As the night wore on, Thaïs proclaimed that it would be a splendid thing for Alexander to avenge the burning of Athens by Xerxes by setting the royal palaces and halls alight, the revenge all the sweeter because it would be inflicted by Greek women. According to Curtius, "the king . . . more greedy for wine than able to carry it, cried: 'Why do we not, then, avenge Greece and apply torches to the city?'" They formed a *comus*, the merry procession of revelers who went out into the streets after many a successful party in Greece and something Alexander had done in the past. As girl musicians played flutes, Alexander hurled a torch to set the buildings on fire, and in some accounts Thaïs threw the second. The blaze flared up, and at first soldiers hurried to the spot to fight the fire, until they realized that the king had started it.[18]

The two stories are not incompatible. Months had been spent stripping out all items of value, but even so there were plenty of small items of gold, such as coins and fittings, buried under the debris when the fire brought down the timber roofs. This suggests that, although the destruction was carefully prepared, it happened suddenly and before everything had been picked bare. A few torches were unlikely to have started a conflagration unless quantities of combustible material had already been arranged to feed the blaze, while hammer blows on some of the sculptures attest to deliberate destruction over a period of time. The balance of probability is that Alexander decided to destroy the royal precincts and made preparations to do the job thoroughly. Perhaps drunken enthusiasm led him to start the fire sooner than planned or perhaps the whole story is another invention.[19]

The occupation of Persepolis showed Darius's weakness and its destruction emphasized his impotence. As a mark of Alexander's overwhelming strength they sent a message to the Persians that further resistance was futile. On the other hand they were fresh and terrible humiliations, inflicted on a sacred place where the bond between god, king, and subjects was confirmed; Alexander's actions could readily provoke outrage and might make it harder for them to accept Alexander as their new ruler. Merely occupying the site had not prompted a flood of surrenders, so perhaps he had little to lose, for it is unlikely that he ever wished to be seen as Darius's successor, and was always ruler by right of conquest. For a Greek audience it was a culmination of the war of revenge, a great achievement by the cities who had allied together at Corinth under the leader they had appointed. When Persepolis burned, Alexander may not have known that Agis was dead and his war over, so perhaps this was a gesture to remind the poleis that Sparta was a collaborator with the "true" enemy, Persia. If he did know that the Spartans were beaten, then he may have wanted to send back news of the great triumph achieved by the Greeks under his leadership. Some sources say he came to regret the destruction and ordered that the fires be brought under control, but the royal precinct was destroyed and never reoccupied, so his concern was probably more for the wider city.[20]

Alexander had sat on Darius's throne, plundered his treasure, and burned his palace. To many in his army it must have seemed that victory was complete.

23

AN END AND A BEGINNING

Yet Darius lived, and in the spring of 330 BC news began to arrive that the king of kings had mustered a new army at Ecbatana, after spending the winter months in the last of the royal cities still under his control. In May Alexander concentrated his own strength and advanced. Some communities resisted him and were stormed, while others capitulated. The burning of Persepolis did not mark any change in his willingness to accept the surrender of noblemen and reappoint them as his own representatives, not least because no Macedonian or Greek could match their local knowledge. The son of the man who had surrendered Susa to him was appointed satrap just like his father, suggesting that he was keener to reward families than concerned that any might gain too much influence.[1]

As Alexander pushed into Media he sent his heavy baggage to the rear and led the bulk of the fighting troops ahead. Reports came in to say that far fewer men had rallied to Darius than the king had hoped, so he had changed his plan and decided to retreat. The Macedonians hurried ahead in the hope of catching him, but when Alexander was three days from Ecbatana, a son of Artaxerxes Ochus—the last strong Persian king before Darius—greeted him. Very little is known about this man, who was presumably too insignificant or young to have perished in the purges preceding Darius's accession. He reported that the Persian king had barely 9,000 men left, and that with these and the 7,000 talents from the treasury at Ecbatana, he had left the city four days earlier and was heading for the series of passes leading through the mountains near the Caspian Sea known as the Caspian Gates.[2]

There was now no prospect of a battle on the scale of Issus or Gaugamela, and when he reached Ecbatana, Alexander released all his Greek allies including the Thessalians, some four years after they had crossed to Asia. Each man was to receive all his back pay, as well as a generous bonus of a talent to every cavalryman and one-sixth of a talent to the infantry, and were to be escorted on the long trek home and then carried in ships back to Greece. Cavalrymen willing to reenlist as volunteers and fight for pay were given a bounty of three talents apiece, and presumably there was an incentive for infantrymen as well. How many men were left overall and the proportion choosing to leave is unclear. Curtius claims that 12,000 talents went on meeting the cost of all this, and that a similar amount was embezzled by the officials responsible for overseeing the process. Arrian tells us that many Thessalians sold their mounts before leaving, and no doubt a high price was paid for these famously good horses, well schooled in a familiar style, which many may still have favored over the lighter Persian breeds.[3]

Alexander still had all of his Macedonians, as well as the Balkan troops, although from now on the role of mercenaries and troops recruited from Asia steadily increased. The first contingent of the latter, including men from Lycia, was soon to join him. Permitting the Greeks to go home fulfilled his role as leader of willing allies who had achieved the promised vengeance over Persia, and would return good numbers of well-disposed men to their home communities with tales of adventure and the tangible rewards of victory. Better to let them go freely than allow resentment to mount at being kept against their will. The Thessalians had played a distinguished part in all the campaigns so far, and the departure of the bulk of them was a loss to the army, although far from a critical one. As far as we can tell, many of the other Greek contingents had acted as garrisons, so were all the easier to replace with mercenaries. All in all the army was militarily little affected by the change, while the cost—even allowing for the corruption—was easily affordable given Alexander's newfound wealth.[4]

Parmenio was ordered to transport all the treasure from Susa to Ecbatana, where 6,000 Macedonian foot and other troops would protect it, and the rehabilitated Harpalus would oversee it as treasurer. Once this was done, the old general was supposed to take the field again with an semi-independent command, but for some reason this never happened. In the meantime Alexander had taken off in pursuit of Darius with the bulk of the Macedonians and other picked troops, including the Thessalian volunteers. For eleven days he forced the pace in his eagerness to catch up, at the cost of numerous stragglers and horses lamed or coming close to collapse. Darius beat them through the Caspian Gates, but more and more defectors came to Alexander, speaking of mass desertions and the collapse of morale. Realizing that he would not catch up for the moment, he gave his men five days to rest and recover. His business did not stop, and while he was camped he chose a Persian nobleman, formerly imprisoned by Darius, as the new satrap of Media.[5]

The Macedonians marched unopposed through the passes of the Caspian Gates, and then paused to forage as the country ahead appeared barren and they seem to have advanced faster than their supplies. More Persian defectors appeared, bringing the news of a coup in Darius's camp. The king of kings was now the prisoner of a cabal of noblemen, led by Bessus, the commander of the left wing at Gaugamela and satrap of Bactria. Alexander put Craterus in charge of the main body and told him to wait for the foraging expedition to return and then follow at a decent rate, while he led out the Companions, *prodromoi*, and infantrymen picked for speed and stamina. Carrying just two days of rations they pressed ahead, keeping on throughout the night and only pausing for a rest at noon the next day. More Persians were caught or surrendered, and they told Alexander that Bessus was acknowledged as leader, since they were now in his satrapy, but that not everyone was happy and that Artabazus—his mistress Barsine's father and one-time exile at Philip's court—had split away with some of the troops, including the remaining Greek mercenaries. Bessus was said to be willing to give up Darius and seek terms if Alexander pressed close, but to flee with him if the chase slackened.

Alexander drove his men onward, again traveling through the night and only stopping at midday at a village where he learned that he was barely a day behind. Discovering from the locals that there was a shortcut "but that the road was desolate for lack of water," he pressed one of them to guide him. Men on foot were no longer able to keep up, so he dismounted 500 cavalrymen and gave their mounts to the pick of the infantry, probably mainly hypaspists and Agrianians, who were to carry their own weapons and be ready to fight as infantry if they encountered trouble. Parmenio's oldest son, Nicanor, and another officer were to take a force of infantry with minimum equipment and follow the route taken by the enemy as best they could, while the rest came on behind them.[6]

As the sun set, Alexander pressed on, allegedly covering forty miles during the night. Horses collapsed and men dropped back, unable to keep up with their leader. Soon after dawn they sighted Persian soldiers straggling along the main route. A handful showed fight and were cut down, while the rest fled as soon as they spotted their pursuers. The chase continued, each side able to see the other, or at least the dust they made. More and more Macedonians dropped back, until only sixty riders remained with Alexander, and still he pressed on. Bessus and the other leaders had hundreds of cavalrymen but no will to fight and perhaps did not realize how few enemies were chasing them. As the Macedonian riders grew closer the Persian nobles decided that Darius was no longer worth keeping. They abandoned all the carts, along with the riches, women, and attendants in them. The captive king's servants were killed, the beasts drawing his wagon crippled, and Darius stabbed repeatedly. Then they fled.

The remaining pursuers were nearly spent as they overran the abandoned camp and in no state to catch the noblemen and their cavalry escort, so at last they halted. A cavalryman searching for water came across a wagon by a spring, its team dead or dying. Inside he found Darius, bound with golden chains. Our sources vary over whether the king was already dead or lived long enough to be given a drink, and a few could not resist claiming that he survived to see Alexander and praise him. A captive Darius might have been useful, especially if he was willing to make formal submission to Alexander and accept him as the new king of Asia. On the other hand a Darius murdered by Persian noblemen was almost as convenient, perhaps even better since Alexander had not had to order his death. He took care to treat the corpse with respect, preparing it as best as possible to be transported to Darius's mother and remaining family so that it received honorable burial. The Macedonian who had attacked Persia, beaten its king in battle, and hunted him into the far east of his empire soon would declare himself his avenger. Much was changing.[7]

Persepolis lay in ruins, Darius was dead, and Alexander and his army had overrun the greater part of the Persian Empire—far more territory than even the most optimistic Panhellenist had ever predicted. Everything suggested that the war of revenge was over, not least the column of Greek allies already partway along the three- to four-month journey back to the coast of Asia Minor. Weary, farther from home than they had ever been before, laden with plunder, and heady with victory, it was natural for Macedonians and other troops alike to conclude that the great expedition was over. Philip had fought campaign after campaign, so his troops came to expect to fight most years and to be away for months, sometimes over the winter. Under his son the intensity of operations increased even further. This was all a major change from the hoplite ideal of brief campaigns, but it had not severed their ties with life away from the army and they had frequently had the chance to return home to see their families and farms. For all their training and discipline, the Macedonians were not yet fully professional soldiers, in the sense that the army was their only life. They fought because they were Macedonians, horse or foot companions of the king, and they received pay and other rewards, including land as their share of victories. The rewards were a great incentive, but at heart they served because it was the duty of a Macedonian to fight for the kingdom.

Ecbatana lay some 2,000 miles from Pella, and Alexander and his men had marched and ridden far more than that distance since landing in Asia in 334 BC, and had fought three major battles, several prolonged and difficult sieges, and many more skirmishes and stormings. A lot of them had taken wounds in the process, and some had died from sickness or the sword, but that was all part of the duty to serve with their king. Reinforcements brought news, and some wrote and received letters, but even the young men given special leave in the winter of 334–333 BC had not seen home for more than three years. Feeling that the war was won and their task complete, homesickness grew, which was not to say that after a break they did not expect their king to lead them on campaign once again, wherever it might be. Rumor spread, as rumors always will in any large group and especially an army, that Alexander agreed and would soon give the order to turn for home. Men started to prepare for the journey, sorting their plunder so that it would be easier to transport.

The strength of feeling among his men may have surprised Alexander, and Curtius claims he wept with frustration at the "envy of the gods" who threatened to stop him before he had completed his conquests. However, his officers assured him of their own enthusiasm for fresh victories, and went to talk to the troops before Alexander addressed a parade of the entire army, or at least representatives who could then convey his words to the rest. His message was simple, logical, and contained just enough truth to help persuade them, for he told them that the victory was not yet complete. The Persians were beaten for the moment, but if the Macedonians marched home then nothing would prevent the enemy from rebuilding his strength, especially while leaders like Bessus were at large. One day in the not too distant future a Persian army might once again invade Greece if they did not finish the job now—a stronger argument for men serving on what was ostensibly vengeance for wrongs committed a century and a half ago than it may be to us. Alexander told them that it would only take a little more effort and then they would be done. The men were persuaded and pressed on with added eagerness to end the war, although if Curtius's claim that the king spoke in terms of days rather than months is true, then they were greatly misled.[8]

Everything suggests that from the beginning Alexander had planned to add territory in Asia to his kingdom and not lead merely a punitive raid. The negotiations with Darius and his refusal of successive offers, including all the lands west of the Euphrates, show his ambitions were grand. If he left a Persian king, whoever it was, at the head of any sizeable kingdom, then the probability was that the war would be renewed at some point in the future, just as he is said to have told his soldiers. Thus conquest of any new territory required the destruction of the Persian Empire to make these gains secure in the longer term. Alexander probably understood this from the start, for the logic is simple enough, and it ought to have been clear to his officers as well. The difficulty lay in achieving this goal, not in the idea itself, and once again we need to remind ourselves just how spectacular and rapid the war had been. Alexander may have dreamed of such success, and was young and self-regarding enough even to expect it, but nothing in recent nor even more distant history foreshadowed it. Any sensible person would have expected a far longer war, perhaps with intervals of negotiated peace before conflict was renewed, much like Philip's campaigns, which in their day had surprised observers by their speed.

Alexander had forced the pace of the war, suffered no truly serious setbacks, and won, which does not mean that it had been easy. Throughout all of this much of his mind and energy was absorbed in fighting the war itself, and this was surely even more true of the rest of the army. Planning for after the victory could wait until that victory had been won. Region by region he appointed satraps, military and financial commanders, including friendly dynasts and factions in Asia Minor, and enlisted locals in Egypt and then the provinces in the heart of the empire, all of it on an ad hoc basis. This was far from being a formal and permanent system of government for the vastly enlarged kingdom he was creating, not least because as yet he did not know what he was creating, and pauses were rare before moving on to the next offensive.

Money was no longer a problem, and unlike Philip, who had soon spent each windfall on ongoing diplomacy and the next war,

Alexander no longer faced any real financial restrictions on what he wanted to do; indeed from now on the only aspect requiring thought was moving wealth to where it was needed. The sums acquired were so great that waste and corruption did not matter. Alexander was also notably generous in gifts, especially to his Companions, and set an example in extravagance. We read of one officer who used silver hobnails in his boots, and another who had sand brought all the way from Egypt for his wrestling practice. The prizes for bravery grew in proportion to the spoils, but all shared in the gains just as they had shared in the toil, as was proper for Macedonians.[9]

The bulk of the army expected to go home when the war was complete. Presumably few, at least of the officers, thought that they would entirely withdraw and abandon all the lands they had taken. Panhellenists had spoken of bringing peace to Greece by letting Greeks live from the produce of estates worked by conquered Asians, and perhaps a few men expected to fulfill this dream. More may have assumed that mercenaries would garrison the new territory and deal with any rebellion or attack from outside, although just like Alexander, few had had much leisure to think in detail of the future; all were consumed by the euphoria of the sheer scale of what they had achieved. They had shown their superiority in battle and in sieges and this was unlikely to change. Yet there were simply not the numbers of soldiers to hold down the newfound empire solely by force, even if all the troops were willing to devote their lives to the task.

Alexander was king of the Macedonians, but they now represented a small minority of the peoples who had submitted to his rule, and Macedonia itself, even after its expansion by Philip, was a small part of the territory he controlled. Philip, and after him Alexander, had become archon of Thessaly and leader of the alliance of Greek cities, as well as king of his own people. More recently Alexander was acknowledged as pharaoh in Egypt and king in Babylon, and had proclaimed himself Lord of Asia, and these represented far more drastic additions to his powers and responsibilities as the ruler of peoples with very different cultures and political traditions. Inevitably this produced a degree of tension between upholding his relationship with his own people—the Macedonians and to a slightly lesser extent Greeks and others who had triumphed under his leadership—and at the same time satisfying the expectations of his conquered subjects, at least to the extent of discouraging them from rebellion. From the start there were fundamental questions about just what it meant to be lord or king of Asia and no easy or obvious answers.

Becoming an Achaemenid was never really practical, since it would be equally abhorrent to his own army after fighting their war of vengeance against the Persian barbarians, as well as to the Persians who could not have accepted the invader as chosen by Ahura Mazda. There is no sign that Alexander even toyed with this idea, and the burning of Persepolis confirmed that it was not a path he chose to take, although he would copy aspects of Achaemenid government whenever he felt it was practical. Before the Persians, the Medes, Babylonians, and others had ruled empires over much of the same area, so there were memories of other "kings of Asia," which helped prepare the way for a new one, established by conquest like all the predecessors. Like the Achaemenids, the successful rulers had delegated a lot of power to the regions, allowing communities their religion, customs, and laws in return for obedience and tribute. Greeks—and as far as we can tell Macedonians—despised easterners as effete barbarians, inferior in every way, and treating them and their traditions with respect did not come naturally to most. One additional reason for appointing Persians and other locals as his satraps was that very few of Alexander's own men spoke any Asian language or showed the slightest enthusiasm to learn.[10]

Alexander combined deeply pragmatic instincts with an even deeper belief that he was special—something his visit to Siwah strengthened—as personally superior to fellow Macedonians and Greeks as he was to everyone else; many things could be justified as long as he wanted to do them. This meant that he did not revolt from the mere thought of adopting some rituals and behavior from Asian traditions in the way that many of his Companions did. A little later, Bessus proclaimed himself king of kings and took the royal name Artaxerxes, adopting the dress of an Achaemenid monarch, most notably the upright tiara. In response Alexander modified his own dress, adopting a two-colored diadem which went around the head unlike the Persian crown, but was still not Macedonian. Trousers were one of the most blatant marks of a barbarian and he remained bare legged like a civilized man, but he did take the white and purple sleeved tunic, which was more Median than Persian. He kept to a traditional Macedonian cloak and hat, the latter with a purple royal band around it.[11]

The experiment with this new style began merely for private meetings with Persians and other locals, before he was sufficiently encouraged to ride abroad in plain view. Senior Companions were given red tunics, like the ones of senior advisors at the Persian court, and were encouraged to use Asiatic saddle clothes and ornaments on their horses. As the advance continued, more Persian noblemen capitulated, and they became ever more prominent at court. Macedonians and Greeks were never displaced or sidelined and remained the overwhelming majority, but the prominence given to so recently defeated "barbarians" was resented in the competitive culture of the court. Over time the king acquired more and more of the trappings of eastern kingship, including a harem with one concubine for every night of the year. This was not simply appropriate for a king in the east, but traditionally was a useful bond with the nobility throughout the empire, because the women came from aristocratic families, for whom it was a source of considerable prestige.[12]

Alexander was changing as he tried to consolidate control over all the conquered lands. There was no sign that he wished to oversee this consolidation in a period of peace and calm, and like Philip he appears always to have been thinking of the next war and the next victory. He was Lord of Asia by conquest, heroic and victorious leader of the Macedonians and Greeks, and to confirm his status he needed more glory. In the short term there was the threat posed by Bessus, whose bid for power could not be permitted to gather momentum. Posing as Darius's avenger as well as the great conqueror, Alexander led his army into the province of Hyrcania. Nabarzanes, one of the noblemen who had murdered Darius, opened negotiations to submit and hand over the capital of the province. This was eventually agreed and he was soon followed by the satrap of Hyrcania, who in due course was reappointed as Alexander's rather than Darius's representative. In contrast, Alexander does not appear to have trusted Nabarzanes, and when he returned to the region without authority he was arrested and may have been executed.[13]

There was very little fighting in Hyrcania. A welcome addition to the court came when Artabazus, father of Alexander's mistress Barsine, arrived, bringing his sons. The 1,500 remaining Greek mercenaries who had stayed loyal to Darius, only leaving his side after his arrest, attempted to negotiate. Alexander demanded unconditional surrender and got it, for they had little choice, and were relieved when they discovered that the harshness shown at the Granicus was not to be revived. Men who had taken service with Persia before the grand alliance of the Greeks at Corinth were allowed to go free, while the remainder joined his army at their existing rate of pay. With the mercenaries were some envoys, including Spartans sent by Agis, and some of these were arrested for a while.[14]

Alexander led a brief campaign against a hill tribe called the Mardi—and the coincidence of the name with the group fought earlier hundreds of miles away caused some confusion in our sources. They could do little more than harass the Macedonians, and the most memorable incident occurred when Bucephalus was among some horses stolen from the grooms watching them. Alexander threatened to ravage the tribe's lands, kill all the men, and enslave the women and children if the horse was not returned. His anger was as obvious as the might of his army, so the tribal leaders swiftly handed over the horse and made full submission.[15]

After Hyrcania, the Macedonians went to Areia, where the satrap Satibarzanes, another of the regicides, handed over the region and was confirmed in his office. He was the first to report that Bessus had declared himself king, spurring Alexander to press on to Bactria, as well as prompting the changes in style noted earlier. Once the army had left, Satibarzanes massacred the officer and forty cavalrymen Alexander had left to support him and began raising the province in rebellion around its capital at Artacoana (modern Herat in Afghanistan). News of this treachery on the part of the defector changed Alexander's plans. Forming a flying column from the usual units, he left Craterus with the rest and covered some seventy-five miles in two days to reach Artacoana. The speed and strength of the response terrified Satibarzanes, who abandoned his own men and fled with a small escort, joining Bessus soon afterward. Some of the men he had left behind fought, one group fortifying themselves on a wooded crag, prompting Alexander to set the trees on fire and burn or asphyxiate them all. Otherwise there were a few reprisals and executions against those still in arms, but most surrendered and in spite of this rebellion another Persian was made satrap.[16]

Rejoining the rest of the army, Alexander resumed the advance, and the Macedonians came to Drangiana. The satrap was another of the men who had overthrown and killed Darius, and he made no attempt at submission and instead fled to India, where he received little sympathy. At some point in the future he was handed back to Alexander, who executed him. For a while the army rested at the regional capital, Phrada (modern Farah in Afghanistan), where an incident occurred that even at the time was shrouded in uncertainty, even though it led to a major change in the Macedonian high command and removed one of the most prominent links to Philip's reign.

Successful commanders tend to have immense self-confidence, which often extends to disparaging others—we need only think of the rivalries between Napoleon's marshals or the less harmful, but still often bitter, relationships between many senior Allied commanders during the Second World War. The Macedonian court set this in a context where the leaders of the expedition spent a lot of time together, often feasting and drinking in an environment where boastfulness was expected, as long as everyone ensured that the king's superiority was not challenged. Humor at Alexander's expense could only be mild, but others could be mocked and for everyone else there was ongoing competition for prestige, favor, respect, and the influence and formal positions these brought. The king was the arbiter, for without a hierarchy and system of promotion every appointment depended on his decision. As the name "Companion" suggests, all of this was very personal, which meant that friendships and disputes could be all the more bitter, and the pecking order was always subject to sudden or gradual shifts, as the balance between family, achievements, and the king's affection changed.

The spark for a major shift was a conspiracy to murder Alexander, formed by a group of otherwise unknown Macedonian aristocrats who presumably had real or imagined cause to seek this revenge on the king. One was named Dimnus, and he confided in his young lover, a youth named Nicomachus, and enlisted his aid. The lad was frightened, and in turn told his older brother, Cebalinus, who was a soldier, possibly in one of the squadrons of Companions, although clearly not of high rank. This meant that he did not have direct access to the king, so he waited outside the royal tent and approached Philotas, Parmenio's last remaining son and commander of the Companions, and told him what he had learned. When nothing seemed to happen, he spoke to Philotas a second time. Again, nothing happened and Dimnus and the other conspirators remained at large, so Cebalinus went to one of the royal pages and persuaded him to pass on the information to Alexander in person.[17]

Parmenio was far away in Ecbatana, on detached duty as had so often been the case under both Philip and Alexander. Of his sons, Hector had died in Egypt, and Nicanor, the commander of the hypaspists, had succumbed to disease just a month or two earlier. Alexander had personally attended to the funeral rites of the former, but in 330 BC the pace of campaigning meant that he had to leave behind a detachment under Philotas to provide this care for the older brother. Both Nicanor and Philotas had played conspicuous roles in all the great battles and many other operations, just as their father had controlled the left wing in all three big battles and fought with great distinction throughout the campaigns. Plutarch calls Philotas a friend of the young Alexander, although notably he came with Philip to reprove the prince after the Pixodarus affair, and was not one of the four close friends subsequently exiled. Since then he had fought bravely and appeared loyal and supportive to the king, for instance persuading him that using Darius's table as a footstool was a good omen. He had also received a generous share of the spoils and enjoyed a lavish lifestyle; Plutarch claims that he had hunting nets twelve and a half miles long. After the capture of Darius's baggage train at Damascus in 333 BC, he acquired a mistress named Antigone, a Greek girl captured and enslaved by the Persians some time earlier.[18]

Philotas was arrogant and boastful even by the standards of the court, which meant that he was not well liked, although in public this was doubtless repressed as long as he remained important. His father is supposed to have warned him about his behavior and his tendency to flaunt his newfound wealth. Other leading Companions, such as Craterus, disliked him personally, as well as envying his command of the Companion cavalry and his favor with the king. During the months in Egypt, Philotas had frequently boasted to Antigone that Alexander's victories had come because of his own and his father's skill and heroism, and had mocked the talk of the king being the son of Zeus. The young woman gossiped, and word reached Craterus, who told Alexander. The mistress was enlisted as a spy, to listen attentively and pass on the pillow talk of her lover.[19]

At Phrada Philotas failed to warn the king of the conspiracy, claiming later that he dismissed it as no more than idle talk from an insignificant and effeminate boy. Alexander took the incident much more seriously. Dimnus was killed resisting arrest or managed to commit suicide, and the others were taken into custody, as was Philotas. His crime was one of omission, for neither Cebalinus nor any of the conspirators claimed that he was directly involved, but Alexander was implacable, egged on by Craterus and other senior Companions including Hephaestion, Perdiccas, and Coenus, all of whom scented an opportunity for their own advancement at the expense of Philotas. It was one thing for the king to dismiss a report of a plot, as he had done with his physician, and quite another for one of his supposed friends not to pass on information and gamble with the king's life. Criticizing Philotas's failure was a way for everyone else at court to prove their own loyalty.

A traditional court of Macedonian citizens was assembled from the army to hear the case, and the king attacked Philotas, mocking him for speaking in educated Greek rather than the Macedonian dialect, even though this was normal among the aristocracy. His failure to tell the king about the conspiracy on two occasions was not contested, and this was enough to ensure his condemnation, especially since Alexander was clearly determined to have this. An ambiguous phrase in a letter from Parmenio was quoted and other slurs mentioned, including his criticism of the king. Philotas was found guilty and tortured, at which point he made a confession, although the precise nature of this is unclear. He was then executed either by being stabbed with spears or pelted with stones. Alexander chose an officer known as a friend of Parmenio for a special mission. Riding fast camels, disguised and with a very small escort, he raced to Ecbatana before news of Philotas's fate could reach the dead man's father. On arrival he gave written orders to the senior officers before going to Parmenio. The old man was pleased to see him, eagerly expecting the proffered letter from his son. As he opened it, Philip's one good general was cut down. When an angry mob of soldiers ran up and threatened the assassins, they had their orders from Alexander read out and the situation was calmed once it was understood that they were obeying the king. The men still demanded an honorable burial for their distinguished commander and a compromise was reached. Parmenio's head was cut off and taken to Alexander, while the rest of his corpse was interred with respect.[20]

Thus ended the life of a man who had contributed a good deal to the success of both Philip and his son. He was about seventy and had survived several regime changes in Macedonia, contributing to Alexander's succession by his acquiescence in the execution of Attalus six years earlier. The truth of the whole affair was hidden at the time, allowing a wide range of interpretations from the same sources. Philotas may genuinely have felt that Cebalinus's talk of a plot was just talk and no more, although it is possible that he did not mind too much if the conspiracy was real and the king was murdered. The plot was clearly real, even if we cannot know what provoked it or whether the men had a successor in mind. Parmenio and his remaining son were powerful and might easily have become the key kingmakers should Alexander die suddenly, and perhaps they even saw this as desirable and were concerned about the king's endless ambition for more conquest. Our sources hint at disquiet over this and the twenty-six-year-old king's new enthusiasm for aspects of eastern style and court ritual, something that would reappear in later conspiracies.

Those who prefer to see a crueler, more calculating Alexander instead depict the episode as an extension of the purge that followed his accession. Philotas provoked him by his arrogance, Parmenio by his frequently opposing opinions, his connection with Philip, and both by the sheer influence of the family, so that the king had been simply waiting for an opportunity to remove them. One tradition has Alexander ghoulishly listening from behind a screen while Philotas was tortured. Alternatively Plutarch saw this as more of a conspiracy against Philotas by rivals at court, who stoked the king's suspicion until he was convinced that his old friend was plotting against him. Curtius adds dark humor to his account, making Philotas whisper to his torturers, "Tell me, Craterus, what you wish me to say."[21]

It was the king's decision to kill the son, and once he had done this it was hard to believe that the father would remain loyal. In the context of Macedonian politics, killing Parmenio was natural, although we do not know whether or not the relatives of convicted regicides were automatically condemned in law or if the assembly of Macedonian citizens passed judgment on the father in his absence. Both deaths were Alexander's decision, and none of the sources suggest that he had to agonize over making it, even if the initiative came from others. As always, Alexander reacted swiftly and ruthlessly to deal with a situation. We cannot say how far the king had created or wished for the situation allowing him to remove Parmenio or if he simply decided as events developed that this was what was needed. Either way, the men died swiftly and they were soon joined by Alexander of Lyncestis, who had been a prisoner for three years since his own alleged conspiracy. Now he was brought before the assembled troops and condemned after a stammering and incoherent defense. However, the assembled Macedonians refused to condemn some brothers accused of conspiracy, one of whom had fled before being arrested, which many took as a sign of guilt. Alexander does not appear to have pressed so hard for these men's deaths, perhaps hoping to display his sense of justice, and the troops may also have wanted to assert their independence, guessing that the outcome was not critical.[22]

Parmenio was popular, widely respected, and lamented by those who had fought under him. Those wishing to see Alexander's hand in everything portray the dismissal of the Thessalians as a deliberate weakening of the general's position by sending away these elite horsemen who had served under his command for so many years. Similarly, that Parmenio was away from the main army performing an apparently minor role can been seen as another step toward his removal. Yet these are not the most natural conclusions in either case, and it was probably simply chance that the events developed at this time, just as it was chance that Nicanor died. None of the ancient authors suggest that there was clear evidence for a conspiracy on the part of Parmenio, and it is surprising that no details seem to have been invented posthumously to justify his death. Similarly, no ancient source claims that Alexander deliberately plotted against his senior general. Parmenio was respected, but he was not an Argead and could not be king. Once he was killed and his male line ended, the army might regret his loss, but it had no reason to act on that regret and oppose Alexander. Alexander was the king, their victorious leader, and they needed him to complete that victory and lead them home to enjoy their glory and spoils.

24

THE UPRIGHT TIARA

The rest anticipated with such eagerness by most of the army proved elusive, and as one war seemed to end another began. Alexander was to fight just one more major battle, and never again attacked a city as large and with such formidable man-made defenses as Tyre or Gaza, where the sieges lasted for months. Even so, he spent most of the remainder of his life on campaign, and fought many, many times in small skirmishes, engagements involving thousands, and especially besieging and assaulting scores of mud-walled settlements. As a share of time, most of the rest of his life was occupied with marching and riding, mile after mile and day after day, sleeping in tents, in modest huts in villages, or occasionally in the grander houses of the biggest settlements. As well as hard travel, combat was a common experience whatever its scale, and he kept on fighting and winning, at the price of adding to his long catalog of wounds. These later years of Alexander's career often lack the clear drama and simple narrative of the grand confrontations with Darius, for more often than not the army split into several columns that then operated independently, not to mention the numerous detachments and garrisons left behind to control conquered territory. In itself this was nothing new, for Philip and Alexander had both split and recombined the army depending on the strategic situation of the time, and big battles were always rare things. What had changed was the scale, for Alexander had substantially more troops under arms than his father had ever mustered, while the distances were far greater, as were the extremes of terrain and climate.

Reforms in the structure of the army reflect this smaller scale of operations, although in some cases details and timings are unclear. After Gaugamela, each *ilê* of Companion cavalry was divided into two permanent subunits with a theoretical strength of about 100 men, and a little later the hypaspists may similarly have reorganized to add an additional level of command. In each case this may have been formal recognition of existing common practice. Within a year the Companions also operated as *hipparchies*, each of two *ilai*, and in due course eight hipparchies were formed, perhaps with a substantial increase in overall numbers of these horsemen, unless each unit was now made smaller. There may have been changes in equipment for some contingents, and a unit of light horse armed with spears or javelins appear around this time—some scholars believe the latter to be locally recruited cavalry, but since the *sarissophoroi* light cavalry vanish at the same time, more likely they had gained a new name and perhaps shorter weapons than the long lances used in the past. Lycian troops arrived in substantial numbers in 330 BC, along with more mercenaries, and over the next few years contingents of cavalry raised in the central and eastern satrapies appear in ever growing numbers. Such men tended to be superb horsemen, their fighting style well suited to the country and warfare of the region, which made them an important asset as well as merely additional manpower. Equally, as with mercenaries from Greece and elsewhere, it was far better to keep restless and warlike men employed as part of Alexander's army rather than letting them wander about taking service against him. As far as we can tell, such soldiers served in separate units, and apart from an additional royal escort of guard formed from Persian nobles, none were given much prominence or status.[1]

From 334 BC Philotas had led all the Companion cavalry, but following his execution in 330 BC Alexander decided not to entrust this responsibility to a single replacement and instead split the command between Hephaestion and Cleitus the Black. The latter was an experienced soldier who had served in many of Philip's campaigns, more recently leading the royal squadron and saving Alexander's life at the Granicus, and the appointment can have raised few eyebrows. In contrast Hephaestion does not appear ever to have led a unit in action, making his promotion a blatant act of faith and favoritism on Alexander's part toward his old friend, whose aggressive loyalty had so recently been proven in the condemnation of Philotas. The Macedonian army was the state under arms—and like the government in general had no fixed hierarchy or system of promotion—so was shaped by the king's choices, which in turn reflected the influence of individuals and families among the aristocracy. While Philotas had some experience leading cavalry units before being appointed to the overall command of the Companion cavalry, he had still been very young for such an important post, and his selection then reflected his father's importance as much as his own record and talent. Arrian attributes the joint command of the elite cavalry as primarily a matter of trust. It is not clear when the hipparchies were introduced, so this reorganization may have occurred at the same time or later.[2]

Although Alexander split command of the Companion cavalry, he kept the hypaspists under a single commander, so fears about entrusting so much responsibility for the troops closest to him was not his only concern, and reform may have reflected the way the cavalry squadrons were being used. Whatever its political or practical advantages, any increase in the number of officers also meant the creation of new permanent posts with all the pay and prestige associated with rank. Alexander is supposed primarily to have taken into account men's service records as he filled these new commands, although no doubt other factors such as family and connections also played a role. The new officers owed their elevation to him, and were visible proof that courage and loyalty to the king would be rewarded.[3]

The relationship between the Macedonians and their king was at heart personal, and found clearest expression in the army, especially for a king who was so constantly and successfully at war as Alexander. Over time the army was bonding with Alexander as leader in his own right and not simply the son and successor to Philip. The intensity of fighting and immense scale of their victories since 334 BC all added momentum and speed to the process, but did not erase the past. Philip had been dead for less than a decade, and many men of all ranks had also shared in his glory and his successes, achievements that were firmly tied to their own pride and self-worth. Yet it is far too simplistic to see an old guard of Philip's men opposed to Alexander's generation, for in both there was a whole range of opinions and allegiances, personal likes, dislikes, and rivalries that needed to be more or less reconciled, or at least kept in balance. Rewards and promotion helped motivate men to keep obeying and fighting for their king, even as the goals of the expedition shifted so profoundly.

There was another side to the coin, and around the same time a special unit of "Disorderlies" (*Ataktoi*) was formed from anyone whose allegiance was suspect. One tradition has Alexander ordering that letters sent home be read and note taken of clear affection for Parmenio or any criticism of Alexander or the ongoing war. Whether or not the new "punishment battalion" was restricted to men of suspect political views or included other offenders, its members were said to fight with exceptional bravery in the hope of redeeming themselves, although no specific instance is recorded of their exploits. The king could both reward and punish, while Philip's fate had shown that even the most successful were not safe from assassination. Alexander's choices of officers were constantly tested by the ongoing campaigning, and any setback or disappointment reflected badly on him. He could not afford to ignore talent and established reputation in favor of blind loyalty, and had to balance each consideration, both to satisfy expectation of good behavior for a Macedonian monarch and maintain morale and effectiveness so that his army kept on winning.[4]

Similarly, his court and government also needed to function sufficiently well to keep his new empire stable, minimize rebellions, and permit him to draw the resources of money, manpower, riding and pack animals, and supplies that he wanted to fuel his campaigns. The focus in the sources and especially in modern scholarship is on the tensions and problems as he tried to balance being king of the Macedonians and "Lord of Asia." These tensions should never be underestimated, for everything had happened so quickly and there was no simple precedent to follow. Some Persian noblemen were willing to serve the new ruler and did so loyally and capably, while others resisted and fought him; there were also those who wavered between the two. We do not hear their side of the story and cannot judge how Alexander's adoption of new costume and customs was seen by the conquered. Some may have found it as distasteful as many of the Macedonians did, if for different reasons, but kept their feelings quiet since his power and dominance were what mattered.[5]

Twin courts and administrations developed and operated in parallel, as Alexander did his best to act as ruler for both the Macedonians and his new subjects. He began to employ Darius's royal seal for correspondence with Asian nobles and communities, keeping his own seal as king of Macedon for Macedonians and Greeks. As far as possible he wanted the existing administration to continue, most of all at local level, so the familiar imagery of Persian rule may have helped, hence at first his new style of dress was reserved for meetings with Asiatic subjects. Although he acquired a harem, unlike the Achaemenids it does not seem to have traveled with him on campaign, given his habitually rapid pace, so presumably it was brought to him only when he planned to settle for a few weeks or more in one place. If selections of concubines rather than the whole harem were with him much of the time then no source mentions the practice, but as so often our sources say almost nothing about things like this. His mistress Barsine may have accompanied him some of the time, and perhaps there were other lovers as well. Darius's mother, daughters, and son had been left behind at Susa some time ago, now that their political importance had lessened. They continued to be treated with every courtesy, and Alexander ordered that the children should receive a Greek education alongside a traditional one, which may be an indication that he was already considering the possibility of taking one of the princesses as a wife at some time in the future. One Macedonian custom is said to have horrified Darius's mother, who was presented with the means to make wool and weave clothes. For her this was a task for slaves and suggested that other degradations would follow, until it was explained that this was a normal activity for Argead women, and that Alexander had clothes made by his mother and sister.[6]

In 330 BC Bagoas, a former favorite of Darius and (like his murderous namesake who had elevated the Persian king to the throne) a eunuch, came to Alexander to negotiate the surrender of Nabarzanes, one of Darius's and then Bessus's most important followers. Handsome, politically supple, and eager to please, the eunuch won the trust of the new king and some sources claim that they became lovers. Bagoas's knowledge of court politics and personalities in recent years was useful, especially as he must have spoken Greek, which would help Alexander to understand men with whom he wanted to work and make the eunuch's importance understandable. Whether there was more than this is impossible to say, and the deep-seated disgust felt by Greeks and Romans for eunuchs may mean that he is mentioned more as a symbol of Alexander's decline into eastern decadence than a reflection of his actual importance. Even so, he is only mentioned occasionally, and then almost always in a general sense rather than being involved in a specific incident.[7]

We cannot say how much luxury surrounded Alexander on campaign and how many courtiers were with him at any time. Wherever he was, he was the king, surrounded by guards and officials, but the level of ceremony and opulence varied, and only for parts of the year was he surrounded by all its pomp. Some aspects of his role continued wherever he was, and Plutarch notes that Alexander was an extraordinarily prolific writer (or, strictly speaking, surely dictator) of letters. It is notable that Alexander got on better with the Macedonian aristocracy while he was on campaign, when everyone was kept busy, had a clear objective and part to play, and the king could set an example of courage and skill. Flashpoints occurred during the lulls in operations, when the army stopped and rested for weeks or months, allowing more of the court to catch up. Everyone was tired while having enough time to resent any favor shown to Persians and other locals, although it should be noted that while Macedonians and Greeks were given the majority of key roles in dealing with the conquered territory, no Persian was appointed to deal with Macedonians or Greeks or appears to have had real influence in matters affecting them. Even so, Persian influences and some Persians were visible, especially during rest periods, and this had not been true just a few years before.[8]

ALEXANDER MARCHED AWAY from Phrada soon after the deaths of Philotas and Parmenio in late 330 BC, although not before he renamed the city Prophthasia (Anticipation) to mark the defeat of the conspirators before they could strike. Heading south he came to fertile agricultural land around Lake Sistan and the valley of the river Helmand. There was no resistance from the locals, the Ariaspians, also known as the "benefactors" for their generosity in feeding the starving army of Cyrus back in the sixth century. Alexander's men were in a much better state, although supplies were always welcome and ready submission as usual prompted generous terms granting the communities considerable self-rule. Curtius claims that Alexander stayed for two months in their territory, while in Arrian's account the Macedonians moved on much sooner, following the line of the river. Around this time Ptolemy, the future king of Egypt, was made one of the king's seven bodyguards, filling a vacancy created when one of the existing members was arrested and executed for alleged involvement with Philotas or the other conspirators.[9]

There was little or no resistance to his main advance, and a succession of peoples submitted, prompting the appointment of a satrap backed by several thousand troops to oversee the area. The man chosen was a Macedonian, which was a break with recent appointments of Asians, although it did not mark a permanent change. A report arrived that Satibarzanes had returned at the head of 2,000 horsemen to raid his former satrapy of Areia, now in the rear as Alexander headed toward Bactria in search of Bessus. A strong detachment was sent under the command of two Companions who were to cooperate with Phrataphernes, satrap of Parthia. Before pressing on, Alexander founded another city bearing his name, Alexandria in Arachosia (modern Kandahar), with a mixed population of locals and settlers drawn from the mercenaries, camp followers, and soldiers rendered unfit for campaigning by wounds or disease. From there he headed toward what is now Kabul along a route well trodden over the centuries.* Another Alexandria was founded, near modern Begram, and the army rested for the rest of the winter.[10]

In late March or early April 329 BC, Alexander resumed his pursuit of Bessus, who was reported in Bactria at the head of almost 10,000 men. In the path of the Macedonian army lay mountains that they wrongly believed to be part of the Caucasus, perhaps connecting with Mount Taurus not far from where the Battle of Issus had been fought. Alexander and his men were already past the lands where Greeks had fairly sure knowledge of the geography, and they were even more reliant on local guides. In fact Alexander was facing a range of the Hindu Kush, not that this really mattered from his perspective, save that even basic reports will have told him that these were higher than any mountains he had so far encountered. There were three passes: the Shibar, which was most frequently used by travelers and relatively easy; the Khawak, which was extremely difficult; and the Salang Pass, which was all but impossible, at least for an army. Bessus had begun ravaging the lands on the far side of the main route, knowing that any army coming through would have few if any supplies left by the time it got that far.

Alexander took the Khawak Pass, where the path climbs to an elevation of some 11,650 feet and the peaks are even higher. Spring was late in arriving, as it seems from analysis of tree rings that for several years around this time the summers were markedly colder than average. Snow and ice lay on the ground, making the going difficult, and never before had the soldiers or animals experienced the thin air of such high altitudes. Food ran short, although terrified villagers in the tiny settlements in their path readily gave all they could at the appearance of so many heavily armed foreign soldiers.

---

* In 1880, during the Second Anglo-Afghan War, Lord Roberts (another short man who rode the "biggest horse he can," if the product of a very different society and age) and his Anglo-Indian Army followed the same route in the opposite direction on their way to Kandahar.

It was not enough. Animals tend to die before men, and the king ordered even more baggage animals to be slaughtered so that they could be eaten. What little wood was available to burn was soon used up, so the meat had to be consumed raw and quickly, before it froze too hard to eat. Tired and hungry, men suffered from frost-bite and snow blindness or became so exhausted that they simply stopped and lay down or clung to trees. If not roused to move on, they would die there, so Alexander set an example of chivvying them on, moving up and down the straggling column and encouraging and yelling to keep them going. Others followed his example and over some seventeen days the army crossed to the far side, where it rested in milder country better supplied with food. The men recovered their strength and waited as stragglers rejoined.[11]

Bessus retreated as soon as he learned that Alexander was over the mountains, and headed for the river Oxus so that he could put another physical barrier between him and his enemy. This meant letting the Macedonians take Bactria, and within days the 7,000 to 8,000 Bactrian cavalrymen who formed the greater part of Bessus's army dispersed and went to their homes in no mood to fight for a leader who had abandoned their families in this way. There was little or no resistance to the Macedonian advance, and communities, including the substantial trading city of Bactra, the capital of the region, all opened their gates to the invaders. All seemed well, and Barsine's father Artabazus was named as satrap for Bactria. There was also the very welcome news of the defeat and death of Satibarzanes, whose head was brought in as proof. In a suitably Homeric style, the former satrap had been killed in single combat by Erigyius, originally from Mytilene, but long since settled in Macedonia, where he had been given lands in Amphipolis and was named as a Companion of the king. One of the young Alexander's friends exiled after the Pixodarus affair, he was substantially older than the others, being now white-haired and elderly according to Curtius. A less satisfying aspect of the campaign was the lackluster, perhaps disloyal conduct of the Persian serving as satrap of Areia, who was duly replaced by a Macedonian.[12]

From Bactra to the Oxus was a journey of some fifty miles, most of it desert, so that just weeks after facing cold and frostbite, the soldiers had to endure the scorching summer heat in a land devoid of water. The advice was to march as far as possible during the night, but the daylight temperatures of over 100 degrees Fahrenheit (about 38 Celsius) still had to be endured. Water supplies ran out faster than expected, and thirsty men turned naturally to wine, whose alcohol left them even more dehydrated, while many horses collapsed and died. As always at times like this, Alexander was at his most inspiring. Two veterans are supposed to have appeared, carrying a little water, which they duly offered to the king. He asked where they had been taking it, and when told that they were bringing it to their sons, Alexander refused to drink any and sent them on their way.

At long last Alexander and the vanguard reached the bank of the Oxus as the sun was setting. He ordered beacons lit on a hilltop to guide the many thousands of men who had lagged behind and tried to organize water and food to be ready for them. Yet some of those already there drank too much too quickly and died as a result—causing more fatalities than in any battle so far according to Curtius. The same author describes how Alexander, "still wearing his cuirass and refreshed neither with food nor drink, stood on the road by which the army was coming, nor did he retire to refresh himself until the whole army had passed by." Even with his army concentrated again, he faced the problem of how to cross the wide river, for Bessus had destroyed or removed all boats in the area. Efforts to make a bridge failed because the bed was too soft even for the piles, and foraging parties failed to find enough timber in the area. Instead, as in one of his first campaigns, he had the men make rafts from tent covers filled with chaff and stitched together. Fortunately there was no opposition, for it took five days to ferry the troops and animals across to the far bank. Some of the army never crossed, for according to Arrian Alexander now discharged the Thessalian volunteers and many Macedonians too worn out to cope with the rigors of campaigning. It was an odd place to do this, after making the same men slog over the Hindu Kush and then through the desert, and Arrian offers no explanation. Perhaps, as in 330 BC, he had waited until he was sure that his opponent had not mustered a field army before deciding that he could reduce his own strength. On the other hand he may have realized that these men were unwilling to go on so let them go rather than let discontent simmer into something worse. If there is any truth to the story then it adds to the paradox of a leader who could drive himself to inspire others at times of extreme hardship, while at other times utterly failing to judge the mood of those he led.[13]

By now Bessus did not have a big army, and soon he had no army at all. In a repeat of his overthrow of Darius, he was now arrested by two of his senior followers, the Sogdian noblemen Spitamenes and Dataphernes, who sent word to Alexander offering to hand over their captive. Ptolemy was tasked with leading several thousand men, including three of the newly introduced hipparchies of Companion cavalry, to fetch the man who had proclaimed himself king of Persia. In later life Ptolemy wrote a heroic account of what followed, as he rode hard to the appointed rendezvous, fearful of an ambush, and secured Bessus without ever seeing the noblemen or their troops because they had left the prisoner in a village. The leaders mattered little since neither had made any move to proclaim himself as king and thus become a challenger to Alexander's right to rule.

Others gave different, rather less dramatic, versions, but all agree that Alexander was delighted and gave instructions as to how the self-proclaimed rival was to be brought before him. Bessus was stripped naked, had a wooden collar put around his neck, and was chained and made to stand by the roadside. Alexander duly arrived in a chariot—importantly a symbol of Persian royalty—and demanded to know why Bessus had turned against his lawful sovereign Darius (who had of course been attacked and hounded to his death by the Macedonians). This treachery was then proclaimed with each stroke of the whip as the former satrap was flogged. Later his nose and ears were mutilated, for a true Persian king was supposed to be perfect physically. Again there are variations in detail over the place and precise means of his execution. What is clear is that Alexander posed as the avenger of Darius and did his best to involve the Persian royal family and the Persian nobility in the punishment of a usurper and murderer. Arrian, in one of his rare criticisms of Alexander, felt that the use of torture and mutilation were signs that the king was succumbing to barbarian influences.[14]

The Macedonian and Greek soldiers of all ranks were tired and a long way from home. Darius was dead, and so was Bessus, the only serious contender to succeed Darius to have emerged. They had made their king Lord of Asia and overrun a great empire, and once again surely felt that the war was finished. Alexander had different ideas.

PART THREE

LORD OF ASIA

329–323 BC

"No matter what he had conquered,
he would not have stopped"

25

THE SWORD AND THE FLAME

India had been in Alexander's mind for some time, and he may now have hoped that the way was clear for him to march in that direction, but for the moment he continued north to the river Jaxartes (modern Syr Darya). Again there was no resistance and the going was easier as he came to Marakanda (modern Samarkand in Uzbekistan), the capital of the satrapy of Sogdiana. This was the furthest extent of the Persian Empire, for the Persians had never established lasting control beyond the river, and when he reached its southern bank Alexander made sacrifices just as he had done beside the Danube in 335 BC. As this was the edge of the Persian Empire, so it would be for his new realm, and he accepted offers of friendship and alliance from the nomadic Sacae from the other side of the river. Alexander and later Greeks and Romans believed that the river connected with the Don in Europe, so this was not merely the edge of empire, but almost the edge of Asia itself. On the far bank of the Jaxartes was believed to be nothing of worth for a conqueror, merely stretches of empty, almost desert-like grassland reaching to the shores of the great seas encircling the three continents.[1]

Persian rule appears to have rested lightly on Sogdiana, Bactria, and the neighboring satrapies. There is some evidence that settlements like Marakanda and Bactra were thriving centers of trade, and that much of the contact with the Sacae to the north and with communities nearby was peaceful, at least by the standards of the ancient world. Yet these regions also boasted a proud warrior culture, and all settlements maintained their walls, so it was not a place without conflict or feud. Alexander and his men had advanced against Bessus and not made war on the population as a whole, which was a major reason why they were not widely opposed. For the locals, the invaders may simply have been passing through and if the identity of their satraps and other overlords changed, everything else would likely remain the same.[2]

This mood changed late in the summer of 329 BC. Near the Jaxartes Alexander founded a new city, Alexandria Eschate ("the farthest," probably near modern Khujand/Khodzhent, formerly Leninabad in Tajikistan). This showed that the invaders planned to stay and involved seizure of land, as well as the movement of population to join the foreign settlers, and may have threatened traditional trade and other communication with the Sacae. Other acts were as provocative. The geographer Strabo tells us that Alexander and his men were disgusted by the local tradition of exposing the dead and dying to be eaten by dogs (nicknamed "undertakers"), so that the ground within their cities was "full of human bones." The Macedonians banned the practice and did everything possible to stamp it out. Interference by foreigners, especially armed conquerors, is rarely welcome, but the invaders were used to getting their way and far too concerned with their own needs to worry about local sensitivities. The fast pace of Alexander's campaigns wore down men and especially horses, and after the grueling crossings of the mountains and desert his army was desperately short of mounts and pack animals. Led by the Lord of Asia, victorious over the vaunted might of Persia, Alexander and his men naturally saw nothing wrong in rounding up and confiscating what they needed from local stocks.[3]

Another incident may have contributed to the nervous mood. Arrian does not mention it, but other sources claim that on the march to the Jaxartes the Macedonians were surprised when one of the communities welcoming them turned out to speak some Greek.

The inhabitants claimed to be the Branchidae, descendants of the followers of a priestly family from Miletus who had betrayed the temple in their charge to Xerxes and been settled here for their protection. In almost the last gasp of the war of vengeance, Alexander ordered his men to slaughter the entire, unresisting population as punishment for this ancient crime. The story may be a myth, or perhaps it was invented as an excuse to justify a deliberate or accidental massacre of a peaceful community, but if there is any truth at all in the tale, then it surely made everyone in the wider area doubt the reliability and good faith of the invaders.[4]

Without warning—at least as far as the Macedonians were concerned—foraging parties gathering supplies were slaughtered or taken prisoner by bands of local warriors, and isolated garrisons were massacred. The rising spread rapidly through Sogdiana and Bactria, encouraged by leaders including Spitamenes and Dataphernes, who had served and then abandoned Bessus. It is impossible to say whether they had always planned this, were dismayed by the signs of permanent settlement, or simply sensed the mood of the local communities and saw an opportunity. A call for local leaders to come to a meeting with Alexander at the city of Zariaspa was interpreted as a ruse to arrest them, which shows the suspicion of his motives and methods. As always Alexander responded with speed and maximum force, made all the more ferocious because of the king's rage at what he saw as treachery, and the anger of soldiers who had thought that the fighting was at last over. The first target was the band responsible for the attack on the foragers, a force that had allegedly grown to some 30,000 men and occupied a formidable position in the mountains. There was no way to outflank the position, so the Macedonians attacked directly into the face of volleys of arrows and other missiles. Many were wounded and the initial assaults failed. Alexander took an arrow in the lower leg, which is said to have chipped the bone, although it is hard to see how an ancient surgeon would have been aware of this, and the injury may have been less serious than our sources claim. It did not stop his men from continuing their attacks and eventually the position was stormed and almost three quarters of the enemy cut down.[5]

As communities declared against him, Alexander ordered his soldiers to make ladders. Over the course of a few days he captured seven "cities" near the Jaxartes, directing some assaults in person while detachments were sent to deal with other communities. Some of these settlements were no more than villages, which fell in a matter of hours to escalade using the ladders covered by heavy volleys from archers and javelinmen. More formidable was Cyropolis, founded by Cyrus, well fortified by local standards and held by the biggest group of warriors. Craterus hurried there to begin the siege, for the place was too strong to be taken by an immediate assault. Alexander joined him a few days later and the assault was supported by engines and artillery, with rams pounding the walls to make breaches.

Then Alexander spotted a dried-up water course that led under the defenses, and sneaked inside at the head of a picked band of hypaspists and Agrianians while the defenders were distracted by the rest of the army. They got in without detection and opened the main gate to let the rest of the attackers through. With great determination the defenders rallied and tried to overwhelm Alexander and his party before they could be properly reinforced. The king was struck on the head and neck by a stone, suffering his most serious injury so far in his career. Ancient surgeons had some awareness of concussion, although none of degrees of brain damage. In the short term he was knocked out, and for some time unable to walk and could speak only with difficulty. Craterus, who had led the charge to join his ruler, was hit by an arrow and it looked as if the Macedonians might be overwhelmed as they stood at bay in the marketplace. Fortunately attacks on the walls themselves succeeded because the defenders were drawn off to deal with the break-in. With little to stop them, more and more Macedonians swarmed into the city. Arrian says that 8,000 defenders were killed, and another 15,000 took refuge in the citadel, only to surrender a few days later as their water ran out. He does not mention their fate, but in the other settlements Alexander's men killed all adult males and enslaved the women and children.[6]

Another town was sacked and then reports arrived that a large army of Sacae was on the far bank of the river and that Spitamenes was besieging Marakanda. Alexander detached a column of 2,000 to 4,000 men, mostly mercenaries, to relieve the city, while the main army labored to build defenses for Alexandria Eschate. This was now critical given the threats it would face, and also surely reflected Alexander's incapacity following his injury. After twenty days the fortifications were in a good enough state to protect the settlers, and after sacrifices and athletic competitions, the army marched to confront the Sacae, who remained on the far bank, shooting arrows and taunting whenever any Macedonians came in range. Alexander remained frail, his orders conveyed in a croaking whisper, but he was as determined as ever to do what he wanted, regardless of difficulty. Sacrifices produced bad omens, and even the diviner Aristander would not change his opinion to please the king.[7]

This was to be an opposed crossing, and alongside the rafts made from hides and tent covers were some that were stable enough to carry light artillery. More catapults lined the bank, just as they had done in Illyria all those years before, and these had a range and force far greater even than the well-made composite bows of the Sacae. One rider was struck by a bolt that penetrated his shield and his armor and knocked him off his horse, and others were wounded. Never having seen such machines before and unable to reply, the Sacae fell back from the bank. A trumpet sounded as a signal for the first wave of rafts to set off, Alexander with them. He formed a line of archers and slingers to keep the enemy at bay—all things being equal, bowmen on foot have a longer range than horse archers—and the artillery helped. Behind this screen units of the phalanx formed up, and no cavalry in the world could break them as long as they stayed in good order. The Sacae kept their distance, staying out of range, and could do no more than watch as Alexander ferried his own cavalry over the Jaxartes.

The crossing must have taken hours, perhaps the bulk of the day, but the enemy did not retire any farther and watched the invaders form up. Alexander sent forward mercenary horse and light cavalry to attack and see what the Sacae did. Their response was a traditional tactic, as the warriors avoided the charge while riding close, loosing arrows and speeding away, forming one or more circles so that the arrows kept coming but the riders were difficult targets, protected by their speed and the clouds of dust thrown up by their hoofs. The Macedonians were heavily outnumbered and the attack soon lost any momentum, soldiers and especially their horses taking wounds from the arrows. Alexander next led forward more cavalry, backed by Agrianians, archers, and other skirmishers, the same formidable combination that had done so well at Gaugamela. This stabilized the combat, keeping the Sacae busy and closely engaged. Next he ordered three hipparchies of Companion cavalry and the squadrons of light horse to charge, and soon afterward led the rest of his cavalry in another attack.

The Sacae, like most Scythians, were fierce fighters and some were heavily armored, but their favorite tactic was to avoid hand-to-hand fighting at first, luring the enemy on until he was scattered and tired. Whether because they had become too closely engaged, their blood was up, or they could not see what was happening amid the dust and confusion, this time they met the charge and were routed. Arrian claims that 1,000 were killed, including a leader, and 150 taken prisoner as the Macedonians streamed after them in pursuit in spite of the searing heat of the day. Curtius simply says that Alexander's men killed many, while losing 60 cavalry and around 100 infantrymen dead, with 1,000 wounded, which suggests that the fighting was heavy. Thirst and exhaustion ended the chase, and many of the victors drank from any pools or streams that they could find. In Alexander's case this led to a violent bout of diarrhea, after which he collapsed and had to be carried back to camp. In the aftermath the king of the Sacae sent an envoy to offer submission, explaining that the men Alexander had fought were freebooters and that it was not his wish to start a war with the Macedonians. Understandably suspicious, Alexander nevertheless judged it convenient to accept the offer of peace, since he and the army were needed elsewhere, a decision quickly confirmed when news arrived of a disaster.[8]

Spitamenes's attack on Marakanda had soon failed, and a sally by the city's garrison cut up a detachment of his men as they withdrew. However, the relief force sent by Alexander did not know this and hurried forward to rescue the town. With the column was a Lycian named Pharnuces, who was fluent in the languages of

Bactria and Sogdiana and knew the area and its leaders well, probably having served Darius. At the very least the other officers were under orders to let him take the lead in dealing with Spitamenes and the rebels, which suggests that Alexander expected the matter to involve far more negotiation than fighting; after all, not long ago Spitamenes had given him Bessus. Yet Pharnuces had little or no military experience, which would make it odd if he was formally in command of the force, and perhaps the king did not make the responsibilities of the senior officers with the column sufficiently clear. Either way Alexander badly misjudged the situation and the ability of the men he put in charge. Since the army had no established system of seniority and the responsibilities of the men involved were muddled, the result was an inept operation.

Spitamenes had local forces as well as 600 Sacae, but probably did not outnumber the expedition by any huge margin. Yet he was focused and skillful, luring the Macedonians on and wearing them out before he turned on them. The details are confused, not least because none of the senior leaders survived to report to Alexander, so we can say little more than that the column was virtually wiped out. More than 2,000 died in the most costly defeat ever suffered by Alexander's army, far more than in any of the great battles, since this time any wounded were finished off by the enemy.[9]

Alexander force-marched to Marakanda with one of his elite columns, allegedly covering some 190 miles in little more than three days. He was still too late, for Spitamenes had already gone, and when he reached the site of the defeat he halted and buried the remains of his men. Rightly or wrongly deciding that communities in the area had helped the rebels, he spent the rest of the 329 BC ruthlessly devastating the wider region, before settling down for the winter at Zariaspa. Substantial numbers of new troops and detachments left behind at one stage or another caught up with the army there, so that the bulk of Alexander's forces and almost all his finest troops were now concentrated in the region; most likely much of the personnel and paraphernalia of court also joined him. Envoys arrived during these months, one from a new Scythian king of the European tribes who offered his daughter in marriage, and another from a ruler suggesting a joint campaign around the Black

Sea. Alexander declined the proposal of marriage alliance and said for the moment his focus was India, but that in due course he would return to Europe and might well embark on the suggested conquest.[10]

Early in 328 BC, Alexander returned to Sogdiana, after leaving substantial garrisons in Bactria. He split his main force into five columns, leading one in person and entrusting the others to Hephaestion, Ptolemy, Perdiccas, and Coenus aided by Artabazus. Any settlement refusing to surrender was stormed and the inhabitants massacred or enslaved. Some of the population was moved to new communities closely controlled and garrisoned by the occupying power. The might of the Macedonian army, even when divided into several mobile columns, was too great for any stronghold to defeat and no single leader emerged to unite the various groups. This was an area of local loyalties, which meant coming together was rare, but equally meant that almost every village had to be dealt with separately. Spitamenes continued to outwit the enemy, swooping down to surprise and massacre an outpost in Bactria, and then raiding the fields around Zariaspa itself. Provoked, a mixed force of mercenaries, recovering convalescents, and even some royal pages galloped out in pursuit. They caught an isolated party and defeated it, only to be then hunted down by Spitamenes and his Sacae. Seven Companions died, along with sixty out of eighty mercenaries. One of the former was the famous musician Aristonicus, an Olynthian who had been a favorite of both Philip and Alexander and now died fighting hard. The king duly paid to have a statue of him erected at Delphi, with a spear in one hand and his harp-like kithara in the other.

This was a far smaller affair than the defeat of the previous year, but it was still a defeat for a king and an army not used to losing even in minor actions. Spitamenes remained at large, striking apparently at will, and although Craterus chased him and inflicted a sharp reverse, killing 150 of the Sacae, their leader and the rest of his men escaped into the barren country, albeit at the cost of much of their plunder. Any of the main columns were too strong for Spitamenes and his men, and they rampaged through more and more of the country, crushing opposition. More and more outposts were established, controlling the population and making it hard for Spitamenes or other raiders to find supplies. The scale was greater, landscape and climate harsher, and the enemy more mobile, but this was war as Philip and Alexander had waged it in Illyria and Thrace, and once again the Macedonians showed that they could adapt and fight in more than one way. For the locals this was extremely traumatic, and the mass slaughter, enslavement, and forced relocation fell heaviest on them, as did the depredations of Macedonians and their opponents alike as they took food and animals to fuel the campaigns.[11]

Spitamenes tried to escape the enclosing net, and after recruiting 3,000 more Sacae, launched another great raid, this time switching back to Sogdiana. He did not get far before he was intercepted by Coenus, who brought a mixed infantry and cavalry force against the mounted raiders. Arrian claims that 800 enemy horsemen were killed for the loss of twenty-five Macedonian cavalry and a dozen infantrymen, and since they drove off the enemy and kept control of the field there were surely many more wounded. Spitamenes no longer seemed so lucky to his subordinates. The Bactrians and Sogdians deserted and surrendered to Coenus, while the Sacae plundered the other contingents' baggage and fled. Spitamenes stayed with them, only to be murdered when they decided that it was better to do a deal with Alexander, who was advancing toward them. Curtius tells the romantic story that the killer was his wife, to whom he was so devoted that he dragged her around with him on campaign. Seeing no end to this hardship, she killed him and took his head to Alexander, who was relieved at the death but disturbed by the idea of a wife slaughtering her husband, so he sent her away. It was not the murder itself but the sex of the killer that bothered him. Greek and Roman men alike were deeply uncomfortable with violence on the part of women, and with killings within families, so if there was any truth in the story it would have troubled Alexander and his officers.[12]

One leader was dead, but there were others, if less famous, and in spite of a second year spent in brutal reprisals, there were plenty of enemies still willing to fight and much of Alexander's army remained split in detachments large and small as it tried to hold down the country. The Macedonian army, filled with tired soldiers who not long ago had believed that the great war was over, had fought, marched, and toiled, defeating enemies in one place only for more to spring up elsewhere. It was a grim business, even by the standards of the ancient world, for as always Alexander forced the pace of operations, perhaps even more than Philip had done. As ever we have no figures for overall losses for the army, although we can be confident that these were far smaller than the huge toll of massacre inflicted on the wider population. Slaughter and death were common, and if the soldiers at times ran short of food, it is likely that some civilians starved as a result of their confiscations. Curtius claims that Alexander let his men loose on a Persian royal game park to kill the animals, which had been preserved for years both for food and to use the hunt itself as an emotional release.[13]

Alexander ordered much of the army to concentrate and spent the harshest of the winter months of 328–327 BC at Nautaca, which probably lay somewhere between Bactra and Marakanda, where he set up court. As always there was much for him to do, including making new appointments, sacking some of his satraps, and replacing them. Barsine's father pleaded old age and was relieved from his post as satrap of Bactria and Sogdiana, although some scholars prefer to see this as no more than an excuse. With insurgency still raging, this was one of the most demanding and dangerous jobs in the empire, and Alexander now gave it to Cleitus the Black, whose record certainly suggested that he was tough enough for the job. It was a promotion of sorts, and since 330 BC the Companion cavalry had so rarely operated together than neither he nor Hephaestion had had much chance to exercise their joint command. We do not know how Cleitus felt about his new office, for he did not live to take it up.[14]

Whenever the opportunity offered, Alexander held the hard-drinking banquets of which he and his father were so fond, as were the Macedonian aristocracy in general. Opportunities came far more often in the lulls between active campaigning, reinforcing the stark difference between these rare intervals and the "normal" experience of marching, fighting, and killing. Our sources portray Alexander's character as changing, generally for the worse, and disapprove of his flirtation with the symbols and traditions of Asian kingship, his greater suspicion of those around him, and a tendency to drink ever more heavily. The last of these was in many ways unsurprising given the drinking culture of the court and the circumstances. Alexander had been at war for all nine years of his reign, crossed thousands of miles, had been wounded several times, and after staggering victories and spectacular plunder, suddenly found himself facing two years of bitter conflict in barren country against opposition he could not pin down and destroy because new enemies seemed to spring up after each victory. The warfare was hard and costly, and the spoils of success very modest after the gold and splendor of great cities. Alexander can only have been tired, frustrated, and unsure how to win and move on to the longed for goal of India. His officers and soldiers of all ranks felt much the same, with the exception that for most a time of rest and a return home offered a far sweeter dream than the invasion of yet another country.[15]

Already frayed tempers were fanned by the plentiful supplies of wine. Complaints and dark humor are a common coping mechanism for those facing dangerous and stressful situations, a safety valve that helps prevent frustration and discontent from coming to a head. Many Macedonian aristocrats were deeply uncomfortable with Alexander's adoption of aspects of Asian costume, the court ceremony, a harem, and eunuchs, and resented the appointment of former enemies to positions of power and honor. The last two years had seen all major commands going to a small circle of royal favorites, most of all Hephaestion, Craterus, Coenus, Perdiccas, and Ptolemy. All were Alexander's men rather than Philip's, friends of his youth and closer to him in age. Hephaestion openly favored all of the king's new policies, and acted on his behalf in many dealings with the Persian nobility. In contrast Craterus was well known for being staunchly Macedonian in speech, dress, and manners, but this in no way diminished Alexander's fondness for him; he is supposed to have said that while Hephaestion was a friend to Alexander, Craterus was a friend to the king. A measure of open disagreement with his policies was acceptable as long as it did not go too far and was accompanied by absolute loyalty. Craterus and the others had shown this in their active role in the deaths of Philotas and Parmenio.[16]

That purge was a warning that even the greatest might fall, but if so it did not end resentment of Alexander's adoption of "barbarian" customs and his insatiable desire for more conquest, nor did it make everyone hide their opinions. Cleitus openly expressed his dislike for the prominence of easterners at court and in the imperial administration, and for the king's changing habits. While it is possible that Alexander decided to make him a satrap in order to send him away, none of our sources suggest this. As always we lack understanding of the balance of power among aristocratic families and their influence at court, so it is conjectural to suggest that the earlier appointment of Cleitus to joint command of the Companion cavalry was a necessary sop to his older officers and advisors, the veterans of his father's campaigns. Equally it may have been a choice based on personal affection and respect for a man with a fine record, the brother of his nurse as an infant and someone who had saved his life. While there was certainly a political dimension to the rise of Alexander's favorites to high command in these years, this was more than blind faith. So far all had performed their new roles at least competently and several had demonstrated considerable talent.

Macedonian tradition surrounded the king with Companions, not mere subjects, so that he was—as the most admired Roman emperors would later strive to appear—the first among equals, rather than a tyrant with absolute power. Much of this was a facade, yet another aspect of the ancient world in which treating individuals and a class with public respect made it easier for them to accept the rule of another. Feasts and drinking parties, the Macedonian version of the more staid Greek symposia, were an expression of this, a proud tradition that they believed showed the great difference between them and the submissive courtiers of a king like Darius. Guests debated, argued, mocked, no doubt within well-understood boundaries, and everyone accepted that drink loosened tongues and that much of what was said need not be taken too seriously. These occasions were common, although it should be said that our sources make more mention of them and of the scale of alcohol consumption in the second half of Alexander's reign. Nearly all passed without incident, which made the night in Marakanda in 328 BC all the more strange and shocking.

The sources differ on the details, and do not tell us how many were present, although it is clear that it was a large gathering, including several of Alexander's favorites as well as Cleitus, other older officers, and some easterners. Plutarch claims that the king had just received a delivery of fruit brought all the way from the Greek world and was eager to share this treat. The guests ate and drank and talked. Many flattered Alexander, something he tolerated readily enough to make it common and ever more extravagant. They compared him favorably to heroes like his ancestor Hercules and the Dioscuri, the heavenly twins Castor and Pollux. There was talk of how far Alexander's victories outstripped all that Philip had achieved. Someone—Plutarch offered two different names— sang verses lampooning Macedonian officers "who had lately been defeated by the Barbarians. The older guests were annoyed by this and railed at both the poet and the singer, but Alexander and those about him listened with delight and bade the singer go on." It is unclear which defeat this was, whether the disaster in 329 BC, the smaller failure in 328 BC, or other actions where perhaps men failed to catch an elusive enemy. In any case, the implication was that setbacks were due to the incompetence or even cowardice of others, so not the fault of the ever victorious king.[17]

"Then Cleitus, who was already drunk and naturally of a harsh temper and wilful, was more than ever vexed," according to Plutarch, and complained that brave Macedonians were being mocked in front of barbarians, and were far better men than those who laughed at them. Alexander asked whether the old warrior wanted to shield his own cowardice—it is not clear whether he meant this as a real insult or it was a botched attempt to turn it all into a joke, something at which his father had been so adept. Given how drunk all the witnesses were, the differences in accounts are all the more understandable and no one may have been sure about what was really said. In reply Cleitus reminded Alexander that he had saved his life, and then many more grievances spilled out. Philip was defended, and perhaps the veteran mocked Alexander's claim to be son of Ammon, and then complained of unending campaigns and toil and the folly of aping customs of the barbarians, with Alexander taking the credit for the sweat and blood of the whole army. Plutarch has Alexander turn to some Greeks and say that they must seem like demigods among wild beasts when they mixed with Macedonians.[18]

Insults flew back and forth and Alexander threw an apple at Cleitus, hitting him. Then he called for his sword, but at least one of those present had been sober enough to hide the weapon, which made the king fear a plot against him. Some tried to calm and restrain him as he began calling the guard to turn out, using the Macedonian dialect rather than pure Greek, which was a sign of urgency. The king turned to a trumpeter and told him to sound the alarm, and when the soldier hesitated and would not act, the king punched him and knocked him down. Another group, Ptolemy among them, hustled Cleitus out of the hall and outside the walls of the settlement. There it might have ended, but Cleitus broke free—or perhaps was mistakenly believed to have calmed down— and went back into the party. "He met with Alexander just as Alexander was calling out 'Cleitus!' and cried, 'Here I am, Cleitus, Alexander!'" The king grabbed a spear from one of the sentries and ran him through, the blow by chance or the habit of training well aimed and killing Cleitus instantly.[19]

The scene recalls the sword-wielding Philip falling at the wedding feast as he bore down on his son, although sadly on this occasion Alexander was not too drunk to walk. These are the only two occasions during either reign when a row at a party produced homicidal intent or indeed any sort of fight, although it is possible that confrontations did occur at other times and those involved were ushered away before any harm was done. Whatever their differences and feelings toward each other, all sources are clear that this was in no way premeditated, and this helps to explain Alexander's sudden swing from rage to horror at what he had done. He was drunk, highly emotional, and also a man devoted to honor and reputation, and while Homer's heroes could be mastered by anger, this was not the behavior of a good king. Propping the same spear or another against the wall, Alexander was about to commit suicide by throwing himself onto its point when he was restrained. For three days or more he stayed in his tent, brooding, lamenting, and refusing food or drink. There is no reason to doubt that his revulsion at his own weakness was not genuine. Alexander killed many men in battle, gave orders for and watched the massacre or execution of tens of thousands more en masse, and plenty as individuals. Yet this was the only murder he committed with his own hands, a spontaneous, drunken act against a man who had not deserved to die.

As the days passed, a succession of visitors tried to soothe the royal conscience. Aristander recalled a bad omen, when Cleitus was summoned to the king in the middle of a sacrifice and was followed by several of the bleating sheep already prepared for the knife. Another tradition had Alexander fail to sacrifice to Dionysus on the day of the feast, even though it was his custom to do so, which seemed fitting since wine was the cause of what had happened. Callisthenes spoke soothingly and may have hinted that Cleitus was at fault for provoking the king. A fellow philosopher, Anaxarchus of Abdera, adopted a radically different approach, berating the king for "weeping like a slave, in fear of the law and the censure of men." He was the king, on earth equivalent to Zeus, who had "Justice and Law seated beside him, in order that everything that is done by the master of the world may be lawful and just." Opinion in the army preferred a live and active Alexander as leader to the memory of a dead officer, however brave, and judged Cleitus wrong for showing such disrespect by arguing with his king so angrily in the first place and then a fool for returning to the feast.[20]

The murder inevitably made life at court a good deal more nervous. Alexander had shown utter ruthlessness in punishing those he felt were plotting against him, but this was different, and while we know that nothing of the sort occurred again, those around him did not have this assurance. It was now dangerous to speak too freely, although judging this cannot have been easy, and the king continued to feast as before with his Companions and friends in the traditional way. Fatigue and the seemingly unending, grinding warfare help to explain the heavy drinking, which in turn made tempers harder to control. The behavior of Alexander and Cleitus does also fit with patterns of post-traumatic stress disorder experienced by modern soldiers, which can cause violent mood swings and difficulty controlling emotions; in the king's case perhaps it was exacerbated by the head injury. All such interpretations are guesswork, and the murder remains as sudden and senseless today as it did all those centuries ago.[21]

26

"POORER FOR A KISS"

After a few days of brooding and self-reproach, Alexander reappeared as his familiar restless self. Although some of the winter of 328–327 BC was spent with the army in winter quarters, the lull in campaigning was brief and operations went on well into the autumn of one year and resumed before winter was over. As usual, even when there was no fighting, the king devoted himself to administration, made appointments, wrote letters, and received delegations. Whether he ever caught up with all the work required to run his vast new empire is impossible to say. Winter weather slowed communications, delaying the receipt of his orders as well as reports coming to him. As ever sources focus on Alexander and say little or nothing about events elsewhere. Bactria and Sogdiana remained turbulent, with many leaders choosing to resist or if possible ignore the invaders, and it is possible that there was trouble elsewhere, including in the heartland of Persia and Media.[1]

At this stage in his campaigns, the accounts of Alexander's activities are confused and often contradictory. Arrian has the king march out early in 327 BC, before the spring thaw, to launch a succession of attacks on enemy strongholds. The first was the Sogdian Rock, a walled town set on high crags and well supplied with food and water. When summoned to surrender, its leaders mocked Alexander, telling him that they were safe from any attack unless he could find "soldiers with wings." The king sought men skilled at mountain climbing from the ranks, offering a lavish prize of twelve talents for the first one to reach the top, with progressively smaller bounties for the others, down to a still substantial 300 gold darics for the last. Some 300 volunteers answered the call and under cover of darkness made the ascent, using ropes and tent pegs as crampons. About thirty fell to their deaths, and Arrian claims the bodies were lost in the snow and never recovered. The others got to the top of a rise higher than the town, and probably outside its walls.

At dawn the climbers shouted out and waved linen flags attached to short spears or staffs they had carried with them. Alexander again summoned the town to surrender, his herald informing the defenders that the Macedonians had found their soldiers with wings. It was a bluff, for the 270 climbers could not be reinforced and were far too few and ill equipped to storm the town, but the shock of seeing enemies was enough and the defenders surrendered. Arrian claims that among the prisoners were the families of many noblemen who were fighting the Macedonians, including the wife and children of Oxyartes, a former supporter of Bessus. He does not mention the fate of prisoners other than the aristocratic women and children.[2]

In contrast, Curtius places the whole episode during the campaigns of 328 BC, calls the place the Rock of Ariamazes after its commander, and does not have Oxyartes's family take refuge there, but in another stronghold. He does have the defenders laugh at Alexander and ask whether he knew how to fly, and tells of the audacious climb by the 300 volunteers, albeit with some different details. The next morning Alexander's men in the main camp blow trumpets as if preparing for an assault to add to the fears of the defenders, who surrender. Ariamazes and his leading supporters are flogged and crucified, while the humbler prisoners were sent in groups to Alexander's newly established colonies as a serf population to work the land for the Macedonian and Greek settlers.[3]

Many scholars prefer Curtius's dating of this incident, although the case cannot be proven one way or the other. Even if Arrian was wrong to place the episode in 327 BC, it is clear that the struggle to dominate the wider region was far from complete in that year. This conflict was prolonged and extremely brutal, so that the execution of leaders and transplantation of the rest of the population would not have been out of character with Macedonian actions elsewhere. There was no enemy field army to smash, no capital to take and no single king like Darius or even Bessus to kill or capture. Instead the focus was much more local. Alexander and his men attacked places that were little more than villages and hunted regional warlords because these were the only targets on offer. Any man who seemed capable of rallying a force of supporters against the invaders was hunted down. Plutarch tells a story of Alexander shooting one leader dead with an arrow. He does not give the context, although a siege seems most likely, and it is significant to see the king employing the bow, a weapon so closely associated with the king of Persia.[4]

Arrian follows his account of the Sogdian Rock with the siege of another mountain fastness, the Rock of Chorienes, named after the nobleman in command. This may have been a title, and elsewhere he is called Sisimithres, while Curtius alleges that following local custom he was married to his own mother with whom he had had a number of children. Once again the defenders mistakenly trusted to the natural strength of their position, since the only viable approaches meant crossing a deep ravine. The Macedonians felled pines and made ladders so that they could get down the sheer side of the ravine and begin making a bridge across it. Soldiers labored in relays, Alexander supervising during the day and other officers taking over during the night so that work never stopped. At first the defenders were scornful, for the task seemed impossible, but as days passed and the mound rose higher and higher, any laughter became strained. Eventually, archers on the siege ramp were high enough to be in range of the wall, while both they and the laborers were protected by wicker screens against missiles shot down at them. The mood inside the stronghold shifted to one of despair.

Oxyartes was by now in Alexander's camp, having surrendered at some point, whether because the Macedonians had captured his family as Arrian maintains, or because the family were besieged with

Sisimithres as some scholars prefer, or simply because he had judged it wiser to join the invaders rather than keep fighting against them. He played the key role in the negotiations that followed, assuring Sisimithres that Alexander and his men would not stop until they captured any stronghold, but that the king welcomed those willing to submit and treated them generously. The town surrendered, admitting Alexander at the head of a strong detachment of hypaspists and opening its ample storehouses to help supply the besiegers. As a reward Sisimithres was confirmed as regional governor.[5]

Oxyartes did even better, for early in 327 BC Alexander decided to marry one of his daughters. Roxane, the "little star," was said to be beautiful, second in all Asia only to Darius's late wife, and just as Philip was supposed to have fallen in love with Olympias, so it was claimed that Alexander was entranced by the teenage girl when he glimpsed her amid a troupe of other young noblewomen presented at a feast. Scholars tend to dismiss this story as romantic invention, even when some at least are willing to speak of his unpredictable emotional responses in the context of the murder of Cleitus. In many ways the marriage fits neatly with Philip's weddings to princesses from bordering peoples and would excite little comment if Alexander had taken one or more wives before this point instead of waiting until he was in his twenty-ninth year. There is no sign that he had developed any great interest in fathering an heir. His mistress Barsine was soon to present him with a son, and if he was looking for an Asian bride then she came from a far more prominent family in Persian politics than Roxane. Yet so did many other eligible women, and as a twice widowed mother of other men's children, Barsine carried too much baggage to make her an obvious choice for his wife. Alexander and Roxane shared no common language, making an attraction based on affection and understanding unlikely. Perhaps Alexander desired her, and this influenced his choice along with practical concerns. As with the majority of political marriages, the bride's feelings were of little or no relevance.[6]

Marrying Roxane was a sign to the noblemen of Bactria and Sogdiana that the conqueror was willing to treat them with respect, confirmed by the subsequent appointment of her father as satrap. At the same time it reinforced the permanence of his control, for a man who married into the local elite was not planning merely to raid and retire. These nobles were thus faced with the same choice as leaders everywhere else since 334 BC—of fighting with little prospect of victory or of submitting in the hope of winning Alexander's favor. Perhaps the wedding helped convince some that the Macedonians and their king could be trusted and were worth conciliating. However, it did not mark any lull in the ruthless operations directed against any sign of resistance, nor did Bactria and Sogdiana instantly become peaceful.

No one records the reaction of the wider Persian elite to Alexander's marriage. Some may have welcomed it, while others wondered at or resented the selection of a bride from such a comparatively obscure family and outside the heartland of Persia and Media. For Macedonians a foreign queen was nothing new, although Roxane and her people may have seemed more alien than their European neighbors. None of this needed matter too much if in due course the king took other wives, one or more of them from closer to home. A late source claims that Roxane was soon pregnant, but that the child was stillborn or perished after a short time. Within a year Barsine gave the king an illegitimate son who did survive and was at least loosely acknowledged without receiving any prominence during his father's four remaining years of life. It is significant that the marriage to Roxane is never prominent and sometimes absent from the many resentments we are told festered among the Macedonians of all ranks. Arrian claims that Alexander's friends shared in his admiration for her beauty, even if this was no more than tact. Had Alexander not died so young without an obvious heir, Roxane and the child she was carrying when he died would probably be a very minor incident in his story.[7]

In 327 BC Alexander had no time for prolonged celebration and festivities. The ceremony involved the bride and groom eating slices from a loaf cut by his sword, a custom supposedly Macedonian. Almost nothing is heard of her until the king's last days, so it is unknown whether or not she ever followed him on campaign in the manner of the Persian king's women. Early in the year Alexander once again led his army into the mountains in another feat of endurance against the altitude and appalling weather, which battered the men with hail. Some died of exposure, others were harried and coaxed along by the king. One story appears prominently in our Latin sources, claiming that an exhausted straggler was brought into camp by Alexander, who helped the much older man off with his equipment and placed him on his own seat next to the fire. Only as the soldier started to recover did he recognize his king and panic. Alexander reassured him, saying that for a Persian merely sitting on the king's seat would have meant death, but for a free Macedonian it brought warmth and life.[8]

Columns chased leaders still willing to fight, killing some and forcing others to submit, while Alexander made sure that his newly founded or refounded settlements were secure. A larger garrison than in any other region was to remain behind when the army left, numbering some 13,500 men, over a quarter of them cavalry, supplemented by the colonists who at the very least could defend their communities, even if some were rendered past active campaigning by age or injury. At the same time large numbers of local warriors were recruited to accompany the army, while 30,000 youths from this area and other satrapies were conscripted to undergo years of military training after the Macedonian manner, which included learning Greek, for this was the language of the army. Thus a significant proportion of those most likely to take up arms against the conquerors were removed to where it would be harder for them to rebel. For the moment military might, conciliation, and the maintenance of strong occupying forces brought sufficient stability to the wider area for Alexander to move on.[9]

Establishing cities, transplanting population, recruiting warriors or potential warriors to strengthen his own forces, fighting relentlessly against active resistance while encouraging defections and rewarding submissions: all of this was familiar from Philip's earliest years securing his enlarged Macedonia and adding to it. Alexander may well have been surprised by the determined hostility he had encountered in Bactria and Sogdiana, but another lesson from Philip's day was that success often took a long time, and that war could flare up again as new leaders appeared among the tribes, for the problem of such a carrot-and-stick approach was that not everyone continued to feel that they had had sufficient carrot, while the wielded stick sowed hatred as well as fear. The army was key to the system Philip had created and Alexander inherited and developed: it grew with each conquest as plunder was turned into pay and reward, and then recruited contingents of the conquered and led them against new enemies.

Alexander had never halted for more than the bare minimum period of consolidation before resuming his advance. That was a reflection of his ambition and impatient nature, but also necessary so that the army could absorb its new recruits and let them share in victories as well as bond them to the king, if not necessarily to each other. The greatest praise and rewards continued to go to the Macedonians. Around this time or during the campaigns in India shields with silver decoration were issued to the hypaspists, earning them the nickname "Silver shields" (*argyraspides*), and the other Macedonians received or purchased ever more elaborately decorated gear. They remained the key striking force of the army, especially in sieges, leading every assault and undertaking the bulk of the labor involved. Yet as the army grew and grew they became an ever smaller proportion of the overall force. Asian contingents were everywhere, with cavalry attached to the hipparchies as separate units, and apart from men from the Persian Empire there were Sacae horse archers from beyond the border. Some sources claim that within a year so, Alexander would command some 120,000 men, although this may reflect men in the wider theater and not those ever concentrated into the field army. The highest estimates would make the Macedonians less than a sixth of this total—far lower than in the earlier campaigns.[10]

In the spring of 327 BC Alexander paused at Bactra while smaller columns went out to chase down recalcitrant leaders, and during this period of rest tension once again exploded in a court uncomfortable with their leader's enthusiasm for Asians and their customs. Persian tradition marked social status by requiring an inferior to perform obeisance, or *proskynesis*, when they met. The ritual varied in proportion to the degree of difference, so that many ordinary people were expected to prostrate themselves before a great nobleman, let alone the king. Where the difference was less, men kissed on the cheeks, while equals kissed on the lips. From the start Alexander's Persian subjects naturally showed this mark of respect to him when they came into his presence, even the noblest bowing and the majority lying on the ground.[11]

Proskynesis revolted Greeks and Macedonians alike. The word is not too strong, for it spoke to a very deep sense of how a free man should behave in a society where honor was so central. Bowing, let alone prostration, were marks of respect reserved for the gods alone, which led to the widespread Hellenic assumption that the Persians worshipped their king as a god. By now, should they have bothered to learn, Alexander's officers would know that this was not true, but that did nothing to alter their unshakeable conviction that the willingness to perform the act was proof of the essentially servile status of even the most aristocratic Persian. Such men deserved contempt, just as they deserved defeat at the hands of free Greeks and Macedonians, and seeing them perform the act to Alexander only reinforced this profound sense of superiority. Sometimes there was open mockery, and we hear of one Macedonian laughing as he called out to a prostrate Persian to get his head down properly.[12]

Yet for the Persians it would be unnatural and disrespectful not to make obeisance to their king, even when that king was a foreign overlord, and they would wonder that this same conqueror was treated so disrespectfully when his own countrymen refused to bow. Thus the two conflicting systems of protocol coexisted as a visible reminder of the distinction between the conquerors and the king's new subjects. Alexander, just as he added aspects of Asian-inspired symbols of office to his costume in an effort to create new marks of kingship recognized by all, decided to introduce a compromise version of *proskynesis* to the Macedonian and Greek members of his court. This was a gentle bow that the king then returned with a kiss.[13]

Care was taken to prepare the court members for the protocol, which was to be introduced at a feast for selected guests. Alexander ought to have known how repellent any hint of obeisance was to aristocrats, suggesting that either he did not care or was confident that the limited gesture would salve their consciences. He was still young, accustomed to getting what he wanted, and lived surrounded by men eager for his favor in a court crammed with

writers competing to eulogize him, so he may have convinced himself that anything he decided must be right and acceptable. One
tradition has Anaxarchus and others arguing that since Alexander's
unprecedented achievements made it inevitable that he would be
worshipped as a god after his death, then they might as well antici-
pate this by granting him divine honors straightaway. Callisthenes
responded fluently and well against this, asking his opponents who
wished to make a god whether they even had the lesser power to
make someone a king.

On the night of the feast, it was arranged that a succession of
senior Companions would pour a libation to the altar of a god
in the room, bow, and then go to Alexander to be kissed. The
presence of the altar may have been another compromise to their
consciences, letting a man feel that his bow was for the god rather
than the king. The lead was to be taken by men who had already
agreed to the ritual. Callisthenes may have been among this group,
or maybe he and the remaining guests were expected to follow
the lead set by the first few to perform it. Instead he poured the
libation, made not the slightest inclination of his head let alone
a bow, and went up to Alexander for the kiss. Busy chatting to
Hephaestion who reclined beside him, the king did not notice,
until the omission was pointed out to him. He pulled back and did
not kiss Callisthencs, who walked away, saying loudly enough to
be heard that he would leave "poorer for a kiss."[14]

Others may have copied him, for his gesture echoed the opinion of the majority. The plan to introduce this limited form of
proskynesis was dropped, so that much about its intention and
form is now impossible to know. Thus we cannot say whether this
limited obeisance was to be reserved for Macedonians and Greeks
or replace the traditional version performed by Asians, at least for
the most important aristocrats. Similarly, there is no mention of
whether it was planned to extend the gesture in this or a more
submissive form to the wider army. The whole episode was badly
judged by Alexander and his advisors, for even if the experiment
had succeeded and the gesture become a part of court protocol, it
was bound to add to the resentment and dissatisfaction of senior
Macedonians and Greeks, who still filled all important military

posts and provided the bulk of his administrators. Nor is it clear that it would have pleased Asian noblemen or satisfied their sense of proper respect to a king. Perhaps time and continued victories would have led all to accept it as normal, or perhaps not. Attempting and failing to introduce the ritual meant the worst of both worlds.

Aristotle judged Callisthenes to be both eloquent and a pompous fool. Callisthenes accompanied the expedition to Asia as historian, and happily wrote fawning accounts of the king's heroism, of the sea making obeisance to Alexander, and the god at Siwah calling him his son. By this time, other authors had far outstripped even this sycophancy, and with the great war of revenge complete, his writings and the Greek audience for them began to matter less. Callisthenes could be caustic when talking about other members of the court and was not popular; he reveled in luxury less than many, which was taken as a rebuke, and was notorious for disdaining invitations to dinner. His public refusal to perform *proskynesis* brought him a sudden popularity with many who shared his view and were glad that he had taken a stand, not least because it meant that they had not been the first to defy the king. Opinion shifted back against him after a demonstration of his oratory at another gathering. Alexander first invited Callisthenes to praise the Macedonians, which he did with skill and enthusiasm. Then, quoting Euripides to say that it was easy for anyone to celebrate the truth, the king challenged him to argue the opposite case. Such exercises were a common form of rhetorical training, and Callisthenes gave an excellent demonstration, arguing that Philip had only prospered because of divisions among the Greeks. His audience took this as an insult, restoring the general dislike of the puffed-up philosopher from Olynthus.[15]

There it might have ended, for Callisthenes was politically insignificant and it did not much matter whether he was liked, but soon afterward there was a serious attempt on Alexander's life. The plot was formed by a group of Royal Pages, and like several of the conspiracies against Argead monarchs, our sources tell a story of injured pride and passionate homosexual lovers. A large contingent of pages had joined the army from Macedonia late in 330 BC, having missed the great victories of the early years. It is not clear whether any pages had been with the king from the start, and perhaps some of those old enough for active service in 334 BC had always been with the expedition and by this time had moved on to adulthood and full military service. By now the tradition going back at least to Philip's day had resumed and pages accompanied the king in the hunt and in battle, and guarded his tent. This gave the conspirators their opportunity.[16]

The trouble was provoked at a hunt, when a page named Hermolaus the son of Sopolis speared a boar that was charging at the king. If the custom was still prevalent, then killing the animal marked a boy's transition to full manhood, allowing him to recline at a feast, and perhaps the excitement when Hermolaus saw his opportunity blinded the teenager to everything else. Alexander was outraged, feeling the boy had poached his kill, perhaps even that the act suggested that he was not perfectly capable of saving himself. Persian hunting tradition reserved the first kill for the king, and reserved any animal he selected as his target and no one else's. No source claims that Alexander introduced this rule, which does not mean that others may not have wondered whether he secretly wished it. As was his right as king, he flogged Hermolaus and added the extra humiliation of depriving him of his horse.[17]

Hermolaus brooded on the insult, confiding in his fellow page and lover Sostratus, who already nursed a hatred against the king for reasons now lost. Four other pages joined them in their decision to murder Alexander because in this incident and more generally he was not behaving as a true king of Macedon should, and was not treating them with honor. Arriving from the far more traditional surroundings of Macedonia so long after the start of the expedition, these teenagers may well have found the changes in the king and his court even more shocking than those who had watched their gradual development. There was grousing in the army and among its leaders, as there always was, but the purge of Philotas and Parmenio and the murder of Cleitus, as well as adoption of Asian dress and the attempt at introducing *proskynesis*, kept adding to the simmering discontent. The boys' fathers all seem to have been officers, but none had an exceptional career, which may have left them dissatisfied and apt to moan in private. Scholars tend to see the political context of resentment among conservative Macedonians as the key motivator and it was surely there, but we should not play down the personal grudges of youths at an age when it is easy to believe in the absolute importance of feelings and beliefs. The personal and political were never separate, for Argead kings were judged on how they treated their Companions and the wider aristocracy.

The plot was well thought out, at least as far as the killing went, and it is harder to say what they expected to happen next; no source mentions any escape plans. After some waiting and bargaining, the conspirators found a night when they alone were the pages scheduled for guard duty. The plan needed all of them, both to ensure that they stayed true, and also because they needed to overpower the king and up to two of his bodyguards who traditionally slept near his bed. Chance intervened when the king failed to return from a drinking party. One tradition said that he was warned by a half-mad old woman who had followed the court for some time and gradually gained a reputation for predicting the future. Whatever the reason, Alexander kept on drinking and did not return during the night. At dawn, a new party of pages arrived to take over the guard duty, but Hermolaus and his confederates found an excuse to linger in desperate hope of getting their chance. The moment had passed, and when Alexander did turn up he praised the boys for their devotion and gave them a reward before dismissing them.

In the days that followed, one of the conspirators cracked under the strain and told his lover, who went to the boy's older brother, who in turn went to the royal tent and managed to speak to Ptolemy. After the fate of Philotas, no one was about to withhold information of a plot from the king. Alexander had the pages arrested and put on trial. Hermolaus's father condemned him, nervous that he would share his son's fate, but the tradition is that the page and his comrades remained defiant to the last, accusing Alexander of failing to behave like a proper king, of not treating his nobles and soldiers well as he used up their health and lives in his unceasing wars. The boys were stoned to death as would-be regicides, and according to Curtius their fellow pages carried out the execution. There is no sign of a wider purge of relatives and the conspirators were too young to have had supporters.[18]

Hermolaus was said to be a pupil and admirer of Callisthenes, but even under torture none of the conspirators said that he was involved. At most his influence was indirect, encouraging the youths to value honor even more highly and praising the murderers of tyrants, none of which differed greatly from the ideas of most mainstream philosophers. For Alexander, Callisthenes's apparent closeness to youths who had dared to attempt to kill him was sufficient, coming on top of the dislike Callisthenes had earned by his refusal to perform *proskynesis*. At some point he was arrested and then held in custody. There was no trial, and one source claims that this was to occur when the army returned to Greece. Accounts of his ultimate fate differ markedly, even when coming from eyewitnesses. Some say he was tortured and ultimately hanged, while others claim that he grew obese and lice-infested during his imprisonment and died of natural causes. Whatever the details, a man once a close supporter and propagandist for the king was imprisoned and died after voicing dissent. For all the victories and all the newfound wealth, Alexander struggled to satisfy many at court.[19]

27

INDIA

I ndia had been in Alexander's mind for some time. Darius I had long ago conquered the Indus Valley, although in the generations that followed it is less clear how far the Persian king's will was actually imposed on the area. Some "Indian" troops had joined Darius III at Gaugamela, albeit probably from the Kabul Valley, for the kingdoms further south by this time appear to have been independent. Nevertheless, India remained the last unconquered territory that could be considered part of the Persian Empire. Stories, even if ill formed and vague, of Hercules and Dionysus winning victories in the area, and of the heroic exploits of the mysterious Babylonian queen Semiramis, all added to the lure, as did the belief that the end of the continent of Asia could not be so very far away. More practically, Indian exiles had come to join Alexander's army and other leaders sent envoys, all imploring Alexander to intervene on their side in disputes with hostile neighbors. Diplomatic activity went alongside the logistical preparations as the army concentrated and began to move south in 327 BC, crossing the Hindu Kush to the Alexandria he had founded near modern Begram.[1]

It took a while for the troops and supplies to muster. Alexander ordered the burning of superfluous transport wagons and the luxuries they contained, beginning with many of his own to set an example. Inevitably the officers suffered the most, at least all those who had failed to make better arrangements for the wealth they had acquired in recent years and insisted on carrying everything with them. While it is doubtful that the army would travel as lightly as it had in the early days, Alexander wanted something sleeker and more mobile than the great processions of a Persian king going to war. He had already sacked and replaced the officer left in charge of this Alexandria for unspecified incompetence, and this was one of several appointments and dismissals. One Companion found to have left his post after being placed in charge was executed. More veterans were discharged to add to the colonists who would help to dominate the area in his absence.[2]

At the start of summer of 327 BC the march resumed, the army divided into two main columns. Hephaestion and Perdiccas went through the Khyber Pass with orders to reach the Indus and prepare a bridge across the great river. En route they were to accept the surrender of each community in their path, or storm them if they resisted. At first all went well, and the diplomatic preparations ensured that there was no fighting. One city rebelled after they had passed, making them turn back and take it after a month-long siege.[3]

In the meantime Alexander led the rest of the army and the bulk of elite units into Bajaur, Swat, and the Chitral Valley, all areas that would more recently lie on the North-West Frontier of British India and remain fiercely independent and prone to violence to this day. Some of the first communities to be reached abandoned their villages and took refuge in hilltop strongholds. Relying on speed, Alexander mounted 800 infantry—probably mainly hypaspists—to reinforce his cavalry and surged forward ahead of his main force. At the first settlement the warriors gathered outside were swiftly routed, but not before they had put an arrow into Alexander's shoulder and wounded Ptolemy and another bodyguard. The king's wound was little more than a scratch: his body armor took the force from the missile. At dawn the next day the place was stormed. Alexander's soldiers slaughtered every man they found but were unable to prevent the bulk

BATTLE OF HYDASPES, 326 BC

Not to scale. This reconstruction is highly conjectural
even by the standards of Alexander's battles.

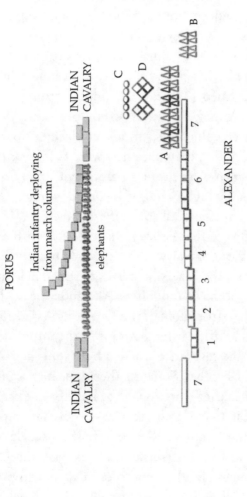

PORUS

Indian infantry deploying
from march column

elephants

INDIAN
CAVALRY

INDIAN
CAVALRY

ALEXANDER

A

B

C

D

1 2 3 4 5 6 7

7

1 = Phalanx Regiment (Meleager)
2 = Phalanx Regiment (Attalus)
3 = Phalanx Regiment (Gorgias)
4 = Phalanx Regiment (Cleitus)
5 = Phalanx Regiment (Coenus)
6 = Hypaspists (Seleucus)

7 = Light infantry
A = Companion Cavalry
B = Companion Cavalry (Coenus)
C = Horse archers
D = Asian Cavalry

of them from escaping into the hills for the Macedonians were too few in number to cut off all escape routes. The village was burned and this dreadful warning helped persuade the next community in the army's path to surrender.[4]

This opening action set the tone for what was to be another brutal campaign against stubborn mountain folk defending their homes. Some fled into the wilds after setting light to their houses, and sometimes they escaped and sometimes they were caught and slaughtered. Ptolemy, whose wound must have been a minor one, was back in action and cut down a chieftain in single combat. A Macedonian stronghold was established on the site of a settlement when the main force caught up, and the pursuit resumed. The sight of many campfires revealed a substantial concentration of warriors willing to defend what they felt was a strong position. Alexander split his men into three columns to attack up different paths, and after a day of hard fighting the tribesmen were defeated. Ptolemy claimed that 40,000 men were captured along with 230,000 oxen, which seems improbably high even if it included women, children, and other noncombatants and all sorts of animals.[5]

Next in the path were the Assacenians, credited with an army of 30,000 infantry, 2,000 cavalry, and 30 elephants. In the event they decided not to face the Macedonians in the open field and split up, returning to their home communities. Alexander headed for the largest town, Massaga, stronghold of the local king Assacenus, who appears to have died a little earlier, perhaps in the initial skirmishing. This meant that the resistance was led by his mother Cleophis and a brother or half brother. Some of their best men came from a contingent of mercenaries who appear to have been experienced professionals who hired out their services to Indian monarchs. Arrian claims that they numbered no fewer than 9,000, but his narrative suggests that this is a considerable exaggeration. A sally against the Macedonians as they entrenched their camp outside the walls ended in a bloody repulse after Alexander deliberately retreated before counterattacking, aiming to kill as many enemies as possible before they could retreat back into the town.

In spite of this the defenders held out for some time, repulsing one assault, but were not really prepared for the artillery and siege techniques employed by the Macedonians. A siege tower was a strange and fearsome novelty as it was pushed up so that archers could shoot down onto the wall. Yet the defenders fought on and drove back another attack launched across a ramp dropped from the tower. At some point Alexander was hit near the ankle by an arrow, although once again this was a very minor wound and he immediately mounted a horse and rode around the siege lines to show everyone that he was fine. The Macedonians kept up the pressure and steadily wore out the defenders, which adds to the impression that their numbers were nowhere near as large as our sources claim. When a prominent leader was killed by a catapult, the defenders sought terms.

The mercenaries agreed to surrender and according to Arrian pledged to take service with Alexander. However, he also claims that they planned to slip away under cover of darkness from the hillock they had occupied outside the walls, for they were unwilling to fight for Alexander against their kindred. Learning of this, Alexander surrounded them and ordered his men to attack, massacring the mercenaries and following up by storming the virtually undefended town. This is the version most favorable to Alexander, as is the modern suggestion that the whole affair was an appalling accident based on misunderstanding. In contrast Plutarch believed that this was deliberate treachery on the king's part, while others add to the pathos of the scene by describing the Indians' wives sheltering behind them, then seizing the weapons of their dead and dying husbands and fighting to the bitter end. Alexander ordered plenty of massacres and mass executions during his reign, and the only thing to mark Plutarch's version of this incident as different is the sense that he broke his word, just as the death of Cleitus is different from anything else as the only murder done in hot blood with his own hands. It was a ghastly incident even by the standards of such savage warfare.[6]

Cleophis surrendered and according to some sources so charmed Alexander that they became lovers and she bore him a child. Modern scholars are understandably skeptical and wonder whether the whole episode—and even her name, which is only given in Roman sources—was inspired by Cleopatra and her affairs with Julius

Caesar and Antony. If she remained in power as is claimed, then this was more likely because she was considered reliable—and from Alexander's desire to encourage other leaders to submit. The siege had cost Alexander twenty-five fatalities, no doubt with many more wounded, so it was surely welcome when soon afterward envoys came offering the submission of the city of Nysa. Either they knew something of Greek customs, or during the negotiations coincidence of their traditions was spotted and turned into the story that their community had been found by Dionysus. It suited everyone to believe the tale, and the discovery of ivy or something much like it growing in the area when it did not in Persia was taken as confirmation. Nysa surrendered and received good terms. Alexander and his Macedonians did not have to fight and could feel themselves walking in the footsteps of a god. A celebration with much drinking marked the occasion when the army reached the town. Alexander was cheered by the thought that this marked the farthest east that Dionysus had gone, believing that his men would be cheered by the thought of going even farther.[7]

This warm welcome and the reputation of their earlier successes did not mean that their advance would be easy, and the next two towns they approached both chose to resist. A sally from Bazira (modern Birkot) was repulsed after heavy fighting, while nearby Ora (modern Udegram) was stormed by Alexander, prompting the defenders at Bazira to abandon their town. Along with others, they took refuge at the high and inaccessible Rock of Aornus (modern Pir Sar) close to the Indus. There was a story of a great hero who had failed to capture Aornus and someone identified this man with Hercules. Alexander chose to believe it and once again a *pothos* or yearning came upon him, this time to succeed where his heroic ancestor had supposedly failed. After securing towns and villages on the river without fighting, he left Craterus with the main body to gather as much grain as they could, while he led the Agrianians, hypaspists, a phalanx regiment, and picked men from the other units, along with archers and some cavalry, back to the Rock. The main track leading up to the heights was difficult to climb and easy for determined defenders to hold against far greater numbers, but as so often luck was on his side. Local men appeared—in some sources an old man and his two sons who lived in a cave—who for a reward told the king of another, less well-known path.

During the night Ptolemy followed these guides with the Agrianians and a detachment of hypaspists, seizing a height where they raised a rudimentary rampart and lit a fire to signal that they had got into position. A day was spent in bitter fighting, as Alexander and his main force tried and failed to break through to join Ptolemy's men, who were holding out against repeated assaults. Alexander found a deserter to carry a message through the enemy position to Ptolemy instructing him to be ready to attack as soon as he heard fighting. The next day the king took the same route that Ptolemy had taken and when the tribesmen engaged him, Ptolemy did as instructed and advanced against their rear. Resistance was determined, but gradually the warriors grew tired as the more numerous Macedonians kept adding fresh troops to the fighting, and by the end of the day they had forced their way through to Ptolemy.

They were now in a position to begin siege works against the stronghold on the heights, but that meant bridging a deep ravine, so work began on a mound next to the hillock seized by Ptolemy. Archers and slingers covered the work parties and on the fourth day another patch of high ground was captured, allowing the mound to be built against it and saving a good deal of labor. Unable to stop the inexorable approach of the assault ramp, the defenders offered to surrender, but according to Arrian they planned to delay until nightfall and then try to escape. Alexander discovered this and removed his pickets to make it easier for them. Once he judged the defenders were leaving, he led 700 men over a weak section of the wall and cut down the enemy as they tried to escape.[8]

The siege was yet another demonstration of the Macedonian army's ability and determination to take any place, regardless of natural or man-made defenses. No refuge was safe, and in the immediate aftermath anyone determined to avoid conquest chose flight instead of defending their settlements. Alexander pursued them, fighting his way through any resistance, and at the same time several other columns actively stamped out any opposition. One leader was murdered by his own men and his head sent to Alexander as a mark of their submission. Other local kings and princes survived the ordeal of invasion and were confirmed in charge of their home communities by Alexander. He chose a Macedonian named Nicanor as satrap for a region embracing all the land up to the Indus. This was a difficult task, and such was the independence of leaders in the area that there does not appear to have been a satrap there under Darius. For the moment the locals were overawed by the power of Alexander and his conquering army, but they were also humiliated by defeat and forced submission, and unaccustomed to strong central authority. As Alexander marched away with the overwhelming bulk of his army, fear of his might began to erode.[9]

Suppressing the region even to this impermanent state had taken the remainder of the year and some of the winter, so it was in the early spring of 326 BC that Alexander rendezvoused with Perdiccas and Hephaestion at the chosen crossing place on the Indus, perhaps somewhere near modern Charsadda. For a month the combined army rested and prepared for the coming campaign, and as so often before reminded themselves of what it meant to be Hellenic by holding games and athletic competitions. This was probably the largest army as yet concentrated in one place, although it may well be that in the field Alexander led with at most some 40,000 men, just as he had done in earlier campaigns, and was always willing to use substantially smaller corps composed of his best troops as a strike force. Boats had been carried in sections or constructed on the spot to make a form of pontoon bridge. (Interestingly Arrian found no description of the method they used to make the bridge in any of his sources, so instead he described best practice in the Roman army of his own era on the basis that the Macedonians may well have done something similar.) As was appropriate for such a great moment, sacrifices were made on both banks of the river to mark the crossing and ensure that the gods would favor the army's march.[10]

This was not an opposed crossing, for diplomacy had already done its work and the invaders were welcomed by Omphis (Abmhi in Sanskrit), the ruler of Taxila, a kingdom in the area of modern Rawalpindi in Pakistan. Usually known as Taxiles as the personification of his kingdom, he preferred alliance to conflict, seeing local threats as more dangerous. More than a year earlier while his father was king, he had persuaded Omphis to send envoys to Alexander in Sogdiana and offer submission. When the old king died, Omphis renewed his contact with the Macedonians as successor, but claimed not to have assumed the throne until Alexander in person confirmed him in the post. While he sent food and supplies to Hephaestion and Perdiccas when they arrived, he declined to meet them; it was only when Alexander arrived that Omphis went to submit in person. Arriving at the head of his court and thousands of warriors, there was nearly a misunderstanding when the Macedonians assumed that this was a hostile army, and the two rulers are supposed to have ridden out to meet each other face to face and only then realized the truth. Lavish gifts of gold were exchanged—Alexander, making sure that he would not be outdone in generosity, handed over 1,000 talents in gold, prompting a few jaundiced comments from Macedonian officers. More importantly Omphis was confirmed as king and was even granted additional territory.[11]

Alexander's right to do all of this relied solely on the power of his army, which the new king could justifiably feel he had harnessed for his own benefit. Neighboring monarchs saw things differently or had simply missed the chance for favorable alliance, and now were disinclined to seek friendship with a foreign warlord who had allied with an enemy. Abisares, who ruled and took his name from Abhisara, a hilly region between the rivers Hydaspes and Acesines, may well have distrusted the invaders from the start, for he had sent warriors to the aid of Ora and later welcomed refugees fleeing from the Macedonians. Porus, ruler of the larger neighboring kingdom of Paurava (from which he took his name), does not appear to have been involved in earlier fighting, although in the past he had allied with Abisares against another leader.

Macedonian envoys went to both kings asking for their submission. Abisares equivocated, refusing to commit one way or the other and saying that he was too ill to attend on Alexander. In contrast Porus openly rejected the appeal (and in one late source even had the ambassador whipped), then mustered his army and marched to the borders of his land. There was talk of Abisares joining forces with him, although in the event nothing happened in time, and as usual Alexander was eager to confront open defiance. By May 326 BC he had marched to the bank of the Hydaspes and could see Porus and his army waiting on the far side. The scene was set for the last great battle of Alexander's campaigns.[12]

PORUS IS AN imposing figure in our sources, brave, honorable, good looking, and large; Arrian and others claim that he was well over seven feet tall, while even the most restrained version says that he was six foot three. Some of this anticipates what happened after his defeat, and some was the desire to have a great hero for the even greater Alexander to face and overcome. In a way he also personified India, a place that Greeks barely knew, so the sheer distance and a desire for the exotic had them interweave all sorts of wild tales. India was supposed to have giant ants whose burrowing brought gold nuggets to the surface; southern India was a land where everyone was fantastically tall and good looking, and where people married solely on the basis of physical appearance. The experience of Alexander's men when they reached India modified this mix of fact and fantasy only a little. They encountered elephants that were huge and fearsome, pythons of immense length, smaller snakes with terrible venom, monkeys, and all sorts of wondrous things. It remained easy to believe in other strange phenomena, and stories grew up over time telling of encounters with them. The tone of our sources when they speak of India is different from that for the earlier campaigns, for even centuries later when more was known, the place remained exotic and was also the place where Alexander had stopped and turned around. Yet for all this difference, Alexander arrived in India as a conqueror and acted there just as he had throughout his campaigns.[13]

Darius III had also been tall and fine-featured, and had still been beaten by the short, tousle-haired Alexander. The Persian monarch ruled over a vast empire and led great armies into battle. In contrast Porus was one dynast among many in the region, lord of a kingdom far smaller in size, resources, and population than Persia; it was certainly not the land of many great cities claimed in our sources. Some hint of this is given in the estimates of the size of his army, which Arrian says included 300 chariots, 4,000 cavalry, 30,000 infantry, and 200 elephants, which is a far cry from the vast host of Persians claimed for Issus or Gaugamela. Diodorus raised the total of infantry to 50,000, chariots to 1,000, although curiously enough places the number of elephants lower at 130, while Plutarch claims that there were just 2,000 horse and 20,000 foot. Overall it is likely that Alexander outnumbered Porus, perhaps by a considerable margin.[14]

Two things gave Alexander pause. The river Hydaspes was wide, deep, and fast flowing from melting snow coming off the mountains and the heavy storms heralding the approach of the monsoon season. This meant that none of the fords were practical, so Alexander sent orders back to the Indus instructing the men there to dismantle the pontoon bridge and send boats overland to him, the larger ones in sections. The other worry was the elephants. Darius had had a small number of these animals at Gaugamela, but if they were used at all they played no significant role in that great battle. Some of the creatures had been captured or given to Alexander since 327 BC, allowing the Macedonians to get a sense of their size and strength. He learned that horses were spooked by the smell and appearance of an elephant, and that only prolonged training could get them used to being around each other. There was no time for him to do this. Porus had a lot of elephants—even the smallest figure claims seventy-five—which were easily visible from across the river as the Indians formed up in battle order on the bank itself, ready to meet an attack.[15]

Alexander realized that this was one problem he could not take head on. Even when the boats arrived and were reassembled, there would not be enough to carry more than a fraction of the army over the river at a time, and the Indians were bound to see them coming and be waiting. At the Granicus Persian horsemen had been poorly suited to defending a bank, but elephants were a different matter. The Macedonian cavalry would not be able to force their mounts onto a riverbank where these terrifying creatures were waiting, and it would be hard for the infantry on their own to fight their way ashore. A direct assault was bound to be costly and stood a good chance of failure, at least until the autumn arrived, when the monsoon would be over and the river level would begin to fall so that the Hydaspes could be forded. Alexander did everything to convince Porus that he was willing to wait the four or five months required, making a show of settling down beside the river and gathering the huge quantities of supplies needed. At the same time patrols scoured the riverbanks to gather information about possible crossing places, and larger detachments were led out by the king or a senior officer to demonstrate at different points of the bank as if about to cross. If they went at night, they made sure to shout orders and battle cries and generally make enough noise to attract the attention of Porus's outposts.

At first the Indians responded by massing ready for battle opposite each demonstration. That meant losing a lot of sleep, and time and again waiting for an attack that never came. Realizing that his men were becoming worn out, Porus decided to stop mustering each time and instead let patrols observe the enemy. There was little else that he could do. Crossing the river would only place him at a severe disadvantage in numbers as well as position. All he could hope for was that Alexander would give up and withdraw, perhaps because it was bound to be difficult feeding his soldiers for so many months. Otherwise it was a question of waiting until the enemy came, and then hoping to defeat the Macedonians before the bulk of their army had crossed. Although he knew that the enemy had won many victories to come to the Hydaspes, he is unlikely to have had much idea of just how determined and skillful Alexander and his army were.[16]

Early on Alexander had found a place to cross where the Hydaspes bent sharply around a headland some eighteen miles from the main camp. Nearby was an island, and both this and the shore were heavily wooded. (In more than two millennia, the course of the river has changed too much for the site to be located.) When the boats arrived they were taken to the spot and reassembled, but kept under cover of the trees. All the while the deception continued, with more demonstrations and a line of piquets established along the bank, who noisily shouted orders and lit fires as if making camp or sending signals. A man who resembled Alexander took his place in the main camp, wearing his armor and clothes and receiving every honor due to the king. How much of this fooled the Indians is hard to say. Porus did not have enough men to defend a long stretch of the river properly, so he waited and watched as best he could. There is no sign that his men noticed unusual activity around the headland.[17]

Alexander left Craterus in charge of his main camp with a hipparchy of Companion cavalry, two regiments of the phalanx, 5,000 troops supplied by his Indian allies, as well as other allied contingents. His orders were specific and recorded in unusual detail. Craterus was not to cross as long as Porus remained in his camp. If the entire Indian army moved off to face Alexander or he heard of the Indians' utter rout, then he was to cross. If Porus divided his army and left some at the main camp, then Craterus was to attempt a crossing, but only if the force opposing him had no elephants. Three phalanx regiments along with the mercenary cavalry and infantry were sent to a point of the river midway between the main camp and the headland, with orders to begin ferrying themselves over the river once they saw that Alexander had engaged the main force. No more is heard of this strong detachment in the subsequent account.[18]

Alexander had with him the royal *ilê* (now usually called the *agema*) and three hipparchies of Companions, backed by horsemen from Bactria and Sogdiana and horse archers supplied by the Sacae and Dahae. His infantry consisted of the hypaspists, two regiments from the phalanx, the Agrianians, and some other light infantry including many archers. Altogether his force amounted to some 5,000 horse and 6,000 foot, and under cover of night they moved into position and brought the boats to the water, supplementing them with rafts improvised from animal skins—perhaps once again tents—packed with chaff. A violent storm hammered the men as they prepared, but at least had the virtue of covering any noise they made. The weather improved a little before dawn, when the first boats and rafts began to make their way across, led by the king in a triaconter, the smallest class of warship but the biggest vessel brought in sections to the spot.

They were visible to the Indian patrols in spite of the darkness, but only when the ships and rafts passed the island did it become obvious that this was more than yet another diversion. Gallopers hurried to Porus with the news, but inevitably this meant a delay before he could react. So far everything was working well for the Macedonians, who landed on shore and sent the boats back for the next wave. It took a while before they realized that they were on another island, so close to the bank that from any distance it looked like a headland. The water separating it from the actual bank was fairly narrow, but so deep from rainwater that it took a lot of frantic searching before they found some fords leading across. Even so the water was chest high for the men on foot and came up to the horses' necks—perhaps because the cavalrymen went across a little upstream to shield the rest and prevent the bank from being churned up more than was necessary. Alexander used the pick of his cavalry to screen the rest as he formed them up. Once this was done, he let the infantry march at a steady pace and pressed on with the cavalry.[19]

What followed is very hard to reconstruct, even compared to Alexander's other battles, for our sources are confused and contradictory. Plutarch says that the fighting was over by the eighth hour and it is vital to remember this when considering what happened next. Alexander crossed at a point some fifteen to twenty miles away from Porus's army. He landed at dawn and then took time getting everyone ashore, finding out that they were on an island, wading through the stream and sorting themselves out before forming up on the far side. Porus also had to muster his men, and then both sides had to march a considerable distance into contact, and then deploy into some form of battle order. All of this is easy to say in a few lines, but in reality took a good deal of time. At the three battles against the Persians—and indeed at Chaeronea—the Macedonians attacked an enemy already formed up in position, even if there was some redeployment. Only at the Granicus and at Issus did Alexander's men advance any significant distance on the day of the battle. The Hydaspes was different. It was essentially an encounter battle, with each side taking up a position and formation chosen in some haste since neither could predict what would happen. It was fought on ground the Macedonians only saw on the day of the battle and much of the time in heavy rain that hampered visibility and thus even participants' understanding of what happened.[20]

The first encounter came fairly soon, when a force of Indian cavalry and chariots was sent by Porus to investigate. Arrian, citing Ptolemy as the most plausible, says that there were 2,000 horsemen and 120 chariots led by Porus's son, but also explains that other accounts claimed that there were fewer; some said that they arrived as the Macedonians were landing. Unlike the scythed chariots used at Gaugamela, these were grand platforms designed as much for spectacle as anything else, and to provide platforms from which to shoot missiles. Drawn by a team of four horses, the large car had space for six crewmen—two of them archers, two shield bearers to protect them, and two drivers who were also capable of throwing javelins. They were not especially maneuverable at the best of times, especially when deployed in large numbers, and on this occasion the rain made the soil so muddy that many simply bogged down.

Alexander was a couple of miles ahead of his infantry and unsure at first whether this was the advance guard of the entire Indian army, but decided to attack, hoping to keep his opponent off balance. He led with his nimble horse archers, who peppered the Indians with arrows before they were ready, and then followed up with a succession of rapid charges by the Companion cavalry. Outnumbered and outclassed by Alexander's veterans, and surprised by the speed of the enemy advance, the Indians were quickly defeated, their leader killed along with 400 of his men. The rest streamed away in flight, leaving all of the chariots broken or bogged down behind them.

Arrian has Porus decide to take his main force against Alexander only after hearing of this setback from some of the survivors, which would mean a considerable delay before he committed the main army. He also says that he was concerned because Craterus's men were embarking in boats on the far bank. If so, this was quite late in the day for him to commit, and implies that Craterus was interpreting his orders quite aggressively and beginning to cross—or at least making a show of doing so—while there were still elephants ready to oppose his landing. Porus could not remain where he was now that a substantial enemy force was over the river. Whether he realized that Alexander was with them or simply guessed that this was the biggest threat, he took the majority of his men off to deal with it, although he did leave some elephants with the men left behind to do their best to oppose Craterus. The main Indian force marched to an area of sandy ground, which it was hoped would allow cavalry and chariots to operate, and began to deploy.

Alexander and his cavalry were visible when Porus ordered his men to halt; presumably there was an obvious route suitable for armies between his main camp and the Macedonian crossing point. Aware that something was happening, the Macedonian infantry commanders doubled their men forward to catch up. None of our sources makes any mention of reinforcements having arrived in the meantime, so claims that by this time numbers had grown are conjectural and unnecessary. Arrian does say that Alexander gave the infantry a period of rest before forming them into a battle line. He and the cavalry demonstrated to keep the enemy from interrupting.

Ancient armies did not move any great distance in battle formation, for this was inevitably wide, slow, and cumbersome, easily breaking up whenever it met any obstacle. Most marched in a narrow column or columns, ideally with the units arranged so that they could wheel into line once they were in position, each unit then forming battle order. Too little is known about Porus's army to judge precisely how it went about such things, but it is unlikely to have been so very different; the Indians were bound to be less well drilled than the Macedonians, so that everything took longer. Porus's intended battle order is described as cavalry and chariots on the wings and a center made up of a line of elephants, each a hundred or fifty feet apart, with the infantry behind the gaps between each animal. This was a wide formation, even if it is based on the lowest estimates for his numbers, and it can only have taken a long time for him to bring his men up to the battlefield in column and then get them all into place. There is a good chance that the line was incomplete before the fighting started, and this helps to explain the disjointed nature of the subsequent fighting.

After resting his men, Alexander massed the bulk of his cavalry on the right, but kept the remaining two hipparchies under Coenus a little back and on his right flank. The infantry were formed with the hypaspists next to the horse, then the three phalanx regiments. Light infantry were in front and on their flanks, and since they were not facing close-order infantry, there were most likely bigger-than-usual gaps between units so that the skirmishers could advance or retire past the pikemen. The Indians did not make any aggressive moves, which reinforces the impression that they were still forming up. Yet there were enough elephants in place for Alexander to be reluctant to engage them, and he ordered the infantry to stay where he had placed them and not advance until the cavalry had routed their counterparts.

Alexander and his own body of cavalry maneuvered, drawing the enemy away from the main body. Before the fighting began, most or all of Porus's cavalry had moved to the Indian left flank opposite Alexander, and may have been acting as a screening force to cover the deployment. Once again the Scythian horse archers went first, streaking forward to shoot at the Indian cavalry who were still in column and not yet formed into line. Arrows added to their confusion, as did the approach of Coenus and his two hipparchies, circling around to threaten their flank or rear. As they tried to deploy ready to meet two threats at once, Alexander charged. Confused and caught at the halt—and some of them perhaps survivors of the earlier rout—many of the Indian cavalry panicked and fled. Some fled toward their own elephants, and this was the sign for the Macedonian infantry to advance. After a while, enough Indian cavalry rallied to launch a charge of their own, only to be beaten for a second time. The whirling melee left Alexander's horsemen in one great mass with little trace of unit formations, but the shapeless crowd remained aggressive and swarmed after the king, attacking the Indian infantry and sometimes managing to close with the elephants.

The fighting where the phalanx met the Indian elephants and infantry was almost as chaotic, combats breaking down into struggles around each of the great animals. Many of the Indian infantry carried a tall bow able to shoot a heavy arrow at short range, but the rain and the slippery ground greatly reduced their effectiveness, and they were outclassed in close combat by the pikemen and hypaspists. In places elephants broke into the phalanx, trampling all in their path. Yet their mahouts, or drivers, and any crew sitting astride the animal's back were clear targets for javelins and arrows, as well as within reach of the long sarissas. They were killed and often this made the elephants stampede, crushing friend and foe alike. Sometimes the phalanx opened lanes between units to let the beasts through, just as they had done with the scythed chariots at Gaugamela, and wherever possible they surrounded and isolated each one. Axes and swords were used to hack at their feet and trunks, javelins and arrows shot or pikes thrust into their eyes. There is a description of elephants retiring like warships backing water, the frightened animals crying shrilly.

Porus was in the thick of the fighting, a giant man on an exceptionally large elephant, but individual heroics could not prevent the collapse of his army. In some sources he was wounded by multiple missiles, finally fainting from loss of blood and even then protected by his faithful elephant. In this version Alexander assumed he was dead and only discovered that the Indian king was still alive when someone started to strip his body. Another tradition has Porus riding off on his great beast, defeated but still unbowed. When Alexander sent King Omphis to seek his surrender, Porus turned at the sight of his hated rival and almost killed him. Only when a nobleman who was a friend was sent did Porus halt and submit. Most versions then have him asked how he would like Alexander to treat him, prompting the answer, "Like a king," which he then explained should be all that his enemy needed to know. Whether or not there is any truth in these stories, Alexander soon not only confirmed Porus as king, but in due course gave him additional territory.[21]

Arrian says 20,000 Indian infantrymen and 3,000 horsemen fell in the battle, including two of Porus's sons and at least one prominent nobleman as well as other leaders, which puts into context the Indian king's willingness to reconcile with his former enemies. As usual, the claims for enemy losses are most likely inflated, although Craterus's men did arrive in time to take over the pursuit from Alexander's weary soldiers, which meant that the chase was in the hands of men who were fresh and eager to play a part. The cost for the Macedonians was 86 infantrymen and some 230 cavalrymen killed, most of the latter from the allied contingents, while Diodorus has 700 infantry and 280 cavalry dead; no one gives a figure for the wounded. Alongside the human casualties, Alexander mourned the loss of Bucephalus, who died of wounds inflicted in the first encounter or of fatigue and disease depending on the account. He was about thirty, so a little older than his rider who would celebrate his thirtieth birthday a few weeks after the battle. Alexander honored his old comrade by founding a city, Bucephalia, on the site of his main camp. Another city, Nicaea (or City of Victory), was placed on the other side of the river, on or near the battlefield itself.[22]

So far the Indian campaign was going very well, and Alexander was eager to press on, believing the shore of the Ocean to be within his reach.

28

VICTORY INTO RETREAT

ost of the month after the battle was spent in rest, sacrifices, and celebration, with the familiar athletic competitions, including an emphasis on horses races. By the time the advance resumed, the monsoon season had begun properly, which meant months of pounding rain storms. Descriptions cannot prepare anyone for the relentless downfall and pervasive damp, rotting clothes and straps, rusting metal, and tracks turning into mud. No one in the army, apart from the local allies, had ever experienced it before. Only occasionally mentioned in our sources, this was the setting for the events of the coming campaign, making everything harder to do and grinding down the spirit of everyone in the army. Diodorus speaks of seventy days of driving rain. It was like nothing any Macedonian or Greek in the army had ever imagined possible.[1]

Craterus was left behind to establish the new cities, while Alexander pushed ahead with the pick of the field army. The methods were familiar and well practiced. At times he detached columns under trusted subordinates to sweep through a wider region. Leaders and communities willing to submit and accept the rule of Alexander were treated mildly. Refusal, and even hesitation if it did not swiftly turn into contrition and surrender, meant being treated as an enemy who deserved to be punished. Thirty-seven "cities" soon surrendered. King Abisares's forces had not arrived in time to join Porus and he quickly submitted, sending his brother with a gift of thirty elephants, albeit risking attack when he failed to appear in person. Eventually Alexander's envoys were satisfied that he was genuinely too ill to travel, and since he died within a year this may well have been true. He was confirmed as ruler of his kingdom, subject to paying annual tribute, but unlike Porus he gained no territory so did not benefit.[2]

The Macedonians crossed the river Acesines (Chenab), leaving a force to protect the crossing and ensure that supplies continued to follow the army. Porus was now sufficiently recovered and trusted to be sent home with instructions to raise men and elephants and return to reinforce Alexander. His cousin and namesake, known in the sources as Porus the "bad" or "cowardly" (kakos), had welcomed the Macedonians before the Battle of Hydaspes, hoping their friendship would give him an advantage over his relative and rival. However, when the other Porus lost but was treated so favorably by Alexander, he realized that this plan was not working. He gathered warriors and fled from the Macedonians, which Alexander took as a hostile act. Hephaestion was given a column and sent to deal with the matter and swiftly accomplished this task. We do not know what happened to "bad" Porus, but his territory was given to his "good" cousin. The whole episode was another good illustration of the dominance of local politics and rivalries in reaction to the arrival of Alexander and his army.[3]

Alexander pushed on and crossed the river Hydraotes (Ravi), and more communities submitted rather than risk fighting the invader. Behind him was a trail of little fortified outposts whose garrisons were there to protect his supply lines. Some of the peoples in his path were less keen to capitulate to the foreign army and began mustering men, at the very least to make a display of their power. They were also enemies of Porus, so his new alliance with Alexander added to their suspicion. The Macedonian king hurried toward them, arriving so suddenly at the first city that they immediately surrendered. A day later he reached Sangala, the main center or capital of the Cathaeans, where men from all over the region were mustering, the majority in a camp formed by three circles of wagons, one inside the other. Alexander attacked, leading with his horse archers and following with the Companion cavalry. When the defenders refused to come out of their wagon laager, he dismounted and led the infantry assault. There was heavy fighting in front of the second line before the Macedonians broke in, at which point the Indians fled inside the city itself.

Settling down to besiege the city, Alexander surrounded it with a rampart, while taking care to suggest that there were weak spots in his line, such as by a shallow lake. Ambushes caught parties trying to escape the encirclement at night and inflicted heavy losses before the surviving Indians managed to flee back into the city. Once the heavier siege equipment arrived, brought by a convoy that also included Porus and his contingent, the assault could begin. It proved easier than expected, the mud-brick wall readily undermined by picks and then captured by men climbing ladders. A massacre followed, with allegedly 17,000 perishing and 70,000 taken captive. Alexander's losses were fewer than 100 dead, with 1,200 wounded, an even higher ratio than usual. Troops were sent to summon other nearby cities to surrender in the hope that this display of power would convince them. Instead the people fled the terrible invaders, which was interpreted as defiance. As soon as this was discovered the Macedonians pursued, killing or capturing all those too elderly or weak to keep up, but the rest had enough of a lead to escape. Alexander demolished Sangala and gave the territory to the communities who had surrendered to him. Then he took his main force and marched to the river Hyphasis (Beas).[4]

It was just another in a long succession of rivers, like so many this army had crossed, and this time there were no hostile warriors watching from the far side. No Greek knew very much about what lay beyond. They knew of more rivers, leading to the Ganges, the greatest of them all, but considered opinion held that the distance was not too great to the edge of India with only the ocean after that. Alexander had come to India believing that he was within reach of the end of Asia, until the locals informed him that India was far bigger than he had thought. Rumors spread of a great kingdom, rich, more populous, and with a huge army including hundreds of elephants. Porus confirmed the story, although he was dismissive of its king, who was no more than the incompetent and obscure heir to great rulers. In truth the Nanda dynasty of the Ganges was in decline and would collapse within a generation, so some of what Alexander learned was accurate. He may or may not have known by now that this realm lay more than 200 miles away, and that even this was not the end of India. Given how far he had come in the last eight years, Alexander still felt it was all within reach.[5]

The king was keen to press on, but his soldiers were not and would go no farther. The Macedonians were well over 3,000 miles from home in a straight line, over 4,000 by even the most direct route for a traveler, and those with him from the start had marched or ridden three times as far at the very least. They had reached the edge of lands that could even remotely have been considered as within the sphere of influence of Persia, and they had fought again and again. Stories of yet more kingdoms and cities lying in their path meant more fighting. Loot no longer mattered since they had all long since acquired so much more than any army had ever done. Like glory and reputation, it was of little value if there was no prospect of returning home to enjoy it. Once again, we should remember that these were not professional career soldiers isolated from the rest of society, as in some ways the Roman army would become under the Principate. At heart this army was the Macedonian people in arms, citizen soldiers serving alongside their king for the good of all, not least their families and communities back home. They now felt that they had been away for too long. Some sources hint that many men feared facing more elephants in battle, although none claim that this was the heart of the problem. They were exhausted, battered by the pitiless rain, and could see no point in fighting on for the sake of more conquest.

In the past, Alexander had persuaded his men to keep going when they were ready to quit: with the appeals to catch Darius, to catch Bessus, to secure their new empire from rebellion and outside threats. The months had turned into years, a few more miles into hundreds, and still there was no shortage of enemies. This was more of a strike than a mutiny. The soldiers did not reject

Alexander and their bond with the king who had led them all this time, who shared the danger and hardship and was generous with praise, promotion, and plunder. They were proud of him and of what they had done. Nor did they refuse a direct order, largely because Alexander had sufficient sense not to issue one. They did not jeer or taunt him, or even appeal, and instead the Macedonians—for it was almost wholly about their feelings and not those of the many allies and mercenaries—gathered in silence.[6]

There is little chance that the speeches in our sources reflect what was actually said, for no one is likely to have recorded it all, and authors by convention invented such things as they saw fit. Alexander no doubt reminded everyone of their victories, promising them that the end was almost in sight because they would soon reach the edge of Asia. No one cheered or said anything, until Coenus came forward as spokesman. He had commanded one of the battalions of the phalanx since at least the start of Alexander's reign and may already have held the post under Philip, so was a veteran like many of the men. Marriage to Parmenio's daughter had not prevented him from condemning Philotas with great vehemence, a demonstration of personal loyalty to Alexander that was rewarded with prestige and numerous independent commands. Coenus once again assured the king of his absolute devotion, which was shared by the men, and explained that they were worn out and homesick.

Alexander failed to persuade them on the first day and tried again on the next day with no more success. He may have lost his temper and said that he would cross the river and advance with just those willing to follow him and let the rest go where they will, to tell everyone that they had abandoned the king. Then he went back to his tent and stayed there for three days, hoping to shame or frighten them into changing their mind. At the end of this time it was clear from his officers that the mood remained the same. Sacrifices were made, which most conveniently showed that the omens for continuing the advance were bad, allowing Alexander to follow the will of the gods and cancel his plan. To mark this frontier of his empire and to intimidate those living outside, he ordered the construction of twelve huge altars. Some sources claim that men were also set to constructing a camp where everything—beds, horse's stalls, and weapons and equipment scattered as if abandoned— was all made unnaturally large to suggest an army of giants. If this really happened then it was an odd counterpart to Greek stories of immensely tall Indians living in the kingdoms to the south.[7]

Late in 326 BC, after so many years of advancing, the Macedonian army turned around and marched back the way it had come. Some scholars argue that this was always Alexander's intention, that he aimed only at securing the former Persian Empire to its very greatest extent, and perhaps had realized that India was far larger than he had thought. In this view the "mutiny" was just what he wanted and had perhaps worked to create, allowing him to claim that he would have conquered the entire world if only his men had not proved too weak. None of this is very convincing. On other frontiers Alexander had made sacrifices, shown his ability to cross any river, and then gone away to campaign elsewhere. There is no reason to believe that he could not have done this at the Hyphasis. The refusal of his men to go on is presented as a failure by our sources, but as a failure for Alexander and not his army, and they show sympathy rather than blame for his exhausted officers and men. This was a far greater dent to his reputation than he would have suffered from simply announcing that the advance was to halt and the army turn around. Alexander was just thirty. Neither he nor anyone else could know that he would never return to this place or march to the lands beyond.[8]

Coenus died within a few months. Some modern scholars have seen this as suspicious and speculated that he was murdered for thwarting the king, but there is not the slightest hint of this in any of our ancient sources. Perhaps it was simply chance, or failing health had encouraged him to speak up for the rest of the army on the basis that he had little to lose. During the strike on the Hyphasis Alexander ordered no arrests, let alone executions or other punishments. His Macedonian Companions, noble and humble, horse and foot, had expressed their united opinion and the king accepted it, at least in the end and after hoping that they would let him have his way. This was how the army and state was supposed to function, which does not mean that Alexander was happy about it all, although the extent of his bitterness is impossible to judge.⁹

For the central message of the Hyphasis was that Alexander remained an Argead king of Macedon. For all that he had gained, for all the trappings of Asian monarchy and his many new subjects, officials, and courtiers, his leadership rested upon the throne he had inherited from Philip. Macedonians were now a small minority of his soldiers, but they were vital for the command structure and still the bedrock of its fighting power. Alexander could not have gone on with just mercenaries and Asian allies, for that would mean becoming no more than a warlord always nervous of his men and officers who would be loyal only as long as it suited them. In spite of their refusal to go on, the Macedonians were his men, tied by kinship, tradition, and patriotism, just as he was their king. At least openly, the retreat from the Hyphasis did not change this relationship, whatever the private feelings of the king and his subjects. Before the year was out he would lead them into battle once more and they would fight and die for him. Soldiers did not start disobeying orders, nor did they expect immediate discharge and the long journey home. They would not go farther, and they wanted to go home with their king and enjoy the fruits of triumph. They were willing to trust that now he would take them there in due course, even if there were some tasks to perform in the meantime.

Alexander and his men returned to the Hydaspes, where work had already begun on a substantial fleet with the aim of sailing down the Indus. Seeing crocodiles on the riverbanks and, later, beans growing that they had last encountered in Egypt, Alexander and many others concluded that the great Indian river was indeed the ultimate source of the Nile, as some Greek geographers had suggested. This offered a chance to join up two parts of his new empire, and the plan to travel down the Indus had been formed at least as early as the defeat of Porus and before he marched to the Hyphasis. As in the past, Alexander often had more than one project in mind, some of which might develop simultaneously under his subordinates. By now Craterus came closest to fulfilling the role once reserved for Parmenio and was given most of the great independent commands. This was a mark of trust rather than a sign that Alexander was weary of his outspoken friend. Rivalry between Craterus and Hephaestion had intensified, and at one point during the Indian campaign an argument turned into violence with both men drawing swords. Alexander rode up and broke the men apart, publicly rebuking Hephaestion before forcing the two men to reconcile.[10]

Alexander was back at the Hydaspes by the end of September 326 BC. With the monsoon over, he remained there as more light triaconters and transport barges were constructed. Estimates of the number of vessels in the fleet range from 800 to 2,000, most of them small. Command was given to Nearchus, one of the friends of his youth exiled by Philip and more recently made satrap of Pamphylia and Lycia. He was one of a number of senior Companions also named as trierarchs, an office copied from the Athenians that made the incumbent responsible for constructing and equipping a warship from his own funds. Alexander's conquests had brought fabulous wealth, but it was not always easy to ensure that coin was available wherever he needed it in sufficient quantities. Lavish gifts to Indian princes seem to have depleted the treasury that traveled with the army, which was one reason for calling on his officers in this way. As important was reinforcing the sense that this was a shared enterprise.[11]

Late in the autumn, after sacrifices, ceremonies, and games, the great expedition set out, with the ships on the Hydaspes and the army marching in two columns, one on either bank. Alexander traveled on board a ship with Nearchus, while Hephaestion and Craterus led the two halves of the army, no doubt happy to have a wide river between them. Arrangements were made for the land forces to follow the best routes, swinging back to rendezvous every few days with the fleet. It was a great spectacle, both the sheer number of ships and the unfamiliar sight and sounds of galleys rowing, which was something never seen or heard before in this region. Then there was the vast host of men, horses, elephants, and other animals traveling down the great river. The figure of 120,000 men for Alexander's forces in India may be realistic for these months, for a large contingent of mercenaries and allied soldiers—although no more Macedonians—had arrived, apart from all the sailors needed for the fleet. Along with the reinforcements came 25,000 panoplies of equipment, so that a good many of the soldiers cut a more dashing figure than they had in their old equipment, worn out by long campaigning and rotted by the monsoon.

There was an air of festival and crowds of locals gathered to watch the departure, singing and dancing in celebration. A cynic might wonder whether they were most glad to see the invaders leave, but this is probably unfair. This truly was a great spectacle, something to remember, and the new cities were left behind with their garrisons, which meant that the invaders were not all leaving. Porus now ruled most of the land from here to the Hyphasis, and unlike other local dynasts including Omphis, no Macedonian or Greek satrap was appointed over him. He proved loyal to Alexander, and perhaps having a strong native king was seen as the best security for the frontier of the empire.[12]

Before the expedition started out the locals had made it clear that the Macedonians were not heading for the Nile and Egypt. Alexander was not deterred, and instead the object became to secure his new empire and reach the point where it met the ocean, some 800 miles away. Before long he wondered whether the sea route from India to the Persian Gulf would offer good communications to connect his widely spread conquests. Traders had used these seaways for centuries, waiting for the winds to change with the monsoon and help them in the direction they wanted to go, but Alexander was thinking of something more permanent and larger scale. This strategic objective went alongside the familiar urge to reach and mark the boundary of his territory whether it lay on empty ocean or desert-like steppe.

Exploration played a far smaller role, tagging along as it had done throughout his conquest. The scholars in his train learned a lot (and like most academics and early explorers inevitably misunderstood a good deal as well) as they traveled according to the military and political demands of the campaigns. They studied plants and animals, as well as natural phenomena. In Bactria the army camped at a spot where oil was seeping to the surface, and decided that they had found a natural occurrence of familiar olive oil. In Asia

Minor they found naphtha and creosote, marveling at how readily it burned. A servant boy at court is supposed to have volunteered to be covered in naphtha and set on fire in the cause of scientific investigation. He somehow survived his terrible burns, and the king undertook to care for the invalid for the rest of his life.[13]

Alexander's fascination with medicinal herbs continued, and in India he found a plant that helped cure Ptolemy from a poisonous snake bite. Yet there is little trace of a deep interest in India itself, although perhaps this would have changed if his army had not stopped at the Hyphasis and he had gone on to conquer far more of the subcontinent. None of our sources mention honors or sacrifice to Indian deities, in contrast to the respect paid to the gods of Egypt and Babylon. There was some interest in Indian holy men, beginning at Taxila, where he and his officers first encountered the men they dubbed "naked philosophers" or in some cases Brahmans. Sadly there are no good Indian sources for this period to provide a view of these encounters from their perspective, while the meeting of the great conqueror and exotic wise men provided such a rich field for embellishment and invention by later Greek writers that it is hard to reach the truth.[14]

There is a nice story of a group of Brahmans stamping their feet time and again during a meeting with the king to remind him that even the greatest ruler truly owned no more than the earth on which he stood—and in which he would soon be buried. Alexander is said to have been impressed by the truth of this, just as he had supposedly admired Diogenes the Cynic at Corinth. Onesicritus, a former pupil of Diogenes who accompanied Alexander, was sent to meet several naked philosophers, and claimed that conversation required no fewer than three interpreters, which made conveying and understanding complex ideas extraordinarily difficult. It is human nature to see a reflection of our own assumptions in others, so he naturally interpreted their beliefs as in keeping with Greek philosophical thought. The rigorous ascetic lifestyle impressed him, not least because it echoed Diogenes, but also other Greeks, as it has impressed many observers throughout history. A man named Shines demanded that Onesicritus strip if the Greek wanted to share his wisdom, and was subsequently persuaded to join Alexander's court—a decision criticized by his peers as abandoning the ascetic life to seek fame and fortune. He was soon dubbed Calanus for his cheerful mispronunciation of the Greek greeting—saying *kale* instead of *chaire*—and seems to have been viewed as little more than a curiosity. The main memory he left among Alexander's entourage came a couple of years later when illness and age prompted him to commit suicide by burning himself on a pyre.[15]

Learning, let alone understanding, was not Alexander's priority as he sailed down the Hydaspes, for as always this was about subjugation. Communities in his path were faced with the usual choice between either accepting his dominance or fighting him. At first there was no resistance, and the greatest danger came when they reached the point where the Acesines and Hydaspes joined, and rapids overturned a few of the light warships. Alexander abandoned his vessel, even though he had never learned to swim, and made it to the bank with the aid of his friends. Some distance from the junction of the rivers was the land of the Mallians and Oxydracans, who had no overall king and formed a loose confederation, sometimes mutually hostile and sometimes willing to ally with each other. They had sent no representatives to meet the invader and now began mustering troops and sending their families to the shelter of walled cities. Alexander soon began planning an attack at what he saw as defiance.[16]

The fleet would press on with much of the army, while several columns drove into "enemy" territory. Alexander had with him half the Companion cavalry, the hypaspists, two regiments of phalanx, the Agrianians, and horse and foot archers, and his was the main attack, moving quickly, while the other groups were to catch anyone trying to evade him. A master of the unexpected, he forced the pace through barren land thought too difficult for an army and caught the Mallians by surprise. Too shocked to organize resistance, many were massacred outside the walls of the first city he reached. His cavalry surrounded the place to prevent any escape, which risked spreading reports of his arrival. Once this was done and his infantry came up, they launched an assault. The outer wall fell quickly, but there was determined resistance at an inner section or citadel and for a while the attackers became confused. Alexander rushed about, urging everyone on and personally led the assault that carried the stronghold, where 2,000 defenders were slaughtered.[17]

Soon afterward Perdiccas reached another community, and when he found it abandoned, chased after the inhabitants, cutting down those who had not yet reached the safety of marshland. Alexander gave his troops a brief rest, then pushed on, missing most of the Mallians at the main ford on the river Hydraotes, but attacking and killing those still making the crossing as the sun came up. He chased after the rest with his cavalry, cutting down many more, and when his infantry caught up he used them to storm another walled village, whose occupants died or were enslaved. With foot and horse he then approached the nearby "city of the Brachmanes" as it is called by Arrian, where many Mallians had taken refuge. The outer wall was swiftly undermined and taken by assault and the citadel stormed after a harder fight, with Alexander the first man up onto the rampart. Some of the defenders set their houses on fire and perished along with their families, as the rest were cut down or enslaved.

After just a day's rest the Macedonians pushed on, finding the next settlements abandoned and sending out parties of light troops to hunt and kill fugitives hiding in woodland. When reports came of an army massing on the far bank of the Hydraotes, Alexander wheeled around and went straight at them. Attacking with only his cavalry, for a while the enemy saw a chance to overwhelm this detachment through sheer numbers, only to break off and flee as the Macedonian infantry arrived. Alexander followed them to a nearby walled town and surrounded it with parties of cavalry to prevent any escape. By the time all of his infantry had caught up it was almost dusk, so he gave the weary soldiers a chance to rest. The next day he launched his assault, leading half the force in person and putting Perdiccas in charge of the rest. They broke in easily, for the defenders did not contest the outer wall and once again fell back to the citadel. There was confusion as the attackers tried to find their way through the maze of narrow streets, and the delay added to Alexander's impatience.[18]

There are hints that his men had shown less aggression in the recent assaults, or at least that the king thought this, for he found them wanting now. Many of the men, especially in units like the hypaspists, had stormed many towns, and if fatalities and serious wounds were relatively small each time, they fell disproportionately on the boldest. All of the army was exhausted, and this campaign was waged at a fast pace even by Alexander's standards, so simple exhaustion was a factor and may have made the men sluggish. Equally, Alexander's disappointment at their refusal to cross the Hyphasis may have rendered him overly sensitive to anything he saw as reluctance. Perdiccas's men were bringing up ladders too slowly for him, although they may simply not have known that the defenders were holding out in the citadel. Alexander grew angry, and with a few of his officers grabbed two ladders, rushed to the citadel's wall, and climbed. The king reached the top and in a moment was on the rampart, slamming his shield into the nearest defenders to knock them off the walkway or killing them with his sword. Seeing their king on his own, the soldiers were so desperate to follow that too many tried to climb the ladder and it broke apart under their weight.

The defenders were holding back, unwilling to face this furious enemy and hoping that someone else would take the risk. Yet up on the wall Alexander was a highly visible target for archers, who began to pepper him with heavy arrows. Three other Macedonians were close behind him, but before they could join their king Alexander leapt down into the citadel, and after these men got up the second ladder also gave way. As so often with the king, his boldness was a mix of instinctive aggression tempered by rational calculation; in this case he would be less exposed inside than high on the walkway. He landed well, near a tree that offered protection at least from one side, and he killed or drove off the closest defenders. For a while—a few minutes at the most and perhaps less—the king of a vast empire fought alone inside an enemy stronghold. Then the other three jumped down to join him.

They fought with swords, threw stones when the enemy would not come within reach, and did their best to catch arrows on their shields. Abreas, an infantryman, perhaps a junior officer with a high reputation for bravery, dropped with an arrow in the face. Alexander took another arrow, probably through the side, which punctured the edge of his lung. Bleeding heavily, he slumped down, although was said to have had enough strength to kill a warrior who rushed at him. The royal bodyguard Leonnatus and Peucestas, who carried the shield of Achilles taken from the shrine at Ilium in 334 BC, both took wounds as they stood over their fallen king, who by now was unconscious. Outside desperate men hammered broken pieces of ladder into the mud brick, using them like crampons to climb the wall. Others pounded at a gate until it gave way. When word spread that the king was down, dead or perhaps mortally wounded, fear turned into blind rage and the Macedonians went on the rampage, killing every man, woman, and child in the city.[19]

Some said that Perdiccas enlarged the king's wound with his sword so that the barbed arrowhead could be removed, producing a fresh gush of blood. Others have Critobulus perform the operation, the same man who had treated Philip's arrow wound at Methone twenty-eight years before. Diagnosis is difficult given differences in our sources and ancient understanding of medicine. It may have been a sucking wound, causing one lung to collapse, although talk of air coming out with blood is not an indication of this, since as the name suggests the flow would be in the other direction. If he was hit in the side rather than from the front, this suggests that the injury was less serious and made it easier in time for the body to heal and the lung to reinflate. The ancient sources make it clear that the wound was serious, and might easily have killed him in the days to come, but they do not suggest that he was permanently crippled. A little later Craterus led a delegation of officers who chided their king for taking too many risks that should be left to others. Alexander preferred the bluff comment of a Boeotian veteran who approached him in the camp and declared that such deeds were "men's work."[20]

For the moment Alexander was weak, needing to be carried everywhere, and rumors spread quickly that he was dead. Back at the camp of the fleet and main army the report caused utter despair; men who had felt they were at last on the way home wondered who would lead them and feared that all the conquered lands were likely to revolt and turn on them. Even a letter written by Alexander was dismissed as a fake. Only when the king reached them, having been carried as gently as possible to the Hydraotes and from there by boat, were their fears allayed. By this time—a few days, if not more—Alexander was conscious and ordered the awning covering him to be removed so that he was visible to those on the banks of the river. He raised an arm and this proof that he was not a corpse prompted a great shout. A litter was waiting for him, but in a display of that implacable willpower that drove him on as hard as it drove everyone around him, Alexander refused this and instead mounted a horse and rode through the camp toward his tent. A little way short he stopped, dismounted, and walked unsupported the last few yards. The cheering continued, and men pressed close to touch him or his cloak as he passed. After this display he had the chance for a proper convalescence.[21]

The Mallians and Oxydracans sent envoys to surrender, bringing with them tribute as a token of their willingness to give Alexander whatever he wanted, and duly supplied the specified numbers of warriors and chariots. There was a pause to organize the territory under the satrap Philip, which included Taxila and all the lands up to the junction of the Acesines and Hydaspes. Then Alexander resumed the campaign, traveling by boat and letting his subordinates carry out his orders. More peoples submitted, others were subdued by force, and the fleet grew bigger as more vessels were constructed, often as part of the tribute paid by his new subjects. He founded another Alexandria on the river to serve as a port. Another satrapy was created, the command given to a Macedonian with Roxane's father as colleague.[22]

After a while they approached the territory of a great and wealthy king called Musicanus, who had not sent envoys to seek peace, perhaps because he was only dimly aware of the approach of these strange foreign invaders. He quickly made up for this by coming in person and acting very humbly, begging Alexander's forgiveness, which was something the latter liked. Musicanus was confirmed in his kingdom, but the goodwill did not last. There was widespread resentment of the invaders, especially among the

Brahmans, whom the Macedonians mistakenly saw as a small sect of philosophers instead of a caste providing warriors and leaders. Resistance spread rapidly.

However much he failed to appreciate the roots of this hostility toward him, Alexander's response was as swift, efficient, and ruthless as ever. Cities were stormed, populations put to the sword or enslaved, until all resistance had been crushed. Musicanus had changed his mind and joined the resistance, so he was brought as a captive to Alexander, who had him crucified. Many Brahmans were massacred or executed in a concerted campaign of terror, and scholars often present the operations in 326–325 BC as the most brutal and costly for the victims ever waged by Alexander and his men. Such a judgment is hard to make, since we never have reliable figures for the populations, let alone the losses and devastation inflicted by the Macedonians. The methods employed were the same ones that they had used for a long time, especially in Bactria and Sogdiana. That does nothing to diminish the horror of these months, and should only remind us that we should feel the same revulsion at similar acts performed elsewhere, whether one community or many suffered.[23]

Alexander's army was too effective and strong for any of the states in its path to defeat, and the price of fighting the Macedonians was appallingly high. Accounts of lightning advances, sieges, and massacres dominate our sources since they inevitably provide more drama and took longer to describe than the submission of leaders terrified into surrender, but the latter were the majority. The king of Patala, the lands around the great delta of the Indus, was one of those who decided that accepting the invader was better than hopeless defiance and in 325 BC came in person to seek Alexander's friendship. There was little fighting in the later stages as the flotilla and army came toward the sea, for they were welcomed as allies and provided with supplies or arrived to find settlements abandoned and no one to be seen. A party sent out to dig wells in a nearby area of desert was attacked by locals who were probably not ever really under the control of the king of Patala, and only chased them off after some fighting. Alexander ordered the construction of major harbor installations and a new fortress at Patala.

In June and July 325 BC a section of the fleet supported by some 9,000 soldiers on land made the final stage of the journey as they investigated the two main branches of the Indus leading to the sea. No local pilots could be found, and there were losses to a sudden storm, which required hasty repairs. Accustomed only to the Mediterranean, the Greeks and Macedonians alike were surprised when an ebb tide left ships stranded on the mud, and some were badly damaged because they were not prepared when the returning tide coincided with strong winds. Yet it was a sign that they were close, and they were guided to an island where they could go ashore and get fresh water. Another twenty-five miles brought them to the sea, with a second island close by. Sacrifices were performed on both islands and Alexander announced that the nature of the offerings and the gods revered were in accordance with the oracle given to him at Siwah by Zeus Ammon. He took his own ship out to sea, where he sacrificed bulls to Poseidon, tipped the carcasses over the side, then poured a libation and threw the golden cup and bowls into the waves. It was six years since he had last seen the sea, and nine since he had sacrificed to Poseidon as he crossed the Dardanelles at the start of his great expedition. Alexander was thirty-one years old and about to start heading westward.[24]

29

SEA AND SAND

Hindsight, and most of all the knowledge that Alexander would never reach his thirty-third birthday, tend to make the moment when he and his soldiers left India into far more of a turning point than it really was, and certainly than it seemed at the time. There is no hint in our sources that he had lost interest in India after his disappointment at the Hyphasis, any more than he had "lost interest" in Egypt or Cilicia when he left them behind. He remained for a year after the refusal of his men to cross the river, and not simply because in due course he was wounded and needed time to recover. Alexander stayed to campaign and conquer, and that was usually the only reason for him to stay anywhere very long. The administration he created was a little different, with heavy reliance on local kings like Porus and Taxiles, but this was a practical decision for a region that had not been under effective control of a satrap for generations, if ever, and in some ways akin to the employment of locals, including Persian noblemen, elsewhere. Alexander also left behind him an officer named Philip as his satrap, backed by troops, mostly mercenaries, as well as the discharged soldiers who settled in the new colonies.[1]

After sacrificing on the islands he returned to Patala, only to set out again almost immediately, exploring the other branch of the Indus to see whether it offered a better route to the Ocean. Meanwhile, the preparations for taking most of his forces back to the heartland of his empire took months and were highly methodical without the slightest trace of rush, as new harbors and other facilities were constructed. His numerous Indian auxiliaries were sent back to their home kingdoms and communities, and the remainder of his troops were split into two land columns and the fleet. Craterus was given the other land force, including the Macedonians earmarked for discharge because of age and failing health. With them went many of the mercenaries and Asian allies, the elephants acquired in India, and the greater part of the baggage and equipment train. This was the slowest-moving column, and it was to march partly retracing routes followed during the advance and rendezvous with Alexander in Carminia in several months' time. It set out first, Alexander once again trusting a subordinate to follow instructions and act on initiative in the months when communications were bound to be slow.[2]

Alexander took the other land force and planned to work with the fleet, following a path that kept as far as possible to the coastline. The ships were ordered to explore the route toward the Euphrates, assuming that the ocean led there and did not prove to be an inner sea facing Africa. Nearchus was tasked with establishing whether Alexander's plan to connect the distant parts of his empire in this way was in fact practical, and later wrote a highly dramatic account of the adventure on which Arrian drew heavily for his own narrative. While Nearchus was inclined to exaggerate his own heroism, the expedition was genuinely a leap into the unknown, for while the route had been used for centuries, there is little sign of much trade employing it at the time Nearchus arrived. Alexander and his men learned next to nothing from the locals, while his own crews came from Mediterranean communities with no experience of these waters. Nearchus claimed that the king was reluctant to let him face such unknown peril, but was finally convinced by his enthusiasm. No doubt he exaggerated, since Alexander was persuaded and the expedition went ahead. It was a gamble, partly into the unknown, but then Alexander had gambled often enough in the past and tended to win.[3]

No source gives us any idea of numbers for any of the three divisions of the great army. It is likely that Craterus's force was the largest, as well as the slowest and most cumbersome. His column included more than half of the hypaspists, old soldiers from Philip's day who were in their sixties, due for discharge and who were felt not to be up to the likely rigors of Alexander's route. Yet the king still had some hypaspists, the pick of the Companion cavalry and the phalanx, along with the Agrianians and the horse archers he had used so effectively in India. While some scholars estimate his force at some 80,000 or more, 30,000 is more likely and 20,000 or less distinctly possible, even if the camp followers are included. The number of ships is likewise unknown, although the bulk of them appear to have been triaconters, the thirty-oared warships he had favored on the rivers. There is no positive evidence that there were also transport ships, and not the slightest indication that Nearchus had vessels to carry large quantities of food and other supplies intended for the troops on land. Nor is it clear that the fleet was anywhere near as large as the one used on the rivers of India; dozens, perhaps scores, of ships are far more probable than hundreds.[4]

This would be a long voyage for such relatively small craft. Unlike transport or supply ships, warships were not solely dependent on their sails and could be rowed for substantial periods, although not at great speed for any length of time and certainly not over the distances envisaged. Thus they would need to sail most of the way, which meant waiting until the end of the monsoon season with its prevailing westerly winds. Usually this ceased by the end of October, after which there was a good chance of better conditions and favorable wind. This at least was something the locals could tell the Macedonians, and was another reason for the delay in setting out.[5]

Alexander had some concept of the difficulties of the route he intended to take, even if he is unlikely to have had too many details. The area to traverse was sparsely populated, with no substantial settlements for most of the distance, and passed through country that was arid or desert. Persian rule had never been enforced tightly there, largely because the effort would not have been worth any gains in revenue or security. At some point stories circulated claiming that Cyrus had marched through this country with an army, and that before him the semimythical Assyrian or Babylonian queen Semiramis had done the same, both forces perishing apart from a handful of ragged survivors. Nearchus claimed that Alexander's *pothos* to succeed where even the greatest leaders of the past had failed came upon him once more. In truth he had little choice about the route once he had decided to send the fleet on its journey and wanted to prepare the way for it.

Doing what was thought impossible certainly did have an appeal for him here as elsewhere, and the naval expedition was part of this. Moreover the region was at least loosely part of the Persian Empire, and a logical addition now that he had added northern India. Going this way also meant that he would lead his men into unconquered territory, advancing rather than merely marching back the way they had come. Craterus had instructions to fight wherever it was necessary or useful to assert Macedonian control, so his march was more than simply a redeployment; for some, it was the start of their long anticipated return home to Macedonia.[6]

The lands in India had only recently been overrun, even in comparison to the rest of Alexander's empire. Throughout history, empire builders tend to face resistance during the initial conquest, and then varying periods and phases of rebellion in the years to come as substantial sections of the population decide that life under occupation is intolerable. Much of Bactria and Sogdiana had soon revolted against Alexander, prompting the long and savage campaigns to suppress the area once again. In 327 BC the Macedonians attacked the hill peoples on their way to the Indus and again achieved temporary dominance. A year later, while Alexander marched against Porus, some of the Assacenians rebelled and killed Nicanor, the man he had made their satrap. Troops were sent to deal with the rising and the area added to the responsibilities of Philip, the satrap of the lands outside Porus's kingdom. Craterus's march back through this country would further reinforce Macedonian control in areas where it remained precarious. Yet in spite of the recent Brahman-led resistance in India, there is no sign of widespread unrest of the type that had spread so quickly in 329 BC. For the moment, at least while the king and large numbers of his best soldiers were present, no one was eager to challenge Macedonian dominance.[7]

Alexander set out from Patala around the end of August 325 BC, knowing that the fleet would not be able to follow for the best part of two months because of the monsoon winds. This was never planned as an operation where land and sea forces would shadow each other, cooperating closely, nor even like the march through India, where Hephaestion and Craterus had regularly looped back to meet the fleet on the riverbanks. Instead, Alexander would prepare a way for the fleet, ensuring that the shoreline was not too hostile, and make ready supplies to assist Nearchus. If there was ever a plan for the fleet and army to meet at any point along the journey, then it can at best have been a loose arrangement, for the speed of each was unpredictable. His intention was to lead the army along a path that allowed him to reach the coast, but he also had to be careful not to strip the shoreline of food as his army passed.

Four months' worth of supplies had been gathered at Patala, and Alexander's column carried large quantities of food with it in a baggage train of carts, pack animals, and probably human porters. Another reason for setting out well in advance of the fleet was to make the most of the seasonal rains, which ought to ensure plenty of water was available, at least at the start of the journey. In his path lay the Arabitae and Oreitae, who had not sent envoys to make their peace, so were considered hostile. Alexander moved fast, once again taking a picked force ahead of the main column. Most of the locals fled long before he arrived, but some were surprised by the sheer speed of the attack and cut down by his cavalry vanguard. The king decided that the main village of the Oreitae was a fine site for a city, and left Hephaestion behind to start work organizing this. Alexander pressed on, and a local army that had gathered to defend a pass melted away before he arrived. Horrified by the violence and strength of the Macedonian onslaught, the local leaders appeared and surrendered.

Alexander was eager to keep going, and since there had been little or no fighting, he was not in the mood for reprisals against the local population. He appointed Apollophanes as satrap for the area, and also left behind Leonnatus—his bodyguard and one of the men who had fought side by side with him inside the walls of the Mallian town—with a strong force including the Agrianians, mercenaries, and allies. Before the army left, parties went out to dig wells for the use of the fleet when it arrived. Even small war galleys like triaconters carried large crews in proportion to their size, making supplies of drinking water a greater priority than food, especially whenever the rowers were required to power the vessel. The satrap and troops left behind were ordered to assist the fleet by securing landing places and supplies, and in the meantime developing the city begun by Hephaestion, which it was hoped would make the population easier to control.[8]

By October Alexander and the main force reached Gedrosia, another region whose people had not seen fit to submit to him. It was a poor area, much of it true desert, but at the start the route was no more difficult than many others the army had followed in the past, and the last weeks of the rainy season ensured that there was sufficient water for his needs. Phoenician merchants traveling with the army were delighted to discover gum from unusually large myrrh trees, as well as ginger grass. There was no resistance, indeed in some areas almost no visible population, but a rugged hill country impassable for transport and difficult for everyone forced the Macedonians inland a good distance away from the sea. Alexander hoped to bypass the difficult high ground and eventually go back nearer to the coastline. With the rains over, water became harder to find, while the searing heat of the day meant that as far as possible they marched only during the night. A patrol was sent to find the coast and search for any harbors or suitable anchorages, as well as water sources. It returned with disappointing news, saying that apart from some desperately poor fisher folk there was no settlement, let alone facilities, nor sign of wells.

After a while, the column came to a less barren area, where some supplies could be foraged. Alexander ordered substantial quantities of food to be set apart in the baggage train and earmarked for the fleet, with the royal seal on each load. With the main force on short rations, the temptation of this hoard proved too great, and while the king was at the head of the column leading them back toward the coast, soldiers, including the guards, broke the seals and gave out the food. It was a breach of discipline, and a mark of desperation on the part of hungry men who saw no sign of relief. Alexander pardoned all those involved, judging that severity was unwise in such understandable circumstances. Another store of food was prepared and sent in an escorted convoy to the coast. Soon afterward a further supply dump was prepared at a different spot, while orders went out for the small local population to gather grain, grind it to flour, and send this so that it would be waiting for the fleet. As far as we can tell, none of these supplies was ever found by Nearchus and his men.

Alexander took sixty days to reach the Gedrosian capital, a place called Pura, and the precise sequence of the journey is unclear. All our sources agree that much of the journey was through desert, where the soft sand made walking difficult and exhausting, and the only water holes were far apart. For once, even Arrian goes into some detail about the sufferings endured by the column as it struggled on, baked by the sun, thirsty, usually hungry, and weary to the point of exhaustion. Traveling as far as possible during the night, sometimes the next water source was more than a manageable distance away. Parched men and horses flung themselves into the pools when they did reach them, and more than a few died from drinking too much too fast or simply fouled the water for the rest. Alexander ordered camps to be made two or three miles short of the water holes to prevent these stampedes and bring back some order.

Even though discipline started to crumble, the army kept going, with the same stubborn determination the men had shown so often before—and a realization that stopping would be simply to await death. Alexander set an example as he always did, his own iron willpower driving him on and making it harder for anyone else to show themselves to be weaker. A story, similar to others told at different times, tells of a group of soldiers bringing him a little water in a helmet. This was all there was, and rather than let everyone see the king drink while they went thirsty, Alexander upended the helmet and tipped it all away. He shared their hardships as he shared the risks of battle, and Arrian claims that for a little while it was as if everyone really had had a drink.

Not everyone's will matched their strength, however, and as strength failed, some dropped to the rear of the column and then fell behind or got lost. All such stragglers died. Arrian compared their fate to men lost at sea. One night the army camped in a dried-up riverbed, a sloppy decision that, rather than ignorance, surely reflected an utter weariness. Storms far, far away in the hills produced a flash flood raging down the gully. The royal tents were swept away, much of the king's baggage lost, as men struggled to swim or wade out of the torrent. Many women and children were drowned, and even the soldiers who survived were left with little more than their weapons. Whatever relief this gave to their thirst was brief, and soon the sun rose again and baked them. Soldiers killed baggage and draft animals to eat their flesh, probably raw or cooked a little in the sunlight because there would not have been wood to burn as fuel unless they also broke up the carts, and that supply would soon have been used up. Packs, equipment, and transport were abandoned, even some of the carts carrying those too ill or weak to walk. Men even started to kill cavalry mounts, claiming that they were lame, and the king again turned a blind eye.

A sandstorm blew up and so changed the landscape that it made the local guides lose their way. Alexander guessed that the army was not far from the coast and took some of the best mounted cavalry left to him and headed due south, guided by sun and star, telling the rest to follow. Men fell out, their mounts exhausted, so that only a handful of riders were with him when they saw the sea. Luck was on his side, and they soon found water, digging out enough new wells so that the rest of the army had plenty to drink as it gradually staggered up. From then on they were able to stay near the coast for the next week and had sufficient water. Things grew easier and finally the army reached Pura, probably late in December 325 BC.[9]

The crossing of the Gedrosian desert was one of the worst ordeals endured by Alexander and his soldiers; Arrian saw it as by far the most severe. However, none of our sources give any numbers for the casualties suffered in these months, apart from Plutarch who vaguely claims that only a quarter survived, but since he is basing this on the totals Alexander allegedly mustered at the height of his campaigns in India, it is not of much use. This has given modern scholars free rein to guess, some even going as high as 70,000 to 80,000 fatalities. Many draw comparisons with other famous disasters, such as Mark Antony's flight from the Parthians in 36 BC, which cost him between a quarter and a third of his army, and most of all Napoleon's catastrophic retreat from Moscow in 1812, which produced an even higher death toll. Neither analogy is appropriate, since for all the severity of the weather, it was pursuit by a strong and vengeful enemy that turned these campaigns into disasters. Alexander faced no enemy in the Gedrosian desert, had suffered no defeat or costly victory before the march began, and had instead started with a confident and well-supplied army. In that sense the deaths that did occur were more futile and can only have seemed tragic, since there was no enemy to overcome.

Alexander's great battles cost his army at most hundreds of dead, and even the defeat in Sogdiana around 2,000. Thus even if the fatalities suffered in the Gedrosian desert numbered in the hundreds, they would have been comparable with Issus or Gaugamela without the glory and achievement of those fights, while a death toll of a few thousand would be more than the enemy had ever managed to kill. Our sources do not suggest any great drop in the number of Macedonian soldiers in the army. Perhaps losses were higher among the allies and mercenaries, as they certainly were among the camp followers. The total number of deaths need not have been anywhere near as high as most modern estimates to have appalled those involved. Alexander and his men had gotten through, as they always got through, losing many of the weakest with the column, and it seems unlikely that the merchants brought much of their prized myrrh with them all the way. In terms of its strategic objective the march proved a failure, since their ability to prepare the way for the fleet was minimal, and most of the supplies and water they prepared and left was never discovered by Nearchus. This does not mean that the original idea was folly, and in the long run the fleet had a much easier time than the army.[10]

Yet things did not begin well, for the monsoon season lasted weeks longer than usual. With Alexander and the vast majority of Macedonian soldiers gone, the fear they had created soon faded and the locals became increasingly hostile to the invaders. Nearchus set out sometime in October, reluctant to wait in case this hostility turned into direct attack. Even so the wind prevented him from getting out of the mouth of the Indus, so he halted, fortifying a camp and waiting another twenty-four days until the wind shifted from northwesterly to southeasterly, and he at last ventured into the ocean. Before long, he found wells and stores left by Alexander and made contact with Leonnatus, who had recently defeated a rebellion of the local people, during which Apollophanes the satrap had been killed. For the moment the Macedonians were back in control, and he was able to aid Nearchus with stores.

From then on the fleet lost contact with land forces. It encountered the inhabitants of the fishing villages seen by Alexander's patrol, and Nearchus claimed that 600 gathered to oppose him if he tried to land. He told of how he stormed ashore, brushing them aside. (The small scale of this engagement is just one indication that the fleet was not very big.) His men found little worth taking, save a few sheep whose flesh tasted salty. Farther along another, slightly bigger community was willing to welcome the strangers and offer them supplies. Nearchus ordered his men to feign friendship before, at a signal, turning on their hosts, killing any who resisted and stripping the rest of all the food they could find. The impact of this voyage on communities along the way was sudden and dreadful, although this was not of any real concern to Nearchus or our sources.

The fleet kept going, and although food ran short several times, Nearchus kept a tight discipline and the fleet always managed to find enough before the situation became truly desperate. An Egyptian-crewed ship vanished near an island and was never found, but otherwise there were no serious losses. A school of whales, larger than any seen in the Mediterranean, caused a momentary panic. Nearchus boasts of how he made his ships row hard toward the animals, shouting and blowing trumpets. The whales dived out of the way, reappearing at a distance, but still close enough for the sailors to see the spouts of water as they exhaled. Luck was with the fleet, not least because the weather was generally kind, and the skill of a Gedrosian pilot helped them a good deal. At times the men rowed or sailed day and night, pressing on in spite of exhaustion, until in January 324 BC, after covering more than a thousand miles, they reached the Persian Gulf and came to the shores of Carmania. It was still some time before Alexander learned that Nearchus and his men were safe.[11]

30

THE RETURN OF THE KING

When Alexander reached Pura he found that supplies of grain had already been rushed to the city, so he gave the army a short rest before it moved on to Carmania and its capital, Ecbatana. After some 200 miles he rendezvoused with Craterus and his wing of the army and with plentiful convoys of supplies and replacement baggage animals prepared for his arrival. The king sacrificed for his column's successful crossing of the desert and held a festival. The celebrations were lavish, food and drink plentiful at long last. Some accounts portrayed the army's progress as a drunken revel, the king and his Companions acting the part of Dionysus and his court, riding on decorated carts and chariots tied together, feasting and drinking. Curtius claims that even a thousand bold enemies could have overcome the entire army as it reeled along in an alcoholic haze. Arrian repeats the tale, but refused to believe it, while modern scholars accept or reject it depending on their attitude to Alexander.

Celebration and letting off steam after the recent hardships are likely enough, but the practicalities of obtaining all that was required for such grand feasting after the loss of so much of the army's transport and the royal baggage in the desert renders the greater excesses improbable. Even so, the reunion of the army was surely a joyful occasion, marred for a while by uncertainty over the fate of the fleet. A messenger who had encountered Nearchus brought momentary hope, then despair when nothing more was heard. Alexander had the messenger arrested, only releasing him when the admiral appeared in person—ragged, filthy and wild-haired, according to Nearchus's own account, so that his friend at first did not recognize him.[1]

Craterus reported that he had encountered rebels during his march, and as instructed had stamped out any sign of resistance. He presented two noble prisoners as a mark of his success. There was news of problems elsewhere, and at Pura Alexander received a letter informing him that Philip, his satrap in India, had been murdered by some of his mercenaries. This was not part of a general rebellion, and Macedonian soldiers had swiftly caught and killed the assassins, so Alexander wrote back instructing Omphis and Porus to manage affairs until he sent a new satrap. There was also discontent among mercenaries and settlers in Bactria and Sogdiana. A false story of the king's death after his wound in India had spread widely and prompted a group of more than 3,000 hired soldiers to abandon the colony where they had been settled and try to make their way home to Greece. Similar rumors flourished as Alexander vanished into the Gedrosian desert, while many of his own men as well as his conquered subjects do seem to have doubted that he would ever return from his Indian expedition.[2]

The journey back from India demonstrated the Macedonians' ability to organize, supply, and move large numbers of troops over vast distances, and none of this should be taken lightly in an era of slow communications and transport. Some of the satraps anticipated the needs of Alexander's men, given the route they were taking, and began to gather and dispatch food supplies before the orders arrived. Others had to be prompted, and Alexander was not satisfied with the response of some of his subordinates, even though it is hard to see what more could have been done. He decided to sack Apollophanes, feeling that the satrap had let him down, and sent the order for this before he learned that the man had fallen in battle. Leonnatus and his men rejoined the main force at some point (by what route we do not know), bringing the news of the rebellion and its defeat with heavy losses.[3]

Soon after Craterus's arrival, a number of satraps and senior officers also joined the king, bringing with them large contingents of troops. Not all received a warm welcome and it was soon clear that Alexander was displeased with several of them. Early on, Astaspes, the Persian Alexander had appointed as satrap of Carmania itself, was suspected of plotting rebellion. According to Curtius, Alexander feigned friendship until he became satisfied that the accusation was valid, at which point Astaspes was arrested and executed. More publicly, charges were made against four of the king's senior officers: Cleander the brother of Coenus; Sitalces and Agathon, both Thracian princes; and Heracon. All were men who had once served under Parmenio and then, on the king's orders, had arranged the latter's killing, an episode that ensured that many disliked them.

Now they were accused of plundering temples and tombs and abusing the native population, including extortion and rape. Cleander was said to have taken a virgin from a noble family, raped the girl, and then when tired of her had given her as mistress to one of his slaves. Witnesses were provided by the accused's own soldiers as well as Persians, and both the king—and our sources—were convinced of their guilt. Cleander and Sitalces were executed, while Heracon was initially spared, only to face similar charges later in the year at Susa, and this time be found guilty and killed. No one tells us what happened to the little-known Agathon, but 600 soldiers—one in ten of the contingent brought by Cleander—were also tried, condemned, and executed.[4]

There were also stories of misbehavior by one of the king's oldest friends. Harpalus, who had fled under mysterious circumstances before Issus, had returned and once again found royal favor in 331 BC and was reappointed as Alexander's senior treasurer. After a period stationed at Ecbatana, he and the bulk of the wealth were moved to Babylon where he lived in extravagant style. Some of his activities were harmless, as he investigated whether plants from Greece could be successfully grown in the city's famous gardens.

Nor was Alexander too concerned about embezzlement, even on a grand scale. More serious was his seduction or rape of local women, and more embarrassing his parading of an Athenian courtesan (*hetaira*), Pythionice, in public and his excessive devotion to her. When she died, he used official funds to build a temple in her honor as Pythionice Aphrodite at Babylon, and a grandiose tomb for her at Athens, which alone cost 30 talents; the bill for both monuments was claimed to be 200 talents. His sorrow was soon consoled when he recruited another Athenian *hetaira*, Glycera, whom he welcomed on the coast of Asia Minor, and instructed the people of Tarsus to treat her as a queen. There were distinctly royal airs about much of what he did, perhaps extending to minting coins bearing his name, and once again it is hard to know what he was planning, for he did not wait to test his friend's reaction to his behavior. Still indulgent and loyal, Alexander is supposed to have disbelieved the accusations made against Harpalus, even arresting his accusers. Only when news arrived that Harpalus had fled to Greece, taking with him 6,000 mercenaries, a squadron of warships, and 5,000 talents, did the king grow angry.[5]

The decision to flee makes it clear that Harpalus did not expect to be pardoned a second time, whether through an awareness of his own guilt or belief that the king was no longer so mild or friendly. He may well have acted before he knew the fate of Cleander and the others, all men who had held positions in the same part of the empire and with whom he had worked, but if not the executions added to his fears. They were not the only deaths ordered by the king in 324 BC. A number of Persian noblemen were executed, one of whom had assumed the royal tiara and proclaimed himself king, and three more were satraps. One of the latter was a local nobleman who had taken over Persis when the man appointed to the province by Alexander died of natural causes; he had maintained order and not shown any sign of hostility. Even so his initiative may have seemed dangerous, and Curtius preserves the story that his open contempt for the eunuch Bagoas caused the latter to engineer his end, under the pretext that he had robbed the tomb of Cyrus. At the same time other commanders and satraps were replaced, some because they had died in office, and others for reasons unknown. One consequence of this was that only a hand-ful of Persians remained in senior posts by the end of the year, and Alexander's administration as well as his military hierarchy was overwhelmingly Macedonian, with a significant number of Greeks.

For some scholars this was a "reign of terror" by a king embit-tered by the refusal of his men to cross the Hyphasis, pained by his wounds, overreliant on alcohol for solace, unable to control his temper, and suspicious of almost everyone around him. Opinion divides over whether this was cold calculation or paranoid suspi-cion, so we sometimes have the king who had needlessly exposed his men to the horrors of the Gedrosian desert, who had killed Cleitus in a drunken rage and ordered countless massacres and executions, steadily losing almost all restraint. This was an Alexander who was angry at his own mistakes and lashed out at the least excuse. Others see it as significant that Cleander was brother to Coenus, who had thwarted Alexander at the Hyphasis, and like Harpalus appears to have come from one of the royal lines of Upper Macedonia. For those who see Alexander as always ruthless, disposing of potential rivals or mere opponents at any opportunity, this was little more than yet another phase in his murderous career, perhaps intended as a smokescreen to distract attention from his recent mistakes and the wasted lives lost in the desert.[6]

Perspective is important. Alexander and his men had overrun the vast and fabulously wealthy Persian Empire in an incredibly short time and kept on moving and conquering more territory. There had been little or no time for consolidation. There was also no great pool of experienced administrators to put in charge of the conquered empire, which was far less familiar and far more het-erogeneous, let alone simply far larger, than the enlarged kingdom and subject allies Philip had hammered together during his reign. Alexander had no precedents to follow when it came to organizing, and could do no more than choose individuals from the senior levels of his army and court, allocate responsibilities, and hope that they learned on the job and coped. As far as possible he kept existing structures in place, whether local, especially city governments, or the bureaucracy of the Achaemenid kings. The Asians who served him were those willing to switch sides after a very short time and serve their conqueror and new master, and were not picked on the basis of talent but because they were willing. None had any great cause to love the new king, apart from gratitude because he chose to appoint or reappoint them.

The Macedonians and Greeks had been raised to despise Persians and all Asians as barbarians, fit only to be slaves, and the defeat of Darius and his great armies can only have reinforced their immense sense of superiority. They were masters over subjects whose language and culture held no interest or value for them, apart from its luxury, wealth, and famously beautiful women. The conquered gained local power as representatives of the new king, and with it the opportunity to satisfy their own ambitions, whether to enrich themselves and their friends or to hurt their rivals. If some were willing to take great or small opportunities to undermine or overthrow the conquerors then that is scarcely surprising.

Close supervision of what his regional officials did was impossible for Alexander. He wrote and received reports and letters, and dispatched orders, but all communication was slow and the king did not have the time to learn and involve himself in everything. As he moved ever farther away, correspondence took even longer or failed altogether. The ability of a Persian to assume a satrapy on his own initiative and then hold it for many months shows how loose a hold Alexander had on his empire. The distances were too great, the time lag of communications too long, and his representatives and the troops under their command far too few for him to police the entire empire closely. For years on end, satraps, garrison commanders, and others were left largely to their own devices. Possession of a few hundred or a few thousand troops, usually mercenaries, permitted them to do whatever they wished locally. That some abused this license is hardly surprising, whether it was the Macedonians and Greeks, whose culture was scarcely one of restraint, or the Asians.

From a purely practical point of view Alexander could not permit blatant abuses of power, which risked provoking the population into rebellion out of anger and desperation, nor attempts to revive a Persian monarchy by local noblemen. A willingness to punish anyone, including prominent Companions, was an earnest expression of his intention to rule fairly. Theft and misuse of his money in itself rarely provoked the king's deepest anger, but he had always reacted very strongly in cases of sexual abuse of women. This may have been from personal feelings as well as a sense that such crimes were especially likely to make his representatives and regime hated. Thus Cleomenes in Egypt was known to have assumed ever greater control of financial affairs and embezzled on a truly grand scale, but he does not appear to have been a sexual predator or murderer and remained in office. Apart from wishing to avoid rather than stir up resistance and rebellion, Alexander was said to be most annoyed by the assumption many had clearly made that he would never return from India. Doubts about his luck and future success, almost as much as disloyalty, angered him.[7]

On balance, there were good grounds for most of the executions ordered in the months after Alexander's return from India. That does not mean that the king's judgment was flawless, his investigations entirely thorough or fair, or that he was not sometimes manipulated by courtiers and prey to his own unwarranted suspicion and distrust. Rebellion by Persian nobles provoked immediate anger, and it was claimed that Alexander personally stabbed one rebel to death with a spear. He wanted to make a stern example and impose his will and control on his empire after years spent far away and only loosely in touch with its heartland. The case for a reign of terror is weak, as is the picture of an unbalanced and vicious king, not least because such a man is unlikely to have limited his murderous impulses to such a relatively small number of victims. He wanted to create fear in his subordinates, and surely succeeded. It is harder to say whether there was a conscious decision to remove the majority of Persians in high office or this simply reflected his greater willingness to trust men that he had known far longer, who spoke his own language and were less likely to rally local support.[8]

Trusting others was never straightforward for any Argead, who knew that he was more likely to die at the hands of someone close to him than a foreign enemy. Alexander had faced at least three significant plots in the course of a decade; these experiences reinforced his fears on this score. (Even if he had engineered the downfall of some of those accused in these cases as some scholars believe, a man inclined to do that was scarcely likely to develop great faith in his Companions and courtiers.) Whatever his feelings toward Cleander and the others, these were all men who knew him well and understood how he expected them to behave, yet they had still abused their positions. So had Harpalus and he was a very close and dear friend. Such men were all the more dangerous because their control of mercenary forces meant that they could only be stopped by a major rebellion of the local population or by dispatching part of his main army to deal with them. Darius had employed many mercenaries, whether Greek, Carian, or from other areas. Some had died, been captured, or either enslaved or recruited by Alexander, and others had escaped to the Mediterranean. That left large numbers of men who never served with the main armies and were instead scattered as garrisons, as well as men who had lost their homes and livelihoods during the course of the wars and become soldiers for hire. Of these, many were hired by satraps and other officials, all with ready access to the profits of conquest, while others turned bandit or marauder.

Alexander issued a decree banning his subordinates from hiring mercenaries on their own authority, and ordered all the contingents they already had to be sent to him and incorporated in the main army. In the case of the Greeks, he soon decided on a simple solution to the problem. The majority of these men were exiles from their home cities, the losers in internal political struggles and wars, not least those campaigns waged by Philip and the Macedonians as they raised allies to power in as many communities as possible. Alexander announced that all were free to return home, with the exception of those guilty of impiety or other serious crimes, and the Thebans whose polis he had abolished. The nature of this decision—whether it was a formal decree or order, or simply an expression of royal will that the cities were bound to feel obliged to accept—is unclear. He did send an envoy to the Olympic Games of 324 BC to announce this and other rulings, and since 20,000 exiles gathered to hear this, word of what was intended had obviously been widely broadcast. Without obvious irony, Alexander stated that, even though he was not responsible for the original exile, in the interest of harmony he would restore them to their homes.

A direct intervention in the internal affairs of every city, since few had no exiles at all, this was in direct conflict with assurances guaranteeing all poleis their autonomy in the alliance at Corinth. The exiles were the rivals of the regimes currently in power, their reappearance an obvious threat to stability, risking the revival of old quarrels. At another level was the question of property, for houses and land owned by exiles, some of whom had been absent for decades, had new owners, raising all sorts of legal questions. As usual, each city reacted individually, their concerns varying. At Athens, whose constitution had long allowed for exile by popular vote, the main concern was with communities it had overcome and colonized in the past, especially the island of Samos; what was to happen to the righteous Athenian settlers if bitter Samians were restored to their homeland? Although news of Alexander's decision was quickly broadcast, there does not seem to have been any detail about the many such questions it was bound to raise, and for the moment this ensured that the inevitable resentment of such high-handed interference was kept in check by respect for Macedonian might.[9]

Harpalus plunged into this volatile situation, arriving off Athens sometime in 324 BC with his ships, soldiers, and treasure. In recent years he had developed a good relationship with the city, sending grain when there were shortages caused by bad harvests and probably by the disruption stemming from Alexander's campaign and the need to feed the ever growing numbers of soldiers in Macedonian service. Grateful for this aid, the Athenians had made him a citizen, but now, nervous of a coup, they refused to admit him, so he went to Taenarum in the Peloponnese, a frequent stopping place for mercenaries seeking employment. Returning to Athens with just three ships, few soldiers, and 700 talents, he was admitted, his money being stored in the city's treasury.

Letters soon came to Athens from Antipater and also Olympias, complaining that Athens was harboring a fugitive criminal and his stolen wealth. The Athenians responded by placing Harpalus under fairly loose arrest, and sending Demosthenes to the Olympic Games to negotiate with Alexander's envoy in the hope of arranging a deal protecting Athens's interests over the matter of the exiles.

Athens and everyone else waited on events, but Harpalus decided
not to wait too long, slipping away from his lax guards to rejoin
his mercenaries at Taenarum. With them he then went to Crete,
only to be murdered by one of his subordinates. Alexander's old
friend and former treasurer was dead, but this short episode would
later haunt the Athenians, for half of his money had vanished from
the city treasury, leading to a flurry of charges against prominent
men accused of taking bribes.[10]

ALEXANDER WAS THIRTY-TWO in the summer of 324 BC, and
it would have been truly remarkable if he and his men had not
changed a lot in the twelve years since he had become king, and
the ten since they had invaded Asia. Even by the standards of the
ancient world they had done a lot of fighting and killing in that
time. By any standards at all they had traveled immense distances,
and the lowest modern estimate would put this at more than
10,000 miles, all the while enduring heat, cold, and monsoon, and
slogging through barren desert and over high mountains. Overall
losses are impossible to know, for there are no figures for the
deaths from disease, which was a far greater risk than fighting in
pre-twentieth-century warfare. For the Macedonians who made
up the core of the army, any deaths came in a community of soldiers who had served and fought together for many years, in some
cases back to the early days of Philip. Many, perhaps the majority,
had taken a wound or wounds, just like their king; even if they survived, they had learned that they were not invulnerable. Alexander
had lost a lot of men he had known well, friends or simply prominent members of his court since his earliest days.[11]

One ancient tradition portrayed Alexander as corrupted by
power, and this is plausible, albeit impossible to prove one way or
the other. He does seem readier to order executions in his later years,
although apart from the delay in killing Alexander of Lyncestis
there had been little trace of any reluctance in his youth. His world
had changed dramatically, from that of the insecure young king not
long returned to favor after exile and heir to a murdered father, to
become the conqueror and lord of Asia. Preparing for the great war

against Persia had absorbed the later years of Philip's reign, and no doubt many of Philip's Companions and men came to share in this big idea, whether as something akin to the dream long preached by the Panhellenists or simply as a great challenge. Yet Macedonia, that weak, unregarded little kingdom until Philip's day, had forced the other Greeks to unite, and then attacked and utterly over-whelmed the great superpower of the day.[12]

Now it was done. Alexander and his army were coming back to the center of Darius's empire as its unchallenged masters. Many things in life are sweeter in the anticipation than the actual achieve-ment, and such a long-held and cherished dream had left little room for thoughts about what came next. So much had been won so quickly, and that owed a lot to Alexander's drive, for it is hard to imagine a middle-aged Philip achieving so much so quickly with-out pausing to consolidate. For the Macedonians, all companions of the king, whether horse or foot, aristocrat or peasant, they had embarked on the great adventure and won more glory and more plunder than anyone could have imagined. Many believed that they were on their way home, something they had sought since Persepolis in 330 BC. At the same time they were physically, mentally, and emotionally exhausted after the years of struggle, hardship, and combat, and it would be natural to feel flat and drained. Something of the same was surely true of Alexander himself: with the great dream fulfilled, if not quite to his fullest satisfaction in India, he had to adjust to the changed world and new ambitions.

Alexander was not short of ideas and plans, focusing next on the Arabian Peninsula, for he had a fresh *pothos* to sail the Euphrates and Tigris and had set in hand major military and naval prepa-rations. First he marched through Pasargadae, where he found the tomb of Cyrus plundered, which was subsequently blamed on the Persian satrap and brought about his execution. At Persepo-lis he is supposed to have expressed regret at his destruction of the palace, but made no attempt to rebuild and instead moved on to Susa. There he held more celebrations, culminating in a grand mass wedding where he took two more wives, Stateira, the eldest daughter of Darius III and his wife Stateira, and Parysatis, young-est daughter of Artaxerxes Ochus. Hephaestion married another daughter of Darius, which pleased Alexander with the thought that their children would be cousins, while Craterus wed one of the Persian king's nieces. Altogether some eighty or ninety of his senior Companions were given aristocratic Persian brides, with generous dowries provided by Alexander and a ceremony conducted in what was felt to be Persian style, the grooms sitting in chairs and drinking a toast, after which their new wives came to sit beside them. Lesser, but still substantial, gifts were given to some 10,000 soldiers who had taken Asian women and started families with them during the course of the campaigns.[13]

No Persian men were given Macedonian or Greek brides. This was no fusion of two races, other than taking many of the most eligible young women of the Persian royal family and elite and giving them to Alexander's officers. Most, like the brides of the king himself, had been given a Greek education to prepare them for this moment, and for Alexander this was a far greater step than marriage to the relatively obscure and definitely not royal Roxane. None of the brides had any choice in the matter, nor were the Macedonians and Greeks in much of a position to refuse the arrangements proposed by their monarch. For them it was a far greater step than it was for him, since as we have seen there is no evidence that any Macedonians apart from ruling kings were polygamous. Only one of the marriages is known to have lasted in the long run, for Seleucus stayed married to Apame, daughter of Spitamenes, the Bactrian leader who had died fighting the Macedonians. In time she became the mother of his heir, as well as giving him two daughters, and he named three cities Apamea in her honor. Otherwise, all of the marriages ended in divorce soon after Alexander's death.[14]

For the moment it was a time of celebration. Golden crowns were awarded to Leonnatus and Peucestas, who had shielded Alexander at the storming of the Mallian stronghold in India, as well as to Nearchus and Onesicritus (who had been with the fleet and may have had more skill as a sailor than Nearchus), and also to Hephaestion and the remaining bodyguards. Peucestas was named as a supernumerary eighth royal bodyguard, and then a little later was made satrap of Persis to replace the executed Persian incumbent.

Encouraged by the king, he was the solitary Macedonian satrap to learn the native language and adopt many local customs, and appears to have been popular with the Persians as a consequence. Apart from the senior officers, Alexander was eager to show largesse to as many of his troops as possible. Apart from the gifts to those with women, he announced that he would pay all outstanding debts owed by anyone in the army. Suspicious that this was a trap, and that those who owed the most would be reprimanded or worse, few came forward. Only when it was realized that their king was sincere did the rest register and see their debts wiped clean. Alexander chided them for doubting his word, claiming that a king always spoke truth, which seems a very Persian sentiment and not something previously associated with the Argead monarchy, especially under the wily Philip.[15]

More misunderstandings and friction followed, through a mixture of poor communication, a growing difference in mindset, and a clumsiness and impatience born of fatigue. Soon after the weddings, 30,000 new soldiers arrived and paraded for the king. While they were drilled and equipped as a Macedonian phalanx, and obeyed commands given in Greek, these were the youths recruited more than three years earlier from the Asian communities. Alexander called them the "Successors" (*Epigoni*), and, perhaps even more tactlessly, an anti-phalanx. His veterans scornfully dubbed them Asian dancing girls, who were fine on the parade ground but had never seen action, and deeply resented the implication that anyone from the conquered barbarian races could ever replace them. Similarly the growing number of Asians incorporated in the hipparchies with the Companion cavalry was resented, as was the creation of a fifth hipparchy entirely recruited from Asians.[16]

Alexander ignored such concerns, if indeed he was aware of them, and busied himself with preparations, sailing down the Tigris out into the ocean and then back up the Euphrates, clearing aside barrages constructed as defenses on both rivers. He had ordered the bulk of the army to join him at Opis in Babylonia. By now the summer was almost at an end, and he chose this moment to announce that he was sending home all the Macedonians who were too old or unfit for rigorous service, much as he had in the past suddenly ordered the discharge of the Thessalians and other allied contingents. These veterans were to be rewarded generously, while the men who stayed with the army would receive so much that they would be the envy of all, including fresh recruits soon to be summoned from Macedonia.[17]

The response was anger at what seemed more like rejection than reward. Macedonians had fought and suffered with their king, and for most the dream of returning home was of Alexander leading them back, not sending them away. Other resentments bubbled—of the recent weddings, of Alexander dressing like an eastern king, of the "Successors" and Asian barbarians so visible in the army—and at the heart of all was the fear that they had conquered the Persian Empire only to lose their own king to the lure of Asia. The mass of soldiers called out to their king for all to go home. He could stay if he liked, and fight his wars with his barbarian soldiers, or with his "father" Zeus Ammon if he liked.

Alexander jumped down from the podium, pointing out men he saw as agitators to his guards. About thirteen were arrested by the hypaspists and led off for immediate execution. The rest were stunned, appalled by the sudden rage, and all shouting died away. Alexander got back up and addressed them. Arrian makes him remind the soldiers of all that they had accomplished under his father—pointedly Philip, not Ammon—and his own leadership, telling them that he had only intended to reward those worn out in service, but that if they chose they could all go home and tell everyone that they had abandoned their king. The words are no doubt invented, but Arrian's sources may well have preserved the essence of what was said. Alexander called the army's bluff, stalking off to the palace in the city and remaining out of sight for two days. On the third day he made a show of summoning senior Persians and Medes, doling out commands and offices to them, even announcing the creation of an elite Asian *agema* as bodyguard, horse and foot companions, and hypaspists.

His Macedonians became desperate, flooding toward the palace, throwing down their arms to show that they meant no harm and demanding to be let in to see their king, begging for his forgiveness and promising to hand over all the remaining agitators. For all their anger at Alexander, for all the resentment of his Asian dress and for employing former enemies as courtiers and soldiers, they were Macedonians and he was the monarch they had followed for so long and with such success. Both bonds ran very deep, far deeper than their anger, which at heart grew from the feeling that the king and his people, most of all his soldiers, should be united. Alexander came out, knowing that he had won, and ironically a Companion asked that like his Persian subjects, leading Macedonians should be named as his kinsmen and permitted to kiss him. The favor was granted and the reconciliation marked by a great feast for some 9,000 guests, mostly from the army. Alexander was in the center, surrounded by his senior Macedonian Companions, next to them the most distinguished Persians, and then the nobles and leading men from other nations; it is unclear where the Greeks fitted into this arrangement. All the key guests drank from the same bowl, while Greek soothsayers and Persian magi made offerings and Alexander prayed for harmony between Macedonian and Persian as partners in ruling the empire.

As he had intended in the first place, the oldest and most worn-out troops were drawn from the ranks to be sent home. There were some 10,000 altogether, and each received all his back pay topped up by a talent. Any wives, concubines, and children were to stay behind, for many of the soldiers had wives and families back in Macedonia, and the sudden introduction of thousands of "barbarian" women and their "illegitimate" children would have been a recipe for trouble in their home cities and villages. Alexander promised to raise the sons, give them a proper education and military training, and send them to their fathers once they came of age, although in fact nothing would ever come of this. Craterus was placed in charge of the column, which showed the importance Alexander attached to it. Aged perhaps in his middle forties, wounds and sickness had taken a toll, and this most trusted of his commanders in recent years was not in good health, which also made the choice appropriate. Another officer, himself an even more elderly veteran, was to accompany him and take over should Craterus die during the march.[18]

At long last, some of the Macedonians were going home. They did not hurry, reflecting their age, weariness, and in some cases infirmity, and perhaps a lingering reluctance to leave the rest of the army and their king after all they had done and seen together. Disturbances in Asia Minor, provoked by the death of a satrap fighting rebels as well as Harpalus's flight, would delay them, forcing some to draw their swords once more, and they had not reached Europe by the following summer. Although they did not know it, most would be called upon to fight again. As 324 BC drew to a close, no one could guess the future, but Alexander was busy shaping new dreams and new ambitions.[19]

31

"AN UTTER LOSS"

E ven Alexander may have struggled to know just what to do
next, for nothing could quite match the simplicity of purpose, romance, and respectable pretext of leading all the
Greeks against Persia, the greatest power in the world. No other
enemy was as great or rich or as hated and despised. There were
many things that he could do, but crowning this achievement was
bound to be difficult, and Plutarch claims that he told friends that
he was at "an utter loss what he should do with the rest of his life."
Settling down to consolidate his control of his conquests and create
a smooth administrative system came less naturally to Alexander
than action, so everyone expected there to be more conquests.
Apart from his longing to excel and surpass even his own achievements, bringing together former enemies to fight side by side with
the victors in new wars was likely to help unite the new empire,
just as the Persian expedition had helped distract Philip's former
enemies in Greece and on his northern frontiers. The Macedonia
created by Philip and honed by his son into such a fearsome power
was geared to war and expansion, military service being the greatest bond between king and subjects, so it would have been hard to
stop even if Alexander had been inclined to do so.[1]

Arabia was just a first step, and a logical one. If never really under Persian control, it was within their sphere of influence and adjacent to their heartland. Another attraction was the trade in luxuries, especially spices, that came from or passed through the region. Alexander is said to have learned that the Arabs worshipped just two gods, and was determined to make himself the third through the might of his conquering army and the justice with which he would then rule. There was also talk of wider plans beyond Arabia, beginning with sending a fleet to circumnavigate Africa, something Herodotus claimed had once been done centuries earlier. After that, Alexander would look to the west, first to Carthage, a traditional rival of the Greeks in Sicily whose links with Tyre had been made plain during the siege. Then perhaps there would be Italy and the rest of Europe. Arrian read of many different projects and could not decide where the truth lay, other than that "none of Alexander's plans were small and petty and that, no matter what he had conquered, he would not have stopped there quietly," always searching "beyond for something unknown."[2]

For the moment it took time and effort to marshal his resources for an offensive in a different direction. Everything was on a grand scale, reflecting the huge change for a king who possessed a great empire, compared to the one who had begun his Asian expedition with an almost empty treasury. Harbor facilities were built in several places along the rivers to accommodate and support a grand fleet. Some of the warships, almost all triremes or larger, were prefabricated on the Mediterranean coast and carried in sections overland to be reassembled. Reconnaissance expeditions gathered more information about the rivers and the coast beyond, as well as helping to train the crews taking part in them. By 323 BC a major reform of the army was in its early stages, which was intended to incorporate 20,000 Asian soldiers, armed with bow, sling, or javelin, into the regiments of the phalanx, depleted as they were by the discharge of the veterans. Based around a sixteen-man file (which was still called a *dekas* or "ten" by tradition), these would have three Macedonians at the front and a fourth in the rear rank, with the Asians in between. An Arabian campaign was more likely to involve sieges, raids, and skirmishes than massed battles, so the structure may have been as much administrative as tactical and seems never to have been tested in action.[3]

As Alexander prepared for his next conquests, he took the army to Ecbatana for the winter, and as usual a lull in operations meant devoting time to politics and administration. In the center of his empire he was more easily accessible and much closer to Greece and Macedonia than he had been for some years. For a while he considered military action against Athens, until news arrived of Harpalus's flight and death along with Athenian assurances of friendship. The pressure put on Athens by Antipater and Olympias was one of the few occasions when the king's representative and his mother were able to work together. The rest of the time they bickered over influence, over patronage, and over the implementation of Alexander's orders, for instance regarding recruitment. Eventually Olympias went to her homeland Epirus, leaving her daughter Cleopatra to dispute with Antipater in Macedonia itself. Alexander said that his mother was wise, for the Macedonians would never stomach rule by a woman. Olympias continued to bombard him with accusations that Antipater was a traitor, plotting to make himself king.[4]

Craterus had orders to replace Antipater on arrival in Macedonia. The latter was by now in his seventies and was then instructed to lead a large draft of new recruits to join Alexander and the main army. Whether or not he was aware of this decision and feared the king might have worse in store for him when he arrived, Antipater sent his son, Cassander, to justify his conduct against any accusations. Perhaps a year or two younger than Alexander, he may have been a frail youth and had not taken any part in the Asian expedition. This left him unprepared for the changes in the king and the new etiquette at court. Seeing some Persians prostrating themselves in *proskynesis*, he burst out laughing, prompting Alexander to bound down from the throne and pound Cassander's head against the wall. Years later the mere sight of a lifelike statue of the king was supposed to have made Cassander quiver and break into a sweat. The incident is unlikely to have helped his or his father's case, but Craterus's progress was slow and matters had yet to come to a head.[5]

Alexander staged more festivals and celebrations, with more than 3,000 performers and athletes coming from Greece to take part. Rest and celebration also meant that he and his officers feasted and drank heavily. Hephaestion developed a fever after one of these parties. For a week he obeyed his doctor's instructions, resting and keeping to a strict diet. Then he felt better, ate a boiled chicken, and drank a lot of wine. There was an immediate relapse, and within a few hours he was dead, before Alexander had heard the news or hurried from the festival to see him. Horrified, the king was said to have lain down, cradling the corpse, refusing to leave for the rest of the day. Whatever the precise nature of their relationship, there is no doubt that Hephaestion played a central role in Alexander's life as his closest and most trusted friend. Whether or not it was ever sexual, the love was deep and genuine, probably rivaled only by his affection for his mother, and perhaps even eclipsing her, for Hephaestion was with him in all the years of war and triumph. Politically, his importance was publicly paraded. He was commander of the senior hipparchy of Companion cavalry— there was no longer a formal post or dual command in charge of the entire force—and had lately been made *chiliarch*, a Greek title for commander of a thousand, but inspired by Persian tradition and effectively the king's senior minister.

In the *Iliad*, Achilles plunged into spectacular grief and mourning when his dearest friend Patroclus was killed, fighting in Achilles's place and wearing his armor because the great hero had refused to do battle after his honor had been insulted. For later generations it was natural to see Alexander's sorrow in the same light, the descendant of Achilles as devastated by the loss of his closest comrade as the heroic ancestor had been. Arrian suggested that both men would have preferred to die before their beloved friend. Perhaps Alexander understood his grief in emotions drawn from Homer, just as he phrased so much of his life through the prism of the *Iliad*. In the past he had taken care to honor the dead, especially the Macedonian dead and most of all any Companions who fell. When Demaratus of Corinth had died of old age on the verge of the Indian campaign, Alexander held a grand funeral, then sent the ashes in an ornate funeral cortege back the thousands of miles to Corinth. As he grew in wealth and power, Alexander's capacity to express any emotion knew fewer constraints. So perhaps did his anger, and some sources claim that he had Hephaestion's doctor executed for his failure.

The grieving for Hephaestion was consciously Homeric, with Alexander cutting his hair and ordering horses' manes and tails to be docked just as Achilles had done. A common feeling for the bereaved is the sense that the rest of the world continues as normal while their personal world has changed so abruptly. Alexander had the power to make sure that the wider world took notice. Diodorus claims that he ordered the sacred flame in each Zoroastrian temple to be extinguished until the funeral was complete, thus extending public mourning to his Persian subjects and either not realizing or not caring that for them this was an appalling blasphemy. The process took awhile, because the corpse was carried in state to Babylon, and there cremated on an immense funeral pyre some 200 feet high and decorated with the prows of warships and other trophies and luxuries. Leading men threw their weapons into the flames. Not long before, a senior Companion named Eumenes had quarreled with Hephaestion and they had been forced to reconcile publicly by the king. At the funeral he was the first to give his finest equipment to the flames, parading his sorrow in the hope of convincing the distraught king that he harbored no ill will toward the dead man.[6]

Alexander sent an envoy to Siwah to consult the oracle over how best to honor the memory of his friend, and was said to be delighted when the reply eventually came that Hephaestion was to receive the cult appropriate for a hero. Achilles had crowned his mourning by plunging into battle and slaughtering Trojans, including Hector, and taking prisoners to sacrifice over Patroclus's tomb. Before winter was over, Alexander sought solace in activity and battle, leading a punitive expedition against the Cossaeans of the Zagros Mountains. This was done with all the Macedonians' familiar speed and savagery, as they divided into several columns and hunted down the mountain tribesmen. New settlements were created in the hope of turning pastoralists into farmers who would be less inclined to banditry.[7]

Early in 323 BC Alexander headed back to Babylon, and the army was met by numerous embassies from all around the Mediterranean, who had either heard or guessed that his attention might be turning in their direction. Arrian lists delegations from Libyans, Bruttians, Lucanians, and Etruscans from Italy, and had read in his sources and was less certain about the presence of Carthaginians, Iberians, and Celts. He was extremely doubtful about claims that there was also an embassy from Rome's Republic. Some came to offer the king gold crowns as marks of his Asian victory, most seeking friendship and some asking for his arbitration in local disputes. There were also plenty of Greek delegations, chiefly concerned with how the return of their exiles was to be managed and controlled. Alexander showed a willingness to be sympathetic as long as the overall spirit of his decision was honored.[8]

Some of this goodwill was a response to the readiness with which many cities introduced the hero cult for Hephaestion, as well as a divine cult for Alexander himself. This had started early on, cities setting up statues and altars to Alexander just as they had done to Philip, often in association with a god. Acceptance of his claim as son of Zeus Ammon was also a good way to secure his favor, whether either father or son took the matter seriously or simply saw it as a formal mark of respect and loyalty. Alongside the decree permitting exiles to return home, Alexander's envoy to the Olympic Games had also expressed the king's desire for some form of divine honors in mainland Greece. This may partly have acted as a reminder of his power, and an encouragement to do whatever he asked. Like all Alexander's inner thoughts, there is no way of knowing whether he had come to see himself as fully divine and not simply in some mystical way special because he was part sired by Zeus Ammon. The impression from Athenian sources is that the reaction in Greece was pragmatic, and they were willing enough to vote for a cult if that is what the king wanted and far more concerned to get concessions from him about more practical issues. Demosthenes is supposed to have said that Alexander could be Zeus and Poseidon if he wanted. There is no trace of any of these cults springing from deep emotion. One fourth century BC source depicted Alexander routinely dressing up as different gods, wearing the horns of Ammon, and even the bow and quiver of the goddess Artemis as he rode around in a chariot, but the general unreliability of the author in question and the failure of anyone else to mention it make it highly unlikely.[9]

––––––––

Ultimately, there is no way of knowing what was in Alexander's mind or the minds of his senior subordinates during his final months. Our sources tell us a little about his activities, which were dominated by preparations for the Arabian campaign scheduled to begin in the summer of 323 BC. Inevitably, they are most preoccupied with a succession of omens foreshadowing what was to come. A little earlier one officer, nervous of his own future and the king's favor, had asked his diviner brother to sacrifice in the hope of learning Alexander's fate and his own. A first sacrifice forecast serious peril for Hephaestion and a second the same danger for the king. His loyalty trumping any fear that his curiosity would seem hostile, the man sent word to Alexander, but the news arrived the day after Hephaestion's death. The king took the warning seriously and thanked the man for his honesty and concern.[10]

During a voyage, Alexander's hat with the royal diadem was blown from his head by the wind. A sailor dived into the river and swam to rescue it, putting the headgear on his own head to keep it dry while he struggled against the current. With the approval of his advisors, Alexander rewarded the man with a talent and then had him flogged (and in some accounts executed) for his presumption in wearing the royal insignia. In the spring as he returned to Babylon, he was warned by the Chaldeans not to approach the city from the usual direction as signs had shown that this would bring him ill fortune. Alexander took the warning seriously, until an attempt to enter via another route proved impractical for the column and he reverted to the usual road. Later, when he had left his throne and gone to get a drink, an unknown man wandered in and sat in his place; the eunuchs were prevented by a Persian royal taboo from touching anyone sitting on the throne, so wailed and beat their chests, but did not remove him. When subsequently arrested, the man claimed under torture to have no idea how he got there or why he had acted as he did. As always, it is just possible that some incidents actually occurred, even if the majority were invented or at the very least embellished in later years. In other respects Alexander was busy and satisfied, investigating, inspecting, and issuing orders, watching warships race on the river. The attack on Arabia was to be a major effort with every prospect of becoming yet another great success, although in fact it was never launched.[11]

The realization that Roxane was pregnant for the second time was another piece of good news for the king, although less important than it would become. In spite of his wounds, Alexander appeared healthy and with every prospect of living on for many years, and had this happened these months would no doubt have been skimmed over as no more than the lull between campaigns. Instead, knowing that his life would soon end, scholars have searched in our sources for any hint about his mood, and when the evidence fails, have speculated. Those inclined to see an Alexander ever more prey to paranoid suspicion paint a picture of a nervous court. From this viewpoint, replacing Antipater and summoning the old man to Persia was a prelude to his denunciation and death for disloyalty, and he must have realized or at least feared this outcome. Yet if this was so, it is odd that Craterus did not hurry to reach Macedonia, leading to further speculation that he was in secret communication with Antipater and probably other senior officers. In this interpretation Alexander's generals were all living in fear of the calculating and ruthless monarch, weary of war but seeing no end to their leader's insatiable lust for conquest.[12]

None of this is impossible—all of it is speculation. Soon after Alexander's death rumors spread of assassination, fueled by the power struggles that followed as rivals tried to blacken their opponents. The most common tradition blamed Antipater, and claimed that his son Cassander had carried poison with him on his journey to court. This was water from the river Styx, which led to the Underworld, ice-cold and always fatal if drunk and so dangerous and hard to contain that he had to hide it in a special compartment hollowed out in a mule's hoof. His younger brother, Iolaus, was already with the king, serving as his cup bearer, and it was he who administered the poison. Six years later, Iolaus had already died, and Olympias had his tomb desecrated, blaming the youth for murdering her son, and others may have chosen to believe it. Modern studies have come to various conclusions, and speculated over whether there was a poison available at the time that would have killed the king in the way described. Others apart from Antipater and his family have been blamed for the alleged murder, acting in concert with Antipater or independently, and one author even decided that Roxane was the murderer, fearing that she would be supplanted by Alexander's new, more distinguished wives. Assassination was a common enough cause of death for any Argead king, so in itself the idea is in no way shocking, although the usual method was an open attack rather than poison. Yet none of the cases for murder or motive are strong, and without better evidence it is far easier to accept that the king died of natural causes, which is the position of the majority of scholars in the field.[13]

Further debate concerns the Royal Journal or Ephimerides, which is quoted by several sources, but only for details from the final year of Alexander's life. This need not mean that these authors had access to the original or a copy. As it stands, the Journal offers a record of his daily activities, and in the selection we have has an emphasis on drinking parties, often naming his host, or claiming that on the next day the king slept late. Alexander's consumption of alcohol may have been less prominent in the full Journal, whose length and coverage is unclear, but the importance given to this in the snippets we have has led to suggestions that the text was tampered with or invented after his death. Portraying the dead king as prone to drunken binges—for instance with five parties in one month, all leaving him badly hungover and barely able to function on the next day—might have been useful to generals seeking power, since it suggested that Alexander had degenerated and that everyone would be better off under a sober leader. Yet fraud seems unlikely, and nor should we judge a Macedonian attitude toward royal revelry by modern standards of behavior. In 324 BC Alexander had granted Caranus his wish to commit suicide by turning his self-immolation into a grand ceremony. Soon afterward, prominent members of the army held a drinking contest as part of a feast, the victor and several others dying as a result. Macedonia's aristocracy, like their Thessalian neighbors, had a hard-drinking culture, alien to southern Greeks, and it is doubtful that they thought less of Philip or Alexander for their drunkenness.[14]

One tradition even had Alexander's final illness beginning after a similar drinking contest at a party, although this is not in the more detailed accounts of Plutarch and Arrian, each claiming to draw on the Journal. On a night at the end of May 323 BC, Alexander attended a party held by Nearchus, drinking and eating heavily. On his way back to the palace he encountered Medius, a Thessalian from Larissa, who persuaded him to join a second party being held in his apartments. Medius is rarely mentioned in a military capacity, but he was a Companion and was accused of being an eager sycophant. Alexander was persuaded and joined in a drinking session until the small hours. Eventually he left, bathed and slept, and the next day once again feasted with Medius, but while drinking a toast with unmixed wine became feverish, cried out, and felt a stabbing pain in his back.[15]

In spite of this he spent the following day once again celebrating with Medius, although because of his fever he slept in the cool of his bathing room. On the next day he made sacrifice as was his duty as king, and Arrian says that he had to be carried in a litter, and spent the rest of the day chatting and playing dice with some of his Companions. In the evening he held a conference with senior officers, discussing the Arabian expedition that was due to begin in three days' time. He slept poorly that night because of his fever, having been carried across the river to the royal gardens. Next morning he bathed and sacrificed. Plutarch says that he spent the day with Medius, while Arrian has him lying in the bathing room and listening to Nearchus tell of his adventures at sea. Probably he did both, but the night was another bad one, with his fever raging. He managed to bathe the next morning, most likely sacrificed, although this is not specifically mentioned, and spoke to Nearchus and other officers to arrange the plan for the fleet's role in the expedition.

The king's fever grew worse, and was especially bad throughout the next day, although he still managed some discussion with his commanders. Things did not improve, and on the following day he had to be carried everywhere, as he bathed and sacrificed. He still spoke to his officers, made decisions about promotions. Significantly, the fleet did not set out as it was scheduled to do. The next morning he again needed to be carried as he went to sacrifice. The same iron willpower that had driven him on over mountains and through deserts made him once again meet with his officers, but there were limits. On the following day he was taken from the gardens back to the palace. The fever was far worse and he was unable to speak. Word spread through the army, and the soldiers wanted to see their king and know whether he still lived. The next day a large number of them were admitted to the palace and allowed to file through his bedroom. Alexander could not speak, although with effort he signaled his recognition by expression and gesture. A group of officers held an all-night vigil in the Temple of Serapis, and asked whether the king should be taken to the temple. The answer from the priests was no, perhaps nervous of being blamed if he died in their precinct.[16]

Alexander spent the remainder of his life in the palace, barely conscious and unable to speak. He died in the evening of the following day. Given the uncertainty about so many details of his life, let alone of his father's, it should occasion little surprise that there is doubt over the date. Most scholars have favored June 10, 323 BC, although others opt for the eleventh or twelfth. He was a few weeks short of his thirty-third birthday and had reigned for a little under thirteen years. The sources do not give sufficient reliable detail for an accurate diagnosis of the disease. This has not prevented a range of suggestions, with malaria one of the most common, but extending to typhoid and a number of rare conditions. Alexander had been thought on the brink of death when he suffered from fever outside Tarsus in 333 BC, and later after his arrow wound in India, just as Philip had narrowly survived bouts of serious illness. Chance played a role on each occasion, and the cumulative cost of successive wounds had made him more vulnerable than in the past, while his heavy drinking made any condition worse. During the course of their campaigns Alexander and his men had crossed through a great range of climates and environments, inevitably coming into contact with unfamiliar bacteria and viruses. No source records losses from disease in the years or hints that Alexander died as part of an epidemic, so he may simply have been unfortunate.[17]

His senior officers must have realized that the illness was serious within a few days, and soon that death was likely. The Mallian arrow wound had given everyone a recent reminder that Alexander was mortal and could die at any time. Men who rise high in any political system, let alone the Macedonian court, naturally gave thought to the future, constantly reassessing their own position and prospects in the case of any likely occurrence. The vast majority could remember Alexander's accession, and a fair few the chaotic years leading up to Philip becoming king. The king's death from battle accident, disease, or plot was always a possibility. At the very least his senior courtiers had several days to adjust to the likelihood that Alexander's death was near. How much the sick man realized is harder to say. It was claimed that he handed over his signet ring to Perdiccas, the bodyguard who had replaced Hephaestion as *chiliarch* (although the senior hipparchy had kept the latter's name and standard as an act of commemoration). A story circulated that in his dying moments Alexander had been asked to whom he bequeathed his empire, and was able to whisper "to the strongest" or "to the most worthy." There was another story that he prophesied that there were to be great funeral games over his corpse, referring to the great wars between his would-be Successors that actually did follow his death. Given that he was unable to speak in the last days, neither of these claims is convincing so cannot be reliable guides to Alexander's mindset.

Perdiccas emerged during the following days as the most prominent of the senior officers at Babylon, whether because Alexander had marked him out in some way or simply reflecting his existing influence. There was no clear successor to the throne. The king's half brother Arrhidaeus was with the army, having been summoned at some point late in Alexander's reign, but had always been considered unfit to rule. Perdiccas backed Roxane's unborn child in the hope that the baby would survive and prove to be both a boy and suited to rule. Nearchus spoke up for Barsine's son Herakles, as an already existing son of Alexander, if an illegitimate one. In either case an infant could not govern, which meant that the king would need guidance by a regent for many years to come, and this man would need to be strong to enforce his will. Nearchus had no significant support in the wider army, which meant that the idea was swiftly dismissed.

The first serious opposition to Perdiccas came from Meleager, commander of one of the phalanx regiments since at least the Battle of the Granicus, who became the spokesman for the bulk of the Macedonian infantry. Reluctant to accept a king Alexander had fathered with a barbarian wife, he proclaimed Arrhidaeus to be a true Argead, son of Philip and already an adult and the natural king. For a while, Perdiccas and most of the other aristocrats left Babylon with the cavalry, until the army was reconciled and for the moment it was agreed that Arrhidaeus and Roxane's child, if a boy, would become joint kings. A formal purification ceremony was held to mark this harmony, and by tradition the soldiers marched between two halves of a sacrificed dog. Sacrifice and parade culminated in the arrest of 300 agitators from the infantry and the murder of Meleager, even though he had taken refuge in a temple.[18]

This was the start of the bloodletting, but the full story of Alexander's "funeral games" is too long and far too convoluted to be told here. A flavor of these decades of strife comes from the fate of many of the key players, most of whom died violently. Perdiccas was killed in a mutiny by his own soldiers during a botched campaign to overrun Egypt. Craterus was thrown from his horse during a battle against an army under Eumenes, and either kicked to death by his own mount or felled by an allied soldier who did not recognize him. Eumenes lasted longer, but failed to win later battles and was eventually given up by his men and executed. Arrhidaeus, or Philip III as he was renamed, was never more than a puppet for others, ruling for six years and four months before his army defected to join a force led by Olympias; he was stabbed to death by his Thracian guards. The apparent vulnerability of Macedonia after Alexander's death, combined with old and new resentments—the exiles' decree a fresh reminder—prompted Athens and many Greek cities to assert their independence. Antipater defeated them in the Lamian War, which was over by the end of 322 BC. Demosthenes, convicted of taking bribes from Harpalus, had returned from exile for the conflict, but fled again after this latest military defeat and committed suicide by taking poison.

This was an era when the royal women played very public roles, leading and inspiring armies. Olympias also killed Arrhidaeus's wife—Philip's granddaughter—Adea Eurydice. The latter's mother, Cynane, was murdered by an erstwhile ally as they took an army into Asia; the act horrified the soldiers and prompted mutiny and the ally's overthrow. Olympias was in turn defeated by Cassander and executed, although he had trouble finding willing execution-ers. Roxane arranged the murder of Darius's daughter Stateira, and played a prominent role as mother of Alexander's son, Alexander IV, although both were essentially figureheads without real power. The boy managed to live until he was about fourteen, on the cusp of manhood and an independence that would have been embarrassing to the dynasts who had come to an uneasy truce. Cassander had held the boy and his mother in comfortable imprisonment for some time, and had them quietly murdered, the secret taking a while to leak out, by which time it no longer really mattered. A year later Cassander arranged the murders of Barsine and Herakles; their willingness to live in virtual obscurity had saved them until they once again were noticed. Alexander's sister Cleopatra was the last to be killed, and the Argead line was ended as new dynasties established themselves.

Cassander was one of the winners, at least for a while, dying of natural causes in 297 BC, after building on the strong position inherited from his father, Antipater, who had earlier succumbed to age and illness in 319 BC. Antigonus Gonatus, who barely figures in the narratives of Philip and Alexander's campaigns, was another general who founded a dynasty, as did Ptolemy and Seleucus, who had both spent more time campaigning with Alexander and been fairly prominent in the later years. It took a while for all of the key players to move from presenting themselves as merely army leaders or regional satraps loyal to the incapable Arrhidaeus and underage Alexander IV and to emerge as kings in their own right. In the longer run three major kingdoms emerged, with the Antigonids in Macedonia, the Ptolemies in Egypt, and the Seleucids in the east, but there were also a number of smaller kingdoms, sometimes dominated by larger neighbors and sometimes independent. Thus Alexander's empire was dismembered, scarcely surviving his death in any way as one unit. Some territory was lost, notably in India where Chandragupta, a man of talent and ambition to match Philip and Alexander, carved out a great kingdom for himself in the last decades of the fourth century BC. Yet there was no widespread drive to independence from the conquerors, and it was not until the second century BC that a new "eastern" empire began to emerge with the rise of the Parthians. While no longer a single kingdom, the bulk of Alexander's empire would remain under rule by Macedonian Successor states for generations to come.

The new dynasties looked to Alexander for legitimacy and prestige, so his image became far more commonly used after his death. During his lifetime Alexander had put his name on coinage, but tended to favor images of Athena or Hercules. Late in life, in commemoration of his Indian campaign, series of coins were minted at Babylon showing him on horseback charging Porus atop an elephant, and on the reverse Alexander standing triumphant, the thunderbolt of Zeus in his hand while Nike, goddess of victory, presents him with a wreath. Other series released at the same time showed an elephant, chariot, or Indian warrior with his tall bow, emphasizing the exotic nature of the defeated enemy. If Alexander felt thwarted by his troops' unwillingness to push farther south in India, he nevertheless chose to celebrate success in this way. Yet the thunderbolt, which Apelles had painted him wielding all those years before at Ephesus, was a rare divine symbol connected with him during his lifetime, not part of a concerted campaign. After his death, the competing factions were far less restrained, using Alexander's image as a badge of legitimacy, and freely depicting him wearing a cap with the horns of Ammon, or as Hercules. In due course most of the monarchs of the Successor kingdoms proclaimed themselves as divine in their own right. Although the Argead line was extinguished, the Successors adopted many of the symbols and behavior of their predecessors.

Alexander's memory mattered, especially now that he was dead, because that meant that it could be manipulated and was unencumbered by the king himself. This meant that some of his unpopular actions could be sifted out to create an idealized figurehead. In the early days, for example, Perdiccas read out to the army a series of plans that he claimed Alexander had intended, ranging from grandiose and staggeringly expensive plans for further campaigns involving vast armies and great fleets, to spectacular monuments for Hephaestion and a tomb bigger than a pyramid for Philip. While he may have been selective in what he told them, and presented it in an unfavorable manner, it is unlikely that he could have simply invented everything. He and the other commanders appear to have been well satisfied when all the projects were rejected by the assembly of soldiers, but the men's love for Alexander remained deep. At the start of the funeral games, all of the best troops were Alexander's men, not least the "silver shields," the survivors of the hypaspists led by Philip and Alexander to so many victories. By the Battle of Gabiene in 317 BC, it is claimed that most of these men were in their seventies, yet they still routed all before them, and, when the rest of their army was defeated, they marched off the field in good order, brushing aside any opposition.[19]

Alexander became a symbol and an inspiration. Just as the Successors battled to prove themselves worthy of the great conqueror's memory and thus of his power, they even squabbled over Alexander's corpse. This was embalmed in the Egyptian style, apparently according to the king's own wishes, although when he expressed the desire is unclear. Plans were made to carry him in state back to Macedonia for burial; presumably this was to be with the rest of the dynasty at Vergina, although it is tempting to suggest that the massive tomb recently discovered at Amphipolis was meant as his final resting place. The sheer scale of this monument dwarfs other Macedonian tombs, and has perhaps its closest parallel in the later mausoleum of the Emperor Augustus, which may well be significant. Not until in 321–320 BC did Alexander's body begin its final journey, only for the procession to be intercepted in Syria by a force sent by Ptolemy, who diverted it to Egypt, claiming that this had been the dead conqueror's intention. Whether or not this was true, he secured the body and either he or his son interred it in a tomb in Alexandria, where it remained, although the location has long since been lost.

Epilogue

TEARS AND A BROKEN NOSE

When Julius Caesar was thirty-eight he was appointed governor of one of Rome's Spanish provinces, which was a reasonably prestigious post for a Roman senator at this stage in a career. It was his first independent command, and he took the opportunity to fight an aggressive campaign against local tribes, winning a victory big enough to secure him the honor of a triumph on his return. According to Plutarch, during a rare moment of leisure during this posting, Caesar read from a history of Alexander—which one, he does not say. To the amazement of his friends, the usually poised and confident Roman governor was very quiet until he burst into tears. When he had recovered sufficiently to answer their questions, Caesar explained that Alexander had made himself king of so many nations at such a young age, while he was older and had so far performed no great deeds. The roughly contemporary Suetonius recorded a variation of this story, which had a younger Caesar on an earlier posting to Spain sighing when he saw a statue of Alexander at Gades (modern Cadiz), and then being spurred on to hurry his own career.[1]

Soon afterward Caesar conquered Gaul in a decade, bridging the Rhine and landing in Britain in the process, and then fought and won the Civil War, becoming sole leader of the Roman Republic and its empire. Plutarch chose to pair Alexander with Caesar as the greatest Greek and Roman commanders and leaders in his series of paired biographies, traditionally known as the *Parallel Lives*. The comparison seemed equally natural to Appian, another Roman citizen of Greek origins and culture who wrote in the early second century AD. No other Roman leader came anywhere near matching Alexander, although some had tried. Pompey was styled Magnus, "the great," and took great pride in wearing a cloak supposedly once owned by Alexander when he celebrated one of his triumphs at Rome. Yet ultimately he lost to Caesar in the civil war, fleeing to Egypt where he was murdered on the orders of a descendant of Ptolemy.

Caesar was the Roman Alexander, or at least the closest the Romans could boast. While ten years to overrun Gaul was impressive, his campaigns could not truly match the sheer scale and fame of conquering Persia. Alexander was not simply "the great" to the Romans, but the greatest, at least when it came to military prowess. Livy, a Roman historian who wrote late in the first century BC, devoted a lot of space to the Second Punic War, when the Carthaginian Hannibal inflicted horrendous losses on the Romans, who only prevailed after a grueling struggle. Hannibal was beaten just once in the open field, at Zama in North Africa in 202 BC, a Roman victory that finally brought the war to an end. A few years later, an exiled Hannibal was at the court of a king of Asia Minor when he met Roman ambassadors, including Scipio Africanus, the man who had bested him at Zama. The encounter itself may actually have happened, and although the reports of what was said must be treated with as much caution as so many of the anecdotes about Philip or Alexander, Livy's version does seem to reflect a widespread Roman attitude. He claims that Scipio asked Hannibal to name the greatest generals of all time. Without hesitation, he placed Alexander first, followed by King Pyrrhus of Epirus (one of the most famous leaders from the second generation of Successor warlords), and then Hannibal himself. Asked what he would say if he had beaten the Romans at Zama, the Carthaginian declared that in that case he should be named first—an answer Livy declared to be typical of Punic artfulness, since it flattered both the speaker and his former enemy.[2]

This is a book about both Philip and his more famous son, but inevitably when it comes to ancient or modern attitudes to them, it is Alexander who receives nearly all the attention. Philip saved a weak Macedonia from dismemberment or at the very least domination by external powers, then built up and expanded his kingdom and its power until he in turn dominated not simply his neighbors, but most of Greece. Thus he created the circumstances that allowed Alexander to hurl himself at the Persian Empire and vanquish it. Without Philip there could have been no Alexander, at least not one who conquered so much so quickly, but in a way the son had little choice. Philip's Macedonia was based on the bond between king and subjects, which was expressed primarily in the form of the army, and his economy—if it can be dignified with the term—revolved around gaining new resources and income, only to spend them in order to expand his power and gain more wealth in the process, funding the next war, and so on. Preparations for the Persian expedition came close to draining the kingdom's wealth, even after all that Philip had done to augment his revenue.

There is not the slightest sign of reluctance on Alexander's part as he led the attack on Persia, and throughout his adult life he reveled in war and conquest. Glory mattered to Alexander, and it is easy to take this for granted and see his personality as the sole driving force in his planning. Certainly, his lust for glory was an important motive and gave an urgency to the wars he fought, but in truth he had little choice. Under Philip, Macedonia fought a campaign almost every year, and most of the time was at war with several opponents, and he passed seamlessly from being the underdog fighting for survival to the aggressor absorbing other communities. That was the way in the Greek world, where alliances were as readily made as broken, and the status and self-esteem of each polis rose or fell as perception of others' power changed. As he became more and more successful, Philip's strength became a challenge to others. Thus the temptation grew to exploit any opportunity to weaken him, which meant that Macedonia and its king could never afford to seem weak or vulnerable.

The balance of power in Greece was fluid, not least because as much or more depended on perception than the real strength of states, and because the balance was always being tested. Cities and factions within them bickered constantly, so there were permanent rivalries and frequent appeals to outside powers for aid. If ever Philip did not intervene, then others might, making them seem stronger and more influential, and the same was true for any other leader or state. As he expanded, he became directly involved with more and more communities over an ever widening area, and perceived as someone willing and able to help those who appealed to him. Unless Greek interstate and internal rivalries came to an abrupt end, then anyone with pretensions to power, whether Philip or Athens or Thebes, had to intervene, constantly needing to display power in order to preserve it.

Philip created a strong Macedonia based around war and expansion, and it is unlikely that he could have stopped waging war, other than to have a brief pause as he prepared for the next one. Being a man of his times, it is doubtful that he even considered the possibility; it was simply natural to dominate or be dominated. Isocrates and the other Panhellenists hoped to export the Greeks' aggressive instinct by conquering Persia, and afterward give all Greeks—or at least all who mattered—land and serfs to ensure such a comfortable life that they would have no need to fight again. The dream was never a convincing one. Under Alexander the conquest was achieved, but relatively few Greeks or Macedonians wanted to live in Asia permanently, and he was not inclined to reduce all Asians to no more than a slave work force, toiling for the sake of their new overlords. The Panhellenists had always ignored the lesson of Sparta, whose helot population was essential to the functioning of the state but was treated so badly that it posed a permanent threat to the city's stability. Alexander made no attempt to introduce anything resembling this on a large scale, which would have been bound to provoke resistance and rebellion.

Alexander's love for Homer and emulation of Achilles, and later even more Hercules and Dionysus, are well known and there is no good reason to doubt that they were important throughout his life. He craved glory and was determined to excel in his achievements. Yet this should not hide the basic truth that he would have been no more able to stop waging war than Philip. On accession he was vulnerable, largely unproven, and at the very least needed to demonstrate that he had the military and political skills, as well as the ruthlessness and sheer luck, of his father. Abandoning the planned Persian war would have risked making him seem weak and lacking in confidence, and as usual the slightest hint of vulnerability was bound to invite other states to test the new king. Destroying Thebes was a warning, but another lesson of Greek history was that deterrents did not last very long if the willingness and ability to repeat the same terrible example was not clear to everyone.

Philip created and Alexander led a Macedonia geared to war and expansion, which meant that neither of them had much choice other than to keep fighting. While Philip was prouder of his diplomatic achievements than his military successes, there is no hint that he did not accept war as both natural and enjoyable, while his son clearly relished battle. On balance the only real chance to break the cycle came when Alexander returned from India. Certainly, many of his officers and soldiers believed that the time was right for, at the very least, a significant pause before the next round of conquest. Financially Alexander was secure, with not simply the looted treasuries of Darius, but the income of tax and tribute from his vast new empire; he did not need another war to pay the expenses of the one he had so recently won.

Yet Alexander did not choose to stop, and only his illness and death prevented the launch of his grand Arabian campaign. It is impossible to know how secure his hold was on the former Persian Empire and the rest of his conquests, whether there was the prospect of widespread rebellion or whether Alexander believed that there was, hence his desire to keep the most warlike part of the population busy fighting for him rather than against him. Here personality was of vital importance, and the sources depict a king with an insatiable longing for fresh and ever greater glory. Some of the same driving forces remained as true as ever, for the loyalty of his subjects was primarily shown by the army, which had never been at rest for any length of time, and was accustomed to victory and the rewards of promotion and wealth it brought. It was a relationship under strain after such unprecedented success and the king's drift away from being first and foremost leader of Macedon and its people to become ruler of an empire with its center in Asia, but it had not wholly broken. Habit was important for them all, not least Alexander, for throughout his life Macedonia had been at war, and as king he had fought and had very little experience of peace, stability, and a life not spent on campaign. The end to constant expansion came only with the Successors, although that did not mean an end to warfare.

Philip and Alexander were men of their times, warrior kings acclaimed by the clashing of weapons against shields by the assembled Macedonians and expected to take risks as they led these men into battle. There is little to be gained by judging them by modern standards, turning them into heroes or villains according to the latest fashion. They lived in a world where it was expected that the strong would expand and dominate whenever and wherever they were able. Democratic Athens was no more peace-loving or any less self-centered and ruthless in its international relations than either Philip or Alexander, nor was any other state or leader. In a world of predators, Philip and his son proved far more successful than anyone else, but their behavior was not fundamentally different. That does not excuse the human cost of their careers, with so many dead, enslaved, or occupied, and only places it in context of the similar aggression by Athens, Sparta, Thebes, countless smaller city-states, as well as the kings of Persia or India.

Comparison between Philip and Alexander as individuals is of little greater value, not least because the evidence for what each man was truly like as a person is so weak and also different in nature. Livy's Hannibal ranks the greatest commanders, and such discussion is common enough among enthusiasts today as well as academics; one way of expressing dislike and criticism of Alexander is to contrast him with Philip and portray his father as the greater statesman or king. Yet the context of each man's reign was different. While Philip showed a greater fondness for diplomacy than his son, this may have reflected his weaker position, especially in the first half of his reign, as much as temperament. Alexander's military campaigns were on far grander scale than Philip's, and his talent as a leader and general are widely accepted even by his critics. From the ancient world onward, it has usually been assumed that the son was the better general, although this is as subjective as Hannibal's supposed judgment. No one can ever know how Alexander would have coped had he become king in the same circumstances as Philip, or how the father would have waged the war against Persia if he had not been murdered. Nothing quite like the Macedonian army had existed before, and with any military revolution it takes time for opponents to understand the new way of fighting and begin to cope with it.[3]

Both men were able, and Alexander won the war planned and prepared by Philip. One of the greatest differences between the two was the starting point of their careers. Alexander inherited so much from his father and made the most of it. Yet Philip's legacy was also a burden, for it meant that his heir had at the very least to equal and ideally surpass his achievements. Anything less suggested weakness, for in a sense power and reputation in this era reflects modern economic analysis, where anything less than strong growth is seen as failure. Weakness invited attack from outsiders, and also from internal rivals, and in Argead Macedonia the latter tended to be far more deadly. Thus whether or not Alexander ever said anything along these lines, there was an inner truth in the story that he lamented news of his father's latest victory. Philip's successes kept raising the bar of achievement for his son in a culture that so cherished competition and glory. If Alexander's pursuit of glory seems extravagant, then he had to do so much before he could hope to match Philip, especially when so many of his officers and soldiers were his father's men. Neither of his own sons lived long enough to face the even greater challenge of living up to Alexander.

Saying this is one thing, but saying what it all meant to Alexander can never be more than speculation. Philip and Alexander remain hazy figures, their true characters impossible to establish, which will not prevent plenty of people from filling in the vast gaps in the sources to create what they wish to see. There is little or no prospect of a dramatic improvement in this situation, however much we might hope papyri will turn up with lost accounts of contemporaries. It is easier to consider the impact these two men had on their world, although even here it is impossible to know what would have happened had they not done what they did.

The most dramatic consequence was the conquest of the Persian Empire, for even though none of the Successors kept Alexander's realm intact, the bulk of it remained under the control of the new Hellenistic dynasties. Achaemenid Persia was overthrown, and at no stage was there any prospect of widespread rebellion expelling the Macedonian and Greek conquerors from the heartland of their empire. Syria, Asia Minor, and Egypt remained Hellenistic in language and culture for more than a thousand years, until at least the end of the Roman Empire there. In the second century BC a Parthian dynasty began to emerge in Persia itself, throwing off Seleucid control and then withstanding Roman imperialism, but even this preserved aspects of the Hellenistic tradition and a significant number of "Greek" cities endured.

In contrast, most of the Indian conquests did not remain under the control of the Successors for very long, a retreat hastened by the rise of Chandragupta. The situation in Bactria is more complicated, although for several centuries coins attest to many kings with Greek names who used Greek titles and slogans. None are dated and few of the rulers themselves otherwise attested, making it impossible to establish a sequence or relationships between these monarchs. Similarly the extent to which these Bactrian kingdoms were fully independent or subject to rule from the Seleucids is unknown. What they do show is the long-term presence of an elite that was at least culturally Greek and employed the Greek language. In northern Afghanistan lies the remains of a Greek city at Ai Khanoum, with Hellenic fortifications, a theater, and gymnasium. Its ancient name is not certain, but it also came to house a palace, treasury, and library (of works in Greek) for one of the Bactrian kings. This was most definitely a Greek community, and there were others including some in India that continued for generations even though they were certainly not part of any Hellenic kingdom. The Greek influence on Ghandharan art was deep, not least in depiction of humans, including the Buddha, although it was not the sole inspiration in this local merging of several traditions.[4]

Alexander was not solely responsible for all of this. Ai Khanoum may have been founded by him or could as easily have been set up by the Seleucids a generation later. The Seleucid kingdom, and the lesser Bactrian dynasties, preserved and probably expanded the Greek presence and influence, as did ongoing trade. All were there for a long time, as were the descendants of settlers and others who came later, whereas Alexander's visits were brief and busy. Yet he began the process, spreading Hellenic ideas as he overran territory and established colonies to control it. Without him it is unlikely that Greek culture and language would have spread so far or had the chance to take root on such a scale. Although the connection is long and not straightforward, it is worth recalling that as well as the Gospels being written in Greek, Jesus is the Greek form of the Aramaic, originally Hebrew, name Joshua.

Aramaic was the convenient language of administration and long-distance communication for the Persian Empire, and it was largely supplanted for these purposes by Greek, which in itself is a reminder that Alexander's empire was the latest in a long series of empires that had controlled a large part of the same territory. In a sense, the Macedonians were just another people from the fringes of this area, who produced a leader or leaders skilled in war with the ambition to take over. Cyrus and his Persians had begun in much the same way, and although they were from Asia the distinction between easterners and westerners, Europeans and Asians, is overdrawn, even if it has roots in Greek ideas. The Persians had granted a fair degree of local autonomy to regional elites and dynasts, who in turn no doubt let many small communities run their own affairs in the same way they had always done. Practical concerns meant that any conqueror, including the Macedonians and Successors, had to do the same. Thus alongside Greek cities there would be traditional villages where people spoke their own language, worshipped their own gods and followed the same customs as their ancestors.

How far the ideas of the occupying power impinged on day-to-day life of the general population can rarely be traced, beyond the obvious demands for tax, alien laws where the matter involved colonists or the ruler, and use of force against open opposition. In the second century BC resistance to efforts to Hellenize the population of Judaea provoked revolt against the Seleucids and the emergence of the independent Hasmonaean kingdom, which lasted into the

Roman period, although it did not reject all aspects of Greek culture. In Ptolemaic Egypt ancient traditions persisted, the bulk of the population living in villages as they had always done rather than creating cities, and there were two distinct systems of law for Greeks and Egyptians. The former was more generous in the rights it granted citizens and more lenient in its punishments and fines. The only path into government and royal favor for an Egyptian was to learn Greek and adopt a Hellenic lifestyle. The longer-term consequences of Alexander's conquests in the east were complex, and it is hard to say whether the populations within these areas were better or worse off as a consequence of what he and his father had done.

In Greece there was less of a cultural change as a result of Philip and Alexander. The Lamian War fought not long after the latter's death was an attempt to return to the days before Macedon's rise, but it failed. Never again would a single city be able to expand its power and influence over so much of Greece, as Athens, Sparta, and Thebes had done, ending a key aspect of what many Greeks considered freedom, particularly when they belonged to one of the stronger states. The interstate jockeying for power was less volatile as a result, although it did not end. Thebes reemerged when Cassander allowed its remaining citizens to restore their polis in 315 BC. Sparta continued to decline, slowly and stubbornly in the Spartan way, while Athens dreamed of glory but was rarely in a position to match the power of any of the Successor kingdoms.

This was a Greece where the rule of kings was accepted as natural and not an aberration, because the Successor kingdoms were too powerful to ignore. No one city ever again produced such a staggering flourishing of art, ideas, and learning as Athens in its heyday, and culture was shaped by royal courts and later the rule of Rome's emperors. The era of the independent poleis had faded, although the idea of the city remained profoundly important throughout the era of Roman rule. If Macedonia's rise under Philip and Alexander had not occurred or been less complete, then the city-states would surely have gone on bickering and vying for power. None had the capacity or inclination to turn itself into the aggressive military machine created by Philip, which makes it likely that none would have maintained a similar level of dominance. Thus the liberty of Greece was curbed by Philip and Alexander, although whether this was a good or bad thing is arguable. A degree of unity and internal peace was brought about by the Macedonians, and under the Romans it became complete. Creativity would flourish once again, notably in the second century AD, although this was a wider phenomenon and not primarily focused on mainland Greece, and was different in nature, shaped by the autocratic rule of the emperors rather than the ambitions of vibrant city-states. Southern Greece lost a good deal of its freedom to Macedonia, and then all of it to Rome, but in both cases the victor embraced the culture of the defeated—Horace's "captive Greece captured the fierce conqueror."[5]

Macedonia itself was the heart of Philip and Alexander's power, providing the core of their army. Philip revived the kingdom, recovering lost territory, adding more, and ensuring that it was no longer threatened by foreign interventions. His reign lasted longer and became more secure than that of any of his recent predecessors. He also made Macedonia wealthier, and was generous in granting land and money to the aristocracy, which also increased in size. The cost was near constant warfare and upheaval as populations were shifted around to found new communities, but overall the kingdom was stronger, more prosperous, and more stable because of his reign. It was also more confident, especially when it came to the elite and the army, and this pride and high self-esteem mattered a good deal in Macedonian, and for that matter Greek, society.

Under Alexander Macedonia went further in every sense. He spent little of his reign there, for even during the two years before crossing to Asia he was on campaign outside the kingdom most of the time. Wealth flowed back home as a result of his eastern conquests, and the combination of this with Philip's gains is evident in the lavish displays of gold and silver in Macedonian tombs. Pride reached astronomical levels as the young king won victories greater than any in Macedonian or Greek history, and it was seen as fit to compare him to Hercules and Dionysus. All threats to the security of Macedonia—whether from Illyrians or Thracians, or the bigger challenges posed by Agis of Sparta and, immediately after Alexander's death, by the Lamian War—were defeated. Macedonia remained strong and rich even when its king was far away and showed little sign of wanting to return in the near future.

The absence of the king for more than a decade was unprecedented. Some of the state traveled with him, in the form of the majority of his Companions and the army, but Macedonia itself was ruled indirectly and was not his priority. Opinion is divided over how much Alexander's campaigns took from Macedonia, most of all in manpower. The ancient sources attest to the participation of at least 30,000 Macedonian citizens in the expedition to Persia, but some scholars believe that many drafts of reinforcements are not mentioned in these accounts and that the number was significantly higher. Estimates of losses also vary, although no one would dispute that the bulk of soldiers never returned home to settle in Macedonia, not least because of the power struggles between the Successors, all of whom wanted as many veteran troops as possible.

The price of Alexander's glory must always be linked with the long-drawn-out "funeral games" after his death, just as the impact of his conquests may owe as much to the Successor kingdoms. Some of the battles between the Successors involved far larger numbers of troops armed and equipped in Macedonian style than either Philip or Alexander had ever led, and the cost was high. Over time, first the quality and then the numbers declined, and this was most marked in Macedonia itself. There were enough men for Antipater to keep control and defeat any challenges from Greece. Later on, armies were far smaller, and by the time of the confrontation with Rome, kings like Philip V or Perseus were incapable of mustering an army matching the size of the expedition launched in 334 BC. It is quite possible that Alexander's campaigns had a significant demographic impact, not least because taking so many men away (after the leave of the first winter for the newly married) meant that their wives had far fewer children than was otherwise likely. Once again, the prolonged power struggles under the Successors reinforced any trend, and it is impossible to isolate the consequences of these from Alexander's campaigns. Apart from the human cost, it is also striking that later Macedonian armies were proportionately weaker in cavalry, which makes it likely that the warfare under Philip and Alexander caused a decline in horse stocks.[6]

Macedonia in later centuries was never again quite as strong as the kingdom Alexander inherited from his father, so some scholars are inclined to praise Philip for raising Macedonia so high and condemn his son for causing its decline. Most do not bother to note that the kingdom was also never again as weak as it had been when Philip inherited it, so Alexander's legacy was far from swept away. Once again, the role of the Successors is also critical, for the fragments of a divided empire were bound to be weaker than the united whole. Philip's success was based on a severe cull of real and potential rivals for the Argead throne. For a man who married so many wives, he produced just two legitimate sons, one of whom was felt incapable of rule until the army became desperate because Alexander had died without fathering an heir at all—since no one could be sure whether the pregnant Roxane would bear a boy or girl. In the past there had always been plenty of Argeads, who were both a source of upheaval as well as ensuring that there was always a new king available. For some this is another reason to criticize Alexander as inherently self-centered, obsessed with his own glory and with no thought to the future after he had gone. While this is possible, it is worth again noting that even if he had fathered a son at the start of his reign and the boy had survived, he would have been just in his early teens in 323 BC, still too young to assert himself. As importantly, Alexander remained young, was healthy until his final illness in spite of his wounds, and could reasonably have expected to live a long life. No one can know what he might have done if he had survived.

Ultimately there can be no simple verdict about either Philip or Alexander—and as stated at the start, it is not the historian's job to judge their moral worth, for that is best left to individual readers. They were strong and successful by the standards of the day, the son so successful that he overshadows his father. Not all ancient commentators admired them, but they were famous. The unmilitary Cicero joked when he camped near Issus in 51 BC, confessing that Alexander was a better general, and then in 44 BC modeled his speeches attacking Mark Antony on those of Demosthenes attacking

Philip, favoring their style over their lack of success. Writing under Nero, the poet Lucan dubbed Alexander mad, although he did not question the sheer scale of his conquests.

That was something many Roman leaders envied. Memory of Alexander prompted the Emperor Trajan to cry, just like Julius Caesar, in this case as he watched a ship setting out from the Arabian Gulf and knew that he was too old to follow it to India. In the third century AD the Emperor Caracalla formed a legion equipped in what he believed to be the same uniform and weapons as the Macedonian phalanx and planned to emulate Alexander when he attacked the Parthians, the Asian dynasty that had appeared in the old Persian heartlands. Over a century later, another emperor, Julian the Apostate, attacked Persia, play-acting the part of Alexander as much as those of famous Roman commanders. Trajan died not long after he had wept, Caracalla was murdered, and Julian was killed in a skirmish which left his army, without obvious successor, stranded deep in enemy territory. No Roman ever equaled the military success of Alexander, let alone surpassed it, although Julius Caesar came close.[7]

Augustus cultivated a youthful image like Alexander and may have been inspired in his mausoleum by the great tomb at Amphipolis, but he had the sense to admit that he was no military genius, preferring to rely on gifted subordinates. When he had defeated Cleopatra, the last of the Ptolemies, and Mark Antony, a man who liked comparisons with Hercules and Dionysus, the great nephew of Caesar went to the tomb of Alexander in Alexandria. After staring for some time, he reached out to touch the mummified corpse—and accidentally snapped off part of Alexander's nose. Asked whether he wished to see the tombs of the Ptolemies, he dismissively said that he had come to see "a king, not corpses."[8]

Alexander achieved immense fame, so much so that books like this one still tell his story more than twenty-three centuries later. Philip made that achievement possible and his own career was remarkable in its own right. Between them they changed Macedonia, changed Greece, and changed the history of the wider world. Whether for good or ill, there is no doubt that they mattered and that their stories are well worth telling, for all that there is so much about them and their times that we cannot know. Neither was unambiguously a good man to say the very least, but the title "the great," if understood as important and not necessarily good, is one that both deserve. They were human beings, like us, if from a different age, as were those around them. Their personalities were often veiled at the time, as is the case with any leader, and are now unreachable; all that Augustus achieved in touching the remains of the famous king was to break the mummy's nose rather than sense some essence of the dead man. The human beings are gone, and the memory of what Philip and Alexander did is all that remains.[9]

APPENDIX 1

The Main Sources

AESCHINES (dates c. 397–322 BC). Athenian politician, who although of comparatively humble stock became a highly influential speaker in the Athenian Assembly. In his early life he performed hoplite service as part of his duties as a citizen, and was later a well-known actor before turning to politics. His surviving speeches include a good deal about Athens, Philip, Alexander, and Macedon, but are clouded by their context of conflict with Demosthenes.

ARRIAN (full name Lucius Flavius Arrianus, dates c. AD 86–160). Arrian came from the city of Nicomedia in Bithynia (modern northern Turkey) and studied philosophy from a young age. A Roman citizen, he attracted the attention of the Emperor Hadrian and was appointed to the Roman Senate, later serving as governor of Cappadocia from AD 131–137, an unusually long term in an important military province. Apart from his interest and writings on philosophical questions, he produced a number of histories, but only his *Anabasis of Alexander* and the short companion piece about India, the *Indike*, have survived in anything more than fragments. He also wrote short pieces describing the tactics he intended to employ with the Cappadocian legions in an engagement with the nomadic Alans, who appear to have withdrawn in the face of his advance, and a manual discussing modern Roman cavalry tactics alongside those of the Macedonian phalanx.

Arrian's *Anabasis* is the most complete, detailed, and sober narrative of Alexander's reign. In recent decades, the traditional faith in his reliability has come under attack, although in each case the critics only argue that sometimes alternative accounts are to be preferred.

CURTIUS (full name Quintus Curtius Rufus; dates uncertain, but most likely wrote under the Emperor Claudius [AD 41–54]). Little is known about Curtius, other than that he was a historian and rhetorician from an aristocratic Roman family. He wrote a ten-book history of Alexander, most of which has survived. Missing are the first two books, which covered the years up to 333 BC, as well as several large fragments, especially from the later years, but it does cover the period immediately after Alexander's death in some detail. The style is highly rhetorical, with long speeches and debates that were surely created by the author as he felt appropriate. It is generally more critical of Alexander than Arrian's work, although the tone varies. Many scholars assume that Curtius made considerable use of the lost history of Cleitarchus of Alexandria, who may have written as early as the late fourth century BC. Cleitarchus's book was extremely popular in antiquity but was criticized for its sensationalist tone and unreliability, which partly explains its popularity. However, it is a mistake to see Curtius as wholly dependent on any one source for he clearly put his own stamp on the subject matter. For instance, rightly or wrongly Curtius does appear to have seen reflections of Roman treason trials in his own era in the disputes within Alexander's court.

DEMOSTHENES (dates 384–322 BC). Widely revered in the ancient world as Athens's finest orator, he was the subject of a biography by Plutarch, and hence more is known about his personal life than is the case for the other sources. Thus Plutarch tells us about the misuse of his inheritance by his guardians, and of his long study and practice at public speaking. A considerable number of speeches also survive (as well as a few attributed to him that were probably delivered by other like-minded speakers), many of which deal with Philip and subsequently Alexander. His passion and skill with words are obvious, although understandably he was not impartial or scrupulously honest when arguing a case. Like Aeschines, Demosthenes's version of events needs to be treated with skepticism, but nevertheless it provides an all too rare contemporary opinion concerning events and personalities.

DIODORUS (known as Diodorus Siculus, or "of Sicily"; dates uncertain, but appears to have written in the middle of the first century BC). A Greek from Sicily who spent a good deal of time in Rome, Diodorus wrote a *Library*, a universal history in forty books going from the earliest times down to 60 BC. Its focus was primarily Greece, with more about the western Greeks of Sicily than is common, and then increasingly on the Roman empire. Only a small fraction of this work survives, but it includes Book Sixteen, which offers the fullest account of Philip's reign, and most of Book Seventeen, which deals with Alexander—albeit with a substantial section missing that covered the campaigns in Bactria. Diodorus also left the fullest surviving account of the early period of the Successors. While important, his style varies considerably, as does his probable reliability, and both may well reflect the sources he used.

JUSTIN (full name probably Marcus Junianus Justinus; dates highly uncertain, with second or third century AD possible, but also a strong case for the fourth century AD). Justin produced an *Epitome* of the lost *Philippic Histories* written by Pompeius Trogus, a Gallo-Roman author who flourished in the early first century AD. Trogus's work was wide ranging, covering some early Near Eastern history but focusing on Macedon and the Successor kingdoms, as well as substantial passages about the Parthians, Rome, Gaul, and Spain. Justin's version is brief, sometimes apparently confused, and raises more questions than it answers, but it is the only source for some years.

PLUTARCH (full name possibly Lucius Mestrius Plutarchus; dates c. AD 50–120, although he may have been born earlier and died later). Plutarch was a Greek from Chaeronea, near the site of Philip's great victory in 338 BC. A Roman citizen, it is possible that he held some posts in imperial service. More certainly he taught and wrote, traveled widely, and spent at least three decades as a priest of Apollo at Delphi. He wrote a collection of *Parallel Lives*, pairing a notable Greek with a notable Roman, and reflects the merging of Greco-Roman culture under Roman rule. Twenty-three pairs survive, although four, including Caesar and Alexander, do not have the introductions and conclusions comparing and contrasting the subjects. His *Alexander* is a major source, and like the other lives concentrates on personal details more than political and military matters, since Plutarch believed these to be more revealing about character. There are also snippets of material in some of the other lives, most notably *Demosthenes* and *Phocion*. Plutarch also wrote on a wide range of subjects, and there is much information contained in these, such as his *On the Fortune of Alexander*.

STRABO (dates late first century BC to first century AD). Strabo wrote a seventeen-book *Geography* that is our best overview of many of the regions where Philip and Alexander campaigned. It contains more useful nuggets of information than narrative, but these are sometimes helpful.

APPENDIX 2

The Royal Tombs at Vergina/Aegae

In 1977 and 1978, a team under Professor Andronikos dug into the great mound at Vergina, now confidently identified as the ancient Macedonian capital of Aegae, "the place of goats." The archaeologists excavated a tumulus within this later mound and found that it contained three tombs. From the location and scale of the burials, these surely belonged to the royal family, and since it is quite possible that one of the occupants is Philip, it is worth summarizing the evidence for the identification.

TOMB I. This was a cist burial, roofed with limestone slabs, and had been broken into and plundered in antiquity—perhaps when Pyrrhus occupied Aegae in 274–273 BC. Cist tombs began to be replaced by vaulted tombs in grander burials around the middle of the fourth century BC. Therefore, some have suggested a date of c. 375–350 BC for Tomb I, and most favor the early part of the range. The occupants were a mature man, a young woman (aged about eighteen based on dental analysis), and a very young baby. The man was unusually tall at over six feet. None of the bones had been cremated. The remains may have been the original corpses or perhaps were deposited later during a reuse of the tomb as a burial place. The wall paintings are akin in quality and style to those in the other tombs, suggesting that the original occupant was royal and probably a ruling king.

TOMB II. Rather than the traditional cist, this was a vaulted tomb, divided into a main chamber and an antechamber. It had not been broken into or otherwise disturbed before excavation. It had a facade with Doric columns and large marble doors. On top of the tomb were traces of burning, quite probably a funeral pyre. The style of both Tombs II and III suggest a date from the middle to the end of the fourth century BC. The occupants were a man, aged about forty to fifty, in the main chamber, and a woman aged twenty to thirty in the antechamber. The man was about five foot seven or five foot eight inches tall and had been cremated. With him were a gold crown, weapons including a sarissa, and armor including a cuirass, shield, and greaves. In the antechamber was an ornate golden quiver in the Scythian style and a cuirass, but disorder suggested that the tomb was finished and sealed quickly and without as much care as might be expected. A painted fresco may well depict a hunting scene with a bearded Philip and a young Alexander. In the remains of the fire on top of the tomb were bones of two men, two horses, and trappings and equipment.

TOMB III. Another vaulted tomb with a similar temple-like facade. The occupant was a boy, aged perhaps thirteen to sixteen, and is usually identified as Alexander IV, who was killed at the age of about fourteen.

Outside the tombs was a shrine or *heroon* for the practice of a heroic cult, like that later awarded to Hephaestion, which would fit for Philip and possibly his father, Amyntas III, but not for Philip's son Arrhidaeus or grandson Alexander IV.

Some of the debate has revolved around the objects found in the tombs, and whether these were too early in style, pattern, or theme for Philip, but none of these theories are decisive one way or the other, so the key is the skeletal remains. The case for the occupant of Tomb II being Philip is based around the age of the male, which fits well. Analysis also suggested damage to the skull, severe enough to have destroyed one eye and thus fitting with Philip's wound at Methone. Difference in size between the two greaves was interpreted as evidence for a leg injury, corresponding to the one Philip had received at the hands of the Triballi. In addition, the pyre above the tomb appears to fit neatly with the execution of the two sons of Areopus, brother of Alexander of Lyncestis, along with their weapons and horses, as punishment for alleged involvement in the assassination.

The female remains in the antechamber present a problem, since it is not known that any of Philip's wives happened to die close enough in time to his murder so that they could be buried with him. The skeletal remains appear too old for Cleopatra, who was killed soon afterward, while it is also assumed that the vengeful Olympias would not have wanted her honored in this way by burial with the king. The bow case and other military items have led to suggestions that this might be Philip's wife Meda, daughter of the king of the Getae, or possibly the poorly attested Scythian wife, daughter of King Atheas. This is based on the idea that either woman may have come from a cultural tradition where a wife might commit suicide to join her husband, but the custom is not well attested, so this remains highly conjectural.

The case against the man in Tomb II being Philip rests upon a reassessment of the fragments of skull, arguing that the traces of the alleged wound injury were in fact caused after death by the cremation process. It should be noted that those who performed the original examination and produced the reconstructions of the corpse's face do not accept this and hold to their conclusions. There is no clear evidence for a leg wound, and the greaves are most likely not a pair in the first place, and reflect the hurried nature of the burial, with whatever equipment was at hand and broadly suitable being added.

If Tomb II is not Philip II, then the only other plausible candidate is Arrhidaeus, which would mean that the woman in the antechamber is probably Adea Eurydice, daughter of Cynane, and thus plausibly accompanied by military equipment, since it is recorded that she was trained to fight by her mother. She and Arrhidaeus were buried by Cassander in 315 BC, some eighteen months to two years after their deaths at the hands of Olympias. A degree of haste in sealing the tomb would make a little more sense in this context than in 336 BC with the burial of Philip. Against this interpretation can be set the painting of a royal hunt, which is easier to associate with Philip II than his son. Nor is there any evidence that Arrhidaeus suffered a face injury, assuming that this has been correctly identified in the skull fragments, while a long delay between death and cremation would make it less likely that the damage was caused by the fire.

In the past, there have been suggestions that the man in Tomb I is Philip's father Amyntas III, but more recently a case has been made that the man in Tomb I is Philip II. This has been based on analysis showing lameness in one knee, and a hole in the bone, which is claimed to be the penetrating wound that caused the injury. Estimates of the age of this man vary considerably, and some suggest someone too young to be Philip. However, one analysis based on the wear of the pelvic bones gave a probable age of about forty-five. It was then argued that the other remains in the tomb are Cleopatra and the couple's infant child, whose sex could not be determined and appears to have been a few weeks old. The age of the woman fits this identification. However, it is unclear how soon after the assassination she and the baby were killed, and whether this happened soon enough for her to be interred. The same assumption that Olympias would not have permitted the murdered woman to share their husband's tomb has also been raised, although it should be said that in both cases this is a highly subjective judgment. It is impossible to say whether or not killing a rival was sufficient to satisfy Olympias, leaving her content for the dead to receive full honors, or to guess Alexander's attitude to such things.

A stronger objection comes from Justin's explicit statement that Philip II was cremated. The man in Tomb I was not cremated and was inhumed, while the man in Tomb II had been burned on a pyre. Justin may have been wrong, which would strengthen the case for Tomb I, but we should beware rejecting a source, however unreliable, simply because it is convenient. It is also impossible to know if Amyntas III had suffered an injury that would correspond with the one observed on the knee of the man in Tomb I. Similarly, it is possible, but utterly unattested, that Amyntas III had an additional wife or lover who died around the same time that he did, perhaps as the result of childbirth. There is also the possibility that none of the bones in Tomb I were original and that the chamber was reused at some later point.

At the moment, certainty remains impossible. The majority of scholars continue to favor the identification of the occupant of Tomb II as Philip II, although this is not universal. This suggests that Philip was of average height and allows us to glimpse his face in the famous reconstruction. On the other hand, if the theory about Tomb I is correct, then Philip was unusually tall. Another consequence might be that some of the equipment found in Tomb II, such as the helmet and cuirass, might actually have been worn by Alexander in his eastern campaigns and subsequently used in his half brother's burial.[1]

Whatever the truth, it is almost certain that the remains found in these tombs belong to close family members of Philip and Alexander.

ACKNOWLEDGMENTS

A BOOK LIKE this takes a long time to write and many others contribute to the process, not least all those scholars who have and continue to work on topics relevant to Philip, Alexander, and their era. Without the inspiration provided by their work this book would be far poorer in every way. As always I must express my heartfelt thanks to the family and friends who have read and commented on drafts of the manuscript, especially Kevin Powell and Averil Goldsworthy. Dorothy King has once again listened with patience as my thoughts developed, and provided inspiration, suggestions, and challenging ideas, doing a great deal to make this a better book. Particular thanks must go to my agent, Georgina Capel, for her enthusiasm and for creating the situation allowing me to take the time to write this book properly. Then I must thank Anthony Cheetham at Head of Zeus for suggesting a book about both Philip and Alexander, as well as Richard Milbank at Head of Zeus and Lara Heimert at Basic Books and their teams for seeing the project through.

BIBLIOGRAPHY

Adams, W. 1999. "Philip II, the League of Corinth and the Governance of Greece." *Ancient Macedonia* 6 (1):15–22.

———. 2002. "The Frontier Policy of Philip II." *Ancient Macedonia* 7: 283–291.

Anson, E. 1989. "The Persian Fleet in 334." *Classical Philology* 84: 44–49.

———. 1996. "The 'Ephimerides' of Alexander the Great." *Historia* 45: 501–504.

———. 2009. "Philip II, Amyntas Perdiccas, and Macedonian Royal Succession." *Historia* 58: 276–286.

———. 2013. *Alexander the Great: Themes and Issues.*

———. 2015. "Alexander at the Beas." In *East and West in the World Empire of Alexander: Essays in Honour of Brian Bosworth*, edited by P. Wheatley and E. Baynham, 65–74.

Antela-Bernardez, B. 2012. "Philip and Pausanias: A Deadly Love in Macedonian Politics." *CQ* 62: 859–861.

Ashley, J. 1998. *The Macedonian Empire: The Era of Warfare Under Philip II and Alexander the Great, 359–323 BC.*

Atkinson, J., E. Truter, and E. Truter. 2009. "Alexander's Last Days: Malaria and Mind Games." *Acta Classica* 52: 23–46.

Badian, E. 1960. "The Death of Parmenio." *Transactions and Proceedings of the American Philological Association* 91: 324–338.

———. 1961. "Harpalus." *JHS* 81: 16–43.

———. 1963. "The Death of Philip II." *Phoenix* 17: 244–250.

———. 1967. "Agis III." *Hermes* 95: 37–69.

———. 1977. "The Battle of Granicus." *Ancient Macedonia* 2: 271–293.

———. 1994. "Agis III: Revisions and Reflections." In *Ventures into Greek History*, edited by I. Worthington, 258–292. Oxford: Oxford University Press.

———. 2000. "Darius III." *Harvard Studies of Classical Philology* 100: 241–267.

———. 2002. "Once More the Death of Philip II." *Ancient Macedonia* 7: 389–406.

———. 2012a. "Conspiracies." In *Collected Papers on Alexander the Great*, edited by E. Badian, 420–455.

———. 2012b. "A Note on the Alexander Mosaic." In *Collected Papers on Alexander the Great*, edited by E. Badian, 404–419.

Barnett, R. 1957. "Persepolis," *Iraq* 19: 55–77.

Bartsiokas, A. 2000. "The Eye Injury of King Philip II and the Skeletal Evidence from the Royal Tomb II at Vergina." *Science* 228 (5465): 511–514.

Bartsiokas, A., J-L. Arsuaga, E. Santos, M. Algaba, and A. Gómez-Olivienca. 2015. "The Lameness of Philip II and the Royal Tomb I at Vergina, Macedonia." *Proceedings of the National Academy of Sciences of the United States of America* 112 (32): 9844–9848.

Baynham, E. 1994. "The Question of Macedonian Divine Honours for Philip II." *Mediterranean Archaeology* 7: 35–43.

———. 1998. "Why Didn't Alexander Marry Before Leaving Macedonia? Observations on Factional Politics at Alexander's Court in 336–334 BC." *Rheinisches Museum fur Philologie* 141: 141–152.

Beggiora, S. 2017. "Indian Ethnography in Alexandrian Sources: A Missed Opportunity." In *With Alexander in India and Central Asia: Moving East and back to West*, edited by C. Antonetti and P. Biagi, 238–254.

Biagi, P. 2017. "Uneasy Riders: With Alexander and Nearchus from Pattala to Rhambakia." In *With Alexander in India and Central Asia: Moving East and back to West*, edited by C. Antonetti and P. Biagi, 255–278.

Bloedow, E. 1994. "Alexander's Speech on the Eve of the Siege of Tyre." *L'Antiquité Classique* 63: 65–76.

———. 2003. "Why Did Philip and Alexander Launch a War Against the Persian Empire?" *L'Antiquité Classique* 72: 261–274.

———. 2004. "Egypt in Alexander's Scheme of Things." *Quaderni Urbinati de Cultura Classica* 77: 75–99.

Borza, E. 1971. "The End of Agis' Revolt." *Classical Philology* 66: 230–235.

———. 1972. "Fire from Heaven: Alexander at Persepolis." *Classical Philology* 67: 233–245.

———. 1979. "Some Observations on Malaria and the Ecology of Central Macedonia." *American Journal of Ancient History* 4: 102–124.

———. 1982. "The Natural Resources of Early Macedonia." In *Philip II, Alexander the Great and the Macedonian Heritage*, by W. Lindsay Adams and E. Borza, 1–20.

———. 1987a. "The Royal Macedonian Tombs and the Paraphernalia of Alexander the Great." *Phoenix* 41: 105–121.

———. 1987b. "Timber and Politics in the Ancient World: Macedon and the Greeks." *Proceedings of the American Philosophical Society* 131: 32–52.

———. 1990. *In the Shadow of Olympus: The Emergence of Macedonia.*

———. 1995. "Anaxarchus and Callisthenes: Academic Intrigue at Alexander's Court." In *Makedonika: Essays by Eugene N. Borza*, edited by C. Thomas, 173–188.

Bosworth, A. 1971a. "The Death of Alexander the Great: Rumour and Propaganda." *Classical Quarterly* 21: 112–136.

———. 1971b. "Philip II and Upper Macedonia." *CQ* 21: 93–105.

———. 1975. "The Mission of Amphoterus and the Outbreak of Agis' War." *Phoenix* 29: 27–43.

———. 1980a. *A Historical Commentary on Arrian's History of Alexander I.*

———. 1980b. "Alexander and the Iranians." *JHS* 100: 1–21.

———. 1981. "A Missing Year in the History of Alexander the Great." *JHS* 101: 17–39.

———. 1982. "The Location of Alexander's Campaign Against the Illyrians in 335 BC." *Studies in the History of Art*. Vol. 10, Symposium Series I: Macedonia and Greece in Late Classical and Early Hellenistic Times, 74–85.

———. 1986. "Alexander the Great and the Decline of Macedon." *JHS* 106: 1–12.

———. 1988. *Conquest and Empire: The Reign of Alexander the Great*.

———. 1996. *Alexander and the East: The Tragedy of Triumph*.

Bowden, H. 1993. "Hoplites and Homer: Warfare, Hero Cult, and the Ideology of the Polis." In *War and Society in the Greek World*, edited by J. Rich and G. Shipley, 45–61.

Braund, D. 1980. "The Aedui, Troy, and the Apocolocyntosis." *Classical Quarterly* 30: 420–425.

Briant, P. 2015. *Darius in the Shadow of Alexander*. Translated by J. Todd.

Brunt, P. 1963. "Alexander's Macedonian Cavalry." *JHS* 83: 27–46.

Bucciantini, V. 2017. "From the Indus to the Pasitigris: Some Remarks on the Periplus of Nearchus in Arrian's *Indiké*." In *With Alexander in India and Central Asia: Moving East and back to West*, edited by C. Antonetti and P. Biagi, 279–292.

Buckler, J. 1994. "Philip II, the Greeks and the King, 346–336 BC." *Illinois Classical Studies* 19: 99–122.

———. 1996. "The Actions of Philip II in 347 and 346 BC: A Reply to N. G. L. Hammond." *Classical Quarterly* 46 (2): 380–386.

———. 2000. "Demosthenes and Aeschines." In *Demosthenes: Statesman and Orator*, edited by I. Worthington, 142–143.

Buckler, J., and H. Beck. 2008. *Central Greece and the Politics of Power in the Fourth Century BC*.

Cahill, N. 1985. "The Treasury at Persepolis: Gift-Giving at the City of the Persians." *American Journal of Archaeology* 89: 373–389.

Carney, E. 1992. "The Politics of Polygamy: Olympias, Alexander and the Murder of Philip." *Historia* 41: 169–189.

———. 1993. "Olympias and the Image of the Virago." *Phoenix* 47: 29–55.

———. 1996a. "Alexander and the Persian Women." *American Journal of Philology* 117: 563–583.

———. 1996b. "Macedonians and Mutiny: Discipline and Indiscipline in the Army of Philip and Alexander." *Classical Philology* 91: 19–44.

———. 2000. *Women and Monarchy in Macedonia*.

———. 2015. *King and Court in Ancient Macedonia: Rivalry, Treason, and Conspiracy*.

Cartledge, P. 2004. *Alexander the Great: The Truth Behind the Myth*.

Cawkwell, G. 1960. "Aeschines and the Peace of Philocrates." *Revue des Etudes Greques* 73: 416–438.

———. 1962. "The Defence of Olynthus." *Classical Quarterly* 12: 122–140.

———. 1963. "Demosthenes' Policy After the Peace of Philocrates." *Classical Quarterly* 13 (1): 120–138.

———. 1978a. "The Peace of Philocrates Again." *Classical Quarterly* 28 (1): 93–104.

———. 1978b. *Philip of Macedon*.

———. 2005. *The Greek Wars: The Failure of Persia.*

Charles, M. 2011. "Immortals and Apple Bearers: Towards a Better Understanding of Achaemenid Infantry Units." *CQ* 61: 114–133.

———. 2012. "The Persian ΚΑΡΛΑΚΕΣ." *JHS* 132: 7–21.

Christesen, P., and S. Murray. 2010. "Macedonian Religion." In *A Companion to Ancient Macedonia,* edited by J. Roisman and I. Worthington, 428–445.

Collins, A. 2014. "Alexander's Visit to Siwah: A New Analysis." *Classical Association of Canada* 68: 62–77.

Corvisier, Jean-Nicolas. 2012. *Battaille de Chéronée. Printemps—338. Philippe II, roi de Macédoine, et le futur Alexandre le Grand.*

Dawson, D. 1996. *The Origins of Western Warfare: Militarism and Morality in the Ancient World.*

Devine, A. 1975. "Grand Tactics at Gaugamela." *Phoenix* 29: 374–385.

———. 1985a. "Grand Tactics at the Battle of Issus." *Ancient World* 12: 39–59.

———. 1985b. "The Strategies of Alexander the Great and Darius III in the Issus Campaign (333 BC)." *Ancient World* 12: 25–38.

———. 1986a. "The Battle of Gaugamela: A Tactical and Source-Critical Study." *Ancient World* 16: 87–115.

———. 1986b. "Demythologizing the Battle of the Granicus." *Phoenix* 40: 265–278.

———. 1989. "The Macedonian Army at Gaugamela: Its Strength and the Length of Its Battle-line." *Ancient World* 19: 77–80.

Devine, D. 1989. "Alexander the Great." In *Warfare in the Ancient World,* edited by Gen. Sir John Hackett, 104–129.

Ellis, J. 1976. *Philip II and Macedonian Imperialism.*

———. 1981. "The Assassination of Philip II." In *Ancient Macedonian Studies in Honor of Charles F. Edson,* edited by E. Borza and H. Dell, 99–137.

Engels, D. 1978. *Alexander the Great and the Logistics of the Macedonian Army.*

Epplett, C. 2007. "War Elephants in the Hellenistic World." In *Alexander's Empire. Formulation to Decay,* edited by W. Heckel, L. Tritle, and P. Wheatley, 209–232.

Errington, M. 1975. "Arybbas the Molossian." *Greek, Roman and Byzantine Studies* 16: 41–50.

Evans, R. 2015. *Fields of Battle: Retracing Ancient Battlefields.*

Finley, M. 1963. *The Ancient Greeks.*

Flower, M. 1999. "The Panhellenism of Philip and Alexander. A Reassessment." *Ancient Macedonia* 6 (1): 419–429.

Fox, R. Lane. 2004. *Alexander the Great.* Updated ed. First published 1973.

———. 2006. *The Classical World: An Epic History from Homer to Hadrian.*

———. 2007. "Alexander the Great. The 'Last of the Achaemenids'?" In *Persian Responses: Political and Cultural Interaction With(in) the Achaemenid Empire,* edited by C. Tuplin, 267– 311.

Fraser, A. 1953. "The 'Breaking' of Bucephalus." *Classical Weekly* 47 (2): 22–23.

Fredricksmeyer, E. 1979. "Divine Honors for Philip II." *Transactions of the American Philological Association* 109: 36–61.

———. 1990. "Alexander and Philip: Emulation and Resentment." *Classical Journal* 85: 300–315.

Fuller, J. 1958. *The Generalship of Alexander the Great.*

Gabriel, R. 2010. *Philip II of Macedonia: Greater than Alexander.*

———. 2015. *The Madness of Alexander the Great and the Myth of Military Genius.*

Gaebel, R. 2002. *Cavalry Operations in the Ancient Greek World.*

Garvin, E. 2003. "Darius III and Homeland Defense." In *Crossroads of History. The Age of Alexander,* edited by W. Heckel and L. Tritle, 87–111.

Green, P. 1991. *Alexander of Macedon 356–323 BC: A Historical Biography.*

Greenwalt, W. 1989. "Polygamy and Succession in Argead Macedonia." *Arethusa* 22: 19–45.

Griffith, G. 1947. "Alexander's Generalship at Gaugamela." *JHS* 67: 77–89.

Grudd, H., et al. 2002. "A 7400–Year Tree Ring Chronology in Northern Swedish Lapland: Natural Climate Variability Expressed on Annual to Millennial Timescales." *Holocene* 12 (6): 657–665.

Guth, D., and D. Guth. 2015. "The King's Speech: Philip's Rhetoric and Democratic Leadership in the Debate over the Peace of Philocrates." *Rhetorica* 33 (4): 333–348.

Hamilton, J. 1956. "The Cavalry Battle at Hydaspes." *JHS* 76: 26–31.

Hammond, N. 1966. "The Kingdoms in Illyria circa 400–167 BC." *Annual of the British School in Athens* 61: 239–253.

———. 1974. "Alexander's Campaign in Illyria." *JHS* 94: 66–87.

———. 1980. "The Battle of the Granicus River." *JHS* 100: 73–88.

———. 1988a. "The King and the Land in the Macedonian Kingdom." *Classical Quarterly* 38: 382–391.

———. 1988b. "The Royal Journal of Alexander." *Historia* 37: 129–150.

———. 1989a. "Aspects of Alexander's Journal and His Last Days." *American Journal of Philology* 110: 155–160.

———. 1989b. "Casualties and Reinforcements of Citizen Soldiers in Greece and Macedonia." *JHS* 109: 56–68.

———. 1989c. *The Macedonian State. The Origins, Institutions and History.*

———. 1990. "Royal Pages, Personal Pages, and Boys Trained in the Macedonian Manner During the Period of the Temenid Monarchy." *Historia* 39: 261–290.

———. 1991. "The Royal Tombs at Vergina: Evolution and Identities." *Annual of the British School at Athens* 86: 69–82.

———. 1992a. "Alexander's Charge at the Battle of Issus in 333 BC." *Historia* 41: 395–406.

———. 1992b. "The Archaeological and Literary Evidence for the Burning of the Persepolis Palace." *Classical Quarterly* 2: 358–364.

———. 1994a. *Alexander the Great: King, Commander and Statesman.* 3rd ed.

———. 1994b. "Literary Evidence for Macedonian Speech." *Historia* 43 (2): 131–142.

———. 1994c. *Philip of Macedon.*

———. 1994d. "Philip's Actions in 347 and early 346 BC." *Classical Quarterly* 44 (2): 367–374.

Hammond, N., and G. Griffith. 1979. *A History of Macedonia.* Vol. 2, *560–336 BC.*

Hanson, V. Davis. 1989. *The Western Way of War: Infantry Battle in Classical Greece.*

———. 1998. *Warfare and Agriculture in Classical Greece.*

———. 2005. *A War Like No Other: How the Athenians and Spartans Fought the Peloponnesian War.*

Hanson, V. Davis, ed. 1991. *Hoplites: The Classical Greek Battle Experience*.

Harris, E. 1995. *Aeschines and Athenian Politics*.

Hatzopoulos, M. 1982. "The Oliveni Inscription and the Dates of Philip II's Reign." In *Philip II, Alexander the Great, and the Macedonian Heritage*, edited by W. Adams and E. Borza, 21–42.

Heckel, W. 1977. "The Conspiracy Against Philotas." *Phoenix* 31: 9–21.

———. 1978. "Cleopatra or Eurydice." *Phoenix* 32: 155–158.

———. 1986. "Factions and Macedonian Politics in the Reign of Alexander the Great." *Ancient Macedonia* 4: 293–305.

———. 2003. "Alexander and the 'Limits of the Civilised World.'" In *The Crossroads of History: the Age of Alexander*, edited by W. Heckel and L. Tritle, 147–174.

———. 2006. *Who's Who in the Age of Alexander the Great. A Prosopography of Alexander's Empire*.

———. 2008. *The Conquests of Alexander the Great*.

———. 2009. "The King and his Army." In *Alexander the Great: A New History*, edited by W. Heckel and L. Tritle, 69–82.

———. 2016. *Alexander's Marshals: A Study of the Makedonian Aristocracy and the Politics of Military Leadership*. 2nd ed.

Heckel, W., C. Willikes, and G. Wrightson. 2010. "Scythed Chariots at Gaugamela: A Case Study." In *Philip II and Alexander the Great: Father and Son: Lives and Afterlives*, edited by E. Carney and D. Ogden, 103–109.

Helama S., et al. 2002. "Supra-long Scots Pine Tree-Ring Record for Finnish Lapland: Part 2, Interannual to Centennial Variability in Summer Temperatures for 7500 Years." *Holocene* 12 (6): 681–687.

Holland, T. 2005. *Persian Fire: The First World Empire and the Battle for the West*.

Holmes, R. 1986. *Firing Line*.

Holt, F. 1988. *Alexander the Great and Bactria: The Formation of a Greek Frontier in Central Asia*.

———. 2006. *Into the Land of Bone: Alexander the Great in Afghanistan*.

Kagan, D. 2005. *The Peloponnesian War: Athens and Sparta in Savage Conflict 431–404 BC*. New ed.

Kaplan, P. 2006. "Dedications to Greek Sanctuaries by Foreign Kings in the Eighth Through Sixth Centuries BCE." *Historia* 55: 129–152.

Kern, P. 1999. *Ancient Siege Warfare*.

Kuhrt, A. 2007. *Persian Empire: A Corpus of Sources from the Acaemenid Period*. 2 vols.

Lendon, J. 2000. "Homeric Vengeance and the Outbreak of Greek Wars." In *War and Violence in Ancient Greece*, edited by H. van Wees, 1–30.

———. 2005. *Soldiers and Ghosts*.

———. 2006. "Xenophon and the Alternative to Realist Foreign Policy: *Cyropaedia* 3.1.14–31." *JHS* 126: 82–98.

———. 2010. *Song of Wrath: The Peloponnesian War Begins*.

———. 2017. "Battle Description in the Ancient Historians, Part 1: Structure, Array and Fighting." *Greece and Rome* 64: 39–64.

Ma, J. 2008. "Chaironea 338: The Topographies of Commemoration." *JHS* 128: 72–91.

Macurdy, G. 1927. "Queen Eurydice and the Evidence for Woman Power in Early Macedonia." *American Journal of Philology* 48: 201–214.

Mader, G. 2006. "Fighting Philip with Decrees: Demosthenes and the Syndrome of Symbolic Action." *American Journal of Philology* 127: 367–386.

———. 2007. "Foresight, Hindsight, and the Rhetoric of Self-Fashioning in Demosthenes's Philippic Cycle." *Journal of the History of Rhetoric* 25: 339–360.

March, D. 1995. "The Kings of Macedon 399–369 BC." *Historia* 44: 257–282.

Markle, M. 1974. "The Strategy of Philip in 346 BC." *Classical Quarterly* 24 (2): 253–268.

———. 1976. "Support of Athenian Intellectuals for Philip: A Study of Isocrates' Letter to Philip and Speusippus' Letter to Philip." *JHS* 96: 80–99.

Marsden, E. 1964. *The Campaign of Gaugamela.*

———. 1969. *Greek and Roman Artillery: Historical Development.*

———. 1977. "Macedonian Military Machinery and Its Designers Under Philip and Alexander." *Ancient Macedonia* 2: 211–233.

Matthew, C. 2015. *An Invincible Beast: Understanding the Hellenistic Pike-Phalanx at War.*

Matyszak, P. 2012. *Expedition to Disaster: The Athenian Mission to Sicily 415 BC.*

McCoy, W. 1989. "Memnon of Rhodes at the Granicus." *American Journal of Philology* 110: 413–433.

McGroaty, K. 2006. "Did Alexander the Great Read Xenophon?" *Hermathena* 181: 105–124.

Mitchell, L. 2012. "The Women of Ruling Families in Archaic and Classical Greece." *Classical Quarterly* 62: 1–21.

Moore, K., ed. 2018. *Brill's Companion to the Reception of Alexander the Great.*

Mortensen, K. 2002. "Homosexuality at the Macedonian Court and the Death of Philip II." *Ancient Macedonia* 7: 371–387.

Mossé, C. 2004. *Alexander: Destiny and Myth.* Translated by J. Lloyd.

Musgrave, J., R. Neave, and A. Prag. 1984. "The Skull from Tomb II at Vergina: King Philip II of Macedon." *JHS* 104: 60–78.

Musgrave, J., and A. Prag. 2011. "The Occupants of Tomb II at Vergina: Why Arrhidaios and Eurydice Must Be Excluded." In Ashmolean Museum's *Heracles to Alexander the Great: Treasures from the Royal Capital of Macedon, a Hellenic Kingdom in the Age of Democracy*, 127–130.

O'Brien, J. 1992. *Alexander the Great: The Invisible Enemy: A Biography.*

Ogden, D. 1996. "Homosexuality and Warfare in Ancient Greece." In *Battle in Antiquity*, edited by A. Lloyd, 107–168.

———. 2011. *Alexander the Great: Myth, Genesis and Sexuality.*

Olbrycht, M. 2010. "Macedonia and Persia." In *A Companion to Ancient Macedon.* edited by J. Roisman and I. Worthington, 351–360.

Pearlman, S. 1957. "Isocrates' 'Phillipus': A Reinterpretation." *Historia* 6: 306–317.

———. 1976. "Panhellenism, the Polis and Imperialism." *Historia* 25: 1–30.

———. 1983. "Isocrates, ΜΑΤΡΙΣ and Philip II." *Ancient Macedonia* 3: 211–227.

Peltonen, J. 2019. *Alexander the Great in the Roman Empire, 150 BC to AD 600.*

Perlman, S. 1985. "Greek Diplomatic Tradition and the Corinthian League of Philip of Macedon." *Historia* 34: 153–174.

Phillips, G. 2004. *Alexander the Great: Murder in Babylon.*

Pope, A. 1957. "Persepolis as a Ritual City." *Archaeology* 10: 123–130.

Prag, A. 1990. "Reconstructing King Philip II: The 'Nice' Version." *American Journal of Archaeology* 94: 237–247.

Price, M. Jessop. 1979. "The Coinage of Philip II." *Numismatic Chronicle 7th Series* 19: 230–241.

Pritchett, W. 1958. "Observations on Chaironeia." *American Journal of Archaeology* 62: 307–311.

Rahe, P. 1981. "The Annihilation of the Sacred Band at Chaeronea." *American Journal of Archaeology* 85: 84–87.

Revermann, M. 1999–2000. "Euripides, Tragedy and Macedon: Some Conditions of Reception." *Illinois Classical Studies* 24/25: 451–467.

Ridgway, W. 1926. "Euripides in Macedon." *Classical Quarterly* 20: 1–19.

Riginos, A. 1994. "The Wounding of Philip II of Macedon: Fact and Fabrication." *JHS* 114: 103–119.

Roebuck, C. 1948. "The Settlements of Philip II with the Greek states in 338 BC." *Classical Philology* 43: 73–92.

Roisman, J. 1984. "Ptolemy and his Rivals in the History of Alexander." *CQ* 34: 373–385.

Romane, P. 1987. "Alexander's Siege of Tyre." *Ancient World* 16: 79–90.

———. 1988. "Alexander's Siege of Gaza." *Ancient World* 18: 21–30.

Sakellariou, M. 1980. "Panhellenism: From Concept to Policy." In *Philip of Macedon*, edited by M. Hatzopoulos and L. Loukopoulos, 128–145.

Schachter, A. 2016. *Boiotia in Antiquity: Selected Papers.*

Schell, J. 2000. "Observations of the Metrology of the Precious Metal Coinage of Philip II of Macedon: the 'Thraco-Macedonian' Standard or the Corinthian Standard?" *American Journal of Numismatics* 12: 1–8.

Scott, M. 2009. *From Democrats to Kings: The Downfall of Athens to the Epic Rise of Alexander the Great.*

———. 2014. *Delphi: A History of the Center of the Ancient World.*

Scullion, S. 2003. "Euripides and Macedon, or the Silence of the Frogs." *Classical Quarterly* 53: 389–400.

Sekunda, N. 1984. *The Army of Alexander the Great.* Men at Arms, vol. 148.

———. 2007. "Military Forces." In *The Cambridge Companion to Greek and Roman Warfare. Vol. 1: Greece, the Hellenistic World and the Rise of Rome*, edited by P. Sabin, H. van Wees, and M. Whitby, 325–357.

Shrimpton, G. 1991. *Theopompus the Historian.*

Sidnell, P. 2007. *Warhorse.*

Spann, P. 1999. "Alexander at the Beas: Fox in Lion's Skin." In *The Eye Expanded: Life and Arts in Greco-Roman Antiquity*, edited by F. Titchener and R. Moorton, 62–74.

Spencer, D. 2002. *The Roman Alexander.*

Stoneman, R. 1994. "Who Are the Brahmans? Indian Lore and Cynic Doctrine in Palladius' *de Bragmanibus* and Its Models." *Classical Quarterly* 44: 500–510.

———. 1995. "Naked Philosophers: The Brahmans in the Alexander Historians and the Alexander Romance." *JHS* 115: 99–114.

Taylor, C. 2001a. "Bribery in Athenian Politics Part I: Accusations, Allegations, and Slander." *Greece and Rome* 48: 53–66.

———. 2001b. "Bribery in Athenian Politics Part II: Ancient Reactions and Perceptions." *Greece and Rome* 48 (2): 154–172.

Thompsen, M. 1982. "The Coinage of Philip II and Alexander the Great." *Studies in the History of Art* 10: 112–121.

Tierney, J. 1959/1960. "The Celtic Ethnography of Poseidonius." *Proceedings of the Royal Irish Academy: Archaeology, Culture, History* 60: 189–275.

Townshend, R. 2003. "The Philippeion and Fourth-Century Athenian Architecture." In *The Macedonians in Athens, 322–229 BC*, edited by O. Palagia and S. Tracy, 93–101.

Tritle, L. 2003. "Alexander the Great and the Killing of Cleitus the Black." In *Crossroads of History: The Age of Alexander*, edited by W. Heckel and L. Tritle, 127–146.

Tronson, A. 1984. "The Marriages of Philip II." *JHS* 104: 116–126.

Unz, R. 1985. "Alexander's Brothers?" *JHS* 105: 171–174.

Van Wees, H. 2004. *Greek Warfare: Myths and Realities*.

Vaughn, P. 1991. "The Identification and Retrieval of the Hoplite Battle-Dead." In *Hoplites: The Classical Greek Battle Experience*, edited by V. Hanson, 38–62.

Walbank, F. 1967. *Polybius II: A Historical Commentary on Polybius*.

Walker, W. Seymour. 1921. "An Outline of Modern Exploration of the Oasis of Siwa." *Geographical Journal* 57: 29–34.

West, A. 1923. "The Early Diplomacy of Philip of Macedon Illustrated by His Coins." *Numismatic Chronicle and Journal of the Royal Numismatic Society* 3: 169–210.

Wheeler, E. 1991. "The General As Hoplite." In *Hoplites: The Classical Greek Battle Experience*, edited by V. Hanson, 121–170.

Worthington, I. 1991. "The Context of [Demades] on the Twelve Years." *CQ* 41: 90–95.

———. 2003. "Alexander's Destruction of Thebes." In *Crossroads of History: The Age of Alexander*, edited by W. Heckel and L. Tritle, 65–86.

———. 2008. *Philip II of Macedonia*.

———. 2014. *By the Spear: Philip II, Alexander the Great, and the Rise and Fall of the Macedonian Empire*.

NOTES

INTRODUCTION: "SOME TALK OF ALEXANDER"

1. No ancient source tells the story of Alexander weeping because there were no more worlds to conquer; this is a modern invention. In Shakespeare's *Henry V*, the king's famous "Once more into the breach" speech, includes the lines: "On, on, you noblest English! Whose blood is fet from fathers of war-proof; Fathers that, like so many Alexanders, have in these parts from morn till even fought, and sheath'd their swords for lack of argument." *Henry V*, act 3, scene 1. In reality, Alexander was only prevented from fresh conquests by his death.

2. Plutarch, *Alexander* 58.4–5.

3. Arrian, *Anabasis* 1.1, preface 1–2.

4. A glance at the bibliography will show my frequent reliance on Bosworth, Carney, Griffith, and Hammond in particular, among many others. There seemed little point after decades of reassessment to refer to the likes of Tarn, whose ideas would now find few if any supporters. That is not to deny the huge contribution to the field made by earlier generations of scholars. Attitudes have changed, and they have not been kind to older interpretations of Alexander, but history by its nature requires constant reassessment of the evidence and our understanding of it.

CHAPTER 1: IN THE BEGINNING

1. Herodotus 8.137 for the story of the origins of the Argeads as exiles from Argos, a claim repeated by Thucydides 2.99.3, 5.80.2; and in general see Hammond and Griffith (1979), 3–11, 27–28, 31–39; for the Aedui see Braund (1980), 420–425.

2. Baby taken to battlefield to ensure victory over Illyrians, see Justin 7.2.8; religious role of king see Hammond (1989c), 21–23.

3. For acclaiming a king by the clash of weapons see Curtius 10.7.13–14, describing an episode after the death of Alexander; on succession see discussion in Anson (2009), 276–286, esp. 277–280.

4. Diodorus Siculus 14.37.6, Aristotle, *Politics* 1311^{b}8–35, with discussion in Hammond and Griffith (1979), 167–168; Archelaus as son of slave, see Plato, *Gorgias* 471a–c.

5. Hammond and Griffith (1979), 167–172, March (1995), 257–282, which challenges the orthodox reconstruction of the chronology.

6. Diodorus Siculus 14.92.3, with Hammond and Griffith (1979), 172–173, and Hammond (1966), 239–253.

7. Diodorus Siculus 14.92.3–4, 15.19.2–3, Isocrates 6.46, Xenophon, *Hellenica* 5.2.11–20, 42, 5.3.1, 3–6, 26, with Hammond and Griffith (1979), 177–178, and Borza (1990), 182–189, and 296–297 on the question of Argaeus.

8. Hammond and Griffith (1979), 14–22 on Upper Macedonian dynasties.

9. Carney (2000), 23–27, and Carney (1992), 169–189, esp. 171–172.

10. Pausanias 8.7.6 where he is said to have been forty-six when he was murdered in 336 BC, and Justin 9.8.1 who says he was forty-seven when assassinated.

11. On the status of the Macedonian royal family see Hammond (1989c), 16–24; Carney (2015), 191–205 gathers the information about education, largely drawn from sources dealing with Alexander the Great. There is very little even then for the early years; dismissing an officer for taking hot baths, Polyaenus, *Stratagems* 4.2.2; cult of Artemis see Christesen and Murray (2010), 428–445, esp. 431.

12. Justin 7.4.5, 7, for Eurydice's children; for malaria see discussion in Borza (1979), 102–124.

13. See Carney (2000), 40–46 on Eurydice, and 46–47 on Gygaea.

14. Plutarch, *Education of children* 20 (14).

15. On Eurydice see Macurdy (1927), 201–214 and references in note 9. Some have doubted that the work containing the Plutarch quote was actually written by this author; see Carney (2000), 269n12–14 for detailed discussion and references.

16. Diodorus Siculus 15.60.3, Justin 7.4.5, 7–8, with Carney (2000), 39–40, 42.

17. Justin 7.5.1, Diodorus Siculus 16.2.2, Plutarch, *Pelopidas* 26, which all differ on details.

18. Athenaeus 1.18a claims that the son of one of Alexander's marshals sat at feasts until he was thirty-five because he had not performed this rite of passage.

19. Philip and Pammenes as lovers in Suidas, s.v. *Karanos*.

20. Plutarch, *Pelopidas* 26.4–5 (Loeb translation).

21. E.g., Worthington (2008), 17–19, Gabriel (2010), 23–28, and Hammond and Griffith (1979), 204–206; importance of these years, Justin 6.9.7, 7.5.3.

22. Diodorus Siculus 15.71.1, Justin 7.5.4, Plutarch, *Pelopidas* 26–27, Marsyas, *Fragments of Greek Historians* 135/6 = Athenaeus 14.629d, Hammond and Griffith (1979), 181–184, Borza (1990), 190–195, Carney (2000), 42–44.

23. Ptolemy is called *epitropos* in Plutarch, *Pelopidas* 27.3, and Aeschines, *On the embassy* 2.29, but king (*basileus*) in Diodorus Siculus 15.71.1, 77.5, and some late lists of kings, see Hammond and Griffith (1979), 183–184; the claim

that Eurydice married Ptolemy is based on a scholiast's comment in Aeschines, *On the embassy* 2.29.

24. Plutarch, *Pelopidas* 27–28, Diodorus Siculus 16.2.6, Aeschines, *On the embassy* 26–29, Nepos, *Iphicrates* 3.2.

25. Aeschines, *On the embassy* 2.28–29.

26. Aeschines, *On the embassy* 2.26, 29.

27. Diodorus Siculus 15.77.5, 16.2.4.

CHAPTER 2: CRISIS

1. Worthington (2008), 15–16; a well-illustrated guide to the tombs is the catalog produced by the Ashmolean Museum *Heracles to Alexander the Great*, notably Musgrave and Prag (2011), 127–130; and Carney, "Tomb I at Vergina and the Meaning of the Great Tumulus As an Historical Moment," in Carney (2015), 91–107.

2. Justin 7.5.5 claims Eurydice murdered Perdiccas, which conflicts with the fuller evidence of his death in battle, but it is the last mention of Eurydice in any source. On the two reconstructions of the skull from Tomb II see Prag (1990), 237–247.

3. Speusippus, *Epist. Socrat.* 30.12, Caryst. Perg. F 1. *Fragments of Greek Historians* 4.356 = Athenaeus 11.506e, with Hammond and Griffith (1979), 188, 206–208, and Worthington (2008), 19–20; Euphraeus, see Plato, *Ep.* 5 = Athenaeus 12.508d.

4. For discussion see Hammond and Griffith (1979), 186–188.

5. Polyaenus, *Stratagems* 4.10.1.

6. Frontinus, *Stratagems* 2.5.19 on Molossia.

7. Diodorus Siculus 16.2.5–6.

8. Justin 7.5.9–10, with Anson (2009), 276–286.

9. Hammond (1989c), 60–70 on the Assembly.

10. For opposing views of whether or not Philip was regent, see also the detailed discussions in Hammond and Griffith (1979), 702–704 rejecting the regency, and Hammond (1994c), 23–24, 40; the Boeotian inscription is *IG* vii. 3055.

11. See Justin, 8.3.10 referring to two half brothers who were later sheltered by the Olynthians, with Hammond and Griffith (1979), 699–701.

12. Hammond (1989c), 69–70 for little use of the title king.

13. Worthington (2008), 23–24 seems unjustified in looking for reasons why Bardylis did not immediately follow up on his success, so proposes an unattested alliance dictated by the Illyrians.

14. Thucydides 2.100, Anaximenes = *Fragments of Great Historians* 72 F4, with useful survey and discussion of this in Matthew (2015), 4–22.

15. For coinage see Hammond and Griffith (1979), 191–193; Alexander I, see Herodotus 5.17.2; Callisthenes, Ps-Aristotle, *Oec.* 2.22 and Hammond and Griffith (1979), 187.

16. Theophrastus, *Hist. Plant.* 5.2.1, and in general Borza, (1982), 1–20, and Borza (1987b), 32–52.

17. Orestae, H&G p. 185, *SEG* 23.471.13; reversion to an older alignment, Hammond and Griffith (1979), 63, Hecataeus, *Fragments of Greek Historians* 1

F 107 in c. 500 BC describes them as Molossian, cf. Strabo, *Geog.* 7 C 326 and 9 C 434; on coinage Hammond and Griffith (1979), 189–193.

18. Satyrus in Athenae 557b.

19. Diodorus Siculus 16.3.1, 3 (Loeb translation).

20. Diodorus Siculus 16.3.2; on the creation of the pike phalanx and the sarissa see Matthew (2015), passim, and esp. 1–91.

21. Plutarch, *Aemilius Paullus* 19.

22. Nepos, *Iphicrates* 1.3–4, with Matthew (2015), 11–19.

23. On casualties among generals see Hanson (1989), 107–116, with a differing emphasis in Wheeler (1991), 121–170, esp. 146–151.

24. Diodorus Siculus 16.3.3–4, with Hammond (1994b), 24–25.

25. Diodorus Siculus 16.3.3–6, 4.2, with Hammond and Griffith (1979), 211–213.

26. Diodorus Siculus 16.4.2–3.

27. Diodorus Siculus 16.4.4.

28. Thucydides 4.126 (Loeb translation).

29. Diodorus Siculus 16.4.4–7, Frontinus, *Stratagems* 3.2, with Griffith and Hammond (1979), 213–214, and Hammond (1994b), 25–27; both accounts assume Bardylis deployed in square from the start, but Diodorus claims that this occurred after the battle had begun.

CHAPTER 3: MACEDONIAN, GREEK, AND BARBARIAN

1. On the issue of whether or not Macedonians were Greek, see discussions in Borza (1990), 77–97, esp. 90–97, and more specifically on language see Hammond (1989c), 12–15 and Hammond (1994b), 131–142.

2. There are plenty of good surveys of Greek history and culture such as M. Finley, *The Ancient Greeks* (1963), or more recently the early chapters of R. Lane Fox, *The Classical World* (2006).

3. Dawson (1996), 47–107, Bowden (1993), 45–61, and in general V. Davis Hanson, *Warfare and Agriculture in Classical Greece* (1998), and H. van Wees, *Greek Warfare* (2004).

4. Herodotus 7.9b (Loeb translation).

5. The literature on hoplite warfare is extensive. In general see V. Davis Hanson, *The Western Way of War* (1989), and the collection of papers in V. Davis Hanson, ed., *Hoplites* (1991).

6. Plutarch, *Pelopidas* 4.

7. On competition and honor see Lendon (2000), 1–30, Lendon (2005), 20–38, Lendon (2006), 82–98.

8. A lively and accessible account of the Persian wars is T. Holland, *Persian Fire* (2005). For the Persian perspective see Cawkwell, *Greek Wars* (2005), 1–138.

9. For the main conflicts between Athens and Sparta in the fifth century see J. Lendon, *Song of Wrath* (2010), D. Kagan, *Peloponnesian War* (new ed. 2005), and V. Davis Hanson, *A War Like No Other* (2005).

10. On Syracuse, see P. Matyszak, *Expedition to Disaster* (2012).

11. For a survey of Greek history from the end of the Peloponnesian war see M. Scott, *From Democrats to Kings* (2009).

12. Xenophon, *Hellenica* 7.5.26–27 (Loeb translation).

13. Hesiod in *Cat. Gyn*, frag. 3, with Borza (1990), 62–63, and Herodotus 7.131; Persian inscriptions see Cawkwell (2005), 46–47, D Pe 1 16 and 17 (Kent 136), D Na 15–30 (Kent 137).

14. Herodotus 9.44–45.

15. It is not clear when he was first called philhellene, see Hammond and Griffith (1979), 101n3; on the Olympic games, Herodotus 5.22. Borza (1990), 110–113 is skeptical, but this seems unnecessary.

16. Herodotus 5.18–21, 8.140, with Hammond and Griffith (1979), 98–103, Borza (1990), 100–103.

17. Borza (1987b), 34–35, and Borza (1990), 108–109.

18. Thucydides 4.102–106, 18.

19. Borza (1990), 139–166 for the careers of Perdiccas II and Archelaus.

20. Solinus 9.13, Pausanias 5.23.1, 10.13.9, Thucydides 2.99.3, with Hammond and Griffith (1979), 103, 149. On the wider context of foreign kings making dedications at Greek shrines, see Kaplan (2006), 129–152; on Euripides see Ridgway (1926), 1–19, Scullion (2003), 389–400, and on later perceptions of his time there Revermann (1999–2000), 451–467.

21. Aristotle, *Rhetoric* 1398a.24.

CHAPTER 4: ALLIANCES AND WIVES

1. Athenaeus 557c; and for Audata, Carney (2000), 57–58

2. Diodorus Siculus 16.8.1, with Hammond (1994c), 27–28.

3. Arrian, *Anabasis* 7.9.2–3, and Hammond and Griffith (1979), 405–428 on integration in army.

4. Diodorus Siculus 16.95.3, and Polyaenus 4.2.9.

5. On Thessaly see Hammond and Griffith (1979), 218–230; 6.4.28 for praise of Jason of Pherae; and Xenophon, *Hellenica* 6.4.33–37 for Alexander's rise to power and murder.

6. Athenaeus 13.557b–e, with Tronson (1984), 116–126, and Carney (2000), 52–58, 60–62.

7. Carney (2000), 62–67.

8. Carney (2000), 27–32, 35–37.

9. On the pages see Hammond (1990), 261–290, and Carney, "The Role of the *basilikoi paides* at the Argead Court," in Carney, (2015), 207–223. The use of the word "pages" is now so well established that I employ it even though boys or youths would be better, although not perfect. These were not the very young children employed as pages in the Middle Ages. The point is well made by Carney (2015), 207.

10. See Mitchell (2012), 1–21.

11. Athenaeus 560f, Polyaenus 8.60, Arrian *Fragments of Greek Historians* 156, F 9.22–23, with Carney (2000), 57–58.

12. Carney (2000), 59–62.

13. Plutarch, *Alexander* 2.1 (Loeb translation); on names, Plutarch, *Moralia* 401, Justin 2.7.13.

14. Story tentatively accepted in Hammond (1994c), 30, and rejected in Carney (2000), 63.

15. Plutarch, *Alexander* 2.3–3.4.

16. Arrhidaeus was considered for a marriage alliance before Alexander, which suggests that he was older, if only by a little: Plutarch, *Alexander* 10.1.

CHAPTER 5: WAR AND ITS PRICE

1. Diodorus Siculus 16.8.2 (Loeb translation); for a detailed overview of the campaign for Amphipolis see Hammond and Griffith (1979), 230–254.

2. Kern (1999), 89–134.

3. Diodorus Siculus 16.8.2, with Kern (1999), 197–201.

4. Diodorus Siculus 16.8.2 for "severe and continuous assaults."

5. E.g., Arrian, *Anabasis* 2.24.4 for 16 dead and about 300 wounded at one siege, and 5.24.5 for 100 dead to 1,200 wounded at another; the wearing-down process for outnumbered defenders is noted by Julius Caesar, *Bellum Gallicum* 3.4–5, 5.45.

6. Cicero, *Letters to Atticus* 1.16.12 (Loeb translation).

7. Demosthenes, *First Olynthiac* 1.8 (Loeb translation).

8. Demosthenes, *Second Olynthiac* 2.6 (Loeb translation), Theopompus F 30 A, and Hammond and Griffith (1979), 237–242 for detailed discussion.

9. Diodorus Siculus 16.8.2; in general for the treatment of captured cities, see Kern (1999), 135–162.

10. Diodorus Siculus 16.8.3.

11. Diodorus Siculus 16.22.3; becoming king, Justin 7.5.9, with Hammond (1994c), 23–24.

12. Hammond and Griffith (1979), 241–246.

13. Plutarch, *Alexander* 3.4–5, and Hammond and Griffith (1979), 246–249.

14. Diodorus Siculus 16.3.7, 8.6–7, and Hammond and Griffith (1979), 246–251; in the early years of Philip's reign Parmenio is said to have arrested and executed a friend of Perdiccas III, Carystius *ap.* Athenaeus 11.508e. This suggests that he demonstrated loyalty to Philip from the start.

15. Diodorus Siculus 16.8.5, 21.1–4, Demosthenes 4.23, 35, with Hammond and Griffith (1979), 250–251.

16. Plutarch, *Alexander* 3.5.

17. Diodorus Siculus 16.8.7; on the status of groups within the community at Philippi, see Hammond (1988a), 382–391; on coinage, see West (1923), 169–210, Price (1979), 230–241, Thompsen (1982), 112–121, and Schell (2000), 1–8.

18. Polyaenus 4.2.10, Frontinus, *Stratagems* 4.1.6; on logistics and speed of movement, see in general D. Engels, *Alexander the Great and the Logistics of the Macedonian Army* (1980).

19. Hammond (1989c), 16–36.

20. Arrian, *Anabasis* 4.13.1, with Carney (2015), 208–210, 214–216.

21. Aelian, *Various Histories* 14.48, Theopompus *Fragments of Greek Historians* 115 F 27.

22. Diodorus Siculus 16.34.4–5, with Hammond and Griffith (1979), 254–258; Polyaenus 4.2.15 on taking away ladders.

23. For full discussion of the stories surrounding this incident, see Riginos (1994), 103–119. The earliest ancient source, or at least citing of early sources, is Didymus, *In Demosthenes* 11.22 col. xii 43–64. Strabo, *Geog.* 7. frag. 22, 22a, 8.6.15 for an arrow shot by a catapult rather than a bow.

24. Pliny, *Natural History* 7.37.124 for the quote; on the skull, see Prag (1990), 237–247, although note skepticism of Bartsiokas (2000), 511–514.

25. Diodorus Siculus 16.34.5.

CHAPTER 6: "I DID NOT RUN AWAY": DEFEAT IN THESSALY

1. On Philip's navy, see Polyaenus, *Stratagems* 4.2.22, with discussion in Hammond and Griffith (1979), 264–267.

2. Polyaenus, *Stratagems* 2.2.6.

3. Diodorus Siculus 16.31.6, although 16.34.4–5, which repeats the fall of Methone, could refer to a later intervention in Thessaly. For differing interpretations see Hammond (1994c), 46, 200n3, and Worthington (2008), 57.

4. Theopompus, *Fragments of Greek Historians* 115 F 49 (translation from Shrimpton [1991]), Demosthenes, *First Philippic* 35.

5. Diodorus Siculus 16.34.1, Demosthenes, *Against Aristocrates* 23.183; Thebans send force to help Persians reconquer Egypt, Diodorus Siculus 16.44.1–2.

6. Polyaenus, *Stratagems* 2.2.22.

7. For Sestus, see Diodorus Siculus 16.34.3; on Adaeus, see Theopompus, *Fragments of Greek Historians* 115, F 249.

8. For Delphi in general, see M. Scott, *Delphi* (2014).

9. For the background and the ensuing conflict in general, see T. Buckley, *Philip II and the Sacred War* (1989), and J. Ellis in *Cambridge Ancient History*, vol. 6, 2nd ed. (1994), 739–742.

10. Diodorus Siculus 16.23.1–25.3, 27.1–31.5 for his narrative of the early stages of the war.

11 Mercenary pay, Diodorus Siculus 16.30.1, 36.1; for Chares, see Theopompus, *Fragments of Greek Historians* no. 115, F 249, and in general Diodorus Siculus 16.33.2–3.

12. Diodorus Siculus 16.35.1, Hammond and Griffith (1979), 267–268.

13. Diodorus Siculus 16.35.2, Polyaenus, *Stratagems* 2.38.2.

14. Diodorus Siculus 16.35.2–3, Polyaenus, *Stratagems* 2.38.2, with Hammond and Griffith (1979), 269–273, suggesting that the presence of artillery reveals Onomarchus's strategy.

15. Justin, *Epitome* 8.3.

CHAPTER 7: THE AVENGER

1. Justin, *Epitome* 8.2, Diodorus Siculus 16.35.3–6; for the use of the laurel and also doubts about the executions, see Hammond and Griffith (1979), 274–277; in contrast Hammond (1994c), 47–48, Worthington (2008), 62–63; killing of prisoners earlier in the war, Diodorus Siculus 16.31.1–2.

2. Justin, *Epitome* 8.2–3; Hammond and Griffith (1979), 277–279, 285–295, and Hammond (1994c), 48–49 on Philip and Thessaly in these years.

3. Justin, *Epitome* 8.2; Worthington (2008), 64–66, Hammond and Griffith (1979), 293–295.

4. Diodorus Siculus 16.37.1–38.2.

5. Demosthenes, *First Olynthiac* 12–13, Demosthenes, *Third Olynthiac* 4, Hammond and Griffith (1979), 283–284.

6. Demosthenes, *First Olynthiac* 13, Worthington (2008), 69–70.

7. Justin, *Epitome* 8.6, and in general, Hammond and Griffith (1979), 304–308, Errington (1975), 41–50, although his argument that Arybbas was expelled from his kingdom at this time is not widely accepted.

8. For the tension between Philip and the Chalcidian League, see Hammond and Griffith (1979), 296–304.

9. Cawkwell (1978b), 77–82 gives a sober assessment of Demosthenes's importance and the Athenian background.

10. Plutarch, *Demosthenes* 4.1–6.3; quote from Demosthenes, *First Olynthiac* 14–15 (Loeb translation).

11. Demosthenes, *First Philippic* 40 (Loeb translation).

12. Demosthenes, *First Philippic* 21–22 for formation of a picked squadron of ten triremes to counter Philip's naval raids; for raiding by Philip's ships, Demosthenes, *First Philippic* 34.

13. Diodorus Siculus 16.52.9, with Hammond and Griffith (1979), 315–321.

14. Philichorus, *Fragments of Greek Historians* 328 F 49–51 for Athenian expeditions, see Cawkwell (1962), 122–140, esp. 130–131.

15. Demosthenes, *Third Philippic* 11.

16. Diodorus Siculus 16.53.2–54.4, with Hammond and Griffith (1979), 321–328.

17. Aeschines, *On the embassy* 2.12–14.

18. Diodorus Siculus 16.55.1–4, Demosthenes, *On the false embassy* 192–195.

CHAPTER 8: PEACE

1. Justin, *Epitome* 8.3–4.

2. Contrast Hammond (1994d), 367–374, arguing for the overall reliability of Justin for this period, with Buckler (1996), 380–386, who is unconvinced.

3. Justin, *Epitome* 8.3; for Cersobleptes's son, see Aeschines, *On the embassy* 81, with Hammond (1994c), 370 noting that the implication is that this would have surprised Athenians.

4. For a survey of Athenian attitudes, see Hammond (1994c), 79–82, 84–89.

5. Diodorus Siculus 16.56.3.

6. Justin, *Epitome* 8.4; in general see Hammond and Griffith (1979), 331–335.

7. Diodorus Siculus 16.59.1–2, Aeschines, *On the embassy* 12–17, 130–133.

8. Diodorus Siculus 16.59.2–3, Aeschines, *On the embassy* 134–135, and discussion in Cawkwell (1978b), 91–97.

9. Aeschines, *On the embassy* 17–20. For a useful discussion of the evidence, see Cawkwell (1978b), 92–95; for the subsequent chronology and background, see Worthington (2008), 86–104, Cawkwell (1960), 416–438, and Cawkwell (1978a), 93–104.

10. Aeschines, *On the embassy* 22–39 and Plutarch, *Demosthenes* 16 for the speeches to Philip; on Halus, Demosthenes, *On the false embassy* 2 (with scholiast), 163, 174.

11. Demosthenes, *On the false embassy* 69 for Philip's ambassadors.

12. Aeschines, *On the embassy* 104–105, 120.

13. Demosthenes, *On the false embassy* 166–167, Aeschines, *On the embassy* 100, 112, and 136–137 on hopes that Philip would deal harshly with Thebes.

14. Demosthenes, *On the false embassy* 139; on presentation of Philip, see Guth and Guth (2015), 333–348.

15. Demosthenes, *On the false embassy* 128, 196–198, Aeschines, *On the embassy* 153, 162.

16. Demosthenes, *On the false embassy* 17–18, 31–32, 121–122, Aeschines, *On the embassy* 94–95, 137.

17. Diodorus Siculus 16.59.2–60.5, Demosthenes, *On the false embassy* 62–63; Justin, *Epitome* 8.5 claims that Philip broke his word to the Phocians and massacred much of the population, but this does not appear even in the hostile Athenian sources, so is probably mere propaganda; on the settlement in general, see Hammond and Griffith (1979), 450–458.

18. Diodorus Siculus 16.60.2–3, Demosthenes, *On the false embassy* 86–90, Aeschines, *On the embassy* 137–142.

19. For arguments that Philip did hope to defeat Thebes in 346 BC, see Ellis (1976), 103–124, and J. Ellis in *Cambridge Ancient History*, vol. 6, 2nd ed. (1994), 751–759, and Markle (1974), 253–268.

20. Buckler and Beck (2008), 259–276, esp. 267–269 offers a very good assessment of Philip's aims and the situation in 346 BC.

CHAPTER 9: THE PRINCE

1. Aeschines, *Against Timarchus* 166–169.

2. Plutarch, *Alexander* 10.1–2, 77.5; for other brothers, see Unz (1985), 171–174.

3. Plutarch, *Alexander* 2.5–3.2.

4. For Lanice, see Plutarch, *Alexander* 4.9.3, Curtius 8.1.21, 2.8–9; tutors, Plutarch, *Alexander* 5.4–5; Leonidas searching for hidden treats, Plutarch, *Alexander* 22.5.

5. Plutarch, *Alexander* 22.5; for Macedonian attitudes to education, see Carney, "Elite Education and High Culture in Macedonia," in Carney, (2015), 191–205; for the suggestion that Alexander had a sheltered childhood, see Gabriel (2015), 17–31, in contrast to those who assume he had a far more active upbringing, such as Fox (1973), 43–67, Green (2012), 35–65, and Cartledge (2013), 47–58.

6. Plutarch, *Alexander* 6.1–5 for the whole story (quotes from Loeb translation, slightly amended).

7. Fraser (1953), 22–23; Plutarch, *Alexander* 61 says that Bucephalus was thirty when he died.

8. Plutarch, *Alexander* 7.1 (Loeb translation) for Philip's comment; for Aristotle, see Plutarch, *Alexander* 7.1–8.4, Pliny, *Natural History* 8.44; Justin, *Epitome* 12.16 claims that Aristotle taught Alexander for five years, but this seems exaggerated.

9. Plutarch, *Alexander* 8.2, 26.1.

10. Plutarch, *Alexander* 4.1–2, Aelian, *Various Histories* 12.

11. Plutarch, *Alexander* 5.1–3, 25.6–8, Plutarch, *Moralia* 331C, Pliny, *Natural History* 12.62.

12. Justin, *Epitome* 8.5–6; for discussion see Hammond (1994c), 109–114 and Worthington (2008), 108–110.

13. Polyaenus, *Stratagems* 4.2.12; on the campaign and the problems of our meager sources, see Hammond and Griffith (1979), 469–474, Hammond (1994c), 115–118.

14. Justin, *Prologue* 8, Diodorus Siculus 16.69.7, 93.4–6, Plutarch, *Moralia* 331B, Demosthenes, *De corona* 67, Didymus, *In Demosthenes* xi 22, col. xiii 3–7; for the wound, see Riginos (1994), 103–119, esp. 115–116.

15. Diodorus Siculus 16.69.8, with Ellis (1976), 137–143 and Hammond (1994c), 118–119.

16. Diodorus Siculus 16.72.1, Justin, *Epitome* 8.6.4–7, Demosthenes, *On Halonnesus* 32, Demosthenes, *Against Olympiodorus* 24, Demosthenes, *Third Philippic* 72, with Hammond (1994c), 120–122.

17. Diodorus Siculus 16.71.1–2, Demosthenes, *On the Chersonese* 2.35, Demosthenes, *Third Philippic* 49–50.

18. Polyaenus, *Stratagems* 4.2.16 for the dogs and 4.2.13 for rearguard action; marriage to Meda, see Jordanes, *Getica* 10–65, Athenaeus 13.557b–e, with Carney (2000), 68.

19. For fuller discussions of Athenian politics during these years see Ellis (1976), 143–147, 148–150, 151–153, Hammond (1994c), 105–108, Worthington (2008), 118–119, Cawkwell (1963), 120–138 and Cawkwell (1978b), 114–131.

20. Taylor (2001a), 53–66, Taylor (2001b), 154–172, Mader (2006), 367–386, and Mader (2007), 339–360.

21. Demosthenes, *On the Chersonese* 44–45 (Loeb translation).

22. Demosthenes, *On the false embassy* 87, 260–261, 294–295, 326, 334, Demosthenes, *Third Philippic* 57–66 and see Hammond and Griffith (1979), 474–484 on the Peloponnese and 496–504 on Euboea.

23. Diodorus Siculus 16.62.1–63.2, Philochorus, *Fragments of Greek Historians* 328 F 157.

24. Demosthenes, *On the Chersonese* passim, esp. 2, 8–20, 23–32, 44–47, with Hammond and Griffith (1979), 563–566.

25. Demosthenes, *On the crown* 136, Demosthenes, *On Halonnesus* 20–23, with Ellis (1976), 143–147 and Hammond (1994c), 106.

26. Demosthenes, *On Halonnesus* esp. 26–30, and Pseudo-Demosthenes, *Philip's Letter*, passim, Ellis (1976), 166–178 and J. Ellis in *Cambridge Ancient History*, vol. 6, 2nd ed. (1994), 768–770, 773–777.

27. Pseudo-Demosthenes, *Philip's Letter* 2–5.

28. Demosthenes, *On the Chersonese* 14–16, Demosthenes, *On the crown* 244, 302, Demosthenes, *Fourth Philippic* 32, Diodorus Siculus 16.54.1–2; in general Hammond and Griffith (1979), 554–570.

29. Diodorus Siculus 16.74.2–76.4, Vitruvius, *De architectura* 10.13.3, with Marsden (1969), 5–17, 48–62 and Marsden (1977), 211–233.

30. Kern (1999), 198–200.

31. Philolochus F 162, Theopompus, *Fragments of Greek Historians* 115 F 295, with Hammond and Griffith (1979), 575–577. Justin, *Epitome* 9.1.6 places the capture of the convoy after a prolonged siege of Byzantium, but this seems less likely.

32. Diodorus Siculus 16.77.2–3; for the dogs, Hesychius Milesius 26–27 (FHG 4.151).

33. Athens's destruction of the treaty, Demosthenes, *On the crown* 71–72, Diodorus Siculus 16.77.2, Aeschines, *Against Ctesiphon* 55; Worthington (2008), 128–135 argues that Philip's letter to Athens in 341 BC was effectively a declaration of war, while Ellis (1976), 179–180 and Hammond (1994c), 131–132 have the Athenians declaring war in 340 BC after Philip had seized the grain convoy.

34. Plutarch, *Alexander* 9.1, with Worthington (2008), 130–131.

CHAPTER 10: OLD AND NEW ENEMIES

1. In general, see Flower (1999), 419–429 for the wide appeal of the idea.

2. Isocrates, *Letter to Philip* 68 (Loeb translation); for Isocrates and his appeals to Philip, see Pearlman (1957), 306–317, Pearlman (1976), 1–30, Pearlman (1983), 211–227, Markle, (1976), 80–99.

3. Isocrates, *Letter to Philip* 73 (Loeb translation), and 56 for Athens's willingness to join Philip.

4. Isocrates, *Letter to Philip* 154 (Loeb translation); concern over Philip risking his life fighting obscure tribes, Isocrates, *Letter to Philip* 1–11.

5. Isocrates, *Letter to Philip* 132 (Loeb translation).

6. Demosthenes, *On Halonnesus* 33–35 (Loeb translation). The speech was probably delivered by Hegesippus in 342 BC; for discussion of Philip's attitude, see Cawkwell (2005), 200–203.

7. Plutarch, *Phocion* 14.

8. Frontinus, *Stratagems* 1, 4, 13–13a for the deception and the negotiations, with discussion in Hammond and Griffith (1979), 579–581, and Hammond (1994c), 134–135.

9. For a good overview of Philip's activities on his northern frontiers, see Adams (2002), 283–291.

10. Hammond and Griffith (1979), 581–584; Darius's invasion, in Herodotus 4.1–2, 86–143.

11. Quote from Justin, *Epitome* 9.1.9, comparing Philip to a merchant.

12. The exchanges between Philip and Atheas only appear in Justin, *Epitome* 9.2.1–13.

13. Justin, *Epitome* 9.2.14–16; cavalry ordered to execute anyone who flees, Frontinus, *Stratagems* 2.8.14.

14. Justin, *Epitome* 9.1.8 for Alexander accompanying Philip on campaign in Thrace.

15. Justin, *Epitome* 9.2.16 if taken literally has the mares sent back to Macedonia.

16. Justin, *Epitome* 9.3.1–3.

17. For the wound see Riginos (1994), 103–119, esp. 116–118, and Gabriel (2010), 12–14, arguing that the injury must have been a flesh wound that missed the bone if the weapon had sufficient power to go on and kill his mount.

CHAPTER 11: CHAERONEA

1. Justin, *Epitome* 8.1.

2. Philolochus, *Fragments of Greek Historians* 328 F 56.

3. Aeschines, *Against Ctesiphon* 3.115–121, Demosthenes, *On the crown* 140–155 provide the bulk of information about the meetings of the Amphictyonic council.

4. Demosthenes, *On the crown* 149 on the alleged naivete of the council members when faced with a polished Athenian orator.

5. Aeschines, *Against Ctesiphon* 125–128; for discussion see Hammond and Griffith (1979), 585–588, Harris (1995), 126–130, and Buckler (2000), 142–143.

6. Justin, *Epitome* 9.3.4, Diodorus Siculus 18.84.2, Demosthenes, *On the crown* 169, with Hammond and Griffith (1979), 589, Hammond (1994c), 144–145, and Worthington (2008), 141–142.

7. Plutarch, *Demosthenes* 18.2–4.

8. Demosthenes, *On the crown* 172–173 (Loeb translation).

9. Demosthenes, *On the crown* 184–185 (Loeb translation, slightly modified).

10. For the full account, Demosthenes, *On the crown* 169–187, which is clearly the principal source for Diodorus Siculus 16.84.2–85.1, and more briefly Plutarch, *Demosthenes* 18.1–4.

11. For Thebes in this period, see A. Schachter, "From Hegemony to Disaster: Thebes from 362 to 335 BC," in Schachter (2016), 113–132, noting the economic weakness of the city.

12. Hammond and Griffith (1979), 590–593; Worthington (2008), 263n28 identifies Proxenos as an Athenian rather than a Theban, contra Hammond (1994c), 147.

13. Demosthenes, *On the crown* 18.216–217, Polyaenus, *Stratagems* 4.2.14, Diodorus Siculus 16.85.5.

14. Polyaenus, *Stratagems* 4.2.8, Aeschines, *Against Ctesiphon* 146, Diodorus Siculus 16.85.3 for strength of Philip's army and 16.85.7 for criticism of Chares's abilities, with Hammond and Griffith (1979), 593–594.

15. Van Wees (2004), 131–150.

16. Plutarch, *Phocion* 16.1–3, Aeschines, *Against Ctesiphon* 3.149–151.

17. On the armies, Diodorus Siculus 16.86.6, Justin, *Epitome* 9.3.9, and for numbers and the battle as a whole, the fullest discussion is Corvisier (2012), 75–80 on numbers; Demosthenes's shield, Plutarch, *Demosthenes* 20.2; on the Sacred Band, A. Schachter, "Boiotian Military Elites (with an appendix on the funeral stelai)," in Schachter (2016), 193–215, esp. 193–198, and Ogden (1996), 107–168, esp. 111–115 are good starting places to the substantial literature on the subject. One of the most obvious practical questions if the stories were literally true is how casualties would be replaced if one of a pair was killed or crippled.

18. The main account is Diodorus Siculus 16.86.1–6, with Plutarch, *Alexander* 9.2, Polyaenus, *Stratagems* 4.2.2, 7; for surprisingly full and detailed reconstructions of the battle, see Pritchett (1958), 307–311, Hammond and Griffith (1979), 596–603, Hammond (1994c), 151–154, Ashley (1998), 153–158, Worthington (2008), 147–151; for more skeptical analysis, Buckler and Beck (2008), 254–258, Ma (2008), 72–91, and Lendon (2017), 39–64, esp. 61.

19. Polyaenus, *Stratagems* 4.2.2, 7, Diodorus Siculus 16.86.1–2. The claim that Philip's men retired to advantageous ground is difficult to reconcile with the terrain today, at least where most scholars have located the battle, but since the landscape may have changed and the favored location be incorrect it is hard to judge the plausibility of the story on this basis.

20. The fullest discussion of the sarissa and its use is Matthew (2015), *passim*; for archers in earlier Greek phalanxes, see van Wees (2004), 172–197, though arguing that they disappear in the fully developed, tighter phalanx of the Classical period, when they were instead deployed behind or on the flanks.

21. Diodorus Siculus 16.86.3–6, Plutarch, *Alexander* 9.2, Plutarch, *Demosthenes* 20.2.

22. Rahe (1981), 84–87, Ma (2008), 75–78, 83–86.

23. Plutarch, *Demosthenes* 20.3, Justin, *Epitome* 9.4.1–4, Diodorus Siculus 16.87.1–3, with discussion in Worthington (2008), 153–154.

CHAPTER 12: LOVE AND PERSIA

1. In general see Vaughn (1991), 38–62, esp. 43–44.

2. Diodorus Siculus 16.88.1–2, Plutarch, *Phocion* 16.3, Plutarch, *Demosthenes* 20.3.

3. Diodorus Siculus 16.87.3, 17.13.5, Justin, *Epitome* 9.4.7–8, Polybius 5.10.1–5 for goodwill felt toward Philip almost 200 years later by many Peloponnesian communities; quote from Plutarch, *Moralia* 177 D. 4; in general see also Roebuck (1948), 73–92.

4. Some claim that Philip wanted to keep the Athenian fleet in existence so that he could use it in his Persian War, e.g., Hammond and Griffith (1979), 570, 619, but if so it is odd that neither he nor Alexander actually made much use of it, cf. Worthington (2008), 155–156 is skeptical, not least because any plans for an eastern war are unlikely at the start of his reign.

5. Hammond and Griffith (1979), 623–646, Perlman (1985), 153–174, Adams (1999), 15–22.

6. Justin, *Epitome* 9.5.1–8, Diodorus Siculus 16.89.1–3.

7. Isocrates, *Letters* 3.3, with Sakellariou (1980), 128–145, Worthington (2008), 166–167.

8. For wider discussion on the decision to go to war with Persia, see Buckler (1994), 99–122, Bloedow (2003), 261–274.

9. Carney (2000), 68–75, who suggests that the desire for heirs was the main motive for the marriage, with Worthington (2008), 172–174, Hammond (1994c), 171–173; Bosworth (1971b), 93–105, esp. 102–103 suggests that the marriage should be seen in the context of power struggles between the nobility of Upper and Lower Macedonia; Heckel (1978), 155–158 explores similar themes while reaching different conclusions.

10. For discussion of internal politics, see Heckel (1986), 293–305, 298 noting how apparently easy it was for Alexander to dispose of Attalus, which does not suggest an especially powerful party of kin and supporters.

11. Plutarch, *Alexander* 9.4–5, with Justin, *Epitome* 9.7.3–4 for a briefer version. If the story is true, then by the same standard Philip with his Illyrian mother would be illegitimate, leading some to dismiss the incident since surely Attalus would not have insulted the king. This implies that the words were clear, correctly heard, and that Philip was touchy about this, none of which need be true, see Hammond and Griffith (1979), 676–678, Carney (1992), 169–189, esp. 174–176, and Greenwalt (1989), 19–45, esp. 41–42.

12. Worthington (2008), 164–166, Townshend (2003), 93–101, Hammond and Griffith (1979), 692–694.

13. Fredricksmeyer (1990), 300–315.

14. As we have seen Plato, *Gorgias* 471B alleged illegitimacy for Archelaus, but this may reflect misunderstanding of Macedonian polygamy; for Caranus/Karanus, Justin, *Epitome* 9.7.3, 11.2.3, with Unz (1985), 171–174.

15. Plutarch, *Alexander* 9.3 for Philip's pride in Alexander.

16. Plutarch, *Alexander* 9.6; Justin, *Epitome* 9.7.7–8 implies Olympias was not at Aegae in 336 BC, but this does not necessarily mean that she was not in Macedonia at all.

17. Carney (1992), 178–179 and Carney (2000), 75–76.

18. Plutarch, *Alexander* 10.1–3. Opinion over this story varies considerably, e.g., rejected by Hammond (1994c), 174–175, but accepted with caution by Carney

(1992), 179–180; Fredricksmeyer (1990), 303 suggests a different chronology, especially for the exile of Alexander's friends.

19. Plutarch, *Alexander* 4.4, 21.4, 22.3, Athenaeus 10.435.

20. Curtius 3.12.16, Diodorus Siculus 17.114.1, 3, with full list of sources in Heckel (2006), 133–137.

CHAPTER 13:
"WREATHED IS THE BULL": PASSION, AMBITION, AND REVENGE

1. Diodorus Siculus 16.90.2, Arrian, *Anabasis* 1.17.11, J. Ellis in *Cambridge Ancient History*, vol. 6, 2nd ed. (1994), 787–789, Hammond (1994c), 167–170.

2. Diodorus Siculus 16.93.3–9, Justin, *Epitome* 9.6.5–8, Plutarch, *Alexander* 10.4; for discussion of the context, see Mortensen (2002), 371–387.

3. Diodorus Siculus 16.94.1, with Antela-Bernardez (2012), 859–861.

4. Diodorus Siculus 16.91.3–92.2; on the timing of the wedding, see Hatzopoulos (1982), 21–42, esp. 38–42.

5. Diodorus Siculus 16.93.3–4 (Loeb translation); on the symbolism of the statues see Fredricksmeyer (1979), 36–61 and Baynham (1994); 35–43.

6. Diodorus Siculus 16.92.5–93.1, 94.2–4, Aristotle, *Politics* 1311b, Justin, *Epitome* 9.6.1–8.

7. Arrian, *Anabasis* 1.25.2, Curtius 7.1.6–7, Justin, *Epitome* 11.2.2; for Antipater, see Heckel (2006), 35–38.

8. In general, Carney (2015), 155–165, Badian (2002), 389–406, Ellis (1981), 99–137.

9. Plutarch, *Alexander* 10.4, Justin, *Epitome* 9.7.1–14.

10. Arrian, *Anabasis* 1.5.4, 25.1, Justin, *Epitome* 12.6.14, Diodorus Siculus 17.2.1, *Fragments of Greek Historians* 148 for the diviner, with Hammond (1994c), 175–179.

11. Diodorus Siculus 17.2.5–6, Curtius 7.1.3.

12. Justin, *Epitome* 9.7.12, Pausanias 8.7.7; for propaganda against Olympias, see Carney (1993), 29–55.

13. Arrian, *Anabasis* 2.14, with Carney (1992), 183–185.

14. Plutarch, *Demosthenes* 22.1–5, Aeschines, *On the crown* 77.

15. Diodorus Siculus 17.3.1–5.

16. Hammond (1994c), 178–182 arguing in favor of identification, with caution in Worthington (2008), 234–241.

17. Diodorus Siculus 17.4.1–3.

CHAPTER 14: THE EXAMPLE

1. Plutarch, *Alexander* 11.1 (Loeb translation).

2. Plutarch, *Alexander* 14.1–3, Plutarch, *Moralia (on the fortune of Alexander)* 331e–f, Valerius Maximus 4.3.4b; for a range of judgments on the authenticity of this story, see Green (1991), 122–123, Fox (2004), 71, Worthington (2014), 127.

3. Plutarch, *Alexander* 11.2, 14.4; Fox (2004), 71–72 is inclined to see the story as a Roman invention.

4. Arrian, *Anabasis* 1.1.4.

5. Arrian, *Anabasis* 1.1.4–13; Green (1991), 125–126 is rather generous to describe "Alexander's inspired foreknowledge" in spotting the enemy plan, but such adulation is common, cf. Worthington (2014), 128 and to a lesser extent Fox (2004), 82; Fuller (1958), 220n2 at least speculates over whether the tactic was novel.

6. Arrian, *Anabasis* 1.2.1–7; Plutarch, *Alexander* 11.5 says that Alexander defeated Syrmus, but Arrian states that the king was at Peuce and not actually present at the battle.

7. Fox (2004), 83 suggests that Xenophon provided the inspiration. For a wider discussion of the influence of the author on the king, see McGroaty (2006), 105–124.

8. Arrian, *Anabasis* 1.2.1–4.5 for the campaign.

9. Arrian, *Anabasis* 1.4.6–8, Strabo, *Geog.* 7.3.8; see Tierney (1959/1960), 189–275, esp. 196 for this theme of fearlessness—more recently made famous by Asterix!

10. Arrian, *Anabasis* 1.5.1–7; for discussion of the campaign and especially where it occurred, see Hammond (1974), 66–87, with criticism and a highly plausible alternative in Bosworth (1982), 74–85.

11. Arrian, *Anabasis* 1.5.8–12.

12. Arrian, *Anabasis* 1.6.1–8.

13. Arrian, *Anabasis* 1.6.9–11.

14. For praise of Alexander, but rightly emphasizing the quality of his army, Worthington (2014), 130, Green (1991), 133–134, Bosworth (1988), 31–32, while Fuller (1958), 226, reserves judgment over strategy, but describes it as "outstanding" that Alexander never lost his nerve in this campaign.

15. Arrian, *Anabasis* 1.5.2–4, 7.1–3, Plutarch, *Demosthenes* 23.1, Diodorus Siculus 17.8.3–7, Justin, *Epitome* 11.2.5–10; Demades, *Twelve Years* 17 supports Justin's details, but is widely considered to have been written much later as a rhetorical exercise, see Worthington (1991), 90–95, but may well have been based on genuine lost accounts of events.

16. Arrian, *Anabasis* 1.7.4–6, Diodorus Siculus 17.9.1–3.

17. Arrian, *Anabasis* 1.7.7–11 emphasizes Alexander's restraint, Diodorus Siculus 17.9.4–5 has initial reluctance change to a decision to make an example of Thebes.

18. Arrian, *Anabasis* 1.8.1–8, Diodorus Siculus 17.11.1–12.5, Plutarch, *Alexander* 11.4–6; on Arrian's treatment of Perdiccas based on his use of Ptolemy's account, see Roisman (1984), 373–385, esp. 374–376.

19. Arrian, *Anabasis* 1.8.8, Plutarch, *Alexander* 11.5–12.3, Diodorus Siculus 17.13.2–6.

20. Plutarch, *Alexander* 11.7–8, Arrian, *Anabasis* 1.9.6–9; in general see Worthington (2003), 65–86.

21. Arrian, *Anabasis* 1.10.1–3, Plutarch, *Demosthenes* 23.1–3, Plutarch, *Alexander* 13.1–2.

22. Arrian, *Anabasis* 1.10.3–6, Plutarch, *Demosthenes* 23.3–24.1, Diodorus Siculus 17.15.1–5.

23. For the impact of the destruction of Thebes, see Green (1991), 146–151, Fox (2004), 87–89, Worthington (2014), 133–135.

CHAPTER 15: THE ARMY AND THE ENEMY

1. Diodorus Siculus 17.7.2–10, Bosworth (1988), 34–35, Green (1991), 138–140.

2. Plutarch, *Alexander* 15.1; Arrian, *Anabasis* 1.10.3 gives the main force as a little more than 30,000 infantry and over 5,000 cavalry. Diodorus Siculus 17.17.3–5 provides the only detailed breakdown of the forces, but even this raises questions. For the following section I have drawn heavily on Bosworth (1988), 259–266, Sekunda (2007), 325–357, esp. 330–333, and the same author's heavily illustrated *Army of Alexander the Great* (1984), Heckel (2016), 260–280, and D. Devine (1989), 104–129, esp. 104–108. The bibliography covering Alexander's army and campaigns found in O'Brien (1992), 307–310 remains excellent.

3. I have followed Sekunda (2007), 331 for the units' sizes, but there are other estimates of the size of the royal *ilê* and standard *ilai*, and it is also possible that the 1,800 Macedonian cavalry in Diodorus Siculus 17.17.4 include some or all of the *prodromoi* as well as the Companion cavalry. Heckel (2010), 260–280, notes that 1,800 divided into eight *ilai* would produce 225-man units; for saddles see Sidnell (2007), 20–21, 35, 85.

4. On role of men in front and rear, see Xenophon, *Memorabilia* 3.1.8, *Cyropaedia* 3.3.41–42, 6.3.27, Asclepiodotus 3.2–5.

5. Bosworth (1988), 259, 262–263, contrasting with Sekunda (1984), 20–21 who believes that the *prodromoi* were Thracians.

6. Engels (1978) remains the fullest study of supply, but needs to be used with a degree of caution since inevitably many assumptions and the subsequent calculations are conjectural.

7. Diodorus Siculus 17.17.5 says that Antipater was left with 12,000 foot and 1,500 cavalry. No other sources gives a number for the troops left behind, although the scale of his resources can be estimated from subsequent campaigns, notably the war against Sparta. It is generally and reasonably assumed that Diodorus only gave numbers for the Macedonian troops under Antipater's command.

8. Justin, *Epitome* 11.6.3–7; in 317 BC the *argyraspides* or silver shields, successors to the hypaspists, were all supposed to be more than sixty years old, Diodorus Siculus 19.41.2, Plutarch, *Eumenes* 16.7–8.

9. Plutarch, *Alexander* 15.1.

10. Diodorus Siculus 17.16.1–4, Plutarch, *Alexander* 15.2–3, Arrian, *Anabasis* 1.11.1–2, with Baynham (1998), 141–152.

11. Livy 8.24.5–13, Strabo, *Geog.* 6.1.5.

12. Arrian, *Anabasis* 1.11.3, Curtius 4.1.39, Justin, *Epitome* 11.7.1, Diodorus Siculus 17.32.1, 118.1, 18.21.2, Plutarch, *Alexander* 39.5, 58.2–3, with Heckel (2016), 35–38.

13. Plutarch, *Alexander* 3.2, Arrian, *Anabasis* 1.11.3–4.

14. Arrian, *Anabasis* 1.11.6, with Anson (1989), 44–49 for the inability of the Persians to prevent the crossing.

15. Arrian, *Anabasis* 1.11.5–6; Homer, *Iliad* 2.701–702 (Lattimore translation) for the quote.

16. Arrian, *Anabasis* 1.11.7–12.1, with Plutarch, *Alexander* 15.4–5, Diodorus Siculus 17.17.6–7.

17. Bosworth (1988), 38–39, Green (1991), 165–168, Fox (2004), 109–115.

18. Diodorus Siculus 17.5.3–6.3, Justin, *Epitome* 10.1.1–3.5, with the detailed discussion by Badian (2000), 241–267 = Badian (2012a), 457–478.

19. Justin, *Epitome* 10.1.1 for Ochus's sons.

20. See Badian (2012a), 458–463.

21. See Cawkwell (2005), 198–206 for discussion of Greek attitudes and actual Persian strength.

22. Herodotus 7.60.1, with general comments on the numbers given by Greek sources and the actual size and organization of Persian armies, see Cawkwell (2005), 237–254.

23. Cawkwell (2005), 255–273; fleet of 400 ships, Arrian, *Anabasis* 1.18.5.

CHAPTER 16: THE RIVER

1. Arrian, *Anabasis* 1.12.8–9, Diodorus Siculus 18.2.2–4, with Garvin (2003), 87–111, esp. 96–100; 5,000 mercenaries under Memnon in 335 BC, Diodorus Siculus 17.7.2, for Mentor and Artabazus, Diodorus Siculus 16.52.4, Arrian, *Anabasis* 7.4.6, Plutarch, *Alexander* 21.8.

2. Arrian, *Anabasis* 1.14.4; cavalry from distant provinces are listed in Diodorus Siculus 17.19.4–5, who gives the lower total of 10,000 cavalry.

3. Engels (1978), 11–36.

4. For the campaign, see Arrian, *Anabasis* 1.12.6–7; one example of this genre of poetry is Horace, *Sermones* 1.8.

5. On the campaign and battle of Granicus, see Badian (1977), 271–293 = Badian (2012a), 224–243, Hammond (1980), 73–88, A. Devine (1986), 265–278, Bosworth (1988), 39–44, Green (1991), 168–181, 489–512, and Heckel (2008), 45–51.

6. Arrian, *Anabasis* 1.13.3–7, and Plutarch, *Alexander* 16.1–2, which also includes the story that Alexander renamed the month because the actual one was considered an unlucky time for a Macedonian king to take the field.

7. Diodorus Siculus 17.19.1–22.6 for his account of the battle; Hammond (1980) convincingly dismisses this version, which has only been supported by a minority of scholars.

8. Arrian, *Anabasis* 1.14.1–16.7 offers the most detailed and convincing narrative of the battle, although it includes some clear errors and leaves unanswered questions; Plutarch, *Alexander* 16.3–8 broadly conforms although there are differences of detail. The claim that the Persian cavalry consisted of distinct ethnic contingents is based on Diodorus Siculus 17.19.4, but given the unreliability of the rest of his narrative must be treated with some caution.

9. For topography I have generally followed Hammond (1980), 76–80, who presents the most convincing case.

10. Alexander conspicuous, Arrian, *Anabasis* 14.4; casualties in lead squadron, Arrian, *Anabasis* 16.4; on Memnon, see McCoy (1989), 413–433.

11. Gaebel (2002), 184–185; thousand coppersmiths, see Holmes (1986), 163.

12. Arrian, *Anabasis* 1.15.6–8; Plutarch, *Alexander* 16.4–5 differs over details, while Diodorus Siculus 17.20.3–21.3 differs even more, and adds drama, with Alexander being knocked down and protected by his men. In such a confused situation slight differences even in eyewitness accounts would be inevitable, while subsequently the story was embellished.

13. On casualties and the aftermath of the battle, see Arrian, *Anabasis* 1.16.2–6; Plutarch, *Alexander* 16.7–8 claims just 34 Macedonian fatalities, which may just refer to the leading squadron of Companions and the infantry near them, with

2,350 Persian cavalry and 20,000 infantry killed; Diodorus Siculus 17.21.5–6 does not give Macedonian casualties, but claims 1,000 dead Persian horsemen, 10,000 dead infantry, and 20,000 prisoners; Justin, *Epitome* 11.6.14 has 9 Macedonian infantry and 120 cavalry killed and a great slaughter of Persians.

14. Arrian, *Anabasis* 1.16.7–17.8, Plutarch, *Alexander* 16.8.

15. Arrian, *Anabasis* 1.17.9–18.2, Strabo, *Geog.* 14.1.23.

16. Pliny, *Natural History* 32.95, 35.85–86.

17. Arrian, *Anabasis* 1.18.3–9.

18. Arrian, *Anabasis* 1.19.1–6; Evans (2015), 1–39 offers a useful survey of the Ionian War with some provocative interpretations.

19. Arrian, *Anabasis* 1.19.7–11.

20. Arrian, *Anabasis* 1.20.1 (Loeb translation), Diodorus Siculus 17.22.5–23.3; Bosworth (1980a), 141–143 is critical, but overestimates Alexander's capacity to maintain something as expensive as a fleet at this stage of the war.

21. Arrian, *Anabasis* 1.23.8, Strabo, *Geog.* 14.2.17, Diodorus Siculus 17.24.2–3, Plutarch, *Alexander* 22.7–10.

22. Arrian, *Anabasis* 1.20.2–23.6, Diodorus Siculus 17.23.4–27.6, the latter giving an especially heroic account of the defense.

23. Arrian, *Anabasis* 1.24.1–2.

CHAPTER 17: THE GORDIAN KNOT

1. Arrian, *Anabasis* 1.24.3 (Loeb translation) for the quote, and in general 1.24.3–6, 26.1–29.8.

2. Arrian, *Anabasis* 1.24.4–5 (Loeb translation); Bosworth (1988), 49–53 and especially Hammond (1994a), 83–94 are rare exceptions to the rule and discuss these operations in some detail.

3. Diodorus Siculus 17.28.1–5.

4. Arrian, *Anabasis* 1.26.5, 27.5–28.8.

5. Arrian, *Anabasis* 1.24.5–6, 29.1–2.

6. Arrian, *Anabasis* 1.25.2–3, 26.5–27.4.

7. Plutarch, *Alexander* 17.2–4, and Strabo, *Geog.* 14.3.9 with Green (1991), 205, Worthington (2014), 157–158.

8. Arrian, *Anabasis* 1.25.1–10, Diodorus Siculus 17.32.1–2, Curtius 3.7.11–15, 7.1.6–9, Justin, *Epitome* 12.14.1, with Green (1988), 202–204, Fox (2004), 144–148, Bosworth (1988), 50–51, Badian (2012), 420–455, esp. 424–427, and Heckel (2016), 24–31.

9. Arrian, *Anabasis* 1.29.3–4; on reinforcements generally contrast Bosworth (1986), 1–12, esp. 2–9, with Hammond (1989b), 56–68.

10. Arrian, *Anabasis* 2.3.1–8, Plutarch, *Alexander* 18.1–2, Curtius 3.1.14–18, Justin, *Epitome* 11.7, with Green (1991), 213–214.

11. Arrian, *Anabasis* 2.4.1.

12. Arrian, *Anabasis* 2.1.1–2.5, Diodorus Siculus 17.31.3–4, Curtius 3.2.1, with Garvin (2003), 87–111, esp. 100–101, 107–108, Cawkwell (2005), 209–210, Hammond (1994a), 90–91.

13. Arrian, *Anabasis* 1.29.5–6.

14. Arrian, *Anabasis* 2.8.8, Diodorus Siculus 17.30.1–31.3, Justin, *Epitome* 11.9.1.

15. Aeschines, *Against Ctesiphon* 3.163–164; for Darius's army and strategy see A. Devine (1985b), 25–38, esp. 27.

16. Diodorus Siculus 17.30.2–7.

17. Arrian, *Anabasis* 2.4.1–6, Curtius 3.4.3–5.

18. Arrian, *Anabasis* 2.4.7–11, 3.6.4–7, Plutarch, *Alexander* 19.1–5, Curtius 3.5.1–6.17.

19. Arrian, *Anabasis* 2.5.1–9, with Hammond (1994a), 93–95, Bosworth (1988), 54–58.

CHAPTER 18: "THEN TRULY THERE WAS GREAT BLOODSHED": THE BATTLE OF ISSUS, 333 BC

1. Arrian, *Anabasis* 2.6.1–2, 7.1, contrasted with Curtius 3.7.1–10 who claims Alexander planned to fight a defensive campaign, with A. Devine (1985b), 29–34.

2. Arrian, *Anabasis* 2.6.3–7, 7.2.

3. Arrian, *Anabasis* 2.7.1, Curtius 3.8.1–17, Diodorus Siculus 17.32.2–4.

4. Arrian, *Anabasis* 2.7.3–9, with quote from 2.7.9 (Loeb translation).

5. Arrian, *Anabasis* 2.8.1–2.

6. On the River Pagas, see the arguments in Hammond (1992a), 395–406, esp. 395–396 and Hammond (1994a), 95–103; on numbers Polybius 12.18.1, Arrian, *Anabasis* 2.8.6, 8; A. Devine (1985a), 39–59, 46–47, suggests that since the mercenaries faced off against the pike phalanx and hypaspists they may have roughly matched them in numbers, c. 12,000, but such estimates cannot be proved.

7. The ancient sources for the battle are Arrian, *Anabasis* 2.8.1–12.1, Polybius 12.17.1–22.7, Diodorus Siculus 17.331.1–35.1, Curtius 3.8.18–20.19, Plutarch, *Alexander* 20.1–5, Justin, *Epitome* 11.9.1–16; of the modern accounts, Hammond (1992a) and (1994a), 95–107 is most convincing, and I have followed his views on many aspects of the battle.

8. 30 stades distance, from Diodorus Siculus 17.33.1, Curtius 3.8.23.

9. Depth of formations from Polybius 12.19.6, citing Callisthenes. This is part of a long digression criticizing Callisthenes's understanding and narrative of the battle, discussed in detail in Walbank (1967), 364–376.

10. Polybius 12.17.5, 22.4 with Hammond (1994a), 98–101.

11. "A beaten man," Arrian, *Anabasis* 2.10.2.

12. Arrian, *Anabasis* 2.10.3 (Loeb translation).

13. Arrian, *Anabasis* 2.10.3–4, with Hammond (1992a), 402, esp. n24; on the Kardakes, see Charles (2012), 7–21.

14. On casualties, Arrian, *Anabasis* 2.10.7.

15. Arrian, *Anabasis* 2.11.8; for an interpretation of the mosaic claiming sympathy for Darius, see Badian (2012b), 404–419. Most commentators tend to see it as a simpler celebration of Alexander's victory and heroism.

16. Arrian, *Anabasis* 2.12.1–2, Curtius 3.11.27, Diodorus Siculus17.36.6, Justin, *Epitome* 11.9.10, and the discussion in Devine (1985a), 55–57, although he is inclined to support the higher total of 1,200 fatalities given by the anonymous Oxyrynchus historian (1798) as "maybe closer to the truth." While possible, this seems unnecessary.

17. "Alexander's bath," see Plutarch, *Alexander* 20.7–8 (Loeb translation).

18. Arrian, *Anabasis* 2.12.3–8, Plutarch, *Alexander* 21.1–3 and Plutarch, *Moralia* 338e, 522a, Curtius 3.12.4–26, Diodorus Siculus 17.36.2–4, 37.3–38.3, Justin, *Epitome* 11.9.14–16, Valerius Maximus 4.7 ext. 2; Stateira's death, Plutarch, *Alexander* 30.1, Diodorus Siculus 17.54.17, Curtius 4.10.18–34, Justin, *Epitome* 11.12.6; see Carney (1996a), 563–583, esp. 563–571.

19. Plutarch, *Alexander* 21.4–22.3, Justin, *Epitome* 11.10.2–3, Curtius 3.13.14, with Ogden (2011), 139–142, Carney (1996a), 571–575.

20. Arrian, *Anabasis* 2.14.1–9, with quote from Loeb translation, Curtius 4.1.7–14, Justin, *Epitome* 11.12.1–2, Diodorus Siculus 17.39.1–2 (who makes the unlikely claim that Alexander concealed the real letter from his advisors and showed them only an invented, far harsher version).

CHAPTER 19: "MANIFESTLY A LARGE TASK": THE SIEGE OF TYRE

1. Arrian, *Anabasis* 2.11.9–10, 12.3–8, 15.1–2, Curtius 3.13.1–17, Plutarch, *Alexander* 24.1–2, Diodorus Siculus 17.35.1–36.1, with Green (1991), 244–245, Fox (2004), 177–178; it is possible that Arrian's approximation and Curtius's more specific figure are duplicates.

2. Plutarch, *Alexander* 22.2, 24.1–2, 26.1; Plutarch, *Moralia* 339E for one officer acquiring a mistress.

3. Arrian, *Anabasis* 2.15.2–5 and Curtius 3.13 who names different envoys apart from Iphicrates.

4. Arrian, *Anabasis* 2.13.1–6, Diodorus Siculus 17.48.1.

5. Bloedow (1994), 65–76, esp. 70 argues that the Persian fleet was already breaking up, but this is hard to sustain, and even if the process was underway this would not have meant that it was obvious to Alexander or anyone else.

6. Contra Bloedow (1994) and Bloedow (2004), 75–99 arguing that the sensible strategy would have been to chase Darius.

7. Plutarch, *Sulla* 38.

8. Arrian, *Anabasis* 1.29.3, Curtius 4.1.35, 5.9.

9. Arrian, *Anabasis* 2.13.7–8, 15.6, Curtius 4.1.15–26, Plutarch, *Moralia* 340c-d, Diodorus Siculus 17.47.1–6.

10. Arrian, *Anabasis* 15.7–16.7, Curtius 4.2.1–15.

11. Arrian, *Anabasis* 2.17.1–18.2; Bloedow (1994) discuss this speech and interpretations of it, although too readily dismiss the logic of some of the arguments.

12. Arrian, *Anabasis* 2.21.4; the main ancient narratives are Arrian, *Anabasis* 2.18.1–24.6, Curtius 4.2.12–4.21, Diodorus Siculus 17.40.2–46.6, which differ in many details but are broadly consistent, while the most thorough examination of the siege is Romane (1987), 79–90.

13. Josephus, *Jewish Antiquities* 11.313–320, 329–339, Plutarch, *Alexander* 24.6–8.

14. Arrian, *Anabasis* 2.19.6 (Loeb translation).

15. Arrian, *Anabasis* 2.20.3 (Loeb translation).

16. Curtius 4.3.21–23, Diodorus Siculus 17.41.7–8.

17. Curtius 4.4.1–5, Diodorus Siculus 17.41.5, Plutarch, *Alexander* 24.1–2.

18. Arrian, *Anabasis* 2.23.2, 5, Diodorus Siculus 17.45.6, Curtius 4.4.10–11.

19. Arrian, *Anabasis* 2.24.4–5, and Curtius 4.4.15–18, including the story of the mass crucifixion.

CHAPTER 20: AN OASIS AND A GOD

1. Arrian, *Anabasis* 2.25.1–3 (quotes from Loeb translation); Plutarch, *Alexander* 29.29.4 tells a similar story, but places it early in the next year, as does Diodorus Siculus 17.54.1–5 and Curtius 4.11.1–18, while Justin, *Epitome* 11.12.1–10 records it as happening during the period in Egypt.

2. For the siege of Gaza, only Arrian, *Anabasis* 2.26.1–27.7 and Curtius 4.6.7–31 provide detailed accounts. The best modern discussion is Romane (1988), 21–30.

3. Arrian, *Anabasis* 2.25.4, Curtius 4.5.10, 6.7, Hegesias, *Fragments of Greek Historians* 142 F5, Homer, *Iliad* 22.396–400.

4. For discussion of the omen, see Romane (1988), 25–26, and for the mining operations 28–29; Gabriel (2015), 45–47 argues that Alexander's injury was little more than a flesh wound, and its seriousness was exaggerated by our sources, but it is hard to be certain.

5. Curtius 4.6.26–29 and Hegesias, *Fragments of Greek Historians* 142 F5.

6. Arrian, *Anabasis* 3.1.15, 2.3–7, Curtius 4.5.13–21; on the journey to Egypt see Engels (1978), 57–61.

7. Arrian, *Anabasis* 3.1.3–2.2, Curtius 4.8.1–6, Plutarch, *Alexander* 26.2–5.

8. The main accounts are Arrian, *Anabasis* 3.3.1–4.5, Curtius 4.7.5–31, Plutarch, *Alexander* 26.6–27.6, Diodorus Siculus 17.49.2–51.4; on the site more recently, see Walker (1921), 29–34.

9. Ptolemy cited by Arrian, *Anabasis* 3.3.5.

10. For discussion, particularly of the method of divination, see Collins (2014), 62–77; the letter to Olympias, Plutarch, *Alexander* 27.5; on the importance of the visit to the wider debate over Alexander's claims to divinity, see Bosworth (1988), 281–284, Hammond (1994a), 126–129.

11. On the importance of the visit see Bloedow (1994), 95–99; on dual parentage, see Ogden (2011), 7–28; Arrian mentions an apparent difference between Aristobulus and Ptolemy over the route taken on the return journey, but this really is of minor importance. Whatever the details, the round trip from the Nile amounted to at least 400 miles.

12. Arrian, *Anabasis* 3.5.1–7, Curtius 4.7.4–5; on Harpalus, see Arrian, *Anabasis* 3.6.4.

13. Curtius 4.8.7–9; Lucan, *Pharsalia* 10.272–275, Callisthenes, frag. 12a, Aristotle, frag. 246 on the Nile, where the inundation was considered a result of heavy rainfall in Ethiopia, see Hammond (1994a), 129.

14. Curtius 4.8.9–11; on the journey from Egypt and supply for the coming campaign, see Engels (1978), 63–67.

15. Plutarch, *Alexander* 29.3–5, Plutarch, *Moralia* 334e, Arrian, *Anabasis* 3.1.4.

16. Arrian, *Anabasis* 3.6.2–3.

17. For a discussion of the problems see Badian (1967), 37–69 and Badian (1994), 258–292, both arguing that the revolt was carefully planned and not doomed to failure.

CHAPTER 21: THE BATTLE OF GAUGAMELA

1. Curtius 4.6.30, Diodorus Siculus 17.49.1.

2. Arrian, *Anabasis* 3.6.7, 3.12.5, with Hammond (1994a), 132.

3. Arrian, *Anabasis* 3.7.1–3, with Bosworth (1988), 79, and Engels (1978), 66–69.

4. Arrian, *Anabasis* 3.8.6, Plutarch, *Alexander* 31.1, Diodorus Siculus 17.53.1–3, Curtius 4.12.13; for discussion of the numbers on both sides, see Marsden (1964), 24–39; for the Apple-bearers see Charles (2011), 114–133, esp. 124–130, underlined the vagueness of our sources, especially about the size of this unit, although opting for 1,000 men.

5. Arrian, *Anabasis* 3.7.3–6, Curtius 4.9.12–21, Diodorus Siculus 17.55.1–6, Plutarch, *Alexander* 31.3–4.

6. Arrian, *Anabasis* 3.7.6–8.7, Curtius 4.9.23–25.

7. Arrian, *Anabasis* 3.9.1–3.

8. Curtius 4.10.8–11.22, and Plutarch, *Alexander* 30.1–7 who places the death of Stateira a little earlier, but has similar detail, Diodorus Siculus 17.54.1–7, and Carney (1996a), 563–583, esp. 569–571.

9. Marsden (1964), 40–42 for discussion.

10. Arrian, *Anabasis* 3.9.3–5.

11. Arrian, *Anabasis* 3.9.5–11.2, Curtius 4.12.14–13.25, Diodorus Siculus 17.56.1–4, Plutarch, *Alexander* 31.3–32.2.

12. Plutarch, *Alexander* 32.3–7 on costume; 33.1–2 on Callisthenes and Aristander.

13. The chief ancient accounts of Gaugamela are Arrian, *Anabasis* 3.11.2–15.7, Curtius 4.13.26–16.15, Diodorus Siculus 17.57.1–60.3, Justin, *Epitome* 14.1–15.14, Plutarch, *Alexander* 32.3–33.7; for analysis see Marsden (1964), esp. 32–64, Fox (2004), 233–243, Bosworth (1988), 80–85, Green (1991), 288–295, Hammond (1994a), 138–149, Griffith (1947), 77–89, A. Devine (1975), 374–385, A. Devine (1986a), 87–115, and A. Devine (1989),77–80.

14. Arrian, *Anabasis* 3.9.7–8.

15. On dust, note the comment by Fuller (1958), 178n2, who recalls drilling on an Indian *maidan* during dry weather, when on one occasion "visibility was reduced to four or five yards" by far fewer horsemen than were present at Gaugamela.

16. 400 cavalry under Menidas based on assumption that these were the troops mentioned in Arrian, *Anabasis* 3.5.1 where the name appears as Meneotas.

17. See Heckel, Willikes, and Wrightson (2010), 103–109.

18. Arrian, *Anabasis* 3.14.3 (Loeb translation).

19. The only narrative is Diodorus Siculus 17.62.4–63.4, with a few details in Curtius 6.1.2–21, Borza (1971), 230–235, and Bosworth (1975), 27–43; a "battle of mice," Plutarch, *Aegisilaus* 15.4.

CHAPTER 22: "THE MOST HATEFUL OF THE CITIES OF ASIA"

1. Plutarch, *Alexander* 34.1–2, Arrian, *Anabasis* 3.16.1–3, Curtius 4.16.16–5.1.12; 4,000 talents, Curtius 5.1.10.

2. Arrian, *Anabasis* 3.16.3–5, Curtius 5.1.17–39, Diodorus Siculus 17.64.3–6; Briant (2015), 61–62 on the tablet.

3. Tablet 330 in Sachs-Hunger Collection, translation from Kuhrt (2007), 447–448, cited with discussion in Briant (2015), 60–64. Anson (2013), 105, 122–126; on striptease dances and the corrupting influence of cities, Curtius 5.1.36–39.

4. Arrian, *Anabasis* 3.16.6–9, Curtius 5.2.1–12, Diodorus Siculus 17.65–66.1.

5. Diodorus Siculus 17.66.3–7, Curtius 5.2.13–15, Arrian, *Anabasis* 3.7–8, Plutarch, *Alexander* 36.1–2.

6. Arrian, *Anabasis* 3.16.10, Diodorus Siculus 17.65.1.

7. Arrian, *Anabasis* 3.17.1–6, Diodorus Siculus 17.67.1–5, Curtius 5.3.1–16.

8. Arrian, *Anabasis* 3.18.1–9, Diodorus Siculus 17.68.1–7, Curtius 5.3.17–4.34.

9. Diodorus Siculus 17.69.1–9, Curtius 5.5.5–24, Justin, *Epitome* 11.14.11–12.

10. Heckel (2008), 82–83, Hammond (1994a), 179–180, although Green (1991), 313 accepts the story; Plutarch, *Alexander* 46.2 (Loeb translation) on the amazons, cf. Curtius 6.5.24–32, Diodorus Siculus 17.77.1–3, Justin, *Epitome* 12.3.5–7.

11. Diodorus Siculus 17.70.1 (Loeb translation), Curtius 5.6.1 (Loeb translation, slightly altered).

12. Diodorus Siculus 17.70.6 (Loeb translation) for quote and 17.70.1–6 for the sack; Curtius 5.6.1–8, and Plutarch, *Alexander* 37.2 for more general description of deliberate massacre in Persis.

13. Diodorus Siculus 17.71.1–8, with O'Brien (1992), 105–106 for a brief description, with R. Barnett, "Persepolis," *Iraq* 19 (1957), 55–77.

14. On the role of Persepolis, see Pope (1957), 123–130, Cahill (1985), 373–389.

15. Plutarch, *Alexander* 37.3, Curtius 5.6.10, with Bosworth (1988), 79, and Engels (1978), 92, 154.

16. Plutarch, *Alexander* 37.2, cf. Diodorus Siculus 17.71.1–2; Strabo, *Geog.* 15.3.9 on varying estimates of the amount; the campaign, Curtius 5.6.12–20.

17. Arrian, *Anabasis* 3.18.11–12 (Loeb translation).

18. Plutarch, *Alexander* 38.1–4, Diodorus Siculus 17.72.1–6, Curtius 5.7.3–7 and 5.7.5 (Loeb translation) for quote, and Athenaeus 13.576d–e.

19. Borza (1972), 233–245, Hammond (1992b), 358–364.

20. Regrets, Plutarch, *Alexander* 38.4; the Greek context, see Badian (1967), 37–69, and Badian (1994), 258–292, with Borza (1971), 230–235, esp. 232–235.

CHAPTER 23: AN END AND A BEGINNING

1. Arrian, *Anabasis* 3.18.10, 19.1–3, Diodorus Siculus 17.73.1, Curtius 6.2.11–14.

2. Arrian, *Anabasis* 3.19.4–5, Curtius 5.13.1.

3. Arrian, *Anabasis* 3.5–8, Curtius 6.2.10, 15–17, Plutarch, *Alexander* 42.3, Diodorus Siculus 17.74.3–4 with slight differences over details and chronology.

4. Reinforcements, Curtius 5.7.12.

5. Arrian, *Anabasis* 3.19.6–8, 20.3–4.

6. Arrian, *Anabasis* 3.21.7.

7. For the pursuit, see Arrian, *Anabasis* 3.20.1–22.6, Plutarch, *Alexander* 42.3–43.3, Diodorus Siculus 17.73.2–3, Curtius 5.13.15–25, Justin, *Epitome* 11.15.1–14.

8. Curtius 6.2.15–16, Diodorus Siculus 17.74.3, Justin, *Epitome* 12.3.2–3, Plutarch, *Alexander* 47.1–3.

9. Plutarch, *Alexander* 40.1.

10. For a useful discussion of these broad issues, see Olbrycht (2010), 351–360, and Fox (2007), 267–311.

11. Plutarch, *Alexander* 45.1–2, Curtius 6.6.2–10, Arrian, *Anabasis* 4.7.4, Diodorus Siculus 18.48.5, with Bosworth (1980b), 1–21, esp. 4–5.

12. Diodorus Siculus 17.77.6–7, Curtius 6.6.8, Justin 12.3.10 for the harem, with some debate over whether it consisted of 360 or 365 women, depending on the length of year in use.

13. Curtius 6.4.12–14, 5.22–23, Arrian, *Anabasis* 3.23.4, 28.2, 4.7.1, 18.1.

14. Arrian, *Anabasis* 3.23.1–9, Curtius 6.5.1–10.

15. Arrian, *Anabasis* 3.24.1–3, Curtius 6.5.11–22, Diodorus Siculus 17.76.3–8.

16. Arrian, *Anabasis* 3.25.1–8, Curtius 6.6.13, 20–34.

17. For the conspiracy, the main sources are Arrian, *Anabasis* 3.26.1–4, Diodorus Siculus 17.78.4, 79.1–80.1, Plutarch, *Alexander* 48.1–49.7, Curtius 6.7.1–11.40, 7.2.11–34 (which is by far the longest, but also influenced by the conditions of Rome in the author's own age), with discussions in Heckel (1977), 9–21, Badian (1960), 324–338, and Badian (2012a), 420–455, esp. 427–432.

18. Plutarch, *Alexander* 40.3, 48.1–3, Plutarch, *Moralia* 339d–f; note also the great wealth given to Parmenio, for instance the house formerly owned by the eunuch Bagoas, which was said to contain clothes worth 1,000 talents, Plutarch, *Alexander* 39.7.

19. Plutarch, *Alexander* 48.4–5.

20. Hammond (1994a), 183–187.

21. Curtius 6.11.18 (Loeb translation).

22. Hammond (1994a), 185 accepts Diodorus Siculus 17.80.1 and Justin, *Epitome* 12.5.3, who state that Parmenio was formally condemned by the assembled Macedonians; Alexander of Lyncestis, Curtius 7.1.5–9, Diodorus Siculus 17.80.2, Justin, *Epitome* 12.14.1; the brothers, Arrian, *Anabasis* 3.27.1, Curtius 7.1.10–2.10. The oldest was Amyntas, who was killed at a siege soon afterward, Arrian, *Anabasis* 3.27.3.

CHAPTER 24: THE UPRIGHT TIARA

1. Arrian, *Anabasis* 3.16.11, 4.22.7, 23.1, 24.1, with Hammond (1994a), 191–192, Brunt (1963), 27–46, Bosworth (1988), 268–273.

2. Arrian, *Anabasis* 427.4; Philotas is attested 1.2.5, 5.9–11 leading units in 335 BC, but otherwise nothing is known of his military experience before being made commander of the Companion cavalry.

3. Arrian, *Anabasis* 3.16.11, Diodorus Siculus 17.65.3.

4. Diodorus Siculus 17.80.4, Curtius 7.2.35–38, Justin, *Epitome* 12.5.5–8.

5. Bosworth (1980b), 1–21 remains an excellent overview and emphasis on the twin courts and administrations, and the dominance of Macedonians and Greeks.

6. Diodorus Siculus 17.67.1, Curtius 5.2.17–19, Arrian, *Anabasis* 3.22.6, with Carney (1996a), 563–583, esp. 571–575, 577.

7. Curtius 6.5.23, 10.1.22–38, Plutarch, *Alexander* 67.7–8, Plutarch, *Moralia* 66d; for skepticism over a physical relationship, see Ogden (2011), 167–170.

8. Plutarch, *Alexander* 41.1–42.2.

9. Arrian, *Anabasis* 3.27.4–28.1, Curtius 7.3.1–3.

10. Arrian, *Anabasis* 3.28.1–4.

11. Arrian, *Anabasis* 3.28.8–10, Curtius 7.3.5–23, 4.22–25, Diodorus Siculus 17.82.2–83.1, with Hammond (1994a), 190–191, Holt (2006), 32–36, citing on

the colder than usual summers Grudd et al. (2002), 657–665 and Helama et al. (2002), 681–687.

12. Arrian, *Anabasis* 3.28.3, 8–29.5, Curtius 7.4.32–40, Diodorus Siculus 17.83.5–6.

13. Curtius 7.5.1–16, with 7.5.16 (Loeb translation) for the quote, with Bosworth (1988), 107–108, Holt (2006), 37–38.

14. Arrian, *Anabasis* 3.29.6–30.5, 4.7.3, Curtius 7.5.19–26, 36–43.

CHAPTER 25: THE SWORD AND THE FLAME

1. Pliny, *Natural History* 6.18, Arrian, *Anabasis* 3.30.6–9.

2. Holt (2006), 45–48.

3. Strabo, *Geog.* 11.11.3, 8, Arrian, *Anabasis* 3.30.6, 10.

4. Curtius 7.5.28–35, Strabo, *Geog.* 11.11.4, Plutarch, *Moralia* 557b, Diodorus Siculus 17 summary 20 (the actual text of this passage has not survived).

5. Arrian, *Anabasis* 3.30.10–11, Curtius 7.6.1–9, and for the wound, note the skepticism of Gabriel (2015), 47–48 who argues that the injury was minor.

6. Arrian, *Anabasis* 4.1.1–3.4, Curtius 7.6.10–27, with Gabriel (2015), 48–51, who stresses the seriousness of this wound.

7. Arrian, *Anabasis* 4.3.5–4.3, Curtius 7.7.1–29.

8. Arrian, *Anabasis* 4.4.3–5.1, Curtius 7.8.1–9.19.

9. Arrian, *Anabasis* 4.3.7, 5.2– 6.2, Curtius 7.7.30–39.

10. Arrian, *Anabasis* 4.6.3–7.2, 15.1–6, Curtius 7.9.20–22, 10.10–14, with Hammond (1994a), 195–197, Bosworth (1988), 113–114.

11. Arrian, *Anabasis* 4.15.7–17.3, Plutarch, *Moralia* 334e–f.

12. Arrian, *Anabasis* 4.17.4–7, Strabo, *Geog.* 11.11.6, Curtius 8.2.13–18, 3.1–16.

13. Curtius 8.1.11–19.

14. Arrian, *Anabasis* 4.17.3, Curtius 8.1.19, with Carney (1996a), 575–577, who dates Artabazus's retirement to 327 BC, Bosworth (1988), 114, Fox (2004), 311–312, Holt (2006), 76–77.

15. O'Brien, (1992), 101–104.

16. Plutarch, *Alexander* 48.5–7.

17. Plutarch, *Alexander* 50.4–5 (Loeb translation).

18. Plutarch, *Alexander* 50.5, 51.2 (Loeb translation).

19. Arrian, *Anabasis* 4.8.9 (Loeb translation); the fullest accounts for the murder are Arrian, *Anabasis* 4.8.1–9.8, Curtius 8.1.20–2.12, Plutarch, *Alexander* 50.1–52.4, Justin, *Epitome* 12.6.3.

20. Plutarch, *Alexander* 52.1–4 (Loeb translation for quotes).

21. Gabriel (2015), 49–50, 118–121, and Tritle (2003), 127–146 for an insightful discussion of the incident in the context of PTSD.

CHAPTER 26: "POORER FOR A KISS"

1. The details and chronology of this period remain unclear. For discussion and one solution favoring a chronology based on Curtius rather than Arrian see Bosworth (1981), 17–39, esp. 21–23 for trouble in the Persian heartland.

2. Arrian, *Anabasis* 4.17.4–19.6.

3. Curtius 7.11.1–29, with discussion in Bosworth (1981), 29–33, 34–35, 38–39. In contrast Hammond (1994a), 198–199 accepts Arrian's chronology.

4. Plutarch, *Alexander* 58.2, and on the fighting in general Holt (2006), 66–84.

5. Arrian, *Anabasis* 4.21.1–10, Curtius 8.2.19–33, Strabo, *Geog.* 11.11.4.

6. Arrian, *Anabasis* 4.19.5–6, Curtius 8.4.21–30, Plutarch, *Alexander* 47.4, Plutarch, *Moralia* 332e, 338d, with Carney (1996a), 563–583, esp. 575–577, and Carney (2000), 106–107.

7. Diodorus Siculus 20.20.1 for Barsine's son. Diodorus's account of this period is missing, but the late summary of his work known as the *Metz Epitome* 70 claims that Roxane bore a son who did not survive.

8. Curtius 8.4.27 for the loaf, 8.4.1–20 for the march in stormy weather, with Frontinus, *Stratagems* 4.6.3, Valerius Maximus 5.1. ext.1a. It is possible that these incidents refer to the crossing of the Hindu Kush, but once again the problems of chronology make it hard to be sure.

9. Garrison left in Bactria and Sogdiana, Arrian, *Anabasis* 4.22.3; Arrian, *Anabasis* 5.11.3, 12.2, 7.6.1, with Bosworth (1988), 271–273.

10. Arrian, *Indica* 19.5, and for all the figures see Engels (1978), 146–152; on the silver shields, see Curtius 8.5.4 with Hammond (1994a), 222.

11. Herodotus 1.134 for the Persian custom.

12. Arrian, *Anabasis* 4.12.2, Curtius 8.5.22, Plutarch, *Alexander* 74.1–2 for mockery of Persians performing *proskynesis*.

13. For discussion of this episode see Green (1991), 372–377, Bosworth (1988), 284–287, O'Brien (1992), 142–145, Heckel (2008), 106–110.

14. Arrian, *Anabasis* 4.20.5–12.7, Plutarch, *Alexander* 53.3–4, Curtius 8.5.5–19.

15. Plutarch, *Alexander* 54.1 for Aristotle's verdict on his relative; for his brief popularity, Curtius 8.5.20, Plutarch, *Alexander* 53.3–5, and for a good discussion of his actual importance see Borza (1995), 173–188.

16. Arrival of fifty pages in late 331–330 BC, Diodorus Siculus 17.65.1, Curtius 5.1.42, with discussion in Hammond (1990), 261–290, esp. 265–268.

17. Carney (2015), 207–223, esp. 212–216, 222–223.

18. Arrian, *Anabasis* 4.12.7–13.7, Curtius 8.6.2–8.20, Plutarch, *Alexander* 54.2–4, Justin, *Epitome* 12.7.2.

19. Plutarch, *Alexander* 55.9, Curtius 8.8.21, Arrian, *Anabasis* 4.14.3.

CHAPTER 27: INDIA

1. Herodotus 4.44 on Darius I in India; Arrian, *Anabasis* 3.8.3, 6 for troops at Gaugamela; Diodorus Siculus 17.86.4, Arrian, *Anabasis* 4.30.4, Curtius 8.11.25 for exiles and envoys.

2. Arrian, *Anabasis* 4.22.3–5, Plutarch, *Alexander* 57.1–2, Polyaenus, *Stratagems* 4.3.10; Engels (1978), 65–66 suggests that Alexander wanted to stop the use of all carts except those needed for essential siege equipment, but it is more likely that he was concerned with excessive and cumbersome luxuries.

3. Arrian, *Anabasis* 4.22.7–8, Curtius 8.10.1–4.

4. Arrian, *Anabasis* 4.23.1–5, Curtius 8.10.5–6.

5. Arrian, *Anabasis* 4.24.1–25.4, with prudent skepticism in Bosworth (1996), 42.

6. Arrian, *Anabasis* 4.25.5–27.4, Plutarch, *Alexander* 59.3–4, Diodorus Siculus 17.84.1–6, Polyaenus 4.3.20, and Curtius 8.10.22–34 (who does not mention the mercenaries).

7. For Cleophis, see Justin, *Epitome* 12.7.10, Curtius 8.10.36; for Nysa, see Curtius 8.10.7–18, Arrian, *Anabasis* 5.1.3–3.4, Plutarch, *Alexander* 58.3–5, Justin, *Epitome* 12.7.6–8, Philostratus, *Life of Apollonius of Tyre* 2.9.

8. Arrian, *Anabasis* 4.27.5–30.4, Curtius 8.11.1–25, Diodorus Siculus 17.85.1–86.1.

9. Arrian, *Anabasis* 4.28.6, 30.5–9, Diodorus Siculus 17.86.2–3.

10. Arrian, *Anabasis* 5.3.5–4.3, 7.1–8.3, Curtius 8.12.4, Diodorus Siculus 17.86.3.

11. Diodorus Siculus 17.86.4–7, Curtius 8.12.5–18, Arrian, *Anabasis* 5.3.5–6.

12. Arrian, *Anabasis* 4.27.7, 30.7, 5.8.3, 22.2, Curtius Rufus 8.12.13, 13.2, 14.1, with *Metz Epitome 56–57* claiming that he had the envoy flogged.

13. In general see Bosworth, (1996), esp. 31–97, Beggiora (2017), 238–254; Porus's height and appearance, Arrian, *Anabasis* 5.19.1, Plutarch, *Alexander* 60.12, Diodorus Siculus 17.88.4, Curtius 8.13.7, 14.13, Justin, *Epitome* 12.8.1.

14. Bosworth (1996), 5–11; Arrian, *Anabasis* 5.15.4, Diodorus Siculus 17.87.2, Curtius 8.13.6, Plutarch, *Alexander* 62.2.

15. Arrian, *Anabasis* 5.9.1–4; for elephants see Epplett (2007), 209–232, esp. 209–216.

16. Arrian, *Anabasis* 5.10.1–4, Curtius 8.13.9–11, 17–21, Polyaenus, *Stratagems* 4.3.9.

17. Arrian, *Anabasis* 5.11.1–2.

18. Arrian, *Anabasis* 5.11.3–12.1.

19. Arrian, *Anabasis* 5.12.2–13.4, Curtius 8.13.22–27, Plutarch, *Alexander* 60.1–3.

20. Sources for the battle, Arrian, *Anabasis* 5.14.1–18.3, Curtius 8.14.1–30, Diodorus Siculus 17.87.3–89.3, Polyaenus, *Stratagems* 4.3.21–22, Plutarch, *Alexander* 60.5–8; modern reconstructions include Bosworth (1996), 15–20, Hammond (1994a), 210–215, Hamilton (1956), 26–31. All assume ordered battle lines and a formal engagement, clearly influenced by Alexander's other three battles.

21. Arrian, *Anabasis* 5.18.6–7, Curtius 18.14.35–36, Plutarch, *Alexander* 60.7–8, Plutarch, *Moralia* 332e, 458b, Diodorus Siculus 17.89.2, Justin, *Epitome* 8.12.1–15.

22. Plutarch, *Alexander* 61, Arrian, *Anabasis* 5.19.4–6.

CHAPTER 28: VICTORY INTO RETREAT

1. Diodorus Siculus 17.94.2, with comments in Green (1991), 461–462.

2. Arrian, *Anabasis* 5.20.1–7, Curtius 9.1.7, Diodorus Siculus 17.90.4.

3. Arrian, *Anabasis* 5.20.6, 21.2–5, Diodorus Siculus 17.91.1–2, Strabo, *Geog.* 15.1.30.

4. Arrian, *Anabasis* 5.21.1–2, 4–24.8, Curtius 9.1.9–36.

5. Arrian, *Anabasis* 25.1, Curtius 9.2.1–9, Diodorus Siculus 17.93.2–3, with Bosworth (1988), 132–133, Hammond (1994a), 218–219.

6. Hammond (1994a), 218–219.

7. Sources for the mutiny, Arrian, *Anabasis* 5.25.2–29.2, Curtius 9.2.9–3.19, Diodorus Siculus 17, 93.4–95.2, Plutarch, *Alexander* 62.1–4, Justin, *Epitome* 12.8.10–17.

8. Discussion in Bosworth (1988), 133–134, Green (1991), 407–411, Fox (2004), 367–372, Heckel (2003), 147–174, Heckel (2008), 120–125, Heckel (2009), 69–82, esp. 80–81, Spann (1999), 62–74, with response in Anson (2015), 65–74.

9. E.g. suspicion raised in Bosworth (1988), 134, Badian (1961), 16–43, esp. 20.

10. Arrian, *Anabasis* 5.20.1–2, 6.1.2–5, Diodorus Siculus 17.89.4–6, Curtius 9.1.4, Strabo, *Geog.* 15.1.29; Hephaestion and Craterus, see Plutarch, *Alexander* 47.6–7.

11. Arrian, *Anabasis* 6.2.3–4, Arrian, *Indica* 19.7, Curtius 9.3.22, with Bosworth (1988), 134.

12. Curtius 9.3.20–22. It may have been now rather than earlier that the hypaspists received their shields inlaid with silver.

13. See Beggiora (2017), concentrating on ethnographic aspects; naphtha, Plutarch, *Alexander* 35.1–5; oil/petroleum, see Arrian, *Anabasis* 4.15.7–8, Strabo, *Geog.* 11.11.5, Curtius 7.10.13–14, Plutarch, *Alexander* 57.5–9.

14. Ptolemy and poison, Strabo, *Geog.* 15.2.7, Curtius 9.8.20, Diodorus Siculus 17.103.3–6. Notably the incident is not included in Arrian's narrative, which drew heavily on Ptolemy's own account so is probably fiction.

15. Useful discussion in Stoneman (1994), 500–510 and Stoneman (1995), 99–114; for Calanus, see Plutarch, *Alexander* 65.5, Diodorus Siculus 17.107.1–6, Strabo, *Geog.* 15.1.68, Arrian, *Anabasis* 7.3.1–6.

16. Arrian, *Anabasis* 6.3.1–5.4, Curtius 9.4.10–14.

17. Arrian, *Anabasis* 6.5.4–6.5, Curtius 9.4.1–5.

18. Arrian, *Anabasis* 6.6.6–8.8, Curtius 9.4.6–8, 15–25, Diodorus Siculus 17.96.2–5, with different chronology and details.

19. Arrian, *Anabasis* 6.9.1–11.1, Curtius 9.4.26–5.21, 6.4–27, Diodorus Siculus 17.98.3–99.4, Plutarch, *Alexander* 63.1–4, Justin, *Epitome* 12.9.1–13, once again with conflicting details.

20. Arrian, *Anabasis* 6.11.1–8, 13.4–5, Plutarch, *Alexander* 63.5–6, Curtius 9.5.22–30, with discussion in Hammond (1994a), 225–226, Bosworth (1988), 136–137, Bosworth (1996), 139–141, Green (1991), 418–422, Fox (2004), 378–382; detailed discussion of the wound in Gabriel (2015), 52–55.

21. Arrian, *Anabasis* 6.12.1–13.3, Curtius 9.6.1–2, Plutarch, *Alexander* 63.6.

22. Arrian, *Anabasis* 6.14.1–15.3.

23. Arrian, *Anabasis* 6.15.4–17.6, Curtius 9.8.1–16, Plutarch, *Alexander* 64.1–65.1 with a probably fictional anecdote where Alexander releases rather than executes captive Indian philosophers, with Bosworth (1996), 133–165.

24. Arrian, *Anabasis* 6.17.4–19.5, Curtius 9.8.28–9.27, Plutarch, *Alexander* 66.1.1.

CHAPTER 29: SEA AND SAND

1. For discussion see Heckel (2008), 122–127; Green (1991), 412 attributes a sudden loss of interest in India to factors beyond his control.

2. Arrian, *Anabasis* 6.20.1–5.

3. Arrian, *Indica* 20.1–11, with Bosworth (1988), 139–140, Hammond (1994a), 231–233.

4. Arrian, *Anabasis* 6.17.3, 21.3–4, 27.3; for claims that the fleet was intended to supply Alexander's troops, Engels (1978), 111–117, who also presumes some 400 merchant ships as part of the fleet; for a more convincing assessment, see Hammond (1994a), 236–239; Green (1991), 435 conjectures 85,000 people in Alexander's land column, including noncombatants, with Engels (1978), 11n57 giving even higher numbers, while Bosworth (1988), 142 suggests at least 30,000, while admitting this was "pure guesswork."

5. Arrian, *Anabasis* 6.3.

6. Arrian, *Anabasis* 6.24.2–3.

7. Bosworth (1988), 140 cites Arrian, *Anabasis* 6.18.1 where well-digging parties were attacked near Patala, but this was limited in scale and it is not clear that there was any fighting after this incident.

8. Arrian, *Anabasis* 21.3–22.3.

9. Accounts of the journey, see Arrian, *Anabasis* 22.4–27.1, Curtius 9.10.8–18, Plutarch, *Alexander* 66.2–3, Diodorus Siculus 17.104.4–106.1, Strabo, *Geog.* 15.2.3–7, Pliny, *Natural History* 12.18.34.

10. Discussion of the Gedrosian desert, see in particular Bosworth (1996), 166–185, and on numbers of Macedonian survivors, Bosworth (1988), 145–146, 267, Hammond (1994a), 233–235, 238–239; for a high estimate of the losses see Green (1991), 435, 558n23, and for a lower, but still in thousands, see Cartledge (2004), 186–187.

11. For the voyage, see Arrian, *Indica* 21.1–33.13, Curtius 10.1.10–12, Diodorus Siculus 17.106.5–7; for discussion see Biagi (2017), 255–278, and Bucciantini (2017), 279–292.

CHAPTER 30: THE RETURN OF THE KING

1. Arrian, *Anabasis* 6.27.1–28.5, Arrian, *Indica* 33.1–36.6.

2. Arrian, *Anabasis* 6.27.2, Curtius 10.1.20; mass desertion in Bactria, see Diodorus Siculus 17.99.5–6, Curtius 9.7.1–11, with Holt (2006), 111–114 and Holt (1988), 82–85.

3. Arrian, *Anabasis* 7.3.4.1–3, 5.5, Arrian, *Indica* 23.5; Arrian, *Anabasis* 6.27.6 on anticipation by satraps of losses in Gedrosia.

4. Arrian, *Anabasis* 6.27.3–5, Curtius 10.1.1–9, 22–42, Plutarch, *Alexander* 68.4.

5. Diodorus Siculus 17.108.4–6, Athenaeus 13.595a–c, Pausanias 1.37.4, with Badian (1961), 16–43.

6. A view strongly advocated by Badian (1961), esp. 16–25; see also Bosworth (1988), 147–148, Green (1991), 436–439, Hammond (1994a), 243–244, Heckel (2008), 135–137.

7. Arrian, *Anabasis* 7.23.6–8.

8. Plutarch, *Alexander* 68.4.

9. Diodorus Siculus 17.106.3, 113.3, 18.8.3–5, Curtius 10.2.4–8, with Heckel (2008), 146–148, Bosworth (1988), 215–228, Hammond (1994a), 256–259.

10. Justin, *Epitome* 13.5.9, Plutarch, *Demosthenes* 25.1–26.2, Curtius 10.2.1, Diodorus Siculus 17.108.6, with Badian (1961), 31–40.

11. For opposing views on losses, see Bosworth (1986), 1–12, Hammond (1989b), 56–68.

12. Even Arrian, *Anabasis* 7.4.3 notes that it was said Alexander became readier to execute on his return from India.

13. Arrian, *Anabasis* 7.1.1–2, 4.4–8, Plutarch, *Alexander* 70.2, Diodorus Siculus 17.110.3, Justin, *Epitome* 12.10.9–10, Plutarch, *Demetrius* 31.5.

14. Bosworth (1980b), 1–21, esp. 11–12, Heckel (2008), 137–140.

15. Arrian, *Anabasis* 7.5.1–6, 6.3.

16. Arrian, *Anabasis* 7.6.1–5, Plutarch, *Alexander* 71.1–3, Diodorus Siculus 17.108.1–3, Curtius 7.5.1, with discussion in Bosworth (1988), 271–273.

17. Arrian, *Anabasis* 7.7.1–7 on exploration of the Tigris and Euphrates.

18. For the mutiny at Opis and its aftermath, see Arrian, *Anabasis* 7.8.1–12.4, Diodorus Siculus 17.109.2–3, with Carney (1996b), 19–44, esp. 37–42.

19. Arrian, *Anabasis* 7.12.4, Diodorus Siculus 18.22.1.

CHAPTER 31: "AN UTTER LOSS"

1. Plutarch, *Moralia* 207D 8 for quote, cf. Aelian *Various Histories* 3.23 emphasizing the sheer scale of his achievement.

2. Arrian, *Anabasis* 7.1.2–4, 20.1–2, quote from Loeb translation.

3. Arrian, *Anabasis* 7.23.1–4, Diodorus Siculus 17.110.2.

4. Arrian, *Anabasis* 7.12.5–7, 14.1, 23.6–8, Diodorus Siculus 18.29.4, Plutarch, *Alexander* 68.2–3, Justin, *Epitome* 12.14.1–3.

5. Arrian, *Anabasis* 7.12.1–6, Plutarch, *Alexander* 74.1–4.

6. Arrian, *Anabasis* 7.14.1–10, Plutarch, *Alexander* 72.1–4, Diodorus Siculus 17.110, 115.1–6, 7–8, Justin, *Epitome* 12.12.11–12, with comments in Bosworth (1988), 163–165.

7. Arrian, *Anabasis* 7.15.1–3, Diodorus Siculus 17.111.5–6.

8. Arrian, *Anabasis* 7.15.4–6.

9. For discussion, see Bosworth (1988), 278–290, Cartledge (2004), 215–227 for good surveys of this vast and irresolvable question; a fragment of the deeply unreliable Ephippus alleges that Alexander dressed up, Athenaeus 12.537e–38b.

10. Arian, *Anabasis* 7.18.1–6, Plutarch, *Alexander* 73.1–2.

11. Arian, *Anabasis* 7.22.2–5, 24.1–3, Plutarch, *Alexander* 73.3–75.1, Diodorus Siculus 17.116.1–7.

12. For a range of views see Bosworth (1988), 158–173, Heckel (2008), 149–152, Green (1991), 471–488, Cartledge (2004), 189–194, Fox (2004), 436–460, O'Brien (1992), 210–228, with one of the most critical in Badian (1961), 16–43.

13. Atkinson, Truter, and Truter (2009), 23–46 provides an excellent overview; G. Phillips, *Alexander the Great* (2004), argues that Roxane was responsible for the murder.

14. Five celebrations in a month, Aelian, *Various Histories* 3.23; for discussion see Bosworth (1971a), 112–136, Hammond (1988b), 129–150 and Hammond (1989a), 155–160, Anson (1996), 501–504.

15. A drinking contest, Athenaeus 10.434a–b; the main accounts are Arrian, *Anabasis* 7.25.1–28.1, Plutarch, *Alexander* 75.2–77.3.

16. The presence of a Temple of Serapis at this date has been claimed as a sign that the Ephimerides are a later forgery, but this is unnecessary, see Anson (1996), 502.

17. For discussion of the various suggested diseases, see Atkinson, Truter, and Truter (2009), 27–32.

18. For a narrative, see Curtius 10.5.1–10.19.

19. Diodorus Siculus 19.41.2, Plutarch, *Eumenes* 16.4 on age of *argyraspides* in 317 BC.

EPILOGUE: TEARS AND A BROKEN NOSE

1. Plutarch, *Caesar* 11.3, Suetonius, *Julius Caesar* 7.1.

2. Livy 35.14.

3. Worthington, *By the Spear* (2014), R. Gabriel, *Philip II of Macedonia* (2010), and R. Gabriel, *The Madness of Alexander the Great and the Myth of Military Genius* (2015) praise Philip to criticize Alexander.

4. For Ai Khanoum, see Holt (2012), 154–164.

5. Horace, *Epistles* 2.1.156–157.

6. For differing views on the manpower implications of Alexander's campaign, see Bosworth (1986), 1–12 and Hammond (1989b), 56–68.

7. Lucan, *Pharsalia* 10.1–52, Cicero, *Letters to Atticus* 5.20.3.

8. Suetonius, *Augustus* 17.3–5.

9. Reception has become a highly fashionable branch of the Classics in recent years and inevitably Alexander attracts a lot of attention. This is not the place to deal with the subject, but an excellent introduction bridging the history and the afterlife is C. Mossé, *Alexander* (2004), while there is now the compendious K. Moore, *Brill's Companion to the Reception of Alexander the Great* (2018); D. Spencer, *Roman Alexander* (2002) and J. Peltonen, *Alexander the Great in the Roman Empire* (2019) look at Alexander's significance in the Roman world.

APPENDIX 2

1. See Chapter 2, notes 1 and 2, along with Hammond (1991), 69–82, Borza (1987a), 105–121, Musgrave, Neave, and Prag (1984), 60–78; for the case for the man in Tomb I being Philip, see Bartsiokas et al. (2015).

INDEX

JO NIXON

ADRIAN GOLDSWORTHY received his doctorate of philosophy in ancient history from Oxford and has taught at Cardiff University, King's College, and the University of Notre Dame in London. The author of numerous books, including *Pax Romana*, *How Rome Fell*, and *Caesar*, he lives in South Wales, UK.